POVERTY AND WELFARE AMONG THE PORTUGUESE JEWS IN EARLY MODERN AMSTERDAM

THE LITTMAN LIBRARY OF
JEWISH CIVILIZATION

Life Patron
COLETTE LITTMAN

Dedicated to the memory of
LOUIS THOMAS SIDNEY LITTMAN
who founded the Littman Library for the love of God
and as an act of charity in memory of his father
JOSEPH AARON LITTMAN
and to the memory of
ROBERT JOSEPH LITTMAN
who continued what his father Louis had begun
יהא זכרם ברוך

'Get wisdom, get understanding:
Forsake her not and she shall preserve thee'
PROV. 4:5

The Littman Library of Jewish Civilization is a registered UK charity
Registered charity no. 1000784

POVERTY AND WELFARE AMONG THE PORTUGUESE JEWS IN EARLY MODERN AMSTERDAM

TIRTSAH LEVIE BERNFELD

London
The Littman Library of Jewish Civilization
in association with Liverpool University Press
2012

The Littman Library of Jewish Civilization
Registered office: 14th floor, 33 Cavendish Square, London W1G 0PW

in association with Liverpool University Press
4 Cambridge Street, Liverpool L69 7ZU, UK
www.liverpooluniversitypress.co.uk/littman

Managing Editor: Connie Webber

Distributed in North America by Longleaf Services
116 S Boundary St, Chapel Hill, NC 27514, USA

Catalogue records for this book are available from the
British Library and the Library of Congress

ISBN 978–1–904113–57–7

Publishing co-ordinator: Janet Moth
Copy-editing: Gillian Somerscales and Philippa Claiden
Proof-reading: Laurien Berkeley
Index of Persons: Tirtsah Levie Bernfeld
Index of Subjects: Christine Headley and Tirtsah Levie Bernfeld
Designed and typeset by Pete Russell, Faringdon, Oxon.

Printed and bound by CPI Group (UK) Ltd., Croydon, CR0 4YY

To the memory of my parents

Max Levie

1920–1979

Reina Lea Levie-van Messel

1918–2001

ACKNOWLEDGEMENTS

MY EXPERIENCE of writing this book was not solely that of an intellectual exercise—of solitary confinement in my study, books and classical music my only companions, punctuated by countless visits to archives and libraries. It also meant meeting people and making friends, at home and abroad, besides being surrounded by an ever-expanding extended family.

The book is the final product of a suggestion made by my teacher, Professor Yosef Kaplan of the Hebrew University of Jerusalem, of a topic for a doctoral dissertation. It was he who directed me towards the poor of the Portuguese Jewish community in the early modern period as a subject in need of exploration, and I was indeed fortunate to have access to his vast knowledge of the field.

I should also like to express a special word of gratitude to Professor Jonathan Israel, who was indefatigable in finding me a publisher, and who introduced me to the Littman Library of Jewish Civilization.

My interest in Jewish history has taken me far afield. Setting out from the University of Amsterdam, and encouraged by Professor Maarten Brands, I recall in particular the stimulating atmosphere of Brandeis and Harvard universities, where I had the privilege of attending the lectures of Professor Benjamin Ravid and of the late Professors Benjamin Halpern and Yosef Haim Yerushalmi. On the other side of the globe, I also benefited greatly from the teaching of the late Professor Haim Beinart at the Hebrew University of Jerusalem. Wherever we meet, in New York, Boston, London, Amsterdam, or Jerusalem, Professor Daniel Swetschinski, scholar and friend, has always shown an interest in my work. His ideas have been a source of inspiration to me.

Back at home in Amsterdam, I discussed my work with three special friends, all historians, during convivial evenings at my house. I should like to thank Dr Lotte van de Pol, Dr Rudolf Dekker, and Professor Marco van Leeuwen for their continued support and friendship. I owe Professor van Leeuwen a special debt of gratitude for offering me hospitality at the International Institute of Social History in Amsterdam, where I could take refuge from the hustle and bustle of daily life at home and spend time writing, thinking, and exchanging views. Hans Blom, Professor Emeritus of Dutch History at the University of Amsterdam, helped me through an impasse in my research and set me back on track, for which I am very grateful.

Many long hours were spent at the Amsterdam City Archives, which became, at a certain stage in my life, my second home. I should like to thank all the staff there, especially Drs Odette Vlessing, and also the many others who were always willing to retrieve mountains of archival sources. At the Biblioteca Rosenthaliana I remember the invaluable help of former curators Dr Frits Hoogewoud and Dr Adri Offenberg. At the Ets Haim Library it was Dr Abraham Rosenberg who answered my questions and provided me with material.

The original text of my doctoral thesis, of which this book is an extended version, was written in Dutch and translated into English by the late Arnold Pomerans and his wife Erica. It was a real privilege to work with them. The present version comprises their text with additions that I wrote in English. Drs Francine Menco-Püttmann, a long-standing family friend, offered invaluable assistance in toiling through the notes and bibliography. The sum total was supervised and edited by the staff of the Littman Library of Jewish Civilization, especially by Connie Webber, Ludo Craddock, Janet Moth, Philippa Claiden, Gillian Somerscales, and George Tulloch. Their craftsmanship, cordiality, and continual support made the burden of writing a book a little lighter.

The list of all my friends in the Netherlands, in other parts of Europe, in the United States, in Canada, and, last but not least, in Israel, who have been at all times so very inspiring, reassuring, and supportive, is too long to name them all here: I thank them all warmly.

My late parents, Reina Lea Levie-van Messel and Max Levie, survivors of many ordeals during the Second World War, instilled in me a sense of hope and perseverance that helps me to cope with the joys and sorrows of life. They provided me with a happy and warm environment and a strong foundation from which to move ahead. It is to their memory that I dedicate this book.

It has always been a struggle to combine work with running a family; often work had to come last, and the progress of my research was delayed. But family life has given me so much in return: my children Michael and Eva are now adults, and all our lives are enriched by Michael and Mila's son, my grandchild Benjamin Jona. I cannot but be thankful for the warmth and joy with which our life is constantly filled.

Above all, I want to thank my partner in life Juri Jacob Bernfeld, whose love and care have been a constant blessing.

Amsterdam, 2012 TLB

CONTENTS

TABLES

Tables appear in Appendix I

FIGURES

Figures appear in Appendix II

NOTE ON TRANSLITERATION AND ORTHOGRAPHY

IT WOULD be an impossible task to standardize spellings in the different languages used by the Portuguese of Amsterdam and the surrounding area, especially since no such standardization existed at the time, in either Spanish, Portuguese, or Dutch.[1] The Portuguese community transliterated Hebrew terms into the orthography of their (Romance) language: so for example the letter *h* representing the final *heh* is rarely found; where *h* does appear, it often stands for a *ḥet* or a *khaf*, but these are not distinguished. Similarly, *shin* and *tsadi* are not distinguished, both being written as *s*. In most cases, we have applied the following principles.

Throughout the book, in both quoted matter and the surrounding text, terms, titles, and names of *ḥevroth* or specific institutions of the Portuguese community have been spelled as they would have been at the time. So we have *beraha* instead of *berakhah*; *escava* instead of *hashkavah*; *haham* instead of *ḥakham*; *sedaca* instead of *tsedaka*; Sidcat Nassim instead of Tsidcat Nashim. For Hebrew terms that are not specific to this community and are still widely used today, however, we have followed a modern transliteration system: *mitsvah* not *misva* or *misvah*; *ḥerem* not *herem*, *tsitsit* not *sisit*, *Rosh Hodesh* not *Roshodes*. Further details of this system appear below.

Personal names are found spelt in a variety of ways in the records, even when referring to the same person. With the exception of names appearing in quoted matter, we have adopted the following approach. The spelling of first names has been standardized on familiar modern forms: so 'Raquel', 'Rahel', and 'Ragel' are given as Rachel; 'Mozes', 'Moises', 'Moshe', and 'Moseh' as 'Moses'; and so on. The Portuguese spelling of last names has been retained as it appears in the sources, except where the same person's last name, or the name of members of the same family, is variously spelt there. Here we have standardized on the most frequently occurring form of that name: 'Acoen Belinfante', for example, is given as 'Cohen Belinfante'; 'Sarfatim', 'Sarphati', and 'Sarfaty' have been standardized as 'Sarfati'.

In adopting this system we have striven to respect the specific tradition of the Portuguese Jewish community of early modern Amsterdam while not erecting unnecessary barriers for the reader.

Where the above considerations regarding spellings used by the Portuguese community do not apply we have adopted a broad approach to transcription, rather than the narrower approaches found in the *Encyclopaedia Judaica* or other systems developed for text-based or linguistic studies. The aim has been to reflect the pronunciation prescribed for modern Hebrew, rather than the spelling or Hebrew word structure, and to do so using conventions that are generally familiar to the English-speaking reader.

In accordance with this approach, no attempt is made to indicate the distinctions between *alef* and *ayin*, *tet* and *taf*, *kaf* and *kuf*, *sin* and *samekh*, since these are not relevant to pronunciation; likewise, the *dagesh* is not indicated except where it affects pronunciation. Following the principle of using conventions familiar to the majority of readers, however, transcriptions that are well established have been retained even when they are not fully consistent with the transliteration system adopted. On similar grounds, the *tsadi* is rendered by 'tz' in such familiar words as barmitzvah. Likewise, the distinction between *ḥet* and *khaf* has been retained, using *ḥ* for the former and *kh* for the latter; the associated forms are generally familiar to readers, even if the distinction is not actually borne out in pronunciation, and for the same reason the final *heh* is indicated too. As in Hebrew, no capital letters are used, except that an initial capital has been retained in transliterating titles of published works (for example, *Shulḥan arukh*).

Since no distinction is made between *alef* and *ayin*, they are indicated by an apostrophe only in intervocalic positions where a failure to do so could lead an English-speaking reader to pronounce the vowel-cluster as a diphthong—as, for example, in *ha'ir*—or otherwise mispronounce the word.

The *sheva na* is indicated by an *e*—*perikat ol*, *reshut*—except, again, when established convention dictates otherwise.

The *yod* is represented by *i* when it occurs as a vowel (*bereshit*), by *y* when it occurs as a consonant (*yesodot*), and by *yi* when it occurs as both (*yisra'el*).

NOTE ON MONETARY UNITS

The main monetary unit in use in the Dutch Republic at the period discussed here was the guilder. One guilder was divided into 20 stivers; 1 stiver (also known as a 'placa' in Spanish and Portuguese or 'plak' in Dutch) was divided into 16 pennies. Thus a sum of money given as 100:6:12 guilders means 100 guilders, 6 stivers and 12 pennies; 9:1 guilders means 9 guilders and 1 stiver.

Some sources give sums of money in Flemish pounds (1 Flemish pound = 6 guilders). These were divided into shillings and pennies (1 shilling = 6 stivers; 1 stiver = 16 pennies). Thus a sum of money given as 858:16:8 Flemish pounds means 858 Flemish pounds, 16 shillings and 8 pennies.

My thanks to Dr Menno S. Polak, Curator Special Collections, University Library of Amsterdam, for explaining to me about monetary units used in early modern Europe.

CHAPTER ONE

SETTING THE SCENE

OUR STORY BEGINS in the towns and villages of Spain and Portugal during the early modern period, as many families and individuals, some after great deliberation, others in great haste, were deciding to leave their homeland to start a new life elsewhere. Their flight marked for them the end of a long period of discrimination, racism, and persecution.

Officially, by the end of the fifteenth century there were no Jews left in the Iberian peninsula. They had been expelled from Spain, from territories under the Crown of Castile and Aragon in 1492 and from the kingdom of Navarre in 1498, and forcibly converted to Catholicism in Portugal in 1497.

Since the pogroms of 1391 Spanish Jews had either gone through a conversion to Catholicism (voluntarily or under duress) or opted to continue living as Jews. The latter experienced periods of calm coexistence and toleration but also hatred and antisemitism. The Spanish expulsion decrees a century later confronted the remaining Jews with an even more harrowing choice: to leave their country of birth as Jews or to stay on at the price of conversion to Catholicism. From that date on, any who remained in Spain had chosen the latter alternative, to gain, in theory at least, equality with other citizens, or had been born into families that had converted earlier; they were known as New Christians or judaeoconversos (henceforth referred to here as Conversos).

The Conversos were discriminated against, not only on religious grounds —on suspicion of secretly adhering to the Jewish faith—but also for a mixture of political and economic reasons and racist prejudice. In their drive to establish a pure Catholic society, various parts of Spain introduced statutes based on the principle of *limpieza de sangre* ('cleanliness of blood'), consigning people with Jewish or Moorish blood and background to an inferior status in Spanish society. These statutes, introduced by the middle of the fifteenth century, institutionalized the distinction between Old and New Christians and tried to prevent the latter from entering various privileged sectors of Spanish society, such as confraternities, guilds, military and religious orders, universities, municipal councils, and governmental positions. The last traces of supposed judaizing tendencies were thought to have been eradicated by the severe persecutions of the Spanish Inquisition, created in 1478, and by the middle of the sixteenth century most New Christians had successfully assimilated into Spanish Catholic society. At this point, however, events took a new turn.

The union of the Spanish and Portuguese crowns in 1580 triggered a massive influx of New Christians into Spain from Portugal. By this time the Spanish Inquisition's attention had shifted from Conversos to Protestants and other heretics, whereas the Portuguese Inquisition, founded in 1536, was still highly and harshly active in persecuting New Christians, the country's former Jews, most of whom had opted to flee to Portugal after the Spanish expulsion decrees. Consequently, in the last years of the sixteenth century New Christians from Portugal, well known for their cohesion and supposed crypto-Jewish activities ever since the forced baptism of their entire community in 1497, moved en masse into Spain to resettle there. Escape from persecution was not their only motive, however, for Spain also offered more attractive economic opportunities, which the new arrivals from Portugal were quick to exploit.

Because of the economic and social success that many of them soon achieved, New Christians from Portugal were regarded with envy by the Old Christian establishment in Spain, while suspicions of crypto-Judaism put the Spanish Inquisition on high alert once more. Renewed accusations were also levelled at Spanish Conversos, many of whom were by now well integrated into society as faithful Catholics, even though some joined the ranks of mystics, sceptics, and atheists, or of those who tried to reform Catholicism from within.

In Spain, the term 'Portuguese' became equivalent to 'judaizer'. Discrimination and fear contributed to the emergence of various terms used to pick them out—'men of the lineage' (*gente de linaje*); those of 'the Portuguese nation' (*la nación portuguesa*) or just 'the nation' (*la nación / a nação*)—while their success in international trade and finance earned them the epithet *homens de negócios*. All these labels were used in an effort to emphasize their inferiority on the basis of their ethnicity and their supposed religious affinity. The harsh persecution of New Christians in Spain and Portugal by the tribunals of the Inquisition in both countries prompted many of them to look for alternative homes. Since well before the expulsion of Jews from Spain, Spanish Jews had been joining Jewish communities in other places or creating new ones. Now many Conversos, both from Spain and from Portugal, followed suit and reverted to Judaism elsewhere; others who fled continued to practise Catholicism once they had settled down in, for example, France or

Antwerp. A Sephardi diaspora came into being, not only in Muslim countries in cities such as Constantinople or Salonika, but also in Christian Europe in cities such as Ferrara and Venice, expanding over time into a worldwide network of settlements, spanning east and west, south and north.[1]

In northern Europe another alternative came into view in the 1580s. Amsterdam, part of the Dutch Republic that had broken free from the grasp of the Spanish Catholic Crown and was embroiled in a fierce war of independence, rapidly developed into an international trading centre and offered all the attractions of a burgeoning economy.[2] Moreover, it was relatively tolerant of dissident views other than those of the privileged Reformed Church.[3] The first Portuguese arrived in Amsterdam at the end of the sixteenth century, and cautiously created out of nothing a Jewish community that quickly became renowned across the world.[4]

The former Conversos, including those of the Portuguese community of early modern Amsterdam, have been called the first modern Jews.[5] As New Christians, they had, despite all the restrictions placed on them, played an active part in Spanish and Portuguese life, absorbing modern European, Iberian, and Catholic cultural norms; in Amsterdam they were able to incorporate these experiences and influences into their newly recovered Jewish character.[6] These Jews of Spanish or Portuguese origin, former Conversos, referred to here for simplicity as Portuguese (as they were also on the peninsula at the time), gained a reputation for immense wealth, elegance, and aristocratic style that commanded respect in their new domicile. It is less widely known that the new immigrants from the Iberian peninsula also included paupers, or that some of the immigrants or their descendants later became impoverished in Amsterdam.

The flight north meant an emotional, a social, and an economic break with the past. Many, in their hurried escape from the Inquisition, were forced to leave their possessions, and worse still their loved ones, behind. Some travelled as family units; others travelled singly or as part of larger mixed groups. Some had been prosperous and were now dependent on charity; others had never known riches, belonging to the lower middle or artisan class. Because of the economic restrictions Amsterdam imposed upon Jews, many were not able to practise their accustomed occupations and as a result were reduced to penury. Women, single or at the head of a nuclear or extended family, were particularly vulnerable, as were orphans, the infirm, and the aged.

Aware of their responsibility for the well-being of their community amid a relatively hospitable people with whom they were anxious to keep on good terms,[7] the Portuguese in Amsterdam built up a welfare system that included provision for displaced persons, and especially paupers, belonging to their 'nation'. However, in the event they had to cope not only with their own compatriots but also with a host of poor migrants from other parts of the contemporary Jewish world, fleeing various combinations of war, persecution, economic depression, and unemployment and lured to Amsterdam by the reputed wealth of the Amsterdam Portuguese.

Terminology: The Definition of Poverty

Any historical study of poor relief inevitably comes up against problems of definition. It rapidly becomes clear from historical research that the concept of 'poverty' does not relate to a universal standard but is applied subjectively, varying with place, time, and social context.[8] In early modern European sources it is rare for paupers to make their own views known; in most cases they have had the epithet 'poor' imposed on them from above. Being 'poor', accordingly, is not merely a reflection of a particular economic status but seems also to be governed by the prevailing social and religious norms of the elite. In this context it is worth mentioning Paul Slack's comment that a perceived increase in poverty in a given society is not always directly due to economic decline but is sometimes the result of the changing conception of what constitutes an acceptable standard of living during periods of relative prosperity.[9]

Caution is therefore necessary in any attempt to compare the degree of poverty in one society with that in another at the same period. When all is said and done, every society applies its own criteria. Moreover, a degree of arbitrariness is unavoidable even if we follow the development of poverty within a single society, if the analysis covers an extended period: for over time, just as the economic order changes, so does the perception of poverty within that society.

When examining poverty and poor relief in the Portuguese Jewish community in early modern Amsterdam, we encounter all these problems and must be correspondingly cautious in our conclusions and comparisons. What was 'poor' for the Portuguese Jews may not be identical with what was 'poor' for German and Polish Jews, or with what was 'poor' in Amsterdam at large. 'Poor' was a label imposed on certain Portuguese and other Jews chiefly by the leaders of the Portuguese Jewish community, who, without any clear definition of what constituted poverty, determined who was eligible for what relief and for how long.

In this study I shall be dealing not only with 'the poor' so defined by the Portuguese community, but also with those who were not eligible for Portuguese communal poor relief. While some poor people received assistance from the Portuguese community, others relied on institutionalized private charities, and others still were supported by relatives and friends. Many people relied on contributions from several sources. Some lived by illicit means (begging, crime, and prostitution).

Nor is this study confined to Jews of Spanish or Portuguese origin, former Conversos who travelled to the Dutch Republic straight from the Iberian peninsula or via a detour through France or Antwerp; mention is also made of those Jews who reached Amsterdam from other parts of the Sephardi diaspora—including North Africa, the Ottoman empire, and Italy—all of whom are referred to here as Sephardi Jews. When I speak of these two groups collectively I often refer to them as Sephardim but mostly use the term 'Portuguese' since it should be borne in mind that the Portuguese Jews of early modern Amsterdam never used the word 'Sephardi' to define themselves. I have also looked at Jews from other 'nations' who appealed to the Portuguese for help, although the German and Polish immigrants who drew poor relief from the Portuguese community will receive only limited attention here as they have been discussed at some length in other studies.[10]

What Precisely Are We Trying to Establish?

I came to the archive material with various questions in mind. We know that the Amsterdam Portuguese community had to shoulder a heavy burden of poverty around the middle of the eighteenth century, and that this problem had also made itself felt at the beginning of the seventeenth century.[11] What happened in the intervening period? What was the cause of the poverty? How many poor people were there, from what backgrounds, and what kind of family units did they live in? How did they manage to survive in Amsterdam? Was the presence of paupers in the midst of the ostensibly wealthy Amsterdam Portuguese community experienced as oppressive by the more prosperous majority? How did the community try to tackle poverty: through expulsion, imprisonment, employment, and/or education, or did it just accept it as an inevitable component of urban life?

Under the influence of humanist thought in the sixteenth century, new ideas on the modernization of poor relief had emerged in many parts of Catholic and Protestant Europe. Their development involved not so much a power struggle between state and Church as a tug of war between coordinated central welfare and private charities. A central welfare agency, as proposed by both Church and secular authorities, would be able to keep better control of a tightly regulated system of poor relief and the necessary financial resources. Towns would have to set a limit on the hitherto uncontrolled influx of migrants in order to ensure their ability to control the behaviour of the poor in their midst. Young paupers were to be prepared for a better future by education and training for useful employment. Anyone capable of working would be put to work, if necessary by force, possibly in workhouses newly set up for that very purpose. To put an end to the swarms of beggars who roamed from country to country in search of the means of subsistence, jeopardizing public order, safety, and hygiene, begging was proscribed, or at most permitted only to those who had no alternative and who were required to obtain special permission.[12]

These new ideas were put into practice in many countries including those of the Iberian peninsula, where, influenced in part by the post-Tridentine Counter-Reformation, Church and state made repeated attempts to centralize, institutionalize, and target appropriate recipients of poor relief.[13] However, these attempts were not always successful and encountered considerable resistance. Old forms of private charity, often organized by independent confraternities, clung obstinately to their independence, opposed the growing interference of state and Church authorities, and strove to maintain their highly individualized form of welfare work.

Welfare in the city of Amsterdam, as in other parts of Europe, was organized along both modern and traditional lines, with a mosaic of different welfare institutions run by various churches, the municipality, guilds, and private initiatives. Travellers from northern Europe visiting Spain and Portugal in the eighteenth century were nevertheless astonished to find a system of poor relief that, though it showed signs of modernization, reflected many more private influences, with a host of confraternities looking after various groups of paupers.[14] Yet had the same travellers also visited the Portuguese community in seventeenth- and eighteenth-century Amsterdam, and in particular looked at the organization of poor relief there, they might well have imagined they were back in the Iberian peninsula. For, in addition to a strictly regulated central system of poor relief, the Portuguese community of Amsterdam also boasted a vast and constantly expanding private welfare sector.

The question then arises how best to characterize the organization of poor relief in the Portuguese community of early modern Amsterdam. Was it specifically Jewish, or was it substantially shaped by Iberian and Catholic influences? Did the organization of welfare reflect modernizing tendencies of the kind that were beginning to make themselves felt in the contemporary non-Jewish world? How did the Portuguese community react to the rise of private charitable initiatives among its members? Was the tension between the two currents unique to the Amsterdam Portuguese community or could the same pattern, with the same intensity, also be discerned in the wider world?

The Amsterdam Portuguese community was renowned in the contemporary Jewish world for its wealth and generosity. Was this a myth or a reality? Were its resources always adequate, or was there any point at which the financial system broke down as it became unable to cope with increasing expenditure on welfare? What were its preferences and priorities in spending on welfare?

A variety of motives prompted people to charitable behaviour. Could the concepts of mutual responsibility and social concern compete with the desire to keep the poor at arm's length and under control? Was charity given to protect the honour of the family or of the 'nation', or was it, rather, a way of enhancing the personal prestige of the benefactor? And to what extent did charitable giving spring from entrenched religious conviction? If charity and religion were indeed closely intertwined in the early modern period, was the urge towards supporting the poor mainly fed by deep-rooted Catholic impulses of *caritas*, or did the Portuguese Jews of Amsterdam act primarily in accordance with Jewish tradition and under the influence of the spiritual and religious currents informing contemporary Judaism?

The Iberian society the departing Conversos left behind them carried pride, honour, and shame high on its banner, was markedly hierarchical, and, as 'purely' Catholic, felt exclusive and superior to dissidents; it kept a strict guard on religious observance, assigned a modest place to women, and had an aversion to menial work.[15] Can we detect similar patterns in the Portuguese community of early modern Amsterdam, especially in respect of the position of paupers and the organization of poor relief?

Paupers were not only found within the ranks of the Portuguese community; there was also a category of poor Jews that operated with a marginal, if any, connection to organized communal life. How large was this marginal group, and to what extent did it resemble the insiders? To what extent did deviant behaviour inside and outside the Portuguese community constitute an obstacle to its stability?

The economic restrictions imposed on Jews in early modern Amsterdam presented many obstacles to them in the labour market. Notwithstanding this handicap, only a relatively small number of Jewish paupers joined the Reformed Church in this period. Was the open avowal of Judaism by the newly arrived Portuguese paupers by and large religiously motivated, or was it largely a consequence of the support offered by the Portuguese community in the form of employment, help during crises, and social comforts, so that socio-economic factors played an important role in winning the newcomers over to Judaism or keeping them loyal to it?

The Jews were dependent on the goodwill of the city governors for permission to remain in the city. Did the municipal authorities impose any conditions when it came to the reception and care of Jewish paupers? Did they erect obstacles to their entry? Was there any attempt to control the influx, and if so, on whose initiative was it made?

Finally, we shall try to put ourselves in the paupers' shoes in order to visualize their everyday life. Was the life of the poor in the Portuguese community of Amsterdam unique in early modern Europe, or did it follow roughly the same pattern that could be found in the world around it? We shall take glimpses inside their dwellings and try, through the few records at our disposal, to follow them at home, at work, in and around the synagogue, upon their arrival and departure, in joy and in sorrow. What sort of people were Sephardi paupers? Were they the rogues and beggars outside the synagogue portrayed by Rembrandt? Or were they, on the other hand, decent people who had been reduced to poverty by adverse circumstances but who had once enjoyed a higher social standing? Or do they defy any overall characterization, representing a broad spectrum of different types?

It is difficult for us to imagine how the poor must have felt upon arrival in what was for them the cold far north. We do not know a great deal about their doubts, their successes, their frustrations, and their sorrows, but they cannot have had an easy time of it, although they rarely gave voice to their qualms. Inevitably, the voices of the more prosperous among the Amsterdam Portuguese speak more strongly through the historical record. I shall try all the same not to let the poor be heard only indirectly through the medium of the upper social stratum, but to allow them to speak for themselves.

Sources

It is not easy—indeed, it is almost impossible—to make the direct acquaintance, as it were, of paupers in the Portuguese community of early modern Amsterdam. Most of the information about them comes to us at second hand. The details of their lives recorded by the officers of the Portuguese community and of the various charitable institutions give us information from the viewpoint of the benefactors and not of the recipients of their largesse. Rabbis would often make references in their sermons and writings to the lot of the poor in the abstract; those who did speak and write of the actual situation of poor people in their community did so chiefly to encourage charitable behaviour among their flocks. I have come across only a few responsa that shed a clear light on the daily life of paupers in the Portuguese Jewish community of the early modern era. Other Portuguese Jewish writers, too, treat charity for the most part as an abstract concept: they may exalt or criticize the benefactors, but do not often examine the position of the poor themselves. Their writings contain hardly any details about everyday life.

The non-Jewish archives present many of the same problems, especially in the testimony of prisoners recorded by clerks in the Confession Books.[16] It is, of course, open to question whether the prisoners were telling the truth. Last wills and testaments also refer to the poor, but are in most cases not written or dictated by paupers. Likewise, in the archives of the Desolate Boedelskamer, the Insolvent Estates Office, we hear the voices of bankrupt individuals only indirectly.[17]

With these limitations borne in mind, use has been made of the following sources. First, the archives of the Portuguese community in Amsterdam contain a wide range of source material.[18] Sources covering the years before 1639 are incomplete, including those relating to the three separate Portuguese congregations of Bet Jacob, Neve Salom, and Bet Israel.[19] Even so, we can already discern the basis of the welfare structure that was built up after the unification of the three in 1639. Our sources outside the congregational records, and above all the *imposta* records (1622–39), provide us with an insight into migratory movements during this early period. The Resolution Books of the united community Talmud Torah after 1639, the so-called *Livros de escamot*, also contain a great deal of information about paupers and the organizations concerned with them. More details are often to be found in the Memorial Books, the so-called *Memorial de advertencias* and the *Livro de memorias*.[20] In addition, the financial records afford us a glimpse of the bookkeeping system of the Portuguese community, including the tax registers and the cash and poor-relief books (journals, *livros grandes, livros longos,* and *livros longos de cuatro contas*). The *livros longos* in particular, which survive from 1663 onwards, are filled with notes about special payments to paupers and help us to follow the ups and downs in claims by poor Portuguese on relief from the community, at least if we have the patience to go through all the lists and notices published year after year. However, even here the details are sparse, giving no more than the place of origin or destination, occupation, activity in Amsterdam, status, and the like of the beneficiaries. Occasionally, though, one gets a glimpse of the reality behind the records: as I turned the pages,

I sometimes came across the scraps of paper on which the paupers wrote their requests for help.

The *livros longos* also contain information on the education offered to the poor, which supplements that to be found in the archives of the Talmud Torah school and the Ets Haim yeshiva.

Welfare arrangements are also mentioned in correspondence between the Portuguese community of Amsterdam and the wider Jewish and non-Jewish world, both within the city and beyond. Some of this correspondence consists of petitions addressed to the city administration, but it also hints at the existence of an international welfare network.

Social assistance is mentioned in the archives of the various private charitable institutions, such as Dotar, Honen Dalim, and Temime Darech (established in the seventeenth century), and Maasim Tobim, Hase Amaharacha, and Meil Sedaca (established in the eighteenth century). The training of orphan boys for entry into the professions is mentioned in the incomplete archive of Aby Jetomim. Writers and historiographers such as Daniel Levi de Barrios and David Franco Mendes provide us with information on this topic that would not otherwise have survived.[21]

I continued my research with the study of letters and diaries written by Portuguese Jews and of other personal documents, educational works, political tractates, ethical bequests, and travel accounts. One occasionally comes across personal records (diaries and letters) written by paupers, but these are very few and far between: for example, we have one extant travel report from a refugee, and a series of letters from a prisoner of war in a camp outside Belgrade who was anxious to find a safe refuge. We can also hear the poor themselves speak in petitions, although the wording is usually influenced by the formal tone in which they had to be written.

Finally, registers of births, circumcision books, *ketubot* (marriage contracts), and burial records afford us telling glimpses of the experiences of paupers in the Portuguese community of early modern Amsterdam over the whole course of their lives.

Non-Jewish archives are sometimes fuller than the Portuguese records. For example, the Dutch Reformed Church in Amsterdam would discuss new candidates for membership, including Jews, at some length. A search of the archives of the Reformed Church and those of the various guilds and other organizations also enabled me to compare the poor relief provided by those institutions with that offered by the Portuguese community.

The Confession Books go into the background of people in custody in some detail. Unfortunately—for research purposes, that is!—very few Sephardi Jews seem to have been imprisoned for criminal activity. The same is true of the archives of the workhouses and houses of correction, that is, of the Spinhuis (spinning house), the Rasphuis (where inmates were put to rasping wood for use in the dyeing industry), and the Werkhuis (workhouse): here too we find only a few Sephardim.

The city tax records mainly concern the more well-to-do. The *ondertrouw* registers—that is, the registers of intended marriage that all those who were not members of the Reformed Church had to sign in Amsterdam—also afford us details about the occupation, country or town of origin, age, and Amsterdam address of paupers. On top of this basic information, they help to reveal patterns in marriage. In the Desolate Boedelskamer we are afforded glimpses of the household effects of bankrupts in detail. The Notarial Archives, finally, contain a variety of disparate information. Here we can study the wills from which, among other things, we are able to learn about the attitude of more fortunate Portuguese to the poor and to charity. We also find a philanthropic outlook in other sources in these archives: agreements between Portuguese and ships' captains show the extent to which the Portuguese community was anxious to bring fugitives in distress, especially those from the Iberian peninsula, to Amsterdam; from commercial contracts we learn about the joint economic activities of husbands and wives, including paupers; articles of apprenticeship cast light on contracts between Portuguese youths and their masters and on the attempts by the Portuguese Jews, particularly through the Aby Jetomim confraternity, to safeguard the future of orphan boys by training them to enter trades and professions.

The last piece in the jigsaw from which we can assemble our picture of poverty among the Portuguese community of early modern Amsterdam is contemporary historiography concerning the city.

With the help of all these sources I tackle my subject as follows. Chapter 2 deals with the arrival in and departure from Amsterdam of poor migrants and the underlying reasons for their movements, examines the admissions policy of the Amsterdam Portuguese community, and casts light on the city's role as a transit port. Chapter 3 examines the structure of the Portuguese community of early modern Amsterdam in respect of numbers, sex, family composition, and financial viability. It attempts to put a figure on the extent of poverty and its development over time. Chapter 4 looks at the organization of poor relief along both centrally controlled and private lines, and tries to establish what cultural patterns were reflected in the structure of Portuguese welfare provision. Chapter 5 examines the financial resources enabling the Portuguese community to make adequate provision for poor relief. Why they chose to do so is the central question addressed in Chapter 6: the motives examined range from a sense of civic responsibility to religious impulses, and from a feeling of concern for others' well-being to a desire to protect a family's reputation or enhance the benefactor's personal prestige. Chapter 7 shows us paupers in their everyday setting, highlighting various aspects of their daily lives. The Epilogue (Chapter 8) attempts to define the most important characteristics of poverty and welfare among the Portuguese community of early modern Amsterdam.

CHAPTER TWO

MIGRATION OF THE POOR

Introduction

The early modern period saw thousands of people, Jews among them, emigrate from their home countries and travel in search of a new life. Some were forced to leave by war, persecution, or economic difficulties; others were attracted by the work made available by new state or mercantile policies. Thus in the pre-industrial era an influx of migrants swelled the populations of many European cities.[1]

Amsterdam was a very desirable destination for these travellers: during the Dutch Golden Age, a period running from the last decades of the sixteenth century up to the end of the seventeenth,[2] the city made a great impression on newcomers,[3] opening its doors wide in an effort to satisfy an urgent need for manpower, not only on the local labour market but also in its army, on the ships of its naval and commercial fleets, and in its overseas territories.[4] For Jews in particular, Amsterdam was more attractive than other European cities. As early as 1627 Haham Saul Levi Morteira confronted his Amsterdam *kahal* with its privileged position and put it in a global perspective:

> Where are the taxes of Venice? The censorship of books that exists throughout Italy? The seizing of children for forced conversions? The sign of the [Jewish] hat? The ghettos? The need to request permission [to remain]? Being shut away at the evil time [Holy Week]? Where is the derision shown towards Jews in Rome, [forced to] go out naked on their holidays, forced to attend their [Christian] services, forced to bow down to the Pope? Where are the blood libels of Poland? Where are the humiliations of Germany? Where are the hours when they prevent us from attending the [commercial] fairs? The entrances through which we may not walk, the wells from which we may not drink? Where is the harsh oppression of Turkey? The poll tax that is levied there? The cruelty of the gentiles? The fire thrown into houses? The deadly tortures connected with the manufacturing of their clothes? Where is the degradation of Barbary? Where is the youngster who will strike an old man? Where are the animal carcases which they compel us to remove from their paths? And much more of the same, that our brothers, the entire house of Israel, suffer throughout their dispersion in exile. But God has brought us out from there.[5]

The leaders of the Portuguese communities of Amsterdam echoed his point in commenting in 1630 on their newly acquired settlement in Amsterdam: 'We are enjoying here more freedom than elsewhere in the Jewish world and must not endanger this place of refuge.'[6]

In principle everyone, Jews included, had free access to Amsterdam—the city turned no one away. Nor did it impose special taxes on Jews of the kind applied in other parts of Europe, threaten them with expulsion, or hamper them with other restrictions, such as a *numerus fixus*. Against this background, the Amsterdam Jewish community was in no position to proclaim a *ḥerem hayishuv* (ban on settlement), forbidding or limiting access to the community. Jews were free to come and go in Amsterdam as they pleased, and they did so. Outside the city, however, restrictions on Jewish residence were the normal practice, with no Jew being able to count on automatic access to, or permission to settle permanently in, a number of Dutch towns. So, for Jews, Amsterdam compared very favourably with the rest of the Dutch Republic and with Europe as a whole.[7]

The city's tolerant immigration policy carried a number of risks, the most obvious of which was that it would be burdened with a large influx of paupers. However, the city seemed undeterred by this, or indeed by the possibility that, in attracting the manpower it needed, it might well also encourage immigrants, their wives, and their children to become dependent upon the local poor-relief agencies. The city did, however, take a few preventive measures from the last decades of the sixteenth century onwards. For example, undesirable elements were banned from the city, and the authorities laid down that all immigrants must have resided in Amsterdam for a specified period before they could claim poor relief from the city or from the Reformed Charity Board. Over time, eligibility for poor relief was made conditional on increasingly long periods of residence, along with more and more stringent restrictions of other kinds.[8]

In fact, all religious groups in the city were expected to take care of their own poor to the best of their ability.[9] Jews in particular had to rely exclusively on their own poor-relief provisions.[10] This condition was clearly stipulated, for instance, when the city approved the by-laws of the Amsterdam Portuguese Jewish congregation in 1670.[11] On that occasion, the city fathers made their approval dependent on the agreement of the Portuguese congregation not to have its poor rely on municipal charity:

> As early as 1638 it was deemed necessary to enter into an accord by which all members of the Jewish Portuguese and Spanish nation undertook to maintain and frequent a church or Synagogue and jointly to support the poor of the Nation . . . and to ensure that their Poor did not become a burden upon the public Purse.[12]

The same rules applied to Ashkenazi (German and Polish) Jews. The first condition the city laid down before agreeing to the merging of the German and Polish congregations in Amsterdam in 1673 was that the congregation about to be formed would 'support their poor regularly Week by Week'.[13]

To refute the charge that its poor would become too great a burden on those among whom they lived, the Portuguese congregation made continual efforts to convince the city of Amsterdam and the States of Holland and West Friesland of its good intentions. Thus they assured the States of Holland and West Friesland in 1693 that 'they had been instructing applicants for poor relief belonging to their Congregation for several Years past, and were continuing to instruct them, to resort exclusively to the Almshouses of their own aforesaid Nation, without any other Almshouse or Magistrate being troubled or involved in the matter'.[14] In the mid-eighteenth century the Portuguese congregation was still assuring the city governors of Amsterdam that 'poor and impecunious Jews, who in our Portuguese congregation make up twice as many family members as the rich, will be maintained and not allowed to become a charge upon the city'.[15]

The city fathers intervened as little as possible in the internal affairs of any tolerated religious denomination. Thus they allowed the Jewish community to wield full authority over its members in settling internal conflicts, running its religious life as it saw fit, and solemnizing marriages following civil registration.[16] When the city did intervene, it was usually on invitation from the Jewish community rather than on its own initiative, although there were some exceptions.[17]

Having said this, the city viewed the Jewish community as a voluntary religious organization, whose authority extended only over its internal affairs: for the rest, Amsterdam Jewry was subject to the laws of the city, the States of Holland and West Friesland and the Republic. Any Jews who broke one of these would be brought before the Amsterdam bench, as confirmed in article 45 of the 1639 unification statutes of the Portuguese Jewish community, which stated explicitly that Jews who fell foul of the public law by engaging in criminal activities could count on no further help from the Portuguese community and must serve their sentences in accordance with the verdict of the courts.[18]

In general, the Portuguese community watched over the conduct of its members and tried to keep them out of the courts.[19] Indeed, it tried to keep on the right side of the municipality in general, seeing this as a prerequisite of the continued existence of its *kehilah*. Apprehension that its very survival was conditional on its perceived good behaviour continued to be voiced up to the eighteenth century, as can be deduced from the wording of a message from the community leaders in 1717: 'The members of the Mahamad would like to stress how important it is in safeguarding our position to avoid complaints and scandals, lest our neighbours come to hate us or make us appear in an unfavourable light. For it is by Divine grace and the good will of the Gentlemen of the government that our presence here is tolerated.'[20] Maintaining law and order was thus one of the chief tasks of the Portuguese community leaders;[21] and one of the means by which they did this was to limit the influx of poor Jews.

The Amsterdam Portuguese *kahal* as a whole was a migrant community *par excellence*. It was largely built on the reception and absorption of immigrants from the Iberian peninsula, but these members of the Spanish and Portuguese nation soon came into contact with newcomers from various parts of the contemporary Jewish world. Some of these were also Sephardim, from North Africa, Italy, and the Ottoman empire, but others were Ashkenazi Jews—from the German states, Poland, central Europe (the *tudescos* and *polacos*), and again from Italy—many of whom also came flocking to Amsterdam. In addition, the city attracted many Italian Jews (*italianos*) in addition to others from the Levant (*levantinos*) and North Africa (*berberiscos*). All of them, for different reasons, were drawn towards Amsterdam.

Evolving Policy on Admission and Relief of the Poor

The entitlement of Jewish paupers to relief from the Portuguese community was never a straightforward matter, and it exercised hearts and minds for two centuries. The lament of Isaac de Pinto, treasurer of the Portuguese congregation in the middle of the eighteenth century, is well known and often quoted: 'Why are we obliged to support the weak from all over the world . . . what would happen if the doors were opened here in Amsterdam to poor Protestants from Europe, Africa and Asia? Would that act, though apparently a charitable one, not seem ridiculous, ruinous and even impossible?'[22] The surviving records of the three Portuguese congregations of Bet Jacob, Neve Salom, and Bet Israel indicate that they were already having to cope with an influx of poor from outside the Iberian countries well before their unification in 1639. The main concern at this time was the provision of grants for maintenance and onward travel. The beneficiaries are rarely identified by both forename and surname—'Jacob Coen and Simao Levy, passers-by' are among the few exceptions.[23] Sometimes there are notes that tell us a little more about an individual's country or place of origin: for example, the records mention 'Jacob de Italia, foreigner', 'a foreigner from Salonika', 'a Venetian woman', and 'another Berber', as well as referring more generally to *tudescos*, *polacos, italianos, levantinos*, or *berberiscos*. Often the notes are even less specific, simply referring to *forasteiros* or *passageiros*.[24]

Unfortunately, we have no records from the early life of the Portuguese congregations—that is, from before 1622—of political decisions regarding the admission of Jews from different parts of the world and their access to welfare. What is clear is that during that year these congregations were hard pressed to look after their poor. A co-ordinating body was therefore set up for the purpose, and the statutes it drew up in 1622 show that all three congregations were unhappy about the unrestricted admission of Jews from all corners of the world—especially when they were poor into the bargain. Coping with so many paupers was well beyond their financial capacity. The resumption of conflict between the Dutch Republic and Spain following the expiry of the Twelve Years' Truce in 1621, and the consequent departure of wealthy Portuguese to other trading centres such as Hamburg and Glückstadt,[25] forced the Amsterdam Portuguese to take special measures for dealing with paupers. It is to this turn of events, together with an outbreak of plague in the 1620s, to which Haham Saul Levi Morteira referred in his sermon of 1627, when he lamented: 'Still we have not learned! Even today we are worse than our ancestors. Did we not see during the good days that confronted us in this city how many conflicts occurred and how many bans were enacted until war and loss of money and pestilence came, Heaven protect us!'[26]

On the basis of the 1622 resolution, many paupers belonging to the Spanish and Portuguese nation who had already settled in Amsterdam were compelled to move to other Jewish centres. The consequent exodus was financed by a newly founded tax levied by the community on import and exports, the so-called *imposta*.[27] Newcomers to the city could count on assistance only if they had arrived direct from the Iberian peninsula. Anyone reaching Amsterdam by means of a detour had to seek shelter elsewhere. This excluded not only potential migrants from Jewish centres but also the destitute who, having just fled from Spain and Portugal to southern France, were planning to proceed to Amsterdam.[28]

These restrictions barring migrants from countries other than Spain and Portugal appear to have been ineffective.[29] During the following years the Portuguese community was faced with increasing numbers of Jews arriving from other regions, and especially with a constant and swelling flood of German Jews—though these Ashkenazim received only limited help from the Portuguese congregation, and attempts were made to direct most of them elsewhere immediately upon arrival.[30] In 1629 the rule that a Portuguese could claim poor relief only if he reached Amsterdam from the Iberian peninsula without any intermediate stopovers was officially relaxed.[31] During the war between Spain and the Republic it was, after all, difficult to travel straight to Amsterdam, and the route to the Low Countries often took a detour, for instance through France.

The Amsterdam Portuguese did not turn their backs on newcomers, then, although it is apparent that the thought crossed their minds quite often, and various precautionary measures were taken over the years. In this respect the 1639 unification statutes by which the three congregations were merged into one constituted an extension of the 1622 regulations governing the admission of migrants. On paper, the Portuguese congregation proclaimed its solidarity with all Jews able to prove Spanish or Portuguese descent, without geographical distinction. In respect of Jews from other nations, a more cautious line was taken. Article 3 of the unification statutes noted 'that this congregation is reserved for Jews of the Portuguese and Spanish nation now living in this city or coming here anew, and that Jewish persons coming here from whatever other nations may also be admitted provided the serving Mahamad sees fit to do so'.[32] This article had clearly been the subject of careful thought. The newly created congregation was deliberately leaving its policy towards non-Sephardim vague. The discretion thus provided for applied first and foremost to Ashkenazi Jews, who had admittedly founded their own congregation in 1635 but still relied largely on help from the Portuguese. The support of poor Ashkenazim continued to rest in part on the shoulders of the Amsterdam Portuguese community until 1670.

As Chapter 5 will show in greater detail, the attitude of the Portuguese to migrants was always—and increasingly—dictated by their own financial strength. As long as the money was there, the influx of poor foreigners was tolerated. Thus, towards the end of the 1640s and during the 1650s, the Portuguese community not only helped to take in destitute Portuguese after the loss of Dutch Brazil, but also admitted Polish Jews escaping from war in eastern Europe.[33]

Yet, as so often happens in both Jewish history and that of the non-Jewish world, 'foreigners' were always treated differently.[34] Gradually the Portuguese congregation found its hands so full with Sephardi paupers that it stopped giving assistance to all other groups. Every year until 1672, and again from the 1690s to the 1730s, the officers of the Amsterdam Portuguese congregation, like those in southern France and London, kept a separate account of assistance rendered to *forasteiros* (further identifying, between 1666 and 1672, payments given to *tudescos*). Such help was often given just once, and was generally intended to move the new arrivals out of Amsterdam immediately.[35] As early as 1660 the Ets Haim yeshiva let it be known that it would henceforth be unable to admit *italianos, tudescos,* or *polacos.*[36] From 1670 the Abodat Ahesed organization ceased to give assistance to Ashkenazi Jews.[37] And in 1697 a new restriction was introduced, for it had been noted that 'many Jewish persons come to this city simply because of the rumour that they will receive assistance from our community . . . which is to the disadvantage of the poor of the Portuguese and Spanish nation'.[38] Making use of the leeway accorded the congregation's leaders by Article 3 of the unification statutes, it was decided to debar Jews of other nations from drawing communal poor relief in order to protect the community's capacity to continue offering assistance to the poor of the Portuguese and Spanish nation.[39]

That capacity was already under strain. Many Portuguese who had been driven from southern France following the 1684 expulsion edict there had arrived in Amsterdam seeking poor relief;[40] Sephardi refugees were pouring in from the Balkans;[41] and a new wave of immigration from the Iberian peninsula was under way.[42] Time and again it became clear that the barrier erected against the tide of poor Jewish immigration was not impermeable. New regulations had constantly to be passed to patch the gaps. Thus it was decided in 1723 that no *tudesco* or *italiano* vagrant could thenceforth be added to the list of *sedaca* beneficiaries.[43]

Eventually, in the mid-eighteenth century the community's disastrous financial situation forced it to depart from Article 3 of the unification statutes stipulating unlimited assistance to all members of the Spanish–Portuguese nation. In a sense, this meant going back to the *imposta* statutes of 1622 with their explicit statement that assistance could be rendered only to paupers who had come directly to Amsterdam from the Iberian peninsula. Solidarity with victims of the Inquisition was explicitly reaffirmed. The restrictions on relief payments went further still: now 'foreigners', except for those coming from Spain and Portugal, would not be eligible for welfare until they had resided in the city for at least six years without being listed on the communal charity lists during that period.[44]

There was nothing unusual about these measures. In fact, in adopting them the Portuguese were only catching up with other community authorities. The city of Amsterdam and the Reformed Church there had been imposing similar restrictions since the 1630s.[45] Even the Ashkenazi community had set a six-year residence qualification as early as 1737, some time before the Portuguese did so.[46] In other European countries, too, both Christian and Jewish communities took a stricter line against poor people wishing to settle and claim welfare payments: the Portuguese community of France, for example, frequently co-operated with the authorities, giving them lists of poor people to facilitate their removal, and even sometimes asking them to act on their behalf to expel fellow Portuguese.

Despite all their good intentions and successive attempts at regulation, then, the Amsterdam Portuguese *kahal* struggled to cope with the growing influx of Jewish refugees arriving in greater numbers than they had anticipated. It was only in the middle of the eighteenth century that they finally reached a solution to the problem in stricter limits on admission.

Where Did the Poor Come From?

In his analysis of the places of origin of Sephardim who settled in Amsterdam in the seventeenth century, Daniel Swetschinski relied on data from the *ondertrouw* registers of the city of Amsterdam, in which all those wishing to marry who were not members of the privileged Reformed Church were required to declare this intention.[47] While bearing in mind the limitations of this source, Swetschinski concluded that the majority of Sephardim who had settled and married in Amsterdam had a Converso background, and had come from Catholic centres in the Spanish and Portuguese empires. His conclusion does not apply, however, if we focus on those people who do not figure in the Amsterdam *ondertrouw* registers and who were granted assistance by the Amsterdam Portuguese community on at least one occasion.[48] These include not only individuals who took up permanent residence in Amsterdam; transients, inasmuch as their place of origin is known, are also covered. Some of these arrived in the city as married couples; others simply solemnized their marriage in a Jewish wedding ceremony;[49] yet others did not marry in Amsterdam at all. We can find all these in the so-called 'long books' or *livros longos* which, from 1663, afford us a better picture of migration as they record more carefully where a newcomer had arrived from at the time when he applied for poor relief from the Amsterdam Portuguese *kahal*.[50]

However, even this additional material does not give us a complete picture. Sources covering the early period, that is, from the turn of the century to 1639, are incomplete. Our research into migration during that period is based on the account books of the three separate congregations and those of the co-ordinating *imposta* authority. These record the arrival and departure of migrants, but information for many years is missing. From 1639 to 1662, as well, the sources fail to provide full information about migration, and we have to make do with occasional notes in the account books. The 'long books' provide a careful record of the arrival of newcomers, but give no supplementary information about people on poor relief already resident in Amsterdam. An additional problem is the fact that some individuals are not always referred to by the same name, or are not referred to by name at all but described only as 'foreigners' or 'transients', with no information on their place of origin. It is also difficult to determine exactly how many genuine Italian Jews drawing money from the community coffers in Amsterdam are covered by the term *italianos*. Similarly, no number can be put to an entry such as 'gente vindo de Bordeos' ('people coming from Bordeaux'). Newcomers supported by private charities have to be left entirely out of account, since no information is supplied on them. From 1700 the picture is even less clear, for the scribes at that time were apparently reluctant to register most newcomers' place of origin, with the exception of those coming from the Iberian peninsula. Yet, even though we are left in ignorance about the country of origin of hundreds of families on poor relief, we can make a reasonable approximation of some figures, especially for the seventeenth century. For this period we can list more than 1,210 families—representing almost as many people as those investigated by Swetschinski[51]—the majority of whom are not from Catholic centres in the Spanish and Portuguese empires.

The extent to which the Portuguese community of Amsterdam attracted migrants is remarkable. The percentage of migrants on poor relief from Jewish centres such as Italy, North Africa, south-eastern Europe, and the Levant (including Erets Yisra'el), increased from around 50 per cent of the total at the beginning of the seventeenth century to about 69 per cent at the end.[52] On average, only 27 per cent of newcomers in the seventeenth century who drew poor relief from the Amsterdam Portuguese congregation(s) and who are not mentioned in the *ondertrouw* registers came to Amsterdam straight from the Iberian peninsula or through France or Antwerp (inasmuch as their place of origin is known). That is a much lower figure than the 71.7 per cent of those who appear in the *ondertrouw* registers.

The new data presented here provide a corrective to our picture of the migration of Jews and Conversos to the Portuguese community of early modern Amsterdam. In addition to people who were able to settle in Amsterdam more or less permanently, the city's Portuguese community included a large number of migrants for whom Amsterdam was, by choice or by necessity, no more than a temporary stopping place.

Wherever they came from, one thing all these migrants had in common was that they had left their country of origin in search of a better life, and had chosen Amsterdam as their temporary or permanent destination. Here many of them became, whether immediately on their arrival or at a later stage, dependent on relief from the Portuguese community. I shall now try to reconstruct how these people fared on their way to Amsterdam.

The Journey to Amsterdam from the Iberian Peninsula

Details of the ordeals that the Portuguese on the Amsterdam *sedaca* list had suffered in the Iberian peninsula or en route were rarely reported in writing, let alone recorded at length in the minutes of the Portuguese community. For the most part, we must content ourselves with brief notes and allow our imagination to do the rest.[53] Occasionally the administrator of the Portuguese community recorded, in addition to the name and perhaps place of origin, such details as the fact that two (named) Jews from North Africa had 'escaped from the Inquisition in Lisbon'.[54] In one case, the words 'da Inquisisao' were added to the name Meir Uziel to differentiate him from another individual with the same name who came from Izmir. The first therefore must have fled the Inquisition on the peninsula.[55] Elsewhere, we learn that 26-year-old Diego Hendriques Pina from Oporto arrived in Amsterdam after having been expelled by the Inquisition.[56] In yet another record we glimpse the ordeal of the orphan girls Debora and Rachel Nunez Bernal as they explain that they, 16 and 14 years old, are the daughters of Abraham Nunez Bernal 'who [in Córdoba in 1655] was burnt alive because of his sanctification of God's name'.[57]

The decision to flee was often made in great haste, and it was not always possible for those escaping to take with them whatever money or property they had—if any: in many cases the Inquisition had confiscated their possessions. Others tried to get their money out of the country, sometimes successfully, using the dense networks of family, friendship, and trade that linked the Iberian peninsula with centres in the Sephardi diaspora: Lucia da Fonseca, who arrived in Amsterdam after four years in prison in Coimbra, found that although her husband had in the meantime died in St-Jean-de-Luz, at least her money was safe in the Amsterdam Bank of Exchange, her family having secured her assets.[58]

In 1622 an informer notified the Inquisition that an estimated 100,000 New Christians (the figure is probably exaggerated) had fled the peninsula with their families and households, heading for Italy, Flanders, France, Holland, and other destinations.[59] Not all set out with the intention of moving so far from their old homes. The travels of many took a fitful course, sometimes with periods of settlement in places that turned out to provide no more than temporary refuge. Of those who left by boat, some found themselves diverted against their will: in 1684, for example, Isabel Maria was at sea heading for Bordeaux, having set out from Lisbon with her husband and three children, 'all of them members of our nation', when they were captured by privateers and carried off to Algiers.[60] Those who chose overland routes also attracted unwelcome attention. On various occasions the Spanish authorities voiced their alarm about the large number of New Christians who, with all their goods and chattels, travelling in carriages or on foot, were trying to reach France through northern Spain; the fugitives often hired guides to help them get to and across the Spanish–French border.[61]

Information about which routes to take and where to stay on the journey may well have been given by word of mouth. We do not know of any itineraries written in Portuguese or Spanish to advise travellers on where to look for support en route, such as existed in Yiddish for Ashkenazi Jews fleeing central and eastern Europe.[62] We do, however, have some information on individual cases. For example, some, such as João Pinto Delgado, wrote down the routes they took.[63] The autobiography of the wealthy de Pinto family records their experiences of fleeing Portugal and travelling to the Dutch Republic, including the route they took and the time they spent living in Antwerp on the way.[64] Others gave information on routes, passages, help received on the way, and chosen destinations in letters. However, for most of the poorer refugees, details of the journey have to be reconstructed from brief notes.

Most poor refugees from the peninsula seem to have travelled in larger groups, a common feature of migration at this time.[65] Time and again the sources record the arrival of large extended families, such as the Peres family in the early decades of the seventeenth century,[66] the 'three poor families from Portugal' in 1719,[67] an unnamed family of nine fleeing the peninsula in 1736,[68] and several families coming from Portugal in 1745.[69]

Some children were related to the adults accompanying them, some were not. One widow arrived from France bringing the Rocha children with her.[70] In 1685 Sara Vaz came from Vila Flor with her granddaughter.[71] Leonarda Nunes took 'a young daughter called Gana', born 'to Christian parents' from Spain 'over here', and 'brought her to Judaism'.[72] David Nunes de Mercado arrived escorting an orphan girl, who had ended up in Prague.[73]

Many also arrived alone in the city, like the widow Ester de Pas arriving from Mogadouro or the 'man from Lisbon'.[74] Patterns of chain migration, an age-old and continuing phenomenon, are also apparent.[75] Sometimes a husband travelled ahead on his own, leaving his wife and any children to follow later. In 1658, for example, Bartholomeus Rodrigues Henriques declared that he had arrived in Amsterdam from Madrid two weeks previously, bringing his son with him but leaving his wife and family in Spain to pack up the household before coming on to join them.[76] Similarly, Bernaldo Lopes, alias Daniel Israel, arrived from St-Jean-de-Luz, having travelled ahead to see how the land lay before bringing his wife and daughters to join him.[77]

Alone or in groups, then, loaded with memories, disoriented and sad, many poor people from the peninsula headed north. On the horizon lay Amsterdam.

The Route: From Portugal, from Spain, and from France to Amsterdam

Direct migration from Portugal to the Low Countries was a constant, if variable, phenomenon between the late sixteenth and mid-eighteenth centuries. The first wave took place between 1580, when Portugal was united with Spain, and the 1640s, at a time when the depredations of the Inquisition in Portugal were at their height and as a result many Conversos fled in search of refuge elsewhere. Economic crises in Portugal at the end of the sixteenth century acted as a further spur to emigration.[78] This became easier when Philip III and Philip IV granted New Christians greater freedom of movement between 1601 and 1610 and again in 1628. Earlier prohibited from moving abroad, so that any who did leave had to do so secretly, they were now allowed to depart for the Spanish and Portuguese colonies (and also for Spain itself, though onward travel to France and the Low Countries was restricted) and to sell their property.[79] Moreover, during the reigns of Philip III and Philip IV victims of the Inquisition were pardoned in 1605, 1627, and 1630. Many prisoners who were released made straight for Amsterdam or other places of refuge.[80] After Portugal shook off Spanish domination in 1640, Portuguese ports were intermittently opened up to Dutch ships, facilitating the movement of Conversos to Amsterdam.[81]

In the latter part of the seventeenth century and the first half of the eighteenth migration from Portugal to Amsterdam continued in response to renewed and intensified persecution by the Portuguese Inquisition.[82] After 1700 destitute families arriving directly from Portugal appear regularly in the records in Amsterdam. In fact, at that time, in a return to the situation prevailing before 1640, more immigrants tended to come from Portugal than from Spain. Around 1700 alone, more than 48 'poor' from Portugal made it to Amsterdam.[83]

Not everyone travelled directly from Portugal to Amsterdam. Many crossed first into Spain, either by sea or over land.[84] Poor New Christians, just like their more fortunate brethren, would have wished to escape persecution by the Portuguese Inquisition and settle in neighbouring Spain where, as mentioned earlier, the persecution of New Christians seemed to have ceased.[85] Spain was, after all, the closest destination to Portugal, socially and culturally as well as geographically, and the country offered good economic prospects. With the rise of the New Christian merchant houses in Spain, many poor among the *nação* in Portugal, isolated and without means, moved to Spain in the expectation of getting help from their wealthier fellows there.[86]

In the second half of the seventeenth century, the numbers of poor people migrating to the Dutch Republic from Spain exceeded those from Portugal.[87] The mass arrival of New Christians from Portugal from the 1580s onwards alarmed the Spanish Inquisition, which began a massive campaign of persecution against all New Christians in Spain, bearing especially heavily on those suspected of continuing to observe Jewish customs.[88] This persecution reached vicious heights in the 1640s after Portugal's achievement of independence and the fall of Olivares.[89] Increasing numbers of Conversos trying to escape the torment of the Inquisition saw no alternative to turning their backs on their homeland.[90] Economic crises and epidemics of disease in the Iberian peninsula in the 1640s and 1650s were additional incentives to leave; also, after 1648, with the Dutch Republic and Spain at peace and communications greatly improved as a result, it was much easier to travel.[91] The influx of poor refugees from Spain intensified in the 1690s and around the turn of the century, continuing through the War of the Spanish Succession from 1702 to 1713. The last great wave of immigrants from Spain without means and in need of support occurred between 1720 and 1730, as they fled 'la ultima gran persecución'.[92] Only in the second half of the eighteenth century did migration to Amsterdam from the peninsula come to a halt.

Whether the refugees began their journey by sea or overland with the help of guides across the Pyrenees, the most obvious route to Amsterdam or other centres was through France. Travelling that way, the migrants would have hoped to pay the cost in stages and perhaps gain support en route. A report from the early 1650s tells us of thirty-six New Christian families who seem to have fled from Madrid into France.[93] In 1673 a spy reporting to the Inquisition in Madrid wrote that many Portuguese living in Bayonne or Peyrehorade had fled through Galicia, where New Christians encouraged them to move on to France.[94] In the 1720s fifteen refugees were arrested by the Inquisition on their way overland from Pinhel in Portugal through Valladolid in Spain to France.[95] As late as 1723, French *lettres patentes* contain information on streams of refugees arriving in France from the peninsula.[96]

Many of these travellers joined groups who had settled in Bordeaux, Bayonne, St-Jean-de-Luz, Peyrehorade, La Bastide, Bidache, and Toulouse, or in more northerly towns such as La Rochelle, Nantes, and Rouen, since the issue of *lettres patentes* by King Henry II in 1550.[97] The vicinity of their old home country and the absence of the Inquisition rendered southern France an attractive alternative.

However, the situation there turned out to be less stable than they had expected—indeed, the arrival of poor New Christians in such numbers itself created a problem of poverty among the Portuguese in southern France.[98] Some of these paupers went back to Madrid to ask for money from the wealthy New Christians there.[99] Apparently there was considerable traffic across the Pyrenees, to the extent that in some families the women and children lived in France while their husbands stayed behind in the peninsula.[100] Rachel Castro, for example, who lived in southern France, seems to have been supported by her husband, who was living in Portugal.[101] Many poor refugees, however, having got as far as southern France, remained there in penury, having no money to move on.[102]

The French authorities responded to this dilemma by paying the poor to move on to various cities in Italy, the Ottoman empire, or northern Europe.[103] This pragmatic decision, reinforced by various political decrees, led to an exodus of paupers from southern France. The Portuguese nation was threatened with expulsion from Bordeaux in 1597 and from Bayonne in 1602. In 1615 all Portuguese were expelled from France by a decree that was never ratified.[104] In 1619 Portuguese were driven from St-Jean-de-Luz.[105] The flow into Amsterdam of poor immigrants from France was therefore particularly great between 1610 and 1620.

The uncertain political situation of the Portuguese already in France did not incline them to encourage the paupers to stay, and they continued to put pressure on them to leave after 1620.[106] More prosperous Portuguese families in southern France were unhappy to see the poor arriving in their midst in such large numbers, viewing their presence as a threat to the position and permanent settlement of Portuguese in France. In 1636 prosperous Portuguese in Bordeaux attempted to rid themselves of the paupers who, over the preceding years, had come to make up the majority of their community in the city. Other sources, too, indicate that Portuguese in France were keen to speed the poor on their way.[107] The presence of the poor in southern France was still being felt in 1661, as can be deduced from a manuscript on poor relief by Abraham de Olivera which appeared in Bordeaux at that time, entitled *Tratado de la hobligaçion que todos tienen de dar limosna a los pobres* (Treatise on the obligation of all to give alms to the poor).[108] The manuscript was probably no mere intellectual exercise but a description of a real and present need.

For many poor people, France often served as an interim stop on the route from Portugal and Spain to Amsterdam. In 1629 the *imposta* board in Amsterdam observed that 'extremely impoverished families continue to arrive here [from Spain] through France'.[109] Among them was Ester de Arauyo, who had moved to Amsterdam from Nantes in 1620, together with her mother; her father had died in 'Guinee', and her mother was paralysed. In Amsterdam, according to her testimony, the women lived 'in penury, misery and distress'.[110]

Seeing their city becoming such a popular destination, the Amsterdam Portuguese community decided to dam the influx from France. Thus, following the promulgation of the 1622 regulations on migrants, letters were dispatched to the leaders of Portuguese centres in France asking them to send no more needy persons to Amsterdam and suggesting that they redirect the poor to, say, Italy or destinations further east. At first that is what was done: thus we read that the widow Catherjna de Leao with two daughters was helped to travel to Constantinople by the 'esmoleres da Bastjda'.[111] Similarly, the orphan girl Branca Lopez used the assistance she received in southern France to travel from there to Pisa.[112] The mother of Eliau, alias M^{el} Alvares, moved with her daughters via France to the Ottoman empire.[113]

Even so, the flow of indigent immigrants from France to the Dutch Republic did not stop, though it did taper off.[114] In 1684 a new wave of poor Portuguese who had been living in France arrived in Amsterdam following the promulgation of the French expulsion edict issued upon the request of the French Portuguese nation. These so-called *desterrados de França* comprised some forty families, out of the ninety-three families expelled. According to the edict, most of them were 'not of any use for commerce', and would be a burden on the host community because of their poverty.[115]

Some of these latest arrivals had been reduced to poverty suddenly. The merchant Fernando Cardoso, threatened with the stake at an auto-da-fé in Toulouse,[116] was forced 'in order to save his life to escape suddenly from France, like so many others of his nation, having had to abandon, in the haste of his departure, his entire family and all his goods and chattels, and having taken away no more than two over shirts and a little travel money'. Cardoso described his journey from Blaye (near Bordeaux) to Flushing on a Dutch ship. From Flushing he travelled through Brabant to Amsterdam, where he was declared a bankrupt in 1690. His warehouse and goods in Toulouse had been confiscated by the king of France, and his escape had left him no time to sell his house and effects in Bordeaux or to collect his debts.[117]

Most of the *desterrados de França* stayed only briefly in Amsterdam: many moved on after a spell, or returned to France once the crisis of the 1680s had passed. With the gradual re-establishment of Jewish communities in southern France and the stabilization of the political situation around the Portuguese in the region during the last decades of the seventeenth century and the beginning of the eighteenth, the Amsterdam Portuguese no longer felt obliged to receive destitute people from that region. Instead, they demanded from the Portuguese in France a more equal relationship—a 'horizontal solidarity', to use the phrase of Gérard Nahon.[118]

The route taken by the poor from Portugal and Spain, often through France and eventually to Amsterdam, whether directly by boat or overland with stops on the way, brought considerable difficulties for many; but to all the refugees it also brought hope and relief, with the prospect of escape from a life of fear and hardship.

Funding the Journey

How were New Christians without money able to escape from the Iberian peninsula and pay for the long journey to Amsterdam? According to the writer Abraham Indaña, lack of funds was one of the main obstacles preventing paupers from leaving Spain and Portugal.[119] There may be some truth in this statement, for the records contain many testimonies of people in Spain who maintain they cannot flee because they lack the means to travel or would not be able to find work elsewhere.[120] Some said they were planning to postpone their departure for Amsterdam or some other destination until they had gathered a small amount of capital.[121] The inability of these people to leave is one of the explanations for the continuing persecution of people accused of judaizing in the late seventeenth and early eighteenth centuries.

Even so, many New Christians, both the already poor and the newly impoverished, did manage to get away to Amsterdam, as is demonstrated by the case of Diogo Henriques. Having been imprisoned by the Inquisition in Toledo and stripped of all his goods and money, in 1620 he fled destitute to Amsterdam, together with his father, who was more than a hundred years old, his sister, and her son. In 1623, Portuguese refugees testified in Amsterdam that the Inquisition had robbed them of all their possessions and that they had arrived in Amsterdam as paupers.[122]

How did the poor get the cash to leave the peninsula? Some kept money in reserve for the journey. Others were helped by wealthier members of the *nação*, for example Fernando Montesinos, who in the 1630s was accused by the Inquisition in Madrid of helping judaizers to flee from the peninsula.[123] With money saved or given, poor refugees could make arrangements with guides, ships' captains, or anybody else with access to means of aid and/or influence.

Some refugees arrived in Amsterdam on 'cash on delivery' terms, the Amsterdam Portuguese community paying off the ships' captains who had brought them. In 1619, for instance, travel and related expenses were paid for a group of people from Bordeaux.[124] In 1633 the Amsterdam Portuguese

Jewish community paid for the journey of a pauper upon his arrival in Amsterdam from Bayonne.[125] In 1668 Samuel Lopes was given money for the fare of the boat that had brought him to Amsterdam.[126] In 1685 the Amsterdam *kahal* paid off the captains who brought over families expelled from southern France.[127] The expenses of Abraham Henriques Lopez's trip from Spain were paid upon his arrival in Amsterdam in 1699, and the same was done for a few other families arriving from the peninsula in this period.[128] Similar payments were made on behalf of people who arrived from Spain and Portugal in Amsterdam in the 1730s and 1740s.[129]

Sometimes it was only the costs of the last stages of the journey that remained to be paid, the rest having been settled by Jewish or New Christian communities or individuals at various points on the way. Portuguese merchants from Amsterdam and other Jewish communities travelling and trading in France, for example, provided itinerants with money, as may be inferred from incidents reported in Rouen in 1633.[130] Abraham Peres and his family required funds to meet the cost only of their journey from Rotterdam to Amsterdam.[131] Again, in the case of a mentally ill person from Bayonne who turned up in Rotterdam, only the boat trip from Rotterdam to Amsterdam was paid for, the rest of the journey having been funded by others.[132]

The Amsterdam Portuguese community did not wait passively for the arrival of refugees from the Iberian peninsula, but was actively engaged in helping Conversos to get away and in making arrangements for their transport to Jewish centres—including financial arrangements. Amsterdam Portuguese often gave ships' captains explicit instructions about which people to collect. In 1603 Manuel Lopes Homem instructed Captain Cornelis Clasen in Amsterdam to take at least six Portuguese individuals—possibly one or two more—to be designated by his clerk, on board his ship in Spain. The captain would be paid upon his return to Amsterdam.[133] A family of six was fetched on similar terms from Aveiro in Portugal. Duarte Fernandes came to an agreement with Captain Michielszoon from Zaandam that the latter would set sail in his ship *De Bontekoe* for Aveiro, where, in addition to a cargo of salt, 'the captain shall moreover be obliged to take on board his ship a family of six persons, or one or two more, to which persons the captain shall surrender his cabin'.[134] In 1613 instructions were issued in Amsterdam to fetch seven or eight Portuguese persons from a Galician port to be specified.[135] In 1617 Captain Cock was instructed by Amsterdam Portuguese merchants to take on board as many passengers as possible in St-Jean-de-Luz, together with their luggage and household goods. He was to provide these passengers with decent accommodation and also with food and drink, and to 'set sail with these people together with the merchandise and commodities he carried, as quickly as possible . . . and to convey them to the city of Amsterdam'.[136] Two years later, after the expulsion of the Portuguese from St-Jean-de-Luz, Amsterdam did its utmost to have as many people fetched from there as was possible.

Not only during the early years of the seventeenth century but in later decades as well, many rescue operations were launched in Amsterdam. In 1635 Moses Levy asked the community of Amsterdam for money to free his mother and sister in Lisbon and help them to come 'to the Jewish world'.[137] In 1669 Moses Nunez Xabe, who had himself arrived from Lisbon with his son in Amsterdam but had then chosen to live in London, appealed from the English capital to Amsterdam for help in rescuing his daughters, who still lived in Lisbon.[138]

Until well into the eighteenth century the Amsterdam Portuguese community continued to be deeply concerned about the fate of Conversos in the Iberian peninsula, and to launch successive campaigns on their behalf. We do not know the story behind the note in the financial records of 1729 that 200 guilders were to be spent on the rescue of the poor coming from Portugal, but it is clear that a rescue operation took place.[139]

We know more about another rescue initiated by Dr Jacob Idanha, who in 1729 walked into the administrative office of the Amsterdam Portuguese community and, in the most dramatic terms, described the fate of his parents and other members of his family in Spain. Having been tortured by the Inquisition, he said, they were now imprisoned in Burgos, 'plunged into idolatry and unable to escape'. Since it was possible to use intermediaries to free the prisoners 'from their slavery and seeing that he himself lacked the means to pay them', he asked the Mahamad for a donation. The administrators favoured the application and made available money from the *cativos* pool. The Amsterdam Portuguese community attached great importance to supporting projects for attracting New Christians to Judaism; but equally, it had no wish to be duped, and so did not hand over the money until all concerned had been saved from *idolatria* and taken to the Jewish community in Bayonne.[140] Similarly, in 1739 the Amsterdam *parnasim* received a written request for a financial contribution towards the release of three persons in Ávila de los Cavalleros in Spain, who were anxious to convert to 'Judesmo' but lacked the means to get out of the country in order to do so. The *parnasim* first made certain that the persons concerned were indeed of the Hebrew nation, and then handed over the money.[141]

While actively seeking to help poor Conversos from Portugal and Spain to make the journey to Amsterdam, the Amsterdam Portuguese *kahal* made no special efforts to attract poor people from the Jewish centres of early modern

Europe or to pay their travel expenses. Nevertheless, many contrived to reach the city and ask for support. Let us see where they came from and how they made their way to Amsterdam.

The Journey to Amsterdam from Other Regions

Italy

The northward migration of paupers from Jewish centres in Italy was driven mainly by socio-economic factors. Most arrived in Amsterdam as single men, though some were accompanied by their families or others who wished to join them. Only exceptionally do we find poor women among these migrants.

Paupers from Italy—Spanish/Portuguese, Ashkenazi, Italian, Levantine, and others—constituted a steady stream of people knocking for help at the doors of the Amsterdam Portuguese community throughout the early modern period. They arrived without any help from the Amsterdam Portuguese from a variety of towns, not only from Venice but also—as Swetschinski discovered in his examination of the Amsterdam *ondertrouw* registers—from Rome, Pisa, Florence, Ancona, Ferrara, Padua, Modena, Verona, Livorno, Turin, and Mantua.[142] Sometimes they were registered by first name and surname, but in most cases the description was somewhat vague: for instance, 'Italian',[143] 'Portuguese Jew from Pisa',[144] or 'Joseph Somsin with his daughter coming from Italy'.[145]

Migrants from Italy were attracted both by rumours of the great wealth of the Amsterdam Portuguese *kahal* and by the economic prospects the Dutch city seemed to offer. As an international trading centre and a transatlantic shipping port, early modern Amsterdam looked a promising alternative to the economically declining Mediterranean world.[146] Poverty was a severe problem among Jews in Italy, many of whom had no work or fixed abode.[147] They could not always gain admittance to Italian towns, nor could they count on poor relief from the Jewish community. As late as 1636/7 Jews were being threatened with expulsion from Venice,[148] and a few years earlier, in 1630, Jews were temporarily expelled from Mantua.[149] In Venice every Jewish newcomer to the city had to register with the Jewish 'Small Assembly', which took its instructions from the Venetian city authorities. Strangers could remain in the city for eight days before registration (plus another eight days if the Small Assembly was unable to convene in the first period), unless they were considered to be undesirable, in which case they were turned away immediately.[150] In Mantua, the seventeenth-century Jewish community had the legal right to limit or to prohibit the immigration of Jews, and as in Venice any considered undesirable could be expelled from the city. The municipal authorities lent the Jewish community their support in enforcing this measure.[151] In the Portuguese community in Livorno, too, the admission of foreigners was strictly controlled by the leaders of the *kahal*, and great care was taken to keep out *jent escandolosa e enquieta* ('scandalous and restless people'). No one was allowed to harbour a foreigner without the written consent of at least three community officers, who decided on the duration of the stay after assessing the *calidade de ditta pessoa* ('quality of each person').[152] In short, Jews could not be certain of being allowed to stay in Counter-Reformation Italy.[153]

It is not possible to follow in detail the coming and goings of all Jews from Italy to and from Amsterdam. Many disappeared from sight after having drawn poor relief in Amsterdam just once. With them, as with so many others, it was perhaps not so much a matter of immigration as of trans-migration. Sometimes their next destination was recorded, together with the cost of the assisted passage.

Until recently, little has been known about the mass influx into Amsterdam of poor Jews from Italy in the early modern period. We now know that the flow increased gradually from 1620 onwards, decreased slightly between 1630 and 1640, but then soared again, reaching a peak between 1650 and 1660, after which it began to ebb, though it never became insignificant. The fact that the migration of paupers from Italy gathered pace and volume after 1622 in particular is remarkable because the Amsterdam Portuguese were at that time doing their very utmost to stem the inflow of paupers from Jewish centres, Italy included. Amsterdam Portuguese paupers were, in fact, being paid to leave for Italy (and other places yet further away).[154] Abraham da Fonsequa left for Italy with eight other people in the winter of 1622,[155] while Sara de Liao decided (or was persuaded) to move to Pisa in the summer of the same year.[156] A year later Abraham Dalvarenga was paid 260 guilders to cover the cost of removing himself, his household goods, and his family to Livorno.[157]

The *imposta* board realized their mistake a few years later, when they noticed that paupers in such countries as Italy, unable to make ends meet, kept returning to Amsterdam. Thus the board admitted in 1628 that 'experience has shown that there is little point in helping paupers to repair to Italy. Not only is damage done as a result to the *imposta*, but it is also detrimental to the poor themselves, who are unable to procure the necessities of life over there. For that reason many of them are returning to this city.'[158] The Amsterdam Portuguese community was, in fact, confronted with a continuous influx of Jews from Italy, despite every attempt to discourage them. They gave the Italian immigrants little assistance in settling in the city, let alone in establishing a separate *kahal*, as, for example, existed in Venice or in some cities of the Ottoman empire,[159] or as German and Polish Jewish immigrants managed to set up later in Amsterdam. Exceptions confirmed this rule, in particular when it came to immigrants able to prove that they were of Spanish or Portuguese descent, or that they were able to make some kind of a living in Amsterdam from their trade or profession. Thus Rachel Fero from Pisa, and Sara Cardoza and her two sons from Venice, were allowed to stay in Amsterdam.[160] Isaac de Imanuel Baruch from Venice settled down permanently in Amsterdam as a diamond-cutter.[161] Abraham Levi had been a Catholic before the Amsterdam Portuguese community took him in from Rome. Born in Novellara, near Reggio, he had been placed in a Jesuit monastery in Rome as a child. For religious reasons ('tanto que teve conhesim^{to} da p^{ra} cauza': 'because he came to the knowledge of the true God, the First Cause' as opposed to the Christian Trinity), he had fled from the monastery. In Amsterdam, he was helped by the community and taken under the wing of Dr Isaac Orobio de Castro.[162]

Of the Sephardim who appear in the *ondertrouw* registers of seventeenth-century Amsterdam, no more than 9.7 per cent came from Italy. However, Jews from Italy made up a much higher proportion—27 per cent—of people on poor relief in that period who did not appear in the *ondertrouw* registers.[163] The difference in the figures highlights the increase at this time in the numbers of destitute people arriving in the city. In some cases, they retreated to the margins of society. We meet some of them in the criminal records, sentenced for minor transgressions or petty crimes. Salomon Levi from Ferrara, for instance, was sentenced to the pillory, two years in the Rasphuis, and six years of banishment because, as a Jew, he had married a Christian woman in the Oude Kerk.[164] Jacob Italiaen from Venice also came up against Amsterdam justice but was found not guilty of complicity in a theft.[165]

Lack of sources makes it difficult to assess the extent of migration of the destitute from Italy in the eighteenth century. On the basis of information from the Sephardi community in England, however, it seems that migrants from Italy, many of whom were poor, continued to travel to the north and west well into the 1700s.[166]

North Africa

The Dutch Republic did a great deal of trade with North Africa, and Amsterdam's close business links with the region greatly facilitated the movement of Jews in both directions.[167] Ships setting sail from Salé (near Rabat in modern

Morocco) heading to Amsterdam often contained Jewish passengers or their belongings.[168]

One of the first rabbis of the Portuguese community in Amsterdam was Haham Isaac Uziel, who had been born in Fez and had later settled in Oran.[169] Haham Jacob Sasportas came from the same area.[170] Many Jewish families in North Africa and Amsterdam were related. Moses Curiel Rosado of Amsterdam had two nieces living in Salé, to whom he left money for dowries.[171] Isaac de Aron Mendes stated on his marriage in Amsterdam that his father lived in Salé.[172] Rachel Montalta mentioned that her husband Isaac Montalto was presently in 'Berberia'.[173] The Querido and Cohen families were among those actively involved in trade and diplomacy between North Africa and the Dutch Republic.[174] Members of the North African Palache family travelled back and forth to the city as merchants and representatives of the king of Barbary: some settled in Amsterdam permanently, others continued to live in Morocco or elsewhere.[175] Solidarity and familiarity with the North African community were demonstrated by the Amsterdam Portuguese community's sending food to 'Nosos Irmaos de Salee' in 1664, when the city was under siege during a period of war, anarchy, and famine, and assisting *berberiscos* arriving in Amsterdam.[176]

Those who came to Amsterdam from North Africa included the less fortunate as well as prosperous trading families, among them descendants of Spanish or Portuguese Jews or Conversos.[177] Some of them carried on the trades of their fathers in Amsterdam or joined their family businesses.[178] Many of those in need from Fez, Salé, and Algiers were supported after arriving in Amsterdam, including those from the Spanish enclaves of North Africa such as Oran.[179] Some had made their way to Amsterdam by indirect routes: for example, a woman from Oran who arrived in 1671 had travelled via Cádiz in Spain.[180] We do not know much about individual paupers from North Africa: many of them received poor relief just once before moving on, and it is difficult to differentiate between them as the Portuguese referred to them by the collective name of *berberiscos*, comprising mostly the original Jewish inhabitants of North Africa.[181] However, although it is difficult to arrive at precise figures, the flow of poor migrants from North Africa was never substantial.[182]

South-eastern Europe and the Levant

Some Jews came to Amsterdam from south-eastern Europe and the Levant. Indeed, arrivals from the Orient were a regular sight in Amsterdam throughout the early modern period. Most came from such cities as Salonika, Constantinople, Izmir, Alexandria, or Sofia, or from the holy cities of Jerusalem and Safed in Erets Yisra'el.[183] Often they are described by the general terms *levantinos* or *turques*, leaving their precise places of origin unrecorded.[184]

The contrast between poverty and economic decline in the Ottoman empire and better opportunities along the Atlantic coast in western Europe would have driven many of the Jews who left south-eastern Europe and the Levant to head north-west.[185] Others came on special missions to collect charity to ease the plight of their home communities.[186]

Most of the *levantinos* stayed only temporarily in Amsterdam and were not absorbed into the community. For example, one Jew from Salonika had his travel expenses paid on his arrival in Amsterdam in 1621 but was compelled to leave again straight away.[187] The same decision was made in the case of a woman who had come all the way from Turkey with her two sons. Although she promised to go to Hamburg and from there to return home, in the end she was given funds to enable her to travel to London.[188] Eli Habilho, on the other hand, a descendant of a famous Levantine family, settled permanently in Amsterdam: having arrived from Jerusalem aged 40 with his wife and one child, he found work as a *shamash* (beadle) for the community.[189] Individuals continued to arrive from the Levant in the eighteenth century: they included Abraham Algalsy from Izmir in 1734 and three passengers from the same place admitted in 1756.[190]

Numbers of migrants from the Ottoman empire were generally not large.[191] The exception was an influx in the latter part of the seventeenth century from a devastating war in the Balkans: because many came from Buda and Belgrade, they were known in Amsterdam as *belogrados*.[192] Accounts of their experiences of the war that destroyed their *kehilah* and their families and turned them into refugees can be found in works by Joseph Abendanon and Moses Cohen.[193] Abendanon described his wretched and drifting existence following his escape from Belgrade in 1688 in his autobiography *Sheloshah sarigim*.[194] He related how he wandered from Belgrade to the *kehilah* of Kromeriz and made his way thence to Prague. Arriving in the winter, he was provided with food and shelter for four months. He spoke highly of Prague's Jewish community, of its scholars, and of the way they took care of him. On leaving Prague in the spring of 1689, he was provided with a carriage and enough food to reach Amsterdam, where he arrived that summer, a year after he had left Belgrade.[195] Here he gained a patron, the Portuguese merchant Joseph Sarfati, who took care of him on his arrival,[196] encouraged him to write about his former teacher Haham Almosnino of Belgrade, found him work, and offered him hospitality and shelter in his home, all of which Abendanon records with appreciation.[197] After living and working in Amsterdam for a few years, Abendanon travelled on to London, where he worked until his death.[198]

Fugitives from the Balkans sought information as they travelled about the best routes to take, the most promising destinations to aim for, and where the best economic prospects seemed to be. Some began their investigations even before they set out. Thus, at the end of the 1680s, Moses Cohen, while still a prisoner of war in Osijek, north of Belgrade, started to make enquiries about a new and permanent refuge after liberation as he wrote to friends in a number of Jewish communities. These letters were delivered by emissaries who visited various *kehilot* to collect money for the prisoners.[199] Among his correspondents was his former fellow townsman Joseph Abendanon, whom he asked for information about his experience of getting to Amsterdam: 'Tell me what happened to you on your journey to Amsterdam. Did you have many expenses? Did you come by carriage? Did each *kehilah* provide you with these things? Will I be able to find work in Amsterdam as a Torah scribe?'[200] Abendanon consulted Joseph Sarfati, and forwarded his patron's somewhat discouraging summary of prospects in Amsterdam to Moses Cohen:

> Life in Amsterdam is very expensive. Prices are very high. It is not certain that you would get support from the Portuguese community. It is very difficult for Abendanon to make a living, even with the writing of *sifre torah*, *tefilin*, and *mezuzot* that are sold for high prices. Some refugees from Belgrade do get by with support from the *midrash* [study house] or some yeshiva. Sometimes they also teach small children and go round all day in circles from house to house. And yet they don't look happy . . . Think about it carefully. Prisoners of war arrive here from all sides every day and I cannot do what I would like to do and what my heart tells me to do. I cannot provide you with enough on which you and your family could subsist . . . May God give you good advice, lead you to a place where you can make a living and help you to get out of the prison-house.[201]

It was clearly difficult for these Balkan Jews to keep their heads above water with the help provided by the Portuguese community. Even private charity, of the kind Sarfati provided for Abendanon and his family, was insufficient, though Abendanon was most grateful to Sarfati, without whose help his life would have been wretched: 'My family and I have already been in his house for eight months. Without his hospitality and benevolence we would starve to death.'[202]

We do not know whether Cohen received a full reply setting out all the logistics of Abendanon's journey. In any case, he was advised to take a different route and it seems that he did just that. In the end he travelled via Buda, Nikolsburg (Mikulov), and Fürth to Venice, where he found work as a proofreader in a printing works.[203]

Abendanon managed to reach Amsterdam with his whole family. In many other cases, however, *belogrados* arrived alone, in pairs, in small groups—children separated from their parents, widows or widowers accompanied by their children, men or women on their own, sometimes still searching for their loved ones.[204] This fragmentation reflected the hardship and often cruelty they had suffered.

One sad case was that of Ester de David Manuel from Belgrade, the wife of Isaac Menasseh, a simple tobacco seller. During the years of chaos and war Ester lost track of her husband. In 1702 she finally arrived in Amsterdam in search of her husband and found him living there. However, he appeared in the meantime to have married Perla Obediente, the widow of Moses Vas Mexicana. He had believed that Ester was dead, various witnesses having made false declarations to that effect. The officers of the Mahamad tried to prevent Ester from appealing to the Amsterdam magistrates and thus bringing the Portuguese community into disrepute. They offered her compensation in the form of a monthly allowance of 3 guilders, the sum that had previously been paid to Isaac Menasseh's second wife.[205] Ester could not bear to go on living in Amsterdam for long. On the charity list for 1704/5, an entry under 15 Heshvan 5465 reads: 'For Ester Menasseh . . . to Belgrade 36 guilders.'[206]

In most cases, poor Jews from south-eastern Europe and the Levant did not settle permanently in Amsterdam. Many left for destinations known or unknown; some returned home.[207] However, the few families that stayed include some that became prominent in the community and left their imprint on Dutch and Jewish society during the eighteenth century and beyond.[208]

The New World

The New World provided Amsterdam with relatively few poor migrants. In 1629 a 'homem de naçao' apparently fled Portuguese Brazil and arrived in Amsterdam, having been robbed on the way, to join a Jewish community.[209] In 1654 several Portuguese Jews returned impoverished to Amsterdam after the Portuguese recaptured the Dutch colony in northern Brazil and ended up on the poor-relief list of the Portuguese *kahal*, which ran special collections for them.[210] One of these was Aron de Aguilar, who fled Brazil in 1654 with his wife and children and arrived in dire poverty in Martinique; here he was helped by co-religionists who gave him shelter, food, and enough money to cover his transport back to Amsterdam.[211]

Brazil was not the only part of America from which Portuguese Jews returned in poverty at the beginning of the 1660s. After unsuccessful overseas expeditions in the West Indies, others came back from, for instance,

Essequibo, Tobago, and Cayenne.[212] In 1661 money was sent from Amsterdam to Essequibo to fund assistance to, and the travel costs of, those returning via Martinique.[213] Captain Harmen Severijnse declared in 1661 that he had 'agreed to convey David Torres and his family together with their baggage in the aforesaid ship from Martten Nicas to this City of Amsterdam . . . it also having been agreed in Martten Nicas to convey Jacob Barrocas with his family and baggage for a fare of one hundred and twenty-five guilders, payment for which he still owes'.[214]

Apart from political or economic problems, family circumstances such as the loss of a spouse forced poor people, especially women, to return to Europe from the New World. Ester Dias da Fonseca, for instance, explained that in 1742 she and her husband 'had been forced by misfortune and adversity to set out on a journey to St Eustatius with her two surviving children in search of a better life and fortune, having been in frugal and reduced circumstances and having had to rely on friends and next of kin to equip them'. Her husband died six weeks after their arrival in St Eustatius. She sold her few possessions on the island, and when that money ran out she issued a bill of exchange payable by her mother in Amsterdam. On the proceeds she travelled to Curaçao, where she had to ask for assistance from the Portuguese community, who finally paid for her return to Amsterdam. There she and her children moved in with her mother.[215]

This relatively small number of cases apart, however, migration between the Amsterdam Portuguese community and the New World tended to be towards America rather than in the opposite direction.

Hamburg and Antwerp

Movement of poor Portuguese immigrants from Hamburg to Amsterdam began in earnest during the second half of the seventeenth century and continued well into the eighteenth, often motivated by economic factors. Isaac Jeseron, for example, left Hamburg in 1706 to make some money in Amsterdam. However, his experience fell short of his expectations: he ended up bankrupt as a result of complications in his involvement in the tobacco trade.[216] Many Portuguese were also driven to leave Hamburg by the increasing hostility shown by the local population towards Jews and the vast increase in the annual tax levied on the Jews by the city authorities in 1697.[217] Amsterdam proved to be one of the most desirable destinations.[218]

Only a very small number of Portuguese paupers in Amsterdam came from Antwerp, traditionally an important refuge for New Christians. Most of them arrived during the last decades of the seventeenth century, when Antwerp's economic decline looked inevitable.[219]

◆

It is clear, then, that people from all corners of the contemporary Jewish world sought out and contrived to make their way to the Portuguese community of early modern Amsterdam. Simply getting there, however, did not mean being able to stay there permanently, or indeed being able to count on continuous assistance from either the Amsterdam Portuguese community or private sources. Many people nevertheless continued to gravitate to Amsterdam. For numerous Jews it was a home port on which they felt that they could fall back at all times, a safe haven in a dangerous world. Nevertheless, many moved on, either soon after their arrival or after a protracted stay, some voluntarily and some under pressure. No matter how hospitable their reception had been, how much care they had been given, and where they had come from, their journeys often continued. The next section will examine where they went.

Emigration from Amsterdam

Year by year Jews passed through the city, intentionally or by chance, staying for an hour, a day, weeks, or months.[220] Amsterdam had long served as a temporary halt and a transit port for migrants of all kinds, and it did so increasingly, and indeed predominantly, for Jews in this period.[221]

Emigration from Amsterdam did not always proceed along straight lines but took various complex routes: we can reconstruct these patterns from the records, especially the various columns of the *livros longos* that provide us with an annual survey of departures from Amsterdam from 1663 onwards.[222] Sometimes the Amsterdam Portuguese served as one more Jewish community on the way where migrants would pause to ask for money and perhaps try to sell or buy some goods before moving on. At other times the community made deliberate efforts to send migrants on to suitable further destinations. The lists of those leaving grow longer as time passes, reflecting the intention of the community to set clear limits on who was allowed to remain.

Most poor Conversos leaving the Iberian peninsula set off across the Atlantic to find work in one of the Dutch or English colonies. Some, however, took different routes, alone or with their families, heading for Italy, France, North Africa, or the Levant or setting out for London or the German states. Wherever their ultimate destination—if indeed they had one—many of these migrants passed through Amsterdam.[223] A similar pattern was followed by non-Jews, who travelled to Amsterdam from different areas, for example the German states, Scandinavia, and the southern Netherlands, before embarking for the East and West Indies.[224]

The paths chosen by some of the poor show the high degree of mobility characteristic of the times.[225] Lacking a permanent home anywhere, they travelled wherever seemed most propitious, by boat, by horse and cart, or on their bare feet, to try their luck. Perhaps the Portuguese community of Amsterdam could give them support, shelter, and work as other Jewish and New Christian communities on their way had done; perhaps they might gain new information: artisans might find leads to more work elsewhere, merchants might form new trading links. How otherwise are we to explain why people should arrive in Amsterdam from Spain on the way to France or Italy?[226] Why would travellers visit Amsterdam on their way from France to Italy or North Africa or the other way around?[227]

These arbitrary routes passing through Amsterdam were one form of migration; another was re-migration. Many poor people leaving the city with some cash given to them by the Amsterdam Portuguese community came back again, once or many more times, circling the Jewish world, using Amsterdam as their staging post.[228] Here we are dealing with the phenomenon known as 'circular migration'.[229] This too involved a complex network of routes, with Amsterdam always at the centre. For example, Moses Lopes Nunes travelled from Spain to Amsterdam, to North Africa, back to Amsterdam, and then to North Africa again.[230] Joseph Benveniste seems to have come to Amsterdam first as an Italian Jew from the Levant; he then moved on to Italy and the Levant and back to Amsterdam again.[231] David Machorro de Leon travelled between North Africa, the Dutch Republic, London, and the Caribbean.[232] David Alvares Torres, Abraham Pinheiro, and Jacob Gabay Correa wandered for decades between Amsterdam, Brazil, Guyana, Martinique, Barbados, Jamaica, and Curaçao.[233] Salomon do Porto frequently travelled between Italy and Amsterdam, eventually settling in Curaçao.[234] Mordecai Lealtad was given help to travel between Livorno, London, and Salé in North Africa.[235] Jona Fresco travelled with his family to Barbados, came back, and thereafter moved between Italy, London, Hamburg, and The Hague.[236]

These are all examples of individuals who moved around the Jewish world from one *kehilah* to another. Others took in non-Jewish as well as Jewish centres on their wanderings. Yosef Kaplan has studied this phenomenon, as have others since.[237] Among this group were poor Jews, including the newly impoverished. One such was Daniel Lopez Silva de Alborado, who travelled repeatedly between Amsterdam and Portugal using Bayonne as an intermediate stop. Having first fled Portugal in 1724 because of 'religion', he settled in Bayonne, but lost part of his savings there and so in 1731 moved on to try his luck in Holland—only to see the rest of his capital disappear in the

Dutch Republic. He therefore returned to Portugal in 1733 with some merchandise, presumably intending to recover his fortunes. However, on his way back to Amsterdam two years later the ship was wrecked and all his possessions lost, including his money, goods, and papers, and he was declared bankrupt. In the end, Alborado's repeated migration to Amsterdam, for a combination of religious and economic motives, did not bring him much prosperity.[238]

With a continuous stream of people arriving in and leaving the city asking for help, the Portuguese community was not content to let these comings and goings take their own course, but actively tried to keep them under control.

Pressure on Migrants to Move On

Intervention in migration was often explicitly stated to be official policy. As early as 1622, the new regulations stipulated that the money gathered by the new *imposta* tax would be channelled to dealing with

> paupers from our Portuguese and Spanish nation, who are left here without any succour or income. Hence it has been decided to help them to travel to countries with Jewish centres, where they can live more easily . . . it being understood that no one must be sent to places closer than the Jewish centres in Italy or Poland.[239]

Sending poor migrants on to Italy and Poland proved ineffective, as noted above: they simply came straight back. Therefore, in 1628 destinations further away were identified, including Greece, Tunis, and Turkey, the assumption being that having once made so long a trip, the migrants would not return.[240] Thereafter, the *escamot* or resolutions of the community mention no major plans to remove Portuguese paupers from Amsterdam (apart from decisions to send away *tudescos* and *polacos*) for more than a century.[241] Then, in the mid-eighteenth century, a colonization project in Surinam was developed which was deemed capable of absorbing one-third of Amsterdam's poor Sephardi Jews. In 1747, accordingly, it was decided to 'send away one third of the paupers, which amounts to 600 persons, for good . . . to be financed from the capital of the *sedaca* . . . up to the sum of 100,000 guilders, of which at least 30,000 guilders would be spent on the purchase and cultivation of land in Surinam or other colonies'.[242]

Unlike other nations in the early modern period, for example Portugal, England, and France, the Dutch Republic never planned for the large-scale 'deportation' of its poor overseas.[243] There was simply too much demand for manpower in its industries, in its armies, on its fleet, and in its various international operations, so that there was no surplus to deport. Nevertheless a few projects did exist, through which orphanages, workhouses, other welfare institutions, and churches relieved themselves of the burden of supporting their poor by providing labour for activities overseas.[244]

The Amsterdam Portuguese community developed a similarly subtle approach. It is clear that the Portuguese did not sit idly by while paupers flocked to their city; had they been passive in the face of the influx, the number of people drawing relief would have been twice as large.[245] On the contrary, it made constant efforts to dam the tide and to divert incomers to other places in order to keep the burden of poor relief within manageable limits, even though it had no legal powers either to debar Jews from the city or to expel paupers. The 1747 plan speaks only of setting up a colony in Surinam consisting of 'persons willing to be sent out to these places'.[246] That is, the leadership recognized that at this point it was not in a position to force people to leave.[247]

In the early part of the period under study here the Amsterdam Portuguese remained aloof from the city authorities in dealing with unwanted paupers. This situation was in sharp contrast to that in other Jewish communities of early modern Europe, where leaders co-operated closely with the local authorities in moving on the poor.[248] In Amsterdam, the police were called in to help only very infrequently. This seems to have been the case with Moses Alvares, who in 1713 was sent out to Livorno: the *kehilah* paid the city authorities to get him on board ship.[249] In 1760, when the community's migration policy threatened to break down with paupers promising to leave and then failing to do so, it finally called on the city of Amsterdam to impose sanctions on paupers refusing to leave, using the agreements to leave signed by the poor that had become common practice by this time.[250]

An example of close co-operation between the Portuguese community and the city authorities in handling recalcitrant poor refusing to leave is the case of Sara Saso, the widow of Ebiatar Cohen da Silva. She was a poor woman, living with her daughter in a room on the corner of Zwanenburgstraat. In June 1759 the Portuguese community gave Sara money to travel with her daughter to New York via London and settle down there permanently. She signed the contract, thereby agreeing to leave. She was to receive 30 guilders in Amsterdam, with the remaining 130 guilders to be paid through the correspondent of the Amsterdam Portuguese Jews in London. Sara took the 30 guilders, but by September that year had still not left; even worse, she was still receiving welfare payments. When she refused to depart, the Portuguese community asked the city authorities to arrest her and send her to New York as soon as possible. The arrest took place, though four years passed—possibly in prison—before she eventually agreed to leave for Curaçao in 1763, by which time she had two children.[251]

Calling in non-Jewish authorities was the *kehilah*'s last resort in influencing and controlling the behaviour of recalcitrant individuals.[252] We may therefore conclude that the Portuguese community was at its wits' end in 1760, having by then used every possible means of dealing with the problem internally.

One way of persuading paupers to leave was to indicate to them by means more subtle than physical coercion that they should not overstay their welcome and that, after a decent interval, they should move on to try their luck elsewhere. Thus poor relief might be granted just once, or paupers given so little help in money or kind that they had no choice but to head for another destination. Migrants from Jewish centres in particular were given this treatment and advised to return home on the basis of the resolution adopted in 1622.[253] Thus Jacob Levy, arriving from Jerusalem in 1683, was forced to return immediately.[254] In 1685 Isaac Rodriguez Nunes landed from Algiers only to be told to return to his port of departure straight away.[255] Rachel Vaya from Italy was also told to return home.[256] Joseph Bunum journeyed back 'pª sua terra' of Adrianopolis, encouraged by the Amsterdam *parnasim*.[257] *Tudescos* and *polacos*, too, moved in and out of Amsterdam at the expense of the Portuguese *kahal*, certainly until 1670.[258] The anonymous group of *forasteiros* or *pobres* also disappeared from view quickly.[259]

The leadership tried various ways to get rid of the poor. The rules on migration were repeatedly adapted in the attempt to keep the influx of paupers as low as possible, and those already in the city were offered attractive premiums to leave, with suggestions that chances of work and a better life were to be found elsewhere, hoping to entice the poor to leave the city. Many examples prove that pressure was used, not only during the seventeenth century but on into the eighteenth.[260]

Sometimes Portuguese leaders accompanied a poor person to the ship and gave money to the captain to cover the costs of taking him or her on to another port.[261] In 1623 Abraham Ger was paid 30 guilders to leave for Livorno 'in agreement with him and the captain of the ship'.[262] Similar deals were made with ships' captains in 1645 to deport Daniel Gomez, who was also to be taken to Livorno, and in 1702 to remove Josua Tuby Valensin.[263] In the aftermath of the expulsion of ninety-three Portuguese families from France in 1684, many returned to Amsterdam; the *kehilah* entered into agreements with ships' captains to take them back again, paying them for the task.[264] One of the jobs of Isaac Oeb, himself a recipient of welfare, was to help people leaving the city: thus he earned a little extra in 1685 to put a 'foreigner' on a ship to 'Berberia'.[265] In 1703 Captain van Meel was paid by the Amsterdam

Portuguese community to ship Mordecai Cohen and Efraim Carvalho off to Surinam.[266]

Another method of applying pressure was to punish unwanted returning migrants with increasing severity. The minutes of the community are full of laments about *tudescos, polacos,* and many others on poor relief who, having been shipped out of the city, kept turning up in Amsterdam again to fall back on the charity of the Portuguese.[267] In an attempt to deter this practice the community often stipulated that, having been paid a certain amount of travel money, the person concerned must undertake never to return to Amsterdam, not to come back within a certain number years, or never to claim poor relief again.

Friends or family were often called in to stand surety in such cases, in a manner reminiscent of the use of so-called *borgbrieven* (letters of guarantee) in non-Jewish society.[268] When Daniel Meçia was sent to Surinam, for example, the money for his passage was given to Abraham Meçia, who undertook to return it if Daniel refused to leave.[269] In a similar case, Abraham Is. Henriques alias Azuby received money to go to London, promising not to return; his brother pledged to return the money if he did not comply.[270] Relations in receipt of welfare who stayed behind could also fulfil this role: Jacob Jessurun was sent to Hamburg and told that if he did not go his mother's monthly allowance would be withdrawn.[271]

The time limits set to deter re-migration varied from six months in the seventeenth century to fifteen years in the middle of the eighteenth. Moses de Castro de Britto received money in 1687 to go to London on condition that he did not return before six months had elapsed.[272] In 1683 Jacob de Ancona and his wife Sara were paid to go to Barbados and not to return within a year.[273] Samuel Roza was sent to Surinam in 1687 and told not to return within two years.[274]

In the eighteenth century, stipulations of this kind became official policy. In despair at the large number of paupers in their midst, the *parnasim* decreed in 1742 that 'any person who has received travel subsidies cannot be admitted to *sedaca* for five years'.[275] In 1748 the period was extended to fifteen years.[276] In the middle of the eighteenth century the records of people sent away included the number of years that must elapse before they were permitted to return. Long lists were compiled under the heading *Despachos para fora da terra* to set out the agreements. So Daniel Athias went to London with money to cover his travel expenses on condition that he did not come back for at least fifteen years;[277] Jacob Garsia left for Bordeaux a week later, together with his son, on the same condition,[278] while Samuel de Paz planned to leave for Curaçao and promised not to come back for twelve years.[279]

Many were also required to promise that they would pay back the money they had been given upon arrival at their destination—perhaps with the help of family or friends there, or from the profits on some business transaction—or whenever God granted them the means to do so. In the *despachos* of the latter part of the eighteenth century certificates explicitly setting out these conditions were printed and signed, but the ideas were put into practice much earlier.[280]

There are many other examples both of the Portuguese leadership's determination to curb immigration and of the frustration of its attempts to control the influx of poor. Often there are no details of why particular individuals were sent away, sometimes for ever. In 1624 Abraham Israel Vaz was ordered to leave for Italy without his family and not to return.[281] Moses Baruch de Liorne was urged to go home (to Livorno) and to promise never to bother the community again.[282] Simha Meatob was given money to leave for London with her husband in 1683 and told never to return.[283] In 1690 Eleasar Hope, Abraham Caza, and Joseph Bivas were sent to Hamburg on condition that neither they nor any member of their families ever returned to Amsterdam.[284]

Sometimes, however, the reasons for sending people away are spelt out. In 1622, for example, Abraham Ger was sent away to Livorno with his wife 'because he was a person the "nation" did not want to reside in this country'.[285] Isaac Morão had acquired a bad name in Essequibo, whence he had just arrived,[286] and was told to take a ship to Martinique straight away. The *parnasim* were obviously keen to get rid of him, for they also made him promise not to remain in Amsterdam.[287] Still, many of these unwanted individuals kept coming back. David Lopes Roldão, arriving from Bayonne in 1677, was advised there and then to return home and was handed travel money for that purpose.[288] A year later he was back in Amsterdam, where he received temporary assistance on several occasions.[289] He was supposed to return to Bayonne in 1679, but did not go.[290] It looks as if he was sent away again in the autumn of 1685 and again told not to return, though only a month later he was sent more specifically through Rotterdam to London.[291] It is not clear whether he left at all: in the summer of 1686 he appeared in the registers again, with a note that he was being sent to Bordeaux.[292] Assuming he did in fact go that time, it had taken the community nine years to get rid of him!

Another example of a tenacious returner is Isaac Sacuto. He was in and out of Amsterdam for eleven years, during which time he was sent to London in 1684 and to Hamburg in 1691.[293] On a third occasion, in 1695, he asked for money to get to Livorno. Losing patience with him, the Portuguese community decreed that if he did not leave permanently this time he would never receive any more money.[294]

Attempts were also made to ensure that mentally ill people did not become too great a burden on the Portuguese *kahal*—an intention stated explicitly in the case of one mentally ill *tudesco*.[295] Such individuals were regularly sent, with or without escort, to Jewish centres in the German states, Italy, or the West Indies: some to specific family members, others merely in the hope that the destination community would look after them. Thus 'o simpleo de Selomoh Pinto' was sent, escorted by the *tudesco* in whose house he had lived, to Ferrara.[296] One 'madman' (*doudo*) was sent to Glückstadt,[297] another was escorted to Wesel by a *tudesco*,[298] and a third was shipped off to Venice.[299] The mentally disabled Diego Lopez Marques, who in 1686 had come to Amsterdam from Bayonne, was destined for immediate return to Bayonne (the ship's captain having already been paid), but fell ill and died before the vessel left.[300] The records also tell us of a 'mad Pole' (*polaco loco*) who, after having been kept on poor relief for two months, was sent abroad in 1663.[301] On another occasion three 'poor idiot women' (*idiotas mais pobres*) were sent out of Amsterdam.[302]

In the seventeenth century only a few, and only Portuguese, mentally ill or mentally disabled paupers were accommodated within Amsterdam. Thus Moses Mendes Carlos was found a place in the Amsterdam madhouse from 1686 to 1687 on the recommendation of the city fathers.[303] Thereafter he too was packed off to relatives, leaving for London in 1688.[304] It is difficult to assess how provision for these people developed in the eighteenth century: we come across many mentally ill taken care of within the community, but cannot judge how many were sent away, as no information on mental state was included in the records of people leaving the city at this time.

Pressure to leave, of whatever kind, was often of no avail, confounded not only by migrants' own recalcitrance but also by unforeseen circumstances. Some literarily missed the boat, as in the case of Isaac Habilho da Fonseca, his sister, and David Naamias Torres, who were to go to Curaçao.[305] Some were unable to set out because they fell ill.[306] Others had bad luck at sea and had to be brought back to Amsterdam—alive or dead.[307]

Voluntarily or under duress, large numbers of poor people left Amsterdam in this period. Many of their destinations have already been mentioned in passing, but it is worth looking at them now in more detail to see if any specific patterns can be discerned in the direction, scale, and timing of emigration.

Destinations and Numbers

Perhaps more than 6,000 individuals passed through the Portuguese community of Amsterdam between 1598 and 1759 and received some payment for their onward journey.[308] Allowing for double counting and the overlap with paupers on permanent or temporary welfare reduces this figure somewhat, but the total remains considerable. It reinforces the conclusion that the Amsterdam Portuguese *kehilah* functioned increasingly as a port of transit for the destitute, whether they came and went willingly or under pressure. Indeed, the Dutch Republic as a whole formed an important centre of transmigration for foreign-born migrants.[309]

Emigrants' destinations are not always recorded in the registers, and the available sources are incomplete; nevertheless some kind of a picture can be drawn. Of the estimated 6,000 who touched down in Amsterdam, most left in the first half of the eighteenth century—that is, in less than a third of the period as a whole. That is by no means surprising, for that period was marked by a significant increase in emigration from the city overall; indeed, throughout the eighteenth century all Europe witnessed massive movements of people, including of Jews.[310]

Emigration reached a peak between 1700 and 1729, with 36 per cent of the total of funded departures taking place during these years. The next segment of the eighteenth century saw almost the same rate, with 33 per cent of the estimated 6,000 leaving between 1730 and 1759. It seems that as time went by the community made ever more strenuous efforts to reduce the numbers of poor in its midst: in the first half of the eighteenth century the rate of expulsion of poor people was several times higher than it was during the seventeenth century.[311] Over the whole of the seventeenth century, less than a third of the total emigrated: 25 per cent between 1670 and 1699, and only 6 per cent during the years 1598–1669—although for this early period the data are less precise owing to gaps in the sources.

More than a third of these migrants—over 2,000—travelled to destinations unknown to us. However, the available information relating to the other two-thirds provides an interesting insight into the different routes Jewish migrants in need took in the early modern period. Breaking down the data into periods gives us a more differentiated picture of migration patterns. Taking the period 1598–1759 as a whole, most of the travellers assisted in Amsterdam opted for Italy; the next most popular destinations were London, the New World, and France. Italy disappeared from the top three only after 1730.[312] The following sections examine why and at what times certain destinations were preferred over others.

Italy

Italy provides an interesting case. Not only was it the focus of the *imposta* board's policy of encouraging emigration in the early years after 1622; it remained both the country of origin of many migrants and also the destination of many leaving Amsterdam for many years thereafter, well into the eighteenth century.[313] Thus, during the last decades of the seventeenth century, many *desterrados de França* as well as *belogrados* opted to travel on to Italy, especially Venice and Livorno. The existence of a separate Levantine Jewish community in Venice must have been a magnet for quite a few migrants, especially for the *belogrados* with their origins in south-eastern Europe.[314] In the eighteenth century, too, Livorno undoubtedly offered many possibilities as a result of its leading place in Mediterranean commerce, and its Jewish community expanded through immigration.[315] In short, Italy sent many destitute travellers to Amsterdam, but was a consistently popular destination for the poor.

The New World

From the second and third decades of the seventeenth century the New World opened up fresh prospects for travellers, not least for members of the Amsterdam Portuguese community and for its paupers in particular. By the next century it had risen to the number one destination for the Jewish poor of the city sent out by the Portuguese community, ranking third between 1700 and 1729 and topping the list from 1730.

Poor Jews from Amsterdam began to migrate to Brazil during the 1620s and continued to do so until 1654, in a trend closely bound up with its short-lived colonization by the Dutch Republic.[316] One of them was Jacob Moreno, who in 1639 was given 12 guilders to go to Brazil with his wife.[317] In the same year David Frances, who had been receiving a monthly welfare payment from the Portuguese community, set off for Brazil.[318] Yet another was Daniel de Campos, who received money to cover his travel expenses.[319] The full extent of the emigration to Brazil is impossible to reconstruct, for lack of source material. It was certainly substantial, as is clear from the 175 Portuguese men who signed the local Portuguese congregation's *escamot* in Recife, Brazil, in 1648.[320] We know, too, that some of these migrants returned to Amsterdam, as various names from Recife crop up again on the Amsterdam poor-relief lists after 1654. Not all of them stayed in Amsterdam, many setting out on new ventures in the West Indies, for instance to Jamaica, Essequibo, Guyana, or Curaçao.[321]

Many more paupers were directed to other destinations in the far west. The registers contain entries detailing payments 'for the poor going to ezequepe',[322] 'for helping paupers to cross to hiziquepe',[323] 'for persons going to yziquiepe, corasau and cayena',[324] and 'for others going to Cuyana'.[325] In May 1660 Francisco van Dalen stated that 'at the beginning of January he had arrived in "Cayanne" on board *The Land of Promise*. Later, another two ships arrived . . . with people who had come hither to set up a colony . . . including many Netherlanders, Portuguese Jews.'[326] Since the latter half of the seventeenth century Curaçao and Surinam (and St Eustatius, to a lesser extent, up to 1781) had been developing into the most important commercial centres in the western hemisphere under Dutch rule, and were therefore among the most attractive destinations for paupers sent from Amsterdam to the New World at the time.[327] From the 1720s onwards Curaçao was the most popular.[328] Surinam was another favoured destination, especially in the second half of the eighteenth century, as a result of the colonization project begun by the Amsterdam community in 1747.[329]

London

In the seventeenth century, there was a minimal level of immigration from London to the Portuguese community of Amsterdam. Emigration to London was a much more prominent trend, especially since the development of a distinct Anglo-Jewish community from the middle of the seventeenth century.[330] In the aftermath of the 'Glorious Revolution' of 1688 the position of English Jews was consolidated even further, and between 1680 and 1695 its Spanish–Portuguese community grew by 50 per cent. At this time London was becoming a leading centre of international trade, and continued to expand in the eighteenth century, overtaking Amsterdam. The relatively stable position of English Jewry, combined with apparently unlimited economic prospects, made London an attractive destination for Jews, rich and poor alike.[331] London was also often used as a way-station en route to the New World.

The early decades of the eighteenth century saw a steep rise in the numbers of poor people arriving in England, not only straight from the peninsula as a result of persecution there, but also indirectly via Amsterdam.[332] In fact, Vivian Lipman has calculated that during the second half of the eighteenth century the biggest contingent of immigrants to the Spanish–Portuguese community of London, nearly a third, came from Holland.[333] Between 1670 and 1699 London was the third most popular destination for poor Jewish travellers from Amsterdam, rising to first place after 1700 and falling only to second place after 1730.

The Spanish–Portuguese Jewish community of London—like its counterparts elsewhere—was less than delighted about the influx of poor refugees from the Iberian peninsula or indeed anywhere else, and made constant efforts to turn away those arriving destitute.[334] In the course of the seventeenth century, and certainly in the eighteenth, complaints from England about the steady stream of impoverished immigrants from across the Channel became increasingly strident. In a letter to the well-connected Rotterdam merchant and ship-owner Joseph de la Penha, dated 1692, the London Mahamad made an attempt to reduce the number of paupers coming from Amsterdam.[335] Some of them were simply sent back to Amsterdam, others dispatched elsewhere.

Some of those arriving in London soon moved on to other places, either following plans already made or simply going where opportunity offered. Often poor migrants travelled through London to reach further-flung destinations more easily. One of these was Gibraltar, in British hands since the War of the Spanish Succession: Abraham Morenu Franco, for example, together with his extended family, travelled from Amsterdam to Gibraltar through London in 1712.[336] The British colonies of Jamaica, Barbados, and New York were also popular goals.[337] Jacob de David Jessurun was sent from Amsterdam to Jamaica, picking up money in London to continue his journey (though in fact he then went back to Amsterdam instead!).[338] Abraham Nunez was also explicitly sent via London to Jamaica ('para Londrez y Jamaica'),[339] while the message given to Joseph Gomes Correa, Isaac de Andrade Velosinos, Abraham Alvarez da Costa, and others was somewhat vaguer: in 1705 they were told to travel to London and from there further on: 'p^{a} ir a Lond^{rs} y passar adiante'.[340]

In 1732 the Portuguese Jews of London came up with the idea of sending poor Jews to the British colony of Georgia in North America as a colonization project. In fact, this scheme may have set the example for the Surinam plan developed by the Amsterdam Portuguese community in 1747.[341]

France

Like England, France rose to economic and political prominence during this period, also overtaking the Dutch Republic by the early eighteenth century.[342] The attraction of France for poor Jewish migrants increased accordingly.

The Portuguese communities in southern France had always been reluctant to absorb poor refugees and offer them much help, co-operating with the authorities to expel them or move them on to other destinations, not only in 1619, 1636, and 1684, but well into the eighteenth century. This attitude reflected their own insecure position both at home and in French possessions overseas.[343] Thus in 1723 a document from Bordeaux relates to families being put on a boat from southern France to the Dutch Republic, as had been done in 1684.[344] Sometimes poor people were sent off to Amsterdam to be shipped to the Dutch colonies.[345]

However, the Amsterdam Portuguese community tried to turn the tide. People still came over,[346] but movements of poor in the opposite direction increased.[347] France often objected to this: in 1747 the *parnasim* of the Portuguese congregation in Bayonne wrote to their colleagues in Amsterdam to express their disquiet about the practice of 'dumping' paupers in southern France. The Amsterdam *parnasim* defended themselves with the assertion that they were not trying to get rid of their poor at the expense of the French community, assuming they were only sending in that direction people who had relatives there or who were able to fend for themselves.[348]

In the end, the policy of the Amsterdam Portuguese *kahal* succeeded: the balance of migration between the two countries was shifting, with the weight of settlement tending towards France—helped, but only in part, by the repatriation of a large number of the so-called *desterrados de França* after 1686.[349] Later, too, more and more poor Sephardim in Amsterdam chose to move to France. Jewish life was opening up there; the country offered relative security and had the benefit of being close to the Iberian peninsula. Above all, economic prospects were good and expanding: Bordeaux, for example, grew to be the country's major commercial centre and an important Atlantic port, offering constantly increasing possibilities to, among others, Portuguese merchants, who played an important role in the city's commercial life.[350] Over the course of the eighteenth century the Jewish population of Bordeaux grew from 500 to 1,500, most of them Portuguese, many of whom may well have passed through Amsterdam.[351]

After 1730 the Portuguese communities in France ranked third in the preferred destinations of Amsterdam's emigrating Jews, after the New World and London.[352]

Hamburg, the German States, and Denmark

Nearer 'home', Amsterdam could send its paupers to Hamburg, to other places in the German states, and to Denmark at small cost.[353] The distances involved were relatively short, making these desirable destinations for the migrants themselves, especially for women.[354] In many other cases these locations served as transit points on the way to south-eastern Europe and the Levant.[355] Hamburg, the German states, and Denmark were more popular in the first decades of the seventeenth century than later on, and were at no time of more than minor importance in taking poor Jews from Amsterdam.[356]

Hamburg's Portuguese community had its own pauper problem too. This is evident from the 1652 statutes by which the three existing *kehilot* merged to form the Hamburg Portuguese congregation of Bet Israel. This merger was intended, among other things, to benefit 'the poor who are present here in such great numbers and who need support . . . and can be given greater assistance by one Mahamad able to bestow greater care upon them like a father'.[357]

Poverty among Portuguese Jews in Hamburg continued well into the eighteenth century.[358] Meanwhile many rich Sephardim left the city in reaction to the anti-Jewish atmosphere and the increase in tax levied on the community. Therefore, neither Hamburg nor the cities of Altona and Glückstadt offered serious alternatives as a final destination for the poor leaving Amsterdam.

North Africa

North Africa, accounting for 2 per cent of emigration in the period 1598–1759, provided migration routes for paupers going both into and out of the Dutch Republic.[359] People were leaving Amsterdam for North Africa continuously during the early modern period. Among them were many *berberiscos* being sent back to their place of origin. Myrna Cohen Berberisco was one of them, leaving for Berberia in 1623.[360] Some went to North Africa to work, like the son of Sara Nunes, who went to Salé to act as an interpreter. Later examples of people moving from Amsterdam to North Africa include the group of nine poor Portuguese families who left in 1703, their travel expenses being covered by the Amsterdam Portuguese community.[361] Yet North Africa's economic and political prospects were never stable enough to make the region a major destination in the search for permanent shelter.

South-eastern Europe and the Levant

Most emigrants from Amsterdam headed west and south, locations to the south-east being less attractive. Nevertheless, as we have seen, in the early part of this period the Amsterdam Portuguese community encouraged the poor to move on to eastern destinations—or to return there: many arriving from south-eastern Europe and the Levant were sent back, including the *belogrados* once peace had, albeit temporarily, returned to the area.[362] However, the political instability and economic decline of the Ottoman Jewish communities towards the end of the seventeenth century and throughout the eighteenth made south-eastern Europe and the Levant an ever less attractive choice for Jews looking for somewhere to settle.[363]

One strand of particular interest is emigration to Erets Yisra'el at this time. With an annual intake of 3 per cent over the whole period, Erets Yisra'el constituted a destination of secondary importance for paupers from Amsterdam.[364] In 1633, during a period when no money was available from the *imposta* to fund travel except for those leaving for Erets Yisra'el, a group of emigrants set off from Amsterdam together for this destination.[365] There would have been another pulse of emigration during the excitement surrounding the mystical messiah Sabbatai Zevi in 1666. We do not know how many people left for Erets Yisra'el at this time, but we do know that the Amsterdam Portuguese merchant Juan de Yllan intended to go out with certain other people, taking fifty poor families with them, and to settle there permanently.[366]

Over time, emigration to Erets Yisra'el continued at a steady trickle. The poor in Amsterdam must have heard of the grim political and economic condition of the country from letters that came back to Amsterdam and from *sheliḥim* (emissaries) passing through and begging for money.[367] Even so, religious motives still prompted people to make for Erets Yisra'el, and references crop up regularly to departures of the poor for the Holy Land—for example, the three women who left for Jerusalem in the eighteenth century.[368] These three were among the many poor Jewish women travelling from one place to another, a phenomenon that deserves a closer look.

Female Migration

Mobility among Jewish women is not unique to the modern period. We know of Jewish women in the pre-modern world who travelled to places distant from their homes,[369] and the phenomenon was a common one in early modern times. One remarkable individual was Doña Gracia Mendes, who as head of a banking firm and trading company moved from Portugal through the southern Netherlands and Italy, finally settling in the Ottoman empire.[370] Many Ashkenazi women wandered through the German states and eastern Europe, arriving in Amsterdam while travelling on business or in search of safe haven and work: the ultimate example of this phenomenon was the businesswoman and diarist Glückl of Hameln.[371] Many non-Jewish women also travelled to Amsterdam, for various reasons, from other parts of the Dutch Republic and beyond.[372]

The situation in the Iberian peninsula was one of the 'push' factors driving women towards Amsterdam. In fact, many of the immigrants from Spain, Portugal, and France who were on poor relief in Amsterdam were female.[373] Why should this have been the case?

These women's motives in setting out for Amsterdam were various—political, personal, social, economic, or religious, often a combination. Some wanted to start a new life elsewhere after the death of parents or husband, perhaps joining family members already resident in the north. Rachel Lopez, for instance, arrived from Cádiz, where her father had died. She probably reached Amsterdam on her own, since on her orphan's petition her parents are still referred to by their Spanish names—Antonio Dias and Maria Lopez—with no mention of their Jewish names.[374] Abigail Mendes arrived in Amsterdam with her son, her husband Jeronimo Almanza having died in San Martin in Spain.[375] Others were participants in chain migration, following family members who had gone ahead.[376] For many women in both the peninsula and France, Amsterdam was an inviting place where they would almost certainly be able to call on assistance, if not from family or friends then through institutionalized sources of welfare.[377]

For New Christian women in the peninsula, arrest by the Inquisition or the fear of it must have been a major impetus behind the search for refuge elsewhere, instrumental as many of them had been in the transmission of Jewish tradition from parent to child.[378] This motive is explicit in the case of Ribca R^{s} Nabaro and the widow Rachel Pereyra, who upon their arrival in Amsterdam and registration for poor relief stated that they had 'come from the Inquisition'.[379] New Christian women would have been eager to reach a Jewish centre like Amsterdam where they were able to profess their Judaism openly.[380] Some may have made the long journey in the hope of finding a Jewish husband.

All these separate push and pull factors made Amsterdam a favoured destination for women leaving the peninsula. As early as 1615 the arrival of widows and orphan girls persecuted by the Inquisition and reduced to poverty was noticed,[381] and in 1618 Amsterdam's Portuguese Jews started to complain about the large number of poor women in their midst.[382] Nevertheless, the stream of female immigrants continued well into the eighteenth century.[383]

The arrival in Amsterdam of these women in ones or twos, or larger groups, reflects the tragedy going on in Spain and Portugal at the time. There were single women, alone or in the company of other women; married women with their children; grandmothers with grandchildren; orphans on their own; widows with nieces—in short, broken families.[384] A sample of the records of payments made to women having arrived in Amsterdam from the peninsula makes the point: 'to Izabel de Campos widow and family coming from Spain';[385] 'to the four women coming from Spain who are on *sedaca* together';[386] 'to Lea and Ribca Rs coming from Spain';[387] 'to some Portuguese women coming from Lisbon';[388] 'to Raquel Henriq^{s} coming from Portugal';[389] 'for the trip of the widows Sara Delgada and Rachel Namias and grandchildren coming from Portugal'.[390] In the charity books of the community, women pass from 'wife of' into 'widow of', without their husbands ever appearing in the community or city's registers.[391] We do not know why, where, and in what conditions they remained behind—if they did. Was it by choice or under coercion? Perhaps they settled down elsewhere. We can only guess at their fate.

The influx of poor women from the peninsula, many travelling via France, was soon followed by a wave of arrivals from Italy, the German states, and Poland, though the majority of these were male. Men and women alike fled from these areas to escape war and hostility at home and in search of economic improvement and shelter. The same motives must also have driven the many *belogrado* women who fled the devastations of war in the Balkans in hope of relief in the city they knew as 'the Jerusalem of the West', joining members of their Balkan community who had gone ahead of them. Quite a large proportion of the *belogrados* were women, who made up between a third and a half (and sometimes even more) of the Jews arriving in Amsterdam from the Balkans in the early 1690s.[392]

Many single female migrants were travelling around Europe in search of their husbands. Some, such as Ester Menasseh from Belgrade, were successful—although in Ester's case the success was a hollow one, for her husband had remarried in Amsterdam. Doña Jurada was another woman who must have come to the city looking for her husband. She arrived from Belgrade with her son Eliau Gaon in 1691,[393] and we know that she lost a child—not Eliau—in 1695.[394] The whereabouts of her husband remain unknown; to the best of our knowledge he never turned up in Amsterdam. Yet there must have been news that he had died by 1696, for in that year Doña Jurada is mentioned as the widow of Isaac Gaon.[395]

Female immigrants formed, of course, a particularly vulnerable group among the Amsterdam Portuguese Jews. Many arrived in misery. Rachel Lopez wrote that she was 'very poor and miserable'.[396] Sara da Fonsequa arrived with four small children in great need.[397] The petitions of women among the *desterrados de França*, forced to flee from France in great haste after the expulsion, also emphasized their poor state.[398] Quickly these women formed a majority of those drawing poor relief, although that disproportion was true of the city population as a whole, as it was in many other cities of early modern Europe.[399] Work was not always available, often badly paid, and frequently not taken up. Jewish partners were difficult to find. Even those orphan girls who were fortunate enough to be awarded sizeable dowries by the Amsterdam-based society Dotar or one of the other charitable foundations often failed to find husbands in the city.[400] All too many were doomed to a life of poverty, isolation, and loneliness.

Emigration from Amsterdam was predominantly male. Men often moved on to new places, either alone or at the head of a family unit.[401] This picture is consistent with that of emigration from the Dutch Republic in general, in which most emigrants were (mainly young and unmarried) men.[402] This tendency was buttressed by official policy in the middle of the eighteenth century, when the Amsterdam Portuguese community directed all unmarried men on welfare between the ages of 20 and 50 to leave the city for other destinations overseas.[403]

Many poor men entrusted their wives, children, or parents to the care of the Amsterdam Portuguese community when they moved on in search of other opportunities. The son of Sara Nunes, who as noted above settled in Salé, left behind his mother, a poor widow, relying on the care of the Amsterdam Portuguese community.[404] Another Sara, the wife of David Henriques Correones, was often left alone while her husband, a courier, travelled around delivering letters. In his absence Sara lived in a small alley, the Lazarussteeg, where she received monthly support payments from the community for nine years in succession.[405] A further example is the wife of Abraham Israel, who had come to Amsterdam from Pisa. From there he moved to Brazil, where he settled until 1654. In 1662 he turns up in Jamaica in search of gold, vanilla, and pimiento; in 1664 he is in London and in 1671 in Barbados. At various times he was back in Amsterdam receiving welfare payments himself, but more often he was abroad, leaving his wife and children behind in the city to be taken care of by the Amsterdam Portuguese *kahal*.[406] Brides at their civil marriage ceremonies often simply stated that their fathers were travelling.[407] Others told the clerks they had no idea about their fathers' whereabouts.[408] In all these cases Amsterdam Portuguese women conformed to the general pattern found in medieval and early modern Europe, Jewish and non-Jewish alike, where many women were parted from their husbands temporarily or permanently.[409]

Nevertheless, poor women among the Portuguese in early modern Amsterdam did travel abroad, just as they had travelled to get there. For the most part these journeys were relatively short, to destinations such as Hamburg, Antwerp, and London.[410] France was popular, too: Ester de Mattos was given money to leave for that country, together with her two children.[411] By the time she left, the expulsion decree had been annulled, and many *desterrados de França* had gone ahead of her. Others departed alone, or with their children and grandchildren, heading south and east, towards Gibraltar, Italy, North Africa, or the Levant.[412] One widow from Bragança in Portugal, for example, left with her son-in-law for Livorno in 1630 after a stay of nine weeks in Amsterdam.[413] Many of the women who left headed west, for example to Surinam, Curaçao, Jamaica, and New York.[414] Some even went round in circles, turning up in Amsterdam more than once: Rachel da Cuna travelled to London and back three times, in each case her travel expenses being covered by the Amsterdam community.[415] Others used Amsterdam as a port of transit and a source of financial support at the same time: Ester Rodrigues moved from Spain through Amsterdam to London in 1722.[416]

Women travelling were always at risk, as is evident from the many examples of women being captured by the Moors or others. Doña Isabel, the daughter of Simão Vaz Monis, fled Lamego in Portugal with her three children on a boat, and was most probably heading for Italy when she was captured; like Isabel Maria, mentioned above, she ended up in Algiers.[417] In 1700 the daughter of Rica Nunes Almeida was taken captive by the Moors, but was brought back safely from 'Berberya' to Amsterdam.[418] Various measures were taken to minimize the hazards. Some of these women may have decided to dress in men's clothes, a protective stratagem adopted by many women travelling by themselves in early modern Europe.[419] Others were accompanied by men for at least part of their journey: thus Aron, the son of Salomon Levy Maduro, accompanied his sister to Salé,[420] and Rachel Nassi's son travelled with her to London.[421] Others, such as the *belogrado* women, sought safety by travelling in groups.[422]

The reasons for female emigration were various. Some had family abroad: thus Sara Diaz left for Jamaica in 1685 to join her son-in-law (and possibly also her daughter).[423] The wife of Riby Juda Leb was given money to travel to Jerusalem, apparently to be reunited with her husband, who was living in the Holy City.[424] Debora Maduro and her mother Hana Levy Maduro sailed out for Curaçao, presumably to join relatives already present there.[425] Some took the initiative to start a family abroad: in 1688 Rica Nunes Almeida sent one of her daughters to get married in Surinam.[426] In 1710 she sent another daughter out as well, perhaps to create a similar opportunity for her too; it is possible that this is the girl who had been taken captive in 1700.[427] Others must have left primarily for socio-economic or personal reasons: the *belogrado* women moved on in search of a better refuge, finding the help offered them by the Amsterdam Portuguese barely sufficient to support them, while many of the French refugees returned home as soon as they were able to do so.

The Portuguese *kahal* did not treat women migrants any differently from men, and put similar pressure on them to leave the city. Those who were not members of the Portuguese *nação* or were unwelcome because of misconduct were most likely to be told to leave, though in some cases no reason is recorded. In 1676 Judith Nunez was sent to London with her family and told not to return; no further details are given.[428] Two years later, the *parnasim* reacted to the petition of the widow Simha Lopez by giving her money to travel to Hamburg, stating that she would receive no further monthly allowances whether she went or not.[429] The case of Sara Saso and her children has been mentioned above.[430]

Many more women arrived in the Portuguese community of Amsterdam and left for unknown destinations. These and all the women like them are part of the global picture of Jews in early modern times, men and women alike, wandering around the world in search of physical survival and peace of mind.

The Migration Balance

The courtyard of the Portuguese synagogue in Amsterdam in the seventeenth and eighteenth centuries must have swarmed with people and resounded with voices in a host of languages: Spanish, Portuguese, Ladino, Yiddish, Italian, German, French, Judaeo-Arabic, Dutch, and perhaps others as well. Having just arrived in the city by ship, by carriage, or on foot, the newcomers would tell their sorry tales and ask the officers of the *kahal* for charity, in person or in writing. We would have little idea of the misery suffered by many of these migrants if we relied exclusively on the testimony of these officers, who in most cases contented themselves with making brief, dry notes, and above all with recording the expenses they had reimbursed or the grants they had paid out.

The Amsterdam Portuguese community adopted a somewhat detached attitude to the steady stream of paupers entering their city. Every new arrival was slotted into the hierarchical system of Amsterdam Portuguese poor relief, which dictated the amount and duration of the relief to be given and also the permissible duration of the applicant's stay in the city and in the *kahal*. Believing that migrants from the Iberian peninsula were superior and of the elect, the *kahal* saw to it that the poor of the Spanish and Portuguese nation were favoured above all others, with especial privileges accorded to those New Christians who had adopted Judaism in Amsterdam. It was to them that the Amsterdam Portuguese felt particularly akin, and they made active efforts not only to support them when they got to Amsterdam, but to help them escape from the Iberian peninsula in the first place.

Their ties to those Sephardi paupers whose families had left the Iberian peninsula centuries earlier, often as professing Jews, were less close. These occupied a lower place in the ranks of privileged paupers, and were subjected to entry restrictions in the eighteenth century. These people reached Amsterdam without assistance from the Portuguese community, as did those one step below them on the privilege ladder, the *italianos*, *levantinos*, *berberiscos*, *passageiros*, *viandantes*, and *forasteiros*. Lower still were the *tudescos* and *polacos*, whose admission en masse finally led to the establishment of a separate *kahal*, although poor relief for them still remained largely in the hands of the Portuguese community until 1670.

A substantial proportion of the destitute entering the Amsterdam Portuguese community in the early modern period did not, in fact, originate in Spain, Portugal, or France, as was assumed until recently, and therefore threatened the carefully guarded Converso character of the *kahal*. This diverse substratum within the Spanish and Portuguese community came chiefly from Italy, North Africa, south-eastern Europe, and the Levant, was granted poor relief for a short time, and then disappeared from sight.[431]

The scale of migration to Amsterdam by Portuguese women from the Catholic world was remarkable. Many of them had left the Iberian peninsula by themselves or at the head of a family. Some had lost those closest to them in dungeons or at the stake, had fled in the hope of being speedily reunited with the rest of their family, or had set out alone in search of a new life in an openly Jewish environment. Many, having made it to Amsterdam, never left. Hence it is not all that surprising that the majority of those drawing regular poor relief in the Portuguese community were women.

The Amsterdam Portuguese community had no legal means of restricting the inflow of paupers to the city or of hastening their departure. Amsterdam was open to Jews just as it was to everyone else: a situation unique in the Jewish world at that time. Relations between the city of Amsterdam and the Portuguese community were not affected by the influx; nevertheless, for two centuries the Portuguese of Amsterdam tried to regulate Jewish migration into and out of the city. Self-preservation, limited work opportunities, fear of social unrest, and lack of financial resources all compelled the Portuguese to convey to the poor more or less subtly that they could not count on permanent assistance and would do well to seek shelter elsewhere.

Setting limits to poor relief was in fact a flagrant breach of the Jewish principle of mutual responsibility, a fact of which the Amsterdam *kahal* was fully aware. As long as there were adequate funds to provide some degree of support, as was the case until the middle of the eighteenth century, the Amsterdam *kahal*, unlike many other Jewish communities, never shut its doors completely on destitute newcomers, no matter where they came from. One reason for this was the constant fear that the Portuguese community might fall foul of the city authorities if it failed to care properly for Jewish newcomers, who might then become a burden on the city, seek alms from the churches, or turn to crime.[432]

Many migrants looked upon Amsterdam not as a final destination but—

sometimes out of choice, sometimes under duress—as a springboard from which to pursue promising new prospects further afield. Many men, alone or accompanied by their families, came and went repeatedly in a pattern of circular migration, pausing on return from each overseas expedition before looking forward to the next adventure. Often these men would set out on their own, entrusting their families to the watchful eye and care of the Amsterdam Portuguese *kahal*.

For the rest, the policy of the Amsterdam Portuguese *kahal* was deliberately geared to sending paupers on to other places, thus reducing the burden they represented at home. Sending migrants to the west, first to Brazil and later to Surinam and various Caribbean islands, was seen as having the double benefit not only of reducing the current burden of poor relief but potentially of yielding economic benefit to the home community, so making it easier to bear the cost of welfare payments.[433] In this matter as in that of supporting new migrants, the Amsterdam Portuguese were selective in deciding who was to be sent on a journey and where, attempting to reserve the new colonies for members of the Spanish and Portuguese nation. They were patently less inclined to send Jews of other nations to these favoured destinations, trying instead to relieve themselves of the burden of support by sending them elsewhere. This policy often failed, with those dispatched overseas often continuing to rely on Portuguese poor relief when settling abroad or returning to Amsterdam. Many non-Portuguese Jews, however, did return home or make a new life in nearby locations such as Hamburg, London, southern France, or the Mediterranean countries.

In short, many Jews felt compelled to turn their backs on the city of *ḥesed, sedaca*, and *gemilut ḥasadim*, to quote the *belogrado* Abendanon, soon after their arrival,[434] one illusion the poorer as they made their way to the next stopping place. The Jewish centres naturally preferred to hand out travel expenses just once rather than look after newcomers time and again, and the land and sea routes across and around Europe must have been crowded with Jews and Conversos trekking from one community to the next, fleeing war, expulsion, and persecution, or in search of a better life.[435] Many of them arrived at some point in the Amsterdam Portuguese *kahal*, to which more and more people applied for travel expenses to other places.

The migration policy of the Amsterdam Portuguese *kahal* was hampered by a lack of powers to regulate the flow of paupers. None of the steps it took to shake off the burden imposed by the poor could stop the growing tide of paupers appealing to it for help in the early modern period. In the next chapter, we shall see how the *kahal* developed demographically, not least by virtue of the increase of paupers in its midst.

CHAPTER THREE

DEMOGRAPHIC OUTLINE

Introduction

Population figures for the early modern period are generally no more than reasonable estimates. This is as true for Amsterdam as for any other city or country. It is even more difficult to put precise figures to demographic trends. The Amsterdam censuses of 1622 and 1795 have given rise to a variety of interpretations. Even though by the end of the sixteenth century both London and Paris were significantly larger in population terms, between that point and about 1670 Amsterdam underwent a spectacular expansion, its population growing from about 30,000 in 1578 to more than 200,000 in 1672. The pace of growth then tailed off, though the number of inhabitants continued to increase to 240,000 in 1735.[1]

Much of this population growth is attributable to a very large influx of immigrants, which included ex-Conversos from the Spanish and Portuguese empires and Sephardi, Italian, North African, Levantine, German, and Polish Jews. Various estimates of the numbers of Jewish immigrants were made in the seventeenth and eighteenth centuries. According to more recent calculations by Jonathan Israel, published in the *History of the Jews in the Netherlands*, Jews accounted for no more than a small proportion of the total population of Amsterdam at this time, rising from just 1.4 per cent (2,400) in 1650 to about 10 per cent (20,335) in 1795. The figures quoted by Israel indicate that at the end of the seventeenth century the Sephardim in the city were for the first time outnumbered by the Ashkenazim, whose ranks were greatly swelled by immigration at the end of the seventeenth century and throughout the eighteenth. Between 1700 and 1750 their number more than quadrupled (from 3,200 to 14,000), and from 1750 to the end of the eighteenth century it grew by another 50 per cent, to around 20,000.[2]

According to my own calculations, Israel's (and before him Nusteling's and Kaplan's) estimates of the Jewish population of Amsterdam in the seventeenth and eighteenth centuries are too low,[3] because they fail to include the presence of paupers (registered or not).[4]

Numbers of poor people are also elusive as it is by definition difficult to determine the extent of poverty. An important count of the Jewish population conducted in 1797 yielded higher totals of Jews living in Amsterdam, namely 20,304 for Ashkenazi Jews and 2,800 for Sephardi Jews. These figures proved to be similar to those arrived at one year later, in 1798, when the numbers of people in each of Amsterdam's different religious communities were counted. In 1799, these same figures formed the starting point for calculating the numbers of poor people within each of these communities. At that time (January 1799), the proportion of Ashkenazim on poor relief was assessed as being no less than 85 per cent, or 17,350 out of the 20,304 souls in the Ashkenazi community, while the proportion of Sephardi Jews on poor relief was said to be 55 per cent (1,530 out of a total of 2,800).[5] Before that date, the numbers of Sephardi and Ashkenazi poor were not assessed with any degree of precision.

That poverty was rife among the Ashkenazim in the early modern period is generally known. Well into the eighteenth century, foreign visitors often contrasted the rich Portuguese in Amsterdam with the poor Germans.[6] How correct was the picture of rich Sephardim and poor Ashkenazim, a picture that has survived for centuries? It is a fact that not only Ashkenazi but also Sephardi Jews, entrenched in their *kehilot* in Amsterdam, had to wrestle with widespread poverty. An economic adviser in Madrid, visiting Amsterdam in 1619, noticed that most of the Jews there at that time were poor.[7] In the historiography of Portuguese Jews, the initial phase (particularly the years 1615–40) and the middle of the eighteenth century are treated as the periods of greatest pressure on the community's resources. Little attention has been paid to the intervening period, though the Amsterdam Portuguese community was, in fact, bent under the weight of poor relief for two whole centuries.

The Scope of Poor Relief

In 1690 the Italian writer Gregorio Leti recorded some of his impressions of a visit to the Amsterdam Jewish community:

> The number of Portuguese Jews is made up of 450 families, apart from a few paupers, whose number can be ignored. Of these families, many enjoy great riches . . . By contrast, the 'Hebrei tedeschi' [Ashkenazim], while including some wealthy persons, albeit very few, and a small number of the well-to-do, are by and large a poor community . . . Portuguese Jews have a proud lifestyle, in the Spanish tradition, while German Jews live much more modestly, as is the German custom.[8]

Although Israel realized that Leti underestimated the number of paupers,[9] his demographic account treats Leti's estimates as a reliable reflection of the condition of the seventeenth-century Portuguese community.[10] For Leti and all other visitors to the Portuguese community in seventeenth-century Amsterdam, the Portuguese poor were apparently invisible. Leti described the contrast in the appearance of Ashkenazi and Portuguese Jews as follows: 'And in their [the Ashkenazi Jews'] synagogue only a few distinguished people are to be found, while in the Portuguese synagogue one rarely encounters anyone who has not paid attention to his appearance.'[11]

Leti's comments suggest that the Portuguese community managed to keep the issue of poverty away from the eyes of the world. It is possible that the Portuguese paupers themselves also tried to hide their condition from outsiders. However, anyone who looks at the early modern poor-relief ledgers of the Portuguese community, and notes the growing lists of people on benefits recorded in them, forms a different picture. In fact, an increasing number of paupers proved to be a growing burden for the Portuguese Jewish community. Let us examine the demographic and social trends more closely.[12]

The numbers of heads of household assessed for tax on general wealth were derived from the so-called *finta* and *promessas* records. The *finta* was a tax on general wealth, levied (and, if necessary adjusted) every two or three years by the charity administrators of the Portuguese Jewish community.[13] It amounted to approximately 2 per cent of the householder's wealth, which had to be handed over annually, in two instalments.[14] We do not know precisely how the administrators set the level of the tax: it could well be that the congregation appointed tax assessors and collectors. In fact, Saul Levi Morteira talks in a sermon of 1641 about well-to-do Amsterdam Portuguese being subject to assessment.[15] A similar practice was followed in various Jewish communities at that time.[16] The *parnasim* reserved the right to enforce payment 'by fines imposed with the necessary severity'.[17] The *finta* applied to all members of the community with general wealth of 100 guilders or more, which included some poor people.[18] Recipients of poor relief and synagogue staff were exempted, while women were rarely made to pay the *finta* until the end of the eighteenth century.[19]

Promessas or *offertas* were promises to contribute money to the Portuguese community's charity box (*sedaca*), made at synagogue services or on other occasions.[20] *Promessa* contributions were voluntary in principle, though social pressure must have been considerable, not only to give at all but also in respect of the level of the contribution. In the eighteenth century, *promessas* seem to have become almost obligatory. From incidents recorded chiefly during that century it appears that people refusing to make a *promessa* could expect to incur severe disapproval and even fines.[21]

Data taken from weekly, monthly, or periodic poor-relief registers indicate how many families were drawing permanent or temporary welfare payments from the Portuguese charity box. The data do not, however, include those paupers who did not draw poor relief from the Portuguese community, but were supported by relatives, acquaintances, or private organizations; nor do they include those leading a marginal existence or transient visitors.[22] Anonymous 'indigents' who drew charity from the community in the eighteenth century, for instance through the *Livro de segredos*,[23] have also been omitted, as have those paupers who, at the end of the seventeenth century and during the eighteenth, received monetary contributions or welfare in kind from legacies and were therefore entered in the pauper registers kept by the *kahal*. Until 1670, large numbers of German and Polish Jews were also supported by the Portuguese community.[24] These Ashkenazim on poor relief have also been omitted from the calculations.

Using these data, six categories were constructed: the number of families paying the *finta* tax; the number of families paying *promessas* only; the number of families paying *finta* and *promessas*; the number of families permanently on welfare; the number of families temporarily on welfare; and the number of families permanently or temporarily on welfare. Overlaps between the *finta* and *promessas* categories and between the category of families permanently on welfare and that of families temporarily on welfare were found to be negligible and have therefore been left out of the calculations.[25] It is not clear how many Portuguese Jewish families were not registered with the community; in any event, they are not included here, being listed neither in the taxation nor in the welfare registers.

Taking into account all these qualifications, the scope of poor relief among the Portuguese Jews of early modern Amsterdam can be represented graphically as shown in Figure 1 (see Appendix II).

What conclusions can be drawn from these figures? First of all, it is clear that the Portuguese community in early modern Amsterdam was not simply composed of very rich people and Leti's handful of paupers. Next, it appears that, in addition to families required to pay the *finta* by virtue of their wealth and families on welfare, there was an intermediate group who were not wealthy enough to have to pay the *finta* but not poor enough to end up on the welfare list.[26]

The number of recorded paupers also varied from one period to another. In times of war or epidemic, in severe winters, hot summers, or economic crises, the number of people on welfare increased. Thus, in 1665/6, when the Dutch Republic fought its second war against the English—and also the period of the turmoil caused by the mystical messiah Sabbatai Zevi—almost half the members (43 per cent) of the Portuguese community drew welfare benefits from the community chests and almost the entire revenue of the *kahal* was spent on poor relief.[27] The open-handedness of the community in this year was apparently occasioned by the turbulence associated with the messianic phenomenon.

In view of all these factors, calculations of the size of the Portuguese *kahal* in the seventeenth and eighteenth centuries, and in particular of the extent of poverty within it, must be treated with circumspection. Certainly, the number of paupers must have been greater than the registers suggest.

The sources I have consulted yield a larger number of Sephardi Jews than Israel, Kaplan, and Nusteling have indicated.[28] I have converted the number of families into the number of individuals, putting the average size of a Jewish family for the eighteenth century (except for *c.*1795) at 4.3 individuals. For *c.*1795 I applied different averages for the size of a family, differentiating between men, widows, other women paying *finta* tax and *promessas*, and all family units on welfare.[29] For the seventeenth century, the average family sizes, for people on welfare and for those paying the *finta* tax and *promessas*, are somewhat different.[30] Taking all sources together, the figures I arrived at exceed those adopted before now.

These calculations cast a new light on the composition of the Portuguese Jewish community in Amsterdam in the early modern period. In the first place, the community seems to have been much larger than Israel, Kaplan, and Nusteling have so far assumed. In my view, the figures arrived at by Isaac de Pinto more closely reflect the actual situation. The latter observed in 1748 that 'during the last twenty-five years the number of contributing members has declined from 629 to 610, while the number of families dependent on *sedaca* has risen from 450 to more than 750'.[31] According to de Pinto, therefore, the Portuguese community comprised more than 1,360 families in 1748, which corresponds to my estimate of 1,360 families *c.*1750. My calculations further yield a total of 1,269 families *c.*1795.

Second, it becomes clear that the Portuguese community of the seventeenth and eighteenth centuries included a much larger number of paupers than has been assumed. Third, the proportion of paupers in the population as a whole kept growing over the years. While in 1650/1 roughly one-fifth (19 per cent) of the community was on permanent poor relief and just under a third (27 per cent) on permanent or temporary poor relief, the percentages in 1700/1 were 27 per cent on permanent poor relief and 42 per cent on permanent or temporary poor relief. In the eighteenth century the proportions rose dramatically: the figures *c.*1730 were 50 per cent on permanent poor relief and 62 per cent on permanent or temporary relief. At the end of the eighteenth century, the proportion on permanent poor relief was put at 38 per cent and that on permanent or temporary poor relief at 52 per cent. The figure of 55 per cent for the proportion of Portuguese on poor relief produced by the census of 1799 thus differs only slightly from my figure of 52 per cent for paupers drawing permanent or temporary poor relief *c.*1795.[32]

The growth of the Sephardi population up to the middle of the eighteenth century largely reflected a growth in the number of paupers: that is, the community was patently growing poorer. The same inference can be drawn from the fact that fewer and fewer male heads of household were required to pay the *finta* tax.[33]

It remains an open question to what extent the percentage of Jews drawing poor relief from the Portuguese community of Amsterdam corresponded to the proportion of paupers in other groups in the city, in the Republic, and in other centres in western Europe. A comparison would in any case be difficult to construct, given that different criteria were applied in different places.[34] Even so, it seems reasonable to suppose that, with between 19 per cent and 27 per cent of its members on permanent poor relief in the seventeenth century and up to half on permanent poor relief in the eighteenth century, the Amsterdam Portuguese community occupied a fairly prominent position in the overall welfare picture. In Amsterdam and other Dutch towns the percentage of people on permanent poor relief in the seventeenth and eighteenth centuries ranged from 8 per cent to 25 per cent.[35] Seen in the light of these figures, the poor-relief census of 1799 does not convey a true picture of the extent of poverty in Amsterdam, as van Leeuwen and others have shown conclusively.[36] Even so, at 38 per cent, the proportion of the Portuguese community on permanent poor relief *c.*1795 was much greater than the 17 per cent on permanent poor relief in the rest of Amsterdam at the time.

In other towns of early modern Europe the percentage of paupers was probably higher than it was in Dutch urban centres. None the less, it did not exceed 35 per cent in most places during the seventeenth and eighteenth centuries, and was therefore lower than the percentage of persons on poor relief found in the Amsterdam Portuguese community.[37] However, if we look at other Jewish communities in the Dutch Republic, the percentages on welfare seem to be broadly similar to those among the Sephardim of Amsterdam. In the middle of the eighteenth century, over a third of the Jewish population of Leeuwarden was on welfare: more than the average in various towns in the Republic, but less than that found in the Amsterdam Portuguese community at the time.[38] In Rotterdam, half the members of the Jewish community appear to have been on welfare at the end of the eighteenth century,[39] mirroring the percentage in the Portuguese community of Amsterdam (though not that found in the Amsterdam Ashkenazi community, where the percentage was even higher).

It is more difficult to compare poverty in the Amsterdam Portuguese Jewish community with situations in other Jewish centres of Europe, simply because we have few concrete figures to go by. We do know, however, that in 1621, 50 per cent of the members of the Jewish community in Rome were dependent on welfare.[40] Indeed, there is mention of 90 per cent of Roman Jews being on poor relief in the seventeenth and eighteenth centuries.[41] In the Mantua Jewish community the pauper problem was less explosive, but there too 60 per cent were on regular or occasional poor relief in the middle of the seventeenth century; the percentage dropped to 25 per cent by the end of that century, but increased again to 38 per cent in 1738.[42] In the eighteenth century poverty was considered the most pressing problem of the London Jewish community.[43] In other European towns and villages, too, poverty seems to have been widespread among Jews in the seventeenth and above all in the eighteenth century.[44]

Such figures as exist for south-eastern Europe and the Levant suggest a broadly similar picture. According to some calculations, between 50 per cent and 75 per cent of the Jewish population in the seventeenth-century Ottoman empire were poor.[45] Other calculations yield slightly different results: for example, 43 per cent of the Sephardi congregation Gerush in Constantinople in the early seventeenth century were said to fall in the lowest tax brackets—along with 92 per cent of the city's Ashkenazi congregation.[46]

In summary, then, it should be noted that poverty in the Amsterdam Portuguese Jewish community was not atypical of the conditions generally prevailing in the Jewish world of the seventeenth and eighteenth centuries. However, the large percentage of Jews on poor relief in other seventeenth- and eighteenth-century European *kehilot* stood out glaringly from the much lower average proportion of paupers in the non-Jewish populations of early modern Europe.

Expulsions, wars, epidemics, and economic crises led to the migration of hosts of destitute Jews looking for new homes in attractive locations. Amsterdam was one of these. However, limited employment opportunities and natural population increase also brought vulnerability and poverty to the Amsterdam Jewish community.

Financial Strength

Between the *molte famiglie con gran richezza* and the *alcune poveri* observed by Leti in 1690,[47] it is possible to fit a whole series of gradations. Much as everyone was assigned a place in early modern Iberian society according to his or her birth, profession, and wealth,[48] so social stratification seems to have been handed down to, and adopted by, the Amsterdam Portuguese community. This is reflected, for instance, in letters and other documents written by Amsterdam's Portuguese Jews. In 1686 Abraham Idaña listed three distinct groups in the Portuguese community: the rich, the middle class, and the poor. He hastened to add—lest the reader gain the wrong impression—that all of them were most well mannered and held in high regard by the Amsterdam authorities.[49]

Sermons, too, extolled the existence of a fixed social order, a system in which everyone had his rightful place. Isaac Vellozino, addressing the *kahal* in 1675 in the Esnoga, the brand new synagogue, compared the Amsterdam Portuguese congregation to the four elements: fire, air, water, and earth. To begin with, there was the most powerful group, the rich. Next came the less fortunate who, in his opinion, also lived a very comfortable life. The third group, he continued, consisted of people who, with their moderate capital and hard application, could still make a respectable living; and the last group was made up of paupers who, plying various petty trades, earned just enough to survive amid their brethren.[50] That hierarchy was also reflected in the way the leaders of the Portuguese community classified their members, from the richest down to the poorest.[51]

Before setting out the relative financial strength of the various groups within the *kehilah*, on the basis of the tax registers, it is worth first considering the value of the guilder and the kind of budget families in the Dutch Republic lived on, the Sephardim included. The purchasing power of the guilder was of course susceptible to inflation. The economic climate, frequently affected by political crises, periods of war, and natural disasters, significantly influenced the cost of living, not least the prices of basic food products. While wages in the seventeenth and eighteenth centuries remained relatively stable, prices increased, especially in the first three-quarters of the seventeenth century and the last decades of the eighteenth. Thus, as time passed, the purchasing power of the guilder diminished, life became more expensive, and poverty increased.[52]

In the early modern period an adult would need 80–100 guilders a year to meet his essential needs, a child 40 guilders.[53] A skilled worker in the Dutch Republic earned around 300 guilders a year.[54] Living with a family consisting of five members, he would have spent 51–67 per cent of his income on food in the period 1638–1749. The remainder would have gone on clothes, fuel (peat and/or wood), soap, and rent.[55]

Many of the less fortunate among the Portuguese Jews lived on similar levels of income. Four Portuguese girls, orphans of a teacher at the Ets Haim yeshiva and self-supporting since the death of their father in 1701, earned 150 guilders a year printing *ketubot*, which comes close to the 40 guilders a child mentioned above.[56] The *ḥazan* (cantor) Abraham Baruch had a salary of 280 guilders, plus free accommodation: more or less similar to that of a skilled worker in the Dutch Republic. However, his family was much larger than the average, consisting of nine people including himself and his mother.[57] No wonder that his salary—as he claimed in 1643—was not enough for him to exist on without a welfare supplement. The Portuguese community intervened, but not lavishly: his salary was increased to 300 guilders.[58]

Some people had to manage with even less: with a yearly income of around 200 guilders, a family in the Dutch Republic in early modern times was teetering on the brink of poverty.[59] Many Dutch Sephardim were in this position, including the widow of the 'sohet & bodek' (ritual slaughterer and inspector of meat) Maimon Haiaia from Salé. From 1668 onwards she was paid 190 guilders a year, including peat and matzah meal, for herself and her five children. This was anything but generous, and she hovered on the verge of poverty.[60] The same situation applies to the widow of Aron Castiel and her family, who in 1729 received a yearly income of 185 guilders, including peat and matzah meal.[61]

Anyone subsisting on an income of below 200 guilders in 1640 would be in even more pressing need of charity to provide for their basic needs; the lives of these people will be examined more closely in Chapter 7.

People from the middle groups would live on larger budgets, usually spending around 500–1,000 guilders a year on food, clothes, rent, taxes, house servants, and expenses during childbirth, sickness, and death. There are many variations here. The grocer Josua Mendes, for example, spent 600 guilders a year in 1725: 500 guilders on household expenses and clothes, 100 guilders on rent.[62] David Franco Drago, a merchant, lived in a larger house together with his wife and nine children—of whom five died between 1681 and 1694—paying 140 guilders a year in rent. His expenditure during this period was higher, amounting to 1,000 guilders a year on household needs, including costs relating to illness and childbirth as well as clothes.[63]

A small group enjoyed much higher earnings and were among the wealthiest in the Dutch Republic.[64] One of them, Antonio Lopes Suasso (also known as Isaac Israel Suasso) was taxed in 1674 on a capital of 231,000 guilders—770 times as much as the yearly income of an average skilled labourer. Suasso's total wealth was valued at 1 million guilders before 1700, which put him among the country's financial elite.[65]

Antonio Lopes Suasso and others like him were, however, the exception rather than the rule. We can gain a picture of the financial capacity of the different elements of the Amsterdam Portuguese community in early modern times by analysing the taxes they paid.

On the basis of the tax register *Kohier van de 200ste penning* (the assessment register for the 0.5 per cent wealth tax levied by the city authorities) it is possible to establish how many Portuguese families were deemed to have wealth over 1,000 guilders. Just 48 households qualified in 1631; by 1674 the figure had risen to 245.[66] In 1675, 450 Portuguese families were considered to be liable to pay the *finta* tax, handing over a minimum of 2 guilders a year. The highest amount paid in *finta* that year was 484 guilders, but payments at that level were rare exceptions.[67] Though the assessment level varied, in general 200 guilders was the maximum annual payment during the seventeenth and eighteenth centuries.[68] As noted above, all Portuguese Jews worth more than 100 guilders were liable to pay the *finta*. From the data used by Vaz Dias and the calculations shown in Appendix I, it is possible to conclude that *c.*1675 approximately 54 per cent of *finta*-payers and 32 per cent of the total number of Portuguese families had wealth amounting to 1,000 guilders or more.[69]

The *Kohier van de Personeele Quotisatie* (personal quota assessment register) for 1742 lists a total of 332 Portuguese households with an annual income of 600 guilders or more. Of these, men headed 279 households and women 53. In short, according to this register, 67 per cent of the male heads of households who paid the *finta* in the middle of the eighteenth century, and 20 per cent of all Portuguese families at that time, had an annual income or general wealth of 600 guilders or more. These proportions echo those in the overall population of Amsterdam.[70]

The sources from 1674 and 1742 use different criteria (one relates to households with general wealth over 1,000 guilders, the other to those with incomes over 600 guilders); also, as noted above, real incomes tend to change over a period of seventy-five years as a result of relative shifts in costs and earnings. Nevertheless, these figures enable some observations to be made about changes in the financial strength of members of the Portuguese community, certainly if we compare the numbers of Portuguese families with incomes or wealth of 1,000 guilders or more. In the period between *c.*1675 and the middle of the eighteenth century, the number of *finta*-paying families with general wealth of 1,000 guilders or more barely changed (245 as against 244—male or female—heads of Portuguese families). As a proportion of the total Portuguese population, however, there was a substantial drop of 14 per cent: in 1742 only 18 per cent of households in the community had an income or wealth of 1,000 guilders or more, as against 32 per cent in 1675.

In short, only a small section of the membership of the Portuguese community registered for tax had an annual income or general wealth of 1,000 guilders or more in about 1750. The great majority—*c.*1675 some 68 per cent, and in the middle of the eighteenth century around 80 per cent— fell below that level. The gulf between a broad base and a narrow top layer, a phenomenon that began to become apparent during the third quarter of the seventeenth century, had therefore widened within the space of seventy-five years. Patterns in the Portuguese community, moreover, did not differ markedly from those in non-Jewish urban centres or in Sephardi communities elsewhere in the diaspora.[71]

Using Daniel Swetschinski's analysis of *finta*-payers in the period 1678–95,[72] we can also infer the financial strength of members of the Portuguese community from their internal tax assessments. That approach conveys a more accurate picture of the structure of the community. I have retained Swetschinski's division into five groups by tax assessment, but have extended the period under review.[73]

From the collected data we can deduce that the great majority (between 60 and 78 per cent) of the Portuguese community in the seventeenth century had general wealth of 500 guilders or less. During the seventeenth and eighteenth centuries, a third to a half of this group, taxed at between 2 and 10 guilders, teetered on the poverty line, if we put that at a general wealth of about 200 guilders.[74] Between 1650 and 1675 the two lowest wealth groups shrank, while the middle[75] and top[76] strata expanded. From 1675 to the beginning of the eighteenth century, the lowest-income group grew larger; when it stabilized over the eighteenth century, the great majority of households (between 79 per cent and 84 per cent), that is, more than in the seventeenth century, still fell into the lowest wealth groups.

The middle group, with general wealth ranging from 550 to 2,500 guilders, expanded from 21 per cent of the whole in 1650 to 31 per cent in 1675.[77] This reflects an increase in prosperity to a peak never again attained.[78] Between 1675 and 1700 this group was nearly halved (from 31 per cent in 1675 to 16 per cent in 1700). Swetschinski also draws attention to this development.[79] From figures for the eighteenth century, however, it appears that this decline did not foreshadow the disappearance of the intermediate group, nor yet a greater polarization between rich and poor. The decline was temporary, and the middle group continued to make its presence felt in the eighteenth century, even though its members made up a smaller proportion of the community: in the eighteenth century around 12 per cent of all Portuguese had general wealth of between 550 and 2,500 guilders.[80]

The rise in prosperity between 1650 and 1675 was also striking in the top group, consisting of those with general wealth of more than 2,550 guilders,[81] which increased from 1 per cent to 9 per cent of the total over this period. Again like the middle group, these highest earners declined in prominence from 1675 to 1700, slipping from 9 per cent to 5 per cent of the total. From 1700 the situation stabilized, and from about 1730 to the end of the eighteenth century this group amounted to between 4 and 7 per cent of the total Portuguese population.

What do these figures tell us about the relative financial strength of the various groups in the Portuguese community? The structure of the community did not fundamentally change during the seventeenth and eighteenth centuries. It is true that from the second half of the seventeenth century the community became more sharply polarized, but for two whole centuries the Portuguese community possessed a stable, almost unchanging base of between 60 and 84 per cent with general wealth of 500 guilders or less. At the other end of the pyramid was a small top layer, which emerged chiefly between 1650 and 1675 and which persisted into the eighteenth century, consisting of the 4–7 per cent of the community with general wealth of more than 2,250 guilders. Between the broad base and the tiny tip there was a small middle stratum, which up to 1700 comprised between 16 and 31 per cent of the total. This middle stratum, with general wealth from 550 to 2,500 guilders, admittedly shrank in size during the eighteenth century, but nevertheless continued to make its presence felt.

Thus the analysis of taxation and poor-relief registers merely confirms the conclusion drawn from the municipal tax data: namely that the Portuguese community in Amsterdam was by no means made up of extremely rich families. Only a narrow top stratum could be called truly prosperous. In the seventeenth and eighteenth centuries, the majority of Portuguese Jews lived modest lives not far from poverty, with a small middle stratum of the relatively comfortable dividing them from the upper crust. In many towns of the Republic, incidentally, the general wealth structure was not very different.[82]

Family Composition

Who were all the different individuals identified simply as 'heads of household' on the long lists so carefully compiled by diligent clerks? That question is difficult to answer, especially in the case of heads of household marked as eligible for payment of the *finta*. Until late in the eighteenth century the tax registers of the Portuguese community were almost invariably confined to men, because until that time female heads of household were in principle exempted from paying the *finta*. The same was more or less true of those too poor to be obliged to pay the *finta* but not so poor that they received welfare, although this category (many of whom would have paid *promessas*) contained a larger number of women than the *finta*-payers. More detailed information about the family composition of those paying the *finta*—and *promessas*—is as yet lacking, and this might well prove a rewarding subject for closer research.

We know more about the group drawing permanent or temporary poor relief from the *kahal*. Not only were men as well as women registered as recipients of *sedaca*, but the notes attached to their records give us some information about their status and other attributes. Thus, in the case of women, the notes may tell us if they are married or widowed. Sometimes we are even told when a wife lost her husband. Moreover, it is often possible to infer whether the individuals concerned are orphans.[83] Finally, there are occasional references to the recipient's place of origin, occupation, and Amsterdam address.[84] The size of a family can often be deduced from the quantity of matzah meal allotted to the head of the household by the *kahal* for Pesach (Passover): in principle every needy person was issued with 8 pounds of matzah meal a year during the seventeenth and eighteenth centuries.[85] In the middle of the eighteenth century, the poor-relief records of the *kahal* grew so bulky and the number of paupers so large that the registration rules had to be tightened. From then on the poor-relief lists expressly recorded the number of persons subsumed under the name of a particular head of family.[86] From the middle of the eighteenth century we therefore have a more detailed picture of the family structure than for the preceding period.

Who exactly was considered eligible for weekly, monthly, or temporary poor relief? In the seventeenth century most of the beneficiaries were migrants: some households were made up of single males, but the majority were single women and small groups, the residue of broken families. In addition there were a number of large families headed by men.[87] In the course of the early modern period, as discussed in Chapter 2, these migrants came to Amsterdam from far and wide, not just from the Iberian peninsula. Some chose to travel on their own, leaving the rest of the family to fend for themselves. Manuel Nunes Carvalho, for instance, fled to Amsterdam for fear of the Inquisition in Oporto in Portugal in 1689 in such a hurry that he was forced to leave his wife and children behind.[88] Jacob Rodrigues Carrion reported that his parents still lived in Spain. Rachel Louzada's mother had also been left behind in Spain. Isaac Baruch's father was still in Portugal, while Rachel Aboab's father lived in Venice.[89] Isaac Albergu from Salé declared that 'his father Moses Albergu [had gone] to Jerusalem, but that he did not know if he was dead or alive'.[90]

The family structure of the migrants in Amsterdam was not always stable, and often unusual: Sara Thomas lived with her grandson;[91] Judith Rodriguez had the sole care of her granddaughter.[92] Judith Valensin had three grandsons living with her.[93] Rachel Semah da Costa looked after the two children of her son-in-law David Cohen de Lara.[94] Sara Lopez Pitta lived at first with her two sons; then a third one joined them; then Sara was abruptly left on her own; and after her death a granddaughter received poor relief in her stead.[95] Abraham Fiqueiroa, having had his house full for years with family members coming and going, certainly since 1649, suddenly found himself on his own in 1670.[96] In 1667 Ester Nunes de Sevilla was the head of a family of five. Within one year, between 1673 and 1674, this family suddenly shrank to two.[97] Abraham Arias's family fluctuated between five and three persons, and was joined by new members just after it had grown smaller.[98] In short, for many people family life in Amsterdam was constantly in flux as family members came and went.[99]

In the eighteenth century the family composition of Portuguese Jews on poor relief in Amsterdam changed. This was probably due to the deteriorating economic situation and the consequent increase in unemployment.[100] The face of poverty was altered, inasmuch as men heading large families now made up the majority of those on the welfare lists. Around 1730 there were four times as many families with a man at their head on regular poor relief as there were in 1700/1.[101] In the period between 1650/1 and 1700/1 women headed between 54 and 64 per cent of the families on some form of poor relief, and between 63 and 83 per cent of those drawing regular poor relief from the *kahal*.[102] In both cases, the figures declined steadily, with the highest percentage in about 1650 and a change from a majority of families headed by women to a minority at some time between 1700 and the 1730s. From *c.*1730 to *c.*1750 the number of female heads of household on poor relief increased once more, but never again constituted a majority, with the exception of single women, who throughout most of the early modern period, apart from the 1730s, outnumbered single men on welfare.[103] A predominance of male heads of household among families on welfare began to set the pattern of the distribution of charity in the Portuguese community during the eighteenth century, during which they made up between 52 and 66 per cent of recipients.[104]

How large, on average, were the households on poor relief? Like those outside the Jewish community, poor households drawing welfare benefits from the Portuguese were generally small: at least a quarter of them in the seventeenth century and roughly one-third of them in the eighteenth century consisted of single individuals. Together with two-person families, these small units made up the majority of households on poor relief in nearly all sections of the period studied here.[105] Large families comprising five or more persons accounted for roughly one-quarter of the total number on welfare in both the seventeenth and eighteenth centuries, while the intermediate stratum, households consisting of three or four people, was the smallest of all.[106]

Small families often consisted of a woman—single, married, or widowed—with perhaps one other person. The larger the family, the more likely it was to be headed by a man rather than a woman. Thus in 1650/1 single men accounted for no more than 6 per cent of one-person Portuguese households on welfare in Amsterdam, while in the same financial year 70 per cent of families consisting of five or more people were headed by men. Here too, a growing trend can be discerned: in 1675/6, 17 per cent of one-person Portuguese households consisted of single men; by 1700/1 that figure had grown to 32 per cent and by the 1730s to 53 per cent, and the percentage continued to fluctuate around the 40 per cent mark during the rest of the eighteenth century. The great majority of large families continued to be headed by men, ranging from 68 per cent in 1700/1 to 92 per cent of households of five persons or more in the 1750s. In families consisting of three or four persons the balance clearly tilted, in particular from 1700, towards the male-headed household, leading to a sizeable majority of families headed by men from the 1730s up to the end of the eighteenth century.[107]

The average number of people in a family on poor relief, deduced from the total quantities of matzah meal distributed annually, varied from 2.6 to 2.9 in the seventeenth century and from 2.0 to 3.2 in the eighteenth century.[108] This low average size is also found in pauper families elsewhere in early modern Europe.[109] The family structure of Portuguese paupers in Amsterdam was therefore not unusual, but conformed to the general picture of paupers in early modern Europe. In the seventeenth century, there was a preponderance of small households headed by women; in the eighteenth century the picture changed as large-scale family immigration, population growth, economic crises, and wars led to greater numbers of men becoming dependent on poor relief. As a result, the face of poverty assumed a different character.

Conclusion

This chapter has drawn a demographic outline of poverty in the Portuguese Jewish community in early modern Amsterdam. It has become clear from examining records of the numbers of people on poor relief that at times the community was larger than used to be assumed. Behind the beautiful façade of prosperity and *grandeza* that the community liked to show to the outside world, the *kahal* had to wrestle with the ever more pressing dilemma of having to look after paupers, who had flocked to Amsterdam expecting to find there a safe and sheltered life, free of persecution, war, and economic depression. By the end of the seventeenth century a third of all Portuguese Jews were drawing permanent poor relief and almost half were drawing either permanent or temporary poor relief. In the eighteenth century, the ratio ran out of control. In the context of the Jewish world of that time, the level of poverty in Amsterdam was not especially striking, although it was much higher than the norm in early modern Europe.

The Portuguese community seems to have been less polarized than has generally been supposed. Great prosperity was found only in a narrow top stratum, but a sizeable middle layer was present in the eighteenth century. Having said that, even during the so-called 'Golden Age' of Amsterdam Portuguese Jewry the great majority of the community lived at best modestly and at worst below the poverty line. In accordance with the Iberian pattern, everyone, from the top to the bottom, was assigned a status and fitted into a hierarchy based on wealth, profession, and family background.

Portuguese on welfare, like other paupers in early modern European society, were often found in small families, mostly headed by women; larger families tended to be headed by men. In the eighteenth century, the character of Portuguese poverty changed. From then on—with the exception of single women—the poor were dominated by men trying to support their families through the economic slump with financial help from the Portuguese community. The next chapter will examine how the Portuguese organized poor relief for the less fortunate in their midst.

CHAPTER FOUR

THE ORGANIZATION OF WELFARE

Introduction

Poor relief was organized on a number of different levels and reflected a variety of cultural influences. It was centralized, yet subdivided. It was institutionalized, yet showed close personal involvement and private initiative. It was hierarchical, yet also mutual. Age-old Jewish charitable concepts could be perceived, yet Iberian and Catholic patterns were also interwoven. Modernity set in, yet conservatism persisted.

Rabbis, mostly recruited from various Jewish centres round the Mediterranean, introduced a traditional Jewish model of social and religious organization when founding the new Portuguese Jewish community in the north. Armed with experiences from their own *kehilot*, they were pleased to put their knowledge and ideas at the disposal of the Amsterdam Portuguese community.[1] The Jewish heritage which they transplanted to Amsterdam was influenced in its turn by factors in both their immediate and more remote surroundings.[2]

It is not surprising, then, that the Amsterdam Portuguese community incorporated many elements of the Sephardi model from Jewish communities in southern Europe and the Orient, above all from Venice.[3] More general references to traditional Jewish models were made in the founding articles of the burial society Gemilut Hasadim in 1643, which make it clear that the organization was based on *ḥevrot* (societies) found in other parts of the Jewish world: *como hay em outras partes*.[4] Thus the Amsterdam Portuguese *kahal* was to some extent modelled on traditional Jewish forms of organization and on the southern European and oriental Sephardi model in particular.

Within the Portuguese community, the Jewish tradition rubbed shoulders with concepts and structures of poor relief characteristic of Catholic and Iberian society brought to Amsterdam by the immigrants as part of their intellectual baggage. Moreover, being modern citizens, some at least of the newcomers must also have been au fait with the latest ideas on poor relief current in early modern Europe and have used some of these ideas when setting up a poor-relief system in Amsterdam. Traces of this cultural encounter can also be found in certain forms of social care dispensed by the Amsterdam Portuguese, who could also see for themselves how novel ideas for poor relief were applied in the Dutch city. The new views on dealing with and caring for paupers must have given even the traditional Jewish community pause for thought and encouraged them to opt for the greater centralization of poor relief. However, in earlier times and then during the Reformation, charity in both Catholic and Protestant Europe came in various forms, on the one hand controlled centrally by Church and state and on the other hand run by individuals and independent institutions.[5] The same two strands of provision were evident in the Jewish world.

Eventually, a strongly centralized system of poor relief emerged in Portuguese Amsterdam, led by an executive that liked to co-ordinate all its activities and to keep a tight rein on the course of events. Alongside this there emerged a growing network of organizations that distanced themselves from the central authority and adopted an independent stance. Last but not least, individual assistance by private donors constituted an important element of charitable activity. Incidentally, it must be noted that charity proceeded not only on a vertical plane, from high to the low, with help being passed down to the indigent by agencies or individuals, but also on a horizontal plane, with many organizations and individuals assisting one another in times of need. Let us look more carefully into this kaleidoscopic welfare system and analyse its most important features.

The Theory: Modern Elements in a Traditional Approach

Centralization versus Private Initiatives

During the establishment of the Portuguese congregations in Amsterdam at the beginning of the seventeenth century, it was taken for granted that poor relief was one of the tasks that fell under the central control of the communal leaders. All forms of basic care were dispensed by the central authority or by one of its subsidiaries. This was, in fact, part of the agreement between the Jewish community and the city government mentioned in Chapter 2. The leaders of the Portuguese community were aware that their obligations to the city included responsibility for ensuring peace and order among their members and keeping the poor under control. This, they believed, was best achieved by a co-ordinated system—which had the incidental benefit of enabling the leaders to keep a closer watch on the morals of the community.

In addition, by centralizing poor relief the Amsterdam Portuguese community aimed to bind its members, many of whom had come into contact with a Jewish community and the public profession of Judaism for the first time in their lives on arriving in the city, more closely to the Jewish faith, and to drive home to them their duty to practise charity. By compelling them to carry out certain tasks and assigning to them various positions in the charitable work of the Portuguese community, it made a strong claim on their loyalty. The community's policy of centralization also ensured control over the financial contributions of its members, on which the whole system of poor relief was based. Not only did a large proportion of the taxes the Portuguese community imposed on its members flow into poor relief, so did the entry fees levied by various organizations directly dependent on the Portuguese community, along with obligatory annual contributions and voluntary donations.

However, the centralization of poor relief was not adopted simply in response to local needs or in fidelity to models of organized Jewish charity elsewhere. The Portuguese community would also have been familiar with the newest ideas on poor relief, based on the belief that a co-ordinated approach was the best way of tackling the problem. A similar trend towards centralization in order to fight poverty and contain disorder can be seen elsewhere in both the Jewish and the non-Jewish world.[6]

The centralization trend made itself felt early on. The first two Portuguese congregations, Bet Jacob and Neve Salom, decided in about 1616 to combine forces in burying the dead, caring for the sick, and fostering education through the Bikur Holim and Talmud Torah societies.[7] In 1622 a co-ordinating body of congregations, of which by that time there were three, was set up: this was the *imposta* board, mentioned in Chapter 2, whose primary task it was to stem the influx of paupers and to hasten their departure, but which also concerned itself with collecting taxes earmarked for this project. In addition, it co-ordinated and centralized various other communal tasks.[8] The merger of the three congregations in 1639 was therefore a logical development that came about in part because of the desire of the Portuguese *kehilot* to take adequate care of their poor.[9]

Many welfare activities were under the direct or indirect control of the Mahamad, an administrative body composed of six *parnasim* and one *gabai* or treasurer. The Mahamad not only co-ordinated all the activities listed in the previous paragraph, but was also the supreme Portuguese Jewish authority. Its members were invariably chosen from the highest strata of Portuguese society, far removed in terms of income and status from the less fortunate. The Mahamad filled gaps in its ranks by co-option, thus ensuring the continuity of its leadership. It also appointed the heads of the community's most important charitable and educational institutions. Election to the administration was therefore part of a closed system, to which the elite alone had access.[10] All executive functions were reserved for individuals who, by virtue of their wealth, paid the highest *finta* taxes. They represented the greatest concentration of power within the *kahal*, with those at the top enjoying priority over all the rest. Moreover, it appeared that the richer you were, the longer you held on to your leading position. This type of aristocratic, oligarchic administration was not confined to Portuguese Amsterdam; a similar structure was the norm in various *kehilot* of medieval and early modern Europe.[11] *Hahamim* such as Raphael Mordecai Malki in seventeenth-century Jerusalem and, before him, Samuel de Medina in sixteenth-century Salonika justified the oligarchic rule of many Jewish communities by their most affluent members on the grounds that those who bore the financial burdens of the community should be given the power to regulate communal affairs.[12] Elitist leadership was also a characteristic feature of the contemporary non-Jewish world.[13]

The Portuguese community handled the organization of poor relief as efficiently as possible, and tried, for better or worse, to cover the entire spectrum of charitable work. Certain aspects of relief it left, either by choice or by necessity, to organizations that ever since their inception had attempted—sometimes, it is true, with the approval of the central organization—to act independently, and continued to do so during the latter part of the seventeenth century and on into the eighteenth. Despite the strong drive for centralized control, private initiatives were by no means stifled. Together, acting in harmony or otherwise, the Portuguese Jews of Amsterdam built up a reputation as a charitable community that itself exerted a strong attraction on outsiders.

Selective Poor Relief

The Portuguese were selective in dispensing poor relief. In that respect they seemed not only to be following precepts deeply rooted in Judaism,[14] but also to be influenced by the selective model of early modern south European society, in particular that of the Iberian society in which they had lived as New Christians.[15] The same principle was reinforced by the new ideas on poor relief current in early modern Europe. From the sixteenth century onwards, the belief had been spreading that the poor could no longer be aided indiscriminately. Poor relief would henceforth have to be confined to those who, through unemployment, illness, permanent invalidity, or old age, could no longer work. The rest—that is, those who, though able to work, preferred to rely mostly on poor relief—would no longer qualify for assistance.

While the Amsterdam Portuguese did not commit their own poor-relief philosophy to paper at any great length, they were able to consult the treatise on the subject written in 1661 by Abraham de Olivera, mentioned in Chapter 2. Though it had been written in Bordeaux, it seems highly probable that the Amsterdam Portuguese were aware of the ideas advanced by Olivera in his *Tratado de la hobligaçion que todos tienen de dar limosna a los pobres*, a title resembling those circulating in the Spanish empire, such as Juan Luis Vives's *De subventione pauperum*, Tomás de Trujillo's *Tratado de la limosna*, and Martín Batista de Lanuza's *Tratado sobre el modo de distribuir y repartir la limosna con discreción, mérito y utilidad*.[16]

Olivera's treatise seemed to address the well-to-do Portuguese living in France, striving to instruct them in the Jewish laws concerning charity and to persuade them to aid the poor. The poor were not all lumped together: Olivera placed paupers into various categories, discussing the differences between them at some length.[17] Thus he distinguished between *pobres menesterosos*, *pobres de solemnidad*, *pobres mendicantes*, and *pobres vergonzosos*. The first group could count on assistance because they did not earn enough by their work to support their families. *Pobres de solemnidad* had no work, or were unable to fend for themselves by virtue of old age or illness. 'Mendicant paupers' roamed through various countries and usually received more money than 'solemn paupers', but had nevertheless to be assisted, though *pobres de solemnidad* were more deserving of poor relief than these transient paupers.[18] Finally there were the 'genteel poor', who had seen better days but had been reduced to poverty by adversity. This group also included those who had never had an occupation and had had a little capital at their disposal, that little having usually gone by the time they reached old age. For that reason this group, too, was deserving of assistance.[19] Thus Olivera differentiated between various groups of indigents but did not deem any of them ineligible for relief.[20]

The Portuguese community of early modern Amsterdam must have applied criteria similar to Olivera's, even though they left us few explicit references to the subject. What is clear is that ethnic and religious background, and financial need, were among the factors taken into account in deciding whether to award relief. Correct and honourable behaviour also became a leading consideration. As elsewhere in Europe, the age-old line between the deserving and the undeserving poor was being drawn once more.[21] Moreover, Portuguese paupers in Amsterdam were granted relief before others, in accordance with the Jewish precept that *sedaca* begins at home. When the *pekidim* and *hahamim* of the Sephardi community of Jerusalem wrote to ask for help in 1752, the Amsterdam *parnasim* had recourse to this principle in their response: 'It is an established fact that, in keeping with the teachings of our famous scholars, we are obliged to look after the poor of our own community first, and to perform the relevant administrative tasks . . . which is why we have decided to limit the above-mentioned subsidy.'[22]

Selection was not, however, taken to extremes. There were extenuating circumstances in many cases that militated against too strict an approach. The *kahal*, confronted with a continuous stream of refugees who needed help and came knocking at their door, could not be blind to the Jewish principle of mutual responsibility when considering those who found it difficult to find work in the Dutch Republic. In the first decades of the seventeenth century there was no alternative source of poor relief for these people, either in Amsterdam or anywhere in its environs, so that Jewish paupers had no one else to care for them.[23]

The result of all this was a relatively flexible poor-relief policy, certainly in the seventeenth century, though paupers of the Spanish–Portuguese Jewish nation, former Conversos, enjoyed clear preference over all others, often receiving supplements to inadequate wages. The unemployed, the ill, the old, and the infirm could all count on assistance. The records analysed in Chapter 2 show that transient paupers were given assistance on arrival and helped to continue their journeys with travel allowances. Similar help was given to paupers who, though adequately trained in a craft or profession, could find no work because of restrictive measures that applied in the city. Also, discreet assistance was given to genteel paupers.

The basic premises on which the Portuguese community selected its poor for relief, then, differed little from those applied by the authorities—national, urban, or ecclesiastical—across early modern Europe. However, the Portuguese also applied rules specifically geared to the character of the Jewish community in general and that of Spanish–Portuguese Jewry in particular.

Criteria for Granting Poor Relief

The selective approach to poor relief was adopted from the earliest days of the Portuguese community. Though the sources we have for these years are sparse, we can infer from them that paupers were assigned a fixed place in the hierarchy. There were several distinct groups of paupers, including those who received assistance on a permanent basis—the *pobres da terra*.[24] Then there were the paupers who were not intended to stay in Amsterdam for long. These were registered as 'strangers', 'transients', or 'paupers assisted to move abroad'.[25]

Not until the adoption in 1639 of the statutes of the newly merged Portuguese community, henceforth known as the Kahal Kados de Talmud Torah, were the conditions laid down that paupers had to meet in order to qualify for permanent poor relief. Good behaviour was mentioned explicitly. A scale of payments was laid down with minimum and maximum levels. Finally, it was stipulated that, having been selected as eligible, the poor who actually received relief were to be chosen by lot: 'Paupers admitted to the *rescodes da sedaqua* [monthly poor-relief list] have to be persons of good repute and behaviour, and will be chosen by *busulo e balas*, no house receiving more than from two to six guilders a month.'[26] These criteria remained unchanged from 1639 onwards.

The Ethno-Religious Aspect

When it came to admitting paupers to poor relief, the Portuguese Jewish community of Amsterdam had to steer a careful course for two centuries while balancing various interests against one another. As mentioned earlier, the crux of its policy was to bind the newcomers from the Iberian peninsula, already united by their common experiences, to Judaism, and to prevent them from turning to other religious congregations in the city or elsewhere, or from backsliding.[27]

This principle was stated expressly in 1639 in the statutes of the newly merged Portuguese congregations, and was also applied when it came to the admission of paupers to permanent poor relief: the Kahal Kados de Talmud Torah was meant first and foremost for members of the Spanish and Portuguese Jewish nation, with the implicit understanding that precedence would be given to the Spanish and Portuguese who had come as Conversos from the Iberian peninsula.[28]

That article was observed to the letter: new members had to establish their antecedents. Refugees from the Iberian peninsula had to prove their Jewish descent; newcomers from Jewish centres had to prove their Spanish or Portuguese roots. These stipulations applied to rich and poor alike. Manuel Nunes from Fundão in Portugal, for instance (who does not appear on the welfare lists), mentioned in his application for circumcision that he was *judeo da nação*. At the end of the application, a witness attested that he knew Manuel as a *judeu de pai e mai* (on both his father's and his mother's sides).[29] The facts set out in the petition of Sara Rodrigues Ferois—her husband had been burned at the stake before she took her son on the long journey to Amsterdam, where she arrived poor and miserable (*pobre e mizerável*) without anything left to her—were apparently not enough reason for the leaders of the community to admit her unconditionally to the *kehilah* and to *sedaca*. Nor did her request to have her son circumcised suffice to admit her to poor relief. At least two witnesses had to testify that they were acquainted with her and her son, and that they knew that both were of the Jewish nation.[30] Rachel

Desaldaña came to Amsterdam as an orphan from Almorox near Toledo, and she too had to testify that she was of Hebrew descent—*desçendente de hebreos*.[31]

By contrast, it was not the Jewish but the Spanish identity that was in question in the case of Moses Forte, *Doctor de Medicina* from Mantua, who in 1729, on the basis of documents signed by the local *hahamim* and confirmed by two notaries, testified that he was of Spanish descent.[32] Refugees from Belgrade described their Spanish and Portuguese background in detail when applying for poor relief. Thus witnesses in 1700 helped Jacob Aubi by declaring they knew his family to descend from a Spanish house, a *caza española*.[33] Isaac Valensin from Belgrade was described as belonging to the Portuguese nation 'from all four sides'—*de nação portugueza de todos quatro costados*.[34] Other Jewish paupers from the Balkans similarly attested their Spanish or Portuguese descent in order to gain acceptance on to the welfare list.[35]

The principle was stressed in the community's 'foreign policy' as well, with a particular commitment being shown towards refugees from the peninsula on their way to Jewish centres. Amsterdam Portuguese continued to make a clear distinction between the help extended to members of the Spanish and Portuguese nation, (ex-)Conversos, and that offered to others. Samuel Ramirez, travelling from Zeeland to Italy, received help 'because he is one of us, a Portuguese whom we are obliged to help and to support'.[36] In 1636, when money was donated for the release of prisoners of war, favourable treatment was accorded to 'Portuguese', to whom 1,000 guilders were allocated, while only 500 guilders was allotted to a group of Jews from Salonika.[37] Similar distinctions were overtly applied when it came to the grant of money to travel on from Amsterdam. Members of the Spanish and Portuguese nation were given larger sums than others to enable them to get to their destinations without too much hardship. Others merely received 'going away' money, just enough to get them out of the city and delivered to London, Hamburg, or wherever they were headed.[38]

The statutes of many independent and semi-independent charitable institutions of the Amsterdam Portuguese community likewise show not only how strong were the ties to, and identification with, the (former) Conversos and their descendants, but the great extent to which Portuguese Jews kept on emphasizing their exclusivity, distancing themselves from other Jews.[39]

The dowry organization Dotar, established in 1615 to provide dowries for poor and orphaned girls, made this preference a basic principle: only orphan girls and poor girls 'of the Portuguese and Spanish nation, Hebrew girls living from St-Jean-de-Luz to Danzig: in France, Flanders, England and Germany' could apply to participate in the lottery for a dowry.[40]

The Honen Dalim loan society, founded in 1625—at which point the Portuguese were the only Jewish congregations in the city—admittedly made statutory loans to 'all needy Jewish persons', but it went without saying (at the time: later this principle was confirmed in writing) that the loans were actually meant for poor Portuguese.[41] The Aby Jetomim orphanage was founded for the upbringing and education of fatherless sons of 'Jews of the Portuguese or Spanish nation'.[42] The Vestiaria dos Talmidim gave priority over other applicants to 'our Portuguese and Spaniards' when distributing clothes to pupils of the Talmud Torah school.[43] The eighteenth-century Portuguese girls' orphanage Mazon Abanot was reserved for orphaned girls who could be shown to be descended 'from our Portuguese and Spanish nation'.[44] The Meil Sedaca society, founded in 1735, issued coats exclusively to paupers of 'our Portuguese and Spanish nation'.[45] Similarly, the Portuguese Jewish old-age home founded in 1749 was reserved for the elderly 'of our Portuguese and Spanish nation'.[46]

Individuals also adhered to these principles. The wealthy widow Abigail Dias da Fonseca set aside a foundation to provide dowries for girls who were related to her or her husband. In the absence of girls who could trace their ancestry to them personally, the funds should be used for dowries for other orphan girls of the Portuguese Jewish nation of the city of Amsterdam.[47] David Imanuel de Pinto gave money to the *cativos* fund on condition it be spent on the rescue of a Spanish or Portuguese Jew only.[48]

In short, Portuguese Jews drew a clear distinction between different kinds of paupers, both in their community and abroad, and were selective in their provision of poor relief. Victims of the Iberian Inquisition, members of the *nação*, received preferential treatment and had at all times unlimited access to the Amsterdam Portuguese *sedaca*. Sephardi Jews from Jewish centres, for whom Spain and Portugal were part of a distant past—for instance, the *belogrados*—were treated with less alacrity and less sympathy. All other paupers had the lowest priority. It was stressed repeatedly that they were to stay in Amsterdam only temporarily. In the eighteenth century, identification with the Spanish and Portuguese Jewish nation, and with those of Converso background, became even more pronounced. This was mostly because of the growing poverty within the Portuguese community, which demanded even stricter criteria for selecting the poor to whom relief would be offered and the exclusion of a greater number of categories.

This selective approach to the poor, based on ethnic and religious principles, was not invented by the Portuguese Jews of Amsterdam. To a certain extent it had always been part of Jewish tradition, as highlighted above.[49] However, it was especially strong and well rooted in the Spanish and

Portuguese empires, where, as we have seen, New Christians were frequently subject to racist prejudice, including attempts to exclude them from public life. There too, charitable activity was influenced by ethnic and religious criteria, introducing a hierarchy of benevolence at home and in the overseas territories.[50] These Iberian patterns were internalized and adopted by the New Christians, as they were by other groups emigrating from the peninsula,[51] and were implanted by the 'New Jews' as carriers of culture in their new home in the north. There they constructed a welfare system that demonstrated similar concepts of exclusiveness and selectivity.[52]

Financial Need

A second criterion was that assistance must go to those who lacked the means to maintain themselves. A definition of the poverty line had existed since post-biblical Judaism, evolving from a fixed level at the time of the Mishnah and Talmud into a more variable one in later periods.[53] In the seventeenth and eighteenth centuries the Portuguese leadership took a flexible stand and set different rates for different people according to different criteria. Little written information on the subject has survived; however, Isaac Vellozino referred to the flexible approach of his community to defining the poverty line when, in a sermon of 1675, he stated that members of the Mahamad supported those who were in need, each 'according to the quality of his position'.[54]

The Portuguese system provided for indefinite distributions to the 'structural poor' in the form of monthly and sometimes weekly payments, but also looked after the 'conjunctural poor' as and when necessary.[55] The 'shamefaced poor', genteel but impoverished, were treated differently and given higher rates than those on the monthly welfare list.

Priority in disbursing poor relief among the Amsterdam Portuguese was often given to single people with no source of income, widows and orphans, those looking for work, and old people. Invalids enjoyed preferential treatment when it came to permanent poor relief.[56] It is difficult to assess the numbers involved, in comparison to the total number on poor relief, but time and again the registrars mention blind, deaf-and-dumb, and crippled people.[57] All in all, most of those on poor relief had strongly fluctuating, declining, or minimal incomes.

As mentioned earlier, maximum and minimum levels of monthly benefit to be paid to any one family were fixed in 1639. These were set at 6 guilders and 2 guilders respectively, and these amounts remained unaltered throughout the early modern period, not even being adjusted to take account of inflation. Nevertheless, sometimes this official scale was ignored and benefits below the minimum or above the maximum were paid.[58] Occasionally, people would receive an amount—more likely to be for a fixed period than as a permanent regular income—far exceeding the maximum, to enable them to return to the standard of living to which they had been used. This exception was often applied to the genteel poor.[59] Conversely, some of the Portuguese Jews who enrolled in the Abodat Ahesed *ḥevrah* after 1670 received allowances below the minimum laid down in the regulations,[60] as did the group of Sephardi refugees from the Balkans.[61] This particular group was registered on a separate list, at least until the first decades of the eighteenth century, and its members were treated as second-class Sephardim.[62]

It is unclear whether the administration of the Portuguese community or of the various organizations and funds disbursing charity looked carefully enough into the financial situation of applicants to establish their true level of need, though we know that the board of Bikur Holim had the task of establishing the state of poverty of candidates before distributing clothes to them.[63] Arbitrary distribution was thought undesirable, and close inspection was the rule here. In fact, given the extent of poverty, the degree of social control exercised was considerable and information about candidates for poor relief easily obtained.

Did the leadership investigate how poor claimants actually were by making home visits?[64] Many municipal and church charities made a habit of visiting paupers in their homes and noting the situation of all who had either registered in person or sent in petitions.[65] It appears that the Portuguese community did much the same, both directly and indirectly. Administrators lower in the hierarchy, such as the *shamashim* responsible for the distribution of welfare, could have seen and judged the depths of poverty among those in and around the households they visited.[66] Perhaps members of the community informed the leadership about the circumstances of the poor, as indeed members of the dowry society Dotar were encouraged to do in respect of the girls who applied to take part in the lottery.[67] Members of other *ḥevrot* were also actively involved in identifying the poor; often they knew candidates for welfare personally.[68] Poor people themselves could also have taken the initiative to point out their destitution in person: in exceptional cases they entered the Mahamad's room to confront the *parnasim* with their misery.[69]

We have no information about how often the *parnasim* themselves visited the homes of the poor. They did have personal acquaintance with the state of the genteel poor, since we know that in the eighteenth century, at least, they went to their houses in person to hand out their welfare payments.[70] However, there could not have been many such visits, seeing that David de Castro Tartas made a special point in the eulogy he delivered in 1675 of singling out the *gabai* Jacob Telles da Costa for visiting the poor in their homes to see their situation for himself.[71] Was his diligence a rare exception? Abraham Pimentel, himself a poor man, voiced strong views on this subject. According to him, the *parnasim* were lax about home visits: 'You never visit the poor in their homes and fail to look properly into their financial situation.'[72] It also remains unclear whether the *parnasim* put the findings of their home visits down on paper; in any event, no such records have come down to us, in which respect the Portuguese differed sharply from the Dutch Reformed Church.[73]

Fraud was certainly practised within the Amsterdam Portuguese community at the time, as it was in many other welfare institutions of the city and elsewhere in the Jewish world,[74] but efforts were made to limit it as much as possible. Lists were drawn up early on and—up to 1639—often exchanged between the three different Portuguese Jewish communities in order to prevent fraudulent multiple claims.[75] Malpractice could never be completely avoided, however: for example, in the 1700s the widow Perla Obediente continued for some years to receive welfare as the widow of Moses Vas Mexicana, despite having married Isaac Menasseh.[76] Also, private *ḥevrot* were careful to avoid duplication of effort: in their provisions we often see measures to prevent the poor from taking benefits from public and private sources at the same time. Thus some *ḥevrot* insisted that their distributions were only for those of the poor who did not enjoy *sedaca* through the *kahal*.[77] Other private organizations tried to co-ordinate their activities with each other: for example, Meil Sedaca took special notice of a similar organization in The Hague in an effort to prevent duplication and dubious claims.[78] Fraud, however, could never be entirely eradicated: in 1752 the Amsterdam Portuguese community mentioned malpractice, or 'abusos', in the distribution of welfare and gave new instructions.[79]

In various cases benefits were increased, reduced, or stopped, for reasons that were not always clearly specified. Thus, in 1663, the Mahamad awarded Rachel Gouvea 50 cents above the 2 guilders a month she had been receiving since 1654 'because of her great need'.[80] The widow of Samuel Pinto found her monthly benefit of 6 guilders, granted in 1654, cut to 4 guilders in 1662 and completely withdrawn in 1667, when the Mahamad 'had positive knowledge that she needed no further assistance'.[81] No explanation at all was given for the cessation of payments to Eliau Henriques, who, having been on the monthly poor-relief list since 1662, was in 1668 declared simply to be *escluido de todo*.[82] The eighteenth-century documents are even less informative. They just drily note the names of poor people who are taken off or added to the poor lists, and those to be subject to an increased or decreased allowance, all without further comment.[83]

Sometimes decisions to cut poor-relief benefits were formulated more explicitly. Thus the son of Pedro Peres had to go without benefits because he had received a bequest from his father.[84] Rachel Calvo de Andrade was taken off the poor-relief list from 1677 to 1679, because her brother was keeping her. When he discontinued his support, her *sedaca* benefits were restored.[85]

Exceptionally, people having left Amsterdam were paid poor relief abroad. These included some abandoned women who pleaded for continuation of assistance while searching for their husbands in other countries.[86] A similar arrangement was developed specifically to aid emigrants to Erets Yisra'el, some of whom were assured by the Amsterdam Portuguese leadership that they would receive support, albeit at modest levels, at the port of destination years later.[87] However, there was considerable disagreement in Erets Yisra'el on this preferential treatment of immigrants from Amsterdam. It attracted criticism from the spiritual leaders of the Jerusalem community, who maintained that charity should go to all in need and not to a particular group.[88] In the great majority of cases, however, relief was stopped when the beneficiary left the city. When Gracia Pinto, for instance, could no longer be found in Amsterdam she was removed from the list as an absentee.[89] When Abraham Rodriguez left for France in 1701 it was explicitly stated he would be taken off the list of beneficiaries of the *sedaca* and Abodat Ahesed, and would no longer receive peat and matzot.[90]

Anyone who married lost their welfare payments, at least in theory, if marriage improved their circumstances or if their new spouse was already on the list.[91] This happened to the niece of Dr Daniel de Prado, Debora Gomez, whose name was removed from the *sedaca* list when she married David Levy Maduro in 1663.[92] The rule applied to men and women alike. Thus Daniel Mendes's name disappeared from the poor-relief registers when he married Reina Israel at the age of 50.[93] In many cases, however, welfare distributions to both partners after marriage must have been made, since the practice was strongly discouraged in a ruling in the middle of the eighteenth century.[94] Both Rachel Alcoser and Jacob Alegem, *belogrados*, for example, remained on the list after they got married in 1696.[95]

Inasmuch as the Portuguese community had any say in the matter, it made members support their poor relatives, attempting in this way to limit the cost of poor relief as best it could. Most of the people we are concerned with here were dependent for their income on the Portuguese community authorities and hence answerable to them. Thus annual deductions were made from the salary of the teacher Jacob Juda Leon Templo for the support of his indigent daughter, who was 'suffering major poverty with three children'.[96] When Isaac Calvo de Andrade was taken on as community *cortador da carne* (ritual slaughterer) in 1684, it was stipulated that he would henceforth help to support his mother, the above-mentioned Rachel Calvo de Andrade.[97] Similar regulations were enforced by the various charitable organizations run by the community.[98] However, support of relatives was not always the result of compulsion: by custom Jews generally provided prompt and generous aid for their poor relatives.[99] That had been the rule throughout Jewish history, and was also true among the Spanish and Portuguese Jews of early modern Europe.

In summary, it looks as if the community leadership kept track of the financial state of its poor in considerable detail, involving family members where possible, either with their co-operation or by force.

Good Conduct

As well as considerations of an ethno-religious and financial kind, acceptable conduct was also taken into account in deciding whether Portuguese paupers were eligible for benefits.[100] Thus the community made the most modern yet also very traditional distinction between the deserving and non-deserving poor. Often witnesses were called in to give information about an applicant's background.[101] It was less usual to hand over letters of recommendation. Only rarely do we come across such papers upon arrival and departure, although the Amsterdam Ashkenazi community apparently did provide its poor with so-called *schooybrieven* upon departure.[102] In the files of the Amsterdam Portuguese community a document was found that tells us about an oral recommendation: in 1684 one woman from North Africa was given money to continue her trip to London on the recommendation of Haham Sasportas.[103] Upon his departure for Curaçao, Isaac Mendez de Crasto got a letter from the Amsterdam *parnasim* declaring he was absolved from the *ḥerem* punishment imposed upon him four years earlier.[104]

When background information was completely missing, the leadership was forced to make judgements itself. Thus Rachel Mendes, for example, was given a dowry because she was *benemerita e pobre*.[105] In 1651 reference was made to the penury of many *pesoas benemeritas de nossa nasão*.[106] Isaac Saragal, a candidate for the post of *shamash*, was praised for his conduct and honesty.[107] The widow of the *shoḥet* and *bodeq* Maimon Haiaia was granted assistance because of her husband's good conduct.[108] The Portuguese community applied this concept well into the eighteenth century: the distribution of proceeds from an extraordinary collection during the severe winter of 1739/40 included *pesoas benemeritas* who were not on the list of usual welfare recipients.[109]

By contrast, misbehaviour or fraud could lead to the threat of, or actual, removal of paupers from the poor-relief list. Jacob Gomez and Joseph Israel, for example, had been handed money in 1645 in order to enable them to return to their country of origin. When it appeared that, after collecting the money, they had failed to depart, it was decided that they would never be given any further assistance, this serving, it was hoped, as a warning to others.[110] In the case of Sara Moron de Luna, things did not quite come to that. The Portuguese elders threatened to withdraw her benefits if she continued to keep Isaac Rodriges de Mercado in her house. Isaac had not acted in accordance with the laws of Orthodox Judaism and had desecrated the sabbath by marrying Sara's granddaughter on that day. Worse still, he was married already.[111]

Not only the Portuguese community itself but also the various charitable organizations stipulated proper conduct as a condition of receiving aid. Candidates for the old-age home Mishenet Zequenim, for example, had to show an unblemished curriculum vitae, demonstrating that they had lived properly and caused no scandals throughout their lives.[112] Moreover, once inside the home, the inmates had to behave with decency, decorum, and honesty in accordance with the codes of good conduct and the *bom Judesmo* of the community.[113] It was not an empty stricture: there were cases of people ejected from the home because of 'improper' behaviour.[114] Meil Sedaca issued coats only to *homems de bem & boms costumems*.[115] The *ḥevrah* Bigde Kodes decided to extend a wardrobe once a year only to a *pessoa benemerita*.[116]

As early as 1615, Dotar laid down in its founding statutes that candidates had to be of good conduct, honourable, honest, and blameless.[117] That principle was applied in practice in 1651, when Dotar refused to provide a dowry for Gracia Franka, who had apparently given birth to a child before getting formally married.[118] The principle of honourable conduct of females had to be stressed several times during the eighteenth century. Often there is mention of cases of decline in female morality. Haham Ayllon sounded a warning about this phenomenon:

> Instead of observing the commandment to be honourable and pure, women nowadays are devoid of all the crowning virtues. Shame on them! For the redemption of Israel depends on their chastity . . . And women now wear their hair so that everyone can see it. The same is happening with their clothes . . . It was always through women, the mothers of the law, that we were redeemed, as in Egypt . . . Make sure that the Holy House is rebuilt, for by it we shall be redeemed.[119]

Not only for the Haham, but also for Dotar, moral behaviour continued to be an issue of concern: in 1747 it emphasized once more that girls would not be eligible for a dowry through Dotar, and would risk losing any already awarded, if 'they trespass[ed] the limits of modesty and chastity that the daughters of Israel should observe'.[120] The warning was clearly necessary: by this time quite a few women were being excommunicated or otherwise punished for becoming pregnant before marriage.[121]

Strictures on moral behaviour not only referred to girls, but also concerned boys. In the 1650s the yeshiva Ets Haim dismissed several students, allowing only those to study and receive scholarships who were well mannered and studious.[122] The boys in the orphanage Aby Jetomim also forfeited their grant and education if they behaved unacceptably. Abraham Pretto, for example, was removed from the list in 1663 for being a rascal, a *velhaco*.[123] Eleasar del Canho was described as a mischievous person, *esqluido por traveso*.[124]

The importance of proper behaviour in the distribution of welfare can also be observed in private charity. In her last will, Ester Rodriguez emphasized her wish to distribute money to the poor after her death, but only to honourable and good people—*por pobres honrados ij gente de bien*.[125] Rachel Belmonte attached stipulations of good behaviour and Jewish identity to her legacy of 500 (Flemish) pounds in shares in the Dutch East India Company, saying it should go to poor relatives of good conduct, born in wedlock, and professing the Jewish religion.[126]

In short, the criteria of good behaviour, honour, and a good reputation, universally accepted and applied within the European elites of the time, were imported by the Amsterdam Portuguese community into their deliberations on poor relief. In this respect as in many others, the approach did not differ greatly from that adopted in other centres of the western Sephardi diaspora or indeed from non-Jewish welfare institutions in general.[127]

Procedures: Petitions and Lots

Even those paupers who met the criteria outlined above were not yet certain of receiving poor relief, for the actual beneficiaries were often chosen by lot.[128] The names of candidates to go into the lottery were frequently taken from petitions through which they applied for welfare, public or private. The same pattern was followed elsewhere in the medieval and early modern world.[129] These petitions seem to have been sent back to the applicants with answers: one of the jobs for which the *shamash* Simon do Valle was paid was the delivery of petitions back to the poor with their answers.[130]

Drawing lots was an old custom, not only in Jewish communities but also in wider European society, especially in the south.[131] Within the Amsterdam Portuguese community a lottery was used not only to choose candidates for welfare, but also in appointments to all kinds of administrative posts. The board of the first Mahamad of the united Talmud Torah congregation, for example, was chosen by lot. Many institutions of the Portuguese community chose their administrative boards by the same method.[132]

Until late in the seventeenth century the drawing of lots for *sedaca*, as laid down in the founding statutes of 1639, was not always applied consistently. Were some paupers granted preferential treatment on kinship or ethnic grounds? Were some in such dire need that they had to be granted relief without question or delay? Or were there occasions when enough money and accommodation was available to grant everyone permanent poor relief without any need for drawing lots?

In 1661, for instance, it was reported that the elders had decided to grant poor relief to a number of named individuals.[133] Later, when several places on the *sedaca* list fell vacant, the precedence of some new candidates was expressly mentioned.[134] In 1676, new candidates were admitted to permanent poor relief after it had been decided which of them were the neediest and worthiest.[135] In these and many other cases there was no mention at all of drawing lots in the decision of the *parnasim* to grant poor relief. Nor did the paupers themselves ask in their petitions to be entered in a *sedaca* lottery.[136]

It was not until 1678 that lots were again mentioned. At that time the Mahamad decided that henceforth all candidates eligible for inclusion on the monthly *sedaca* list would, in keeping with Article 32 of the statutes, be chosen by lot. From this time on, all who entered the monthly list by other means would be excluded.[137] What was the reason for this shift in policy? Had poverty become less grave or less widespread? Had less money become available to cope with greater poverty, so that the system was forced to choose candidates by lot? Or was it the intention to put an end to patronage? It is difficult to answer these questions. An explanation of the community leadership's decision is suggested by the statutes of the private organization Mayafu Pehameha Benealim, which used a lottery only when it had too many applicants and too little capital, while warning its board not to be influenced by personal affections.[138] Up to 1678, apparently, there was enough money to distribute to the poor.

Even after 1678, however, the communal welfare lottery does not appear to have been used in all cases. In 1679, just one year after the drawing of lots had been stipulated, widows were being accepted without the drawing of lots on the basis of their urgent need and lack of other income.[139] In 1680 the board of the Portuguese community decided to admit some new people, including widows and orphaned boys and girls, to the monthly poor-relief list on the basis of 'their dire need and the fact that, apart from the protection of

God, they have no other support'.[140] In the eighteenth century, too, the lottery was rarely applied among the community's poor. One exception is the procedure followed to divide the money from the estate of the late Jacob Mazahod: a shortage of funds necessitated the drawing of lots among the poor on the lists of the *sedaca* and of Abodat Ahesed.[141]

Elsewhere, among the private poor-relief institutions of the Amsterdam Portuguese, we come across the choice of welfare recipients by lot more frequently, not only in theory but also in practice. This method was used by Dotar, the candidates humbly asking for admission to the lottery every time they applied.[142] The board of Meil Sedaca, too, chose candidates for the issue of coats by annual lot.[143] Lots were also the preferred method of choosing residents for the Portuguese Jewish old-age home.[144] The *ḥevrot* Hase Amaharacha and Kisuy Ros used the same procedure, as did Quetonet Bat Codes.[145]

In brief, although the choice by lottery of candidates for various positions in the Portuguese community was a generally accepted principle, when it came to the selection of applicants for poor relief that principle was ultimately ignored. This departure may be attributed to the pressing need of the candidates and probably also to the intercession of interested parties. However, choice by lottery was more commonly practised in the private welfare sector.

Domiciliary versus Institutional Care

Most Portuguese paupers were supported in their own homes in the seventeenth century. For them, there were as yet no almshouses, hospitals, or old-age homes. With the exception of the workhouse for Ashkenazim, the Portuguese community in seventeenth-century Amsterdam had no intention of institutionalizing poor relief. There were several reasons for this.

First, it must be remembered that many Portuguese in early modern Amsterdam had come down in the world, often having lost their capital in the Iberian peninsula. These genteel poor were used to private care and service at home and would not have expected to be taken into institutions.[146] Moreover, Portuguese paupers in early modern Amsterdam were often no strangers to their more fortunate brethren. Many among both poor and rich were connected by family bonds and/or ties of friendship. Partly for this reason, and partly also because of shared experiences in the Iberian peninsula or elsewhere in the Sephardi diaspora, the early modern Portuguese community still enjoyed a high degree of solidarity. This was reflected in a preference for poor relief given in the home and for mutual assistance. For the time being at least, the means to finance this enterprise were available.

Then again, the setting up of almshouses, hospitals, and old-age homes would have drawn attention to the existence of poverty within the community, when the intention clearly was to hide from the outside world the growing problem presented by poverty among the Portuguese.[147]

Also, the community preferred to keep beggars or criminals outside the community, and if possible out of the city, rather than sanction their presence by locking them up in local institutions. One exception must be noted here, namely the initiative of the Portuguese community to open the workhouse Abodat Ahesed in 1642, not for Portuguese but for German and Polish paupers. Even so, this was intended as only a temporary solution.

The situation changed somewhat in the eighteenth century. By now the Portuguese community had gained a certain position in the city, but poverty within its ranks had increased in extent and changed in character. The poor now outnumbered the well-to-do, and the gap between the two groups had widened. Some Portuguese were noticed begging in the streets, to the great dismay of the Portuguese leaders.[148] It was also becoming increasingly cumbersome to continue rendering assistance to all paupers in their homes. Institutionalization offered a more efficient way to keep watch over the morals of the poor, their observance of Jewish laws, and their orderly behaviour, and often provided better accommodation and care.[149]

Thus the Portuguese community felt that the time was now ripe for setting up special houses for paupers, for old people, and for orphans, the better to increase its control over them. Thus we see the establishment in the eighteenth century of a Portuguese Jewish almshouse, a Portuguese Jewish old-age home, a Portuguese Jewish girls' orphanage, and a Portuguese Jewish home for problematic youngsters.[150] However, a large section of the poor continued to rely on domiciliary poor relief, paid through the official channels of the community or by private organizations, both at this time and much later: it was cheaper, and less embarrassing for the poor themselves.

Poor Relief in Practice: Communal and Private Provision

Needy people were not particularly interested in theories of poor relief. What mattered to them first and foremost was survival, which meant getting help in hard times. Admittedly, it was important to them what criteria were being employed, what agencies they could approach for help, and what they could expect from them, not only in the Portuguese community and its subdivisions but also in the private arena. Let us therefore examine how poor relief was applied in practice at various levels.

Communal Care

Portuguese and other eligible Jews could draw on the central poor-relief fund of the Portuguese community for benefits, disbursed at monthly or other regular intervals, that would give them a basic 'survival kit'. The Portuguese community, united since 1639, gradually co-ordinated its tasks further, creating a network of activities covering the entire spectrum of poor relief, on a pattern characteristic of traditional *kehilot* in early modern Europe. Paupers were able to ask for assistance both from the central authorities of the Portuguese community and from subsidiary organizations supervised by the Mahamad.

The aid received included monthly benefits,[151] quarterly benefits during Jewish holidays,[152] travelling expenses,[153] ad hoc poor relief in emergencies,[154] and assistance during illness, including burial costs after death.[155] In addition, they received rent subsidies twice a year,[156] and were issued with matzot for Pesach,[157] with peat,[158] with clothes,[159] with study material in the form of textbooks,[160] and with ritual objects for use in the practice of the Jewish religion such as *talitot*, *tsitsit*, and *tefilin*.[161] In addition to all these provisions, the community administered the *cativos* fund and another fund for the poor in Erets Yisra'el, as noted above.[162]

Apart from the distribution of peat, matzot, and clothing and the infrequent handouts of bread and ritual objects, poor relief was mainly given in cash; this was in contrast to the practice of other poor-relief agencies in Amsterdam, which normally dispensed charity in kind.[163] As noted above, the payments remained constant over two centuries, so that the vulnerability of paupers grew substantially in lean years.[164]

Poor relief, whether in money or in kind, was delivered at home, so that Portuguese paupers did not have to wait in line in the synagogue complex or elsewhere.[165] Most of the other welfare institutions in the city, including that of the Ashkenazim, required the poor to queue up for handouts.[166] For the Portuguese it was a matter of style and *grandeza*: the community and its poor were not to be put into an awkward, shameful position. It was also a way of keeping the extent of poverty in the Portuguese community hidden from the outside world.

As the number of paupers grew, not only did the administration become more efficient, it also started to differentiate more sharply between the different groups of paupers. Poor relief was divided into various categories, every pauper being assigned to a specific list with the help of selective criteria.[167] Over time, this system became more elaborate. In 1667/8, there was a poor-relief list for monthly handouts and one for holiday payments. The chronically ill who received no monthly benefits were put on special weekly lists. All *pobres da terra* could count on help in case of emergency. People who were leaving Amsterdam also received assistance. In addition, as shown in Chapter 2, special provision was made for *forasteiros* and *tudescos*. Rent subsidies were entered on yet another list, as was the distribution of matzot and peat.[168]

By the end of the seventeenth century, changes had been made not only in the scope of poor relief but also in the selection of recipients, and paupers could be found entered on all sorts of separate lists.[169] At the beginning of the eighteenth century, the administration was simplified and welfare to Portuguese paupers was divided into just four categories: *despachos de peticoens de povres, despachos de urgencias extraordinarias, despachos de povres pª fora deste çidade*, and *gastos gerais*.[170]

In addition to the assistance to paupers handed out directly by the Portuguese community, certain relief activities were increasingly delegated to subsidiary organizations. Their administrative bodies were appointed by, and answerable to, the Mahamad; that is, to the highest authority in the Portuguese community. The Mahamad thus not only delegated duties, but also enforced their effective implementation and ensured the involvement and financial support of the members of the various subsidiary bodies, on whose activities it kept a vigilant eye. However, it could not prevent private welfare initiatives from being established and expanded. These sometimes filled gaps in the official system and sometimes overlapped with it, on both accounts much to the dismay of the central leadership, which slowly lost sight of, and control over, the full picture.

Education of Paupers

Learning, and especially the study of Judaism, has always been considered one of the cornerstones of Jewish life, and was accordingly a central feature of the Portuguese community in early modern Amsterdam.[171] Religious education here, as in other centres to which former Conversos had fled, had an additional dimension. Most of the newcomers had had only limited access to Jewish learning: so the leaders of the Amsterdam Portuguese community were faced with the formidable task of acquainting them fully with Judaism, teaching them the law, and turning them into fully fledged Orthodox Jewish citizens.[172] The importance attached to education in Judaism as a fundamental element in the building of a Jewish community in Amsterdam may be gathered from the fact that a religious school was one of the first organizations the community set up. In 1616 the Bet Jacob Portuguese congregation proudly declared that 'our *kahal*, Bet Jacob, has been practising the *misvah* of *talmud torah* [the study of Jewish law] from its inception'. That same year the administration of the Talmud Torah school was assumed by the

Portuguese communities Bet Jacob and Neve Salom, which henceforth ran it jointly for the furtherance of Jewish education.[173] The rabbis of the Portuguese Jewish community continued to emphasize the study of, and immersion in, Jewish learning. In his *Thesovro dos dinim*, published in the middle of the seventeenth century, Rabbi Menasseh ben Israel reminded his congregation that 'every Jew, poor or rich, young or old, healthy or sick, is obliged to devote himself to the study of the Holy Law . . . on a set part of the day and night'.[174]

Many adults were initiated into Judaism through study groups, some of which also had charitable objectives. They generally sent their sons for religious instruction to the Talmud Torah elementary school. Some of these children continued their study in the upper classes of the Ets Haim yeshiva;[175] others went to learn a profession straight away, while a third group was sent to city schools for further secular education, often to be completed at one of the Dutch universities.[176]

Instruction took place at home as well as in schools. Many better-off Portuguese families, as elsewhere in early modern Europe, had their children taught at home by private tutors. The influence of wealth on education could be felt here, as Haham Saul Levi Morteira, in his discourse on the advantages of wealth over poverty, had observed as well: 'the wealthy person is prepared by his parents for study, generosity, largesse and others of the most praiseworthy virtues'.[177] Shabtai Bass, a Jew from eastern Europe who stayed in Amsterdam between 1679 and 1684 to learn the printing trade, described in 1680 how 'every father, when the boys are back at home, employs a teacher, who instructs them in the writing of Hebrew and in other languages, goes over with them what they have learned at school, instructs them in the composition of verses and poems, guides their education, and teaches everyone those subjects that interest him'.[178] The records offer many examples that reinforce Bass's observations: Abraham Israel Suasso employed Samuel Texera in his home *pera la buena educación de mis hijos*;[179] also, *belogrados* were hired as home teachers for young children.[180] However, it was not only wealthy individuals who employed teaching personnel; sometimes the community took the initiative in private instruction as well. Thus, in 1689, Daniel de Lara was hired to instruct the nephew of the *shamash* Azuby for four months,[181] and in 1713 the Portuguese community paid Abraham Fidanque to act as a private teacher to the sons of Cardozo.[182]

The remainder of this section is devoted to an analysis of the facilities that the Portuguese community provided for the children of their paupers, helping to equip them with a secular, religious, and professional education.

Education of the poor was considered important in Amsterdam, as elsewhere in Europe at the time, not only as a tool to improve the opportunities of the young and so to take the new generation out of poverty but also as a means of social and religious control.[183]

Poor boys in the religious schools were provided not only with education but also with food, clothing, *tefilin*, *tsitsit*, and *talitot*. Books were distributed among them: in 1742 the printer Salomon Levy Maduro was instructed by the community to provide twelve books in 'Ladino' for the poor.[184] Students desirous of continuing their studies in the Ets Haim yeshiva were eligible for bursaries, for which purpose a fund was set up in the 1630s.[185]

Apart from religious studies, secular education was also given to poor Portuguese boys.[186] The community employed teachers to instruct them, usually for three hours a day, in addition to the six hours all the boys of the community received at the Talmud Torah school.[187] Officially, the secular curriculum consisted of arithmetic and the reading and writing of Portuguese.[188] Dutch, French, and the principles of commerce were not taught, if we are to believe Isaac de Pinto's critique published a century later.[189] From the interrogation of the pupils of Daniel Ribera and Daniel de Prado, teachers at this pauper school in 1658, it appears that in their classes education in the basic skills and in Latin went hand in hand with heated discussions of philosophical and theological questions: some turmoil surrounded these two teachers, both of whom took a highly critical approach towards Orthodox Judaism.[190]

Teaching poor boys was not a respected profession and, although many of the teachers seem to have been highly educated, was badly paid, as indeed their counterparts were in non-Jewish circles in the Republic.[191] The teacher Daniel Abudiente was apparently a poor man and was recompensed for his educational services by being granted a monthly welfare payment.[192] Many teachers combined their educational work with other careers. Abraham Machorro, for instance, was also a copyist, played the flute, and helped to bake *matzot shemurot* for the Portuguese community.[193] Despite the poor remuneration, the secular education of paupers was taken very seriously by the *parnasim*, and was strictly supervised.[194]

Early in the seventeenth century and also towards its end, just one teacher was employed in the Portuguese community for the secular instruction of poor boys.[195] Between 1663 and 1673 five to seven teachers were appointed annually, each in charge of a class of about eleven children. After 1673 the number of teachers providing pauper education was reduced to three, and the classes were expanded to an average of fifteen pupils. From 1679 no more than two teachers were employed, and from 1687 just one teacher was given the task of providing education for poor boys—those on *sedaca* poor relief as well as all other paupers.[196] Whereas seventeenth-century secular education of poor Portuguese, as in the better schools in the Republic and elsewhere in Europe, originally displayed a distinctly structured character, involving several classes and teachers, by the end of the seventeenth century that structure had disappeared and just one teacher was employed, teaching poor pupils of various ages in a single class.

The reason for this change was not only the need of the Portuguese community to economize, but more importantly the diminishing number of children who attended these lessons. Thus while about eighty pupils attended pauper school in 1665, by 1675 their number had shrunk by over a half to thirty-seven.[197] Clearly, despite the increase in the number of paupers at the end of the seventeenth century, there was falling interest in the secular education of indigent pupils.[198] This tendency continued throughout the eighteenth century. Growing poverty probably meant that these children had to work from an early age, relying on poor relief and sometimes living disreputable or even criminal lives, as frequent complaints suggested.

One of the obstacles to getting poor children out of poverty was the failure of the Portuguese community to offer them a good professional education which would have prepared them for a better future. These children might then have been kept off poor relief, thus saving the community money in the long run. The independent Aby Jetomim organization took on that task, but was not so much interested in educating the poor as in teaching boys who had lost their fathers or had to cope without parents.

Most of the poor children started schooling at the age of around 5 and continued until after their barmitzvah. Then they went on to vocational training, if they had the necessary funds or if, as orphans, they were assisted by the orphanage Aby Jetomim. No provision for professional education was made for any other poor boys. Thus many had no alternative but to go to work, inside or outside the Dutch Republic, as soon as their school education was over.[199] Before the eighteenth century there were enough job vacancies in the tobacco, diamond, and sugar industries, where poor boys could acquire a variety of practical skills. Abraham Bassan, for instance, went to school for around eight years from the age of 5, and became a tobacco-spinner's labourer.[200] Untrained boys could sometimes find work in territories overseas such as Brazil, Surinam, and Curaçao.[201] David Habib received secular schooling for seven years and then left Amsterdam for an unknown destination.[202] Many boys must have managed to maintain themselves in this way without overburdening the community.

The Portuguese provided no educational facilities for girls until the last years of the eighteenth century, apart from the girls' orphanage which operated from 1734.[203] This was largely because Portuguese girls and women generally remained in the home, in keeping with the Iberian tradition. Young girls were kept indoors as much as possible, and married women too usually operated in the background.[204]

Nevertheless, the general level of literacy among Portuguese women was quite high.[205] More prosperous and educated families probably had their daughters taught at home.[206] This was also common practice in affluent non-Jewish Dutch circles, although rich Dutch girls often attended a school as well.[207] Through home education many rich Portuguese girls were enabled, after marriage, to make their way into trade and industry.[208] Some of them even mastered the Hebrew language. The seventeenth-century Portuguese community also boasted several women poets, writing in Spanish.[209]

Even so, there were girls from wealthier or more educated families who did not even know how to write their first names.[210] That was true particularly of Portuguese brides from poorer families.[211] But even these girls had had some education. Vocational work was certainly taught, both individually and in small groups, in order to prepare them for work in various sectors, as was the practice in the non-Jewish world.[212]

Given the tradition of seclusion, it was difficult for Portuguese women who had not been born and reared in an Orthodox Jewish environment to reach out for information on Judaism, although many of those who arrived from the Iberian peninsula had not been completely cut off from the faith. In fact, as Conversas, they had often been essential for the continuation of Jewish education on the peninsula. Haham Ayllon referred to this matter in a sermon he preached in 1723:

> In the past, women were ever devoted to the service of God . . . It was devout women who appreciated God's word, who wanted to enter the Holy Land. At all times, they observed the Law; even during the persecutions in Spain and Portugal they held fast to their faith and risked their lives and possessions by instructing their children in the word of God.[213]

In Amsterdam many among them continued along this path and instructed their children 'in the fear of God and according to the Laws given through Moses to Israel'.[214] Once in Amsterdam, Portuguese women could freshen up and enrich their knowledge of Judaism by reading books such as Menasseh ben Israel's *Thesovro dos dinim*, which addressed the *señoras* of his community and taught them the laws of Orthodox Judaism that most concerned women.[215] Thus it was mostly through education and training at home and the reading of books, not yet through an established school system, that girls and women, poor and rich alike, could take the opportunity to learn and prepare themselves for their lives and careers within and beyond the boundaries of the family and community.

The education of Portuguese paupers failed to encourage upward mobility. In most cases, successive generations of the same families received poor relief, with little change in their level of training or qualification or in their living standards. The early modern Portuguese policy with respect to the education of paupers ultimately proved fatal to the community and certainly showed few signs of foresight. Many young people were found lacking education and training, relying on poor relief and living disreputable lives. That is why in the middle of the eighteenth century Isaac de Pinto was so scathing in his denunciation of the state of the pauper education provided by the Portuguese community. Poor children, he contended, did not receive a proper education. He pleaded for the opening of vocational training institutes. As an alternative, he suggested placing the educational facilities of the Portuguese Jewish orphanages for boys and girls under the supervision of the Portuguese community and opening them to all paupers. The administration of the community apparently accepted his suggestions and tried once more, in 1751, to persuade people on welfare to send their children aged 5 to 13 to the religious and secular schools of the community.[216] However, these appeals were not very effective. The state of Jewish pauper education at the end of the eighteenth century showed few signs of improvement and school attendance within the Amsterdam Portuguese community remained relatively low.[217]

Care of Orphans

Jewish writings include countless references to the special care and attention owed to orphans.[218] The Talmud holds the Jewish community responsible for the care of poor orphans in particular, and urges it to assist them, to help give girls away in marriage, and to provide them with the means of gaining financial independence.[219] The Amsterdam Portuguese *kahal*, like many other Jewish communities, took this injunction to heart and went out of its way to provide special assistance to those who had lost a father or both parents.

Care of orphans in the Portuguese community of early modern Amsterdam was addressed not only as a biblical commandment, but as a very acute problem. As will have become clear from the preceding chapters, the family composition of Amsterdam Portuguese society was strongly influenced by conditions in the Iberian peninsula, and by the vast migratory movement of this time that extended to the furthest corners of the world. Some husbands and fathers stayed behind in the Iberian peninsula as their families went on ahead, or set off abroad, temporarily or permanently, leaving families behind. Not only in Amsterdam, but elsewhere in the Sephardi diaspora as well, a large number of families were now headed by women, while many children were left on their own. It was considered a matter of primary importance to save or win over these children for Judaism, enable them to live honourably, provide them with the necessities of life, give them a proper education, teach them professions, and finally lead them to marriage.

One way of helping orphans was through the monthly, weekly, and ad hoc distributions from the charity box of the community. Another—for boys, at least—was to admit them to the community's schools. Thus community poor relief provided for their basic needs.[220] It is noteworthy, however, that most of the other initiatives for orphan care circumvented the official channels of the community and came from the private sector.

In the first place, many orphans were cared for and housed with families.[221] According to the Talmud, taking in orphans was a most laudable thing to do:

> Whoever brings up an orphan in his home, Scripture ascribes it to him as though he had begotten him . . . 'Happy are they that keep justice, that do righteousness at all times' [Ps. 106: 3]—Is it possible to do righteousness at all times? . . . This refers to a man who brings up an orphan boy or orphan girl in his house and enables them to marry.[222]

Many other orphans were cared for through the establishment of independent, private *ḥevrot* or through the bequests of individuals. Particular institutions worth mentioning are the bridal organization Dotar, which provided dowries for poor and orphaned girls from 1615; the orphanage Aby Jetomim, which from 1648 devoted itself to the upbringing and education of orphaned boys;[223] and the girls' orphanage Mazon Abanot, set up in 1734.

Dotar was established in order to draw poor girls into the Jewish world and help them to stay there, supported and firmly rooted. It did this by providing them with the prospect of a dowry for marriage to a Jewish bridegroom, thus continuing the chain of Judaism. It was also motivated by an enduring preoccupation with the honour and virtue of unmarried girls, a familiar attitude in the Iberian peninsula and in early modern Europe at large; thus it also served as an important bulwark against prostitution and other immoral behaviour by Portuguese women.[224]

Dotar seems to have been modelled on a society set up by the Ponentini Jews in Venice.[225] The provision of dowries was rooted in the Jewish tradition and was present in medieval Jewish Spain.[226] However, Dotar also resembled institutions found in the contemporary Catholic world. Here, too, people were concerned that girls might not be able to get married for lack of funds, thus putting their honour and reputation at risk.[227] Societies and foundations providing dowries played an important role in southern Europe. The statutes of Dotar read like a Jewish version of those adopted by non-Jewish organizations in southern Europe.[228] Some of the inspiration for the establishment of Dotar must therefore also have come, either directly or indirectly via Venice, from the Catholic environment.[229]

Dotar had a hierarchical structure. The closer a girl's family ties to members of the organization, the greater her chance of receiving a higher dowry. In that sense, Dotar was in fact a mutual aid society.[230] No one, however, was allowed to become a member for the sole purpose of increasing the chance of obtaining a larger dowry for their daughters or nieces. For that reason it was decided in 1632 not to enrol any paupers as members.[231] In 1635 another resolution to that effect was passed: 'There will no longer be accepted as members those who hope to profit from the advantages that membership bestows.'[232]

These provisions highlight the elitist character of the society. Indigent Sephardim who could not claim to be related to members of the Amsterdam Portuguese establishment were shunted into subordinate positions. *Belograods'* orphan girls in Amsterdam, for instance, participated in the lottery for a dowry, but only for relatively small sums, since none of them could claim to be related to a member of the society.[233]

There was an international dimension to Dotar's work, as it provided dowries for orphaned girls and poor young girls not only in Amsterdam but also elsewhere, mostly in other parts of the western Sephardi diaspora. In 1667, for example, Clara de Almeida applied from Bayonne to the administrators of Dotar in Amsterdam, referring in her petition to the dramatic sufferings of her family: 'To the honourable administrators and treasurers of the holy confraternity of orphaned girls: Clara de Almeida, resident in Bayonne, an orphaned girl without father or mother, the daughter of Francisco Rodriguez Almeida, whose family has suffered so much in Cordoba and sister of the martyr Isaque Dalmeida Bernal, who perished in Santiago in Galicia, sanctifying God's name.'[234]

In Amsterdam itself, however, the situation of orphaned girls was far from bright. It became clear that many were finding it impossible to get married for lack of a dowry. For that reason, it was decided in 1657 that from then on girls living in Amsterdam and other parts of the Dutch Republic, Hamburg, and Glückstadt merited preferential treatment in the dowry lottery over girls from elsewhere. This decision was based on Jewish law, in which priority is always given to the poor of one's house/city.[235] The problem remained unsolved, however, with girls often waiting in vain for their dowries for years. This may perhaps have been why Rica Nunes Almeida had her daughter marry in Surinam, and why other orphan girls were going abroad.[236]

Private individuals tried to fill this gap by making provision for dowries either in their lifetimes or in their wills. Joseph Henriques Sequeira supported the preference of Dotar since the 1650s in giving priority to local orphans and poor girls. He founded a bridal foundation under his own name, yet under the authority of Dotar, to allow Spanish and Portuguese girls living in the city to draw a lot for a dowry once a year.[237] The widow of Isaac de Prado decided to set up a foundation of her own independently of Dotar with the aim of providing poor orphaned girls with dowries.[238] They were not the only ones: many more of the wealthier Amsterdam Portuguese, both men and women, following the cultural norms of southern Europe, decided to provide for dowries for Portuguese Jewish girls in the city and beyond.[239]

Orphaned boys were helped by the *ḥevrah* Aby Jetomim.[240] The society was founded during a contentious dispute following the break-up of the Gemilut Hasadim *ḥevrah*, and as a show of defiance towards the central administration. Originally, it was not particularly co-operative in its attitude towards the Portuguese community, but ultimately it fitted in with Portuguese social life, while preserving its independence until the early nineteenth century.

In its purpose, structure, and procedure, Aby Jetomim resembled, to a certain extent, organizations in the Iberian peninsula and could have been modelled on them, although the so-called 'Padre de Huérfanos' there was a paid supervisor—an individual, not an institution—who oversaw and co-ordinated the care for orphans, both boys and girls, putting them into orphanages or with host families, and looking for work for the boys.[241] There may also have been models in the city of Amsterdam itself, which had several institutions for the assistance of orphans.[242] Similar bodies were to be found elsewhere in Europe.[243]

Aby Jetomim not only served as a shelter for orphans among the Dutch Sephardim but was also highly regarded for accepting orphans from abroad.[244] It also offered opportunities to orphan boys from the Sephardi diaspora already present in the city, for example sons of the *belograd os*.[245]

We should see the early modern orphanage more as a fund than as an institution where orphans were taken care of day and night. The first building for that purpose was not opened until the beginning of the nineteenth century.[246] Before then, orphaned boys were looked after privately, as had been traditional in Jewish communities in the past,[247] with the cost of housing, food, clothing, and medical attention being repaid to their carers.

Aby Jetomim provided both elementary and more advanced religious education. A building was at first rented, later purchased, to house its yeshiva, with a proper teaching staff and a *shamash*. Here, not only could students immerse themselves in the study of Jewish texts, but ordinary members of the *ḥevrah* could join in the studies as well.[248] Boys were also provided with elementary secular education.[249] In the eighteenth century, besides Portuguese, orphan boys were also taught French and Dutch, something the general secular education in the community did not provide.[250] After primary education, orphan boys could continue their religious studies on a higher level, or they could opt for vocational training, which was run privately, much as it was in the rest of Amsterdam and elsewhere in Europe.[251] In such cases, the orphans were apprenticed to master craftsmen for several years. These might be Sephardim, Ashkenazim, or Dutch Christians. The apprentices were trained variously in Jewish studies, as religious leaders; in trades, as booksellers, cashiers, bookkeepers, or brokers—in wool, spices, jewellery, cocoa, and coffee; in crafts, as diamond-cutters, bookbinders, or wigmakers; and in medicine, as barbers or surgeons.[252] The choice of occupation for Sephardi orphan boys differed markedly from that for non-Jewish orphans: the latter mostly chose trades implying physical labour and skills.[253]Aby Jetomim often reimbursed travelling costs, thus enabling the boys to earn their living outside the Republic. For some, passage was paid for settlement abroad as a substitute for covering the expenses of vocational training.[254] Others were assisted to leave the city after finishing their training. These opportunities were similar to those given to non-Jewish boy orphans to leave the Dutch Republic.[255]

One orphan, Eliau Lopes, ended up as *haham* of the Portuguese community in Barbados.[256] Many others left for Barbados and other destinations in the West (Surinam, Jamaica, Curaçao) and also for North Africa, France, Italy, England, Antwerp, Hamburg, and Jerusalem.[257] Thus Amsterdam educated and exported to other parts of the Sephardi diaspora not only religious leaders but also professionals in trade, crafts, and medicine.

The financial records of Aby Jetomim give us some indication of how many boys received help in money or in kind (clothing, food, textbooks, travelling expenses, education, professional training), disbursed annually over a period of three to six years.[258] The support they received appears to have been comprehensive. On the other hand, it is clear that this private organization, probably like many others, provided assistance for no more than a small number: thus Aby Jetomim supported just twelve boys from 1648 to 1651; twenty-one orphaned boys in 1677; and no more than thirty-seven boys by 1757, that is, a century later.[259] To see these figures in perspective, we must remember that the Portuguese community in 1675 included 313 unmarried boys aged 13 and over, of whom no more than twenty-two, that is 7 per cent, received assistance from Aby Jetomim.[260]

Like many other private organizations, Aby Jetomim was involved in a variety of activities. This *ḥevrah* was not only an orphanage but also a mutual aid society: in case of illness, members were expected to look after one another, and in cases of death, the *ḥevrah* shouldered the task of accompanying their mortal remains to the Portuguese cemetery at Ouderkerk aan de Amstel.[261] At first it also gave shelter to poor Jews of Portuguese or Spanish background, and to Italian foreigners, but this activity was dropped later on.[262]

Aby Jetomim played a model role in the Amsterdam Portuguese community, and beyond it as well. Until well into the eighteenth century the community continued to praise the level of education and the progressive curriculum provided by the society.[263] In addition, Aby Jetomim was a unique and innovative phenomenon in the contemporary Jewish world. Never before had a Jewish orphanage been established, and this one served as an example for the founding of other Jewish orphanages elsewhere.[264]

Mazon Abanot, the girls' orphanage set up in 1734, followed the example of Aby Jetomim—*a Imitaçam da gloriosa e pia Irmandade de Abi-Jetomim.*[265] By this time, poverty had struck the community to such an extent that the initiators complained of seeing 'some orphaned girls go[ing] begging from door to door scantily dressed, a scandalous thing and most discreditable for so glorious a *kahal*'.[266] All the activities of Mazon Abanot—education, work, feeding—were concentrated in one building. Even so, up to the nineteenth century it was mostly a 'day-care' centre. The girls did not stay overnight, and on holidays did not have to attend.[267] Women took care of daily administration and supervision, but this is not to say that the girls' orphanage was entirely in female hands. The initiative was taken by men, and ultimate authority remained in their hands; financial matters were controlled by a male treasurer,[268] and a male *shamash*, appointed by the founders and the treasurer, was in control of the collection of money, which he handed over to the treasurer.[269]

In common with many other Amsterdam Portuguese organizations, Dotar among them, admittance took place according to an established hierarchy: preference was given to orphans related to members, in a specific order.[270] There were other similarities between this organization and others. One was the ethnic–religious component: candidates for admission, administrators, and other personnel should all be descended from the Spanish and Portuguese Jewish nation.[271] Good conduct was also stressed, with girls being warned in advance of admission that proper behaviour was an important condition of acceptance.[272] Once in the orphanage, a vigilant eye was constantly kept on their conduct, and indeed also on that of the female personnel.[273] Acts of indecency against 'honour' and 'modestia' would be severely punished.[274]

Girls could enter the orphanage between the ages of 6 and 8 and stay for a maximum of six years up to the age of 14; this was a shorter period of stay than that applied in the Amsterdam city orphanage for girls.[275] The importance of educating the orphans was frequently stressed.[276] They were taught to read, apparently in Portuguese.[277] Writing was not mentioned. As in other girls' orphanages, in Amsterdam and elsewhere, the children learned to sew and knit.[278] Orders for garments came from members of the Portuguese community, and the girls' work was remunerated.[279] The most important part of the curriculum was education—at least, that is what it said: 'sobre tudo'—but what this involved was not specified, except for concepts like 'indoctrination and instruction into the fear of God'. For this and other aspects of education and training a widow was employed as a 'mestra'.[280]

Besides education, the girls were provided with food and clothes and received monthly allowances. When they left, they were often given some clothes and money to take with them; this was common practice among the various girls' orphanages of the city, as it was elsewhere in early modern Europe.[281]

Mazon Abanot was never a large institution. It started out with seven orphans in 1734 and grew to accommodate nineteen in the middle of the eighteenth century, but dropped back to five at the end of the century.[282] The obsession with the morals of girls betrayed Iberian influences. Yet the orphanage was also an example of a modern welfare institution, imitating others of the time across Europe, in which girls learned not to sit idle but to work, to behave honestly, and to practise good manners.

Care of Paupers in Sickness and Death

Caring for the sick and the dying had been a fundamental duty of Jewish communities since time immemorial, as the London Sephardim acknowledged in 1678: 'It is a general virtue of all the congregations of Israel, in all the places where they dwell, to establish and form a Hebra, which shall practise the meritorious and urgent charity which is due to the sick and dead.'[283] On settling in Amsterdam, the Portuguese were quick to apply this principle, as other groups were doing across the early modern world.[284] Bikur Holim was the first organization to emerge in the Amsterdam Portuguese *kahal*. Set up in 1609, it worked first in the three separate congregations, then as a co-ordinating body, and finally as a subsidiary of the united Talmud Torah congregation.[285] All members of the Portuguese community were expressly asked to join it and to support it financially.[286]

Societies with similar objectives to Bikur Holim, and often with the same name, were found in Jewish communities in Spain from the thirteenth century. These Spanish organizations had also been set up in order to tend the sick and help to bury the dead, but were quite often run independently of the organized community.[287] In the *kehilot* of Egypt, Italy, and the German states too, there appeared organizations with identical names and objectives.[288]

Despite the lack of source material, information on the activities of Bikur Holim during the early period can be distilled from notes registered in the *imposta* files and in those of the three congregations. In case of illness it provided the sick with doctors, surgeons, and nurses; it also distributed medication, food, and clothes to the poor among them. It took care of burial arrangements and sent representatives to accompany family mourners to the synagogue.[289] The historian Daniel Levi de Barrios confirms these points, adding that visiting the sick was a duty for rich and poor alike.[290] Saul Levi Morteira fills out the picture, indicating in his sermons that in the early period Bikur Holim also took care of the professional education of poor boys and provided dowries for poor girls.[291]

According to the revised articles of 1639, at this point the society shifted its emphasis from caring for all the sick to aiding the poor in illness, especially those on regular poor relief.[292] Membership of Bikur Holim was open to all married members of the Portuguese community and anyone unmarried above the age of 20.[293] Members were fined if they failed to perform duties delegated to them by the officers of the organization.[294] The society continued to arrange funerals for rich and poor, but as the range of activities undertaken by Bikur Holim expanded, certain tasks were eventually delegated to a new set of organizations. From 1643 onwards, for example, activities around burial were delegated to Gemilut Hasadim, a separate organization that in 1648 was taken under direct control by the central community administration.[295]

Bikur Holim, as an organization for looking after the poor at times of illness and death, had limited powers. Ultimately it was the central administration of the Portuguese community that did the work of co-ordination and supervision.[296] The community board also appointed and instructed doctors, surgeons, and pharmacists.[297] The medical staff were not exclusively male: some women (on welfare) were appointed as its assistants, especially in treating the poor.[298]

The strict supervision of Bikur Holim and its staff by the *parnasim* was intended to ensure the proper treatment of the sick, to cut expenses, to counter misuse of provisions, and to prevent complaints from, and dissension among, the poor.[299] Above all, it ensured compliance with the rules of the city authorities and professional guilds concerning health and medicine.

There was no Portuguese Jewish hospital in Amsterdam until the nineteenth century.[300] This is quite remarkable, given that Jewish communities elsewhere had set up hospitals in the Middle Ages and in the early modern period, some of them, though not all, dependent on the *kahal*.[301] The Spanish–Portuguese Jewish community in London, for example, ran a hospital of its own from the middle of the eighteenth century.[302] However, in most cases the Amsterdam Portuguese continued the tradition of domiciliary care that was common practice among both the more well-to-do and the genteel but poor Conversos on the peninsula, although even there the 'Portugueses' set up a hospital in Madrid in 1606.[303]

Only in exceptional cases did Jews seek admission to the municipal hospitals, and the records show Ashkenazim doing so more frequently than Sephardim. One Ashkenazi Jew died in the city hospital in 1624, being buried later at the cemetery in Ouderkerk.[304] Any Ashkenazim who fell ill while imprisoned were taken to a municipal hospital. Thus Abraham Salomon from Cracow was transferred to the Gasthuis (municipal hospital).[305] Salomon Jacobsen from Prague, 'being ill was sent to the Gasthuys', too.[306] However, members of the Portuguese Jewish community also found their way to the municipal hospitals—among them the Pesthuis, Lazarushuis, and Dolhuis—especially when contagious illnesses were diagnosed. Sara Doelzarne was taken to the city Pesthuis in 1628, as was Sara Mulatto de Algarvo.[307] Some Portuguese were hospitalized in the Lazarushuis.[308]

Cases of Portuguese Jews entering the municipal hospitals, however, were very rare, for a number of reasons. To begin with, the Portuguese community was supposed to pay for the services provided, which could become too costly. Second, it was well known and recognized that Jews had a duty to look after their own poor. Third, it was difficult to observe ritual and religious laws in non-Jewish institutions, a point of great concern to the Portuguese religious leadership. *Hahamim* of the Portuguese community, for instance, decided in 1734 that a person, not mentioned by name, could only be sent to the Dolhuis (madhouse) if food for him was prepared at home.[309] Finally, the Portuguese had sufficient medical expertise and personnel to deal with illness within their own community. In fact, one Portuguese Jewish doctor left Amsterdam because there were so many Portuguese physicians there that he was unable to find work in the city.[310] For all these reasons, tending the sick poor and watching over the dying remained by and large domiciliary activities.

The mentally handicapped and mentally ill were also cared for at home until late into the eighteenth century, if they were not sent out of the city.[311] The city hospital for the mentally handicapped, the Dolhuis, had hardly any Portuguese inmates.[312] Sometimes what passed for a psychiatrist was consulted ('D^{r} dos locos').[313]

The adequacy of the nursing organized by the community for paupers is open to question. The fact that in 1639 reforms were needed 'to provide better help for the sick paupers of our nation' suggests that the prevailing system was not entirely satisfactory.[314] The statutes adopted in 1639 were expanded over time, and reference was frequently made in the revisions to assistance for sick paupers who were not covered by the monthly *sedaca* relief. In 1662, for instance, money was given to sick paupers who were not drawing regular poor relief and hence 'suffering terrible deprivations'.[315] In times of crisis the numbers of poor and sick people increased significantly and health-care provision seems to have been unable to keep up.

Sources continued to stress that the demands of caring for the sick and the poor were beyond the capacity of Bikur Holim. In the second part of the seventeenth century, doctors, surgeons, and apothecaries for the poor were offered permanent employment by the community authorities.[316] Before that time, doctors had largely worked for Bikur Holim in a freelance capacity.[317] The reason given for the change was that sick paupers were not getting adequate help.[318] From that time on there were two doctors permanently employed by the community to look after the poor; in the eighteenth century their number was increased to three.[319]

Bikur Holim apparently took constant pains to look after sick paupers as best it could. Since it had originally taken upon itself the full care of the sick, as was normal for welfare institutions of early modern Europe,[320] with the Portuguese community pulling most of the strings, we must interpret the growing number of private health-care organizations and mutual aid societies in the middle of the seventeenth century and later not only as reflecting a growing demand for care in the safe environment of like-minded people, and a desire, based on a sense of honour and social status, not to be dependent for health care on a central poor-relief organization, but also as a response to the inability of the Portuguese community to provide adequate care for its sick paupers.[321]

Distribution of Clothing

Clothing the poor was another duty prescribed in the rabbinic literature and practised—on both a private and an institutional level—by Jewish communities since ancient times.[322] It is referred to in the inventory of the goods left by

Salomon Doria in Amsterdam in 1660, 'all of whose clothes and linen were given to the poor according to the custom of the Jewish nation'.[323] Like other charitable activities, the practice of distributing clothes to the poor was not confined to the Jewish community; in the Christian tradition, it is considered one of the seven works of mercy.[324] In both traditions, the donation of clothes to the poor had a spiritual aspect and was viewed as an aid to salvation.[325] Abigail Abarbanel, for instance, on her deathbed in Amsterdam, made this clear when she instructed her husband to pass her clothes and linen over to the poor 'for her soul' (*por su alma*).[326]

Clothing the Portuguese poor was also institutionalized early on through the so-called Vestiaria, an organization found within each of the three Portuguese congregations until 1639.[327] The traditional distribution of clothing to the poor usually took place during the Hanukah festival, items handed out including socks, shoes, capes, coats, skirts, and fabric.[328] In cases of particular need, paupers were also issued with clothing at other times in the year; many refugees, for example, were handed clothing immediately upon their arrival in Amsterdam.[329]

In 1639 Vestiaria became part of Bikur Holim.[330] A *parnas* of that society was charged with the administration of the Vestiaria subdivision, while the physical distribution of clothing was left to the six administrators of Bikur Holim. Thanks to the statutes of 1639, we know quite a bit about the tasks of Vestiaria at this time. Co-ordination through Bikur Holim was promoted even further in the 1660s and 1670s, when the issue of clothing for pupils, originally a task of the Talmud Torah school,[331] was entrusted to a special administrator who worked in close collaboration with the Vestiaria subdivision and was finally incorporated as the seventh administrator of the board of Bikur Holim.[332] The reason behind this decision was most likely a financial one. In 1660 there were complaints about the small sums collected for Vestiaria in comparison with other similar bodies, most probably chiefly the one associated with the religious school, the so-called Vestiaria dos Talmidim.[333] Competition for limited funds had begun to impede the achievement of charitable aims. It was at this point that, centralization of welfare being at risk, the competition between independent *ḥevrot* was reduced as much as possible through a statement of the Mahamad requiring its approval for the foundation of any new institutions.[334] However, private initiative continued to hamper the centrally co-ordinated Vestiaria effort.

As poverty increased rapidly during the eighteenth century, the centralized effort was not sufficient to clothe the poor. By then the situation had worsened to the extent that 'many paupers of our Spanish and Portuguese nation walk in the streets without proper clothes and suffer the cold of severe winters, there being no one to protect and cover their bodies', in the words of one of the new organizations, Meil Sedaca, created in 1735 to take charge of the distribution of cloaks.[335] It was not the only initiative in this field. Many more *ḥevrot* were established for similar purposes. As early as 1723 Gracia Alvares referred to a brotherhood that distributed clothes to women.[336] There was also the above-mentioned *ḥevrah* Mayafu Pehameha Benealim, established in 1739 to provide shoes to the poor, which in 1745 changed its name to Quetonet Bat Codes and its aim to supplying linen shirts to the poor in need.[337]

Thus, while the Portuguese community resisted the establishment of competing clothing agencies in the seventeenth century, it apparently dropped its objections in the eighteenth century (as long as they officially asked for approval from the central authorities), allowing Meil Sedaca and many other organizations to respond to the needs of the ever-growing mass of the poor. Meanwhile it continued to run its own Vestiaria. The principle behind its relaxation of control seems to have been *force majeure*: in permitting independent initiatives in the distribution of clothing and in other fields, the Portuguese community once more acknowledged its inability to control *sedaca* on so large a scale from the centre and accepted the inevitability of outside help.

Loans and the Portuguese Variant of the Monte di Pietà

Early modern Europe saw the advent of pawnshops, which appeared first in fifteenth-century Catholic Italy. Their object was to help the poor with loans at no or very low rates of interest in order to alleviate their plight and so reduce the likelihood of disorder. In fact, these so-called *monti di pietà* were established in particular to challenge Jewish loan banks, which, according to various Catholic authorities and religious orders, charged excessive rates of interest, draining the Christian population's resources, drawing them into poverty and, in their eyes, committing usury.[338] The situation was quite different in Venice, where the *monti di pietà* were run not by Christians but by Jews, in response to the request of the Venetian authorities for loans to be made available at low interest rates to the poor of the city; this concession on their part was part of the price they paid for permission to reside in the city.[339]

In 1625 the Portuguese Jews of Amsterdam established a loan bank in their community to serve their own poor. It was named Honen Dalim, but was also known in Spanish as the *monte de piedad*—and referred to thus by the historians de Barrios and Franco Mendes[340]—and as the Lombardo Judaico.[341] Generally speaking, Honen Dalim was an imitation of the pawnshops, based on the southern European model, that were increasingly appearing in northern Europe, for instance in Nuremberg, in the sixteenth century.[342] In the city of Amsterdam a pawnshop was opened under the name of Lommerd in 1614, some ten years before the Portuguese variant. Here, too, the interest charges were kept low 'to spare the poor and outcasts from all sorts of improper usury'.[343]

However, the specific inspiration for Honen Dalim must have come from Venice itself, the home city of its initiators, the *hahamim* Saul Levi Morteira and David Pardo.[344] These two learned men must have encountered the *monti di pietà* in the Venice ghetto and decided to set up a similar institution in Amsterdam, naming it *a pia dadora de pobres*.[345] Traditionally Jews consider lending money to the poor as the highest form of charity.[346]

One reason for founding Honen Dalim was the plague that ravaged Amsterdam between 1623 and 1625.[347] Such crises stimulated the communal desire to respond with practical solutions and restore order. Indeed, many of the victims during this episode of plague were Portuguese Jews.[348] In addition, there were religious motives associated with responses to disasters such as the plague: by opening a pawnshop to serve the Portuguese Jews of Amsterdam, the founders hoped 'to assuage the wrath of God . . . now that we see so much sickness caused by our sins'.[349] 'A pious bequest', they continued, 'would rescue us from death, it is said in the Holy Scriptures.'[350] The bank was established 'as an atonement for our lives', said Saul Levi Morteira in a sermon delivered in 1656, a year after another outbreak of plague had raged in Amsterdam.[351] Elsewhere in Jewish Europe, too, *ḥevrot* emerged as a form of penance during or immediately after disasters. In Verona a *ḥevrah* was formed in response to the plague of 1632, while a pious confraternity emerged in Rome after an outbreak in 1656.[352]

References to sinfulness, remorse, and repentance after a disaster were not exclusive to Judaism, but were a widespread phenomenon in early modern Europe. One resident of Amsterdam, for instance, was heard to say during the plague of 1664 that 'we shall henceforth practise justice and charity and walk before God in meekness and humility'.[353]

The Amsterdam Portuguese *monte de piedad*, unlike the pawnshops in the city, adhered to the principle of lending money free of interest, as Jews are not allowed to charge interest on loans to other Jews.[354] Only small amounts could be lent: the maximum was originally set at 20 guilders, later increased to 40 guilders.[355] The period over which articles could be pledged was set to match that laid down by the municipal pawnshop. In both instances, loans could not be extended beyond one year, after which unredeemed pledges were put on public auction by both institutions.[356] Idaña, an Amsterdam Portuguese Jew, had this to say in a letter he sent to a friend in Madrid in 1686:

> Here there is a luxurious building known as the Lommerd, where they lend money to anyone wishing to borrow sums ranging from very small to very large, against five per cent interest a year . . . The Jews, too, have a pawnshop for their paupers, but the value of the pledges may not be above fifty guilders and no interest is charged on the loans, and the pledges have to be redeemed within a year, or else they are sold by auction.[357]

The Portuguese pawnshop was under the control of the central Portuguese administration.[358] After 1639 the united Portuguese community took closer charge of moneylending, now also known by the name of *emprestimo*, and appointed an administrator every year for that purpose.[359]

At first the Amsterdam Portuguese pawnshop was not housed in a separate building, money being lent to people in the homes of the administrators.[360] Pledges, however, were sold at the Portuguese synagogue.[361] Only by the end of the seventeenth century was the pawnshop housed within the synagogue complex.[362] This development and the employment of a paid official gave tangible form to the increasing centralization and institutionalization of this part of the community's charitable work.[363]

The pawnshop was evidently very popular, not only with Portuguese but even more with other paupers in the city. After all, it was the only place in the city where money could be borrowed free of interest. Not surprisingly, complaints reached the *parnasim* that loans were often made to people other than Spanish or Portuguese Jews. To put a stop to this practice, a declaration was issued in 1676 stating emphatically that loans were reserved for members of the Portuguese community.[364] Even so, pledges from borrowers who were patently not Portuguese or Spanish were taken to the Portuguese pawnshop by intermediaries until well into the next century. This may be inferred from the fact that the Portuguese community had to reiterate its views on loans in 1759.[365]

We know little about what kinds of articles were commonly pledged. The founding statutes of Honen Dalim stressed that it was contrary to Jewish law to pledge bedding, used linen, mattresses, or tools to pay off debts, but one year later this restriction was slightly eased.[366] We know that jewellery, (prayer)books, (ceremonial) objects, and clothing were handed in as pledges. For lack of source material, we cannot say much about the extent of pawnbroking or about whom among the Portuguese poor it served over the course of time. However, in view of the pledges given, it seems likely that the pawnshop did not attract the utterly destitute, but rather the genteel poor.[367]

Applications for membership of Honen Dalim grew markedly, the list of members expanding from about seventy-five men and women in 1625 to about 700 in the 1670s.[368] Socio-religious considerations must have played an important role in this development, especially in view of the successive outbreaks of epidemic disease that hit the city over the course of the seventeenth century. Appeals by rabbis like Morteira may well have done the rest.[369]

The pawn bank Honen Dalim was not the only way in which Portuguese Jews could borrow money. They also used the city loan bank, apparently pledging pawns for higher sums than the maximum set by Honen Dalim. Here Portuguese Jewish families who had fallen on hard times could go to present their pawns anonymously, thus avoiding shame within their own community: this option was resorted to more and more frequently as a growing number of Portuguese Jews found themselves in financial difficulty in the course of the eighteenth century.[370]

There were other ways, too, of getting credit, such as the more informal tactics used by Hester Lindo and her daughter Mariana. For eight years they bought bread, butter, and other groceries on pledge in a store belonging to a non-Jewish lady, borrowing money there as well and ending up in debt.[371]

There must also have existed private Jewish loan banks in Amsterdam. We know very little about these apart from occasional reports, for example of one run by a lady called Francisca Lopes, offering money in exchange for pawns to other Portuguese in the city.[372] Later on, most private pawn banks were suppressed.[373] However, there were other private initiatives. Josua de Prado, a rich Portuguese Jew, lent Joseph Levi, the husband of his former German Jewish housekeeper, a set of tools for use in a tobacco-spinning plant. The loan was ultimately changed into a gift, thus serving as a gracious charitable act. Moreover, it was quite common for Portuguese Jews to take loans from family and friends within their immediate environment.[374]

In addition, there was the more formal option of taking a loan through the charity box of the community. This also helped the poor by offering direct loans without interest. The practice was followed in many other European *kehilot*,[375] and was copied in newer Sephardi communities established towards the end of the seventeenth century, such as those in France.[376] These loans could be larger than those given through Honen Dalim, often ranging from 100 to 250 guilders.[377] The money was not given without assurances, however: charity of this kind, in the form of a loan, had to be repaid to the Jewish community. One way of securing repayment was to take it out of the deceased person's estate after his death.[378] Another was to wait until better times, hoping that the debtor might get back on his feet: Samuel Hamiz Vaz, for example, was given 66 guilders on condition that he would pay it back if

God were favourable to him.[379] The money given through the *despachos* to poor Jews leaving for other countries was often given on the same conditions, stipulated in the agreements signed by those departing.[380] *Ḥevrot* such as Aby Jetomim and the old-age home Mishenet Zequenim also requested repayment of costs disbursed in charity when the beneficiaries were able to do so.[381] Repayments could also be made out of salaries: the *ḥazan* Abraham Baruch, who in this capacity was on the community's payroll, asked the *imposta* board for 60 guilders in 1633 and promised to pay back 7.10 guilders at the beginning of every Hebrew month (Rosh Hodesh).[382] Isaac de Eliau Cohen Belinfante was advanced a loan of 200 guilders, in view of his great need, after he gave the names of four people to act as guarantors of repayment. The amount was to be deducted from his salary.[383]

Thus the poor in need of loans had a range of options, several based on long-standing Jewish traditions. They could have recourse to family, friends, or the nearest shop; or they could turn to the community's *sedaca* box, the city loan bank, and some charitable associations established by Portuguese Jews, not least its very own pawnshop, Honen Dalim. This was not only an exemplary Amsterdam foundation, incorporating early modern elements, but also an imitation of southern European institutions, especially those present in the Jewish ghetto of Venice.

The Abodat Ahesed Society and the Workhouse for Ashkenazim

Alternatives to imprisonment for the destitute, so-called 'houses of correction', were never set up with the intention of housing Portuguese Jews. There was no question of the Portuguese community putting its own paupers into a workhouse, and there are no suggestions in the records of the early modern period that the poor of their nation should be 'corrected' by being provided with the means of livelihood by manual labour. This once again emphasized the perceived difference between Portuguese paupers and the rest, and staked out the boundaries within which the Portuguese community cared for its poor. That tells us something about the nature of Portuguese paupers at the time, and even more about the image their community wished to present to the outside world: superior to other Jews, exclusive, elevated, the true aristocracy of the Jewish people.[384]

Nevertheless, the community leadership decided that other Jews did indeed need 'correcting' and so established an institution for that purpose: the workhouse Abodat Ahesed, which was founded in 1642 and lasted until 1670. Thus the community showed itself to have been aware of and influenced by the latest ideas about welfare, according to which the poor should be 'improved' by work, to keep them on a normal, respectable path and to preserve them from mendicancy, prostitution, and criminality.[385] The Portuguese had seen similar institutions set up in the city of Amsterdam, for example the Spinhuis and the Rasphuis, both of which were established at the end of the sixteenth century.[386]

Abodat Ahesed was in principle intended for 'poor Jews of whatever nation, willing to acknowledge the necessity of providing for themselves by their work'. In practice it was aimed at the Ashkenazim from the German states and Poland.[387] Its establishment was a response by the Amsterdam Portuguese community to an increasingly serious problem that they felt urgently required solution. More and more poor Ashkenazim, flocking to Amsterdam in the wake of wars or persecution, or in search of gainful employment, were found begging in the streets and alleyways of Amsterdam.[388] Many ended up in one of the city's penal institutions, such as the Rasphuis or the Werkhuis, where they were put to work to pay off their fines for begging.[389] The fact that Jews were unable to observe Jewish ritual laws and other commandments and prohibitions in these non-Jewish institutions was a source of constant irritation for the leaders of the Portuguese community.[390] Beyond that, the Portuguese wanted to protect their reputation as an honourable community. Therefore, they tried to curtail begging by Ashkenazi Jews, so as 'to prevent scandal and annoyance to the inhabitants of the country and the magistracy'.[391]

Few archives of the Abodat Ahesed workhouse have come down to us, so that we know little about the identity of its inmates. We do, however, know that some 200–300 Ashkenazim were held there between 1642 and 1669.[392] This population was mixed, including men, women, and children, some in families and some on their own.[393] The number of young children was apparently considerable,[394] as may be inferred from the resolution passed one month after the opening of Abodat Ahesed that they should be gathered together and found shelter elsewhere with the help of members of this *ḥevrah*.[395]

We do not know the precise location of the building, but we do know what went on inside, for it was laid down in the founding statutes that master craftsmen were to be employed to teach various trades by which the inmates could earn a living.[396] The work mainly involved the processing of wool and cotton—spinning, weaving, and carding[397]—with the object of selling the finished products and accumulating the proceeds.[398] A co-ordinator was employed to supervise the work.[399] In addition, there were internal managers whose job it was to maintain order, prevent unruliness among the many inmates, and ensure observance of Jewish law.[400] To manage the running of the organization the Portuguese community appointed six further administrators, each of whom took turns, for a week at a time, in visiting the building to ensure that all the rules were being observed.[401] A treasurer saw to the finances.[402] Special help was reserved for the sick. If enough capital was available, money would also be set aside for clothing the poor and for rendering whatever other help was needed.[403]

The institution seems to have been strictly run, in accordance with specific rules drawn up to fulfil these objectives. Its funding came from various sources. At its foundation, the Portuguese community raised a loan of 2,400 guilders from its members, and it was possible to become a member of Abodat Ahesed by paying a joining fee of 10 guilders. Together with donations, this produced an initial capital of 4,225 guilders.[404] The Portuguese community supported the organization further with an annual contribution of 600 guilders.[405] In addition, the money collected in the plates passed round every Rosh Hodesh for the benefit of *tudescos* was distributed to the sick and the poor by the administrator of Abodat Ahesed;[406] house-to-house collections were also run to raise additional funds for it;[407] and one or two individuals are on record as having bequeathed money to the organization.[408]

Abodat Ahesed functioned as a workhouse for just twenty-eight years. Over this period, the enthusiasm shown by members of the Portuguese community for helping Ashkenazim in this way declined,[409] and at the same time the Portuguese community found itself unable to accommodate the increasing numbers of destitute German and Polish Jews in its workhouse. Begging Ashkenazim were (and remained) a familiar sight in the streets of Amsterdam. Even after 1642 many warnings were issued to Portuguese not to give money to *tudescos* who went begging from door to door.[410]

Despite the existence of Abodat Ahesed, many *tudescos* and *polacos*, including many children, went on being caught for begging and brought into the penitentiaries of the city of Amsterdam.[411] Portuguese leaders still had to go into the Amsterdam Rasphuis and Werkhuis to ensure, by paying the workhouse authorities, that these people were not put to work on the Jewish holidays.[412] In addition, they often managed to have inmates released, again in return for payment or on certain conditions. Daniel Pinto must have been a regular visitor in the city's Rasphuis and Werkhuis in the 1650s and 1660s. Sometimes he and other delegates from the Portuguese community would go there by themselves; at other times they were accompanied by a member of the Ashkenazi community. Thus Pinto went to the Rasphuis with Abraham Barents in 1663 to obtain the release of a 10-year-old Jewish boy who had been begging in the streets. His mission was successful: the boy was let out on condition that he left the city with his mother.[413] Other Portuguese, too, were involved in such negotiations. Samuel de Souza paid 100 guilders bail in 1662 for Netel Wolf, a 40-year old Jewish woman from Cracow.[414] In 1658 Isaac Brandon intervened on behalf of Salomon Davidts, aged 28.[415] The Rasphuis and the Portuguese community also collaborated in sending Jewish inmates to locations in the German states and Poland: in 1639, for instance, after consultations between the two bodies, a group of forty-five *tudescos* was sent off to Danzig.[416]

The Abodat Ahesed society also removed *tudescos* and *polacos* from the city.[417] We may take it that many of the inmates of the Abodat Ahesed workhouse were forced to leave, just as inmates of the Rasphuis and the Werkhuis were sent away.[418] Apparently it was not the intention of the Portuguese community to keep the Abodat Ahesed workhouse open to all comers for permanent residence in Amsterdam.

The end of provision for poor Ashkenazim through Abodat Ahesed came in 1670. At that time the Portuguese asked the ever-growing Ashkenazi community to see to the support of indigent members itself.[419] Intervention by the Portuguese community on behalf of Ashkenazim in the Rasphuis and Werkhuis then almost ceased: only seldom did the Portuguese *parnasim* go to visit the Rasphuis, the rare exceptions usually being to secure the release of Portuguese inmates.[420] After 1670 the mediators for Ashkenazim there were mostly members of the Ashkenazi community,[421] as the Portuguese community distanced itself from the care of German and Polish Jews.

Abodat Ahesed continued to exist after 1670, but no longer as a workhouse. From this date the interest on the capital was used to help Portuguese paupers who were not on monthly poor relief.[422] In that way some of the poor could bypass the strict selection procedure for official welfare payments and receive sums of money outside the formal scale. These were people for whom assistance constituted a welcome addition to their earnings. The barber Joseph Pereyra, for instance, was paid 3.10 guilders extra a month in this way.[423] Benjamin Mendes, a teacher in the pauper school, was given similar treatment.[424] Abraham Dias served at this time, among other things, as *shamash* in the Gemilut Hasadim yeshiva, and could make good use of a supplement to his yearly salary of 48 guilders.[425] Students such as Abraham Cohen de Lara and Samuel Ramirez were only able to subsist with the help they received from Abodat Ahesed.[426]

In addition, Abodat Ahesed proved a godsend to people who failed to gain acceptance on to the *sedaca* list via the usual selection procedure. Some people accepted for poor relief by Abodat Ahesed in 1670 were known to be of poor repute, which rendered them ineligible for regular *sedaca*. Sara Lumbrosa, for instance, was registered with Abodat Ahesed although she had been a member of the Reformed Church for a time.[427] The name of Judith Henriques de Sanlúcar also appeared on the list: her reputation had been tarnished by her son, Abraham Vaz, who had been excommunicated in about 1661 and was therefore denied access to the Portuguese community.[428]

Thus, although Abodat Ahesed had ceased to be a workhouse, it continued as a *ḥevrah* for the assistance of poor Portuguese for the rest of the seventeenth century and throughout the eighteenth. It provided monthly relief for paupers and was able in that way to attract and assist people who would otherwise have languished in even deeper misery or who would have turned their backs on the community.

Shelter for Strangers

The Amsterdam Portuguese community did not maintain temporary shelters or guest houses in which visitors could stay for a fixed period, although such institutions had always had their place in Jewish and non-Jewish society.[429] The existence of a special shelter would only have served to prolong the stay of visitors and temporary residents, to attract even larger numbers of them, and to draw the attention of outsiders to their presence. For all these reasons, the Portuguese community opted to house visitors in private homes, and where possible to persuade them to leave the city as soon as possible. Thus, for example, Isaac Henriques from Mallorca was given food and lodgings on his arrival, but was sent off to Italy a few months later.[430]

Not only Portuguese, German, and Italian Jews, but Dutch Christians as well earned good money by giving house room to transients on behalf of the Portuguese community.[431] The same pattern was adopted in Portuguese communities elsewhere: for example, in St-Esprit in southern France in 1735 people were paid by the community to take in *forasteiros* and *passageiros*.[432]

There was clearly no adequate centrally controlled system for the care of strangers, so that such help had to come from other quarters. This is why so many private organizations listed the care of strangers as their main objective, or cared for 'foreigners' as a sideline, especially during the seventeenth century. Even though at that time, and later, 'foreigners' were not tolerated in the Portuguese community for long, Portuguese Jews privately showed enough compassion to hold out a helping hand to them for a brief spell and did not ignore them completely. In 1642 Menasseh ben Israel mentions Acnasat Orhim as a *ḥevrah* for the care of strangers.[433] Aby Jetomim, in addition to helping to educate the young, also provided hospitality for poor strangers until the middle of the eighteenth century. With its stipulation that it would put up 'foreigners' at its own expense for three days and three nights, this *ḥevrah* closely resembled De Bayert, a temporary public refuge in Amsterdam, where needy transients could also take shelter for three days and three nights.[434] The Amsterdam Portuguese leadership adopted similar principles: when in 1699 the wife of Juan de Mendoza, accompanied by her ten children, arrived in Amsterdam from Portugal, Gaspar Henriquez Pereyra was paid to take her into his house for three days, after which she was supposed to continue her journey to London.[435]

Identical rulings could be found abroad, in both the Jewish and the non-Jewish world: travellers in Portugal, for example, were allowed to take shelter in lodging-houses for three days.[436] Foreigners in the Jewish community of Pisa were not allowed to remain for more than three days without the consent of the municipality.[437] In 1674 the Spanish–Portuguese community of London forbade persons of the nation to intercede on behalf of foreigners.[438] From 1710 onwards it especially resisted the arrival of Jews from North Africa and Italy, who were required to leave the country after a stay of three days.[439] In the Portuguese communities of southern France a term of three days was also set as the maximum for which 'vagabonds' were allowed to stay and take charity.[440]

In addition to Acnasat Orhim and Aby Jetomim, other private *ḥevrot* were also involved in the reception of the stream of Jewish immigrants. 'Passengers' received small handouts from Abodat Ahesed,[441] and the Gemilut Hasadim yeshiva, founded in 1665, also gave money to *forasteiros* from time to time.[442] The yeshiva and *ḥevrah* Honen Dalim, founded in 1667, included in its statutes provision for the care of strangers, and more particularly of the sick among them, who were to be provided with doctors, medicines, and financial assistance.[443] Maskil el Dal, set up in 1673, as well as looking after its own members, took care of *pobres forasteiros* not eligible for poor relief from the Portuguese community.[444] Sahare Sedek, founded in 1678, not only gave alms to the poor but also distributed food to *forasteiros*.[445]

In the eighteenth century the picture changed. Of course, we still find people earning extra money through the community by accommodating foreigners.[446] However, with the poor now an overwhelming presence in the city, the attitude of the community to strangers was less accommodating. De Pinto spoke on its behalf of the strain placed on the obligation of hospitality, maintaining that giving to a stranger what belongs to a brother is not charity but injustice.[447] Even though the rule of a maximum three-day stay for foreigners had been in place earlier, it cannot have been applied consistently, or perhaps was not made an official rule, for de Pinto found it necessary in 1748 to insist once more that poor foreigners should be expelled after three days: 'It should also be borne in mind that *parnasim* in all *kehilot* have the right to expel all mendicant strangers who do not live an orderly life, after three days.'[448]

A similar mood was apparent among the various private *ḥevrot* established in the eighteenth century: references to the accommodation of foreigners were almost absent or, where they existed, were taken out.[449] The growth of poverty consequent on economic decline and wars, and new restrictions in welfare allowances pushed forward in the 1740s, did the rest: the Amsterdam Portuguese community became less open-minded and hospitable, its immigration policy more strict. As a result it became less attractive to foreigners and began to lose its international stature and reputation as a benevolent and welcoming community.

Other Forms of Organized Private Poor Relief

A Kaleidoscope of Private Enterprise

During the second half of the seventeenth century and well into the eighteenth the centrally controlled welfare system had to cope with an ever-growing number of organizations in the private sphere, some of which have already been mentioned. Many were at least partly motivated by the search for spiritual fulfilment and devoted some part of their effort to religious study, with charity as an additional component.[450] Some required from their members a commitment to mutual aid for protection against life's hazards. Frequently set up after a natural disaster, an eruption of spiritual enthusiasm, a new wave of immigration, a war, or an economic depression, together they provided an important supplement to the centrally run Portuguese poor-relief administration.[451] De Pinto maintained in 1748 that without this private help the ever-growing mass of the poor would have died of hunger, thirst, and cold.[452]

How can we explain the rise of the various *ḥevrot*? The Portuguese community had at first managed without most of them, but was gradually confronted with a growing number of societies that assumed some of its functions or overlapped with its own provision. One explanation for the extensive spread of such societies may have been a growing doubt about the inability of the Portuguese *kehilah* to perform all its tasks adequately.[453] Another is that private arrangements spared many from the ignominy of enrolling their names in the Portuguese poor-relief registers. The increasing numbers of genteel poor, striving to match the living standards of their social peers, would not ask for help and could thus best be assisted unobtrusively; some even took preventive action and ensured they would have access to help in case of need by joining a mutual aid society or other *ḥevrah*.[454] In this way they protected their honour and self-esteem.

Then again, private welfare has always been an important supplementary element in Jewish society. There are plenty of examples of similar organizations in Jewish Spain, Italy, and the Levant, among other areas.[455] The emergence of pious societies with a charitable dimension may also be closely linked to patterns existent in southern Europe at the time.[456] Iberian society was itself increasingly organized into socio-religious confraternities, mutual aid societies, and professional guilds.[457] The patterns of all these organizations could have served as models in Amsterdam. Also on the peninsula, charity often functioned as a means to do penance, and many organizations were set up to this end;[458] many Portuguese Jews in Amsterdam, following the same trend, felt the need to set up *ḥevrot* in which they could atone for their sin of having professed Catholicism in the Iberian peninsula through a combination of the study of Judaism, prayer, and donations to charity.

A further religious motive was related to the spiritual currents, such as Lurianic kabbalah, that had spread throughout the Jewish world. Groups of adherents felt the need to get together, study, and fulfil *mitsvot*, thus striving to end the Jews' captivity and bring about their redemption. There was good reason why Sabbatai Zevi, the mystical messiah, had a vast following in the Amsterdam Portuguese community.[459] Sabbatian controversies and messianic mysticism did not come to an end in 1666. In the aftermath of this episode the Jewish world still had to brave many storms caused by pro- and anti-Sabbatian factions and messianic currents.[460] Also, the eighteenth century saw the establishment of many pious organizations that stressed the importance of charitable works. Paame Dalim, set up in 1756, referred to a famous phrase in *Pirke Aboth* (Ethics of the Fathers) in citing charity as one of the foundations on which the world rests, combining welfare with the study of the 'Divina Ley';[461] and for the founders of Mishenet Zequenim in 1749, charity was one of the most important means of attaining redemption.[462]

The social diversity of the Amsterdam Portuguese who poured into the city as part of the great stream of immigrants also explains the emergence of a host of different organizations in which various elements among them could feel at home.[463] Immigrants had been torn from their familiar surroundings and had had to leave friends and loved ones behind. Although persecution must have been a common denominator, there were considerable differences in background, outlook, and mentality. Most of them must have felt the need to join forces with their peers, as a kind of substitute extended family.[464] In this connection, it is interesting to note that these associations were by no means driven by common economic concerns. Rich and less fortunate people alike could be found in one and the same organization. It is plain that motives other than financial were at work.

Tensions within the Amsterdam Portuguese community were responsible for the emergence of even more organizations.[465] In its early days, such conflicts had led to the establishment of a third Portuguese congregation alongside the two existing ones, Bet Jacob and Neve Salom.[466] A similar phenomenon occurred in respect of private charity. Aby Jetomim appeared as an independent organization after a conflict with, and the resignation of, various members of the Gemilut Hasadim society, which fell under the official control of the Portuguese community in 1648.[467] At issue in this case was compliance with, or resistance to, the central authority. The emergence of Honen Dalim in 1667 was the result of a quarrel in the Temime Darech society which had been set up two years earlier;[468] what precisely caused the split in this instance is not altogether clear. It is even more difficult to reconstruct the background of strife in other *ḥevrot*.

Documents relating to organized private charity among the Portuguese Jews of early modern Amsterdam are difficult to find. In some cases only the statutes of the various organizations have survived; in a few cases further information can be traced. The historian Daniel Levi de Barrios left only a superficial account of this type of charitable activity, and his eighteenth-century colleague David Franco Mendes did little more. We can nevertheless judge there to have been around sixty different confraternities among the Amsterdam Portuguese Jews in the early modern period.[469] They may be grouped into several different categories. First, there were at all times among the Amsterdam Portuguese societies devoted exclusively to study.[470] More often, however, associations combined religious study with charitable activities. Others were intended to function exclusively as mutual aid societies. Many societies were multi-functional, combining study, charity, and mutual aid. Finally, some—especially in the eighteenth century—were devoted entirely to charitable action.

The size of these different private organizations varied. Study associations, whether engaged in charitable activities or not, were generally small. Meirat Henaim (founded in 1643) had fourteen members in 1683 and Keter Torah, established in the same year, had seventeen.[471] Mutual aid societies were larger, reflecting the great need for such organizations. Honen Dalim had 156 male and female members in 1683, while Temime Darech and Maskil el Dal each had about 270 members that same year.[472] Fewer data are available for the eighteenth century: the figures for Hase Amaharacha and Meil Sedaca indicate memberships varying between 90 and 200.[473] The numbers are quite modest compared to those of Ets Haim, Dotar, Mishenet Zequenim, or the loan bank Honen Dalim, each of which had more than 400 members in the early modern period.[474]

Study groups were more often than not supervised by a spiritual leader, sometimes assisted by one or more students.[475] Different groups concentrated upon different works of Judaism. The orphanage and yeshiva Aby Jetomim had a large library of Jewish literature at its disposal.[476] Under its first *rosh yeshivah*, Haham Isaac Aboab da Fonseca, members of Neve Sedek studied Talmud and Maimonides (the Rambam), besides giving money to the poor of the brotherhood.[477] Other associations were less specific about their curriculum, saying only that members were supposed to study the 'holy law' or simply learn (*meldar*) together.[478]

Private organized charity for the poor and the sick was provided in many forms, including money, food, clothes, firewood, beds and bedding, medical assistance, deathbed rituals, and personal care. Distributions in money or in kind were given once a year or more often, to a single person or to many at once; some were aimed at specific subgroups like females or the elderly. The scope of the various charitable activities of these private organizations is difficult to assess: de Barrios and Franco Mendes, for example, give no figures concerning the help to the poor. The *ḥevrah* Masmiah Jesuah is said to have spent one-tenth of its income on the general poor, and nine-tenths on those of the poor who came to the yeshiva to study.[479] Other documents are equally uninformative: all we know of Tikvat aJesuah is that it provided meat and bread to the poor; we have no information about how many of the poor were eligible for this assistance.[480] The same holds true for Honen Dalim and Resit Hochma, which gave out butter and vegetables as well as bread.[481] Similarly sparse is the documentation on Michse Leani'im, which provided beds for the poor,[482] Migdal Oz, which distributed first blankets and later meat and bread,[483] and Paame Dalim, which handed out shoes.[484]

Mutual aid societies offered reciprocal support at times of illness, old age, infirmity, and death. Such societies had been a familiar feature among Jews and Christians alike since the Middle Ages, and so it is no surprise that they existed in Portuguese Jewish Amsterdam. They provided assistance for people who, out of a sense of honour and shame, did not wish to be associated with poor relief from the communal *sedaca*, and preferred to associate with people of their own kind. They were especially popular among the Portuguese as Jews were not admitted to most of the trade and craft guilds, and were thus deprived of the security that guilds generally provided in the Dutch Republic and elsewhere in this period.[485] As poverty grew over time, more and more of these mutual aid societies sprang up. In many cases the coverage they offered to members against misfortune was backed up by access to particular medical professionals.[486]

Some of these societies added the study of Jewish law to their general welfare and mutual aid provisions: examples were Temime Darech, set up in 1665, and Resit Hochma, founded in 1682.[487] The yeshiva and *ḥevrah* Honen Dalim took care of sick men and women and provided them with assistance to cover burial costs when they died; from 1704 it also distributed bread to poor widows.[488] The eighteenth century saw the rise of similar multi-functional organizations. Maasim Tobim, for example, was established in 1707 not only as a yeshiva but also as a society to take care of sick people in need, with doctors to tend to them, and money, linen, blankets, and medicine to be distributed among them. A conflict among its members led to the foundation of a new society called Somer Holim, which stressed the importance of keeping watch over its poor members and of deathbed confession.[489] Hase Amaharacha was established in 1713 with the main purpose of distributing firewood to the poor. A year later, however, it was also making gifts of firewood to its own members, thus acting as a mutual aid society too.[490]

Several associations, especially those established during the eighteenth century, were set up out of concerns about how Portuguese Jewish society was to cope with the ever-growing numbers of poor in its midst, and did not include yeshivot. Thus it was explicitly noted in its statutes that Meil Sedaca should not be turned into a yeshiva, its income being solely meant for distribution of cloaks to the poor.[491] Roffe Holim was established solely to help the sick poor of the Portuguese nation, including its own members,[492] while Oneg Sabat focused entirely on the distribution of bread and oil every Friday.[493] However, even in these cases religious motivations cannot be completely ruled out. In making these particular gifts, Oneg Sabat must have had the intention of enabling the poor to fulfil the religious duty of celebrating the sabbath. On certain specific days members of Hase Amaharacha would get together, study, and pray.[494] Also, provision was often made for religious ceremonies around burial, specifically for the members of each *ḥevrah*.[495]

Youth Confraternities

It was not only adults who for various reasons were involved in the dispensation of private charity. Young Portuguese Jews too organized themselves for charitable work. The emergence of youthful confraternities is in line with similar trends in both Jewish and non-Jewish society elsewhere, particularly in Italy, since the fifteenth century.[496]

A need seems to have been felt for ways in which the younger generation could fill a spiritual vacuum by means of prayer, study, and charity. Basic education at home and in the community's schools may well have inspired young people to continue both work and charitable activity, convincing them that 'the world cannot exist without the study of the Holy Law and charity'.[497] In 1760 Selomoh Saruco of The Hague, *ḥazan*, *haham*, and formerly private tutor to the children of the Suasso family, wrote a treatise entitled *Caminho de Vidas* for his own seven children, the eldest of whom was 8 at that time; in it he stressed the importance of benevolence to those around them—poor people and strangers, and especially orphans and widows.[498] A century earlier Ishack de Matatia Aboab had written a treatise for his children in the same vein.[499]

Charitable work by the young may well have been initiated as an attempt by adults—either fathers or spiritual leaders—to guide young people, during the period between their finishing school and marrying, and even beyond, into a serious and God-fearing path of life, preparing these youngsters for their future tasks as active members of the Portuguese community.[500] Often, it looks as if the initiative was taken less by the young themselves than by adults who steered them towards such institutions: it is often older men who, on behalf of the youngsters, request the Portuguese community to approve or sign the founding statutes of these groups.[501]

We know little more about Amsterdam youth societies than what we have been told by Saul Levi Morteira, Daniel Levi de Barrios, and David Franco Mendes and what we can read in some eighteenth-century documents relating to the various groups.[502] Haham Saul Levi Morteira describes a study circle set up by his students to read ethical literature during winter evenings analysing the work *Kad hakemaḥ* by Bahya ben Asher.[503] Others concentrated on study of the Talmud or the *Shulḥan arukh*.[504]

There were quite a few of these societies in the early modern period—around twelve in all—which makes them significant enough to merit some attention here. A few of them were purely religious in character and concentrated exclusively on the study of Judaism: this applied to Tipheret Bajurim (founded 1670), Hateret Bahurim (1737), and Keter Torah (1745).[505] However, most also had a charitable objective. These included several founded during the last decades of the seventeenth century in particular, for example Sahare Sedek (1678), Keter Sem Tob (1679), and Bahale Tesuba (1680, or possibly 1666).[506] Prior to this there had been no provision for organized, religiously motivated, charitable action by the young in the Amsterdam Portuguese community. Only upon reaching the age of 20, or after marriage, did most of them qualify as potential members of a *ḥevrah*.[507] Yet even after this age young adults in their twenties tended to seek out each other's company: instead of joining the older generation in their associations, they tended to prefer studying with their peers in a yeshiva such as Keter Torah.[508]

It is possible that the later societies were modelled on the earlier, but that tells us nothing about why they appeared when they did. The stated purpose of Bahale Tesuba, namely 'to awaken sinners, filling them with the fear of the Lord and making them submit to the Law', makes it clear that the intention was to bring young people back to the serious study of Judaism.[509] In fact, in the 1670s and especially during the course of the eighteenth century there was a growing lack of interest among the young generation in Jewish studies. Pupils were expelled from Ets Haim because of improper behaviour, causing disturbances, and lack of interest. The new initiatives may have been an attempt to change this tendency.[510] Often, the statutes of the new societies exhort the youngsters to behave decently and not to be provocative or cause disorder.[511]

The establishment of youth societies went on well into the eighteenth century. The 1740s alone saw the foundation of Hateret Tipheret, Kisuy Ros, and Honen Dal; some were set up even later, for example Haberim Magsibim in 1764.[512] Their members varied in age for the most part between 12 and 20.[513]

As well as fostering the study of Judaism, these societies must have contributed to imbuing the young with a positive attitude towards Jewish traditions in general and to charitable activity in particular. Spiritual leadership was provided by Orthodox figures, including the *hahamim* Saul Levi Morteira and Jacob Sasportas, and former Ets Haim students such as Joseph Franco Serrano or David Nunes Torres.[514] In the eighteenth century the Orthodox Belinfante and Siprut di Gabay families from Belgrade (whose ancestors were educated at famous Balkan yeshivot and whose own sons were taught at the Ets Haim yeshiva in Amsterdam) seem to have been actively involved as leaders and participants in various religious societies for the young.[515]

These groups generally met on free days or afternoons, in the evenings, on the sabbath, or during the Jewish holidays.[516] Sometimes, like the adult societies, they met in family homes; often they were allowed to use the classrooms of the various yeshivot, for example Ets Haim or Aby Jetomim. The average membership of these societies was around thirty-five, so homes had to be large to accommodate them.[517] For generations, the Bueno de Mesquita family opened their house for meetings.[518] The members of Haberim Magsibim were hospitably received in the house of Eliasib Netanel Sarfati,[519] and the boys of Resit Daat would gather in the house of Abraham Penso Felix.[520]

In addition to studying, most of these young people spent time and effort caring for the poor. As with many other private associations, we do not know precisely how this form of poor relief by the young worked in practice. De

Barrios and Franco Mendes simply refer to 'helping the poor', 'burying the dead at their [that is, the members'] expense', and 'providing shelter and distributing food to strangers'.[521]

Eighteenth-century documents offer a little more detail. Grants to the poor consisted of clothes or food.[522] Distributions were not frequent—once or twice a year—and not extensive: Kisuy Ros, for example, gave only one hat and jacket to one poor person, once a year;[523] Hateret Tipheret gave hats and wigs to the poor twice a year.[524] Procedures were similar to those of the adult societies: charity had to be requested through petitions and recipients were frequently chosen by lot.[525] Often, the members were personally involved in handing out the charity themselves.[526]

Little is known about the background of these boys. The members of Tipheret Bajurim came from rich families and later became prosperous themselves.[527] Young people in other societies, too, were mainly recruited from families that were rich or intellectual, or both.[528] In Catholic youth societies in sixteenth- and seventeenth-century Italy there is also a growing trend towards aristocratization.[529] If charity was to be provided, money was needed, and this required the involvement of the more prosperous families. There were exceptions: most of the younger members of Bahale Tesuba were not wealthy, being enrolled in classes for education of the poor or registered on the charity lists themselves.[530]

The involvement of young people in study and charity, whether on their own initiative or at the urging of their superiors, shows an effort to stimulate continuous commitment and loyalty to the basic principles of Judaism. Such enterprises also encouraged young people not to remain passive, but to learn responsibility for and sensitivity to the ever-growing social, economic, and spiritual problems present in their immediate environment and thus prepared them for the leadership tasks awaiting them in adulthood.

Charity by and for Women

The *ḥevrot* set up to help Portuguese Jewish women in early modern Amsterdam deserve special attention here. Women did not initiate the establishment of these organizations,[531] nor were they included on the supervising boards, as noted above in the case of the orphanage Mazon Abanot. The position of Portuguese women in the Amsterdam *ḥevrot* was even more restricted than that of their counterparts in southern Europe, where sisterhoods, initiated and managed by women, did exist, though there too they played a minor role in a society dominated by male confraternities.[532] Here again, we notice the influence of southern European society on patterns established in the north. However, Jewish influences should not be ruled out altogether. In many *ḥevrot* of the Jewish world of that time women assumed a passive role, although Jewish women in Italy or the German states, and even those in the Ashkenazi community of Amsterdam, did establish *ḥevrot* of their own.[533]

Notwithstanding their subordinate position, Portuguese Jewish women in Amsterdam were often members of, and actively engaged in, the various charitable associations founded by Portuguese men. The orphanage Aby Jetomim could serve as an example for the seventeenth century, and the orphanage Mazon Abanot and the old-age home Mishenet Zequenim for the eighteenth.[534]

Even though the establishment and administration of organized charity was mostly a men's affair—and in a few cases men even received preferential treatment[535]—much charitable initiative was directed towards poor women and girls: single females including orphans, married women, and widows.

Widows in particular were in a vulnerable position. They accounted for between 14 and 37 per cent of women on welfare over this period, proportions similar to those in the non-Jewish world.[536] Some of them had never been on welfare before and fell into difficulty suddenly. Moses Gedalia, for example, had been able to keep his family off the charity register by his work as a tobacco spinner, but after his death his widow 'had to rely on the synagogue for support', as she declared.[537] Even the widows of professional men such as doctors and apothecaries were not always able to escape the poverty trap, as is clear from the cases of the widow of Dr Benjamin de Sea and the widow of the apothecary Jacob Coronel.[538]

It is in the eighteenth century that we see the greatest expansion in *ḥevrot* set up to help poor women of the Spanish and Portuguese nation, paralleling developments in the Iberian peninsula,[539] and also the increase in number of other charitable *ḥevrot*. The first decade of the eighteenth century, during the War of the Spanish Succession, saw the establishment of the house for poor elderly women, in imitation of similar houses for women existing in southern Europe.[540] Also, the Honen Dalim *ḥevrah* and yeshiva changed its statutes at this time, in 1704, adding to its activities the distribution of bread to poor widows.[541]

Then, in the 1730s, when the resources available for welfare dwindled, four *ḥevrot* were established to help women. Berit Salom and Mispat Abanot (both founded in 1730) paid a sum of money every week for four weeks to women who had given birth to girls.[542] Sidcat Nassim was set up in 1733 to assist poor women during times of illness.[543] The foundation of the girls' orphanage Mazon Abanot in 1734 has already been mentioned.

The 1740s were marked by harsh winters, wars, economic distress, and cutbacks in official poor relief.[544] Right at the beginning of the decade, the severe winter of 1739/40 had already prompted the Portuguese community to make a special collection for relief of hardship.[545] Two more *ḥevrot* were founded in the following years to help women: Hesrat Nasim in 1741 and Quesut La Ebion in 1748. Both concentrated their activities on the distribution of clothes: the first on shoes and socks, the second on skirts.[546] The second half of the eighteenth century saw more new foundations: for example, Parnasad Almanot, both yeshiva and welfare society, distributed money among poor widows of the Spanish and Portuguese Jewish nation.[547]

The help extended to women represents a progressive development for an impoverished female constituency lacking other means and not willing to be helped, or insufficiently helped, through the official channels of the community. It also reflects the obsession with female well-being, honour, and status that was characteristic of southern Europe and brought from there to the north.[548]

Charity for the Elderly Poor

The elderly poor among the Amsterdam Portuguese were not considered to merit attention as a separate group until the first decade of the eighteenth century. In this closely knit community, with strong family ties and feelings of mutual solidarity, the older generation would ordinarily have been looked after as a matter of course. However, by the eighteenth century this traditional support network could no longer be relied upon.

Although old-age homes among the non-Jews in Amsterdam and elsewhere had been established much earlier than this,[549] institutions for the elderly among the Portuguese of Amsterdam were not established until the eighteenth century. In 1708 Isaac Abrabanel Arede gave a house named Rehobot for the accommodation of elderly women of the Portuguese and Spanish nation in need.[550] In 1750 a Jewish old-age home by the name of Mishenet Zequenim was founded, several months after the establishment of the *ḥevrah* of the same name in 1749.[551] The reason was obvious, as set out in the organization's statutes: 'It was a disgrace for so resplendent a nation to see sad and tired people walk about the streets, begging for food.'[552] Probably many youngsters had left for better opportunities abroad, often with the encouragement of the community, leaving behind increasing numbers of elderly detached from any family structure or support.

Admittance to Mishenet Zequenim was managed through a hierarchical system that gave priority to existing members.[553] People applied for enrolment as members not only from Amsterdam and from other places in the Dutch Republic, such as The Hague, Naarden, and Maarssen, but also from abroad—from Bayonne, Bordeaux, Hamburg, London, and Surinam.[554] New regulations introduced in 1753 restricted entrance to widows and widowers on their own, aged 60 years or over, belonging to the Spanish and Portuguese nation, but in practice the old-age home was meant for and populated by men only.[555]

Life within Mishenet Zequenim was governed by strict rules and behaviour was assessed year by year, good conduct being a condition of continued residence.[556] Medical care was taken care of by the charity's own nurses and doctors.[557] Attention was also given to the inmates' religious life. The sabbath and holidays were duly celebrated,[558] and a yeshiva was provided soon after the home's foundation on the initiative of the *ḥevrah* Temime Darech, which transferred its yeshiva, its capital, its personnel, and all its other assets to Mishenet Zequenim in an amalgamation of the two organizations.[559]

The statutes of Mishenet Zequenim show many features characteristic of welfare provision in the Amsterdam Portuguese community: the ethnic–religious conditions for acceptance of administrators, members, and inmates; the insistence on, and supervision of, lifelong good conduct; the hierarchical structure of admittance; and the international dimension.

The *Kahal*'s Response to Private Charitable Initiatives

The *kahal* looked upon the development of private charities with disfavour, particularly when it came to the founding of independent societies. On the other hand, it must have felt supported in its care of the poor by the activities of the various private organizations, certainly if it had some control over them. Time and again, the *kahal* stressed the fact that its consent must be obtained before a new *ḥevrah* could be founded.[560] The authority of the *kahal*, in particular as a body ensuring public order and supervising the good conduct and religious diligence of its members, was at stake. The Portuguese community preferred to keep the reins in its own hands, not least to control fraud, co-ordinate cash flow, and ensure that expenditure could be met. This, it believed, could best be achieved by administering charity directly or through societies subordinate to the *kahal*. As soon as money began to pass through channels outside its control, there was always the danger that the financial burden on the community, and official poor relief in particular, would become unsupportable. That would have put the very existence of the Portuguese *kahal* at risk.

One reason for the tremendous expansion of private welfare provision in this period might be an aversion on the part of members of the community to paying ever higher taxes to support the expenditure of a communal authority to which they were not entirely committed. The Amsterdam Portuguese were quite keen to help the poor. It was certainly cheaper than paying taxes—which also forced them to reveal their financial circumstances, including the extent of their assets, and to be subject to arbitrary decisions by the community leadership. It is entirely possible that this feeling was widespread, as indeed is suggested by the terms of a warning from the *kahal* in 1766 that 'anyone who spends part or all of his taxes on a pious deed and distributes the sum he owes to taxes to the poor is alike unto a thief. For he is stealing money from God. He will incur the same punishments.'[561]

Nevertheless, private welfare provision, whether in co-operation with the *kahal* or not, was a major supporting pillar of an all-embracing effort to support the plight of the poor, both in the present and in generations to come.

Conclusion

Poor relief in the Amsterdam Portuguese community seemed at first to be a united effort, developing in a single direction and run by a well co-ordinated administration. Traditional patterns, copied from Jewish communities in southern Europe and the Orient, were intended to provide the basis on which Amsterdam's system could be established, built up, and supported. Despite the division of the community, first into two and later into three separate Jewish congregations, until 1639 poor relief was increasingly provided by a central administration. Indeed, care of the poor was one of the main reasons for the fusion of the three *kehilot*, enabling them to combine forces in coping with the growing influx of their impoverished brethren. In case of financial need, sickness, or death, the Portuguese now had a buffer on which they knew they could rely.

Over time, poor relief in the Portuguese community underwent various reforms and expansions, but the basic help provided through all the subsidiary bodies remained under the control of the highest administrative organ of the Portuguese community. It was recognized that the socially disadvantaged had to be supported adequately if their participation in the new Jewish experiment in the north was to be guaranteed; also, they had to be kept under control and in line with the law if the social stability of the community was to be preserved.

However, Portuguese poor relief did not merely serve a social purpose—namely helping to reduce the wretchedness of the poor and supervising their behaviour—nor was it a simple expression of international solidarity among Jews. Support was extended to the former New Christians, fleeing from the Inquisition, displaced and often robbed of their possessions, in order to bind them permanently to the Portuguese *kahal* and to Judaism. In a sense the same was also true of the more fortunate members of the community, who, by virtue of membership of and participation in the various charitable organizations controlled by the Portuguese community, became more closely involved with the *kahal* and guaranteed its further existence by their financial support.

Centralization of poor relief, a fairly new phenomenon in early modern Europe, helped to co-ordinate the various charitable activities, optimizing the care of the poor and keeping it under control. The Amsterdam Portuguese Jews, being integrated European citizens, were aware of these ideas and tried to adapt them to their own environment.

The system of poor relief built up and maintained by the Portuguese community with so much care quickly developed cracks. Not even when it came to poor relief could the Portuguese be forced to adopt a rigid new system; instead, they continued to use patterns in Amsterdam with which they had been familiar in the Iberian peninsula or elsewhere in the diaspora. As the number of immigrants in Amsterdam increased, so did the social diversity of the Portuguese population. Those who shared a particular place of origin or a common experience preferred to keep company with others like themselves, and organized relief for themselves and for others as they saw fit. Moreover, in this way individual groups could fill in the gaps in the centrally administered poor-relief system according to their own needs and preferences.

The Portuguese in early modern Amsterdam were also influenced by spiritual and religious currents in Jewish thinking. They banded together in societies that, in addition to studying, tried to atone and repent for sins with charitable work. They evinced a highly developed notion of expiation that not only sprang from tendencies within Judaism but also reflected the Catholic background of the former New Christians. Charity was expected to make up for a great many sins.

By accepting the existence of private organizations as they sprang up, and on so large a scale, Portuguese Jewish poor relief fitted seamlessly into patterns that, despite innovative ideas about poor relief, were well established in contemporary Europe, particularly in the south. In that way, the Portuguese demonstrated once again how thoroughly immersed they were in the surrounding society.

The organization of Portuguese Jewish poor relief in early modern Amsterdam was a mixture of modern and conservative, traditional Jewish and Iberian Catholic, spiritual–religious and practical–realistic, centralized and individualistic elements.[562] Charity, no matter in what form, was a remarkable, ramified enterprise and constituted an important aspect of the life of Portuguese Jews in early modern Amsterdam. The next chapter will turn to the financial infrastructure that supported all this charitable endeavour.

CHAPTER FIVE

FINANCING CHARITY

IT GOES WITHOUT SAYING that in the fight against poverty, nothing can be done without money. This was as true in the early modern period as it is today. In times of peace and prosperity the Portuguese community of early modern Amsterdam took a more tolerant and generous line towards the reception and care of paupers, while in periods of war and economic malaise it tended to be stricter and less lavish in its support.[1]

Financing charity within the Amsterdam community was never easy. Poor relief was constantly at odds with a rule in the 1639 unification statutes that the annual expenditure of the *kahal* should never exceed its revenue.[2] This injunction was repeated time and again in the so-called *Livro de escamot*, the Resolution Book, but still expenditure exceeded income on countless occasions;[3] and the greatest area of expenditure for the *kahal* during the seventeenth and eighteenth centuries was poor relief. Private welfare proved to be an indispensable help, saving paupers and relieving the burden on the official sector where public means failed. An analysis of the finances of both public and private welfare provision will help us to understand this crucial underpinning of welfare policy.

The Public Sector

Income and Expenditure

The balance of income and expenditure was recorded by means of an impressive bookkeeping system.[4] As the community grew, so did the accounting system, expanding from a set of slim journals at the beginning of the seventeenth century to a series of thick, heavy, main and subsidiary ledgers during the eighteenth century, giving evidence of a growing bureaucracy. In addition to managing its own funds, the Kahal Kados de Talmud Torah increasingly handled the capital of private individuals.[5]

Two summaries were issued every year, the first covering mainly internal developments, the second all foreign and private transactions, such as annual remittances to people living in Erets Yisra'el. Payments earmarked for aid to *cativos* were also included in the second survey.[6] The following discussion is based particularly on the internal income and expenditure account, also known as the *sedaca* account (*kupat sedaca*), under which heading, as in other *kehilot*, all financial transactions involving the synagogue were entered.[7]

The income of the Portuguese Jewish community in early modern Amsterdam was used predominantly for internal purposes. In other words, it served mainly to cover the costs of running the Portuguese community in general and those of poor relief in particular. The latter could take almost half the budget, sometimes more.[8] The situation was similar in other Portuguese communities of the early modern period—for example, between 1669 and 1677, 33 per cent of communal expenditure in the Spanish–Portuguese community of London went into poor relief[9]—and in the wider world as well: expenditure on welfare in the Dutch Republic also rose as high as 50 per cent or more.[10] Only the continuous manipulation of income and expenditure and repeated recourse to capital reserves enabled the Portuguese Jewish community in Amsterdam to weather this period.

Expenditure

As described in Chapter 4, poor relief gradually ramified out into a large network of compartments, into which everyone could be fitted according to background, need, status, moral conduct, or family size, and then be paid weekly, monthly, or several times a year, in money or in kind. Welfare expenditure also covered costs incurred by other organizations connected directly to the *kahal*: those involved in caring for the sick (Bikur Holim), in attending to and burying the dead (Gemilut Hasadim), and in clothing the poor (Vestiaria), and those of the *ḥevrah* Abodat Ahesed.[11]

Expenditure other than poor relief that was also entered in the *sedaca* account covered the payment of synagogue and school staff, maintenance of the synagogue complex (repairs, cleaning), lighting (wax and oil), maintenance of the Ouderkerk cemetery, the repayment of loans, the distribution of legacies, annuities, property taxes, and the annual remittance by the Portuguese community to the almoners of the municipal charity.

Ever greater amounts were drawn from the capital of the Portuguese community in order to balance income and expenditure in the *sedaca* account. In the seventeenth century, the deficit varied from 280 guilders in the year 1691/2 to 9,414 guilders in 1657/8.[12] In the eighteenth century higher totals were reached as the annual deficit soared, especially after the wars and economic crises of the 1740s. The second half of the eighteenth century, and the last quarter in particular, did not show much improvement.[13]

In the seventeenth century welfare expenditure fluctuated around half the entire income of the *sedaca* account; in the eighteenth century it often exceeded 50 per cent, accounting for 62 per cent in 1699/1700 and 82 per cent in 1740/1. The cost of welfare increased by a multiple of approximately 4.7 between 1650/1 and 1740/1, both in nominal and in real terms. Thanks to the strict economies introduced in the 1740s the cost was reduced to 51,948 guilders in 1793/4, a fall of more than 25 per cent in nominal value and of about 30 per cent in real value in relation to the 1740s; even so, welfare expenditure remained high at 63 per cent of the communal income on the *sedaca* account. The increasing impoverishment of the Portuguese community, which began in the seventeenth century, seemed inescapable despite the various steps taken to address it.[14]

Sources of Income

The Amsterdam Portuguese community coped with income shortfalls in much the same way as traditional *kehilot* had done for centuries.[15] Here too there were direct and indirect taxes, the relative levels of which varied over time. As noted above, the Portuguese community and its spiritual leaders exerted pressure on its members to pay taxes to enable the *kahal* to meet its expenses on welfare.[16]

First there was the *finta* tax levied on general wealth. Then there were the indirect taxes. The international trading activities of many Amsterdam Portuguese invited the taxation of imports and exports—of general merchandise, silver and gold, diamonds, pearls, amber, and jewellery—and of financial transactions, insurance policies, agents' fees, and later also the buying and selling of stocks and shares. The tax on all these activities, the so-called *imposta*, levied at varying rates, was introduced in 1622 in order to boost revenue and to ease the burden of poor relief.[17] Before the last quarter of the seventeenth century in particular, *imposta* proceeds were appreciable; indeed, up to the 1670s this tax in most cases brought in more than the *finta*.[18] The yield from the *imposta* was added to other forms of revenue and used to meet the community's expenses.

In levying a tax on kosher meat, the Amsterdam *kehilah* followed the traditional practice of other *kehilot* of taxing consumer goods associated with ritual practices.[19] From the beginning of the seventeenth century this tax too was used to meet the costs of poor relief.[20] This source of revenue gradually became one of the most important contributions to the total income of the community.[21]

Then there were the *promessas* and *offertas* made during services in the synagogue and yeshivot. People were shamed into making *promessas* throughout the seventeenth and eighteenth centuries: in 1661, for example, a call was made for *promessas* to alleviate the very great poverty—*a grandissima pobreza.*[22] Like those failing to pay the *finta,* the names of all who defaulted on their promised contributions were put on lists displayed on the synagogue wall.[23]

As was also customary in traditional *kehilot,* money for distribution to the poor was collected during the various festivals marking the cycle of the Jewish year.[24] Thus at Purim appeals were made in the synagogue for contributions to the poor.[25] The elders also ordered special collections during emergencies (war, epidemics, especially hot summers and severe winters, and so on).[26] In addition, contributions were sought at set times to certain organizations directly dependent on the *kahal,* each of which had a collection day of its own.[27] Beyond that, collection boxes were placed in the synagogue complex, where any member of the congregation could contribute at any time to *ḥevrot* associated with the *kahal* in accordance with the obligation to support the poor.[28] Finally, there was a weekly round on Friday afternoons, before the start of the sabbath: community officials would go from one Portuguese house to the next with boxes, the so-called *caixinhas de sestas fereiras,* allowing the inhabitants to join in the *mitsvah* of *sedaca.*[29]

Almost every new wave of needy incomers gave rise to special collections to raise extra money.[30] What is striking here is the difference in the treatment accorded to Sephardim from the West as opposed to those from the East. When refugees expelled from southern France arrived in Amsterdam in 1684/5, the *kahal* held a collection and provided the families with generous support in the form of money, clothes, shelter, and medical care. When Sephardi refugees arrived from the Balkans around five years later the Amsterdam Portuguese Jews, feeling less affinity with this group, did not set up a special collection for them, and the amount spent on them was much lower.[31]

Going around with poor boxes and gathering money through collections were not practices exclusive to the Portuguese Jewish community of Amsterdam.[32] Collections for the poor were a characteristic feature of early modern Europe. In the Dutch Republic, for instance, collectors were constantly circulating, both inside the churches and from house to house, accumulating sizeable sums of money to alleviate the needs of the poor and other distressed people at home and abroad.[33]

Legacies left by members to the congregation also helped to increase the assets of the Portuguese community. From the last quarter of the seventeenth century and during the course of the eighteenth, the returns on investment of this capital, known as the Cabedal Codes ('Sacred Capital'), continued to grow. In 1675 the total value of legacies stood at 119,103 guilders.[34] By the middle of the eighteenth century it stood at 545,245 guilders, nearly five times as much.[35]

Fines, rental income from property, and money accruing from the administration of private funds were the final contributory elements in the community's income.[36]

From this total, all the expenses of the Portuguese community, including the costs of poor relief, had to be paid. The balance was awaited anxiously every year and announced in the synagogue.[37]

Fluctuations in Income

Figure 2 (see Appendix II) shows the growth in the income of the community up to 1730. From 1675 to 1700 it increased by a factor of 1.6, in both nominal and real terms. Growth was even more pronounced in the first quarter of the eighteenth century, when it nearly doubled. Figures for the late 1730s and early 1740s indicate that there was something of a crisis, with income declining and the deficit on the *sedaca* account (relating to welfare payments and all other items) rising sharply as economic depression and war made themselves felt. By the second half of the century income had declined further in real terms.[38]

In the seventeenth century, taxes, above all the *finta* and *imposta*, together with *promessas*, were the most important sources of revenue for the Portuguese community: in 1675, 70 per cent of income consisted of contributions in the form of taxes and donations. By the middle of the eighteenth century the proportions had changed: *finta*, *imposta*, and *promessas* together accounted for about 40 per cent, while the income from capital and the tax on kosher meat had increased to a combined total of 45–50 per cent, as shown in Figure 3 (see Appendix II).

The community's income looks considerable, but was often insufficient to cover its expenses. In the seventeenth century, the leadership of the Portuguese community decided to increase the level of taxation on the members. Declining income from the *imposta* was invariably offset by an increase in *finta* taxation. The yield of *finta* and *imposta*, particularly in the seventeenth century, was inversely proportional.[39] Whenever the *imposta*, which reflected the balance of trade, provided the necessary income, the *finta* could be kept low. Between 1640/1 and 1663/4, the *imposta* generated a high, if fluctuating, yield. After that, the level still fluctuated but fell perceptibly (see Appendix II, Figure 4). During the first half of the eighteenth century there was still an absolute increase of revenue from the *imposta*, but thereafter the level declined steadily.

The explanation of the fluctuations in income from the *imposta* lies chiefly in unstable trading conditions. An additional factor is the increasing reluctance on the part of Portuguese Jewish merchants to share their trading profits with their community. In the eighteenth century, many Portuguese seem to have conducted their international trade through accounts held outside the Republic, thus misleading the Amsterdam Portuguese administration about the extent of their dues to the community.[40] The elders, aware of this type of tax evasion, tried to maintain the income from the *imposta* by issuing a continuous stream of orders to its members, laying down guidelines for paying this tax and extending the statutes. The administration also threatened members continually with fines and penalties in cases of tax evasion. Thus they declared in 1675 that 'all dues have to be paid to *sedaca* on pain of *herem* . . . Everyone must reconcile his debt to this *imposta* with his conscience, with all the obligations, good intentions and punishments of *berahot* and *herem* of our Sacred Law.'[41] A century later, the threats sounded even more ominous. In 1776 the administration was still stressing that 'all members are obliged to hand over to the *imposta* board, every year before *sabat hagadol*, what they owe from trading on foreign accounts. Anyone infringing this obligation and concealing any earnings, however small, is inviting the strictest punishments of *berahot* and *herem* of our Holy Law.'[42]

When the revenue from the *imposta* fell short, members of the Portuguese community found their income being taxed more heavily. Thus the *finta* rose steadily from the 1650s, with extra demands being made, for instance, in 1666 to cover the losses in *imposta* revenue caused by the Second Anglo-Dutch War:

> The worthy Gentlemen of the Mahamad met in the company of Señor Haham Isack Aboab and the worthy adjutants to discuss the reform of the *finta*, to be applied provisionally for a year. In this way, aid to the poor can be continued and other assistance and the necessary costs of this congregation can be covered. The community is facing difficulties because of the war and the suspension of trade. For that reason, the above-mentioned consultation, necessitated by the shortfall of revenue from the *imposta*, was held. Unanimously, and in keeping with the statutes of the nation, it was decided to proceed to the reform of the *finta*.[43]

Income from the *imposta* declined sharply again in 1672 as a result of the declaration of war on the Dutch Republic by the united front of France, England, Münster, and Cologne.[44] On top of that, the building of the new synagogue entailed extra costs, and at the same time the war was responsible for reducing more people to poverty. The *finta* tax had consequently to be increased,[45] and income from that source more than doubled as a result.[46]

During the last decade of the seventeenth century, in about 1695/6, increases in the *finta* were again resorted to as the chief means of balancing the *sedaca* account.[47] At the time, the Portuguese community found itself in difficulties resulting from the War of the League of Augsburg[48] and the continuous inflow of refugees, chiefly from the areas around Buda, Belgrade, and Sarajevo. It justified its unpopular measures as follows:

> Because of the large deficit in the *sedaca,* which occurred despite the various reforms of the poor-relief lists . . . it was decided unanimously that all members shall contribute an extra half *finta* and lend an entire *finta* . . . This has to be paid promptly before *Roshodes Nisan.* Anyone having failed to pay by then will no longer be admitted to the *Esnoga* . . . this in order to relieve poverty and to preserve our Holy Community.[49]

The 15 per cent increase in *finta* taxation introduced in 1742 continued to be enforced up to the end of the eighteenth century. This tax reform was part of a set of measures intended to raise income and reduce expenses during the period of crisis in the mid-eighteenth century. By that time, the yield from the *imposta* had declined so sharply that there was no longer any significant relationship between *finta* and *imposta.*[50] At the end of the eighteenth century the number of male *finta* contributors declined owing to a combination of increasing poverty and rising numbers of male taxpayers emigrating. To preserve the *finta* revenue while keeping the tax burden within reasonable bounds, it became essential to begin taxing the wealth of women, much of which was based on the investment of capital. While women were assessed for the *finta* only very occasionally before the end of the eighteenth century, at that point widows (and, apparently, some other women) started contributing to this tax routinely. With this increasing number of contributors, income from the *finta* grew significantly.[51]

The sale of kosher meat underwent a spectacular growth, particularly during the first half of the eighteenth century: between 1700 and 1730 the value of tax gathered on sales of meat grew by a factor of about four, in both nominal and real terms, from 6,986 guilders to 25,176 guilders.[52] A combination of growing tax pressure on the sale of kosher meat and the increase in the consumption of meat by a growing number of Portuguese Jews as a result of rising standards of living (especially up to the 1730s) meant a sharp rise in income from the *carniseria* (meat hall).[53] That the *parnasim* were well aware of the importance of this source of income may be inferred from the many instructions they issued to members of the Portuguese community to buy their meat exclusively in their own community and not to obtain it elsewhere.[54] The same inference may be drawn from the strict supervision by community leaders of the organization of the meat hall and of the quality and price of meat sold, and their regular emphasis on, and revision of, the rules.[55]

During the second half of the eighteenth century, part of the income from the *carniseria*—anything in excess of 15,600 guilders—went into a reserve fund (together with the income from the *imposta* and from fines). This reserve fund was set aside specifically to cover exceptional costs in providing poor relief.[56]

Income from *promessas* rose from 5,173 guilders to 16,866 guilders between 1675 and 1730, more than tripling in both nominal and real terms. For about half a century from 1700, *promessas* brought in more revenue than the *finta*. The decreasing revenue from this source during the second half of the eighteenth century reflects a general economic decline, but also less personal involvement in organized communal life, while in the earlier period the opposite must have been the case.

In the eighteenth century, returns on the successful investment on a growing amount of capital accounted for between a quarter and a third of the overall income of the Amsterdam Portuguese community and did not fall far below the combined income from the tax on kosher meat, the *finta*, and *promessas*.[57] The Amsterdam Portuguese community rarely invested its capital in property, favouring stocks and shares—particularly, in the seventeenth century, in the States of Holland and West Friesland and the Dutch East India Company.[58] In the eighteenth century foreign investments were added, for instance in the Bank of England, the (British) East India Company, the South Sea Company, and later also in the German states.[59] In that respect, the investment policy of the Portuguese community barely differed from that of the urban elite of the Dutch Republic, which tied its fortunes not only to the prosperity of its own country, but also to the shifting international situation.[60]

In the last quarter of the seventeenth century, legacies formed an important part of the community's assets: in 1700 the total credit balance stood at 286,391 guilders, of which 189,005 guilders in legacies represented 66 per cent of the total.[61]

In the eighteenth century, there was a marked change in these relations. During the first half of that century, the legacies amassed in the Cabedal Codes grew threefold in nominal and real terms, from 189,005 guilders in 1700 to 545,245 guilders in 1750/1.[62] However, by that time this fund made up no more than 39 per cent of the community's total capital, much lower than the percentages prevailing in 1675 or 1700.

For the leaders of the Kahal Kados de Talmud Torah—as for the leaders of non-Jewish charitable organizations in the city—capital reserves constituted a last buffer in times of crisis and an important pillar of poor relief. In the case of the Portuguese community, however, their significance went further, guaranteeing the continued existence of the community in Amsterdam.[63]

In the eighteenth century, fears about the erosion of the capital grew rapidly, with good reason. The deficit had been growing continuously since the late 1730s and the capital had had to be tapped in increasing amounts. The financial mainstay of the *kahal* was under grave threat, forcing the elders of the community to rethink their approach to welfare. Their anxiety may be gathered from a letter sent by the States of Holland and West Friesland in 1748, in reply to a request by the Portuguese community for exemption from taxes, summarizing the worries of the community as follows:

> that the applicants for that very reason (the generosity of the Contributors being inadequate), had to call upon their churches' endowment funds . . . And whereas the Supplicants were for once unable to provide their Poor with what is needed to sustain them and to save them from destitution, however prudently they set about it, all their funds will shortly have run out and be depleted, unless the Supplicants be afforded some relief through our benevolence.[64]

As noted above, the capital had grown substantially in the first half of the eighteenth century; however, during the second half of the century, though relatively stable in nominal terms, its real value declined by about 30 per cent owing to inflation (most of the decline occurring during the last decade of the eighteenth century).[65] This decline was the result not only of a falling off in private donations to the Portuguese community, but also of the economic crisis of 1772/3, the pronounced fall in the value of shares in the Dutch East India Company, the bankruptcy of the Dutch West India Company at the time of the Fourth Anglo-Dutch War, and the vicissitudes in the aftermath of the French Revolution all of which severely undermined the financial position of the Portuguese community.[66]

Reforms to the Financial System

As we have already seen, early modern Portuguese Jews felt a strong sense of international solidarity with other members of their 'nation', especially (former) Conversos. The spiritual and secular leadership of the Amsterdam Portuguese often stressed the religious commands of hospitality and mutual responsibility, and constantly reminded its congregation that they were all in exile and should all be seeking redemption.[67] It was in part religious motives of this kind that made the community leaders reluctant to place too many restrictions on the influx of paupers. However, they did not want to see completely unlimited disbursement of poor relief either. While the community sought to tread this uneasy line, the number of paupers kept growing. Thus, in the middle of the eighteenth century, Isaac de Pinto, taking stock of the situation, concluded that concern for others had run wild. In his *Reflexoens Politicas* (1748), de Pinto, treasurer of the Portuguese community at the time, set out his attitude to poor relief, blaming unforeseen circumstances and not the administrators of the past for the current plight:

> In other republics, abuses by those in charge of public affairs are usually blamed on the administrators. These men are self-serving and sacrifice the public interest to their own . . . In the administration of our finances, no malpractice has ever been detected. The intention, will and concern of the directors have always been impeccable, virtuous and unselfish: driven by Divine zeal and fear, they have always endeavoured to perform their work of *caridade* as best they could. But however great the concern and devotion of our worthy predecessors, they were unable to foresee certain matters. Time alone could teach that.[68]

By the time de Pinto was writing, the ratio of paupers drawing poor relief to contributing members had reached dramatic proportions. According to de Pinto, 'we, four hundred paying members, are expected to care for about eight hundred families, who live and die at our expense'.[69]

It is beyond dispute that, from the very beginning of its history, the leaders of the Amsterdam Portuguese community were aware of the problematic situation brought about by poor relief, though they may not have realized that poverty would assume such large proportions. They did, however, appreciate the need to take control of the problem and to keep it within reasonable bounds. As they continuously watched the relationship between expenditure and income, anxious about the maintenance and indeed the continued existence of the Amsterdam Portuguese *kahal*, they were particularly concerned about the rising cost of poor relief. Various ways were tried of keeping it down. Over time, the organization of poor relief was slimmed down, paupers were sent elsewhere, a stricter admission system was imposed, staff expenses were cut, and limits were set to the budget. Income had already been maximized: the contributing section of the Portuguese community had to pay ever-increasing taxes, was urged to make larger donations, had its contributions checked, and, if found to be falling behind in its obligations, was severely rebuked and fined. Whenever necessary, loans were taken out. In the middle of the eighteenth century a reserve fund was set up as a buffer, designed to prevent the depletion of the capital of the Kahal Kados de Talmud Torah.

The following sections examine what the various reforms of income and expenditure entailed and what effects they eventually produced.

Tax Increases and their Effect

The increasingly swingeing taxes on property, trading profits, and the consumption of meat, and the growing pressure to donate money through *offertas*, elicited strong reactions. In the middle of the eighteenth century, de Pinto referred to the intolerable tax burden as something approaching tyranny.[70] Other Portuguese before him had voiced similar complaints.

The problem caused the Portuguese community much anxiety. The possible exodus or defection of wealthy Portuguese was likely to trigger off a downward financial spiral and might well lead to the break-up of the community. This fear was not unfounded: some taxpayers tried to resign from the community and refused to honour their debts. On several occasions, the help of the city of Amsterdam was sought to endorse and emphasize the Mahamad's authority over the Portuguese community.

Tension among the contributing members of the community seemed to reach a peak at the beginning of the 1670s, following the obligatory extra taxes and loans and the calls for voluntary donations. This is vividly illustrated by the Isaac Penemacor affair. In the spring of 1675 Señor Penemacor, a rich merchant, mounted the *teva* of the stately Esnoga to ask God and the Portuguese community to forgive him for the scandal he had caused.[71]

At the beginning of the 1670s, it seems, Isaac Penemacor had raised objections to the high tax burden imposed upon him and his family. He had not only refused to pay his own taxes, but had been able to rally more than a hundred families behind his protest. After the elders of the Portuguese community threatened to excommunicate the recalcitrant taxpayers, the protesters gave in; but Isaac Penemacor himself remained adamant. Despite all attempts by the Portuguese community to bring about a change of heart, he declared that he would resign from the community and refused to pay his dues. It ended in a scuffle. Penemacor and a son who hastened to his assistance set about the *parnasim*, whereupon Penemacor was excommunicated. Finally, however, he bowed to pressure and did his public penance the next day at the ceremony in the Esnoga.[72]

The elders must have feared the disintegration of their community threatened by the resignation of members. Five years earlier, there had already been the threat of a split in the wake of the del Sotto affair.[73] In the settlement of that affair, a resolution was entered in the minutes of the Portuguese community to the effect that the city of Amsterdam confirmed and guaranteed the authority of the Portuguese community; now, for the same reason, a similar resolution was entered immediately after the *termo* referring to Isaac Penemacor.[74] This resolution made specific reference to the chaos in the community caused by individuals who flouted the authority of the elders. Once again the city of Amsterdam authorized the Portuguese community to have recourse to all the punishments at its disposal, including the *ḥerem*, in disciplining its members. The community claimed that only in this way could it maintain its authority and ensure the support of the poor.[75]

The fear of an exodus of prosperous Portuguese, which would leave the poor unprotected, remained acute until far into the eighteenth century. It comes through clearly in the following plea of the Portuguese leadership in 1753 against the idea of the creation of a ghetto, on the grounds that it would restrict the physical living quarters for Jews and influence their quality of life, possibly prompting the rich to leave:[76]

> and where shall the rich and prosperous Portuguese Jews who, from time to time, arrive here from Spain, Portugal and elsewhere, set up home? Do the Supplicants desire many of the Portuguese Jews who have already established themselves here, to betake themselves to other Towns and Locations? What would happen to the poor and indigent Jews who already account for twice as many families in the Portuguese community here as the more prosperous do, yet have never been a burden to the City? And who are already a heavy burden on the prosperous Portuguese Jews, which would become absolutely impossible to bear were some of the prosperous families to leave (only to be received elsewhere with open arms).[77]

In the event, no complete exodus of prosperous Portuguese ever took place during the eighteenth century, notwithstanding the tax pressure. Admittedly, there was a drop in the number of male contributors, from 453 *finta*-payers in 1735 to 329 at the end of the century. However, by constant adjustments, the elders were ultimately able to guarantee sufficient income from taxes and to keep taxation at a reasonable level, even though the share of taxes in the total revenue decreased from 82 per cent in 1675/6 to 62 per cent in 1750/1, and finally to 58 per cent in 1793/4.[78]

The Creation of a Reserve Fund

A new method of financing poor relief was the introduction in 1750 of an 'augmentation' or reserve fund, the so-called Fundo de Augmento. This fund was meant to serve as a buffer between annual income and expenditure, and to prevent depletion of capital.[79] It was launched with a credit from the capital account and thereafter replenished annually with new legacies and the anticipated current-account surplus.[80] From 1755 onwards, income from the *imposta*, from fines, and from increased meat-hall revenue were added to ensure adequate income and cover the cost of poor relief. After a few years any surplus would be channelled into the 'Sacred Capital' or Cabedal Codes account, as a result of which that capital would be increased; this capital would remain untouched and be safeguarded for the future.[81] The plan failed to produce the expected results. The deficit in the current account continued, income diverted to the reserve fund being too small to offset the shortfall in the current account and the cost of *despachos* (exit visas). Contrary to expectation, money had constantly to be withdrawn from the capital account in order to top up the reserve fund.[82]

A new institution had thus been created that proved unable to function independently and to balance its books, so that it had to be fed from other sources. The reserve fund failed to act as the intended buffer and was simply another stumbling block in the poor-relief administration of the Kahal Kados de Talmud Torah.

Cost-Cutting Measures

Alongside tax increases, the Portuguese community made efforts to bring down expenditure in the eighteenth century. To this end cuts were made in staff remuneration and spending on synagogue maintenance, but the overriding focus was on the introduction of a more efficient and restrictive welfare system. This process had begun in the seventeenth century, but was greatly refined in the eighteenth.

Restricted Admission and Redirection of Paupers

In his *Reflexoens*, de Pinto gives the impression that, until the middle of the eighteenth century, the Amsterdam Portuguese community provided poor relief for all destitute applicants.[83] Poverty is admitted to have been a problem at the beginning of the seventeenth century, but is said to have been dealt with at the time. It then went more or less unremarked until the middle of the eighteenth century, when surprise at the number of paupers became widespread and a seemingly original solution was devised, namely to send these paupers elsewhere.

This view has to be modified. The early admission policy of the Amsterdam Portuguese community was far less tolerant than was later claimed. This question has already been examined in detail in Chapter 2, where it has been established that the early modern *kahal* did not grant all indigent Jews unlimited and permanent access to poor relief. On the other hand, it did not issue a *ḥerem hayishuv* (ban on settlement) against Jews from elsewhere and never collaborated with the Dutch authorities to expel the Jewish poor en masse, as community leaders did in other parts of Europe. It was no doubt partly for those reasons that poor Jews poured into the city from every direction. From 1622, if not earlier, the Portuguese attempted to manage this flow by the subtly limited admission of paupers and their continuous redirection to other places. We need only turn to the oldest documents of the Portuguese Jews in Amsterdam to appreciate this. The *imposta* archives and the *livros longos*, too, bear out the existence of a restricted admission policy and the constant departure of paupers, many of whom had barely set foot in Amsterdam before they were sent on their way elsewhere.[84]

Even so, the Portuguese community did allow the situation to get out of control. We must agree with de Pinto that the measures the community took were not nearly drastic enough, compared with those taken in other Jewish communities: the leadership of the Portuguese in southern France, for example, set absolute limits—a *numerus fixus*—on the numbers of poor who would be allowed to stay and receive support within its communities.[85]

By contrast, too many paupers remained in Amsterdam at the expense of the *kahal*. Admittedly those drawing poor relief included a large number of women, many of them widows, and sick and elderly people, who were difficult to turn away. The fact that a resolution had to be passed in the middle of the eighteenth century to redirect elsewhere indigent unmarried males between the ages of 20 and 50, however, does suggest that the policy was not very effective, then or later. Many paupers preferred to remain in Amsterdam and if necessary to draw poor relief there.

Meanwhile, the early modern *kahal* was too preoccupied with attempts to boost revenue by further tax increases to attend to the problem of how to limit poor relief. Only when paupers started to pose a physical and economic threat was admission to Amsterdam further restricted, as noted above. In 1670 German and Polish Jews were definitively excluded from the system of Portuguese poor relief. Seventeen years later all but Portuguese Jews were declared to be ineligible, though it is an open question to what extent this decree was enforced.[86] That brings us to the restrictive measures taken during the first half of the eighteenth century (in 1723, 1742, 1747/8, and 1750).[87] Lack of employment in Amsterdam forced the Portuguese community to turn its back on important potential contributors of income, thus risking its own existence and undermining its financial strength.[88] Despite all these measures, the community continued to be weighed down by a disproportionately large number of paupers until the end of the eighteenth century. Not even so comprehensive a plan as that proposed by de Pinto was able to turn the tide.

Budget Cuts

The burden of charity was largely placed on the contributing sector of the Portuguese community, to whom the appeals for charitable contributions were mainly addressed. We hear no more than occasionally of attempts to generate revenue and to limit expenditure in other ways. Such attempts were, however, certainly made.

One of them, made in the middle of the seventeenth century, concerned paupers who had died in Amsterdam without leaving any immediate heirs: their assets were to be returned to the Portuguese community by way of repayment of the benefits they had received. This measure was applied on a limited scale and remained in force until well into the eighteenth century.[89] Poor-relief lists were controlled more closely than before and pared down.[90] Staff salaries were frozen.[91] However, all these measures did not add much to the coffers and had little effect on outgoings.

Not until the eighteenth century were more sweeping measures attempted to keep the poor-relief budget within bounds. In 1704 it was decided that no more than 45,000 guilders a year could be paid out in benefits.[92] No attempt was made to keep strictly to the letter of the law in this matter, however, and in 1707 an extra 3,000 guilders was added to the supposed maximum.[93] It proved of no avail in the long run: limits were regularly exceeded.[94] Whenever the shortfall became too great, new plans were made to reduce expenditure, as happened in 1723, 1728, and 1742, and between 1747/8 and 1750.[95] Despite all its good intentions, the Portuguese community ended the eighteenth century with a bill for expenditure (in real terms) almost twice as large as that laid down in the budget adopted in 1704.[96]

The rise in the number of paupers and the consequent increase in costs forced the Portuguese community leaders to reorganize and slim down the system. In 1704 that meant simply that no one could any longer draw advances on poor-relief payments.[97] In 1723 benefits were frozen for six years.[98] From the 1740s Amsterdam did not make things easy for newly wed couples: it was only after four years of marriage that people could apply for *sedaca*, and then only if husband and wife both qualified for poor relief.[99]

In 1742 the salaries of synagogue staff were cut.[100] From then on, new staff could only be hired for a year at a time.[101] Economies were also introduced in the sickness benefit sector.[102] Donations to Erets Yisra'el were curtailed.[103]

To ensure compliance with these regulations, inspection was stepped up, not least in order to prevent fraud. We have already noted that fraud occurred on a limited scale in the seventeenth century. However, when the number of paupers reached a peak at the beginning of the eighteenth century, abuses became difficult to control. There were frequent allusions to fraudulent practices. As a result, the administration of poor relief had to be reorganized. By this time the community had lost any general overview of the situation, the attempt to register the increasing mass of paupers having apparently led to chaos in record-keeping. Treasurers were instructed to keep a closer eye and control the lists, and were required to register paupers personally. This was done for the express purpose of 'preventing fraud and of avoiding the least suspicion of it'.[104]

On all applications for assistance, age, family, and (where applicable) year of marriage had to be stated. All *shamashim* were obliged on resigning their function to provide an accurate and complete list of the births and deaths of all those entered on the *sedaca* and Abodat Ahesed lists. In order to secure the removal from Amsterdam of all single men between the ages of 20 and 50, a list of all young men who had reached the age of 20 had to be compiled: the findings were to be copied into a special book to ensure they did not escape the attention of the Mahamad. Finally, a precise check on community finances had to be kept at all times.[105]

Seeking Concessions from City and Province

The Portuguese community also tried to cut costs by asking the mayors of Amsterdam and the authorities of the States of Holland and West Friesland to relieve them of certain excise duties. To that end, the community kept a sharp eye on the position of other denominations. Thus the 'incoming documents' of the Portuguese community include letters patent granted by the States of Holland and West Friesland to, for instance, the 'United Waterland and Flemish Mennonite Congregation' and the Lutheran congregation.[106] In petitions that the Portuguese, too, handed in on several occasions, they accordingly quoted examples of exemptions granted to other denominations, noting in one case 'that your Honours were gracious enough to grant concessions in respect of Impost on Peat to Public Houses of Worship and even to those of the Mennonite and Lutheran Congregations'.[107]

In response to such requests, Amsterdam and the States granted the Portuguese community exemption from taxes on peat and matzah meal (in 1681, 1693, and 1748) and from ground tax on the synagogue complex (from 1675 to 1734 and after 1748).[108] A joint approach by the Portuguese and Ashkenazi congregations in 1750 to gain admittance for Jews to a number of guilds, and hence to create jobs for their paupers, did not prove successful.[109]

Cost-Cutting Measures: In Conclusion

The measures taken during the second half of the seventeenth century and into the eighteenth brought about no more than temporary reductions in expenditure and in the number of people on poor relief. Despite all its efforts, ultimately the Kahal Kados de Talmud Torah failed to shed the pauper burden.

Nevertheless, the system of poor relief continued for two centuries. The Portuguese community was able to hold its own, to keep its head financially above water, and to continue supporting the poor. This was largely thanks to the members, who, certainly until 1750, guaranteed the survival of their community. Apart from paying taxes, making voluntary contributions, and responding to various collections, they also provided the community with much-needed support in the form of bequests. However, despite all its plans, the Portuguese community ended the eighteenth century in a pitiable state.

Little was left of its former grandeur. Two centuries of poverty management and the financing of poor relief admittedly kept it from complete collapse, but proved ultimately of no avail.

The Private Sector

An account of public support for poor relief is only part of the picture of the charitable work of the Portuguese community. Private charity constituted an important supplement to the charity dispensed through the official channels, offering the burgeoning mass of paupers alternative sources of assistance.

The stream of private funds pouring into the coffers of the Portuguese community constituted, in addition to taxes and various collections, a welcome source of supplementary revenue. Part of it also benefited various charitable institutions, some (but by no means all) of which were dependent on the *kahal*. Some of it went straight to the paupers, their families, or their friends without involving either the official *kahal* or the various *ḥevrot*. The following sections examine the financial mechanisms by which private charity operated.

The Contribution of Individuals to Public Poor Relief

As noted earlier, bequests from Portuguese Jews were of great assistance in the *kahal*'s efforts to build up its capital. We know that more than 100 Portuguese left the community some 120,000 guilders between 1639 and 1675 (an average of around 1,200 guilders per donor, rising to an average of 1,400 guilders per donor between 1725 and 1799), thus substantially augmenting the Cabedal Codes.[110] Bequests specifically directed to Erets Yisra'el and *cativos* are included in this figure, in so far as such donations were channelled through the Portuguese community and recorded in its account books.

Bequests to Erets Yisra'el were fairly common. Often, the money was earmarked not only for paupers there but also for the establishment of yeshivot. David Vaaz, for instance, allocated 8,000 guilders in 1649 for the establishment of a yeshiva in Jerusalem and Abraham Israel Pereyra 22,000 guilders for one in Hebron in 1659; in his last will of 1647 Moses Franco Drago left 6,000 guilders for another yeshiva in Jerusalem, while Jacob Pereyra set aside 40,000 guilders in 1693 for *esguerim* (study houses) in Jerusalem and Hebron.[111]

Quite a few Jews outside Amsterdam were deeply involved in the Amsterdam *kahal*. Thus in 1665 Lea Caanet not only gave money to the Portuguese community in Hamburg, where she died, but also remembered the

Portuguese community in Amsterdam.[112] From Brazil, David Senior Coronel sent 6,000 guilders in 1641 for charitable work among Portuguese Jews in Amsterdam.[113] The 40,000 guilders Jacob Mazahod bequeathed to the Amsterdam Portuguese poor in 1718 came from England.[114] Even from the peninsula contributions were made to the Amsterdam *kahal*.[115]

The average donation of 1,200 guilders to the Portuguese community in the seventeenth century and 1,400 in the eighteenth is less than that made to other poor-relief institutions in the city.[116] Nevertheless, the charitable contributions actually made by Portuguese individuals are likely to have been much higher than the average of 1,600 guilders donated by the non-Jewish philanthropists of Amsterdam between 1725 and 1799.[117] This is because many donations were not recorded in the books of the Portuguese community but entered in separate accounts, as happened for instance with 46,000 guilders granted by Abraham Israel Pereyra.[118] Finally, we have not yet taken account of all the donations made to a whole range of charitable societies, whether associated with the *kahal* or not, which fell under the direct financial control of these societies. Thus donations to Ets Haim went straight to that *ḥevrah* and are not included in our figures of 1,200 or 1,400 guilders. To what extent donations to the various charitable societies raised the average figure will be discussed below.

Private Support for *Ḥevrot*

As elsewhere in both the Jewish and the non-Jewish world, a great deal of private money went not into the funds of Portuguese community and its suborganizations but straight to various charitable societies.[119] *Ḥevrot* such as Ets Haim, Dotar, Aby Jetomim, Temime Darech, Maskil el Dal, Honen Dalim, and Mazon Abanot were often mentioned in wills.[120]

As far as it has been possible to establish, of all these *ḥevrot* Ets Haim and Dotar received the highest amounts. While Dotar was still the richest *ḥevrah* in 1675, it was soon overtaken by Ets Haim,[121] whose 'holy capital' stood at 55,000 guilders at the end of the seventeenth century, a fraction more than that of Dotar at the time. In the eighteenth century Ets Haim far outstripped Dotar: by 1790 its capital amounted to 161,584 guilders, while Dotar's capital had reached only 65,500 guilders.[122] The difference in fortune was partly, though not solely, to do with the relative growth in membership: Dotar stood at around 400 members in 1688 and grew to around 540 in the middle of the eighteenth century;[123] Ets Haim, on the other hand, with approximately 200 members in the 1680s, had almost 800 by the 1750s.[124] While Dotar was able to record just seven legacies between 1614 and 1700, Ets Haim received 127 between 1637 and 1700.[125]

Apart from donations, Ets Haim also garnered income from other sources, such as *promessas*.[126] Then there was the Ets Haim collection box, mentioned earlier, which was placed alongside those of the *sedaca* fund, Bikur Holim, and the Talmud Torah school. From 1637 one such box stood in the Bet Jacob synagogue, but another was also given a fixed place in the united synagogue.[127] Thus, thanks to the numerous donations and other income, Ets Haim built up a large fund of capital, something on which the Portuguese community could call for other than educational purposes. Bequests to Ets Haim between 1637 and 1700 averaged around 433 guilders, a lower figure than the average donation to *sedaca*.[128] Often the donors to both were the same individuals, who gave money to Ets Haim as part of a suite of charitable bequests. Taking this into account, we arrive at an average donation of 1,633 guilders to *sedaca* and Ets Haim combined: already higher than the corresponding figure for charitable donations by non-Jewish philanthropists in Amsterdam in the eighteenth century.

Dotar demanded a high membership fee, namely 120 guilders, but membership was hereditary, so that each family only had to pay it once.[129] Candidates for membership were selected and admitted by ballot.[130] These provisions gave the society an exclusive character, so that it attracted a wealthier membership. Dotar received interest on money it lent to individuals and to the Portuguese community.[131] The creation of the *imposta* in 1622 would not have been possible without a loan from Dotar, which at the same time charged interest on that loan. Until 1639 Dotar supported all three separate Portuguese congregations,[132] and after 1639 the united Amsterdam Portuguese community continued to rely on Dotar's financial support. Dotar itself was able to increase its capital with the interest on loans advanced to the community.[133]

On the other hand, Dotar also missed out on some potential sources of income: *promessas* were often used to make donations to orphan girls, but that money went straight to the beneficiaries and not to the Dotar capital fund.[134] In addition, dowries were often provided directly by families or by the independent foundations, bypassing Dotar and thus depriving it of funds.

Aby Jetomim was also mentioned in numerous wills.[135] Capital for the education of boys was acquired not only from donations but also by an enrolment fee of 20 guilders and a monthly contribution of 10 stivers.[136] According to de Barrios, some eighty men and women left money to Aby Jetomim in 1683.[137] We have few other sources for determining the precise number and size of the donations. Most gifts seem to have fallen in the range from 25 guilders to 50 guilders. The average was thus lower than that for Ets Haim, but it should be noted that here too the donations were generally part of a package of gifts for various purposes.[138] We know little about the capital of this society, except for the 10,000 *pesos* mentioned by de Barrios in 1683.[139]

Even less information has come down to us about the financial structure and membership of many other *ḥevrot*, for most of which we have only the statutes. This applies to those established in the seventeenth century as well as to those set up in the eighteenth. The various sections of these statutes refer to income through joining fees, monthly dues, special collections—within the institution itself and/or through house-to-house collections—production, fines, *offertas*, legacies, and investments. Expenditures, besides those related to welfare in money or in kind, were made on personnel (*shamash*, students, *rosh yeshivah*), on the printing of membership lists, and on books, paper, and collection boxes.[140]

As observed earlier, most of the *ḥevrot* discussed here were relatively small operations. However, they could draw for funds on a constituency that went beyond their own membership, often to include all members of the Portuguese community, since members of different *ḥevrot* went with their *caixinhas* (collection boxes) around the houses of the whole community.[141] Even so, the rewards were modest: Hase Amaharacha began with an income of 40 guilders in 1715, growing to 250 guilders in 1737,[142] while Meil Sedaca had a yearly revenue of around 250 guilders in 1754.[143] By contrast, Ets Haim and Dotar had amassed capital of over 50,000 guilders well before this date. Nevertheless, small though they were, the abundant presence of an ever-growing number of *ḥevrot* providing welfare alongside that available through the public system must have met a need, offering comfort and support to the poor.

Direct Assistance to Paupers by Individuals

In addition to poor relief dispensed on a public level and by private organizations, Portuguese Jews also practised charity without affiliation to any particular institution, but purely for individual reasons and on personal initiatives. From the available information it seems that the private charitable sector was large and its assistance to paupers significant in scale.

Preference was often given to impoverished family members, to be assisted there and then or at some future date, in Amsterdam, in the Sephardi diaspora, and even on the Iberian peninsula. Some of the money came from Amsterdam, some of it from outside, and the amounts involved varied considerably. In 1666 Rachel Pinta left a relatively small amount, 200 guilders, to her most needy relatives.[144] Abraham Israel Pereyra, on the other hand, gave 24,000 guilders in 1659 for the support of poor family members;[145] and even he was outdone in 1699 by Abraham Israel Suasso, who set aside 30,000 guilders for poor relatives.[146] The sums reserved for dowries, chiefly for relatives, also varied. Abigail Dias da Fonseca left 12,000 guilders in 1703 for this purpose.[147] Sara Torres reserved 200 guilders and 100 guilders respectively in 1693, destined for the orphan daughters of Daniel Bernal.[148] After helping their own relatives, individuals' next priority was supporting unrelated paupers of their nation, with help for destitute Jews from a different background coming last. Here too there are great discrepancies in amounts given or bequeathed to the poor, fluctuating from 50 guilders to more than 5,000.[149]

The Scope of Charitable Bequests

Wills help us to gain a good idea of the background of the donors by allowing us to relate the size of their donations to other factors such as financial strength, marital status, sex, and state of health. The following paragraphs are based on the examination of thirty-eight wills made by Portuguese Jews in seventeenth-century Amsterdam and fifteen from the first fifty years of the eighteenth century: fifty-three in all, involving fifty-seven testators (twenty-nine men and twenty-eight women), comparing the factors noted above.[150] It turns out that most of these individuals were in poor health when they signed their last will and testament.[151] Just over half (twenty-nine: 51 per cent) were male—single, married, or widowed. Sixteen of the women (28 per cent of the total number of testators) were widows.[152]

It is not easy to determine the relationship between the size of the charitable bequest and the testator's total assets. Most wills fail to give us precise information about the value of the latter.[153] Only where that value is known can the percentage donated to charities be calculated, and then only if the size of the donation is stated precisely and is not expressed in vague terms. In the case of Sara Torres, widow of Abraham Roiz Torres, it is possible to determine what percentage of her total assets went into charitable gifts: in 1693 she was worth 3,723 guilders, 270 guilders or 7 per cent of which she donated to charity.[154] In the case of Abigail Abarbanel, the wife of Pincas Abarbanel, it has been possible to compute that she left 3 per cent of her fortune to charities in 1666, while the charitable donations of Isaac Alfarin were put at about 4 per cent of his estate in 1682.[155] Finally, Rica da Silva, widow of Samuel Haim de la Parra, in 1717 left around 1 per cent of her entire assets to charity: an amount of 350 guilders out of an estimated total of 36,000 guilders.[156]

These percentages, ranging from 1 per cent to 7 per cent, come close to those calculated by Gérard Nahon for Portuguese wills in Bayonne and were higher than those found among contemporary Catholic and Protestant donors, whose charitable gifts ranged from 1 per cent to 4 per cent.[157] The size of the donations was closely linked to the donor's sex: most bequests of more than 5,000 guilders were made by men. Even though many Portuguese women had immense fortunes, far larger than their dowries (if they were married), some had used up a large part of the property left to them by the time they died or preferred to leave it to their families. In general, we may infer that Portuguese men had more money than women and that they used that capital to make their biggest bequests, either in their middle years or when they were aware of being near to death.[158]

The size of the bequests in relation to the respective wealth of the donors varied. This comparison applies only to men, because, as noted earlier, little tax information about women is available for the early modern period. Thus, of the total of twenty-two men for whom data could be traced, eight from the lowest tax group donated money to the poor. Donations of men from all tax groups ranged from below 50 to over 5,000 guilders, with predictably the lowest contribution made by men from the lowest tax group. Charitable bequests by the two highest income groups—41 per cent of the wills examined here—started at a much higher level, namely 401 guilders. Most bequests by this group were greater than 2,000 guilders, while five testators from the two highest tax groups (55 per cent of the testators belonging to the highest two tax groups) donated over 5,000 guilders.[159] The richest Portuguese thus made the largest financial contribution to the charitable institutions of their community. However, less affluent Portuguese Jews also gave fairly large amounts to charities.

Conclusion

Financial support for poor-relief institutions in the Portuguese community continued for two centuries. That was made possible by a combination of measures: a constant process of ad hoc adaptation and revision; extracting promises of legacies from the rich; the productive investment of capital; and, finally, taking out loans from other charitable institutions and from individuals.[160] The problem of poverty continued to be a central feature of life in the Portuguese community of Amsterdam until well into the eighteenth century. The unremitting influx of paupers was a continuous source of worry to the community, and poverty was an unending topic of discussion, particularly in times of crisis, when the means to cope with it were clearly inadequate. Curbing expenditure and stimulating income became the basis of financial policy. Although the growing tax burden increased the risk both of losing affluent existing members of the community and of failing to attract the well-to-do from other parts, more income had to be generated by higher taxation both of assets and of income. It became less and less possible to count on contributions from trading profits.

Private charity constituted an important supporting element in the reception and relief of the poor. Where public poor relief was inadequate, private *ḥevrot* and individuals filled the gap. However, neither plans for reform by the official institutions of the Portuguese community nor the expansion of private charity could stop the decline in the community's financial position.

While we have information on many different charitable donations, it is impossible to put a figure on the overall charitable contributions of the early modern Amsterdam Portuguese community, not least because so much money reached the poor from outside official channels, or was never recorded, or both.

A great deal of money for charitable purposes was donated by the private sector. Men such as Abraham and Jacob Pereyra or Abraham Israel Suasso, to mention just three extremely wealthy individuals, contributed amounts far beyond the average. Contributions to charity were, however, not confined to the elite, but came from various income groups. Much the same happened in other religious denominations.[161] By and large, it would seem that the average contribution donated by non-Jewish philanthropists was far exceeded by that made by Portuguese Jews.

In most cases, family came first when bequests were being made.[162] Next in line were members of the Spanish–Portuguese nation, (former) Conversos: in Amsterdam, in the various towns in the diaspora, and back in the Iberian peninsula. The variations in the size of charitable bequests show that it was not so much individual wealth that determined the amounts given to charity as a variety of motives, which the next chapter will examine.

CHAPTER SIX

THE MOTIVES BEHIND CHARITY

A charitable gift is usually motivated not only by a desire to ease the plight of the poor, but also by one or more of a variety of factors to do with the donor's background. Portuguese Jews of early modern Amsterdam made donations for a wide range of motives that, as their circumstances and perspective shifted, became more or less salient over time and were reflected in an increasingly diverse pattern of charitable giving.

Charity Sustained by Piety

The driving force behind much charitable activity was religious: above all, a strong desire to do penance for sins and save souls—one's own and others'.[1] This tendency reflected not only the influence of Jewish tradition, but also Christian (and Islamic, for that matter) experience and practice: in the words of Yaacov Lev, 'monotheistic sacred charity, whether Jewish, Christian, or Islamic, displays many features common to them all'.[2] Indeed, the terminology used by the Portuguese was in keeping more with the Catholic than with the Jewish framework.[3] In their wills, Portuguese Jews referred much more frequently and in more outspoken terms than the Ashkenazim to charitable acts as a means of doing penance and expressing remorse.[4] Amsterdam Ashkenazim, who had been born and reared as professing Jews and so did not have to make a religious about-face, were far less wont to speak of salvation, sins, and resurrection. True, as death approached they too turned their attention to charitable acts, but their benevolence was not explicitly formulated in terms of doing penance or the salvation of their souls.[5] Having said that, members of all three traditions were aware of a multitude of sins for which charity might help atone.

Religious attitudes to charity were constantly reinforced by the study of sacred books, the sermons of the spiritual leaders,[6] and the appeals of the lay authorities, all of which made frequent allusion to caring for the poor, extending hospitality, and taking responsibility for one's neighbour in the context of one's religious duties.[7]

The reading of works of an ethical and religious character was greatly encouraged within the Portuguese community. Many traditional writings with charity as a theme were translated into Spanish and Portuguese to make them accessible to the congregation.[8] One example, which was actually published twice in seventeenth-century Amsterdam, was *Libro intitulado 'Obligacion de los Coracones'* (Book entitled 'Duties of the Heart') by Bahya ibn Pakuda, a fundamental treatise on Jewish ethics originally written in Arabic in eleventh-century Spain.[9] The aim of the editor, who in 1609/10 translated an edition of the book that had been published in Constantinople or Salonika in Spanish using the Hebrew alphabet into a Spanish text using the Roman alphabet, was to help his readers 'to imbibe the doctrine of this sacred book and to dwell in a blessed state for evermore'.[10] Later, in 1669/70, Samuel, the son of Isaac Abaz, produced a Portuguese version (*Hobat Alebabot. Obrigaçam dos Coraçoens*) that was designed to serve 'for the benefit of our nation' and to be 'useful for all who, with pious intent, wish to devote a few hours of their free time to the reading of this precious book'. Abaz, as he stressed in his foreword, intended the text to deflect readers from vain and profane books. They would then be able to devote their leisure to improving their souls with the reading of these godly documents.[11]

Reference works and compendia produced to serve as signposts on the road to Judaism and as quick introductions to the principles of the Jewish tradition for former Conversos—both adults and children—were widespread and often found in the private libraries of Portuguese Jews.[12] One of these was *Menorat hama'or*, a reference work by Ishack Aboab written in Hebrew in fourteenth-century Spain, and since 1629 also obtainable in Spanish under the title of *Almenara de la luz* ('Candlestick of the Light'), referring to the key principles of Jewish life as seven lights on a seven-branched candlestick. A Spanish edition printed in Amsterdam appeared in 1707/8.[13] *Menorat hama'or* was written for everyone—children, men, and women, the deaf and the blind—as Aboab made clear in his introduction. The *Almenara de la luz* treats charity (*limosna*) as part of the third light, the *luz tercera*, and divides its seventh tract into hospitality to strangers, assistance to paupers, and the collection and distribution of money for poor relief.[14]

A handbook written in Portuguese from which Portuguese Jews in Amsterdam could learn more about Jewish laws in general and charity in particular was the *Thesovro dos dinim* by Menasseh ben Israel, which contained a concise summary of all the Jewish laws.[15] Charity is discussed in the chapter entitled 'Tratado da Esmola e seu mericimiento',[16] which sets out Maimonides' eight levels of charity. The reader is also told that he must treat the poor with respect, how much charity he should give, and who has precedence when it comes to alms. Menasseh explained that the family (starting with one's own) must be considered for gifts before the local poor, captives before other paupers, paupers in the Holy Land before paupers from other parts of the world, and so on.

The *Tratado de la hobligaçion*, written by Abraham de Olivera in Bordeaux in 1661, also gave well-to-do Portuguese advice about charity and their duty towards the poor:

> We consider it the true faith and doctrine to give to the poor and to perform other pious works in this world. It is the best way of laying out money for the salvation of one's soul. For it is certain that God records in the book of life all the good deeds a man has done in this world . . . The more good a man tries to do by giving to the poor and lending to the needy, the closer he will draw to God. That he can only achieve in two ways, namely fearing God and giving to the poor. For we can take no gold or other jewels with us from this world, except for the Law and good works. Anyone leaving much behind in this world and sharing it out imperfectly will find little to enjoy in the next world. By giving generously to the poor and performing more good deeds than bad, a man can reach God and earn a reward from his divine hand. If he leaves his possessions in this life to the poor, true advantage and reward will accrue to his soul.[17]

These and similar works could certainly be found in the libraries of Ets Haim and other yeshivot, which naturally contained all the fundamental Jewish writings.[18] Beyond the realm of formal education and religious practice and the exhortations of community leaders, teachers, and rabbis, it would also seem that training in charitable work was an important item of domestic concern. Thus many parents enjoined their children to live virtuous lives, instructed them about their responsibilities towards paupers and strangers, and told them how best to perform charitable acts. To that end the children were advised to read a number of Hebrew, Spanish, or Portuguese ethical treatises. We know this from the instructions Ishack de Matatia Aboab gave to his children in 1685: namely to read not only entertaining books, useful arithmetical manuals, books on general education, and historical treatises, but also books of a more ethical and religious tenor, such as the above-mentioned *Hobat Alebabot* or *Menorat hama'or*. He told his children to be kind to the poor, to practise as much charity as they could afford, and to match it to the 'quality' of the recipients—a term he did not define, but which probably included various elements such as moral conduct, financial need, health, and family background.[19]

Charity has been a subject of sermons since time immemorial. There is plenty of evidence from elsewhere in the Jewish world of the early modern period, especially from addresses to Jewish congregations in Italy, that rabbis did a great deal of preaching on *sedaca*, repentance, and rewards for good deeds in the hereafter. The same phenomenon can be observed in the non-Jewish world of this period.[20]

In Portuguese Amsterdam, too, the *hahamim* frequently spoke about charity and the condition of the poor. Sometimes they mentioned specific communal problems, but more often discussed charity in general terms. Even so, preaching about charity as a Jewish principle was a way of indirectly referring to current social problems.[21]

Saul Levi Morteira stands out as a *haham* who did not confine himself to generalities in his sermons but also brought up topical problems, both discoursing upon the different forms of charity in general and confronting his congregation with the actual state of affairs in their community. While it is hard to be sure whether his views and those of other spiritual leaders were shared by the lay leaders of the community—a standard problem in analysing and extrapolating from sermons[22]—he (and others with him) certainly criticized the lack of charity among contemporary Portuguese Jews. As early as 1622 he attacked the ostentation of rich Portuguese who had begun to neglect their financial obligations to the community and who would give nothing to charity:

> They forget that some of their brothers have no bread at all for themselves or their children. It would be better for them to spend their money inviting the poor and providing them with food and other necessities. But they curse the poor and spend their money on trivial luxuries that can do them no good, giving money again and again to men who mock them as soon as they leave their homes . . . Such is our way today. All of us complain and weep about hard times, but when we get something we spend a fortune on banquets with wine. The same is true of all the other unnecessary things.[23]

Almost twenty years later—in 1641—he returns to the same theme: 'In this category of vexation are those who do not give a penny to charity. Day and night they weep if any assessment is placed upon them for a true religious or humanitarian need, but afterward they spend a fortune on superfluous jewellery and clothing.'[24] Other spiritual leaders also stressed the need to give to charity. On the dedication of the Portuguese synagogue in 1675, Isaac Vellozino must have been thinking specifically of poor members when he impressed upon his audience that 'caring for the poor was the most direct path to God'.[25] Haham Isaac Aboab da Fonseca was said by David de Castro Tartas to have called for succour to the poor on many occasions and to have brought up the subject of poverty among seventeenth-century Portuguese in his sermons.[26]

Charity was also discussed in connection with donations for Erets Yisra'el. It was not only Amsterdam rabbis who pleaded for help to the poor and wretched in the Holy Land, as Morteira did in 1627, at a time of particular distress for Jews in Jerusalem, and on other occasions;[27] *sheliḥim* from the Holy Land also spoke of the penury endured by Jews in Erets Yisra'el, asking for help through sermons and other channels.[28] These emissaries told the Portuguese that support for study in the Holy Land was likely to speed the coming of the messiah, not to mention the merit charitable Portuguese would accrue by contributing to the Jews' redemption in this way. Thus Hesqia da Silva, a *shali'aḥ* from Jerusalem, stressed in the *sermon moral* he delivered in 1690 that the study of Jewish law serves God only if it is not simply treated as a theoretical subject but also extended to the practical sphere, for instance in the performance of pious acts.[29] He had, after all, come to Amsterdam for the express purpose of collecting money for Erets Yisra'el.[30] Under his influence, the Portuguese merchant Jacob Pereyra decided to found a new yeshiva in Jerusalem.[31] Sending money to Israel, thus enabling those living there to devote themselves to study and prayer, was considered the best way of hastening redemption.[32]

The Portuguese, then, were frequently reminded of their Jewish duty to give *sedaca*. The relationship between the rich and the poor was remarked upon, with emphasis on the advantages available to the rich if they used their wealth for pious purposes. The Catholic Church uttered many similar exhortations. However, the glorification of poverty that was characteristic of much Catholic preaching and literature was rejected entirely and trenchantly repudiated by scholars including Haham Saul Levi Morteira. Although he criticized the arrogance and conspicuous consumption of some of the rich community members, Morteira stressed the importance and desirability of wealth as compared to poverty. Affluence, given by God as a reward, enables a person to fulfil the commandments more easily and to establish a peaceful, healthy, and devout society, in which due consideration and help are given to the weak and the poor.[33] In other Sephardi centres, for example those of Jerusalem and Salonika, spiritual leaders stressed the importance of wealth in the same tone. Affluence not only determined one's position and status within a community, but was also a powerful instrument to help the poor.[34]

Haham Abraham Cohen Pimentel spoke along the same lines in Amsterdam's Keter Torah yeshiva. He informed his audience in 1688 that a rich man could save his soul and share in the glory of the hereafter by making charitable donations, while the poor were often unable to do so:

He [the rich man] can perform such splendid deeds as helping paupers, giving away orphans in marriage, ransoming captives, helping the sick to recover, supporting *midrashim* [houses of study], embellishing the house of God, and performing other pious and meritorious works. The poor for their part lack the money to do so. Moreover, by giving financial support to a pauper, a rich man will both save his own soul and keep the pauper from sinning. For the poor will not have to resort to theft and to making false declarations. Thus the rich man not only maintains the pauper physically, but also helps his soul. With financial support, the rich can bring the poor to the study of the Law and of learned subjects. With the rich man's money, the poor can gain knowledge and in that way live a worthy life. That life can be attained through the study of the Divine Law.[35]

David Nunes Torres, a preacher in the Aby Jetomim yeshiva, also stressed the fact that affluence was beneficial if used for charitable purposes. In his eulogy to Sara de Pinto, he told his audience: 'The pinnacle of possessions is to give them away. Capital cannot be consumed unless there is enough to spend. Thus the soul attains the peak of perfection and imitates its Maker.'[36] Here as elsewhere, *sedaca* was not presented as a topic for theoretical debate: it was assumed that the audience would put its principles into practice. Cohen Pimentel was quite specific in listing ways of performing charitable acts as well as referring to its significance in general terms.

The secular arm of the Portuguese community was just as vocal as the religious leadership in airing the subjects of charity and poor relief, and driving their responsibilities home to members of the community. Socio-religious terminology was woven into the texts in which the lay leaders of the early modern Portuguese community, most likely on the instigation of the spiritual leaders, called upon their people to act charitably.[37] We saw in Chapter 4 how this kind of language was used when a loan bank was opened in 1625 and people were urged to make contributions to it.

Armed with quotations from the Hebrew Bible and from rabbinical texts, the elders played on the conscience of the congregation and also spurred them on to *sedaca*. Exile would persist, they maintained, if people disregarded the *mitsvot*, for example by failing to pay taxes to fund support for the poor. This argument may have been inspired by a rabbi, perhaps Morteira, who constantly emphasized the concept of exile in Amsterdam, no matter how difficult it was to impress this idea upon the well-to-do Portuguese in the city.[38] He also stressed the need of taxation for welfare purposes.[39] This line of thought is clearly expressed in the following declaration of the *parnasim* from 1654:

In many places in our Holy Law it is written that we are obliged to come to help our poor brothers in their need . . . because of the very great and urgent need which righteous persons of our nation display day after day, asking for monthly relief and other forms of assistance, and evincing their need in a continuous stream of petitions. It is our wish to render all possible help to these people. The yields of the *promessas* and the returns from the *imposta* have, however, declined severely. Yet this type of *misva* [i.e. *mitsvah*] must not be ignored, for that is why God keeps us in exile.[40]

The lay leadership reinforced the message in other ways. For example, it tried to direct its members to Orthodox Judaism and the strict observation of its rules, not least in order to guarantee income for charity. A great effort was made to uphold moral behaviour and combat transgression.[41]

We have already noted the unprecedented financial crisis that faced the secular leaders of the community in the eighteenth century. At this time the ratio of members on poor relief to contributing members had grown so steeply and so far that the very existence of the Portuguese community was at stake. The common will to support the Portuguese congregation had slackened. Successive economic crises had eroded the wealth of some Portuguese, sent others to more promising lands, and prompted a third group to retire from active public life. The community leadership devised various strategies in the attempt to stem this downward trend, but seemed to be losing its grip on its members. The *hahamim* rallied to the support of the temporal leaders in an attempt to turn the tide, with sermons repeatedly denouncing the behaviour of their community, whose religious commitment could no longer be relied upon. Haham Ayllon put his finger on the problem in a sermon delivered in the early 1720s:

If we believe that God is present in the Holy Esnoga, why do we not concentrate on prayer instead of talking business? And when the *ḥazan* recites the blessings, why does no one answer 'amen'? We have numerous yeshivot, so why do we not frequent them? We say that we keep the sabbath and the holy days, but that is no more than a sham. For we keep doing nothing but business. Our sins grow by the day. Where does it all spring from? Because we no longer believe in the Holy Law, our exile continues and our redemption is deferred.[42]

The admonitory tone obviously failed to make an impact, for spiritual leaders were still dwelling on the decline of the commitment of their members in the middle of the eighteenth century. Haham Abraham Haim de Meza, for instance, was revolted by the deficient social, religious, and charitable attitudes of his congregation:

An idle life (in which men do nothing) in the midst of riches, feasts and other domestic pleasures, is a sea of depravity . . . for it is better to work virtuously and to be a slave of God than a free but idle man, one who endangers his good name. Teach us to turn our back on a pernicious life of idleness.[43]

Do you know why your sons are disobedient and scorn the education you give them? You are the cause . . . because you defraud paupers, proselytes, orphans and widows, because you despise sacred things, because you show little respect in the house of God, are disorderly, desecrate the sabbath, do business on the holiest day to increase your wealth.[44]

Copying bad examples has forever been the instrument of our misery, of the exile of the Israelite Nation, of the destruction of our Holy Land, of the castigation of our Kingdom and finally of the destruction of the Temple.[45]

It is high time God's people walked in virtue, righteousness and charity so that all the nations shall imitate us and say of us that this is a people deserving of praise, of blessings, and of having its virtuous paths followed.[46]

Haham Abendana de Britto, for his part, called for the restoration of the good name of the nation, not least as a charitable institution:

Let us desist from them [sins] and let us preserve the glorious repute of being the most honourable, the purest and the most charitable of nations. I have come to the end of my sermon. I trust in the benevolence of this K.K. [Kahal Kados], hoping that they have heeded my warnings with love . . . I have no doubt that we shall feel impelled to change ourselves and to amend our shortcomings. In that way, the Divine goodness will be moved and our protracted exile brought to an end.[47]

Secular and spiritual leaders together tried now, as before, to influence the way in which charity was practised. Although it is difficult to discover precisely how great that influence was, they clearly went out of their way to impress on their members that it was their religious and social duty to perform charitable acts and to welcome and support strangers. In books and addresses, in the yeshivot and in the synagogue, Portuguese could learn all there was to know about the subject. At any rate, poverty was something everyone knew about: the Portuguese could observe it all around them. What was the effect of such knowledge? To what extent and with what attitudes did the Portuguese apply *sedaca* in practice?

Inspiration in Action

In 1671 Abraham Israel Pereyra succinctly put into words why he thought it sensible to give money to the poor. Many Portuguese thought and acted like him, in the prime of life or in the face of death. 'The practice of charity is a fruitful activity . . . there is no better remedy for sin than charity. In mortal danger, the intercession of this same charity wards off death. As the Wise King said: "Righteousness [charity] delivereth from death."'[48] Paupers in Amsterdam, as in other Jewish communities, often referred to this verse in Proverbs when appealing for charity.[49] Thus Ester de Caceres, widow of Abraham de Caceres, asking that her daughter be admitted to the Dotar lottery, pleaded: 'I, Ester de Caceres, widow of Abraham de Caceres . . . beg you to admit my daughter Raquel to the lottery, whereby you will be doing God a great service . . . and your life will be prolonged . . . as the verse puts it: righteousness [charity] delivereth from death.'[50]

Charitable donations for pious reasons were often made upon the approaching death of the donor himself or of one of his relatives. In this type of charitable act, the motivation was not so much succour for the poor as succour for the soul of the donor. Such gifts were generally conditional: that is, the beneficiary—perhaps the Portuguese community, perhaps a particular *ḥevrah*—had to do something in return.[51] They might help the dying with deathbed rituals, as in the case of Miriam Alvares, who left the *ḥazan* Manuel Abenatar 50 guilders for his help in saying prayers beside her deathbed.[52] Others paid the community, the religious leadership, or various *ḥevrot* to say prayers for the peace of the donor's soul, on various occasions and in several locations, just once or several times every year.[53] Such stipulations were also common among Catholics at the time. Thus the *misericordia* of Bahia agreed at the beginning of the eighteenth century to say 2,000 masses a month in return for legacies.[54] Closer to home, in Amsterdam itself, Roman Catholics also left money to say masses for the souls of the deceased.[55]

Frequently the community was specifically asked to distribute alms to the poor: for example, during the cycle of mourning following the donor's death, this might be done on the day of the burial, after completion of the seven days of *shivah*, on the thirtieth day after the burial, or at the end of the first year following the death, or at all of these times.[56] Thus certain paupers, specified by forename and surname, received money through the *shamashim* of the community from Jacob de Pinto in memory of his mother in 1685.[57] The widow and son of Isaac Israel Suasso charged the Portuguese community in 1686, eleven months after his death, with the distribution of 800 guilders to the poor.[58] Haham Isaac Aboab da Fonseca, named as executor of the will of Sara Alvares, was instructed by her to distribute her bequest among the poor.[59]

To ensure the salvation of the soul of the deceased, requests were also made to have a *lampeda de continuo* (*ner tamid*, or eternal light) lit in the synagogue.[60] The cost of the oil and the glass was borne by the family.[61]

The donor also took central place in the stipulations attached to the will of Abraham Nahar, whose bequest to the Portuguese community reflected his religious and spiritual motives and had certain conditions attached to it. For instance, the congregation was expected to recite blessings for him in the synagogue during his life and to say prayers for his soul after his death.[62]

Pious motives were also enshrined in the donation for *obras pias* from Abraham Israel Pereyra in 1659. In 1662, Isaac Israel Otsen donated 6,000 guilders to the Portuguese community, to be used 'for several causes that shall not be specified here'. The annual returns on investment of this sum were to be paid back to him after deduction of 10 per cent for Amsterdam Portuguese paupers, to whom he also made a direct gift of 150 guilders. He, too, referred to death and to the salvation of the soul, stipulating that, should he die before he had the chance to make a will, the money should be divided between eleven causes 'for the sake of his soul'.[63]

Charitable institutions profited from the urge to satisfy religious needs. Many Portuguese who came into contact with openly professed Judaism and Jewish concerns for the first time in Amsterdam took a strong interest in promoting Jewish education. Haham Salomon Salem from Belgrade referred to this support when he delivered a sermon in the eighteenth century admonishing his congregation to live a pious life:

> Look at the virtuous among our forefathers who came from Spain and Portugal. They risked their lives for the glory of God and sheltered under His Divine wings. They abandoned their important positions and property and came over here in the fear of God, with much devotion and great virtue. How greatly they exerted themselves, with what fiery devotion and pure feelings to keep the banner of our Holy Law aloft . . . founding holy study groups (instead of those for playing cards) to cause the Tree of Life [i.e. Ets Haim] to prosper, to make it blossom and to pick its fruits.[64]

As noted in Chapter 5, the seventeenth and eighteenth centuries saw a great deal of support for Ets Haim, not only among Portuguese Jews in Amsterdam but also from their co-religionists abroad. Among the reasons for this was the fact that the yeshiva, like the synagogue and many other *ḥevrot*, offered opportunities to say blessings for the living and prayers for the souls of the dead. Impelled by these and other religious motives, many Portuguese remembered Ets Haim in their bequests, especially as they neared death.[65] In his testament, Dr Benjamin Musaphia explained the background of his donation of 10,000 guilders to the Ets Haim brotherhood in 1677:

> I beg all Israel to release me from a heavy obligation . . . When I was unsure about how to make a livelihood, I raised up my eyes unto Heaven and said unto God that if it should ever happen that I acquire riches, I would dedicate ten thousand guilders to the propagation of Thy holiest law, devoting the proceeds to maintain those who study Thy holy law. God heard me . . . So my soul did penance and continues to dwell here in Amsterdam.[66]

Aby Jetomim, the Jewish orphanage for boys, was another favourite target for charitable bequests. The duty to care for orphans is a constantly recurring theme in the teachings of the rabbis. Here again, legacies were often made on condition that *escavot* (memorial prayers) be said. Samuel Oeb, for instance, donated 30 guilders to the 'Irmandade dos orfons' to have the *escava* said on all possible occasions.[67]

That charitable activities and donations by Portuguese in early modern Amsterdam were closely bound up with concepts of repentance and redemption is clearly demonstrated by the fact that in 1665/6, the year of the expected crowning of Sabbatai Zevi as the messianic king, the collection for the poor was disproportionately large in comparison with most other collections. Passions had risen to fever pitch, the community living in a state of ecstasy as redemption neared. Here, a clear link between charitable giving and the fervour aroused by the imminent appearance of the messiah, with the expectation that salvation was at hand, provides one more illustration of the relationship between *sedaca* and the religious motives of the Portuguese Jews in Amsterdam's Golden Age.[68]

Many Portuguese Jews of the seventeenth century were concerned about life in the hereafter as they approached death. For them, charity was a form of penance intended to guarantee the repose of their souls. Religious impulses seem also to have prompted many donations given and bequests willed in the midst of life. A different picture emerges at the end of the seventeenth century and during the first half of the eighteenth. Many documents from these years show that Portuguese Jews were slowly adopting a more detached attitude towards religion and the organized community. References to such concepts as sin, penance, and exile, either on their own or in relation to pious gifts, though still continuously used by the *hahamim* in the city, do not appear as frequently in the vocabulary of the Amsterdam Portuguese citizens, now less attached to Orthodox Judaism and less troubled by an Iberian heritage that in many cases belonged to a distant past.

Rabbis from Erets Yisra'el were appalled at what they saw in Amsterdam. In 1690 the *shali'aḥ* Hesqia da Silva, on being asked to remain in Amsterdam and serve as a leader there, declined the invitation, commenting on the behaviour of the Portuguese Jews of the city: observing what Jewish law forbids and permits would embitter the lives of the Amsterdam Jews, he said, and their frivolity and mores would embitter his life no less.[69] In 1707 Rabbi Moses Hagiz wrote down his impressions as follows: 'The communities [in Amsterdam] were blessed with Divine abundance . . . but due to a diminution of Divine Providence they are being turned into dry wells . . . their money is disbursed for sinful pursuits—consorting with women, riding magnificent carriages, consuming rich food and building homes and courtyards.'[70]

Portuguese Jews couched their bequests in religious terms less and less frequently. Many private donations to paupers, private charitable funds, and institutions were made with hardly any reference to religious factors. Thus, when setting up his fund in 1708, Josua de Prado did not mention spiritual and religious motives explicitly, but merely stipulated that the proceeds from the 500 Flemish pounds invested in the Dutch East India Company 'be distributed from time to time by the said universal heirs and executors among such persons as their conscience tells them must be counted among the needy'.[71] In 1723 the will of Gracia Alvares instructed her husband, Isaac de Jongh, 'to distribute annually to poor and needy persons food to the value of fifty guilders', but the bequest was not formulated in religious terms and made no mention of the solemn rites connected with her burial.[72] In other wills, too, we find little reference to religious ideas, welfare, or the spiritual leaders of the Portuguese community as beneficiaries or administrators of legacies. Wills of this period are often purely legal documents, full of financial formulas, with the emphasis on provision for the testator's family.

Sometimes, as before, charitable donations to the *sedaca* box of the community are made conditionally, but now the required action is less often the saying of prayers or the lighting of candles for the sake of the donors' souls and more often that the *parnasim* act as executors of their will and administrators of their capital.[73] Conversely, in some cases the *parnasim* were even expressly excluded from playing any part in administering the estate of the deceased.[74]

There were exceptions, of course, and these were mainly Orthodox Jews or those who had arrived recently from Catholic areas. One such was Rica de Leon alias Maria Pereyra, wife of Moses de Leon alias Roque de Leon, who had apparently come to Amsterdam in 1710. In her will made later that year she expressed her strong adherence to Judaism and made bequests to a variety of charitable activities for Jews, as well as giving grants to the poor of Erets Yisra'el and a synagogue in Jerusalem.[75] A few other wills of this period also used terms like 'penance' and 'repentance': in 1731 Judith Rodrigues Carrion, widow of David de Daniel Rodriguez, is said to have regretted her sins;[76] in 1717 Aron de Pinto and Abigail de Gracia Nunes Henriques prayed for God's forgiveness of all their sins;[77] and in 1733 Judith Machado, widow of Samuel Abarbanel Souza, also expressed repentance.[78]

Likewise, the various study groups and other societies that sprang up throughout the eighteenth century, often with a connection to some kind of charitable work, are permeated with religious ideas, expressed through biblical texts or other references to Judaism in their charters.[79] The influence of an Orthodox core, often actively involved in the initiative and running of the association, can be detected here, trying hard to bridge the gap between the frivolous lifestyle of quite a few Portuguese and the stringent rules of

Orthodox Judaism.[80] The *hahamim* of this period preached in the same tone, which in turn was adapted for their own purposes by the administrators of the Portuguese community, as for example in their complaint of 1733 that they 'had always been encumbered with paupers who, for our sins, descend upon us from all parts of the world'.[81]

Thus, as time went by, a certain degree of secularization entered the charitable enterprise, and a growing gap emerged among the Amsterdam Portuguese between a secular and an Orthodox approach to life. The same conclusion can be derived from an analysis of the objects of charity, to which we now turn.

The Family as the Main Object of Charity

In keeping with the Jewish tradition and in line with welfare trends in early modern Europe, poor relief was rendered first and foremost to relatives—at the time or in the future, in the Iberian peninsula or in Amsterdam or elsewhere in the Sephardi diaspora.[82] Such charity was not intended merely to enable paupers to cope in the present; capital was often set aside for future generations. We do not deal here with reservations about the wisdom of entrusting funds solely to a Jewish institution, though the Portuguese were only too well aware of the vagaries of Jewish history, and some explicitly registered their concern about the future of a Jewish community in Amsterdam.

Their sudden fall from great wealth to poverty was still fresh in the memory of many Portuguese. Some had lost all their possessions in their attempts to escape from the Inquisition. Stories of flight and loss were not only passed on by word of mouth but often committed to paper as well. In her will, Gracia Senior tells us that she was able to take with her no more than a small part of her money, essential for her travels, when she escaped from the Iberian peninsula.[83] Abigail Levi Gomes made it clear in her will, written in Amsterdam, that she had had to leave all her valuable documents in Spain after she and her son were arrested by the Inquisition, even though she apparently managed to take some of her capital out of the peninsula.[84] Consequently, some Iberian Jews, though not themselves reduced to poverty, came face to face with it in their family circles, in the Iberian peninsula, in Amsterdam, and elsewhere.[85] By keeping control of their assets in the present, they were trying to protect their own livelihoods and those of their descendants as best they knew how. The ownership and preservation of capital proved an important weapon in the fight for survival, in building up a new existence in a foreign country, and in restoring lost status.

There was good reason why some individuals emphasized that if ever the community had to move from Amsterdam, their capital would have to accompany it to its next destination. Permanent residence in Amsterdam, seen in the light of the experience of Jews in general and of former Conversos in particular, was not something to be taken for granted. Gracia Senior, who in her flight from the Inquisition had had to abandon possessions in Spain, Portugal, and Brazil, instructed the Amsterdam Mahamad 'in case of changes occurring in this country, which God forbid, to sell all her paper investments, and to invest her money where they think it is safest'.[86]

Against the background of this survival strategy, Portuguese Jews in Amsterdam and elsewhere were deeply devoted to the well-being of their families, poor or otherwise. Many gave financial support to specific family members, either in the normal course of their lives or as they neared death.

Abraham de Pinto, for example, was generous in granting funds to poor relatives in Amsterdam and other places, sending money first from Antwerp and later from Rotterdam. According to his son Isaac, he

> did not know how people like Aron Cabessão and Isaac de Pina were related to him, but since they were needy he always helped them generously. Many years earlier he sent Isaac de Pina a regular monthly allowance from Antwerp. He always assisted Cabessão and his brother, and succoured them in their need. As long as I can remember he always gave generous help to Isaac Delgado, who was married to his first cousin Rica Delgado, and sent him a monthly allowance from Antwerp. He provided a dowry for their daughter Ester Vaz and also for their daughter-in-law Rica Nunes. In addition he spent a large sum of money on Isaac Cabessão. On three occasions he provided him with the capital needed for trading in Hamburg and a large monthly allowance, which continued for as long as he lived. He married off the latter's three daughters and provided dowries to which I contributed as well. My uncle David de Pinto also played a part in all these charitable endeavours.[87]

Isaac Vaz Henriques helped his family in Amsterdam on the spot. Thus he reported in 1693 that he had 'housed his sister and brother-in-law and their eight children for four years together with the claimant's mother, providing them, while his brother-in-law was ill and unable to earn a living for his above-mentioned wife and children, with food and clothing including linen, wool and everything they needed during those four years'.[88] Pedro Pires declared a weekly grant to support his children, out of paternal love, because they were poor.[89] Joseph Nahemias Torres donated money to a poor cousin in Livorno to help alleviate the poverty of the cousin's mother.[90]

Many more were surrounded by poor family members in Amsterdam or elsewhere. In her will, drawn up in 1636, Ester Pinta asked that the proceeds from part of her estate be paid annually to her *pobres parentes*. On her deathbed, she mentioned four persons by name.[91] Johebed de Casseres made express mention of a poor relative in Bayonne who was to be remembered in the distribution after her death. She also set aside the proceeds from part of her capital for the *pobres de su nacion*; preferential treatment was to be given to her relatives, whom she also mentioned by name.[92] Abraham Israel Suasso supported several relatives including two nieces, one of them a widow. Each received 400 guilders a year, which was to be paid to them for the rest of their lives even after his death, so that they, 'so close to his heart', did not fall on hard times.[93] Jacob Gutierez Gomes kept his mother and his two sisters after his father's death.[94] Rehuel Labat, recognizing that his younger brothers' share in the inheritance of their mother was not enough to support them, 'out of brotherly love and affection' granted each of them 1,000 guilders.[95]

A few individuals continued to support family in the peninsula: for example, Abraham Israel Torres, in Amsterdam, set aside half his fortune for his little daughter of 9, who was living in Osuna in Spain.[96] Fernando Montesinos, having settled in Antwerp, was said to have given a lot of money to his 'judaizing family' in Spain.[97]

Often specific conditions were attached to these donations. In many cases, the money would be given only if the individual or family left Spain, or Catholicism, and came to the Jewish world; Rachel Pinta bequeathed a legacy to her sister, living in Madrid, on this condition.[98] Rica de Leon expressed her disgust at Catholicism and her love for Judaism by making a gift to a niece, who was a nun in a convent in Toulouse, subject to strict conditions: the niece would lose her right of inheritance if she did not, within four years, come to profess the Jewish faith openly in a country where this was permissible.[99] Many others, in Amsterdam and in other parts of the western Sephardi diaspora, made similar conditions and were prepared to support relatives who had stayed behind in the peninsula only if they left and professed Judaism openly elsewhere.[100]

There was also a movement of funds in the opposite direction: from families living on the peninsula to their poor fellows outside it.[101] Jacob Semah Cortissos, Dr Daniel Semah Aboab, and Moses Orobio de Castro let it be known in 1707 that a person, not further defined, was withdrawing from the poor-relief list because he was being supported by a cousin in Spain.[102]

Foundations were also established and capital set aside to protect donors' families from poverty, both at the time and in the future. Many rich people attempted in this way to insure themselves against misfortune and to preserve the good name of their families. Abraham Israel Pereyra, for instance, set aside 24,000 guilders for this purpose. He reserved the proceeds from 8,000 guilders for the support of poor relations, and that of 6,000 guilders for young students in his family who immersed themselves in the study of 'our Holy Law'.[103] He further specified that the second sum could also be used for 'the greatest of *misvot*', namely the ransom of any members of his family who might be taken prisoner.[104]

In establishing funds specifically to provide dowries for poor orphaned girls in general and poor female relatives in particular, Portuguese Jews were continuing not only an ancient Jewish tradition but also a custom widespread in Mediterranean Europe.[105] The beneficiaries were often mentioned by name and were by no means all in Amsterdam. In the will Gracia Senior made in 1673, money for dowries was set aside for relatives in Amsterdam, Venice, Verona, Corfu, and Aleppo.[106] On his deathbed in Amsterdam, Joseph Nahemias Torres provided dowries for his nieces not only in Amsterdam but also in Livorno and Lisbon.[107] Abraham Israel Pereyra allocated the proceeds of 10,000 guilders from his family fund to provide dowries for respectable orphaned girls among his or his wife's relatives.[108] Miriam Alvares reserved some of her capital for dowries for her nieces, not only in Amsterdam but also in Italy (with the exception of one who had become a nun).[109] Private initiatives in establishing dowry funds in the Sephardi diaspora were not exclusive to Amsterdam's Portuguese Jews: Portuguese girls in Amsterdam also received dowries from relatives elsewhere. We know, for instance, of a dowry fund created by Joseph Soares of Smyrna, who left part of his fortune to provide dowries for poor girls in Amsterdam, giving priority to those who were related to him.[110]

Many of these special funds were set up in such a way that at the time of their creation they were not assigned to any specific person, but were intended to provide for poor relations of the donor at some future date. In 1627 Joseph Nahemias Torres set aside 400 *livras de grossos* for the giving away in marriage and support of 'parentas minhas e de minhas mulheres'.[111]

It was not long before these forward-thinking donors were proved wise, as poor members of once-prosperous families emerged to claim the benefits. In 1688 Isaac Delgado, a relative of Sara Cohen de Herrera, was given a scholarship to Ets Haim based on the wording and intention of her legacy to the yeshiva.[112] In 1712 Abraham, the son of Aron Alvares, received—as his mother had done before him—one-third of the proceeds of the 5,000 guilders reserved by Miriam Alvares in 1678 for relatives lest poverty ever afflict her own or her husband's family,[113] because he was very poor ('muy nesesitado') and the nearest blood relative of the testatrix.[114] In 1742 the *parnasim* as executors of the last will of Rachel Medina Chamis received a passionate petition from Moses Chamis Vaz, a nephew of Rachel.[115] He described himself as being in a disgraced and deplorable state, extremely sick and confined to bed, without the necessary food and drink to feed him and his inconsolable wife, who helped him day and night. He requested a gift of 100 guilders from the estate of his aunt Rachel, for which his brothers' permission was required; this they gave, and the grant was made.[116] Money was also distributed from the Abraham Pereyra foundation to poor family members in the course of the eighteenth century.[117]

In making provision to help impoverished members of formerly prosperous families, either immediately or in the future, the Portuguese Jews of early modern Amsterdam were not only remaining loyal to a valuable principle in Jewish tradition; they were also showing their extreme sensitivity to concepts of honour, shame, status, and reputation. It was of the utmost importance to them that family members should never sink into a miserable and shameful condition; if they fell into difficulty, their problems should not be known to the public at large but should be dealt with through family trusts and legacies. In this way the status of upper-class families in the established social hierarchy would remain intact and the continuation of a class-conscious society be guaranteed.[118]

The Civic Sense, Trust, and Charitable Gifts

The Portuguese community, in running its centrally organized charitable enterprise, had an agenda of its own. It tried as far as possible to keep a hold over its members, the better to ensure the maintenance of public order: in this way the poor were both looked after and kept quiet. That agenda also served the Portuguese citizen, who could leave charitable work to his community with trust and a good conscience and feel that he was doing his civic duty. Consequently, through the seventeenth century and into the early decades of the eighteenth the Portuguese community's secular and spiritual leadership was showered with donations and instructions to distribute money, thanks to which it was able to take care of its paupers. The *parnasim* were often named as executors of wills or even appointed sole heirs of testators' estates.[119] All this gave the community as an institution power, both financially and spiritually.

Not all the money donated to the Amsterdam Portuguese community went into the general *sedaca* fund, earmarked for poor relief or otherwise.[120] Bequests were also made to various charitable societies controlled by the Portuguese community, for example the Bikur Holim society for visiting the sick.[121] By making donations to causes under the control of the Portuguese community, Portuguese Jews expressed their faith and trust in the ability of that community to perform its duties satisfactorily. A sense of civic and social responsibility channelled through the Portuguese community continued to make itself felt up to the early part of the eighteenth century.

Moreover, during periods of difficulty Portuguese Jews sometimes lent their community extra support. Thus Abraham Nahar made his donation of 70 *libras de grossos* (420 guilders) in the early 1630s, at a time of extreme scarcity and crisis, during which, as he put it, 'honourable people have fallen on hard times'.[122]

The Portuguese considered it their civic duty to carry out this job responsibly, believing that this would be conducive both to the maintenance of public order and to the continued existence of the Portuguese community in Amsterdam. Poverty was hidden from the view of outsiders, and the elders, with or without the connivance of the municipal authorities, could remove undesirable elements from the city. In the eyes of many early modern Amsterdam Portuguese, common responsibilities were best discharged by mutual consultation and effort.

However, as we have already seen, private charity, not under central control, was an important competitor to public provision from the outset: personal donations had always gone hand in hand with central charitable contributions.

Money also reached the poor without passing through any public Portuguese institutions. Many people urged their relatives, men and women alike, to put aside money for poor relief in their wills, as if they did not trust the Portuguese community to perform that duty. This was partly out of a desire to be in control of their charitable donations, the better to emphasize their independence. In 1623, for example, Brites Tomas instructed her son-in-law Samuel Abravanel to divide her clothes among her relatives and the poor after her death.[123] In 1662 Moses de Oliveira gave a similar instruction, telling his brother to distribute 120 guilders among the poor.[124] Four years later, in 1666, Abigail Abarbanel asked her husband to give away 125 guilders for the sake of her soul,[125] and in the same year Rachel Pinta appointed her husband as her heir and instructed him to distribute money among the poor during the three years following her death.[126] In 1676 Branca de Pas asked her mother to distribute alms,[127] while Ester Rodriguez, in her last will of 1710, charged S^{a} Sara de Natan Curiel with the division of a sum of money among the poor.[128] Similarly, in 1750 Aron Jessurun left instructions to his wife to distribute money to the poor during the year after his death.[129]

Wills making private charitable bequests often prohibited intervention by anyone other than the executors: this was expressly stated by Josua de Prado, who instructed his executors to distribute money among the poor, adding that 'they were not accountable to any persons whatsoever'.[130] His mother used much the same terms when arranging the distribution of alms to poor girls: 'provided only that the Executors listed below shall be pleased to approve . . .

when and who and how much shall be raised and distributed on each occasion; without their being held accountable to anyone'.[131]

On the other hand, the leadership of the Portuguese community was often requested to help manage individuals' assets and to arrange the distribution of private means. It was, for instance, appointed heir to the property of Isaac Alfarin.[132] It also played an active role in the distribution of money from the estate of Jacob Mazahod in the early eighteenth century.[133] Isaac Abrabanel Arede, too, involved the community leadership in the management of his estate in 1708, when he placed three properties in the Nieuwe Keizersgracht, Amsterdam, at its disposal for the setting up of the almshouse Rehobot for poor and elderly women.

If we are to believe the rabbis, the benevolence of the Portuguese in early modern Amsterdam left much to be desired. The wealthier among them were said to care little about the fate of the poor, keeping them at arm's length while revelling in their own idle and frivolous existence. How can this picture be reconciled with the huge increase in the number of charitable initiatives and legacies made to the Portuguese community up to the early eighteenth century? The resolution of this apparent contradiction lies in the widening gap between public and private poor relief. The fact that so many new charitable institutions were created in the eighteenth century bears witness to the numbers of Portuguese becoming impoverished at this time, and also to a changing pattern in the provision and objects of poor relief. Private charity was often dispensed to friends and members of well-to-do families who had fallen on hard times and preferred to receive help from their relatives or neighbours rather than to go cap in hand to the community and have their names displayed in the poor registers. No wonder that the community records increasing numbers of paupers absent from the *sedaca* lists or enjoying preferential treatment by being named in full in a 'secret' register only in order to spare them public shame.[134]

Here we can detect a clear shift in emphasis. While the Portuguese in the seventeenth century rallied round their community and allowed it to shoulder the major burden of poor relief, in the eighteenth century charitable provision apparently tried to shed this impersonal image: donors, lacking trust in the institutional leadership and often scorning communal efforts, increasingly worked instead as individuals or through small organizations. The downward spiral in receipts from *promessas* made during services in the synagogue points at a similar tendency: commitment to organized community life was ebbing.

Private initiative took over—as was also happening in Spain, where social care in the early modern period, and especially during the eighteenth century, was provided through an extensive network of confraternities.[135] The main impetus was the urge to alleviate the need of those who were nearest: family, friends, and members of the 'nation', (ex-)Conversos, whether in Spain and Portugal, en route out of the peninsula, in Amsterdam, or living outside the borders of the Dutch Republic. One motive was to keep up the honour and reputation of the nation; another was to hide from wider view the increasing impoverishment of the Amsterdam Portuguese community. On both these counts, distrust and anxiety about increasing poverty, which the Portuguese community as a central institution seemed powerless to stem, prompted many eighteenth-century Portuguese to take private charitable initiatives.

While private charity chose increasingly to part company with public *sedaca*, the latter nevertheless remained an important pillar of poor relief. A sense of civic and social responsibility continued to make itself felt in the eighteenth century as a motive for charity, but assumed new forms of expression.

Prestige

In making charitable donations, then, Portuguese Jews were variously acting out of a desire for personal salvation and concern for the fate of their families; helping to maintain public order by ranging themselves behind the Portuguese community leadership as responsible citizens; and fighting poverty by private acts of charity. In addition to all these motives was the prestige factor: a charitable gift could also be made in order to raise the donor's social status.[136]

Individual Portuguese were often praised by name for their generosity. Such acknowledgements may be found frequently in written works, in the minutes of the *kahal* and of charitable institutions, and in the preamble of rabbinical sermons. Thus David de Castro Tartas extolled the charity of Isaac Penso in his *Sermões* in 1675 on the occasion of the dedication of the Portuguese synagogue.[137] Daniel Levi de Barrios lauded the charitable behaviour of those who gave him the financial backing he needed to publish his books; it is not clear whether these backers made their generosity dependent upon his mentioning their names when they agreed to give him their support.[138] Baron Manuel de Belmonte, representative of the Spanish Crown in the Republic, was known as the 'grande amico de' poveri', and enlarged his standing and prestige in the city by handing out money generously to both the Jewish and non-Jewish poor of Amsterdam.[139]

Although, as previously observed, the donations made by the Pereyras for yeshivot to be set up in Erets Yisra'el had first and foremost a religious purpose, it must not be forgotten that those yeshivot would also perpetuate the family name.[140] The same pattern can be found in the grants given to found scholarships, motivated by piety but also establishing a continuing reminder to both the administrators and the recipient of the prominence of the benefactor. Many charitable institutions and funds were set up for this very purpose, prestige being closely bound up with charitable deeds. The de Prado, Lopes Suasso, Belmonte, Dias da Fonseca, and Henriques Sequeira foundations could serve as examples.

Individuals' prestige was also enhanced by contributing generously on the sabbath and holidays, when Jews offered gifts during prayers and on ceremonial occasions to various *ḥevrot* and other charitable ends. Honour and pride were important motives for *promessa* contributions, as they were in the Purim service when the plates, the *tasas*, were passed round the synagogue and people could show off their wealth and generosity. A similar process may have been at work in house-to-house collections, when community officials or those of the private *ḥevrot* knocked on doors to solicit contributions.

Ḥevrot also gave individuals the opportunity to enhance their prestige by having their names included on (printed) lists of members and legacies.[141] A hierarchy operated here as well: Mishenet Zequenim, for example, reserved different columns for different legacies, related to their size.[142] Mazon Abanot had four different lists for various classifications.[143] Even today we can admire the wall tablets in the former Ets Haim yeshiva, now the winter synagogue within the Snoge complex, where separate lists record the names of male and female members of Ets Haim and of those who left a legacy to the *ḥevrah*.[144] These individuals certainly succeeded in perpetuating their memory and prestige.

Conditions attached to charitable bequests were also often designed to raise the status of the donor, for example by stipulating the saying of *misheberah* and *escavot*, which would constantly remind people of the donor.[145] Another way to attract attention to a bequest was to make it conditional on representatives of the beneficiary organization accompanying the corpse to its last resting place. Such bequests recalled the practices of medieval brotherhoods, which often paid their last respects to the deceased by following his coffin in a long cortège.[146] Thus, in Amsterdam, Gracia Senior left money to Aby Jetomim with the express wish that the orphan boys accompany her mortal remains to the Bet Haim (cemetery).[147] Rachel Belmonte no doubt had the same objective in mind when she not only left a grant of 2,000 guilders to the same *ḥevrah* but also expressed her wish that 150 guilders be distributed to the orphans on the day of her funeral.[148] The greater the number of people witnessing the solemnity, the more impressive the ceremony and the higher the regard for the deceased.

It was also a great honour to serve on the board of a charitable institution. In the early modern period posts in public charities were the most prestigious, although some individuals—especially in the eighteenth century, as commitment to organized communal charity ebbed—declined to serve in this role.[149] Private associations offered an alternative and gave many middle-class individuals the opportunity to attain an importance and status in administration that they would never be able to reach within the official *kahal* or did not wish to see confined to a select few.[150] In line with the tendency towards detachment from the official community in the eighteenth century and the advantages of the private *ḥevrot*, an increasing number of Portuguese Jews offered their services as administrators of private charities.

All these observations demonstrate that prestige played an important role in motivating people into charitable activities, whether these took a private or an institutionalized form.

Social Concern and Mutual Responsibility

The Portuguese not only had their own experiences of flight from the peninsula freshly engraved on their memories but were also confronted day after day with an influx of the destitute, each of whom had some harrowing story to tell; and they learned from third parties what was happening in the world around them. Thus gifts to the *cativos* fund represent an expression of a bond with other Jews (and Conversos) and a concern for their fate in the wider world. There are hundreds of documents relating to help given through the *cativos* fund to individuals and institutions in distress in the contemporary world. Sometimes this help was provided in the form of unilateral action by the Amsterdam Portuguese community or by some of its members. More often it was part of an international aid programme, in close co-operation with leaders of other Jewish communities of early modern Europe.[151] Donations to the Terra Santa organization express a similar attitude of solidarity.[152]

Mutual responsibility towards fellow Jews was a subject much discussed—in the synagogue, in the various *ḥevrot*, and in books. Haham Saul Levi Morteira stressed the importance of hospitality as an important religious concept: 'That is why God scattered his people to the four corners of the earth: so that wherever one Jew goes to change his residence, he will find his fellow Jews established. This will make his journey easier, for all will help each other, thereby facilitating their survival in exile.'[153] Not surprisingly, charity was informed by a sense of social compassion and responsibility for brethren who were suffering, including the poor, whom the Portuguese community felt obliged to receive and to give a reasonable start in their new surroundings, in keeping with the precepts of Jewish law.

The question remains to what extent Portuguese Jews of early modern Amsterdam took a personal interest in the fate of the poor. Arguments on this subject broke out as early as the seventeenth century. The generosity of the Amsterdam Portuguese was widely praised, and the leaders of the Portuguese community themselves boasted that poor Jews from everywhere flocked to Amsterdam because they could be certain of receiving assistance there.[154] The writer Abraham Idaña, writing from Amsterdam to a friend in Madrid, called the poor-relief organization of the Portuguese community a miracle of benevolence.[155] In his preface to the book *Sefer avak soferim* by Abraham ben Levi Cuenque, which he published in Amsterdam in 1704, Netanel Foa praised his uncle and brother-in-law Joseph Sarfati, who was said to keep open house for passers-by.[156] In a eulogy, Saul Levi Morteira spoke highly of Dr David Masiah for his help to the poor and the sick, his assistance to widows and girls in distress, and his provision of food to prisoners.[157] Many other Portuguese Jews made direct donations to the poor, being sincerely and personally involved with their fate.

The initiative to establish the various private welfare organizations, and the effort involved in sustaining them, must also have fostered a sense of group identity and responsibility towards the poor. The administration of these *ḥevrot* and the distribution of welfare through them often involved close contact with the recipients, which must have prompted some feelings of sympathy.

Many paupers themselves bore witness to the help they received on arrival. Thus Joseph Abendanon, arriving in Amsterdam as a pauper from Belgrade, praised the hospitality of his patron, Joseph Sarfati.[158] Rabbi Moses Rivkes, too, gave voice to his gratitude, describing his arrival in Amsterdam in 1655, on a ship with refugees from Lithuania, in the introduction to his *Be'er hagolah*: 'The mercy of the Sephardi sages and magnates was aroused and they acted towards us with charity and grace, spending much money to give every one of us much shelter and food. They covered our nakedness and they put a bundle of money in the hands of each of us.'[159]

However, critical voices were heard as well. In his *Espejo de la Vanidad del Mundo* (1671), Abraham Israel Pereyra, for instance, compared the poor relief provided by his community unfavourably with that dispensed by the Amsterdam municipality. He took a highly negative view of the attitude of his prosperous brethren towards the poor: many of them, he believed, did not really care about the latter, showed them little consideration, and ignored their own obligations. By contrast, Pereyra praised the *tudescos*, who, as he said, did open their houses day and night to strangers, not just to one or two, but to all who came.[160] Jacob Sasportas could confirm the charges of Pereyra, since he, arriving in Amsterdam from North Africa in 1647, had felt 'like a stranger in the land, a guest who had come to spend the night'.[161] Haham Morteira's critical comments on the attitude of wealthy Portuguese Jews towards their poorer brethren, noted above, fit in neatly with the picture drawn by Pereyra.

There was indeed little interaction between rich and poor among the Amsterdam Sephardim. As time passed, the gap between the two groups grew wider; social mixing and upward mobility were very limited. These patterns reflected those prevailing among the Conversos in the peninsula, where sometimes solidarity between rich and poor was similarly hard to find.[162] Many rich Conversos would have considered it unimaginable to become friendly with someone from a lower rank living on charity.[163] A wealthy New Christian merchant living in Madrid encapsulated this feeling of superiority over the poor among his group when he remarked that others should not confuse him with poor illiterate traders, even though they were 'Portuguese'.[164]

We have seen that some of the Amsterdam Portuguese clashed with their leaders about their financial obligations and refused to give money for *sedaca*. Antonio Alvares, alias Joseph Israel Alvares, provides us with another example: in his last will he refused to give more to the *sedaca* funds of the community because in his opinion he had already given enough when the synagogue was built.[165] Joseph Abendanon admittedly praised his own patron, but did not think particularly highly of the assistance the Portuguese community provided overall.[166] Many of his fellow *belogrados* had no choice but to leave the city soon after they arrived, disillusioned with the meagre assistance offered by the Amsterdam Portuguese.[167] The same pattern could be observed in respect of many other Jewish refugees.

Solidarity with poor migrants was often readily shown as long as they did not stay in town too long, as Studemund-Halévy also observed in Hamburg.[168] Once they had been there a while, however, the Amsterdam Portuguese Jews showed less interest and consideration. They seemed to prefer the idea of keeping the problem of poverty at arm's length, as contributions to the *cativos* fund attest.

Taking these often contradictory attitudes together, it is difficult to define the attitude of Portuguese Jews to charity in early modern Amsterdam. What is certain is that they spent considerable sums of money on the poor—certainly no less than other denominations and often much more, in quantity and perhaps also in quality if we are to believe the assertion by Morteira in one of his sermons that the welfare afforded by the Amsterdam Sephardim was of a higher quality than that provided in their non-Jewish environment.[169]

Even so, not all Portuguese left money for charitable purposes in their wills. Of those who did, many referred not to specific paupers but rather to the poor as an abstract concept. Did this mean that the more prosperous Portuguese saw the poor as an anonymous group, an amorphous mass, with whom they had little if any contact? This may have been the case with some. Such a mode of reference certainly points at the existence of clear boundaries between rich and poor.[170]

Some of the more prosperous Portuguese, however, did genuinely reach out to the poor in their community, holding out a helping hand in particular to those closest to their heart. Poor of the Spanish–Portuguese Jewish nation, former Conversos, were considered members of an extended family, with whom they had shared a common past. Responsibility towards them, as opposed to poor from other Jewish backgrounds, was given top priority. Richer Portuguese took pride in the well-being of their poorer brethren, second only to those of their blood family: Abraham Israel Suasso instructed that 'if there be no paupers in the family, the proceeds of the capital shall go to the poor of my nation'.[171] Joseph Senior left his capital to the poor of the community if his heirs should die out.[172] The wills of Rachel Belmonte, Rachel de Prado, and Abigail Dias da Fonseca contained similar provisions.[173]

There are many cases of testators concerned to ensure that money from their estates would reach the poor of the Spanish and Portuguese nation in particular and strengthen their community in the city. Josua de Prado left large bequests for this purpose, singling out Ets Haim and Dotar for the purpose.[174] He specifically recognized the pressing need of the Spanish and Portuguese poor, expressly stating that his executors should insist that the distributions take place in timely fashion, so the poor should not suffer unnecessarily.[175] Isaac Abrabanel Arede made sure the poor had somewhere to live with his legacy of three houses in 1708. Rachel de Spinosa Henriques, a single woman, continued the legacy made by her mother, setting aside the revenues from the rental of one of her houses in the Zandstraat, originally bought by her father, to distribute yearly to the poor of her nation.[176] Although her will gave priority to provision for her family, it also represents a strong commitment to the poor of her community and nation, in present and future times. She singled out one poor person, the widow Sara de Tolosa, who was also on the community poor-relief list, adding 50 guilders a year to her meagre income.[177] The 'political reflections' which Isaac de Pinto wrote in

1748 on poor-relief policy reflected a similar concern for the poor of his nation.

This commitment to the poor had also existed on the peninsula: despite the arrogance of a few, many well-to-do New Christian families gave charity to poorer members of their group. In fact, the Inquisition accused rich New Christian merchants in Spain of helping 'Portuguese of their nation', citing this practice as proof of their loyalty to Judaism. Rich Conversos also helped some of their poor brethren to flee the country, returned to them money they had kept hidden for them during their imprisonment, and paid ransoms to liberate those sentenced to the galleys or to wearing the penitent's *sanbenito*. Yet this dependence also created considerable tension between rich and poor.[178] This pattern of parallel support for and distancing from the poor thus existed both in Amsterdam and on the peninsula.

In summary, it is legitimate to argue that social concern and mutual responsibility were concepts deeply rooted in the consciousness of Portuguese Jews of early modern Amsterdam and had an international dimension. Benevolence was not extended comprehensively to poor Jews from all backgrounds and origins, but in most cases was directed preferentially to the poor of the Spanish–Portuguese nation, former Conversos.

This is not to say that relations between rich and poor within the Amsterdam Portuguese community were warm or close. Just as the relationship between the two groups on the Iberian peninsula was often characterized by distance, in occupation, income, and status, so this pattern was transferred to the community's new centre in Amsterdam. Here too the attitude of rich to poor remained in most cases impersonal and detached.

Conclusion

According to Bahya ibn Pakuda, there are five aspects to human benevolence. First of all there is the benevolence of fathers towards their children. Then comes the benevolence of the master to his slave. Third, there is the benevolence of the rich to the poor, by which the former seek to reap heavenly rewards. Fourth, some people come to the aid of their fellows to earn a good name, honour, or worldly rewards. Finally, the strong show kindness to the weak because they feel compassion for them and are moved by their condition. If we look at all these aspects, we discover that none is completely devoid of self-interest.[179] The view of this Jewish philosopher may be easily adapted to the situation of the Portuguese community in early modern Amsterdam.

Here, too, we find various forms of benevolence and charity. Honour and prestige, going hand in hand with feelings of solidarity and mutual responsibility, a desire to act on these feelings, and strong pious motives, prompted the Portuguese Jews of this period to set aside capital for charitable purposes. They did so out of concern for themselves and their immediate family and community, and for the future of the whole Spanish–Portuguese nation, not just in Amsterdam but also in other centres of the Sephardi diaspora, and even among members of the nation in the Iberian peninsula. While some Portuguese practised charity mainly for religious reasons, hoping to be rewarded in the hereafter, others simply could not bear to witness their neighbours' misery and were moved more by social than religious concerns. There was also a third group who considered it their duty to donate money trustfully to their community to enable it to do its job. In that way they kept their distance from the poor, while helping to preserve peace and order. Yet others sought by their donations to maintain or improve their standing in the community. Finally, many put private interest first and were mainly concerned to preserve their own wealth, status, and reputation or those of their families, now and in the future, in Amsterdam and beyond. Often, a mixture of motives was at work.

A change of emphasis also occurred over the period. In seventeenth-century Amsterdam, a well-to-do Portuguese community shouldered the organization of poor relief in many ways and discharged its responsibility for receiving and assisting the poor and for maintaining peace and order. Portuguese Jews supported poor relief as a civic duty and because they felt responsible for their neighbours, as well as for reasons of prestige. In addition, they often made charitable gifts, either in the normal course of life or as they neared death, for religious motives.

By the end of the seventeenth century, however, Portuguese religiosity was tapering off—a trend loudly deplored by the *hahamim*—and Portuguese Jews were also becoming less and less involved in the life of their community. Their charity, however, did not decline as a result; on the contrary, it grew. Charitable grants still had religious connotations, but rising poverty, even among the better-off families of the community, called for a collective effort not only through the official channels but also, and to an ever greater extent, by the private sector. Individual Portuguese increasingly took the reins in their own hands, not least in the attempt to maintain their prestige and to gain a hold over the administrative machinery by which charity was disbursed.

Poverty in Amsterdam, as in the world outside, was viewed more and more as a social problem, a threat to public order and to the renown of the proud Portuguese nation. Out of social concern and fear for loss of status and honour, yet without entirely losing the religious context, the Portuguese tried to find a way to alleviate the plight of the poor in their community. Charity was and remained of topical interest, but continually changed in character.

CHAPTER SEVEN

THE DAILY LIFE OF THE POOR

Introduction

The voice of the poor is only seldom heard, but occasionally it breaks through, as here: 'Embittered, busy with temporal cares and the difficulties of making a livelihood, earning hardly enough for his needs and troubled by other domestic concerns.' These are the words of Hiyya Coen de Lara, describing the precarious economic position of a rabbi in the middle of the eighteenth century.[1] Thus far the poor have spoken too little for themselves; mostly they have had light shed upon them from above. In this chapter I shall try to redress the balance, though the task is a difficult one.

Sometimes fragments of information about a pauper lie buried, scattered in the literature. More often we hear a pauper's voice, directly or indirectly, in petitions like that of Coen de Lara quoted above, written on small scraps of paper which frequently lie neglected, sometimes torn, between the sand-blotted pages of the poor-relief ledgers of the Portuguese community or hidden in the files of the various welfare organizations.[2] Through them we are brought face to face with the many crises affecting Sephardi paupers during their lives: as refugees, as heads of young families, as widows or orphans, as the infirm, the disabled, or the elderly.[3]

Occasionally we learn something about their descent into poverty. In a discussion between two women, one of them, Sara, dwells on the discrepancy between the former wealth of her parental home in the Iberian peninsula and her present status in Amsterdam, where she toils away as a domestic servant.[4] Clara Franca Serrana must have had a brighter past, too. Once a wealthy widow, she gave her daughter a dowry of 8,700 guilders out of the estate of her late husband Joseph Franco, and in the 1620s was involved in financial transactions at the Bank of Amsterdam.[5] Thirty-five years later, in 1659, this same Clara Franca Serrana was found on the welfare list of the Portuguese community, where she remained for the ten last years of her life.[6] The orphan Ester Fonseca, reaching Amsterdam from Livorno, experienced a similar regression, setting out in her petition how she had grown up in great prosperity in her parents' home but had now been reduced to poverty: 'Ester Fonseca from Livorno, now living in this city, is an orphan girl, without father and mother. She enjoyed a wealthy youth, when her parents were still alive, but now she is in a miserable state without any means.'[7]

Men did not always have an easy time in Amsterdam either. Salomon Levy Maduro, who worked in a print shop, was struggling to support his family: 'Salomoh Levi Maduro begs you for the sake of God, Whose servants you are, to help him rent a house. He is suffering great hardship with five small children.'[8] The writer Daniel Levi de Barrios explained in a petition how he had mismanaged his finances and now had problems: two books on which he had worked for two years had not been approved by the *haham*, and as a result his income had dwindled.[9] Isaac Ledesma, a student in the Gemilut Hasadim yeshiva, argued in his petition that his annual pay of 47 guilders was inadequate. He asked for an increase in view of the *necesidade e pobreza que padesia* (the need and poverty he suffered).[10]

The sick and the elderly also asked for aid. The blind Isaac Perez, for instance, begged the Dotar association to admit his daughter to the lottery and emphasized his own depleted state: 'Ysaque Perez, blind, very old, sick and poor, has a daughter by the name of Rachel, and begs you to be so kind as to admit his daughter to the lottery.'[11]

Often the supplicants mention the suffering they endured before arriving in Amsterdam only in passing. One such identified herself as 'Ribca Enriques de Acosta, a resident of this city, former wife of Isaac de Leon, by whom she has a daughter named Abigail de Leon, fifteen years of age, who has always been in my company, suffering great misery and hardship, to which the blessed Lord is a witness.'[12]

Others tell us a little more about themselves and about the world they left behind. Thus Francisco Nietto reported that it took him four weeks to travel from Lisbon to Amsterdam, where he joined the Portuguese Jewish congregation. His father, he says, was burned at the stake in Baya in Portugal.[13] Manuel Nunes explained that he had recently arrived from Portugal, after much suffering (*mtas penas e trabalhos*), by which he referred to his persecution at the hands of the Inquisition.[14]

Most paupers, however, failed to leave any personal records and do not appear on these petitions. Others deliberately sought anonymity under the cover of genteel poverty or in other ways.[15] Nevertheless, despite the general lack of information, it has been possible by putting bits and pieces together to assemble a picture of the Portuguese poor as they went about their daily business in early modern Amsterdam.

Housing

From the end of sixteenth century, Jews, rich and poor, Sephardi and Ashkenazi, settled mainly among non-Jews, in the eastern part of Amsterdam, the so-called Jewish quarter.[16] Few paupers lived in the houses that lined the canals in this district; most crowded into other streets, large and small, or into one of the many alleyways found in the city.[17] Here they lived not too far away from their more prosperous brethren in their exclusive canal-side homes.[18]

The precise addresses of people drawing poor relief cannot always be retraced with certainty. Data from the *ondertrouw* registers and other sources do, however, provide some good indications, although they do not always give the correct street or alley, often referring only to a wider area.[19] Thus Daniel Rois lived in 'Floyenburg', but it is not clear in what street.[20] Judith Obediente lodged in 'Uylenburg'.[21] In the Portuguese archives the addresses of paupers are found on only one poor-relief list, that compiled in 1653. The accompanying notes are rather vague, which makes it difficult to pinpoint the addresses of the beneficiaries: 'round the corner from/next door to master Abam', 'in Ysidro's street', 'round the corner from Torto the baker', 'in Abrao Preto's street', 'in the fields', 'in Osorio's side-street', 'in Lazarussteeg'.[22]

However, there are also more specific references. Apart from Lazarussteeg, which according to the 1653 *sedaca* list contained sixteen Sephardi families, welfare recipients also inhabited a number of other alleys, including Markensteeg, Steenvoetsteeg, and Turfsteeg.[23] Streets that recur frequently in the addresses of both paupers and other Portuguese are Staalstraat, Zwanenburgerstraat, Lange Houtstraat, Korte Houtstraat, St Antoniebreestraat/Jodenbreestraat, Batavierenstraat, Leprozenstraat, Weesperstraat, and Joden Houttuinen.[24]

Many houses in this area had been divided into rooms and rented out as such. Whole families would often live in no more than one or two rooms.[25] This practice was common among many of the less well-off Portuguese, not only those on poor relief. In Vlooyenburg, for instance, Abraham de Mercado lived in the front room and Abraham Nunes de Carvalho in the back room of the same house. Neither name appears on the poor-relief lists, but both fell into the lowest taxpaying category.[26] A similar pattern can be found among Sephardim on poor relief. Thus Judith Peixotta lived in a room in Abraham Curiel's house,[27] while the orphaned girl Sara Coena occupied a room in Daniel Nunez's house.[28] In 1688 Joseph Carchas took a room in Leprozengracht.[29] Aron Hesqia Querido stated in 1698 that he was living 'in a passage' in Zwanenburgerstraat, and Isaac Vas's address in 1696 was 'a cellar' in Jodenbreestraat.[30]

It is not always easy to tell what the interior of a pauper's home looked like and how it was furnished. Often it came down to the basics: mattresses, pillows, blankets, chairs, mirrors, tables, and some utensils. Ester Barrocas was perhaps an exception in owning an oven for Pesach, sabbath candlesticks, and five Ladino books as well, her possessions amounting to a value of 133 guilders.[31] However, the household effects of Jacob Argas Henriques in Batavierenstraat around the same time, in 1688, were worth only 9.19 guilders, including some valueless paintings.[32] Abraham Bassan's house, an annex to his tobacco shop, was found, on his being declared bankrupt in 1698, to contain household goods worth 250 guilders. When he was bankrupted again in 1702, he had obviously come down in the world and must have been forced to sell many of his possessions, for his household goods at that time were worth no more than 35 guilders.[33] Few of the poor owned articles totalling more than 100 guilders in value; the bleak furnishings of their homes would have been similar to those of other people of few means in the Republic,[34] but of course radically different from the homes of more prosperous Portuguese, whose household goods were valued at vastly higher sums.[35]

Many paupers were granted two rent subsidies a year.[36] This amounted to about 12 guilders a year on average,[37] and was enough to cover part or occasionally all of the rent, depending on the kind of dwelling, its location, and the period at which the payment was made.[38]

When there was any spare space in their homes, Sephardi paupers, like other poor at the time,[39] earned a little bit extra by putting up travellers, poor refugees, or, on a longer-term basis, mentally and physically disabled people. They did so either on their own initiative or on that of third parties, or as part of organized drives by the Portuguese community and various *ḥevrot*.[40]

The extended family occupied an important place in Jewish society in general, as Grossman has argued.[41] In the early modern period it was more usual in southern and eastern Europe than in northern and central Europe for several generations of a family to live together.[42] A similar situation existed among the Sephardim in Amsterdam, although the opposite was sometimes true among the wealthy, as Saul Levi Morteira disapprovingly noted: 'A man who is alone with his wife, or even a single man, lives in a large house with unnecessarily spacious rooms. Such people waste their money . . . this is not befitting a people living outside its land, in the land of its enemies.'[43]

Even though there was clearly a marked contrast in the housing situations of rich and poor, the picture is not entirely black and white in respect of how much space people had: people at all points on the wealth spectrum lived sometimes in small units, sometimes in large family groups. Thus Rachel and Lea Abenhacar, grandmother and aunt, charged with bringing up the six children of the widower Joseph Mendes da Costa, lived at the latter's home, where they were given free board and lodging in return.[44] Josua de Prado had only his mother living with him.[45] In contrast, Isaac Vaz Henriques and his mother lived with his sister, her husband, and their eight children.[46]

A newly married woman and her husband would often make their first home in the bride's parents' house. A case in point was the daughter of Jacob Juda Leon.[47] The mother of Ester Dias da Fonseca, who was to marry Aron da Fonseca, agreed to take the newly wed couple into her home for a period of three years 'as is the custom among the Jewish nation'.[48] This practice was indeed common all over the Jewish world, but was also widely used in non-Jewish families in southern Europe.[49]

Many married women also lived with their families while waiting for their husbands to join them. Ilona Gomes, for example, lived with her family in Amsterdam until her husband was released from prison in Portugal and made his way to the city.[50] Ester Dias da Fonseca and her children moved in with her mother after her return from St Eustatius, where her husband had died. As this example makes clear, it was not only families headed by men that were joined by Portuguese women; many female heads of household, rich and poor alike, also took in family and friends, both male and female.[51]

Children on their own were often boarded out in private arrangements with families, mostly relatives or acquaintances, as was normal practice in Jewish communities of pre-modern and early modern times.[52] The mother of Dr Daniel de Prado remained behind in Amsterdam to care for her grandchildren after her son left the city and moved to Antwerp.[53] The da Rocha girls were said to have lodged with their uncles Benjamin da Rocha and Isaac Furtado while their father travelled on business between North Africa and the New World.[54] Even though Mazon Abanot, the girls' orphanage, bought a house, the girls stayed there only during the daytime, spending the nights with their mothers or with host families.[55] Boys were treated likewise. One was kept in the house of Jacob Ergas,[56] another in that of Moses Roiz, who also cared for Rachel de Castro's son.[57] Abraham de Leon had two boys in his home while their relatives went to Rouen.[58] Mordecai Juda Rodriguez was able to supplement his teacher's salary by taking an orphaned boy into his house.[59] Sometimes, as noted earlier, boys at the orphanage Aby Jetomim were housed with their teachers and supervisors, who were paid for providing this service.

Finally, many broken families and single persons in this complex social environment lived together in pairs and groups, thrown together by circumstances and mutual convenience.[60] Keeping within the protective environment of the Jewish community, in the vicinity of other members of the *nação*, the poor took refuge in small houses in main streets, side streets, and alleyways, in rooms or in cellars, together with relatives and friends or anyone else in need of a home, sharing the rent among them as best they could. It was from this environment that they would set out and attempt to make a living.

Money and Work

Poverty among the Sephardim of early modern Amsterdam had many causes. Some Conversos had been poor from the very beginning, in their lives in the peninsula: a few maintained before the Inquisition tribunal that they had always been poor and that neither they nor their parents had ever owned goods.[61] One Portuguese woman taken up by the Inquisition was a beggar.[62] From the beginning of the seventeenth century many poor Portuguese were spotted in Castile, having travelled over the border from Portugal in search of work among their more fortunate brethren.[63] We have already seen that some rich Conversos gave gifts or loans to 'portugueses y portuguesas pobres'.[64]

The Inquisition had also left many without means. Some had had their goods confiscated;[65] some who were once prosperous had come out of the inquisitorial prisons impoverished.[66] Those who fled the country often left with only very few belongings. In a request of 1623 one group of Portuguese Jews in Amsterdam maintained that they had been robbed by the Inquisition and the ministers of the king of Spain, arriving destitute in Amsterdam as a result.[67]

In Amsterdam itself, changes in the economic climate and periods of war led to unemployment and bankruptcies. In addition, natural disasters like epidemics and severe climatic changes had serious consequences for families with modest means. On top of all this, personal experiences also came into play: some people just had bad luck, were not successful in their work, or became burdened with debts, large families, illness, or a combination of all these.[68]

The restricted labour market for Jews in Amsterdam created many additional difficulties and often required substantial adjustments on the part of the incoming Portuguese. Even before leaving the Iberian peninsula, many Conversos realized that there were limited openings for Jews in Amsterdam.[69] The city's Jews were officially debarred from membership of most of the guilds, and were not allowed to open shops selling anything other than tobacco, fats and oils, groceries, and alcoholic drinks.[70] Although the regulations were not always strictly observed and sometimes freely interpreted,[71] the restrictions contributed to the further impoverishment of the Amsterdam Portuguese, as summarized by Haham Morteira:

> For indeed our profits and our sustenance this day are all achieved in a miraculous manner, due to the small size of the funds we brought from our land, because of the large number of obstacles inherent in exile, which prevent us from engaging in many areas of business and trades, due to the envy of the Gentiles and their hatred towards us. All of these are hindrances and major causes of our impoverishment. Yet despite it all, we have not lacked and we will never lack sustenance without being dependent upon another people.[72]

Thus even those who had a profession or trade could not necessarily pursue it in Amsterdam, and not even the highly educated could count on finding employment. Many complained that they were forced to take more menial work in Amsterdam than that for which they were trained. Some struggled to make any kind of living in Amsterdam and roamed the streets dejectedly, eventually leaving either temporarily or permanently to seek work elsewhere. Fernando Gil de Espinosa told inquisitors in 1669, when he was 22 years of age, that he had left his home in Amsterdam because he could not find work there.[73] Román García returned to Spain in pursuit of a debt 'because his own wife and child were suffering poverty [in Amsterdam] and he could not return to Amsterdam without collecting what was owed to him'.[74]

In the eighteenth century, with ever more Jews looking for work and economic conditions becoming harsher, the guild restrictions were felt particularly keenly. The Portuguese and Ashkenazi communities had good reason to make common cause against these constraints, and in the middle of that century dispatched a joint petition to the Amsterdam authorities asking them to admit Jews to all the guilds in order to increase their opportunities to work and hence to reduce poverty. To buttress their argument, the *parnasim* argued that England was now successfully competing with Amsterdam to attract skilled and expert workers: while only 'indigent and useless families' were gravitating to the Portuguese community of the Dutch Republic, 'those Jews fleeing the Inquisition who have some means or skills to gain their livelihood in a respectable manner have taken refuge in England and other places, where they can make a living in a most acceptable manner'.[75] Over the years, the economic opportunities and prospects of Amsterdam Portuguese Jews thus entered a perceptible downward spiral.

In the Iberian peninsula quite a few Conversos practised professions that demanded capital, skill, and education.[76] Some had been active in international trade and industry and belonged to the prosperous middle class.[77] Others had been shopkeepers or small merchants.[78] Many had been trained for various professions. Dr Daniel de Prado was a physician and teacher in Amsterdam, having attended an Iberian university.[79] Jacob Israel came from Spain to Amsterdam as a poor barber (*barbeiro pobre*), a trade he must have learned in the peninsula.[80] Among those on poor relief in Amsterdam we find an astrologer, also educated in Spain or Portugal.[81]

The Conversos from the peninsula who became 'New Jews' in Amsterdam also included artisans, mainly of the more highly skilled type. Abraham Dias was a trained gold- and silversmith when he arrived in Amsterdam.[82] Abraham Rodrigues had been a tailor in Seville.[83] Two workers in gold and leather from Lisbon were employed in the same capacity by Amsterdam merchants.[84] Others had been seamstresses, silk workers, weavers, or shoemakers.[85]

Finally, many had worked in the peninsula as pedlars or in menial jobs, often as well as receiving charitable handouts. The New Christian widow Beatriz Rodríguez, for example, supported herself with manual work ('la labor de las manos'), income from a small deposit, and charity from some richer New Christians; she frequently took out small loans, giving a ring as a pledge.[86] Isabel María Suárez Suerra was working as a servant when she was condemned for secretly observing Judaism by the Inquisition of Llerena in 1722.[87]

The distribution of professions among the former Conversos in Amsterdam seems to have been quite similar to that in the peninsula, and more balanced than Swetschinski has suggested (he proposes that occupations connected with trade accounted for 81 per cent), although lack of adequate information makes it difficult to arrive at precise figures.[88] Only now and then do we learn something of the professional background of the paupers from the summary notes attached to their names or other brief comments. What is clear is that they were a very varied group.

How did Portuguese Jews on poor relief obtain work? Some succeeded in plying their old trades in Amsterdam, and some of these were helped to do so by the Portuguese community, for example by being provided with the tools of their trade. Jona Fresco, for instance, received carding machinery (*huas cardas*) from the Portuguese community to enable him to process wool.[89] Moses Israel Ger Ingrez was given assistance to buy instruments for fitting books with locks.[90] Vaguer indications include such comments as that a particular individual from Lisbon was being helped with his profession—*aoque veo de Lxa pa ajuda de seu oficio.*[91] Some people were given help regularly by the Portuguese community to pay for their business travels.[92] Others received money to buy them admission to a guild, among them goldsmiths, cobblers, and tailors.[93]

Many were trained or retrained for new professions. Occupations connected with commerce, medical science, Jewish studies, and some crafts must have offered prospects of work at home or abroad, for why else would orphans have been trained, as they were, for those professions?

The Portuguese community administration and the various *ḥevrot* were major employers. Apart from rabbis, cantors, and beadles, there was an increasing need for teachers, both religious and secular.[94] *Soferim* were needed for writing, copying, and translating Hebrew texts, for correspondence, and for inscribing Torah scrolls and *mezuzot*.[95] *Ketubot* had to be printed.[96] Then an eye had to be kept on the *kashrut* of the meat and bread and the preparation of food for holy days.[97] Ceremonial objects had to made and repaired.[98] Staff were also needed to attend and maintain the *mikveh*.[99] The loan bank had to be administered.[100] There was a call for people to keep and guard the synagogue and the cemetery.[101] And, somewhat ironically, as time passed assistants to tend to the needs of the poor themselves were in great demand.[102]

Medical care was an important concern of the community, which along with various *ḥevrot* offered certain services of this kind to people on welfare, as noted in Chapter 4. This provision depended on the abundant numbers of people with the necessary training and experience—doctors, pharmacists, surgeons, and barbers, many assisted by women.[103] The *nação* also had midwives of its own.[104]

Charitable institutions, such as the old-age home, the girls' orphanage, and the almshouse Rehobot, also provided work for the poor, especially in the eighteenth century.[105]

Nursing was mostly provided within the community, organized both by the central administration and privately: people of North African origin and from the Balkans and the Orient were often recruited for this task, as well as German and Italian Jews, or, less frequently, non-Jews.[106] Poor non-Jewish people in other parts of the city also made a living this way,[107] as indeed did less fortunate Portuguese with a Converso background, some of whom had done so in the Iberian peninsula. When Amsterdam was hit by plague in 1664, as it had been in 1655, and 'many prominent persons . . . fled from the city, Jews in particular . . . taking refuge in Beverwijk in large numbers',[108] the *parnasim* remaining in the city employed a Portuguese pauper, Daniel Lopez Rison, to tend the 'sick of our nation' who had succumbed to the plague and to take measures to bury them should they die.[109] Elsewhere in the city other people were appointed to perform similar tasks.[110] Daniel was obviously unable to cope alone, and over the following month eight more people were employed to look after the victims of the plague, all of them picked from poor-relief lists, some with a Converso background, others of North African or Ashkenazi origin.[111] Benvenida Halaca from North Africa, for example, did not mind the hard and dangerous work. After all, it was very well paid, providing a valuable addition to her meagre income: she helped to tend the sick during this epidemic and washed the bodies of people who had succumbed to the plague.[112]

The pattern persisted. In the latter part of the century many Balkan Jews turned to this type of work, tending to the sick and dying: men such as Salomon Levy, Joseph Crespo, and Juda Alva, and women such as Doña Jurada, Paloma Vidal, and Judith Alcoser.[113] However, Portuguese Jews on welfare also continued to contribute. Thus, in 1661, Rachel Lopes assisted at the deathbed of Abraham Israel Torres.[114] Eliau Nunes Leao watched at a sickbed for two nights.[115] Isaac Bentancor, who had been sent out to Guyana and had returned, accepted a job watching over Isaac de la Penha in 1679.[116] Debora Guedelha looked after the blind Rachel Sega, apparently for fourteen years.[117] Gideon Henriques assisted Abraham Valverde in 1692.[118] In the eighteenth century, when poverty became much more widespread, even more of the poorer Portuguese took on nursing jobs. The wife of Abraham Fernandes de Paz, for example, took care of Ester Fernandes da Costa, while Ribca Ribeyro assisted Lea Castiel.[119] Mordecai Rodriguez took Abraham Carillo into his house and looked after him.[120] Isaac Franco helped Benjamin Preto; Samuel Teixeira was paid to take care of the sick Abraham Israel do Valle.[121] In the same period Debora Vintura apparently ran a small infirmary at her home, taking in sick people and caring for them like many other women of her time, both in the city and elsewhere in Europe.[122]

Care for those of the mentally handicapped who stayed in the city rather than being sent away was mostly entrusted to private individuals—in the seventeenth century, especially to Ashkenazim. Thus Moses Carillo was put under the care of a *tudesco* from 1663 onwards.[123] Portuguese Jews were also found among these carers early on, but become more prominent in this role in the eighteenth century. In 1619 Jeremias Masaot—and his widow after him—rented out accommodation for many years, for a payment of 30 guilders a year, to a mentally handicapped woman, Fereira Douda.[124] In 1734 Samuel Palache was paid to put up 'Loca Ferra' in his house, while Josua Busnach took care of five mentally ill women from 1753.[125] Twenty years earlier, in 1734, this same Josua had taken care of Salomon Romero, who had lost his mind.[126] Rachel Mendes da Costa Nahar let her house in Roeterseiland in Amsterdam to the treasurer of the Portuguese Jewish community and lodged mentally handicapped Portuguese in it, four in separate units (*hokken*: apparently, closed huts) within one room and one in a *hok* in the attic.[127]

Thus many Portuguese men and women found work in the various areas of Jewish life based on the synagogue, its affiliated institutions, and independent organizations. But there were also opportunities elsewhere, beyond the community.

First of all, industry needed workers, especially the sugar, tobacco, diamond, silk, and chocolate-manufacturing industries.[128] In these sectors there were no guild restrictions, which explains why so many poor were employed as labourers in the sugar refineries and as tobacco spinners, silk weavers, and diamond-cutters.[129]

Second, the several flourishing Hebrew printing works in Amsterdam provided a host of employment opportunities.[130] We have already met Salomon Levy Maduro and Joseph Abendanon, who worked in this field. The latter, who had trained in Belgrade as assistant to Haham Joseph ben Isaac Almosnino and had thus been immersed in Hebrew and Jewish tradition, was not only welcomed into Joseph Sarfati's home but was also offered employment in his printing works.[131] It is no wonder that other Jews from the Balkans and the Levant with similar backgrounds found work in this industry.[132]

People drawing poor relief also worked at various crafts. Some, such as Abraham Dias, were employed as goldsmiths.[133] Others found employment as silversmiths,[134] coppersmiths,[135] decorators,[136] tailors,[137] cobblers,[138] pastry cooks,[139] candle makers,[140] and mattress makers.[141]

Women did a great deal of needlework, either at home or elsewhere, work that could be done as an extension of normal domestic activity, as it was by non-Jewish women across early modern Europe.[142] The domestic inventories of Portuguese Jews in Amsterdam often included spinning wheels as well as the pillows women used while knitting.[143] Portuguese women were seen knitting at the doors of their houses, close to the light.[144] Rachel de Andrade sewed clothes for Rachel Sega de Espanha.[145] The daughters of David Lobado made and repaired clothes for the inmates of the old-age home.[146] The orphans in Mazon Abanot were employed to do similar work. Wealthy Portuguese families, however, had most of their clothes made by Dutch tailors.[147]

Some Portuguese kept taverns or coffee houses: Abraham Zuzarte ran a coffee and chocolate house where his brother-in-law Isaac Ramos worked as a waiter.[148] Many Portuguese also tried to make a living as shopkeepers.[149] Rachel Preto had a tobacco shop;[150] Josua Furtado had a 'cruydeniertiewinkeltje' in the 'Voorhuys' of his house in 'Corte Houtstraat', where he sold oil, sugar, cacao, and flour.[151] His business was not a great success, however. In 1683 he was noted as being without means of support,[152] and he was periodically on the charity list.[153] In 1670 he made a trip to Hamburg funded by the community.[154] He was paying the *finta* tax in 1690, but by 1700 was no longer on the list of *finta*-payers,[155] and from then on he appeared on the monthly list of welfare payments by the Portuguese community—a clear case of an impoverished Portuguese Jew.[156]

Others made a living by trading in a variety of products, such as 'snuff and flax',[157] tobacco,[158] mattresses,[159] fabric,[160] oil,[161] candles,[162] and groceries.[163] One such trader was Emanuel Vaes de Oliveira.[164] He dealt in all sorts of goods, including sugar, spices, groceries, almonds, soap, oil, bed linen, and lace. In 1692 he went bankrupt, blaming the collapse of his business on the debts he had contracted earlier, on bad times, on the wars, and on his many serious illnesses.[165]

There were also musicians among the Sephardi paupers. Isaac Nunez and Abraham Pereyra are described as 'muzicos'.[166] Abraham Oeb Peres worked as a troubadour in the area known as Marken.[167] Moses Oeb seems to have earned his living playing the trumpet.[168] Other people on welfare found additional income as translators: the son of David Ano Bueno translated papers from Latin into Dutch,[169] while Joseph Cohen from Belgrade was known as a 'master of languages'.[170] Another option for people of few means was working as a courier:[171] Ereira delivered letters from Jerusalem,[172] and the Delgado family carried letters sent to and from the western Sephardi diaspora: London, France, and Surinam.[173] There are also a handful of references to people working as soldiers.[174]

Quite a few Portuguese supplemented their income by letting lodgings to refugees, travellers, and children.[175] Aron Italiaender apparently ran a sort of hostel, taking in overnight guests on production of a voucher from 'the Jewish nation', and was paid by the Portuguese community for his services.[176] Many others offered the same kind of service. The widow of Salomon Farques supplemented the poor relief paid to her and her children with the money she received for putting up travellers, including Isaac Calvo on his way from Hamburg to Bordeaux.[177] Abraham de Leon was also given money for accommodating travellers, in this case two boys on their way to Rouen.[178] In 1685 Judith Tobar y Oliveros was paid to take into her house a mother and child of the *desterrados de França*.[179] Mordecai Agoa Branca offered 'posada' to, among others, two 'levantinos' on one occasion and '3 pobres' on another.[180] Salomon Sanches likewise accommodated short-term lodgers: he took children into his home during holidays, for which he received a fee.[181] For Moses Alva, taking lodgers was a continuous source of income: in 1689 he, together with Daniel Perez, was paid for accommodating *sheliḥim* from Belgrade;[182] around 1699, as we saw earlier, he was sheltering large families who had fled from Portugal; in February 1702 he gave house room to two foreigners; and in March the same year he took in two poor people from abroad.[183] Isaac Talano was also paid for looking after travellers. For six weeks in May and June 1688 he had Moses Gaon from Verona in his house,[184] and later he helped Isaac Oeb and Isaac Moreno to accommodate *belogrados*.[185] Di° Mendes was also involved in this work, on a smaller scale: in 1629 he let a room to a blind woman from Hamburg, for which the *imposta* board footed the bill.[186]

For the most part, the Portuguese left heavy manual labour to others, in Amsterdam as in the peninsula. That sort of work was considered degrading within the strictly hierarchical framework of aristocratic Iberian society.[187] Anyone who wanted to be considered noble in Spain should abstain from manual work and surround him- or herself with an abundance of servants, even if they were totally unnecessary, as Guerrero Mayllo put it.[188] One Portuguese woman even took a servant to attend to her in the prison of the Inquisition.[189] The Amsterdam Portuguese Jews, rich and poor alike, had a similar 'passion for domestic servants'.[190] Simon Gomez de Paz was on the community's charity list, but still had his *mulatto* and black servants at home.[191]

He was not the only one. Some Portuguese brought their servants with them to Amsterdam—and indeed to other parts of the Sephardi diaspora—so used were they to having their own staff.[192] In 1695 Maria de Baillot came from southern France to Amsterdam in the service of Abraham Mendez da Costa and Judith Mendez Salazar. Later she moved on to London in the service of their son.[193] Ester Malbrancq, spinster, served for more than twenty-six years as a 'camenier' and maid for Marie Anne Josephe Therese de Partes, a former Christian, now a Jew, with whom she had travelled from Brussels to The Hague.[194] Rica de Leon brought a *mulatto* woman (*Angela a mulata*) with her to Amsterdam.[195]

Many mentioned *mulatto* and black servants; others employed non-Jewish inhabitants of the city or *tudescos* and *moriscos*.[196] Sephardim from south-eastern Europe, the Levant, and North Africa were also hired for menial jobs. Among them was *belogrado* Jacob Alegem, who told the municipal officials at his wedding in 1696 that he had been a manual labourer in Belgrade and continued to work as such in Amsterdam.[197]

In some cases, especially in the eighteenth century, we find Amsterdam Portuguese working in domestic service or as cleaners, cooks, and labourers. Even in the Iberian peninsula some lower-class women had worked as domestic servants, wet-nurses, cooks, or housekeepers, including some of the more privileged functions within a household.[198] In her last will Judith Henriques called herself the 'domestique' of Madame Reyna Mendes da Silva.[199] In 1699 Abraham Dias took over the cleaning work previously performed by the daughter of Jan Duyts,[200] and David Rodrigues was Daniel Fresco's porter in 1709.[201] Samuel Henriques Faro was in the service of Daniel Pinto in 1707.[202]

It should be kept in mind, however, that servants of Portuguese descent often enjoyed preferential treatment and status. Sara de Tavora was living and working in the house of Gracia Senior, but apparently she did not do the heaviest work, since a 'tudesquita' was employed there as a maid.[203] Ester Pimentel, another Portuguese woman, worked as a cook for Isaac del Sotto's family.[204] Sara de Palma acted as a housekeeper within a Portuguese family serving in the house of the Teixeira family in The Hague, but higher in the hierarchy than the non-Sephardi servants.[205]

There are no records of Portuguese who drew poor relief dealing in second-hand goods. This seems to bear out the remark by a leader of the Portuguese community in 1753 that members would rather be on the dole than trade in old rags.[206]

Many Portuguese, like other paupers in the city and elsewhere in Europe, combined various jobs or changed from one to another to keep their heads above water.[207] In 1674 Abraham de Jacob Zuzarte described himself as a tobacco merchant.[208] Earlier, upon his first marriage in 1670, he had been registered as a schoolmaster. Was he the same man who in 1665, as we saw above, was running a coffee and chocolate house?[209] Moses Bassan registered as a tobacco spinner on his marriage. When he was declared bankrupt in 1706, however, it appeared that he had run a shop 'on the corner of Houtstraat', selling oil, playing cards, raisins, currants, and almonds.[210] Abraham Bassan also reported a range of occupations, saying that since 1682 he had been

> earning his keep . . . as a tobacco-spinner's labourer . . . which helped him to feed his family until the year 1695. When he remarried, he continued with his spinning job as before, but to maintain his family he also kept a kind of tavern so as to feed and keep those of his four children old and new as are still alive and also himself and his wife.[211]

As we have already seen, restrictions on the admission of Jews to the labour market added to the difficulties of finding work. Jobs were scarce and competition was fierce. People boasted of their prowess as workers and played up any extra advantages they could lay claim to. Once father and mother had found employment, attempts were made to preserve their jobs for the children. Thus a particular job would be handed on from father or mother to son (or son-in-law) or daughter (or daughter-in-law) and then on to their child, and so on for generations, guaranteeing the family income and continuous employment.

A case in point was that of Abraham Dias. As *shamash* in the Gemilut Hasadim yeshiva, he asked the board of the yeshiva to employ his son-in-law Samuel Marques as his assistant, with the stipulation that Marques would take over Dias's job upon the latter's demise.[212] In the event, things did not go as he had planned: David Fernandes, Dias's brother-in-law, took over the job after Dias's death, having persuaded the board of the yeshiva that they would be doing a 'work of great *charidade*' in appointing him because he would undertake to pay over half of his earnings to the widow of Abraham Dias, his sister.[213] As a result, the post of *shamash* passed to the Fernandes family: in 1746, ill and at an advanced age, David Fernandes asked to have his son appointed as his successor and had his request granted.[214] However, the Dias family did not completely disappear from the yeshiva: Dias's son Isaac, who had been a student there, returned as a *rosh yeshivah* of Gemilut Hasadim in 1736.[215] Earlier, in 1713, he had graduated as a physician in Harderwijk, and so was also able to work as a doctor, both privately and in the employ of the community.[216]

Another *shamash*, Simon do Valle, also safeguarded his position and that of his descendants by proposing Isaac Saragal, his granddaughter's fiancé, as his successor. Saragal was a poor man or, as Simon put it, had no means (*como lhe faltavao os meyos*).[217] When this Isaac Saragal died, Simon do Valle, now 'very old and almost blind', persuaded the Mahamad to appoint Jacob Lopez Silva, the new husband of his granddaughter Sara, Saragal's widow, in Isaac's place.[218]

In 1703 Abraham Lopes Arias acquired the right to supply candle wax to the *kehilah*. His mother-in-law, the widow of Abraham Nunes, had petitioned the Mahamad to that effect. The actual work of making the candles was done by his—blind—father-in-law and later by the widow herself.[219]

Another widow who fought to keep income and work in the family was Rachel Israel Fernandes: in 1662 she asked that, because of her *extrema necessidade e aperto*, her eldest son be allowed to take over her late husband Samuel's post as 'sohet e bodecq'.[220] Twenty-three years later, in 1685, her son was at long last appointed assistant in the *carniseria*,[221] but another twenty-two years passed before, in 1707, he was allowed to take over her late husband's post of *cortador* (ritual slaughterer), by which time the widow herself was 'in extreme need'.[222] Thereafter, at least, this family had an ensured income for generations in the butchery trade.

The social structure of people on poor relief seemed to be stable, with a great emphasis on continuity, as was the case among paupers outside the Portuguese community.[223] Most people from poor families chose their partners from their own social class and only rarely married into richer Portuguese families.[224] The same families sometimes applied for charity from one generation to the next, temporarily or permanently. Some, however, had new opportunities through education and openings at home or abroad and were able to rise out of poverty. The tax register of 1742 includes a few families whose parents or grandparents had been on the dole: evidence that the younger generation had attained a modest yearly income, enough to enable them not to be dependent on others.[225] Such cases of upward social mobility were rare, though: time and again the same names crop up generation after generation in the poor-relief registers, side by side with those of impoverished, formerly well-to-do families.[226]

Appeals for Help: Petitions

The many Portuguese forced to seek credit or support from the Portuguese community, independent organizations, relatives, and friends made their requests either orally or, more frequently, in writing. These 'petitions' were an accepted way of asking for help, as the Amsterdam Mahamad noted when it observed in 1651 that 'many deserving people ask to be admitted to the monthly welfare distributions, while others state their continuous need in petitions'.[227]

Petitions were written for many purposes, not only to ask for money. Many Conversos, for example, submitted petitions on their arrival in Amsterdam asking for permission to be circumcised, citing their Jewish antecedents.[228] Others wrote offering their services: Dr Daniel Gabriel de Anauia professed himself willing to give medical attention to the poor in a written application in which he presented his curriculum vitae and set out his work experience in some detail.[229] Many people applied for help to independent organizations through petitions.[230] Dotar is a famous example, its archives containing myriad examples of these small pieces of paper.[231] This practice of submitting written petitions was common elsewhere in the Jewish world and beyond.[232]

No instructions about how to frame requests for assistance have been found in the early Resolution Books kept by the Portuguese community. At that time the extent of poverty was still manageable; the community knew who its paupers were and was in control of welfare payments to them. In 1748, however, in order to keep a check on the ever-growing mass of paupers, many of whom were no longer known in person to the administrators, the Portuguese community issued guidelines on writing applications for *sedaca*. A candidate for poor relief was now expected to specify his or her age and family situation and, if married, state for how long.[233] Unfortunately no eighteenth-century applications along these lines have been found.

Petitions by paupers tended to be written in stilted phrases, sometimes using a fixed formula, and were not generally signed by the petitioner.[234] The text was not always chosen or written by the applicant himself.[235] There were probably some individuals in the community who made it their special business to compose petitions, though sometimes a relative or friend of the petitioner did the job. Poor women, especially, were often totally or nearly illiterate.[236] Ester da Rocha was one of these, as is clear from her *ondertrouw* declaration.[237] Her petitions to Dotar were signed with her name,[238] but in the same hand as the petitions themselves. Those who were sick or otherwise disabled, like the blind man Isaac Perez, would also have their petitions written by somebody else. Sometimes the petitioner would sign a petition written on his or her behalf: an Ashkenazi woman described as 'Ester the wife of the musician' could certainly not have written her petition herself, for it was formulated in the Portuguese language, but it was signed in Hebrew letters using a different ink.[239]

The tone of petitions to the Portuguese community and the various organizations was often insistent yet humble.[240] This reflects the anxiety of petitioners both to present themselves as loyal servants of the *kahal* or the *ḥevrah* and to paint their misery in the starkest possible colours.[241] It also reflects the distant relationship between the Portuguese leadership and its subjects, including those dependent on welfare, indicative of the widening gap between rich and poor. Not only did the petitioners address the leadership in a very solemn, polite, and submissive way; many ended their requests with pledges to pray for their well-being, in an attempt to forge a bond between giver and recipient.[242]

'To the worthy Parnasim and Treasurer of the Holy Talmud Torah Congregation [the Kahal Kados de Talmud Torah]', starts the request by Salomon Levy Maduro.[243] 'Most Worthy Parnasim of the holy brotherhood for orphans', begins Isaac Perez.[244] Ester Fonseca 'implores the *parnasim* of Dotar to bring in her lot, together with those of other orphan girls and will pray to God for your life and good fortune'.[245] Dr Anauia declared in his petition that he was willing to submit to the 'authority of the *Senhores parnasim* and treasurer . . . may God grant you many prosperous years', and signed himself 'Yours ever obediently'.[246]

Paupers knew perfectly well how best to persuade their more fortunate brethren to be charitable and often used religious language in their attempt to manipulate the feelings of the addressees. We have already seen how Ester de Caceres, the widow of Abraham de Caceres, wrote in such terms when asking that her daughter be considered for the Dotar lottery.[247] Sara Abravanel sent a heartbreaking petition to the leaders of Dotar with the same object, ascribing her poverty in the city to her sins ('por meus pecados'), stating that she had lost her son of 21, who could have helped her, and appealing to the administrators' religious duty to pity the fate of widows and orphans.[248]

Similar themes appear in the petition of Ribca Enriques de Acosta, also addressed to Dotar. Imploring the administrators to admit her daughter to the lottery, she wrote of her God-fearing behaviour, her sins, the *mitsvah* to protect orphaned girls and widows, and the benefits that might accrue from its observance:

> Ribqua Enriques de Acosta . . . always living a God-fearing life with due respect and deference, begs you to use your great benevolence and clemency and to admit my daughter to the lottery, which is a great *misvah* [i.e. *mitsvah*] and much valued in the eyes of the blessed Lord, as I am without any means to protect her because of my sins and I pray the Divine Majesty with humble supplications for your life and increase, that He may grant you many years for protecting orphaned girls and widows. May the Lord of the world reward you well. She undertakes to pray to the Lord for your life at all times.[249]

While those petitions that have survived tell us something about the relationship between the people in authority and their supplicants, they reveal very little about the specific material background of the petitioners. The details of their physical, social, and material circumstances are usually left out of consideration, at least, it seems, until 1748.[250] Most petitions of the poor to the Portuguese administration were generally devoid of details, representing their plight only in vague terms.

The petitions are, however, often more specific in respect of the assistance requested. For example, Gracia Sacuta, a single woman, wrote:

> Worthy parnasim, worthy treasurer of this holy congregation, which it may please God to multiply
>
> Grasia Sacuta asks you for the love of God to be so gracious as to send me some peat. I have been without peat throughout the winter. So I beg you to have compassion on this poor woman. May God's blessing be upon you. And salom.[251]

A message on a torn shred of paper written by a woman called Bassan, a widow with five children, tells of her hunger and that of her children and asks for chicken.[252] In another, Raphael da Silva asks the *parnasim* for a rent subsidy.[253] Samuel Lopes Henriques requests matzot.[254] Debora Jessurun asks for the fare to the Terra Santa.[255] Abraham Monsanto's wife asks for financial support because her husband was gravely ill.[256]

In exceptional cases, a petition was recorded in the Resolution Books of the Mahamad, often to note a permanent arrangement. To confirm the appointment of Daniel Montesinos as a *shamash* in 1621, the *parnasim* of Bet Israel attached his petition, in which Montesinos applied for the job maintaining he had no other work and no other sources of income.[257] The petition of Jacob Alcalaim, who was ready to leave for Erets Yisra'el to dedicate his life to the study of the Holy Law, was likewise copied into the Resolution Book in order to record a permanent arrangement. Being 'muito pobre', he had requested and been awarded part of the annual distribution for the poor in Erets Yisra'el.[258]

Sometimes, in the absence of petitions, it is possible to reconstruct them from other documents. An example is the decision of the Mahamad in 1657 to appoint Joseph Pardo as *ḥazan* of the *ḥevrah* Bikur Holim and procurator of the *misvot* (funeral director). It appears from the record of this decision that Pardo had sent in a petition in which he had referred with pride to the merits of his late father, Haham David Pardo, who at the end of his life, eleven days earlier, had pleaded with the leadership to help mitigate the hardship suffered by his wife by letting his son continue the tasks relating to death and burial that David Pardo had formerly performed.[259] For the most part, however, all we have to go on are entries in the cash books, where requests granted were noted, giving the name of the petitioner, the amount paid out, and occasionally a brief account of the reason.[260]

In addition to—or instead of—submitting written petitions, paupers also applied for assistance by word of mouth. Occasionally, petitioners sought out the house of the treasurer to ask for money.[261] Others were ushered into the board room of the Portuguese community so that they could offer their petitions personally and give additional explanations of their problems to the seven *parnasim*, although that was the exception rather than the rule.[262] Rachel Haiaia, for instance, took her five children to the board room of the Mahamad in order to drive home the extent of her poverty. The board seems to have grasped her 'extreme need . . . being with five small children' when they were 'brought face to face with them'.[263] Rachel de Sea, too, the daughter of Dr Benjamin de Sea, appeared in person before the Mahamad to tell the *parnasim* that she was entitled to a legacy from the estate of Lopo Soares on the basis of her family connections with the testator.[264] The widow of Daniel de Campos apparently managed to make her way into the board room in 1725 to impress her great poverty (*muyta nesesidade que padessa*) on the gentlemen inside.[265]

In some cases assistance was given unprompted by any kind of petition. One of the highest forms of *sedaca* is giving without having to be asked.[266] Sometimes a particular pauper's situation was so wretched and so well known that no application was needed. In that case, a record was made to the effect that assistance was agreed in the absence of a petition. In 1669, for example, Moses Berberisco received 1.4 guilders while recovering from illness, although he did not submit a petition for help.[267] In 1668 Gerson Bar Efraim Italiano was given unsolicited assistance because he was found to have an ailing wife.[268] When Ribca Levy Alvares arrived in Amsterdam from Nice in 1669, her dire condition was so obvious that unsolicited assistance was offered through the *parnas* Abraham da Vega.[269] Abraham Zacuto received unsolicited help because his bed and clothing had gone up in flames.[270]

As we have already seen in several contexts, many of the poor were inhibited by honour and a sense of shame from applying for assistance. Others had no choice. Aron Gomes had tried vainly to escape from the poor-relief trap. On declaring his bankruptcy, he added a summary of all his reverses and showed what exertions he had made to overcome them. Sadly, he had to conclude that there was no way out. 'At present', he ended his account, he was 'in so bad a state' that he was 'forced to accept poor relief'.[271]

The *kahal* was well aware of the sensitivities of the Portuguese poor and tried to find ways to act with discretion. To protect the reputation of paupers drawing official poor relief, from the seventeenth century onwards some of them were registered anonymously or placed on separate lists under the headings of *secretos, vergonhozos,* and *encubertos* (secret, shamefaced, and concealed).[272] When many respected families lost their fortunes in the eighteenth century, a special book was opened for them. This *Livro de segredos* contained the names of those who, while receiving assistance from the *kehilah,* did not appear by name on the normal poor-relief registers and were thus not generally known to be paupers.[273] Extreme secrecy was ensured: only the *parnasim* knew who the recipients were and how much assistance they were given. This would be handed over in person by a single *parnas.*[274]

Apparently it was also sometimes possible to apply for assistance in secret, as is shown in the applications for charity from the estate of Jacob Mazahod. His heirs protected the reputation of several beneficiaries of his will by placing their names on separate lists, reserved for those who did not appear on the common poor-relief registers but who had nevertheless applied for help in *piticoims secretas.*[275] The strictest secrecy was also ensured in distributing assistance from the fund set up by Abraham Nahar. This bequest was intended to benefit the genteel poor, that is, for those in his Bet Jacob congregation who were not widely known to be poor. Petitions were explicitly ruled out: any pauper who asked for assistance by handing in a petition or by other means was immediately disqualified from help by the fund.[276]

Once reduced to receiving poor relief from the Portuguese community, most—but not all—paupers tried to get out of that trap, with or without help from their families. This eagerness to be free of welfare payments shows the degree of shame involved in agreeing to receive official charity. Isaac Namias declined a second handout of peat in the winter of 1676/7.[277] Jacob Zuzarte's wife had her name removed from the monthly poor-relief list.[278] In 1672 Isaac de Pina was granted 3.3 guilders but refused to accept any more aid on principle.[279] Aron Rodrigues Pereyra also declared that he needed no further assistance.[280]

No matter how requests for poor relief to the Portuguese community were made—on the petitioner's own initiative, by the *parnasim*, or by third parties—all decisions to grant or withhold aid were taken by the board of the *kahal*, by the administrators of the various charitable organizations, or by private benefactors. Paupers could apply to all these sources.

The Level of Poor Relief

Was the Portuguese community a generous benefactor? We can try to find the answer to this question by comparing the level of poor relief paid by the Portuguese community with that paid by non-Jewish charities in the city. The 1750s have been chosen because this decade was used in a previous study of the level of poor relief provided by other charities. Ad hoc poor relief, private donations—in so far as these are known—bursaries and study material, travelling expenses, and payments for sickness and burial costs have not been taken into account. Extra payments of these kinds by the various Christian denominations have also been left out of the comparison, although they were undoubtedly made.[281]

It turns out that poor relief provided by the Portuguese community in the 1750s, at an average of 78 guilders a year for a family with two children and 95 guilders a year for a family with four children, was above the level of municipal poor relief. Yet it was lower than that granted by the Reformed Church, the Mennonites, or the Remonstrants, who gave a minimum of 97 guilders a year to the first group and a maximum of 220 guilders a year to the second. The level of poor relief provided by the Portuguese community was therefore no more than average and by no means exceptionally high in relation to other denominations in the city. However, it must be noted that the Portuguese community was more generous in providing poor relief in the seventeenth century than it was in the eighteenth, when benefits were cut back as part of a general retrenchment.

Poor relief generally came to much less than the annual income of a skilled labourer, which, as we have seen, fluctuated around 300 guilders, and thus constituted no more than a supplement to wages or income from other sources.[282] That was as true of benefits provided by the municipal and church charities as it was of poor relief handed out by the Portuguese community.

How the Portuguese poor managed on their earnings and welfare payments can be seen from the following case studies. These include men and women, single people, and heads of families. There was no such thing as a standard grant: every payment was calculated and disbursed according to a variety of criteria. As we have seen, some paupers did all sorts of work to supplement their relief money; with others we are in the dark when it comes to supplementary earnings. Those who were handicapped, either mentally or physically, were unable to work and so could not earn anything. In every case, women, with or without children, were paid the highest benefits, although their total annual income remained minimal. However, in no case do we have complete information about incomes—from work, loans, the Portuguese community, the various charitable organizations, relatives, and friends—in Amsterdam and beyond. Some of the beneficiaries may even have had reserves of their own.

Let us begin with Ester de Andrade. She lived alone with three children, having apparently lost all trace of her husband since 1640, though there is a hint that he may have been in Brazil.[283] From then until her death in 1652 she was supported by the Portuguese community.[284] In addition to her poor relief she had several other sources of income. From 1648 she worked for the community, helping in the preparation of kosher bread.[285] She also looked after invalids: first a deaf, mentally ill woman, the sister-in-law of Isaac de Pina,[286] and then a deaf woman from Tunis.[287] Notwithstanding these various jobs she undertook for the community in order to support her family, in 1648/9, that is, the period from Pesach 1648 (5408) until Pesach 1649 (5409), her total income was just 106.10 guilders, which placed her below the poverty line.[288] Perhaps her husband sent her a little money from abroad or her family in Amsterdam helped out.

Poverty continued to dog the family for another generation. Ester's daughter Rachel did not lead a very happy life either, although it started well: she drew a dowry of 300 guilders in the Dotar lottery,[289] and six months after her mother's death she married Abraham Calvo, an orphan from the Aby

Jetomim orphanage and a student in the Ets Haim yeshiva.[290] However, three years after the marriage her husband died, leaving her with two little boys to look after.[291] From her mother she took over the care of the deaf woman Ester Coen a Surda, which brought her 7.10 guilders every three months.[292] She also inherited her mother's work in the bakeries, and specifically the *mitsvah* of setting aside a piece of dough (the *ḥalah*).[293] She received poor relief from the Portuguese community intermittently from 1656 to 1677. Then her brother helped her for two years, until 1679.[294] When his help came to an end, she was put back on monthly poor relief, this time continuing to receive the regular payments until 1683.[295] Her sons Jacob and Isaac learned to read and write at the pauper school as well as apparently studying at the religious school.[296] Isaac then became an apprentice bookbinder for Gerrit Huygen in Amsterdam, thanks to the good offices of Aby Jetomim.[297] Jacob apparently settled permanently in Curaçao, where he earned a good living by means of, among other things, the slave trade.[298] Rachel's poverty was temporarily relieved for three years from 1684, when her son Isaac was employed as a butcher by the community on condition that he supported his mother.[299] The community then paid him an annual salary of 700 guilders, and he had a supplementary income from his work as bookbinder and other activities.[300] We do not know whether the stipulation attached to his job was the only reason why he supported his mother, but in any event that support proved temporary, and from 1687 Rachel had to go back on poor relief. Her sons, the grandsons of Ester de Andrade, seem, thanks to the education they received and better prospects abroad, to have escaped the poverty trap, while the women of the family, in this case Ester and Rachel, had to wage a constant battle against penury.

Another woman on poor relief was Sara Buena de Moura. She was supported for a decade, heading a large family from 1660 to 1665 as the wife of Abraham Bueno de Moura and then from 1665 as his widow. We know very little of her husband's whereabouts. The family, apparently from Fronteira in Portugal,[301] fluctuated in size: in 1660 it consisted of five members, a year later there were nine, and from 1662 to 1664 eight. In 1665 Sara's husband died in Amsterdam,[302] and for the following two years the widow presided over a family of seven members, including herself. Our calculations do not include special donations, distributions of clothing and the like, or any possible supplementary earnings brought in by Sara, so the total household income may have been higher than her annual relief payment of 110.50 guilders, which was certainly no fortune and in fact plainly inadequate to support a large family.[303] Nevertheless, Sara's children were able to get the better of their plight: not one of them appeared on the later poor-relief registers. We encounter her three children in the community's records: one was a merchant, another a translator and a board member of the *ḥevrah* Honen Dalim.[304]

Rachel Sega de Espanha was a blind single woman who came, as her name suggests, from Spain. She lived in lodgings.[305] In 1663/4, the year in which poor relief was first introduced, because of her handicap she was granted 10 guilders a month, more than the statutory monthly allowance, which along with other small payments brought her income up to a total of 139.05 guilders, probably the maximum she could count on as a single woman.[306]

Abraham Dias, whom we have already met, was a gold- and silversmith and practised various aspects of his trade.[307] He originated from Valladolid in Spain and is referred to as a Spanish Jew in the records.[308] We do not know when he arrived in Amsterdam or whether he came straight there from Spain, but we do know that he drew poor relief from 1661.[309] He was deeply involved in Amsterdam Portuguese Jewish life and was active in several aspects of it. In 1667, for instance, he was one of the men behind the establishment of the Honen Dalim society.[310] He was paid for guarding the synagogue and later for cleaning it; in the *kehilah*, sometimes with one of his sons, he helped in the preparation of special foods such as *ḥaroset* and *shemurim* for Pesach or assisted the *shamash* of the synagogue.[311] He also served as *shamash* in the Gemilut Hasadim yeshiva.[312] Finally, he worked as a supervisor of the baking of kosher bread.[313]

Abraham was married twice,[314] and his family grew steadily. In 1660 it probably consisted of three people,[315] in 1668 of four,[316] from 1672 of six,[317] and from 1678 of seven to eight.[318] We do not know in what order his children were born, but we do know for certain that he had four sons and two daughters in 1677.[319] He lost children in 1664, 1675, and 1682.[320] In 1683 his daughter Ribca married Moses Dias from Badajoz, probably a cousin,[321] who was admitted to the printers' guild in 1692[322] and printed work for the community.[323] Ribca supplemented her husband's income by sitting with sick people.[324] Abraham's second daughter, Sara, was married a year after Ribca: her husband was a baker, Moses Fernandes from Livorno. They apparently lived with Abraham at first.[325] Some years later, by which time she was a widow, Sara became impoverished, and submitted a petition requesting the Mahamad to appoint her son David as *cortador de carne*.[326]

We know that two of Abraham Dias's sons were taught to read and write Portuguese, and also learned arithmetic at the expense of the Portuguese community.[327] All four of them also studied at the Talmud Torah school and Ets Haim yeshiva.[328] One son, Jacob, left for Barbados in 1680.[329] Another,

Isaac, we have already met: he became a doctor and served as head of the Gemilut Hasadim yeshiva.[330] Besides his work in these capacities he had other sources of income as well: he delivered flour to the community for the process of baking matzot and was paid for giving sermons in the synagogue.[331]

To supplement his wages Abraham Dias also drew poor relief, although at first not on a monthly basis. At a later stage, from 1670, he received 2.90 guilders a month from Abodat Ahesed,[332] and was given additional sums during particularly hard times and periods of illness, and to pay for the burial of his children.[333] Our estimate of his annual income is based on the figures for 1671/2. For lack of information, special relief for illness, funeral costs, clothing, and education have not been taken into account for this particular year. Nor do we have any further details about other work Abraham may have done and other possible sources of income. In 1672 his family consisted of about six people—father, mother, and probably four children—and there may have been some subsidiary income which prevented the family from being reduced to penury. The total amount from the sources we know about thus reflects the household's minimum income, which, at 131.90 guilders, was certainly not high.[334]

Daniel Lopes Arias was also the head of a large family, sharing a home with his wife, two daughters, and four sons.[335] Like Abraham Dias, he had a number of different occupations. Among other things, he worked as a teacher in the Portuguese community, instructing young boys of the *kahal* in reading and writing Portuguese as well as in arithmetic.[336] In 1673 he was appointed *shamash* to the Maskil el Dal society.[337] He was also one of the inspectors supervising the baking of kosher bread.[338] In addition, he helped in the preparation of *shemurim* for Pesach.[339] In 1655 he married a girl who drew a dowry of 250 guilders from Dotar.[340] His wife helped to augment the family income by nursing the sick.[341] He himself took out sickness insurance with the Temime Darech society.[342] His sons studied in the Ets Haim yeshiva.[343] Characteristically of this class and time, his daughter Sara had hardly any education. When signing the *ondertrouw* register, she could not write her name in full and so used just the first two letters of her first name. One of Daniel's sons went to Surinam in 1685, his fare paid by the Portuguese community.[344]

Despite all his industry, Daniel was unable to make ends meet without support from the Portuguese community. In the year 1672/3, his family of eight received a total income of 229.50 guilders (not including a monthly grant from Ets Haim to one of his sons, Abraham). This was barely enough to keep the family above the poverty line.[345] Later we come across the name of Daniel's widow on the charity lists.[346]

The level of annual relief in these examples varies—depending on the size of the family and their personal situation—from 69.90 to 139.05 guilders a year, which, though higher than the averages computed for the middle of the eighteenth century and similar to the level of poor relief provided by the Reformed Church in 1750, is still far from lavish.[347] A handicapped single woman who could count on no other income was granted the highest rate of poor relief. A man heading a large family could, with his earnings and help from the Portuguese community, count on a minimum income of 229.50 guilders a year, but still remained mired in poverty. He may, however, have had additional reserves that we do not know about, and aid from relatives, friends, and private institutions may well have helped people like him to stave off starvation.

It seems clear from both the general discussion and the specific examples cited here that Portuguese paupers in the early modern period must, in addition to working, have tapped many other sources of funds in order to make a living. Help from the Portuguese community was inadequate as a sole resource: it was impossible to survive in Amsterdam without other support. It is for that reason that the Portuguese community was so keen to get rid of people who could not summon up sufficient extra help or income—for example, David Gomes from Bayonne, who in 1677 was directed to return to his place of origin because he could not sustain himself in Amsterdam.[348] If this was not done, the community feared, poverty was likely to generate violence and criminality.

Protest and Misbehaviour

Ostensibly, Portuguese paupers in early modern Amsterdam were quiet and well behaved, awaiting the decision of the community on whether to grant them poor relief with passive resignation. Yet they did not always show particular gratitude, and some were in fact given to agitation and conflict. Although criticism from people on poor relief was frowned upon, a few of them ventured to speak up. The community leaders were not amused.

A case in point is Isaac Oeb Peres, a welfare recipient in the last twenty years of the seventeenth century, at which time he was probably in his fifties and sixties. He erupted in 1680, during celebration of the Purim holiday. At this time paupers were given money, but the Amsterdam community had its own procedure: the poor were strictly forbidden to ask for cash themselves in the synagogue, this task being reserved for the elders, not only to preserve the anonymity of the poor and the benefactors, but also to maintain order.[349] The procedure was carefully laid down. In a strict hierarchical sequence, which kept growing with all the subdivisions of *sedaca*, *parnasim* would pass plates around collecting contributions for the poor, for the synagogue staff, and for various charitable institutions.[350]

Oeb repudiated the system. In the courtyard of the synagogue he declared that he did not give a fig for the authority of the Mahamad, which he considered incapable of running poor relief efficiently. In future he would ask the congregation itself directly for money during the Purim collections. His outburst—according to the report of the *parnasim*, 'couched in loud and shameless terms, in the presence of the greater part of the Kahal'—was punished with a public rebuke and a fine of 50 guilders.[351]

During the eighteenth century the protests grew louder. In a petition to Señor Parnas Vega in 1724, Abraham Pimentel, overwhelmed by poverty, is said to have threatened the *parnasim*. He wrote about the miserable situation he found himself in with two sick children, and rounded on the Portuguese poor-relief administrators, alleging that 'you only help infamous characters, asslickers, brothel keepers, whores and thieves, and have little interest in assisting paupers who are in real need of help'.[352]

Agitation continued throughout that century. The *parnasim* were harassed on quite a few occasions, although the precise cause of most of these incidents is unclear. In any case, around 1750 the Portuguese community appealed for help to the municipality. Implicitly acknowledging the need to quash trouble within the *kahal*, the city governors replied that,

> having been informed by the Parnassins of the Portuguese Jewish Nation that they are frequently insulted by members of their church, it has been resolved to prevent such Insolence by decreeing . . . that those who Injure or Insult the said Parnassins in their official capacity, at or outside their meetings, will be punished by being put on water and bread for a period of time or dealt with otherwise depending on the Exigencies of the Case, the aforesaid Parnassins having been provided with Extracts to be read out in their church.[353]

The case of Josua Habillo Benveniste in 1752 was one of those that were handled in close cooperation between the Portuguese *parnasim* and the municipality on the basis that he posed a threat to the community. A married man with several children and grandchildren, and receiving welfare payments from the Amsterdam Portuguese *kehilah*, he was excommunicated because, in his words, 'he found himself among different women'. He repented and, since he wanted to leave the city to seek a living elsewhere, the leadership decided in 1747 to give his wife 100 guilders to cover their travel expenses, not to return in five years.[354] However, he returned before this period had expired and tried to coerce the Portuguese leaders into reinstating him on the charity lists by threatening to revenge himself on them. His dangerous and deviant behaviour was reason enough for the city authorities to intervene in support of the Portuguese authorities, and they expelled Habillo Benveniste from Amsterdam permanently, banning him from ever returning to the area under jurisdiction of the city.[355]

Another crisis took place in 1764, when, on the basis of the Habillo Benveniste resolution, the Portuguese community asked the city bailiff to arrest and imprison David Alascar, who was in receipt of poor relief and was a man 'of very vexing behaviour', and to act 'in accordance with the exigencies of the case'.[356] It appears that David Alascar was continuously pestering the *parnasim* and other community officials and moreover refused to apologize to them in the synagogue.

In 1767 there was unrest in the Rehobot almshouse, with the inmates at each other's throats.[357] Similar confrontations had occurred elsewhere in earlier periods: in a responsum in sixteenth-century Salonika, Samuel de Medina criticized the poor for ingratitude in behaving wickedly and without appreciation for the generosity of the well-to-do who paid their taxes, rather than showing obedience and appreciation towards those in authority.[358]

In spite of it all the Amsterdam Portuguese community managed to keep peace and order among the poor, although there were occasional cases of violent behaviour, either at home or in the street: in 1658 Rachel Abarbanel and her son were arrested for 'doing mischief' and kicking windows near the St Antonispoort;[359] Rachel Maimona and her daughter were brought before the police for causing grave damage in someone else's house.[360]

Others simply did not want to follow the rules and procedures of the Portuguese Jewish community, as is also evident from the cases noted by Yosef Kaplan in his studies on deviance and excommunication.[361] Young boys were expelled from school or lost scholarships. Other rebellious paupers were summarily punished with a fine, by withholding poor relief, or by threatening or imposing excommunication. Any ban on a poor person was usually imposed for a short time only: this was often enough to force the wrongdoer to repent, since his welfare allotment was at stake. Often the ban, with its concomitant loss of relief payments, was transmuted into a small fine in order not to endanger the material condition of the individual involved or, especially, that of his or her family.

A case in point is Daniel Rachao. Twice he was subject to *ḥerem*, for a short period only, the first time because he wrote mockingly about Judaism.[362] During the periods involved he did not receive charity, but welfare to him and his family resumed soon after the bans were lifted.[363]

As a last resort offenders could be expelled from the city, with or without the intervention of the municipal authorities. This is what eventually happened to Rachel Maimona. A few months after her confrontation with the Amsterdam police mentioned above, the *parnasim* gave 'La Maimona' money, in Amsterdam and again in Rotterdam, to pay for her passage for Bordeaux.[364] This practice of sending troublemakers away was not always successful, at least initially. In 1658 Baruh Vidal Munhon was banished from Amsterdam for twelve years. When, after an absence of just two years, he returned from Essequibo on the eve of Pesach, he was given permission to spend the week of the festival in Amsterdam. It was made clear to him, however, that he had to leave the city after that.[365]

Those of the poor who proved to be good and submissive members of the Portuguese community were spared social isolation and an uncertain material existence. For poor newcomers, certainly if they were Portuguese, that community was their first port of call for social, cultural, and economic benefits.[366] Poor Sephardim had little alternative in Amsterdam. The Ashkenazi community was much poorer and provided less poor relief. A Portuguese, in any case, would not apply to them. And the city of Amsterdam gave no assistance to Jewish paupers.

The suspicion with which the Reformed Church treated Jewish paupers and questioned the validity of their claims hardly encouraged poor Jews to join its ranks, although many poor from the Catholic and Lutheran communities in Amsterdam seem to have joined the Reformed Church, attracted by its generosity in handing out alms.[367] Nevertheless, a few Portuguese Jewish paupers did convert to the Reformed Church in the city in order to increase their chances on the labour market—although they could not always be sure of receiving poor relief if they did. Thus the former monk and priest Dr Isaac de Rocamora, who had become a Jew in Amsterdam, weighed up the pros and cons of joining the Reformed Church. In the end, financial assistance from the Portuguese community won out over an uncertain future among the Reformed. In 1650, the church council took this decision concerning Dr de Rocamora: 'His acceptance cannot be lightly resolved upon, seeing that we have often been deceived by people of his ilk . . . moreover, he seemed discontented when he made his application as if he had counted on assurances of financial support.'[368]

It is well known that, among the different religions of early modern Europe, conversion was a very sensitive matter that aroused a great deal of anger towards renegades.[369] The issue was especially sensitive among ex-Conversos, for whom Christians were the enemy, the people who had ruined their lives in their country of origin. Thus converts such as Sara Lumbrosa learned the hard way that joining a Christian congregation would bring down fury on their heads and condemn them to social isolation. According to the church council, her conversion to Christianity forced her to 'suffer disgraceful insults [from the Portuguese Jews], who spat at her out of their windows, and abused her, calling her a dog and a pig'. In addition, the church council reported that 'it is found that Jewesses abused her for having turned into a dog or for following a dog's law, that Rijcka, her daughter, was encouraged by certain Jewish women to kill her mother or rob her because of her conversion to the Christian religion'.[370]

Portuguese paupers thus had good reason for adhering to Judaism in Amsterdam and for submitting meekly to the Portuguese oligarchy. Moreover, in addition to official assistance from the Portuguese community they could also appeal for aid to private sources. It did not take long to weigh up the pros and cons.

We cannot therefore be certain about the sincerity of paupers who adopted Judaism in Amsterdam. It seems reasonable to conclude that some were motivated to join the Amsterdam Portuguese *kahal* and to obey its rules less by religious conviction than by material considerations. The same motivation explains why the Sephardi paupers voiced so few protests, and why no more than a handful dared to turn to Protestant institutions or to return to the Catholic faith their forebears had been compelled to adopt in the peninsula.[371]

Life on the Fringe

Besides the majority of paupers who seem to have been relatively obedient, submissive, and well-behaved, there were a small number who remained on the fringes of society. Some never joined the congregation. Others registered at first but turned their back on the organized community after a while.[372] Some of these unaffiliated Jews quietly integrated into Dutch society and disappeared from sight; some, though not well off, were never on poor relief or under the supervision of the Portuguese Jewish community, turning instead to less acceptable and respectable ways of making a living. They can be found in the criminal records of the Dutch Republic, the so-called *Confessieboeken*, or Confession Books, of the Judicial Archives.[373]

There is ample information available on Jewish crime in the Dutch Republic. The historians Sjoerd Faber and Florike Egmond conducted extensive research on the subject, showing that the Ashkenazim in particular played a prominent role in Dutch crime, especially in offences against property. However, their research barely touched on the Sephardim. Assuming it was poverty that drove the Ashkenazi Jews to illicit behaviour, they left what they viewed as the wealthy Portuguese Jews out of the picture.[374]

I have traced sixty-eight cases involving Sephardim in the *Confessieboeken* for Amsterdam and the vicinity, thirty-one (46 per cent) in the seventeenth century, and thirty-seven (54 per cent) in the eighteenth, most of them concerning crime against property.[375] It is a small group compared to the number of people on poor relief in the Amsterdam Portuguese Jewish community in this period (between 5 per cent and 7 per cent of the two groups together).[376] It is also a smaller proportion than that of Ashkenazim who turned to crime. The ratio of Ashkenazim to Sephardim in Amsterdam between 1650 and 1700 varied from 1:2 to 1:1.25. After that, the Jewish population of Amsterdam consisted of more Ashkenazim than Sephardim, with a ratio of on average about four Ashkenazim to one Sephardi.[377] However, in the period from 1680 to 1795 the ratio of Ashkenazi to Sephardi involvement in crime was 40:1.[378] The judicial records elsewhere in the Dutch Republic also show a majority of Ashkenazim among Jewish perpetrators of crimes, with Sephardi involvement much less evident.

For an example of who these errant Sephardim were, let us look at the case of Isaac Lopes de Luna. In 1673 he was interrogated before the court at Dam Square in Amsterdam and said he was 15 years old. It was a period of warfare and he served in the Dutch army under Lieutenant Colonel Fullana, an ex-Converso.[379] Isaac had come to Amsterdam from Livorno, Italy. There was nothing strange about that: as we have seen, many poor Jews took the same route in early modern times, attracted by the prospects of the Dutch Republic in general and a metropolis like Amsterdam in particular, to say nothing of the reputation of the Amsterdam Portuguese Jewish community for wealth and hospitality. However, unlike most of his fellow poor Jews, Isaac seems to have spent most of his life on the margins of Portuguese Jewish and Dutch society. He appears in the *pinkasim* (minutes) of the Amsterdam Portuguese Jewish community only once as the recipient of charity.[380] He seems to have been well informed, though, about 'who was who' in the Portuguese Jewish community and might have been personally in touch with several Portuguese Jews.[381] At any rate, he managed to survive in the Dutch Republic, working—or at least claiming to work—as a perfumer and tobacco worker,[382] but mostly through illicit means: by stealing and robbing in Amsterdam, in other cities of the Dutch Republic including Rotterdam, Delft, and The Hague, and abroad in Hamburg and England. As the judges in The Hague noted, he was surrounded by 'notorious male and female thieves, living in idleness and waste, behaving dishonestly'.[383] Except for a few Portuguese Jews, his companions were mostly Christians.[384] He frequented prostitutes, but also had a long-term relationship with Bregje Henricks, a Christian woman born in Amsterdam, whose husband was alive and well. Bregje preferred Isaac and assisted him in his robberies in the Republic and abroad, enjoying the proceeds together with him.[385] In the verdict of the judges, Isaac had broken the law on several counts, since it was forbidden for him as a Jew to have sexual relations with Christian women.[386] It was also forbidden to live with a married woman, which as adultery was also a punishable offence.[387] Isaac's criminal record stretched over seventeen years, from 1673 to 1690, and would certainly have gone on for many more years had he not been sentenced to death and hanged in The Hague in 1690.[388]

What does this case tell us? As a Sephardi Jew in the Dutch Republic, Isaac Lopes de Luna was not living in isolation. He apparently knew some prominent and less prominent Portuguese Jews and was officially registered in the poor-relief books of the community, albeit only once. For him, apparently, the community still served as a frame of reference. In addition, he was professionally and privately in touch with non-Jews, and well able to live outside the authority and control of the Amsterdam Portuguese Jewish community. He obviously came to the Dutch Republic for economic reasons, in the first instance as a soldier without other skills, and learned the trades of perfumer and tobacco worker later. The lure of profit, however, attracted him to criminal activities, since poor relief combined with work would not bring him prosperity.[389] Not only had he arrived from far away, his activities were not restricted to the Dutch Republic, demonstrating the high mobility and international range of the Dutch Sephardim, rich and poor alike. Finally, as his lack of connection to Judaism and his relationships with Christian women show, the Jewish religion did not play an important role in his identity.

Is Isaac Lopes de Luna typical of the Sephardim on the margins of the Dutch Republic?

Networks of Crime

Most people like Isaac were only loosely connected to the Amsterdam Portuguese Jewish community in the early modern period. No more than a handful of them were in the poor-relief or taxation registers of the Amsterdam Portuguese Jewish *kahal*.[390] A few turned to the Reformed Church, where they applied for assistance. One such is Samuel Aboab, alias Antonio Sanches de Pas. The Reformed Church found him to be 'short of provisions' and 'in dire need'.[391] Some would try both sources;[392] however, they were the exception rather than the rule. Most criminals operated on the fringes of Amsterdam and provincial society and preferred to give the official institutions a wide berth.

Like their Ashkenazi brethren, Sephardi criminals almost never operated on their own.[393] Some had one or more accomplices from their own circle.[394]

It was rare, though not unknown, for Sephardim to co-operate with Ashkenazim. Sephardim also co-operated with non-Jews in informal associations.[395] It is unclear whether there was a fixed hierarchy in these enterprises, although Sephardim do seem to have played important if not pivotal roles in various small groups.[396]

Most Sephardi delinquents at this time were young men aged between 15 and 40. In the seventeenth century only a minority of these Sephardim were born in Amsterdam. Most of them, like Isaac Lopes de Luna, were first-generation immigrants.[397] This changed in the eighteenth century, when more and more delinquents were Amsterdammers, although just as many came from other regions, some having been expelled, some simply attracted by the opportunities of the Dutch Republic. Their registered places of origin included other towns in the Dutch Republic, the German states, Antwerp, France, Italy, and North Africa. Portugal, the Orient, England, and the West Indies were added as places of origin in the eighteenth century.[398] These areas reflect the migration routes of the Sephardim in the early modern world.

In the Dutch Republic, female involvement in crime was relatively high.[399] However, not very many Jewish women were involved;[400] the criminals usually left their women and children at home. This is consistent with the sheltered position Sephardi women generally occupied in their community.[401] The same comment could also be made of Jewish women in general, although more Ashkenazi women were active as assistants to their menfolk or as independent criminals.[402]

Whether these transgressors were male or female, born in the city or elsewhere, poverty must have implicitly or explicitly played a role in their offences. Not only does it seem the most likely explanation, it was often explicitly mentioned during interrogations. Eliasar Bassan's sentence was commuted 'out of pity for his poverty'. Isaac Peritie from Paris was apparently a beggar, though 'never caught begging in Amsterdam, but only outside the city'.[403] Judging from her own words, Rachel Cardoose, who was caught stealing, also committed her crime because she was poor.[404]

References to poverty were far more commonplace in the eighteenth century, reflecting its increasing incidence among the Amsterdam Sephardim at the time. The cases of Abraham Pimentel, Josua Habillo Benveniste, and David Alascar have already been mentioned. Mordecai Gabielje claimed he had 'violated his banishment from this city due to poverty, so as to make an honest living', and Moses Cohen was described as a 'brazen beggar'.[405] Manuel da Sylva, accused of attacking people on the street, admitted he was supported by 'Jewish charity',[406] and Sara Abiatar was said to have murdered her children due to 'poverty, grief and debt'.[407]

Ordinary jobs did not earn these delinquents much of a wage, and many of them had large families to support.[408] That must have been why some people severed their ties with any religious organization and earned a living outside the law.

Such occupations as they had were not always specified. Some belonged to the lower middle class and worked as small independent businessmen, for example shopkeepers, publicans, or street vendors.[409] Quite a few were skilled workers—diamond-cutters, barbers, tobacco spinners, hatters, bombazine workers, cobblers, or candle makers.[410] Some were unskilled workers, especially in the eighteenth century.

Women often did lowly work as washerwomen and maids.[411] Others ran brothels in their homes, where Jews could meet 'Christian women'.[412] While in Amsterdam, as elsewhere in the Dutch Republic, the judicial archives make many references to Ashkenazi women working as prostitutes, mentions of Portuguese prostitutes are few and far between.[413] One of them was Gracia Baruch, who confessed that, since being divorced from her husband David Athias in Amsterdam, she had made a living as a whore.[414]

We find brothel keepers among the men too, alongside publicans, ships' cooks, sailors, porters, menservants, and street musicians, reflecting the downward social mobility and growing poverty among the Amsterdam Sephardim at the time.[415] These men often combined several trades or pursued them in turn.[416] This pattern of employment coincides with that of most of the paupers in the Portuguese Jewish community in early modern Amsterdam.[417]

Unlike Ashkenazi crime, which occurred in both urban and rural environments,[418] criminal Sephardim were mostly active in the cities. Indeed, it was only in the cities that they could find fellow Sephardim—business partners and dealers, practising and non-observant Jews—to provide the infrastructure for their activities. Crime was committed on the streets or in warehouses, shops, and private homes, which were often adjacent to businesses. The most common items stolen were money, gold and silver (including jewellery), textiles (linen, lace, wool, damask, silk, clothes), and food products (cacao, chocolate), all of which could easily and quickly be sold or exchanged at pawnshops or in other shops or sold to goldsmiths, silversmiths, and other Jewish or Dutch traders.[419]

Sephardi Jews, like their Ashkenazi counterparts, also moved abroad to commit crime, taking no account of geographical borders. The Ashkenazim mainly operated on the eastern routes, towards central and eastern Europe and back, whereas the Sephardim concentrated on the routes between southern Europe and the north, actively commuting between Amsterdam, other cities in the Dutch Republic, Brussels, Ghent, Paris, and Spain, though also taking in Hamburg to the east and England to the west.[420] Antonio del Castillo, alias Abraham Santier, a comrade-in-theft of David Moreno in Amsterdam, shuttled between the Jewish and Catholic worlds, travelling around Spain with stolen Dutch merchandise.[421] Networks and international trade and migration routes were thus used not only by the well-to-do merchants among the Portuguese Jews, but also by the poor operating outside the law.

Some offenders were arrested and sentenced just once. The tobacco spinner Jacob Asoubie, for example, stole money at the Amsterdam fair in what seems to have been his only offence.[422] Many others, however, were repeat offenders, a common feature in the Dutch underworld. Over a period of three years Aron Sanches, a diamond-cutter who was about 20 years old, ended up in Amsterdam's prison twice for brawling, theft, and indecent assault. Jacob Moreno committed a string of offences over a period of thirty-three years, from 1682 to 1715. He was tried not only in Amsterdam, but also in Middelburg and Dordrecht.[423]

Most of the Sephardim referred to above had no declared religious affiliation. Unlike their Ashkenazi counterparts, those Sephardim who turned to crime did not identify themselves as Jews as a matter of principle.[424] Delinquent Sephardim did not participate in the religious life of the Portuguese Jewish community. Some changed their religion—once or more than once; some just did not want to be affiliated with any institutionalized community. The brothel keeper Manuel Mercado lived with a Christian mistress, with whom he had eight children.[425] Isaac Fidanque, found guilty of bankruptcy and adultery, was born a Jew, but became a Christian at the age of 28.[426] After her divorce, Gracia Baruch left Amsterdam for Brussels and converted to Catholicism, which she said lost her the esteem of her friends.[427] Sara Jacobs Mettera told the judges in Amsterdam that she had been a Christian in Hamburg before she became a Jew in Amsterdam, but joined the Lutheran community there later.[428] Her son took the same religious route, but was apparently rejected by the Lutheran community after he was arrested. He said that the first thing he would do on his release would be to renounce the Jewish faith.[429] David de Solis was released on the condition that he sail for Brazil—which in 1675 meant also switching to a Catholic environment.[430] For Sephardim on the margins of society, religion did not really matter.

In brief, although they kept their distance from official community circles, Sephardim involved in crime seem to have had social and professional connections with their fellow Sephardim and with non-Jews as well. In fact they were more familiar with both those groups than with the Ashkenazi underworld. Apparently, acculturation to the Dutch environment was not a phenomenon exclusive to the Portuguese Jewish elite of the Republic, but also applied among the lower strata of the Dutch Sephardim.

Solidarity

Unsurprisingly, the Amsterdam Portuguese Jewish community rarely interceded with the courts on behalf of criminal Sephardim. Only occasionally did it try to get them released from prison.[431] Individuals acting on their own initiative would also take steps to deal with criminal elements, often by contriving to have them expelled from the country or thrown into prison rather than being allowed to return to the community. For example, 'several Jews' arranged for a letter of safe conduct to Tunis for Jacob Moreno,[432] and friends of Abraham Herera applied to have him put into jail and then released on condition that he would take a ship to the Dutch East Indies.[433]

In general the community was only too glad to be rid of criminal elements and wanted nothing to do with them. After all, in accordance with the statutes of 1639, the community authorities were obliged to dissociate themselves from the case once a member of their *nação* had been caught by the magistrate. Practical experience clearly played a part in the framing of the relevant article, for as early as the beginning of the seventeenth century (and as late as the latter part of the eighteenth century) the city was intervening in disturbances or criminal acts committed by members of the Portuguese congregation, expelling the culprits from the city or throwing them into prison.[434] Often the city acted at the express request of the Portuguese community.[435] In 1636, for instance, the Portuguese community advised the city council to have all Portuguese miscreants who caused disturbances in the city deported to the East Indies; other, later, such cases have already been mentioned. The city helped to ensure that the reputation of the Portuguese community was not permanently besmirched and that its good name in Amsterdam was preserved.[436]

Happy as it was to get rid of troublemakers, however, the community did look after the wives and children of the excommunicated, the exiled, and the imprisoned. The children of Isaac de Casseres, for example, were supported when they fell into great need after the imprisonment of their father.[437] Assistance was given to the daughters of Samuel Aboab the moment their father got into trouble for spying for the Spanish Inquisition.[438] The wife and children of the 'devil of Vlooyenburg', who was not only unfaithful to his wife but, like Aboab, also engaged in espionage,[439] were also supported by the Portuguese Jewish community.[440] The *kahal* provided assistance for the wife of Juda Cohen Berberisco after her husband's excommunication and departure for Italy.[441] The Portuguese community, as the responsible authority, thus gave these women and their families a chance to preserve their honour in a protected environment, to keep their children on the right track, and to ensure their (Jewish) future.

Conclusion: A Motley Crowd

Paupers in the Portuguese community came in all shapes and sizes. On the one hand there were those who depended for their income partly or wholly on the Portuguese community and accordingly kept a low profile. Then there were the agitators and other people with deviant attitudes, over whom the Portuguese community still exerted some authority. They might have their poor relief cut, be excommunicated from the community, or be expelled from the city. Finally, the community also included a small nucleus of impecunious people who, independent of every institution, felt wonderfully at home in the non-Jewish criminal circuit, maintained various contacts with it, and knew how to hold their own in it. The Portuguese community had hardly any hold on this group and preferred to keep its distance from them, afraid as it was of compromising its own honour and reputation. This last group was tenuously, if at all, associated with the *kahal* and many of its members had no religious affiliation of any kind. They frequently ended up in prison, in the workhouse, or on the scaffold, or were expelled for many years or indeed permanently from the city and province.[442]

Our sources provide no more than a limited view of the daily life of Sephardi paupers in early modern Amsterdam. However, small pieces of information gleaned here and there enable us to fill in pieces of the picture.

What were the most important characteristics of the Sephardi poor? Their life differed to some extent from that of other paupers in the city, with quite a few characteristic features of its own. In their small houses, rooms, and cellars, Sephardi paupers, men, women, and children, just like other indigents, searched desperately for a survival strategy. By all accounts they constituted a varied group, originating not only in territories under Spanish and Portuguese rule but also in centres of the contemporary Jewish world, each carrying his or her own cultural baggage. The idea that Amsterdam's Portuguese community was particularly generous may have been misplaced in an absolute sense, but the city nevertheless held out hopes of a better life for many outsiders. The reservoir of well-to-do Portuguese in Amsterdam, who provided many paupers not only with financial assistance but often with work, at home or overseas, exerted an enormous attraction on contemporary European Jewry.

In Amsterdam, the poor among the Portuguese Jewish community ranged from the highly educated to the illiterate. On the one hand there were those whose sense of honour debarred them from asking for poor relief, and on the other there were those described as inveterate beggars. There were men and women; large, complete families and fragmented units; and there were people left completely on their own. Some were healthy or young or both, others old or sick or both, with all sorts of variations between them. Many applied for poor relief no more than occasionally; others relied permanently on outside help.

The poor relief provided by the Portuguese community constituted no more than a supplement to income from work, private funds, and legacies, and help from friends, relatives, private charity, and other sources. Sephardi Jews who had no access to these sources, or who missed out in other ways, found themselves forced to seek their fortune elsewhere sooner or later.

Women, highly protected in the Iberian tradition, constituted a high proportion of those on permanent poor relief, especially in the seventeenth century. Some had come over on their own from their country of origin, having been widowed, abandoned temporarily or permanently, or unable to find a suitable marriage partner. Whether educated or not, they were involved in various branches of the Portuguese economy.

The economic restrictions placed on Jews in Amsterdam determined the range of occupations open to them. With the help of 'an economy of makeshifts', to use Olwen Hufton's term, they engaged in a wide range of activities to make ends meet.[443] When employment was scarce in Amsterdam, some tried their luck overseas or sent their children abroad.

There was keen competition in the labour market, so that anyone who had a job was anxious to keep it. On the other hand, some occupations were considered to be beyond the pale, thanks to the persistence of Iberian cultural prejudices. Those who refused to do such work, for example trading in second-hand goods or street vending, were apparently supported by their superiors, that is, by the leaders of the Portuguese community, and also by relatives and friends, who preferred to assist those of their less fortunate brethren who received too little poor relief by supporting them in Amsterdam or helping them to procure work outside the Republic rather than forcing them into what they considered unacceptably inferior occupations.

This protective attitude on the part of the Portuguese elite also had a reverse side. By strict supervision of behaviour and selective admission to poor relief, the upper stratum of Portuguese society tried to keep its paupers under control and to hide their poverty from the outside world. This explains why the decision-making process in the granting of poor relief was rarely recorded.

Petitions requesting help generally show us paupers who treat their superiors with humility, obedience, and respect. After all, they were seeking a benefit and had to satisfy the selective criteria. Hence in the early modern period the poor thought it best to avoid misconduct, dissension, or protest. In Amsterdam, poor Sephardim had hardly any alternative if they were to escape social isolation, an uncertain material future, or expulsion from the city. That is why the great majority of them chose to participate in the life of the Portuguese community. Their conversion to Judaism was thus probably based less on purely religious considerations than on socio-economic factors.[444]

Yet not everybody was prepared to be subservient to the elite. Protest among paupers gradually swelled in the seventeenth century and grew even louder as the eighteenth century progressed. Side by side with those drawing poor relief, there was also a group who preferred to live on the fringes of society and managed to keep their heads above water in that way.

The majority of the poor who were able to survive in early modern Amsterdam within the Portuguese community must not be imagined as the beggars or vagrants Rembrandt so often painted.[445] Although poor relief was far from lavish, wages and supplementary forms of assistance clearly enabled paupers to survive, most of them without being forced to live a marginal existence.

CHAPTER EIGHT

EPILOGUE

THIS BOOK has focused on poverty and welfare in an early modern Jewish community of world renown. Many subjects have passed under review. Although the story centres on one city, it does not begin and end in Amsterdam, or indeed in the Dutch Republic, for it has international ramifications.

We have looked at the slow but steady process of migration of poor people into the Amsterdam Portuguese community from early in the seventeenth century to late in the eighteenth. This was a time of high mobility across the western world, of people coming and going, including many Jews and (former) Conversos circulating from the Iberian peninsula throughout the Sephardi diaspora, travelling in Europe, the Levant, North Africa, and the New World, often with Amsterdam as the hub of their journeys. These continuous movements were not a phenomenon unique to the Jewish world, but were characteristic of the behaviour of many people in pre-industrial Europe.[1]

The Jews arriving in the city included nuclear families but also broken units, each with a history of its own, and single individuals. Overall, more Jews from other regions than Conversos from territories under Spanish and Portuguese rule came to the Portuguese community of Amsterdam; but people belonging to 'the nation', *a nação portuguesa e espanhola*, wherever they came from, were generally allowed to join the community as permanent members, whereas those of other 'nationalities' remained peripheral. All these new arrivals were drawn by the city's reputation. This renown was not undeserved. Speaking in relative terms, Amsterdam formed a heaven in the contemporary Jewish arena: no ghettos, no *numerus fixus*, no collective tax; religious freedom in a rising centre of global economic activity, where prosperity had created a rich upper class, among the Portuguese Jews as in the wider city. This glowing image inspired many poor Jews and Conversos everywhere to pack up and go to see it for themselves. In Amsterdam there was hope: hope for work, in the city and overseas; hope for material well-being; hope for freedom and an existence without fear; hope for a Jewish life without limitations. Religious impulses thus went hand in hand with socio-economic motives in the desire of many Jews and Conversos to settle in Amsterdam.

The influx of poor people rapidly posed severe problems for the Portuguese of Amsterdam that became more serious as time passed by. The rising tide of poverty took the leaders of the community by surprise. It had never intended to create a reception centre to which all Jews would have unrestricted access, and certainly did not intend to provide permanent support for the Jewish poor from all over the world. It did indeed help those in distress, especially on their first arrival. It considered many cases individually and kept its doors open to those seeking help, at least officially, until the middle of the eighteenth century. In this respect the Amsterdam Portuguese community was much more liberal than any other Jewish or Christian community at the time. And if the official channels could not or would not listen to the pleas of the poor and help them, there was always the ever-growing range of private welfare organizations they could try. Moreover, there were private individuals who were inclined to spend a part of their fortune on the poor. All of these people and organizations were motivated to help, in principle. Yet from an early stage the welfare system also built in limits to stem the tide, even though these restrictions were not far-reaching enough to keep the quantity of the poor manageable and in reasonable relation to the size of the community.

In his address to the Portuguese leaders in Amsterdam in 1642, Menasseh ben Israel praised the welfare system of his community: 'You are not the heads and leaders of just another *Kehilá*, but of one of the most famous that is known in the *Galut*. Just look at the *misvot* [i.e. *mitsvot*] and *Hebrot* with which it is enriched . . . these help a whole class of poor in life and death.'[2] The fame of welfare provision among the Amsterdam Portuguese was certainly well deserved when it came to the level and range of poor relief provided for refugees from the Iberian peninsula, by both the public and the private sectors. It was for them, after all, that the community had been established and them that it was intended to accommodate; and the community made continuous efforts to preserve its Converso character, which was not a natural fact but a matter of will, requiring constant vigilance. This selective sense of solidarity was very much in evidence in matters of welfare, where different criteria were applied to claimants from different ethnic backgrounds. The traditional Jewish principle of mutual responsibility was applied here with a clear bias: non-Sephardi Jews were excluded or, at best, received inferior treatment. Surprisingly, a further bias was also evident within the Sephardi milieu, with poor Portuguese from territories under Spanish and Portuguese rule or the western Sephardi diaspora receiving superior treatment to that accorded to the Sephardim setting out from the south-east and the Levant. Anyone who did not meet the requisite criteria was, in effect, shown the door and covertly or overtly sent out of the city. This kind of selectivity was not confined to Sephardi Jews in early modern Amsterdam: both in the period under study here and earlier, similarly discriminatory practices were applied in other parts of the Jewish world. Christian churches, too, did not always extend poor relief to paupers from other denominations and backgrounds.

Charitable behaviour, public and private, was determined by many factors. Religious impulses remained the most important throughout the early modern period. Besides the basic values of Judaism, in which help for fellow Jews was an imperative, the community was eager to keep ex-Conversos loyal to the community and the Jewish faith, to prevent them choosing an existence on the margins of Jewish society or leaving it altogether, for example by joining the Reformed Church, returning to Catholicism, or staying aloof from any religious denomination. Rationality was another driving force: the community was obliged to adopt a strategy of control to keep internal order and to maintain its position vis-à-vis the city authorities. The Portuguese establishment thus made a point of camouflaging poverty in its ranks, the better to keep up appearances towards the outside world and to maintain its status in the city.

The Portuguese in Amsterdam shared a sense of civic responsibility: they knew that social order was an essential condition of their community's survival and supplied the administration with the financial tools to establish and maintain it. Portuguese Jews of early modern Amsterdam were also impelled by a concern for the well-being and honour of the family and that of the 'extended' or substitute family formed by the *nação*, (former) Conversos. Prestige, always important to Portuguese Jews, was another significant motivation in matters of *sedaca*.

The community and its members, together and separately, through an ever-widening network of charitable organizations, built a welfare system that took shape along Jewish lines but was also inspired by early modern ideas and practices on poor relief and drew on certain Iberian and Catholic influences. The result can therefore be characterized as a mixture of modern cultural features within well-established, traditional patterns.

Welfare provision among the Portuguese in early modern Amsterdam is thus best seen as a socio-cultural phenomenon characteristic of Iberian and early modern European society, rather than as one based purely on traditional Jewish conceptions. It reflects a deeply entrenched and long-lived cultural continuity rather than any radical Jewish structure imposed from above, as Yosef Kaplan has demonstrated.[3] At their best, in respect of charity as in other areas, Portuguese Jews in early modern Amsterdam constituted a patchwork culture, to use Daniel Swetschinski's term,[4] drawing on elements from a wide variety of sources.

Indigents among the Portuguese Jews of early modern Amsterdam were atypical of paupers of this period, as generally depicted. Even though institutionalization gained purchase over time, many of them were genteel paupers and assisted discreetly by means of domiciliary care, preferring to hide class-consciously behind a façade of grandeur. Honour and a sense of shame played a significant role here. In terms of education and occupation, these paupers ranged from highly educated persons to unskilled labourers.

One remarkable feature of the poor in the Amsterdam Portuguese milieu is the prominence of women, until recently hardly considered. This should not come to us as a great surprise: in many cities of early modern Europe women made up the majority of the recipients of charity. Even so, the proportion of Portuguese women on poor relief was exceptionally high. The reasons for this were manifold: as a key group in the effort to perpetuate Jewish tradition in the peninsula, women were consistently persecuted by the Inquisition and many fled in fear of it, as well as out of the desire to live openly as Jews. Also, economic opportunities for men outside the Dutch Republic led to many women being left on their own in the city, dependent on welfare. Finally, there was a limited supply of Jewish partners and a lack of financial resources to enable couples to start out in married life. That explains the large number of dowries on offer and other welfare institutions set up specifically for women, in the attempt to solve an acute social problem. Their position was rendered even more vulnerable by the high degree of protection that women enjoyed within the Amsterdam Portuguese community, as they did in the Iberian peninsula: this left them ill-equipped to earn their own living when they had to.

The poor relief provided by the Portuguese community was not exceptionally generous, at least when judged by Amsterdam standards, nor was it granted permanently to all poor people. A reasonable standard of living could be maintained by combining income from work or other sources and drawing on all sources made available to those meeting the criteria for eligibility. The system was hierarchical and elitist, presided over by a closed, wealthy caste who ran a strict regime. Supervision of morals was keen and every form of deviant behaviour punished. Those who lacked the necessary contacts with, or goodwill of, the Portuguese establishment could not count on anything more than minimal assistance; the *kahal* preferred to wash its hands of them, ever more readily as time passed and the Portuguese community became increasingly hard pressed to render permanent assistance to a growing army of the poor with the limited resources it had at its disposal.

Thus for many poor people the reality was considerably less rosy than they had expected. The economic restrictions the city had imposed on Jews only served to make their lives more arduous. Portuguese Jews were also hampered by the attitude to work they had brought to Amsterdam from the Iberian peninsula, which made many of them reluctant to do heavy, dirty, lowly, or servile work; this insistence that others do the least attractive jobs further restricted their options in the labour market. In the course of the eighteenth century, however, this trend slowly changed, partly as rising poverty made such scruples an unaffordable luxury, partly because for many second- and third-generation immigrants the Iberian heritage and culture belonged to a more distant past.

Only a very few paupers turned to begging, prostitution, or criminality. That situation was, in a sense, kept alive artificially by the strictly selective policy designed to keep out undesirable elements, a policy also adopted in many other parts of the Jewish world.[5] Rich and poor alike had an interest in the smooth running of poor relief and depended on each other in achieving this. The poor, for their part, were waging a struggle for survival and needed the rich to support them. With adequate help and the creation of work opportunities, they could look after their own existence and safeguard the future of their children.[6]

It has proved difficult to probe the feelings of these paupers and to place them in three-dimensional clarity against the background of the Amsterdam 'Jewish district'. This is, of course, the constant frustration of historical research on the poor. We can hear them appealing for help in petitions, sometimes obsequiously, sometimes insistently. They tell us at times about what they had been through or about the desperate situations in which they found themselves. Many must have hankered after their former prosperity. Occasionally we catch glimpses of their frugal existence inside their cramped dwellings in the narrow streets, alleyways, and passages of the city. We also gather that poverty was not always crippling. We watch them here and there at their various jobs, in their workrooms, in their shops, inside the walls of the Portuguese synagogue, or simply at home, searching for the best survival strategy. A few managed to climb the ladder to a higher social status, though most did not. A third group decided to leave a community that could not fulfil their dreams and continue their search elsewhere.

Meanwhile, by the middle of the eighteenth century, the Amsterdam Portuguese community had lost its international attraction as a place of refuge. By this time the community, overloaded with people on welfare, was only a poor shadow of its former glory and had lost its reputation as a city of *ḥesed, sedaca,* and *gemilut ḥasadim* throughout the contemporary Jewish world.

TABLES

Table 1

Heads of family drawing poor relief, not given in the Amsterdam *ondertrouw* registers, by place of origin, 1598–1699

Place of origin	1598–1639		1640–69		1670–99		Total no.	Aggregate %
	No.	(%)	No.	(%)	No.	(%)		
Portugal	>12	(11)	>14	(3)	>10	(2)	>36	3
Spain	8	(7)	>79	(18)	40	(6)	>127	11
France	>18	(16)	55	(12)	81	(12)	>154	13
Italy	>34	(30)	147	(33)	145	(22)	>326	27
New World	3	(3)	>35	(8)	16	(2)	>54	5
N. Africa	>10	(9)	>35	(8)	43	(7)	>88	7
SE. Europe & Levant	>12	(10)	31	(7)	243	(37)	>286	24
Erets Yisra'el	4	(3)	11	(3)	23	(3)	38	3
Hamburg	8	(7)	21	(5)	24	(4)	53	4
Antwerp			1		6	(1)	7	
London	>3	(3)	9	(2)	5	(1)	>17	1
Other	1	(1)	6	(1)	17	(3)	24	2
Total known	>113	(100)	>444	(100)	>653	(100)	>1,210	100

Note: Ashkenazim from the German states and from eastern Europe are not included. I did not calculate, specify, and compare numbers and places for the eighteenth century, because of the severe lacunae in the data on places of origin.

Source: SAA entry no. 334, nos. 3–6, 9–10, 13, 17, 172–4, 215–20.

Table 2

Portuguese brides and grooms registering their marriage at City Hall, by place of origin (other than Amsterdam), 1700–1800 (numbers)

Place of origin	1700–29		1730–59		1760–89		1790–1800		Total
	M	F	M	F	M	F	M	F	
Portugal	55	27	39	26	16	6	1		170
Spain	36	21	32	31					120
France	47	38	32	25	14	2	6	3	167
Italy	57	19	43	11	16	6	12	1	165
New World	24	7	15	10	12	6	5	1	80
N. Africa	20	2	18	1	3		2		46
SE. Europe & Levant	14	7	6		7	1	2		37
Hamburg, German states, Denmark	66	70	32	23	16	7	3	3	220
Southern Netherlands	5	13	4	2					24
London	19	24	9	19	8	8	5	2	94
Dutch Republic[a]	7	35	28	28	18	28	4	3	151
Gibraltar			7	1	4	3			15
Avignon			3						3
Batavia						2			2
Cochin	1								1
Vienna	1								1
Sweden							1	1	2
Total	352	263	268	177	114	69	41	14	1,298

[a] Other than Amsterdam.

Key: M = males; F = females

Source: Verdooner and Snel, *Trouwen in Mokum*.

Table 3

Portuguese brides and grooms registering their marriage at City Hall, by place of origin (other than Amsterdam), 1700–1800 (%)

Place of origin	1700–29		1730–59		1760–89		1790–1800		Aggregate
	M	F	M	F	M	F	M	F	
Portugal	16	10	15	15	14	9	2		13
Spain	10	8	12	17					9
France	13	14	12	14	12	3	15	21	13
Italy	16	7	16	6	14	9	29	7	13
New World	7	3	5	6	11	9	12	7	6
N. Africa	6	1	7	0.5	3		5		4
SE. Europe & Levant	4	3	2		6	1	5		3
Hamburg, German states, Denmark	19	27	12	13	14	10	7	21	17
Southern Netherlands	1	5	2	1					2
London	5	9	3	11	7	11	12	14	7
Dutch Republic[a]	2	13	10	16	16	41	10	21	12
Gibraltar			3	0.5	3	4			1
Avignon			1						
Batavia						3			
Cochin	0.5								
Vienna	0.5								
Sweden							2	7	
Total	100	100	100	100	100	100	100	100	100

[a] Other than Amsterdam.
Key: M = males; F = females

Source: Verdooner and Snel, *Trouwen in Mokum*.

Table 4

Heads of family receiving money from the Amsterdam Portuguese community to emigrate, by destination, 1598–1759 (numbers)

Destination	1598–1639	1640–69	1670–99	1700–29	1730–59	Total
France		4	>97	224	75	>400
Italy	47	>34	291	549	52	>973
New World	6	31	217	271	115	640
N. Africa	3	7	47	77	9	143
SE Europe & Levant	2	3	78	93	14	190
Erets Yisra'el	27	12	46	63	7	155
Hamburg & German states	21	17	>151	172	25	>386
London	1	5	201	609	96	912
Flanders			9	15	11	35
Gibraltar				13		13
Ireland				2		2
Denmark				5		5
Poland				3		3
Naples					4	4
Dutch Republic[a]				12		12
Unknown	>79	>57	>353	41	1,539	>2,069
Total	>186	>170	>1,490	2,149	1,947	>5,942

[a] Other than Amsterdam.

Source: SAA entry no. 334, nos. 3–6, 9–10, 13, 17, 172–4, 215–23, 969–70.

Table 5

Heads of family receiving money from the Amsterdam Portuguese community to emigrate, by destination, 1598–1759 (%)

Destination	1598–1639	1640–69	1670–99	1700–29	1730–59	Aggregate
France		3	6	10	4	7
Italy	25	20	20	25	3	16
New World	3	18	15	13	6	11
N. Africa	2	4	3	4		2
SE. Europe & Levant	1	2	5	4	1	3
Erets Yisra'el	14	7	3	3		3
Hamburg & German states	11	10	10	8	1	7
London	1	3	13	28	5	15
Flanders			1	1	1	1
Gibraltar				1		
Ireland						
Denmark						
Poland						
Naples						
Dutch Republic[a]				1		
Unknown	43	33	24	2	79	35
Total	100	100	100	100	100	100

[a] Other than Amsterdam.

Source: SAA entry no. 334, nos. 3–6, 9–10, 13, 17, 172–4, 215–23, 969–70.

Table 6

Sex ratio of foreigners on poor relief, by origin, 1598–1699 (no. of women per 100 men)

Place of origin	1598–1639	1640–69	1670–99
Portugal	140	100	—
Spain	100	130	200
France	125	187	65
Italy	3	15	14
New World	33	28	17
N. Africa	50	6	38
SE Europe & Levant	9	3	26
Hamburg	34	12	41
Antwerp	—	—	80
London	—	29	—

Source: SAA entry no. 334, nos. 3–6, 9–10, 13, 17, 172–4, 215–20.

Table 7

Number of Sephardi Jews in Amsterdam and their percentage of the city's population, 1650–*c*.1795

Year	No. of Sephardi Jews in Amsterdam	% of total population of city
1650	1,990 (1,400)[a]	—
1675	2,713 (2,230)[a]	1.4
1700	4,017 (3,000)[a]	1.76
c.1730	4,554 (3,000)[b]	1.90
c.1750	4,583 (2,800)[a]	1.92
c.1795	4,003 (2,800)[c]	1.86

[a] Figure in parentheses according to Israel (see 'sources' below).
[b] Figure in parentheses for 1725 according to Israel.
[c] Figure in parentheses according to Bureau of Statistics (no data in Israel).

Sources: See calculations in Table 8 below. See further Israel, 'The Republic of the United Netherlands', 100; Vaz Dias, 'Amsterdamsche Jodenkwartier', 32; M. van Leeuwen and Oeppen, 'Reconstructing the Demographic Regime of Amsterdam', 87. For the years 1650 and 1675, the calculations in Nusteling, *Welvaart en werkgelegenheid in Amsterdam*, apps. 1.3 and 2.1, have been used. The figures for Amsterdam's population in 1700–95 are based on the data in M. van Leeuwen and Oeppen, 'Reconstructing the Demographic Regime of Amsterdam'.

Table 8
Number of Sephardi families paying taxes or drawing poor relief, 1640/1–*c*.1795

Year[a]	Paying tax			Drawing poor relief			Total	% of Sephardi population on relief	
	Finta	*Promessa*	Overall	Permanent	Temporary	Overall		Permanent	Any
1640/1	185	113	298	56	90	146	444	13	33
1644/5	250	93	343	75	49	124	467	16	26
1650/1	308	134	442	115	46	161	603	19	27
1655/6	331	181	512	123	61	184	696	18	26
1660/1	373	164	537	135	86	221	758	18	29
1665/6	377	139	516	150	144	294	810	18	36
1670/1	382	173	555	160	78	238	793	20	30
1675/6	450	64	514	141	98	239	753	19	32
1680/1	442	35	477	154	101	255	732	21	35
1685/6	441	84	525	169	152	321	846	20	38
1690/1	417	100	517	223	137	360	877	25	41
1695/6	423	109	532	278	121	399	931	30	43
1700/1	478	175	653	299	166	465	1,118	27	42
c.1730	453	83	536	702	163	865	1,401	50	62
c.1750	417	199	616	517	227	744	1,360	38	55
c.1770	406	172	578	478	187	665	1,243	38	53
c.1795[b]	489	122	611	480	178	658	1,269	38	52

[a] 'Year' here refers to the bookkeeping year, which started each spring after the Passover holidays and ended just before them.

[b] Figures include widows and other women (160 in total) charged the *finta* tax since 1791.

Source: SAA entry no. 334, nos. 172–6, 179, 277, 288, 290, 974–6.

Table 9

Finta-paying and non-*finta*-paying families in relation to the total number of Sephardi families in Amsterdam, 1650/1–*c*.1795

Year	Total families[a]	Not liable to *finta*		Heads of family assessed for *finta*, by assessment of general wealth (guilders)									
				100–500[b]		550–1,250[c]		1,300–2,500[d]		2,550–5,000[e]		5,050 and over[f]	
	No.	No.	(%)	No.	(%)	No.	(%)	No.	(%)	No.	(%)	No.	(%)
1650/1	603	295	(49)	176	(29)	92	(15)	33	(6)	7	(1)	0	
1675/6	753	303	(40)	153	(20)	130	(17)	104	(14)	41	(6)	22	(3)
1700/1	1,118	640	(57)	241	(22)	112	(10)	70	(6)	37	(3)	18	(2)
c.1730	1,401	948	(68)	192	(14)	133	(9)	52	(4)	37	(3)	39	(3)
c.1750	1,360	943	(69)	200	(15)	109	(8)	51	(4)	24	(2)	33	(2)
c.1770	1,243	837	(67)	173	(14)	99	(8)	65	(5)	32	(3)	37	(3)
c.1795[g]	1,269	780	(61)	247	(19)	98	(8)	58	(5)	34	(3)	52	(4)

[a] *Finta*-paying families and families on poor relief registered with the Portuguese community.
[b] Corresponding to an annual *finta* tax of 2–10 guilders.
[c] Corresponding to an annual *finta* tax of 11–25 guilders.
[d] Corresponding to an annual *finta* tax of 26–50 guilders.
[e] Corresponding to an annual *finta* tax of 51–100 guilders.
[f] Corresponding to an annual *finta* tax of 101–208 guilders.
[g] Figures include widows and other women (160 in total) charged the *finta* tax since 1791.

Source: SAA entry no. 334, nos. 173–4, 176, 179, 277, 288, 290.

Table 10

Heads of family with a *finta* tax liability of 2–10 guilders, 1650–1790

Year	Number	Of which assessed at 2–4 guilders[a]	
		No.	%
1650	176	86	49
1675	153	50	33
1700	241	123	51
1733	192	76	39
1750	200	89	44
1770	173	70	40
1790	161	55	34

[a] A *finta* liability of 2–4 guilders corresponds to a general wealth of 100–200 guilders, assuming 2% as the basis of assessments made by the *parnasim*. In the early modern period, the poverty line fell at an annual income of about 200 guilders.

Source: SAA entry no. 334, nos. 173–4, 176, 179, 288, 290.

Table 11

Households on poor relief (temporary or permanent) by sex of head of family, 1650/1–*c*.1795

Year[a]	Families on relief	Head of family		Ratio of male to female heads
		Male	Female	
1650/1	161	58	103	36 : 64
1675/6	239	107	132	45 : 55
1700/1	465	215	250	46 : 54
c.1730	865	571	294	66 : 34
c.1750	744	452	292	61 : 39
c.1770	665	420	245	63 : 37
c.1795	658	407	251	62 : 38

[a] 'Year' here refers to the bookkeeping year, which started each spring after the Passover holidays and ended just before them.

Source: SAA entry no. 334, nos. 20, 173–4, 176, 216, 220, 974–96.

Table 12

Households on permanent poor relief by sex of head of family, 1650/1–*c.*1795

Year[a]	Families on permanent poor relief	Head of family: Male	Head of family: Female	Ratio of male to female heads
1650/1	115	20	95	17:83
1675/6	141	48	93	34:66
1700/1	299	110	189	37:63
*c.*1730	702	447	255	64:36
*c.*1750	517	268	249	52:48
*c.*1770	478	276	202	58:42
*c.*1795	480	262	218	55:45

[a] 'Year' here refers to the bookkeeping year, which started each spring after the Passover holidays and ended just before them.

Source: SAA entry no. 334, nos. 173, 176, 216–17, 220, 974–96.

Table 13

Size of families on poor relief (temporary or permanent), 1650/1–*c.*1795

Year[a]	Families on relief	No. of people in household: 1		2		3		4		5 or more	
		No.	(%)	No.	(%)	No.	(%)	No.	(%)	No.	(%)
1650/1	161	47	(29)	40	(25)	28	(17)	15	(9)	31	(19)
1675/6	239	72	(30)	48	(20)	38	(16)	22	(9)	59	(25)
1700/1	465	111	(24)	125	(27)	85	(18)	51	(11)	93	(20)
*c.*1730	865	295	(34)	162	(19)	144	(17)	88	(10)	176	(20)
*c.*1750	744	270	(36)	180	(24)	99	(13)	78	(11)	117	(16)
*c.*1770	665	235	(35)	135	(20)	75	(11)	67	(10)	153	(23)
*c.*1795	658	244	(37)	134	(20)	71	(11)	71	(11)	138	(21)

[a] 'Year' here refers to the bookkeeping year, which started each spring after the Passover holidays and ended just before them.

Source: SAA entry no. 334, nos. 173, 176, 216–17, 220, 974–6.

Table 14

Families on poor relief: sex of family head, by size of household, 1650/1–*c*.1795 (%)

Year[a]	No. of people in household									
	1		2		3		4		5 or more	
	M	F	M	F	M	F	M	F	M	F
1650/1	6	94	33	67	43	57	60	40	70	30
1675/6	17	83	46	54	42	58	59	41	75	25
1700/1	32	68	32	68	52	48	61	39	68	32
c.1730	53	47	70	30	71	29	80	20	80	20
c.1750	41	59	56	44	75	25	80	20	92	8
c.1770	41	59	65	35	72	28	74	26	87	13
c.1795	42	58	65	35	65	35	81	19	86	14

[a] 'Year' here refers to the bookkeeping year, which started each spring after the Passover holidays and ended just before them.
Key: M = males; F = females

Source: SAA entry no. 334, nos. 173, 176, 216, 217, 220, 974–6.

Table 15

Deficits reflected in the *sedaca* account (community income and expenditure on welfare and other items) of the Portuguese community, 1648/9–1793/4 (guilders)

Year[a]	Deficit	Year[a]	Deficit	Year[a]	Deficit	Year[a]	Deficit
1648/9	2,954	1665/6	6,302	1683/4	1,600	1727/8	10,583
1652/3	828	1666/7	749	1686/7	1,498	1739/40	14,017
1653/4	946	1667/8	1,576	1691/2	280	1740/1	26,880
1656/7	6,895	1668/9	1,633	1693/4	4,869	1741/2	31,708
1657/8	9,414	1672/3	3,674	1694/5	4,260	1747/8	8,279
1661/2	1,082	1673/4	3,289	1696/7	2,815	1748/9	4,282
1662/3	3,384	1681/2	293	1697/8	3,927	1775/6	22,296
1664/5	3,145	1682/3	5,247	1698/9	306	1793/4	19,412

[a] 'Year' here refers to the bookkeeping year, which started each spring after the Passover holidays and ended just before them.

Source: SAA entry no. 334, nos. 239–42, 246–8, 251, 254.

Table 16

Proceeds of *finta* and *imposta*, 1640/1–1697/8 (guilders)

Year[a]	*Finta*	*Imposta*	Year[a]	*Finta*	*Imposta*	Year[a]	*Finta*	*Imposta*
1640/1	4,659	5,016	1660/1	5,746	9,751	1680/1	9,864	2,214
1641/2	4,923	5,859	1661/2	5,666	8,895	1681/2	9,290	1,446
1642/3	5,320	6,761	1662/3	6,128	8,417	1682/3	9,034	2,846
1643/4	5,593	6,353	1663/4	5,632	12,122	1683/4	9,409	1,394
1644/5	6,405	7,318	1664/5	5,680	5,897	1684/5	9,541	2,146
1645/6	6,609	5,965	1665/6	5,669	5,518	1685/6	9,847	2,555
1646/7	7,179	7,531	1666/7	9,713	7,774	1686/7	10,087	2,057
1647/8	5,589	8,674	1667/8	6,099	5,777	1687/8	10,241	1,441
1648/9	3,894	8,374	1668/9	5,867	6,488	1688/9	10,136	1,645
1649/50	4,049	10,939	1669/70	5,767	5,284	1689/90	9,845	1,691
1650/1	4,205	9,365	1670/1	5,673	6,954	1690/1	9,769	3,638
1651/2	4,466	9,613	1671/2	5,468	7,004	1691/2	9,637	2,710
1652/3	4,388	6,865	1672/3	5,684	2,491	1692/3	9,771	1,865
1653/4	4,267	7,829	1673/4	5,188	3,704	1693/4	9,704	1,222
1654/5	4,429	8,852	1674/5	11,832	5,574	1694/5	9,599	2,751
1655/6	4,782	9,196	1675/6	13,833	2,410	1695/6	14,982	2,352
1656/7	4,935	9,779	1676/7	14,204	1,747	1696/7	9,798	2,118
1657/8	5,041	7,814	1677/8	12,356	1,762	1697/8	9,738	2,933
1658/9	5,349	7,877	1678/9	10,440	1,326			
1659/60	5,478	7,546	1679/80	10,523	2,144			

[a] 'Year' here refers to the bookkeeping year, which started each spring after the Passover holidays and ended just before them.

Source: SAA entry no. 334, nos. 172–6.

Table 17

Yearly yield of *promessas*, 1650/1–1654/5 (guilders)

Year[a]	1st collection[b]	2nd collection[b]	Total
1650/1	3,056	3,926	6,982
1651/2	2,801	3,725	6,526
1652/3	4,654	3,865	8,519
1653/4	3,384	4,011	7,395
1654/5	3,314	4,656	7,970

[a] 'Year' here refers to the bookkeeping year, which started each spring after the Passover holidays and ended just before them.

[b] The taxes were collected twice a year, first before the Jewish New Year, then again before Passover.

Source: SAA entry no. 334, nos. 172–4.

Table 18

Sedaca account: community income and deficit in relation to expenditure on welfare and other items, 1730/1–1749/50 (guilders)

Year[a]	Income	Deficit in relation to expenditure	Year[a]	Income	Deficit in relation to expenditure
1730/1	90,480	9,438	1740/1	83,959	26,880
1731/2	81,428	13,033	1741/2	78,108	31,708
1732/3	95,099	7,689	1742/3	79,097	6,778
1733/4	95,542	5,163	1743/4	76,220	7,464
1734/5	94,117	4,421	1744/5	85,031	78 credit
1735/6	91,167	5,411	1745/6	78,796	8,318
1736/7	92,358	9,932	1746/7	79,535	9,095
1737/8	88,251	7,000	1747/8	80,201	8,279
1738/9	90,221	10,627	1748/9	75,737	4,282
1739/40	87,108	14,017	1749/50	86,770	4,285 credit

[a] 'Year' here refers to the bookkeeping year, which started each spring after the Passover holidays and ended just before them.

Source: SAA entry no. 334, nos. 247–8.

Table 19

Portuguese testators leaving money to poor-relief institutions of the Amsterdam Portuguese community, 1600–1750, by state of health

State of health	No. of wills	Percentage
Healthy	13	25
Fair	4	7
Ill	30	57
Unknown	6	11
Total	53	100

Source: Last wills of Portuguese Jews in Amsterdam, recorded in the notarial archives and the archives of the Amsterdam Portuguese community for the period 1600–1750, all of them located in SAA.

Table 20

Portuguese testators leaving money to poor-relief institutions of the Amsterdam Portuguese community, 1600–1750, by marital status and sex

Marital status and sex	No. of wills	Percentage
Unmarried woman	3	6
Married woman	5	9
Widow	16	30
Unmarried man	4	8
Married man	13	24
Widower	8	15
Married couple	4	8
Total	53	100

Source: As for Table 19.

Table 21

Portuguese testators leaving money to poor-relief institutions of the Amsterdam Portuguese community, 1600–1750: size of donations, by sex

Donation (guilders)	Men	Women	Married couples	Total
1–50		1		1
51–100	1	3		4
101–200	2	1		3
201–300	1	3		4
301–400	2	3		5
401–500	2	3		5
501–1,000	4	2	1	7
1,001–2,000	1	2		3
2,001–3,000	4	2	1	7
3,001–5,000	1	1	1	3
Over 5,000	7	3	1	11
Total	25	24	4	53

Source: As for Table 19.

Table 22

Portuguese testators leaving money to poor-relief institutions of the Amsterdam Portuguese community, 1600–1750: size of donations, by taxation class (*finta*)

Donation (guilders)	Annual tax (guilders)					
	2–10	11–25	26–50	51–100	Over 100	Total
1–50	1					1
51–100	1		1			2
101–200	1		1			2
201–300						
301–400	1	1				2
401–500	1			1		2
501–1,000		1				1
1,001–2,000	1					1
2,001–3,000			1	1		2
3,001–5,000					2	2
Over 5,000	2			3	2	7
Total	8	2	3	5	4	22[a]

[a] Of the Portuguese testators, I was able to find the *finta* tax data of twenty-two males only.

Sources: SAA, entry no. 334, nos. 172–80 (*manual*), and as for Table 19.

Table 23

Sedaca account: community income and welfare expenditure, 1640/1–1793/4 (guilders)

Year	Community income	Welfare expenditure	Expenditure as % of income
1640/1	17,803	7,189	40
1650/1	25,682	14,897	58
1675/6	30,410	13,013	43
1699/1700	48,133	29,679	62
1729/30	90,871	57,748	63
1740/1	83,959	68,932	82
1750/1	81,790	42,447	52
1775/6	75,985	50,869	67
1793/4	81,980	51,948	63

Source: SAA entry no. 334, nos. 239, 240, 242, 248, 254.

Table 24

Comparison of yields of the *nedava* among the Amsterdam Sephardim in 1665/6 with yields of *nedavot* on other occasions (guilders)

Year	Context	Yield	Year	Context	Yield
1638	Illness	240	1665/6	Sabbatai Zevi	8,345
1638	Illness	619	1674	Time of war	380
1655	Poor from Brazil	3,697	1685/6	Support to French refugees	4,692
1656	Poor from Brazil	1,406	1693	Illness	312
1656	Epidemic of plague	1,016	1727	Illness/hot summer	4,008
1657	Support to Polish refugees	3,947	1741	Time of war/extreme need	1,798
1662–3	Cold, harsh winter	3,229			

Sources: *1638, illness*: SAA entry no. 334, no. 17, p. 67; *1655/6, poor from Brazil*: SAA entry no. 334, no. 174, p. 89; ibid., p. 145; *1656, plague*: SAA entry no. 334, no. 174, p. 136; *1657, Polish refugees*: SAA entry no. 334, no. 240, p. 53^v; *1662/3, harsh winter*: SAA entry no. 334, no. 174, pp. 537–40; *1665/6, Sabbatai Zevi*: SAA entry no. 334, no. 174, pp. 724–7; *1674, war*: SAA entry no. 334, no. 174, p. 1011; *1685/6, French refugees*: SAA entry no. 334, no. 175, pp. 305–16; *1693, illness*: SAA entry no. 334, no. 176, p. 148; *1727, illness/hot summer*: SAA entry no. 334, no. 246, p. 38; *1741, war/extreme need*: SAA entry no. 334, no. 180, p. 42. Compare also the collections made by non-Jewish institutions in Amsterdam in the 18th century, whose yields were mostly lower (M. van Leeuwen, 'Liefdadige giften', 434–8).

Table 25

Average value of poor relief paid by various charities *c.*1750, by size of family (guilders)

Charity	No. children in family		Form of relief
	Two	Four	
Municipal charity (NZ Huiszittenhuis)[a]	57	94	Money, bread, butter, peat
Municipal charity (OZ Huiszittenhuis)[b]	59	75	Money, bread, butter, peat
Reformed Church	97	136	Money, bread, peat, rent subsidy
Catholic Church	70	112	Money, bread, peat
Mennonites	122	140	Money, peat
Remonstrants	175	220	Money, peat, food
Portuguese Jewish community	78	95	Money, peat, matzot, rent subsidy, clothes

[a] The Nieuwezijds Huiszittenhuis was a municipal outdoor poor relief institution situated in the newer part of 17th-century Amsterdam.

[b] The Oudezijds Huiszittenhuis was a municipal outdoor poor relief institution situated in the older part of 17th-century Amsterdam.

Sources: M. van Leeuwen, Schoenmakers, and Smits, *Armoede en bedeling*, 9 (col. relating to 1750); SAA entry no. 334, nos. 249, 736, 970, 974, and 1187, 1752/5512.

Table 26

Annual income of Ester de Andrade at the head of a family with three children, 1648/9 (guilders)

Item	Amount
Poor relief, 4 guilders per month	48.00
Festivals (four)	13.00
Matzot	5.60
Peat	9.50
Total poor relief	76.10
Income from work and other sources	30.00
Total income	**106.10**

Source: SAA entry no. 334, nos. 173 and 239, 1648/9.

Table 27

Annual income of Sara Buena de Moura at the head of a family of seven members, 1667/8

Item	Amount
Poor relief, 5 guilders per month	60.00
Festivals (four)	14.50
Rent subsidy	16.00
Matzot	9.00
Peat	11.00
Total poor relief	110.50
Income from work and other sources	0
Total income	**110.50**

Source: SAA entry no. 334, nos. 174 and 215, 1667/8.

Table 28

Annual income of Rachel Sega de Espanha, a single blind woman, 1663/4

Item	Amount
Poor relief, 10 guilders per month	120.00
Festivals (four)	7.00
Rent subsidy	6.00
Matzot	1.85
Peat	4.20
Total poor relief	139.05
Income from work and other sources	0
Total income	**139.05**

Source: SAA entry no. 334, nos. 215, 174, and 240, 1663/4.

Table 29

Annual income of Abraham Dias and his family, consisting of six individuals, 1671/2

Item	Amount
Poor relief, 2.90 guilders per month[a]	34.80
Festivals (four)	10.50
Rent subsidy	10.00
Matzot	7.20
Peat	7.40
Total poor relief	69.90
Income from work and other sources[b]	62.00
Total income	**131.90**

[a] From Abodat Ahesed.

[b] As *shamash*, goldsmith and silversmith, and baker.

Sources: SAA entry no. 334, nos. 19, 294, 216, 1671/2.

Table 30

Annual income of Daniel Lopes Arias and his family, consisting of eight individuals, 1672/3

Item	Amount
Poor relief, 4 guilders per month	48.00
Festivals (four)	11.50
Rent subsidy	12.00
Matzot	9.00
Peat	15.00
Total poor relief	95.50
Income from work and other sources[a]	134.00
Total income	**229.50**

[a] As *shamash* and teacher; wife's work.

Sources: SAA entry no. 334, nos. 174, 216–17, 240, and 1052, 1672/3.

Table 31

Numerical relation of Ashkenazim and Sephardim in Amsterdam, 1650–*c*.1795

Year	Ashkenazim	Sephardim	Ratio of Ashkenazim to Sephardim
1650	1,000	1,990	1:2
1675	1,830	2,713	1:1.5
1700	3,200	4,017	1:1.25
1725	9,000	—	
c.1730	—	4,554	
c.1750	14,000	4,583	3:1
c.1795	*c*.20,000	4,003	5:1

Sources: As for Table 7.

FIGURES

Figure 1

Scope of poor relief among the Portuguese Jews of Amsterdam, 1650/1–*c.*1795

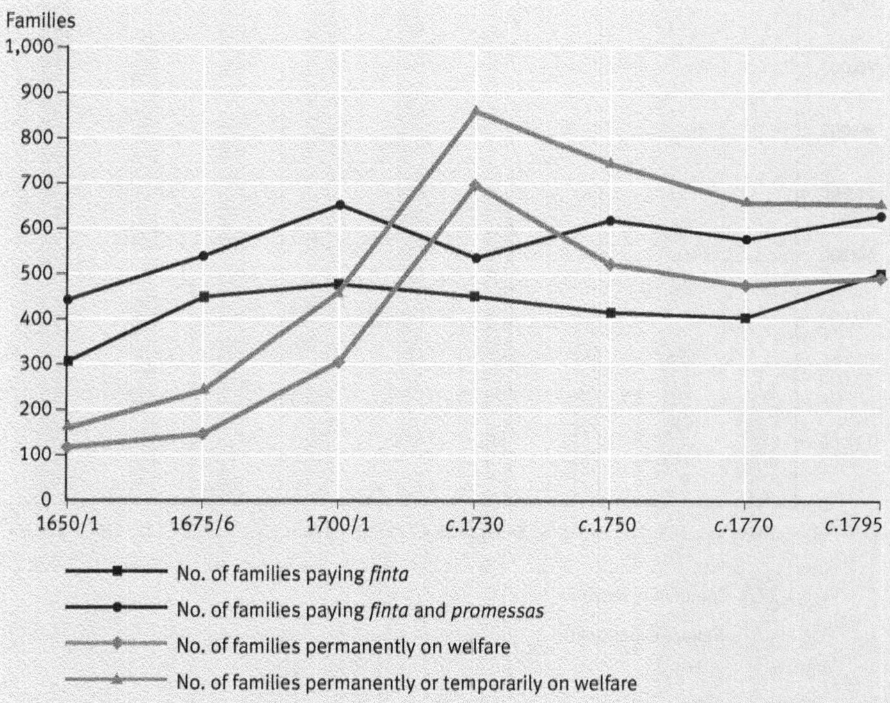

Source: SAA entry no. 334, nos. 172–6, 179, 277, 288, 290, 974–6.

Figure 2

Sedaca account: community income and welfare expenditure, 1640/1–1793/4

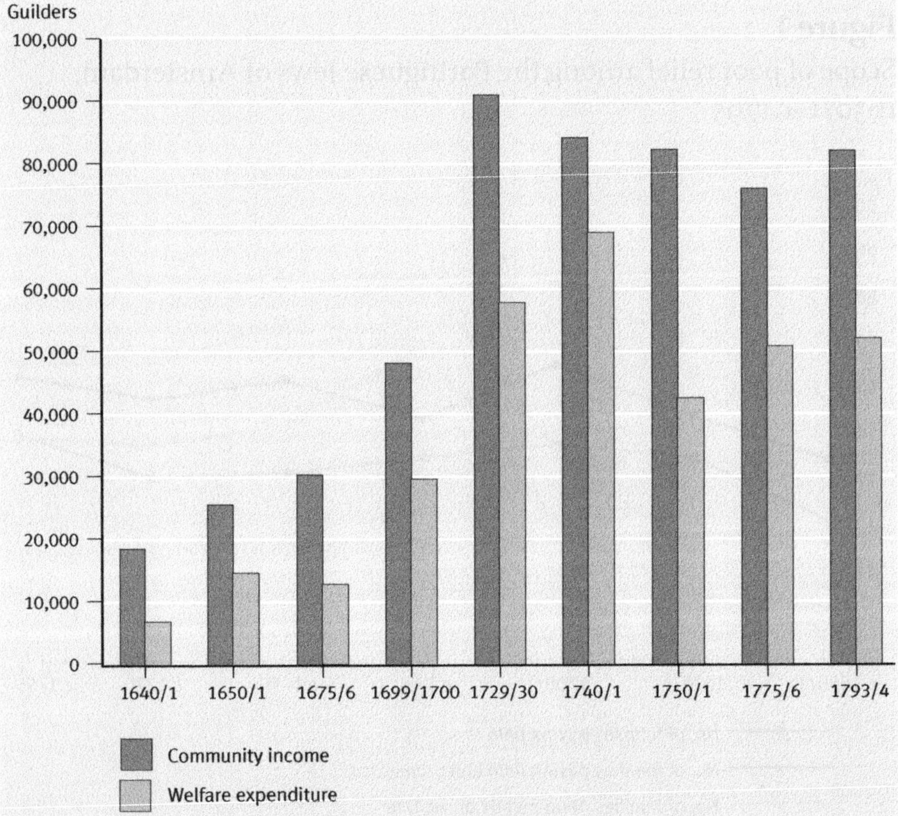

Source: SAA entry no. 334, nos. 239–40, 242, 247, 249, 254.
See also Levie Bernfeld, 'Financing Poor Relief', 101.

Figure 3
Sources of income, 1650/1–1793/4

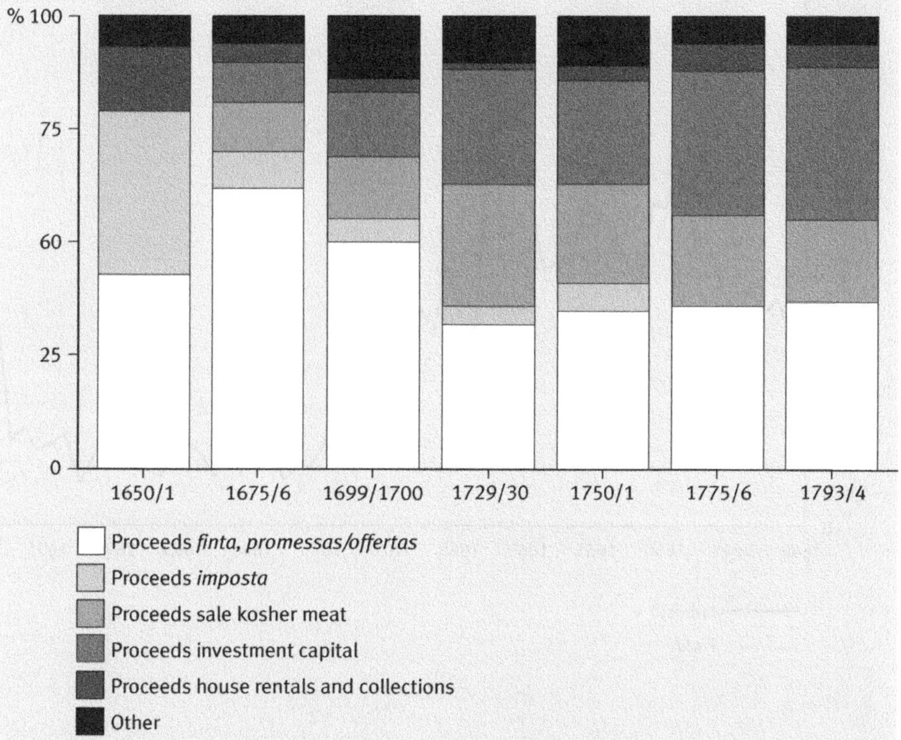

Sources: SAA entry no. 334, nos. 173–6, 179, 181, 183, 186, 239–40, 242, 247, 249, 251, 254. See also Levie Bernfeld, 'Financing Poor Relief', 100, 102.

Figure 4

Yields of *finta* and *imposta*, 1640–1695

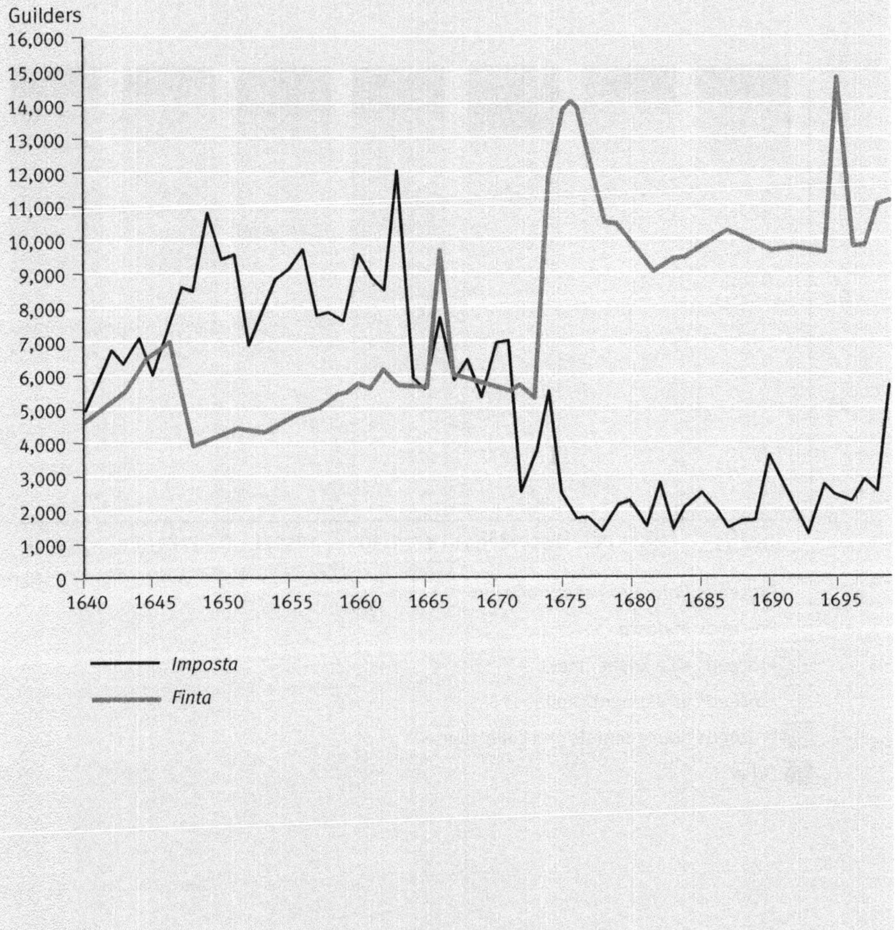

Sources: SAA entry no. 334, nos. 172–6, 179, 277, 288, 290, 974–6.
See also Levie Bernfeld, 'Financing Poor Relief', 100, 102.

APPENDIX III

FOUR BIOGRAPHICAL STUDIES

INFORMATION on most members of the Portuguese community in Amsterdam in the period treated in this book is fairly limited, sometimes consisting only of brief passing references. However, while we can catch only glimpses of some individuals, in a few cases we can put together at least the outline of a life. This appendix presents biographical summaries of four men whose experiences illustrate some of the main themes studied in this book, especially that of migration, which is the focus of Chapter 2.

David Machorro de Leon

The life of David Machorro de Leon gives us some idea of the movement of Jews between Amsterdam and North Africa. In about 1678 David, then aged about 15, arrived in Amsterdam from Salé accompanied by his younger sister Luna. His father, who used occasionally to visit Amsterdam, died at about this time in Salé.[1] Perhaps he intended that David should take over his trading activities. Relatives of David and Luna had moved to Amsterdam earlier,[2] and helped with David and Luna's reception and integration. In 1679, a year after their arrival in Amsterdam, Luna married Joseph Hazan from Turkey.[3] In 1671, while still in Salé, she had been granted a dowry by the international Dotar organization, based in Amsterdam.[4] All she had then to do was wait for a suitable partner, who turned up, not in Salé, but in Amsterdam. David earned money by, among other things, guarding the synagogue and helping to prepare for Passover. In addition he received poor relief.[5] His mother had remained in Salé.[6] Meanwhile he travelled to and from Amsterdam: to Salé in 1679, and to London in 1680.[7] A few months later the circle was closed when he returned to Amsterdam from Salé once more,[8] before leaving for London again in 1681.[9] All his travel from Amsterdam was paid for by the Amsterdam Portuguese *kahal*.[10] While he was in Amsterdam he received poor relief from time to time.[11] In 1684, at the age of 20, he married Ribca Levy Maduro, daughter of Salomon Levy Maduro. His mother did not come over for the occasion.[12] The couple received a dowry of 400 guilders through Dotar.[13]

After his wedding he took his 'familia' to Salé, but not permanently.[14] He continued to travel: in 1686 he and his family went from Amsterdam to Jamaica,[15] and in 1687 from Amsterdam to Algiers.[16] In 1690 he was given money for a wedding ring, his old one having been lost in a pawnshop.[17] In 1692 we find him on a list of those drawing regular poor relief in Amsterdam,[18] and in 1696 his daughter Sara competed for a dowry from Dotar, just as his sister from North Africa had done twenty-five years earlier.[19] He and his family seem finally to have settled in Curaçao. From that island, his daughters Hana and Sara tried their luck with Dotar from 1698 onwards.[20] Machorro de Leon's migration ran in circles between Amsterdam, North Africa, and the Caribbean, with Curaçao as his final destination.

Joseph Benveniste

Joseph Benveniste was a great traveller. In 1665 he apparently arrived in Amsterdam from the Levant as an Italian Jew, for he was given the nickname of 'Frankite'. Six months later he was given money to move to Venice. After another three years, in 1668, he came back to Amsterdam, this time from Cairo. Receiving no more than sporadic relief at first, he seemed to grow poorer and poorer. From 1670 he was accordingly granted monthly poor relief until his death three years later.[21] His travels to and from Amsterdam took in Italy and the Levant.

Jacob Gabay Correa

Jacob Gabay Correa lived and worked in Brazil until 1653, probably with his family, and was a member of the Portuguese community in Recife.[22] Returning to Europe from Brazil impoverished, he drew poor relief in Amsterdam from 1652 to 1655.[23] His wife, too, was granted assistance, which may indicate that her husband was away from time to time.[24] The family had at least five members,[25] and during this period one of the daughters tried to obtain a dowry.[26] In 1658 Gabay Correa apparently moved on again. Having been promised two slaves, a man and a woman, he travelled to Guyana, probably with his family, since his wife, too, vanished from the poor relief registers.[27] By 1664, however, he was back in Amsterdam again. In 1661 his daughter Ribca drew a dowry of 400 guilders from Dotar, and three years later she was married in Amsterdam.[28] Between 1663 and 1664 his son Abraham was being taught in the pauper school run by the *kehilah*.[29] In 1664, after his daughter's wedding, Gabay Correa returned to Guyana. The Portuguese community granted him funds to travel to the tune of 70 guilders, together with a further 70 guilders in poor relief.[30] Two years later, in 1666, Jacob's presence in Amsterdam is mentioned again, together with the fact that he had received 1 guilder in poor relief. There is no further mention of him in the Amsterdam Portuguese archives. It is believed that he died in Jamaica in 1695.[31]

Gabay Correa's activities were focused mainly on the west, using Amsterdam as his base for expeditions at first to Brazil, later to Guyana, and finally to Jamaica.

Salomon da Rocha

Salomon da Rocha's wife Ribca Furtado seems to have died in 1663, leaving him with two daughters, Sara and Ester.[32] He travelled a great deal—to Surinam, to other colonies in the west, and to North Africa. He was in Surinam in 1659,[33] and then in North Africa between 1667 and 1669.[34] A year and a half year later he returned to Amsterdam, apparently because of ill health.[35] He went back to Surinam in the summer of 1669, having taken about six months to recover.[36] He had a bad reputation in the colony, and the Portuguese community there succeeded in refusing him admittance through a request, dated 1669, directed to the governor there. He was ordered to get out of the country as soon as possible.[37] It is not known whether he returned home immediately, but we know that he was in Amsterdam in 1674.[38] He apparently returned to the West Indies, since we know that he died there in 1684.

Salomon da Rocha seems to have been the only person in the colony of Essequibo who knew how to process vanilla beans, a key ingredient in the production of chocolate: to get his raw materials he travelled in 'Pomeroon and Barima', from where he sent the vanilla out of Surinam secretly, bypassing the monopolistic control of the Dutch West India Company.[39] It seems that he was not well off since there is no trace of him on the tax lists, though he does appear in the charity records of the Amsterdam Portuguese community; in addition, we know that his daughters in Amsterdam were receiving welfare.[40] Da Rocha seems to have died in Essequibo.

GLOSSARY OF TERMS AND NAMES

Abodat Ahesed Work of Mercy: name of a *ḥevrah* set up within the Amsterdam Portuguese community as a workhouse for Ashkenazim; after 1670 its function changed to distributing money to the poor of the Portuguese Jewish community

Abodat Akodes Holy Worship: name of a *ḥevrah* that tried to maintain the dignity of funerals by ensuring that the officials responsible were dressed in black

Aby Jetomim Father of Orphans: name of a *ḥevrah* set up as the Portuguese Jewish boys' orphanage; it also acted as a yeshiva and undertook other charitable activities such as offering shelter to refugees

Acnasat Orhim Hospitality; Accommodation of Guests: name of a *ḥevrah* that provided accommodation to Jewish travellers arriving in Amsterdam

arvit Evening prayer

Asuta Habraya Friends of Health: name of a *ḥevrah* that assisted teachers of Ets Haim (and later also their widows), and students receiving monthly payments to study, during periods of illness

ba'ale torah Scholars well versed in Jewish tradition

Bahale Tesuba Penitents: name of a *ḥevrah* for youngsters, enabling them to combine religious study with acts of charity such as helping the poor and bearing the cost of paupers' funerals

beraha Term used by the Amsterdam Portuguese as a euphemism for punishment

Berit Salom Covenant of Peace: name of a *ḥevrah* that helped poor women who had just given birth to daughters

Bet Israel House of Israel: name of a Portuguese congregation in Amsterdam before 1639

Bet Jacob House of Jacob: name of a Portuguese congregation in Amsterdam before 1639

Bigde Kodes Holy Garbs: name of a *ḥevrah* that distributed clothes to the poor

Bikur Holim Visiting the Sick: name of a *ḥevrah* that concentrated primarily on the provision of care for the sick poor; it also took care of funeral arrangements and offered practical support for mourners

bodeq Inspector of ritually slaughtered meat

carniseria Hall where ritually slaughtered meat is sold

cativos Name of the organization within the Amsterdam Portuguese community (and of similar organizations in many other communities in the Sephardi diaspora) which aimed to free Jews from captivity, including New Christians on the Iberian peninsula and in other territories under Spanish and Portuguese rule on condition that once liberated they joined a Jewish community outside the Iberian peninsula. The word *cativos* is also used to define the prisoners themselves

cohen, pl. ***cohanim*** See *kohen*

congregante Non-taxpaying member of the congregation and those on welfare, who did not have the right to vote

cortador da carne Ritual slaughterer

derashah, pl. ***derashot*** Sermon

Dotar ('Santa companhia de dotar orphans e donzelas pobres') Name of a *ḥevrah* that was (and still is) based in Amsterdam but in the early modern period operated internationally, providing dowries to orphans and poor young girls throughout the Sephardi diaspora

escama, pl. ***escamot*** Resolution passed by the community

escava, pl. ***escavot*** Prayer for the repose of the soul of the dead

esguer (***hesger***, lit. 'enclosure'), pl. ***esguerim*** Small study house

Esnoga Synagogue

Ets Haim Tree of Life: name of a *ḥevrah* that supported students of the community yeshiva

finta Tax on general wealth

forasteiro Foreigner

gabai Treasurer

galut Exile, diaspora

Gemilut Hasadim Benevolence: name of the community burial society; also the name of a yeshiva

gemilut ḥasadim The quality or concept of benevolence

ger, pl. ***gerim*** Convert to Judaism, proselyte

Haberim Magsibim Listening Companions: name of a youth society that combined religious study with acts of charity, and particularly the distribution of bread

haham, pl. ***hahamim*** (lit., 'a wise person') Sephardi title for a rabbi, as a scholar of Jewish law

ḥalah Special bread eaten on the sabbath and Jewish religious holidays; also referring to the piece of dough, set aside and burnt or given to the *kohanim* around the ceremony of baking kosher bread and other dough-based products

ḥaroset Condiment of nuts, fruits, and spices eaten ceremonially on the first night of Pesach, and in the diaspora on the second night too

Hase Amaharacha Woodpile Arrangement: name of a *ḥevrah* distributing firewood to its own members and to the poor

Hateret Bahurim Crown of Young Men: name of a youth society for religious study

Hateret Tipheret Crown of Beauty: name of a youth society that combined religious study with charitable acts such as distributing hats and wigs to the poor

ḥazan, pl. ***ḥazanim*** Cantor

ḥerem Excommunication

ḥerem hayishuv Ban on settlement: an ordinance prohibiting new members from attaching themselves to a Jewish community

ḥesed Kindness

Hesrat Nasim Support to Women: name of a *ḥevrah* that distributed shoes and stockings to poor women

ḥevrah, pl. ***ḥevrot*** [Holy] society formed for charitable, educational, and religious purposes

Honen Dal Pitier of the Poor: name of a youth society that combined religious study with charitable actions, such as the distribution of linen to the poor

Honen Dalim Pitier of the Poor: name of the communal loan bank; also the name of a yeshiva and charitable society that took care of the sick and assisted poor widows

Honen Dalim–Resit Hochma Pitier of the Poor–Beginning of Wisdom: name of a *ḥevrah* in which religious study went hand in hand with charitable activities, particularly distributing food to the poor

Jadrech Anavim He Will Guide the Humble: name of a *ḥevrah* set up by people originating in Belgrade, combining religious study with support for the helpless and poor of Belgrade

kahal, kehilah, pl. ***kehilot*** Congregation

Kahal Kados de Talmud Torah The Portuguese community of Amsterdam after 1639, formed from the merger of the three congregations existing before that date: Bet Jacob, Neve Salom, and Bet Israel

kashrut Dietary laws

Keter Sem Tob Crown of Good Reputation: youth society that combined religious studies with charitable deeds towards the poor

Keter Torah Crown of the Torah: religious study society, established in the seventeenth century (as distinct from the youth society of the same name set up in the eighteenth century with a similar aim)

ketubah, pl. ***ketubot*** Marriage contract

Kisuy Ros Covering for the Head: youth society that combined religious studies with charitable deeds, in this case the distribution of hats and jackets to the poor

kohen, pl. ***kohanim*** Descendants of Aaron, first high priest of Israel, and as such having certain ritual functions and subject to certain ritual regulations

lampeda de continuo See *ner tamid*

Leqah Tov Good Learning: name of a *ḥevrah* concentrating on religious study in a small group

levi, pl. ***levi'im*** Member of the tribe of Levi and as such having certain ritual functions

livros longos, livros longos de cuatro contas Names given to the records held by the Portuguese community in Amsterdam of poor relief disbursed

Maasim Tobim Good Deeds: a yeshiva that was a centre both for study and for charitable activity directed at taking care of the sick

Maasim Tobim–Sidcat Nassim Good Deeds–Charity for Women: name of a *ḥevrah* that provided health care for the poor (men as well as women)

Mahamad Governing body of the congregation

Malbis Arumim Clothing the Naked: name of a *ḥevrah* set up by the Portuguese Jews in The Hague to help the poor (including those among the Portuguese Jews in Amsterdam) and distribute clothes

Mamlechet Coanim Kingdom of Priests: name of a religious study society

Maskil el Dal Enlightener of the Poor: study and mutual aid society which, besides looking after its own members, also took care of those 'foreign' poor (*pobres forasteiros*) not eligible for poor relief from the Portuguese community

Masmiah Jesuah The Pronouncement of Salvation: name of a *ḥevrah* that combined religious study with assistance to the poor

matzah, pl. **matzot** Unleavened bread traditionally eaten on Pesach

matzah shemurah Matzah made under strict rabbinical supervision from the time of harvest and throughout the production process; widely used on the night of the *seder* and throughout Pesach by the more punctilious

Mayafu Pehameha Benealim How Beautiful Are Thy Feet with Shoes: name of a *ḥevrah* that provided shoes to the poor

Mazon Abanot Nourishment for the Girls: name of the Portuguese Jewish girls' orphanage

Meil Sedaca Cloak of Charity: name of a *ḥevrah* providing cloaks to the poor

Meirat Henaim Illuminating the Eyes: name of a religious study society that also provided assistance with funeral-related activities

Menahem Aniim Consolation of the Poor: alternative name for the *ḥevrah* Honen Dal (*see above*)

Mesib Nefes Refreshment for the Soul: name of a Portuguese Jewish hospital (including an old-age home for women) set up in the nineteenth century

mezuzah, pl. ***mezuzot*** Parchment scroll containing specific biblical texts that is affixed to the doorpost of the rooms in a Jewish home

Michse Leani'im Covering the Poor: name of a *ḥevrah* that combined religious study with charitable activities, in this case providing beds for the poor

midrash, pl. ***midrashim*** Study house

Migdal Oz Tower of Strength: name of a religious society that also acted as a charitable organization, distributing blankets and later meat and bread to the poor

mikveh Ritual bath

minyan Quorum of ten men needed for communal prayer

misheberah First word of a prayer recited in the synagogue to ask for blessings under a variety of circumstances

Mishenet Zequenim Support for the Elderly: name of the old-age home for men

Mispat Abanot Justice for Girls: name of a *ḥevrah* that distributed money for four weeks to women who had given birth to daughters

misva, pl. ***misvot*** *Mitsvah*; also used among Sephardim to mean 'funeral'

mitsvah, pl. ***mitsvot*** A biblical commandment of action (or inaction); also (by extension) a good deed

morisco A Catholic convert of Islamic origin in Spain or Portugal

mortalhadeyras Female makers or repairers of shrouds for the dead

nação (Port.)/***nación*** (Sp.) Nation; the term often used to designate the Spanish–Portuguese 'nation' of Jewish descent

nedava, pl. ***nedavot*** Donation; gift; offering

ner tamid The eternal light in front of the Holy Ark in the synagogue

Neve Salom Dwelling of Peace: name of a Portuguese congregation in Amsterdam before 1639

Neve Sedek Dwelling of Justice: name of a *ḥevrah* in which religious study was combined with charity, giving money to the poor among its members

Oel Ishack Tent of Isaac: name of a *ḥevrah* for religious study

offerta Promise to contribute money to Portuguese Jewish charities (also *promessa*)

***ondertrouw* register** Municipal records in which the intention to marry is listed; all those who were not members of the Reformed Church were required to set down their intention in this way

Oneg Sabat Enjoyment of the Sabbath: name of a *ḥevrah* that distributed bread and oil to the poor every Friday, before the start of the sabbath

Paame Dalim Steps of the Needy: name of a *ḥevrah* that combined religious study with charity, distributing shoes to the poor

parnas, pl. ***parnasim*** One of the six leading figures of the Portuguese Jewish community who, together with the treasurer (*gabai*), made up the governing body of the congregation (Mahamad); the term was also used of those who were elected to lead sub-organizations within the community, such as the health-care organization Bikur Holim or the community school Talmud Torah.

Parnasad Almanot Livelihood for Widows: yeshiva and welfare society that distributed money among poor widows

passageiro Passer-by, transient

pekidim Officials appointed specifically to gather gifts for the Jews in the Holy Land

Peri Ets Haim Fruit of the Tree of Life: name of a small study society

pinkas, pl. ***pinkasim*** Record book / minutes

Ponentini Western Sephardi Jews of Venice

promessa See *offerta*

Quesut La Ebion Righteousness to the Poor: name of a *ḥevrah* that distributed skirts to poor women

Quetonet Bat Codes Holy Garment: name of a *ḥevrah* (previously known as Mayafu Pehameha Benealim) that supplied shirts to the needy

Rehobot Name of a poor house accommodating elderly women

[rol de] rescodes da sedaqua Monthly poor-relief list

Resit Daat Beginning of Faith: youth society that combined religious study with supporting the poor

Resit Hochma Beginning of Wisdom: name of a *ḥevrah* that combined religious study with supporting its own members in case of illness

rimon, pl. ***rimonim*** Finials placed on top of the staves of the Torah

Roffe Holim Doctor of the Sick: name of a *ḥevrah* devoted to helping the sick poor, including its own members

Rosh Hodesh First day of the Jewish month

rosh yeshivah Head of a yeshiva

Sahare Sedek Gates of Justice: name of a study society that was also active as a charitable organization, giving alms to the local poor and food to 'foreigners' (*forasteiros*)

sedaca Charity; also the community's charity chest

seder Jewish ceremonial meal that marks the beginning of the holiday of Passover

sefer torah, pl. ***sifrei torah*** Torah scroll

shabbat, pl. ***shabbatoth*** Sabbath

shali'aḥ, pl. ***sheliḥim*** Emissary from Erets Yisra'el, seeking assistance for the Jewish community there

shamash, pl. ***shamashim*** Beadle

shemurim See *matzah shemurah*

Shevet Achim Dwelling of Brothers: name of a small study society

shivah First seven days of mourning

shoḥet Ritual slaughterer

Shulḥan arukh Halakhic codex by Joseph Karo

Sidcat Nassim Charity for Women: name of a *ḥevrah* that helped poor women in times of illness

sofer, pl. ***soferim*** Jewish ritual scribe

Somer Holim The Guarding of the Sick: name of a *ḥevrah* that maintained a vigil over members who were sick and took deathbed confession as an important aspect of its activities

takanot Regulations drawn up by the Jewish community

talit, pl. ***talitot*** Prayer shawls

Talmud Torah Learning of the Law: name of the Portuguese community of Amsterdam from 1639, and also the name of its school

tefilin Phylacteries

Temime Darech Straightforward People: name of a mutual aid *ḥevrah* that combined religious study with sick care for its own members

teva Desk from which the Torah is read in the synagogue

Tikvat aJesuah Hope of Redemption: name of a *ḥevrah* that combined religious studies with charitable activities, in this case the distribution of meat and bread to the poor

Tipheret Bajurim Splendour of Youths: youth society involved in religious study only

Tora Hor Light of the Torah: name of a religious study society

tsitsit Fringed ritual garment; also the fringes of the *talit*

tudesco Ashkenazi Jew, used especially of those from the German states

Vestiaria dos Talmidim Clothing of the Pupils: name of a *ḥevrah* that provided clothing for students at the Talmud Torah school and Ets Haim yeshiva

viddui Ritual confession of sins

yad Ritual indicator, used to point to the text during the Torah reading from the parchment Torah scrolls

yahid, pl. ***yehidim*** Paying member of the congregation with the right to vote

yeshiva Institution for the full-time study of Jewish texts by men

NOTES

For abbreviations used in the notes, see page 489.

Note on Transliteration

1 See Swetschinski, *Reluctant Cosmopolitans*, pp. xi–xii.

1 Setting the Scene

1 For Jews and Conversos in the Iberian peninsula see e.g. Baer, *A History of the Jews in Christian Spain*; Caro Baroja, *Los Judíos en la España moderna*; Domínguez Ortiz, *La clase social*; id., *Los Judeoconversos*; Azevedo, *História*. For the writings of Haim Beinart on this subject see Beinart Kaplan, 'Bibliography' (Heb.); see further Netanyahu, *The Marranos of Spain*; Lea, *A History of the Inquisition*; Kamen, *The Spanish Inquisition*; Yerushalmi, *From Spanish Court to Italian Ghetto*, ch. 1; Gampel, *The Last Jews on Iberian Soil*; Y. Kaplan,'Between Christianity and Judaism'; Bodian, *Hebrews of the Portuguese Nation*, ch. 1. For an overview of the lives of ex-Conversos living in the Sephardi diaspora of early modern Europe see the sources cited by contributors to Beinart (ed.), *Moreshet Sepharad*. Historiography and differences of opinion in this field are discussed in Y. Kaplan, *An Alternative Path to Modernity*, 1–28; Nahon, 'Les Marranes espagnols et portugais'; Oliel-Grausz, 'L'Histoire des juifs séfarades'; Novinsky, *Cristãos novos*, 3–22; Roth, *A History of the Marranos*, pp. vii–xix (Salomon's introduction); and Saraiva, *The Marrano Factory*. For the most recent discussion of the term 'early modern' in Jewish history see Ruderman, *Early Modern Jewry*, 1, 9–10, 191–206, 220–6, who applies it to the period between the expulsion of Jews from Spain in 1492 and the days of institutionalized and politicized emancipation from the 1780s. My research covers the period from the end of the 16th century to 1750, with some trends followed up to *c.*1795, just before the political and economic emancipation of the Jews in the Netherlands in 1796; here I tend to follow Jonathan Israel, who, in *European Jewry in the Age of Mercantilism* (1–3), locates the early modern period between 1550 and 1750.

2 Israel, *Dutch Primacy*; id., *The Dutch Republic*; Schama, *The Embarrassment of Riches*; Vries and van der Woude, *The First Modern Economy*; Frijhoff and Spies, *1650 Bevochten eenheid*; Deursen, *Plain Lives*.

3 On tolerance in the Dutch Republic and early modern Europe see Nierop and Po-Chia Hsia, *Calvinism and Religious Toleration*; Berkvens-Stevelinck, Israel, and Posthumus Meyjes, *The Emergence of Tolerance*; and B. Kaplan, *Divided by Faith*.

4 For an overview of historiography on Dutch Sephardi Jewry see Y. Kaplan, 'A Generation of Progress', and, further, Blom, Fuks-Mansfeld, and Schöffer

(eds.), *History of the Jews in The Netherlands*, chs. 2–4 and the bibliographies on pp. 399–416 and 441–80.

5 Yerushalmi, *From Spanish Court to Italian Ghetto*, 43–4; id., 'Conversos' (Heb.). Yosef Kaplan has written extensively about this characterization of the Amsterdam Portuguese Jews: see his *From Christianity to Judaism*, esp. the epilogue, and his 'The Portuguese Community of Amsterdam in the Seventeenth Century between Tradition and Change', 'The Self-Definition of the Sephardi Jews of Western Europe', and 'Gente política'.

6 On the absorption by (ex-)Conversos of Spanish concepts such as purity of blood, exclusivity, and honour see Yerushalmi, *From Spanish Court to Italian Ghetto*, 40–1, 357–8, 386; Y. Kaplan, *From Christianity to Judaism*, 173–5; and id., 'Political Concepts', 56–62. See also Swetschinski, *Reluctant Cosmopolitans*, and Méchoulan, *Hispanidad y Judaísmo*.

7 Swetschinski, *Reluctant Cosmopolitans*, ch. 1; Y. Kaplan, 'Gente política'.

8 Slack, *Poverty and Policy*, esp. ch. 1; Blockmans, 'Circumscribing the Concept of Poverty'; Beckerman, 'The Measurement of Poverty'; Sen, *Poverty and Famines*.

9 Slack, *Poverty and Policy*, 5–6.

10 For studies on the Ashkenazim see the following by Yosef Kaplan: *From New Christians to New Jews* (Heb.), ch. 4; 'Relations between Spanish and Portuguese Jews'; 'Amsterdam and Ashkenazi Migration'; and 'The Portuguese Community in 17th-Century Amsterdam and the Ashkenazi World'.

11 R. Cohen, 'Passage to a New World'; Swetschinski, *Reluctant Cosmopolitans*, 181–7; Bartal and Kaplan, 'Emigration' (Heb.).

12 For poor relief in early modern Europe in general see Geremek, *Inutiles au monde*, *La Potence ou la pitié*, *Les Fils de Cain*, and *Geschichte der Armut*; Jütte, *Poverty and Deviance*; Lis and Soly, *Poverty and Capitalism*; Mollat, *Études* and *The Poor in the Middle Ages*; Pullan, *Poverty and Charity*: Riis, *Aspects of Poverty*; Safley, *The Reformation of Charity*; and Woolf, *The Poor in Western Europe*. For France see Davis, 'Poor Relief, Humanism and Heresy'; Fairchilds, *Poverty and Charity in Aix-en-Provence*; Gutton, *La Société et les pauvres*; Hufton, *The Poor of Eighteenth-Century France*; and Norberg, *Rich and Poor in Grenoble*. For Spain see Flynn, *Sacred Charity*, which has an extensive bibliography, and Martz, *Poverty and Welfare in Habsburg Spain*. For Italy see Black, *Italian Confraternities*; Cavallo, *Charity and Power*; and Pullan, *Rich and Poor in Renaissance Venice*. For England see Beier, *The Problem of the Poor*, and Jordan, *Philanthropy*. For Holland see Bos, *'Uyt liefde tot malcander'*; Gerwen and M. van Leeuwen, *Studies over zekerheidsarrangementen*; Groenveld, 'For the Benefit of the Poor'; Kooijmans, *Vriendschap*; M. van Leeuwen, *The Logic of Charity*; McCants, *Civic Charity*; Manen, *Armenpflege in Amsterdam*; Parker, *The Reformation of Community*; Prak, 'Armenzorg 1500–1800'; Spaans, *Armenzorg in Friesland*; Swaan, *In Care of the State*; van der Vlis, *Leven in armoede*; and Wijngaarden, *Zorg voor de kost*. For Nuremberg see Strauss, *Nuremberg*. For Geneva see Kingdon, 'Social Welfare'. For Zurich see Wandel, *Always Among Us*.

13 Flynn, *Sacred Charity*, ch. 4; Martz, *Poverty and Welfare in Habsburg Spain*, ch. 2.

The Council of Trent was a 16th-century Council of the Roman Catholic Church. It convened between 1545 and 1563 as a reaction to the upsurge of Protestantism. Besides condemning Protestantism, it set out plans to reform the Catholic Church from within. In the aftermath of the Council, during the so-called Counter-Reformation, the Catholic Church launched a counter-offensive against Protestantism. Besides implementing internal reforms, including some concerning poor relief, it attempted, with militant, missionary, disciplined, and uncompromising religious fervour, to retain and extend its influence.

14 See Flynn, *Sacred Charity*, 112, 117, and her extensive bibliography on poor relief in Spain (pp. 184–91); Rumeu de Armas, *Historia de la previsión social en España*; and Callahan, 'Corporate Charity in Spain'.

15 Bennassar, *The Spanish Character*; Casey, *Early Modern Spain*; Defourneaux, *Daily Life in Spain*; Domínguez Ortiz, *La sociedad española*; Kamen, *Spain 1469–1714*; id., *The Spanish Inquisition*.

16 On these so-called *Confessieboeken* see S. Faber, *Strafrechtspleging*.

17 On the Insolvent Estates Office see Moll, *De Desolate Boedelskamer*, and Oldewelt, 'De Desolate Boedelskamer'.

18 See Pieterse, *Inventaris*.

19 On the background of the emergence of the three Portuguese communities, in 1602 (Bet Jacob), in 1608 (Neve Salom), and in 1618 (Bet Israel), see Y. Kaplan, 'The Jews in the Republic', 117–20.

20 The Resolution Book recorded decisions taken on many matters. Besides the terms of the agreement on the union of 1639, it includes the resolutions taken by the united community Kahal Kados de Talmud Torah; the elections of the administrators and other personnel of the community; and the statutes of the various organizations that depended directly on the community leadership. The Memorial Books (both the *Memorial de advertencias* and the *Livro de memorias*) also recorded resolutions of the community together with admonitions, but in most cases these were decisions and admonitions that seemed to be of minor importance to the Mahamad and therefore were not recorded in the Resolution Books—mostly matters of everyday concern. Here too the establishment and statutes of various charitable and pious semi-independent organizations were recorded and confirmed by the *parnasim* of the *kahal*.

21 On de Barrios's historiography see Pieterse, *Daniel Levi de Barrios*; on that of David Franco Mendes see Franco Mendes, *Memorias*.

2 Migration of the Poor

1 Moch, *Moving Europeans*, chs. 1–3; Canny (ed.), *Europeans on the Move*; Kleinschmidt, *People on the Move*, ch. 3; Ruderman, *Early Modern Jewry*, ch. 1: 'Jews on the Move'.

2 For periodization of the Dutch Golden Age see Israel, *The Dutch Republic*, 231, 593.

3 See the writings of Gregorio Leti, as cited in Israel, *Diasporas within a Diaspora*, 490–1.

4 Lucassen and Penninx, *Newcomers*, 21–36, 49–54, 56–7; Lucassen, *Dutch Long-Distance Migration*; id., 'The Netherlands'; Vries and van der Woude, *The First Modern Economy*, 46–80; Lottum, *Across the North Sea*; Kuijpers, *Migrantenstad*; Hart, *Geschrift en getal*, 115–81; Knotter and van Zanden, 'Immigratie en arbeidsmarkt'; Moch, *Moving Europeans*, 29–31.

5 Cited in Saperstein, *Exile in Amsterdam*, 135–6, 402–4. 'Deadly tortures connected with the manufacturing of their clothes' could refer to torture suffered by delegations from the Salonikan Jewish community who delivered fabric to the sultan of the Ottoman empire (the fabric was used to make uniforms for janissaries). After 1535 these deliveries replaced a tax in cash on Salonikan Jewry, but over the years the quota of free deliveries of fabric was increased, placing a heavy burden on the community. A few years after Haham Saul Levi Morteira's sermon, for example, a delegation from the Salonikan Jewish community met the sultan to request relief from this burdensome tax. The request was rejected; the leader of the delegation, R. Yehudah Covo, was hanged and the other delegates were imprisoned, being released only after payment of a heavy fine.

6 SAA entry no. 334, no. 13, p. 62, 5 Tishrei 5391.

7 For an overview of the position of the Jews in early modern Europe see Ruderman, *Early Modern Jewry*; Israel, *European Jewry*, and, for the Sephardi Jews in particular, id., *Diasporas within a Diaspora*. On residence issues see Swetschinski, *Reluctant Cosmopolitans*, 185; Rabinowitz, *The Herem Hayyishub*; Baron, *The Jewish Community*, i. 367, ii. 5–6, iii. 91, 95, 98, 101; J. Katz, *Tradition and Crisis*, 85, 89–90; for Italy see Simonsohn, *History of the Jews in the Duchy of Mantua*, 108, 120–1, 125–6, 501–2, 522–3; for Livorno see Trivellato, *The Familiarity of Strangers*, 77, 99. In central and eastern Europe the admission and accommodation of poor beggars by the Jewish community or by government authorities were not automatic and access was quite limited (Shulvass, *From East to West*, 44–5, 54–6). On the expulsion of the poor in eastern Europe see Baron, *The Jewish Community*, ii. 323–5. For the position of Sephardim in the Ottoman empire see A. Levy, *The Sephardim in the Ottoman Empire*, 49. On the *ḥerem hayishuv* and other restrictions in France see Nahon, *Les 'Nations' juives portugaises*, 3–7, 13–17, 186–8; id., 'La Nation juive portugaise en France', 358–61, 382; id., 'From New Christians to the Portuguese Jewish Nation', 339; id., 'Los *Cristianos Nuevos*', 604–5; Szapiro, 'Le Sud-Ouest', 235–6; Malino, *The Sephardic Jews of Bordeaux*, ch. 1. For restrictions on poor Jews entering England and its Jewish communities see Hyamson, *The Sephardim of England*, 39, 82; Endelman, *The Jews of Georgian England*, 167–70; R. D. Barnett, 'The Correspondence of the Mahamad', 4–5; Picciotto, *Sketches*, 40; Kochan, *Jews, Idols and Messiahs*, 109; D. S. Katz, *The Jews in the History of England*, 181; Gaster, *History of the Ancient Synagogue*, 21–2, 149; Samuel, 'The First Fifty Years', 35. For tolerance in the Dutch Republic see Swetschinski, 'From the Middle Ages to the Golden Age', 59–77. For restrictions within the Dutch Republic see Zwarts, 'De Joodse gemeenten'; Reijnders, *Van 'Joodsche Natiën' tot Joodse Nederlanders*, ch. 4; Bolle, *De opheffing*, 19–20; Huussen, 'Legislation on the Position of the Jews', 54–5.

8 Prak, 'Armenzorg 1500–1800', 63; M. van Leeuwen, 'Amsterdam en de armenzorg', 154–5; M. van Leeuwen, Schoenmakers, and Smits, *Armoede en bedeling*, 5; Everts, *De verhouding van kerk en staat*, 61–2; Deursen, *Bavianen en Slijkgeuzen*, ch. 6; Groenveld, 'For the Benefit of the Poor'.

9 Groenveld, 'For the Benefit of the Poor'; Kuijpers, 'Een zeventiende-eeuwse migrantenkerk'; Manen, *Armenpflege in Amsterdam*, 54, 61, 64; Prak, 'Armenzorg 1500–1800'; Spaans, *Armenzorg in Friesland*, 228–329. Gregorio Leti describes how Jewish communal poor relief was meant to keep the Jewish poor off the streets and prevent them from begging from Christians (cited in Israel, *Diasporas within a Diaspora*, 507–8).

10 For a discussion on the relations between the Portuguese community and the city authorities of Amsterdam concerning poor relief see Levie Bernfeld, 'Financing Poor Relief', 89. On the position of the Catholic Church in Amsterdam regarding the poor see J. Faber and M. van Leeuwen, *Amsterdamse katholieke bedeelden*, 18–21.

11 As the result of a conflict between the *parnasim* and the del Sotto family in 1670, the governors of the city were invited to confirm the unity of the Portuguese community and prevent separation. On the 'del Sotto affair' see Swetschinski, *Reluctant Cosmopolitans*, 252–9; Ancona, 'De Portugese gemeente', 286; Hagoort, 'The del Sottos'.

12 *Handvesten ofte privilegiën*, ii. 473–4, 17 Nov. 1670, 14 May 1683; Swetschinski, *Reluctant Cosmopolitans*, 186–7.

13 SAA entry no. 334, no. 118, file 4, p. 524 [probably 1673]. See also Sluys, 'Hoogduits-Joods Amsterdam', 330.

14 This statement was made in connection with a request for tax exemption on 8,000 tons of peat: SAA entry no. 334, no. 986, pp. 1–3, 18 Apr. 1693.

15 SAA entry no. 334, no. 87, file 20, 1753, *Remonstraçoems e rq^{a} aos^{sres} Burgames^{trs}*.

16 Huussen, 'De joden in Nederland en het probleem van de tolerantie', 118–19; Reijnders, *Van 'Joodsche Natiën' tot Joodse Nederlanders*, 18–33; Swetschinski, *Reluctant Cosmopolitans*, ch. 1.

17 SAA entry no. 334, no. 22, pp. 182–3, 8 Av 5511; ibid., no. 66*a*, 18 Jan. 1760. See also Y. Kaplan, 'The Social Functions of the Herem'.

18 SAA entry no. 334, no. 19, p. 25/110, 22 Tamuz 5399. As was explicitly stated, the Portuguese community did not want to have anything to do with criminal cases and left them to the jurisdiction of the city, mostly without any effort to intervene. A similar regulation had been enacted earlier by the administrations of the three Portuguese communities existing before 1639 (ibid., no. 13, p. 101, 25 Tamuz 5393).

19 Y. Kaplan, 'The Social Functions of the Herem'.

20 This warning from the leadership of the Portuguese community relates to an instruction not to trade in Dam Square on Sundays: SAA entry no. 334, no. 21, p. 141, 3 Elul 5477.

21 On the constant and rigid social control exerted by the Portuguese leadership to

establish the ideal of *bom Judesmo* among its members see Y. Kaplan, 'Gente política'.

22 Pinto, *Reflexoens*, 6; on de Pinto as a merchant, economist, and philosopher see Nijenhuis, *Een Joodse Philosophe*, and Wijler, *Isaac de Pinto*.

23 SAA entry no. 334, no. 9, p. 2, 5376.

24 'Jacob de Italia forasteiro . . . f 1,–' (SAA entry no. 334, no. 172, p. 231, 11 Tishrei 5404); 'forasteiro de Salonique' (ibid., no. 5, p. 120, 1 Av 5381); 'a veneciana . . . f 1,10' (ibid., no. 174, p. 50, 19 Nisan 5414); 'outro berberisco . . . f 2,–' (ibid., no. 9, p. 2, 5376); for *tudescos*: 'Tudescos aquen se derao os anos passados . . . turba' (ibid., no. 173, p. 20, 1 Kislev 5408); for *polacos*: 'polacos . . . f 51:10' (ibid., no. 215, p. 72, 6 Av 5424); for *italianos*: '3 judeos italianos e hu de mantua' (ibid., no. 17, p. 37, 10 Nov. 5391/1630); for *levantinos*: 'Judeus levantinos . . . f 15,–' (ibid., p. 28, 24 May 5389); for *berberiscos*: 'esmola . . . a berberiscos por orden do maamad . . . f 10,–' (ibid., no. 3, p. 90, 6 Nisan 5383); for *forasteiros*: 'por 8 dias mais dos 3 forasteiros' (ibid., no. 5, p. 183, 4 Adar 5382); for *passageiros*: 'passageiro . . . por orden dos ss^{res} do maamad . . . f 0:18' (ibid., no. 215, p. 317, 23 Adar 5430).

25 Israel, 'The Changing Role of the Dutch Sephardim', 37–40; Weber, 'Were Merchants More Tolerant?', 83.

26 Saperstein, *Exile in Amsterdam*, 133–4. The events to which Morteira refers also include the conflict of 1618 within the Bet Jacob congregation that resulted in the creation of a new congregation, Bet Israel, and the enforcement of bans on a number of individuals, e.g. that on Uriel da Costa in 1623.

27 SAA entry no. 334, no. 13, pp. 3–9, 24 Shevat 5382. See also Swetschinski, *Reluctant Cosmopolitans*, 182–3; id., 'The Portuguese Jewish Merchants of Seventeenth-Century Amsterdam', 357–67; Vlessing, 'New Light'; and ead., 'The Portuguese Jewish Merchant Community'.

28 SAA entry no. 334, no. 13, pp. 8–9, 24 Shevat 5382, art. 29 (also cited in Swetschinski, *Reluctant Cosmopolitans*, 182–3); ibid., p. 10 [(?)after 26 Shevat], 5382.

29 SAA entry no. 334, no. 13, p. 50, 2 Tamuz 5389; ibid., p. 54, 10 Feb. 5390; ibid., pp. 58–9, 7 July 5390; ibid., p. 66, 1 Shevat 5391.

30 SAA entry no. 334, no. 11, p. 4, 5388: 'f 195,16 . . . esmolas particulares e p. ajuda de aluger das cazas e encaminhento dos tudescos'; ibid., no. 17, p. 59, 5396/15 June 1636: 'f 377,6,8 . . . que tanto despendeo no seu tempo com emcaminhar tudescos . . .'; ibid., p. 59^{v}, 5396/20 Aug. 1636: 'f 290,4,2 . . . que tantos despendeo com pobres tudescos no encaminhar'; ibid., p. 62^{v}, 5397/21 July 1637: 'f 571,1,14 . . . q tanto despendeo com encaminhar tudescos'. In 1638 the Portuguese communities and the Ashkenazi community co-operated in sending away *tudescos*. The Portuguese provided the money, leaving the organization to the Ashkenazim: 'f 283,4,8 . . . que pagou . . .dos esmoleres dos tudescos pera se emcaminharem p^{a} Polonia e mais prasas' (SAA entry no. 334, no. 17, p. 65^{v}, 13 June 5398); 'f 194,18 . . . que pagou aos esmoleres . . . de encaminhar tudescos' (ibid., p. 65^{v}, 12 July 5398). See also the following by Y. Kaplan: 'Amsterdam and Ashkenazi Migration'; *From New Christians to New Jews* (Heb.), ch. 4; 'Jewish

Refugees' (Heb.); and 'The Portuguese Community in 17th-Century Amsterdam and the Ashkenazi World'.

31 SAA entry no. 334, no. 13, p. 50, 2 Tamuz 5389.

32 SAA entry no. 334, no. 19, p. 1^{v}/78, 28 Adar II 5399; also published in Pieterse, *Daniel Levi de Barrios*, 156.

33 SAA entry no. 334, no. 174, p. 145, Rosh Hodesh Nisan 5416: 'nedaba feita para soccorrer os Pobres do Brazil'; for help to refugees from Poland in 1657: SAA entry no. 334, no. 240, p. 53, 16 Adar 5417: 'pa o que rendeo a nedaba para os de Polonia'.

34 For the low position accorded to foreigners in the hierarchy of welfare among the Jews of medieval Egypt see M. Cohen, *Poverty and Charity*, ch. 2; for the perception and treatment of New Christians in the Iberian peninsula as strangers see Graizbord, *Souls in Dispute*, 37–8.

35 SAA entry no. 334, no. 215, p. 15, 19 Nisan 5423–7 Nisan 5424: 'Despachos de petticões de pobres forasteiros'. In this section the *parnasim* registered not only the names of people who were given money to leave, but also general expenses to 'foreigners'. From 1666 onwards Ashkenazi Jews are mentioned separately in this section: 'Despacho de peticões de forast^{ros} e tudescos' (ibid., p. 160, 14 Nisan 5426–6 Adar 5427). In 1672, apparently after the ending of support to Ashkenazi Jews, this section was taken out (ibid., no. 216, p. 116, 5432). One year later a more general section was included under the heading 'Despacho depitoins com pezoas que vem, e sahem fora da terra' (ibid., p. 147, 7 Iyar 5433–7 Nisan 5434). This section registered all new arrivals in the city who asked for help from the Portuguese community. In addition, all individuals are noted who left the city with money given by that same community to cover travel expenses. From 1693 in these sections we again meet the word *forasteiros*. The new influx of Jews in the 1680s and 1690s apparently made it necessary to distinguish between Portuguese Jews and 'foreigners': 'Despacho de forasteiros e de pesoas q se vão para fora da terra' (ibid., no. 219, p. 167, 20 Nisan 5453–18 Adar 5454). Here support is recorded to all 'foreigners' and to individuals who left the city with an allocation of money for travel. In the 1730s the term *forasteiros* disappeared completely from headings of migration records, to be replaced by the more general *despachos p^{a} fora*, listing all those going abroad, either immediately after a short visit or after a more prolonged stay in the city: see e.g. SAA entry no. 334, no. 969, pp. 265–6, 5493–4, and ibid., pp. 314–15, 5494–5. For similar accounts in the Spanish–Portuguese community of 17th-century London see Diamond, 'The Community of Resettlement', 147–8. We also come across the same terminology among the Sephardim of southern France (and elsewhere). In the financial administration of St-Esprit in 1735, for example, we find *passageiros* and *forasteiros* being supported (Nahon, *Les 'Nations' juives portugaises*, 150–1). In the same community in 1784 we find expenses being described as 'distributions ordinaires & extraordinaires tant aux pauvres de l'endroit qu'aux étrangers de passage' (ibid. 233); see further Oliel-Grausz, 'Portugais et tudesques', 35.

36 SAA entry no. 334, no. 1052, p. 28, 12 Heshvan 5421.

37 SAA entry no. 334, no. 19, p. 613, 14 Adar 5430. Control in this respect does not appear to be waterproof and *tudescos* sometimes did take advantage of Portuguese *sedaca*. For gaps in the law see SAA entry no. 334, no. 21, p. 242, 3 Nisan 5481; ibid., p. 306, para. 2, 27 Sivan 5483; ibid., p. 453, 20 Tevet 5489; ibid., no. 22, p. 168, para. 3, 8 Heshvan 5509.

38 SAA entry no. 334, no. 20, p. 230, 1 Elul 5457.

39 Ibid. A similar rule was later adopted in Bordeaux in 1736, under which only Spanish or Portuguese poor were admitted to the roll of charity, and German, Levantine, and Italian Jews, and Jews from Avignon, were excluded: Nahon, '*Los Cristianos Nuevos*', 604–5.

40 SAA entry no. 334, no. 217, p. 489, 24 Adar II 5445; ibid., no. 218, pp. 75–80, 3 Elul 5445–Rosh Hodesh Nisan 5446. See also Nahon, *Les 'Nations' juives portugaises*, 3–4; Szapiro, 'Le Sud-Ouest', 233; Cardozo de Béthencourt, 'Le Trésor des Juifs Sephardim'. The Portuguese nation of southern France apparently took the initiative in this expulsion of ninety-three families: see Nahon, 'Los *Cristianos Nuevos*', 604–5; Israel, *Diasporas within a Diaspora*, 267–8. The decree of expulsion might also have been influenced by a fresh influx of immigrants from Portugal at that time due to the policy of the Portuguese king (Azevedo, *História*, 326).

41 See e.g. SAA entry no. 334, no. 219, p. 2 [5451]; for the reception of these Balkan Jews in Amsterdam see Levie Bernfeld, 'Confrontation entre l'Orient et l'Occident'.

42 See the arrival of immigrants from the Iberian peninsula detailed in SAA entry no. 334, nos. 219–21.

43 SAA entry no. 334, no. 21, p. 306, 27 Sivan 5483.

44 At first, in 1742, the limit was set at three years (SAA entry no. 334, no. 22, p. 144, para. 2, 28 Adar II 5502). In 1748 it was raised to six years (ibid., p. 168, para. 3, 8 Heshvan 5509).

45 For the criteria of the Amsterdam Reformed Church see Groenveld, 'For the Benefit of the Poor', 192–208. In 1634 this church distributed poor relief only to those who had been resident in the city for six months. In 1647 it extended the qualifying period to a year, in 1651 to two years, in 1701 to four years, and in 1759 to six years (SAA entry no. 376, no. 7, p. 83, 28 Dec. 1634; ibid., no. 8, p. 150, 5 Dec. 1647; ibid., no. 8, pp. 378–80, 23/30 Nov. 1651; ibid., no. 17, pp. 169–74, 17/24 Nov. and 8/15/29 Dec. 1701; ibid., no. 24, pp. 421, 427, 436–7, 439, 441, 443, 1/15 Feb., 22/28 Mar., 12/26 Apr., 3 May 1759). For criteria concerning the admission of the poor to the Lutheran Church of Amsterdam see Kuijpers, 'De zeventiende-eeuwse migrantenkerk', 309–16. In 1626 the welfare institutions of the municipality of Amsterdam required a minimum of two years' residence before one could receive charity (SAA entry no. 343, no. 1, Register van Keuren: '*Extract uit het Keurboek*', p. 73, 27 Jan. 1626); see also M. van Leeuwen, 'Amsterdam en de armenzorg', 154–5. For selection and exclusion in Christian communities elsewhere in Europe see the essays in Safley (ed.), *The Reformation of Charity*.

46 *Handvesten ofte privilegiën*, ii. 483, para. 25, 11 Oct. 1737.

47 Swetschinski, *Reluctant Cosmopolitans*, 67–8.

48 See Appendix I, Table 1.

49 Often a Jewish ceremony was considered sufficient and couples did not bother to register their marriage with the civil authorities. Ribca de Aron Musaphia married Moses Musaphia in 1675 without registering (SAA entry no. 334, no. 1144, p. 225, 22 Nisan 5435). In 1655 Daniel Lopes Arias married Rachel, daughter of Abraham Rodrigues, again without registering his plans to marry with the city authorities (ibid., no. 1143, p. 248, 2 Nisan 5415). It could well be that some Portuguese, used to religious wedding ceremonies in the Iberian peninsula, felt that a religious ceremony was sufficient. Perhaps there was also an aversion among the Portuguese Jews of Amsterdam to the registration of marriages at City Hall: on the basis of their experience in the peninsula they might have felt it wiser to keep their distance from the authorities and might have been afraid to be entered in official registers. Fear could have played another role in that some marriages involved an alliance between Jews and non-Jews, which was forbidden by Amsterdam law. For more on this issue see Reijnders, *Van 'Joodsche Natiën' tot Joodse Nederlanders*, 29–30. Sometimes Portuguese Jews were summoned to City Hall to pay a fine for failing to observe the law on civil marriage (SAA entry no. 334, no. 17, p. 28, 27 May 5389; ibid., p. 29, 20 July 5389).

50 For these *livros longos* see SAA entry no. 334, no. 215 ff. These cash books seem to have been introduced in the 1630s (ibid., no. 17, p. 63^v, 20 Dec. 5398/1637: 'como consta do livro longo'), but were only preserved from 1663 onwards.

51 See Appendix I, Table 1; Swetschinski (*Reluctant Cosmopolitans*, 68, table 2.1) notes 1,383 foreign-born individuals (i.e. born outside the Dutch Republic) registering their marriages at City Hall; I have recorded 1,147 foreign-born individuals (born outside the Dutch Republic) who so registered in the 18th century (see Appendix I, Table 2).

52 In the 17th century some 27% of the migrants on poor relief, for instance, came from Italy and another 34% came from south-eastern Europe and the Levant, Erets Yisra'el, and North Africa. Non-Jewish immigrants mostly came from countries much closer to the Dutch Republic, such as Scotland, Scandinavia, the German states, and the southern Netherlands. Lucassen describes these countries as forming 'concentric circles' around the republic. Lucassen, 'The Netherlands', 183–5; see also Lottum, *Across the North Sea*.

53 Sometimes the record includes a place of origin, often to distinguish between two individuals with the same name. Also, the surname might reveal something about the place of origin, though this was not always the case: Chaves: 'Ester de Chaves' (SAA entry no. 334, no. 175, p. 112, 1 Nisan 5440). Baeza: 'Abraham de Baeza' (ibid., no. 217, p. 56, 11 Nisan 5437). Almeida: 'David Franco Dalmeida' (ibid., no. 218, p. 242, 14 Tishrei 5449). Soria: 'Ester de Soria' (ibid., no. 216, p. 130, 25 Tishrei 5433).

54 SAA entry no. 334, no. 17, p. 8, 23 Apr. 5383: 'a dous judeus berberiscos que aqui vierao saido libres da inquisicao de Lisboa . . . f 25,–'. Earlier, in 1616, we come across a *berberisco* in Amsterdam who had escaped the Inquisition; he left Amsterdam to continue his journey (ibid., no. 6, p. 2, 19 Nov. 5377/1616: 'berberisco que veio da Inquisição'). On the presence and activities of Jews from North Africa on the Iberian peninsula see Beinart, 'The Movement of Jews from Morocco to Spain' (Heb.); Israel, 'The Jews of Spanish North Africa'; García-Arenal and Wiegers, *Entre el Islam y Occidente*. On contacts between Conversos on the Iberian peninsula and the Jewish world beyond it, the circulation of books with Jewish content in the peninsula, and people from outside the region teaching Judaism throughout the peninsula see López Belinchón, *Honra, libertad y hacienda*, 361–4; Muchnik, 'Des intrus'. Azevedo, *História*, 374 n. 3, mentions judaizers from southern France penetrating Spain in order to influence the New Christians living on the peninsula.

55 SAA entry no. 334, no. 219, p. 101, 20 and 27 Nisan 5452.

56 SAA entry no. 5061, no. 292, p. 131, 4 Oct. 1619.

57 See the petition of Debora and Rachel Nunez Bernal (SAA entry no. 334, no. 946, D 79 [apparently 1660]). In 1655, on the occasion of the death of their father Abraham Nunez Bernal and their uncle Marco Bernal, a collection of lamentations appeared in Amsterdam dedicated to the victims (*Elogios*; Roth, 'Abraham Nuñez Bernal'). Illustrations in Kistemaker and Levie [Bernfeld] (eds.), *Êxodo*, 15–16.

58 Vaz Dias, 'Een blik in de marranenhistorie', 109; see also the case of Eliasar de Solis, ibid., and that of Manuel Cortizos de Villasante (as mentioned in Yerushalmi, *From Spanish Court to Italian Ghetto*, 30 n. 44), an influential Portuguese at the court of Philip IV. He died on the peninsula in 1651, when inquisitorial proceedings against him had just begun. In the inquisitorial documents it was written that he had transferred a fund of 600,000 *escudos* to the Amsterdam community to hold for him in trust.

59 Cited in López Belinchón, *Honra, libertad y hacienda*, 365.

60 SAA entry no. 334, no. 24a, p. 65^r, 13 Tamuz 5444.

61 Beinart, 'Exodus' (Heb.); Millás Vallicrosa, 'Emigración masiva'; Domínguez Ortiz, *Política y hacienda*, 131; Lea, *A History of the Inquisition*, iii. 271, 277–9, 304; Contreras, *El Santo Oficio*, 592. In 1619 the Inquisition warned that the borders of France should be guarded to prevent New Christians fleeing the country (López Belinchón, *Honra, libertad y hacienda*, 365); nevertheless, New Christians kept crossing the border into France until the end of the 18th century (Szapiro, 'Le Sud-Ouest', 244; Israel, *Diasporas within a Diaspora*, ch. 7). Many migrants travelled long distances by foot in the early modern world (Moch, *Moving Europeans*, 43).

62 Important terms from Hebrew were translated into German, Italian, and Latin to help the travellers (Shulvass, *From East to West*, 28–9). On routes to Erets Yisra'el described in different travelogues and letters see also David, 'Fifteenth and Sixteenth Century Pilgrim and Immigrant Journey Routes', and Adler, *Jewish Travellers*. For information given to migrants in general and travel reports see Moch, *Moving Europeans*, 16; Kleinschmidt, *People on the Move*, 163–4.

63 Révah, 'Autobiographie d'un marrane', 54–6, 85, 88, 93–4: his route led him from Lisbon to Antwerp, back to Rouen, then to Antwerp again, all as intermediate stops on the way to bigger cities like Amsterdam.

64 Salomon, 'The "De Pinto Manuscript"'.

65 Moch, *Moving Europeans*, 40, 81.

66 Abraham Peres and his large family arrived in Amsterdam in 1629, sick and destitute. Apparently they had no money or other resources at their disposal and were in great distress. The community helped out with bedding and clothes. Doctors were hired and medication was distributed (SAA entry no. 334, no. 13, p. 51, Rosh Hodesh Av 5389: 'Abraham Peres E familia Vindo de novo a f 8 p mez. fora ho q se gastou Com Sua Dezembarqassão'; ibid., no. 17, p. 29, 2 Sept. 5389; ibid., p. 31, 8 Dec. 5390; ibid., p. 32, 13 Jan. 5390; ibid., p. 35, 19 Mar. 5390/1630).

67 SAA entry no. 334, no. 221, p. 293, 11 Heshvan 5470.

68 SAA entry no. 334, no. 970, p. 10, 4 Tishrei 5497: 'por frete de 9 pesoas vindas de Portugal . . . f 120'; ibid., 9 Heshvan: 'por resgatte de roupa de 9 pessoas vindas de Portugal f 50'.

69 SAA entry no. 334, no. 970, p. 567, 3 Tevet 5506.

70 'A hua Viuva que veheo de França co filhos Rocha': SAA entry no. 334, no. 172, p. 107, 1 Kislev 5401.

71 'Sara Vaz Villaflor' (SAA entry no. 334, no. 20, p. 91, Nisan 5445); 'Sara Vaz Villa Flor e sua neta': ibid., no. 217, p. 525, 5445.

72 SAA entry no. 5061, no. 311, p. 156^{v}, 11 July 1656.

73 The girl was the daughter of David da Silva (SAA entry no. 334, no. 175, p. 118, 1 Tamuz 5440).

74 SAA entry no. 334, no. 215, p. 4, 23 Nisan 5423. For the man from Lisbon see SAA entry no. 334, no. 17, p. 46^{v}, 10 Apr. 5393.

75 On this phenomenon see Moch, *Moving Europeans*, 17.

76 SAA entry no. 5075, no. 2205, Not. A. Lock, pp. 357–8, 2 Sept. 1658.

77 In 1616 his daughters tried their luck with the Amsterdam-based dowry organization Dotar (for more on this *ḥevrah* see Chapter 4), applying from their residence in St-Jean-de-Luz; their father was already in Amsterdam by this time (SAA entry no. 334, no. 1141, p. 47, 5376: 'das tres filhas de Bernaldo Lopes alias Daniel Israel, morador nestas e as ditas em Jan de Lus com sua may'). Bernaldo Lopes became a member of Dotar in 1617 (ibid., p. 81/65, 26 Nov. 5378/1617). His daughters also seem to have been in Amsterdam in that year. They were all supplied with dowries from Dotar: SAA entry no. 334, no. 1141, p. 38/53, 15 Adar 5376; ibid., p. 62, 12 Shevat 5377; ibid., p. 85, 5378: '2 filhas de Daniel Israel . . . donzellas, q ten pay abitantez nesta villa'; ibid., p. 99, 15 Adar 5378; ibid., p. 102, 19 Nisan 5378; ibid., p. 110, 5379: '1 filha de Daniel Israel'; ibid., p. 163, 5481; ibid., p. 164, 5382; ibid., p. 168, 5382; no. 1142, p. 9, 5383; ibid., p. 29, 5384; ibid., p. 43, 5385; ibid., pp. 61 and 69, 5386; no. 1142, p. 88, 6 Elul 5387. One daughter, who married Juda Haim (from Italy?), left for Hamburg, where her husband worked as a *ḥazan* (cantor) and perhaps also as a *haham*. She was finally buried there (Sárraga, 'Early Links', 38–46). Her daughters, granddaughters of Bernaldo

Lopes, also participated in the Dotar lotteries. One of them, Judith, obtained a dowry in this way in 1649 (Sárraga, 'Early Links', 40–1).

78 Lea, *A History of the Inquisition*, iii. 265–6, 273–4, 278–9, 281–2, 290; Azevedo, *História*, chs. 4–10, and the chronological table on pp. 497–9; Swetschinski, *Reluctant Cosmopolitans*, 60–2, 69–75, 87, 90. For poor immigrants from Portugal in this period see, from Beja: 'David Pinto de Beja . . . f 15' (SAA entry no. 334, no. 4, p. 426, 2 Iyar 5381); 'Mancebo de Beja . . . f 1,10' (ibid., no. 17, p. 35, 8 Apr. 5390/1630); from Bragança: 'Veuva de Braganca' (ibid., p. 33, 5390/1630).

79 Lea, *A History of the Inquisition*, iii. 271, 277–8; Azevedo, *História*, 184, 186–90.

80 Lea, *A History of the Inquisition*, iii. 269–70, 273–4; Swetschinski, *Reluctant Cosmopolitans*, 61, 99, and the sources mentioned there; Domínguez Ortiz, *Política y hacienda*, 128, 130; Azevedo, *História*, 158, 184–90; Kamen, *The Spanish Inquisition*, ch. 13.

81 Israel, *Diasporas within a Diaspora*, ch. 10; Azevedo, *História*, chs. 6–8. In this period we find people coming from Portugal, for example from Távora: 'V[a] de Eliasar de Tabora' (SAA entry no. 334, no. 173, p. 206, 7 Kislev 5412); 'A mulatta de Tabora' (ibid., p. 234, 5412); and from Guarda: 'Abraham Frois de Guarda' (SAA entry no. 5075, no. 2226, Not. A. Lock, pp. 367–8, 14 Feb. 1668).

82 For the influx of migrants from Portugal in the second part of the 17th and the first half of the 18th centuries see those registered in SAA entry no. 334, nos. 215–23 (covering 1663–1729), and nos. 969–70 (covering 1729–59). The relative tranquillity in the years during which the Portuguese Inquisition was suspended (1673–81) was followed by years of fierce persecution which triggered a continuous flow of refugees, especially after the expulsion in 1683 of those condemned for secretly adhering to Judaism (Azevedo, *História*, 283–4, 289–301, 310–23, 326, and the chronological table on pp. 497–9); see further Azevedo, *História*, chs. 8–10; Israel, *Diasporas within a Diaspora*, ch. 18; Janin-Thivos Tailland, *Inquisition et société*, 18–19; Torres Veiga, 'Uma longa guerra social'.

83 See the following examples in SAA entry no. 334: 'a familha de Medina vindo de Lixboa f 20' (no. 220, p. 13, 11 Tishrei 5460); 'Fr[co] de la Penha e sua m[er] vindo de Lixboa f 10' (ibid.); 'Diego Brandão e sua enteada com sua fam[a] vindo de Lixboa f 45' (ibid.); 'a Mosseh Alva por poizada e comida q deu 15/d a Gaspar Marques e sua familha 8 Pessoas vindas de Port[l] (ibid., p. 14, 28 Tishrei 5460); 'a d[o] Alva p. Poizada e Comida de Diego Brandão e sua familha . . . 12 Pesoas 2 dias e mais a 2 pesoas 6/d todos vindoz de Portugal f 17:17' (ibid.); 'a Gaspar Marquez vindo de Portugal por aluguer de caza f 18' (ibid.). In 1728 documents in Amsterdam mention the large number of families newly arrived in the city, having fled Spain and Portugal (SAA entry no. 334, no. 21, p. 425, 25 Shevat 5488: 'y a grande cantidade de familias q acudirao de Espanha y Portugal de novo'). The Amsterdam *ondertrouw* registers in the first half of the 18th century also show a large percentage of people originating from Portugal (see Appendix I, Tables 2 and 3).

84 Lea, *A History of the Inquisition*, iii. 237, 266–7, 277–8; Azevedo, *História*, 205. One potential immigrant from Portugal to Spain was Eliau, alias M[el] Alvares. In

1622 he tried to travel by boat from Lisbon to Seville, but was taken prisoner of war by the Moors in Morocco. Money for his release was collected in Amsterdam (SAA entry no. 334, no. 10, p. 82, 3 Feb. 5382: it is interesting to note that Eliau described himself as a circumcised Jew).

85 Azevedo, *História*, 205; Lea, *A History of the Inquisition*, iii. 277–8, 302–3; Kamen, *The Spanish Inquisition*, 287–92.

86 Domínguez Ortiz, *Los Judeoconversos*, ch. 4; López Belinchón, *Honra, libertad y hacienda*, 267, 273, 295–6, 372. A large group of poor immigrants from northern Portugal established themselves in Castile in the 1640s and 1650s and joined those who had gone there earlier. Francisco Torres, for example, was said to have helped many poor members of his family in Estepa and Osuna, who were 'observing the Law of Moses' (Lera García, 'La última gran persecución', 94); see also Contreras, *Cristianos de España*.

87 See Appendix I, Table 1; see also Swetschinski, *Reluctant Cosmopolitans* 62–4, 77–8, 120, and Israel, 'Sephardic Immigration'. For immigrants on welfare in Amsterdam see, from Madrid: 'Judica da Costa de Madrid' (SAA entry no. 334, no. 173, p. 49, Rosh Hodesh Av 5408); from Ocaña: 'Sara Vas de Ocaña' (ibid., no. 174, p. 251, 11 Adar II 5418); from Sanlúcar: 'Judica Henriques de S Lucar' (ibid., no. 216, p. 159, 5433/4); and from Utrera: 'Ester Vale de Utrera' (ibid., no. 215, p. 336, 5429/30).

88 López Belinchón, *Honra, libertad y hacienda*, 317; for the policy of Olivares towards the Conversos see Elliott, *The Count-Duke of Olivares*, 117–19, 300–4, 449; Escamilla-Colin, 'Juifs et l'Inquisition'.

89 López Belinchón, *Honra, libertad y hacienda*, table 5 (p. 341), shows the intensity of the Inquisition's activities in the years 1645–65, reaching a peak in this period between 1653 and 1656. See also Schreiber, 'Cristianos Nuevos de Madrid', and, for periodization of the activities of the Inquisition towards Conversos, Escamilla-Colin, 'Les Juifs et l' Inquisition'.

90 Caro Baroja, *Los Judíos en la España moderna*, ii. 50. López Belinchón (*Honra, libertad y hacienda*, 404) speaks of an intense wave of migration from Spain after the 1650s.

91 Israel, 'Spain and the Dutch Sephardim', 42–3. On the journey of Christobal Mendez, alias Abraham Franco y Silvera, fleeing the Iberian peninsula across the Pyrenees into France and on to Amsterdam in the winter of 1649/50 see Trivellato, *The Familiarity of Strangers*, 34–5.

92 On the situation in Spain around the War of the Spanish Succession and the inquisitorial repression of the 1720s see Kamen, *The Spanish Inquisition*, 301–2; Caro Baroja, *Los Judíos en la España moderna*, vol. iii, chs. 2–4; Martínez Millán, 'La persecución inquisitorial'; Lera García, 'La última gran persecución'; Israel, *Diasporas within a Diaspora*, ch. 18. For examples of poor refugees from Spain in the 1690s, for those leaving just before, during, and immediately after the War of the Spanish Succession, and for those fleeing the inquisitorial persecutions of the 1720s see the following in SAA entry no. 334: 'Para hua familha q veo de españa' (no. 219, p. 23, 23 Iyar 5451); 'Ester Henriquez de Espanha' (no. 219, p. 19,

10 Adar 5451); 'Ab. Robres de Leao vindo de espanha' (no. 219, p. 89, 11 Tishrei 5453); 'para cobertores para os que vierão de espanha' (no. 219, p. 94, 5 Tevet 5453); 'a Mosseh Alvares de Espanha' (no. 219, p. 391, 13 Kislev 5459); 'a Moseh Rodrigues y a Raquel Rodriguez vinds despa' (no. 220, p. 55, 25 Nisan 5460); 'Jacob Fernandes despanha' (no. 220, p. 87, 25 Nisan 5460); 'Rahel Rodrigues de Espanha' (no. 220, p. 88, 15 Elul 5460); 'A David Henriquez vindo de Toledo' (no. 221, p. 18, 1 Shevat 5465); 'Daniel Rois de Espanha' (no. 222, p. 73, 3 Heshvan 5475); 'Isaac de Almeyda desp[a]' (no. 223, p. 173, 29 Shevat 5485); 'Ab. Moreno despaña' (no. 223, p. 381, 3 Elul 5488); 'Ab. Ramos despania' (no. 223, p. 381, 5 Av 5488); 'Samuel Teixeira despana' (no. 223, p. 382, 9 Shevat 5489); 'orfans Grasia de Espanha' (no. 969, p. 81, 9 Nisan 5490). Between 1720 and 1735 there was also an increase in Sephardi emigration from the peninsula to London as a result of the growing severity of the Inquisition: see Lipman, 'Sephardi and Other Jewish Immigrants in England', 41–2, who mentions a number of *vindos de Portugal*; for the escape of fifteen Converso families from Lisbon to London in 1726 see R. D. Barnett, 'Diplomatic Aspects of the Sephardic Influx', 213.

93 Israel, *Diasporas within a Diaspora*, 264.

94 Nahon, 'Bayonne', 50. Fernando Montesinos also fled over land: after he was set free by the Inquisition, having paid the fines demanded and being banned from Ocaña in the summer of 1656, he fled with his extended family via Burgos and Vitoria towards Bayonne in France and from there via Paris to Antwerp (López Belinchón, *Honra, libertad y hacienda*, 403).

95 Israel, *Diasporas within a Diaspora*, 582.

96 These *lettres patentes* of 1550, received from Henry II, king of France, gave merchants and other Portuguese New Christians the same rights enjoyed by other foreigners: the rights to settlement in France, to the acquisition of goods, and to participation in commerce and industry. Up to 1723 these letters were given to them as New Christians, not as Jews, and protected them from persecution by the Inquisition. Yet the *lettres patentes* did not constitute a guarantee against expulsion: they had to be continuously reconfirmed, as they were in 1723. See Szapiro, 'Le Sud-Ouest', 224–5, 234; Nahon, 'The Impact', 171; id., 'Bayonne', 38–9, 48, and n. 13; id., 'Los *Cristianos Nuevos*', 598; id., *Les 'Nations' juives portugaises*, 35–9, June 1723.

97 Portuguese New Christians were given permission to live and work in the region around Bordeaux (Szapiro, 'Le Sud-Ouest', ch. 4, 223–53; Nahon, 'Bayonne', 41–4). In 1574, 1656, 1723, and 1776 the licence was issued again. Instead of using the term New Christians, the *lettres patentes* of 1723 mentioned them as Portuguese Jews for the first time. After 1776 no geographical limitation was imposed (Nahon, 'From New Christians to the Portuguese Jewish Nation in France', 336–41); see also the case of Samuel Palache, who in 1607 fled the Iberian peninsula to settle in St-Jean-de-Luz (García-Arenal and Wiegers, *Entre el Islam y Occidente*, 10).

98 Graizbord, 'A Historical Contextualization', 289, mentions an inquisitorial spy observing in 1660 that most of the former Iberians in Bayonne lived on charity.

The poverty problem lasted well into the 18th century: for example, in Bayonne in 1718 there were as many poor people to be supported as there were people who contributed to the community (Szapiro, 'Le Sud-Ouest', 236; Nahon, 'Los *Cristianos Nuevos*').

99 López Belinchón, *Honra, libertad y hacienda*, 265, mentions that these poor people threatened that they would reveal the (Jewish) identity of the rich if they didn't give them money.

100 Huerga Criado, 'El problema de la comunidad judeoconversa', 479–80. It was known that Francisco Torres of Spain supported poor members of his family in France (Lera García, 'La última gran persecución', 94). Apparently trips between Bayonne and the peninsula were very frequent in the early modern period (Nahon, 'Bayonne', 51).

101 Nahon, 'Los *Cristianos Nuevos*', 595.

102 Graizbord, *Souls in Dispute*, 68; Nahon, 'Bayonne', 52.

103 In Rouen in 1634, for example, João Pinto Delgado is said to have exhorted New Christians to go to Amsterdam (Roth, 'Les Marranes à Rouen', 147–8).

104 For a survey of the vicissitudes of the Portuguese in France see Nahon, 'From New Christians to the Portuguese Jewish Nation in France', and the literature mentioned in the notes there; id., 'Pour une approche', 38–9; Szapiro, 'Le Sud-Ouest', 223–33; Swetschinski, *Reluctant Cosmopolitans*, 79–81.

105 In the years 1616–19 large numbers of refugees arrived in Amsterdam from St-Jean-de-Luz and the surrounding area. See e.g. 'Comadre de St. Jean de Luz' (SAA entry no. 334, no. 6, p. 2^{v}, 2 July 5376/1616); 'David de Casseres de St. Jean de Luz' (ibid., p. 194, 5377/1617); 'O Judeu de St. Jean de Luz' (ibid., p. 193, 5378); 'Duas molheres vindas de St. Jean de Luz' (ibid., no. 9, p. 18, 5378); '3 ff^{as} de Isack Jessurun q aquy se sirconsidou . . . donzellas q ten pay habitantez en JandaLuz' (ibid., no. 1141, p. 85, Adar 5378); 'Das pessoas que vierao de Jaunes de Luz' (ibid., no. 4, p. 15^{v}, Ta'anit (the fast of) Tamuz 5379). See also Nahon, 'Bayonne', 44; Israel, *Diasporas within a Diaspora*, 247; on judaizers in St-Jean-de-Luz see Webster, 'Hebraizantes portugueses'.

106 An example of the precarious situation of the Portuguese in France in the early 17th century is the case of Rouen in 1633: see Swetschinski, *Reluctant Cosmopolitans*, 79–81; Roth, 'Les Marranes à Rouen'; Muchnik, 'Du catholicisme'; Israel, *Diasporas within a Diaspora*, ch. 7; see also n. 130 below.

107 Detcheverry, *Histoire des Israélites de Bordeaux*, 59, 62; Szajkowski, 'Population Problems', 95–7.

108 Olivera, *Tratado de la hobligaçion* (1661).

109 SAA entry no. 334, no. 13, p. 50, 2 Tamuz 5389.

110 'Ester de Arauyo moca orfam filha de Sarah Israel . . . veuva, vindas de Nantes a sta tr^{a} e de Dr^{te} de Arauyo (que) morreo em Guinee faz saber a Vs Ms a m^{a} Pobreza desamparo e neçesidade com q passa com sua May entrevada e sem remedio pello que lhe he necessario pedir A Vs Ms que por amor do S^{or} a admittão aas sortes das orfans desta S^{a} Hebrah no que reçebera Esmola e . . .' (SAA entry no. 334, no. 1151, p. 10, 5380).

111 SAA entry no. 334, no. 10, p. 82, 3 Feb. 5382.

112 Apparently she had been ill during her journey and arrived in Pisa much later than expected. Although the term of her dowry had expired she could still, after her arrival in Pisa, withdraw her lot of 300 guilders, drawn on Dotar in 1617, since it had been established that her trip to the Jewish world had been delayed because of her illness. In Pisa she married Isaac Montalto (SAA entry no. 334, no. 1142, p. 23, 22 Aug. 5383).

113 SAA entry no. 334, no. 10, p. 82, 3 Feb. 5382.

114 Swetschinski, *Reluctant Cosmopolitans*, table 2.5 (p. 80). For more on poor refugees from France between 1622 and 1680 see 'Viuva, vinda de Franca' (SAA entry no. 334, no. 5, p. 179, Rosh Hodesh Adar 5382); 'As mosas da Rochela' (ibid., no. 10, pp. 1 and 8, 5393–4); 'A Mello de Nantes' (ibid., no. 172, p. 4, 24 Nisan 5399); 'Veuva de Abrao Lopes de Ruao' (ibid., no. 173, p. 27, 20 Adar 5408); 'Rifica e Sara e Rahel, f^{as} de Jacob Sedikario de Rouen' (ibid., no. 1143, p. 180, 5410); 'Sara Nunes, orfa de Ruao' (ibid., no. 174, p. 86, 14 Adar II 5415; ibid., p. 143, 22 Adar 5416; ibid., p. 198, 16 Adar 5417).

115 Nahon, *Les 'Nations' juives portugaises*, 3–7, 20 Nov. 1684 (the date of the promulgation of the French expulsion edict).

116 Szajkowski, 'An Auto-da-Fé against the Jews'; Blumenkranz, *Documents modernes sur les Juifs*, 384.

117 SAA entry no. 5072, no. 692, p. 50, 3 Nov. 1690.

118 Nahon, 'Los *Cristianos Nuevos*', 606. For more on relations between the Portuguese communities of Amsterdam and those of southern France, including those concerning the migration of the poor, see Nahon, 'Rapports'. For the position of Portuguese in southern France see Graizbord, 'Becoming Jewish'.

119 Teensma, 'Fragmenten', 153.

120 See the declarations of Juan Carlos López Redondo and the Villegas family: López Belinchón, *Honra, libertad y hacienda*, 400 n. 11.

121 For the poor financial condition of many victims of the Inquisition during this period see Israel, *Diasporas within a Diaspora*, 579–80.

122 SAA entry no. 5075, no. 383A, Not. J. and N. Jacobs, p. 31, 10 Feb. 1620; ibid., no. 646A, Not. S. Cornelisz., p. 427, 24 Feb. 1623, published in *Studia Rosenthaliana*, 23/2 (1989), 205; Vaz Dias, 'Een blik in de marranenhistorie', 77.

123 In addition he was accused of collecting alms in Castile for Jewish orphanages in Amsterdam (even though there were no such institutions among the Jews in Amsterdam at that time) and of having rented a house in that city where he could reside after fleeing the peninsula himself. One individual accused him of supporting Jewish immigrants, and of sending money (the author speaks of 'Jewish alms') to members of his family in Bordeaux for Yom Kippur (López Belinchón, *Honra, libertad y hacienda*, 329–30, 360, 364–5, 378).

124 'p^{a} ajuda de frete . . . vinda de Baion' (SAA entry no. 334, no. 4, p. 130, 29 Av 5379); 'Frete e gastos de certa gente vindo de Bordeos' (ibid., p. 131, Elul 5379).

125 SAA entry no. 334, no. 17, p. 47^{v}, 15 Aug. 5393/1633: 'pobre de Bayonne plo frete

. . . f 32,12'; ibid., p. 32, 13 Jan. 1629: 'p^{a} o frete q vinha desempenhado hum mansebo barbejro vindo de bordeoz . . . f 24,–'.

126 SAA entry no. 334, no. 215, p. 264, 12 Tishrei 5429: 'a Semuel Lopes p. hum Socorro p^{a} pagar obarco q o trouxe . . . f 3:10'.

127 SAA entry no. 334, no. 217, p. 489, 24 Adar II 5445.

128 SAA entry no. 334, no. 220, p. 9, 2 Tamuz 5459: 'Abram Henriquez Lopez pa ajuda do frette desp^{a} the aquy f 50'; ibid., p. 15, 14 Heshvan 5460: 'a Soiza p. resto de frettos de Diego Brandao e Gaspar Lopez e fam^{as} f 22:10'.

129 In 1730 the travel expenses for eleven individuals were paid, and in 1731 for eight people, all of them travelling directly from Portugal (SAA entry no. 334, no. 969, p. 28, 1 Nisan 5490; ibid., p. 118, 28 Tishrei 5492); at the same time the expenses of eight Spaniards travelling to Amsterdam via Lisbon were met (ibid., p. 162, 28 Tishrei 5492). In 1732 a further six people had their expenses paid to travel to Amsterdam via Lisbon (ibid., p. 176, 14 Heshvan 5493). In 1736 the same procedure was followed for a further nine individuals travelling from Portugal to Amsterdam; an additional amount was provided to transport their clothes (ibid., no. 970, p. 10, 4 Tishrei and 9 Heshvan 5497). In 1745 money was given to help families arriving from Portugal (ibid., p. 567, 1 Tevet 5506). In 1746 the travel expenses of two Portuguese arrivals had to be met, and they also had to be taken care of (ibid., p. 569, 2 Shevat and 13 Feb. 5506: 'p. Gasto q se fes com os 2os Portugeses q vierão p. fretes e mantellos 4 semanas . . . f 379'; 'gastos q fizierão com os 2° Portugueses f 947:5'; 'p. gastos feytos p^{a} d^{os} Portugueses f 87:11'). These may perhaps have been the same 'two Portuguese' who several months later were sent away from Amsterdam (ibid., p. 443, 25 Tishrei 5507: 'Isaque Pensa de Portugal . . . f 3'; ibid., 2 Heshvan: 'Isaque Mendes de Portugal . . . f 20').

130 Révah, 'Autobiographie d'un marrane', 87, and Bodian, *Hebrews of the Portuguese Nation*, 143. For poor people arriving from Rouen see SAA entry no. 334, no. 217, p. 270, 11 and 22 Tishrei 5442: 'A hun moso de Ruao por nome Montezinos'. A memorandum, dating probably from the third quarter of the 17th century, shows how the poor from Bourg St-Esprit received support from their brothers in Holland and England (Nahon, 'Les Rapports des communautés judéo-portugaises de France avec celle d'Amsterdam', 61).

131 SAA entry no. 334, no. 17, p. 29, 20 and 22 July/2 Av 5389: 'por frete de Rotr^{dam} do Pobre Abraham Peres e sua fam^{a}'.

132 SAA entry no. 334, no. 218, p. 116, 19 Sivan 5446. In the late 17th and early 18th centuries other Portuguese communities—for instance that in London—paid the travelling expenses of refugees on arrival (R. D. Barnett, 'The Correspondence of the Mahamad', 4 and n. 2; id., 'Diplomatic Aspects of the Sephardic Influx', 216).

133 SAA entry no. 5075, no. 96, Not. J. F. Bruyningh, p. 100^{v}, 23 Oct. 1603; published in *Studia Rosenthaliana*, 3/1 (1969), 113–14.

134 SAA entry no. 5075, no. 258A, Not. J. Meerhout, pp. 16^{v}–17, 1 July 1610; published in *Studia Rosenthaliana*, 5/1 (1971), 118–19.

135 SAA entry no. 5075, no. 131, Not. J. F. Bruyningh, pp. 155^{v}–156^{v}, 4 July 1613; published in *Studia Rosenthaliana*, 6/2 (1972), 237.

136 SAA entry no. 5075, no. 147, Not. J. F. Bruyningh, pp. 29^{v}–31, 1 Feb. 1617; published in *Studia Rosenthaliana*, 11/1 (1977), 84; also cited in Bodian, *Hebrews of the Portuguese Nation*, 141 and nn. 39–40. See also the agreement, in 1649, between a Portuguese Jew from Amsterdam (Jacob Chilon) and a Dutch skipper to take Maria Nunes with her three children and her belongings from Oporto to Amsterdam (Vaz Dias, 'Een blik in de marranenhistorie', 109).

137 SAA entry no. 334, no. 12, p. 11, 5395; ibid., no. 9, p. 187, 5395.

138 SAA entry no. 334, no. 215, p. 265, 2 Adar II 5429: 'A Mosseh Nunez Xave em Londres p. o Valor de f 40: de banco . . . p^{a} se lhe concederão p. os Ss^{res} do Mahamad p^{a} ajuda de trazer aly de Portugal 2: filhas p. os coais se pagou neste dia ao parnas Abraham da Vega'. Moses Nunez Xabe had been in Amsterdam before and had been given charity. See SAA entry no. 334 no. 215, p. 192, 5426–7: *nedavot*; ibid., no. 174, p. 732, 20 Adar 5426: 'Nedaba feita neste Kahal p^{a} Socorro de pobres . . . q se repartio por duas vezes . . . Mosse Nunez Xabe f 20,-/f 12:12'; ibid., p. 201, 5427: matzot for him and his son; ibid., p. 207, 5428: *nedavot* (here it is written in the margin that he left the city—'foise'). The money was spent on a good cause. In 1685 the daughters must have been taken out of Portugal: we meet Abigail, orphan of Moses Nunez Xabe, applying for a dowry through Dotar, not from London but from Hamburg (SAA entry no. 334, no. 1144, p. 327, 5445; ibid., pp. 362, 371, 383, 413, 5448, 5449, 5450, 5453; ibid., no. 1152, p. 372, 1685). This Abigail married in Amsterdam in 1693 (SAA DTB 698, p. 183, 6 Nov. 1693: 'David Alvarenga van Lisboa Coopman, weduwnaar van Sol Alvarenga op de Houtgracht en Abigail Noenes Xave van Lisboa oud 35 jaar woont als voorn. Ouders doot. Geass. met haar zwager David Noenes Henriques').

139 SAA entry no. 334, no. 969, p. 13, 24 Elul 5489. On the efforts of Jews in other centres of the Sephardi diaspora—often through intervention of the authorities under which they resided—to rescue New Christians from the Iberian peninsula in the 1720s see Trivellato, *The Familiarity of Strangers*, 52–3.

140 SAA entry no. 334, no. 25, p. 18, 4 Nisan 5489.

141 SAA entry no. 334, no. 25, p. 249, 7 Heshvan 5500. Also here it is stipulated that the promised amount will be paid only if Raphael de Paz and his children become members of the Jewish community of Bayonne. See also, on the help given to prisoners in San Sebastián in 1751, ibid., no. 249, p. 65, 3 Tevet 5512: 'que pagou por letra para asistensia dos prisioneiros em S^{n} Sebastian . . . f 97:2'.

142 *Ancona*: 'Jose Biar de Ancona . . . f 2:10' (SAA entry no. 334, no. 218, p. 243, 5 Kislev 5449). *Ferrara*: 'Baruc Cohen de Ferrara . . . f 2:10' (SAA entry no. 334, no. 215, p. 117, 11 Tishrei 5426). *Florence*: 'Mosseh Florencia p^{a} irse a Roma f 2' (SAA entry no. 334, no. 219, p. 317, 7 Tevet 5457); 'Eliezer Gaon vezinho do Monto de S. Sevin estado de florensa p^{a} Italia . . . f 12:12' (ibid., no. 218, p. 243, 17 Adar II 5449). *Livorno*: 'mansebo de Liorne . . . f 6:12' (SAA entry no. 334, no. 17, p. 53^{v}, 30 Jan. 5395/1635); 'Un forasteiro de Liorne . . . f 1:10' (ibid., no. 216, p. 10, 15 Elul 5430). *Mantua*: 'Judeo de Mantua . . . f 1:04' (SAA entry no. 334, no. 17, p. 38, 3 Jan.

5391/1631); 'Ome de Mantua . . . f 10' (ibid., p. 41, 24 Aug. 5391/1631); 'A os de Mantua p[a] se irem . . . f 7:10' (ibid., p. 37, 10 Nov. 5391/1630); 'a outro italiano q chama o Zacarias de mantua . . . f 2:10' (ibid., no. 218, p. 243, 17 Adar 5449). *Modena*: 'Jacob Levy e Seby de Modena Ytalianos . . . f 2,–' (SAA entry no. 334, no. 217, p. 7, 30 Av 5436). *Padua*: 'Hu Velho Italiano de Padua . . . f 3.–' (SAA entry no. 334, no. 5, p. 184, 5382). *Pisa*: 'Judique Israel de Pisa' (SAA entry no. 334, no. 1141, p. 136, 5380); 'Mansebo de Piza para cazamento de irma . . . f 20,–' (ibid., no. 9, p. 18, 5378); 'Pobre que veio aqui de Piza . . . f 6,–' (ibid., no. 17, p. 38, 30 Jan. 5391/1631). *Rome*: 'Forasteiro de Roma . . . f 1:16' (SAA entry no. 334, no. 217, p. 112, 20 Tamuz 5438); 'Mordocay de Roma . . . f 1,–' (ibid., no. 174, p. 281, 11 Tishrei 5419). *Turin*: 'A hum italiano de Turin p. hum socorro em mão do Haham Aboab . . . f 5,–' (SAA entry no. 334, no. 215, p. 269, 27 Sivan 5428). *Venice*: 'Italiano de Veneza . . . f 0:12' (SAA entry no. 334, no. 216, p. 11, 12 Tevet 5431); 'A hum forasteiro pobre de Veneza, Samuel Salom . . . f 1:10' (ibid., p. 10, 29 Iyar 5430); 'Homem talmid de Veneza . . . f 3,–' (ibid., no. 172, p. 85, 10 Iyar 5400). *Verona*: 'Mosseh Gaon de Verona e may . . . f 34' (SAA entry no. 334, no. 218, p. 242, 16 Sivan 5448).

On immigration from Italy see also Swetschinski, *Reluctant Cosmopolitans*, 83.

143 'Italiano . . . f 0,6'(SAA entry no. 334, no. 5, p. 161, Kislev 5382).

144 'Judeu Portugez de Pisa' (SAA entry no. 334, no. 4, p. 139, 29 Tishrei 5380).

145 'Ao dito Josseph Somsin vindo com sua f[a] de Italia . . . para se hir p[a] alemania' (SAA entry no. 334, no. 218, p. 15, 23 Shevat 5446; ibid., 28 Adar 5446).

146 See Bonfil, 'History of the Spanish and Portuguese Jews in Italy', and the literature mentioned there; id., *Jewish Life in Renaissance Italy*; F. C. Lane, *Venice*, 400–2; Pullan (ed.), *Crisis and Change*; Sella, *Italy*; Black, *Early Modern Italy*, chs. 1 and 3; Revel, 'Au XVIIe siècle'; Israel, 'The Jews of Venice'.

147 Malkiel, *A Separate Republic*, 141–2.

148 Ravid, *Economics and Toleration*, and id., 'The Venetian Government and the Jews'.

149 Simonsohn, *History of the Jews in the Duchy of Mantua*, 135, 138–43. The Amsterdam Portuguese communities helped the Jews of Mantua with the sum of 2,250 guilders (SAA entry no. 334, no. 17, p. 37, 27 Oct. 1630/5391).

150 Malkiel, *A Separate Republic*, 152–4.

151 Simonsohn, *History of the Jews in the Duchy of Mantua*, 132–3.

152 Toaff, *La nazione ebrea*, 583–4 (para. 75, 26 Oct. 1670) and 601–2 (13 Adar Rison 1677).

153 Black, *Early Modern Italy*, 39; Israel, *Diasporas within a Diaspora*, chs. 1 and 2.

154 SAA entry no. 334, no. 13, pp. 7–8, para. 25, 24 Shevat 5382. For an overview of emigration to Italy in this early period see Appendix I, Tables 4 and 5.

155 SAA entry no. 334, no. 17, p. 1, 27 Feb. 5382.

156 SAA entry no. 334, no. 17, p. 5, 18 Aug. 5382.

157 SAA entry no. 334, no. 13, p. 28, Aug. 5383.

158 SAA entry no. 334, no. 13, p. 45, 21 Av 5388.

159 For Jewish communities in Italy see Malkiel, *A Separate Republic*, 13–15, 101–11; on Venice see Israel, 'The Jews of Venice', and Bodian, 'Amsterdam, Venice'; for Jewish communities in the Ottoman empire see Hacker, 'Sephardim in the Ottoman Empire'; A. Levy (ed.), *The Jews in the Ottoman Empire*, 1–97; M. A. Epstein, *The Ottoman Jewish Communities*; Ben-Naeh, *Jews in the Realm of the Sultans*.

160 For Rachel Fero de Pisa see SAA entry no. 334, no. 13, p. 54, 10 Feb. 5390; for Sara Cardoza see e.g. SAA entry no. 334, no. 1142, p. 26, 23 Jan. 5384; ibid., p. 219, 5396; ibid., no. 172, p. 4, 24 Nisan 5399; ibid., p. 316, Sukkot 5416.

161 Isaac de Imanuel Baruch (SAA DTB 687, p. 273, 10 Nov. 1668) married a daughter of the Pardo rabbinical family, Rachel Josephs Pardo; see also Bloom, *Economic Activities of the Jews of Amsterdam*, 41 n. 35. Isaac was in receipt of welfare in the last seven years of his life. He was still young, between 31 and 39 (see welfare distributions over the years 5433–41, e.g. SAA entry no. 334, no. 216, p. 142, 5433, distribution of matzah meal; ibid., no. 217, p. 268, 3 Elul 5441); two of his daughters died in the same period (ibid., no. 216, p. 195, 17 [Adar] 5436; ibid., no. 217, p. 197, 7 Adar II 5440). As well as being a diamond-cutter he also earned some extra money helping with the preparation of special foods for Pesach (ibid., p. 153, 5439). After Isaac's death his widow was supported by the Portuguese community from 1679 to 1683 (see e.g. ibid., no. 217, p. 195, 29 Kislev 5440; ibid., no. 175, p. 236, Rosh Hodesh Heshvan 5444; ibid., no. 19, p. 830, 11 Adar II 5440). From 1683 she was taken off the monthly welfare list since she was paid a salary equal to half her niece Ribca's income for helping Ribca, who had been appointed to assist at the *mikveh* (SAA entry no. 334, no. 24a, p. 64^{v}, 13 Iyar 5444). One of Isaac and Rachel's children, also called Ribca, applied to Dotar for a dowry in 1685, but it took nine years for it to be granted, in 1694. A year later she married Isaac de Josua Sarfati (ibid., no. 1144, pp. 326, 334, 5445–6; ibid., pp. 420, 434, 5454–5). The dowry had a value of 1,000 guilders with an additional 200 guilders given as *promessas*.

162 SAA entry no. 334, no. 217, p. 61, 12 Tamuz 5437. On the life and work of Dr Isaac Orobio de Castro see Y. Kaplan, *From Christianity to Judaism*.

163 Swetschinski, *Reluctant Cosmopolitans*, table 2.1 (p. 68). In the 18th century 13% of Portuguese Jews whose families originated in Italy registered their intended marriage with the authorities of the city of Amsterdam (see Appendix I, Tables 2 and 3); for the figure of 27% see Appendix I, Table 1.

164 SAA entry no. 5061, no. 319, pp. 245^{v}, 246, and 250^{v}, 26 Mar. and 1 May 1671.

165 SAA entry no. 5061, no. 311, p. 194^{v}, 1 Nov. 1656.

166 Lipman, 'Sephardi and Other Jewish Immigrants in England', 42–3; R. D. Barnett, 'The Correspondence of the Mahamad', 4.

167 García-Arenal and Wiegers, *A Man of Three Worlds*; Swetschinski, *Reluctant Cosmopolitans*, 85, 129; Chouraqui, *Histoire des Juifs en Afrique du Nord*, 128; Israel, 'The Changing Role of the Dutch Sephardim', 38–9, 'The Jews of Spanish North Africa', *Diasporas within a Diaspora*, chs. 5, 9, 13, and 'Jews and Crypto-Jews', 9; Hirschberg, *A History of the Jews in North Africa*, vol. ii, 220, 224–7, 262–7; Corcos, 'Les Juifs au Maroc et leurs Mellahs', 96–8; Goulven, *Les Mellahs de*

Rabat-Salé, 131–6. See also trade contracts in notarial deeds, published in *Studia Rosenthaliana*, 1/1 (1967): 110–11 (22 July 1597) and 120–1 (23 June 1598); and 33/1 (1999): 85 (1 Oct. 1626), 86–7 (2 Nov. 1626), 88 (6 Nov. 1626), 89 (9 Nov. 1626), and 91 (18 Nov. 1626).

168 On Salé see Israel, *Diasporas within a Diaspora*, ch. 9. On Jewish passengers boarding ships to Amsterdam see ibid., 294, 297. For 1679 see SAA entry no. 334, no. 24a, p. 50^{v}, 22 Elul 5439. For the shipping of the goods of Rachel de Figeiroa see ibid., no. 218, p. 249, 4 Tishrei 5449.

169 On Fez and Oran see Gerber, *Jewish Society in Fez*; Tourneau, *Fez in the Age of the Marinides*, index s.v. 'Jews'; Chouraqui, *Histoire des Juifs en Afrique du Nord*, 161–2; Hirschberg, *A History of the Jews in North Africa*, vol. ii, index s.v. 'Fez, Oran'; Israel, *Diasporas within a Diaspora*, ch. 5; Schaub, *Les Juifs du roi d'Espagne*. For more on Jews in North Africa see Gerber, *Jewish Society in Fez*; Barnai, 'The Jews of Spain in North Africa'; Benbassa and Rodrigue, *Sephardi Jewry*, pp. lii–liv; Israel, 'The Jews of Spanish North Africa'. On Uziel see Hirschberg, *A History of the Jews in North Africa*, vol. ii, 63; Ancona, 'De Portugese gemeente', 223–4; Barrios, *Triumpho* (Biblioteca Rosenthaliana copy, RON A 5252), 435–54 [pencil] ('Vida de Ishac Huziel'); Pieterse, *Daniel Levi de Barrios*, 58, 60, 63; *Encyclopaedia Judaica*, xx. 449–50.

170 On him see *Encyclopaedia Judaica*, xviii. 66–7; see also Goldish, *Rabbi Jacob Sasportas*.

171 SAA entry no. 334, no. 119a, file 17, Not. J. Oli, 18 Oct. 1678: 'legateerde ofte prelegateerde noch aen Jaël ende Abigael, ongetrouwde Dochters van wijlen Moses Cohen dazevedo, daer Moeder aff is, de voorn. sijne Suster Hester cohen dazevedo, tegenwoordigh sijnde tot Salle in Barbarijen, tot haerlieder houwelijx goed . . . yder van haer beyde, een'.

172 SAA DTB 696, p. 265, 18 Mar. 1689.

173 SAA entry no. 334, no. 19, p. 216, 28 Kislev 5407.

174 García-Arenal and Wiegers, *A Man of Three Worlds*, 38–9; Maziane, 'Entre Salé et les Provinces-Unis', 261–2; ead., *Salé et ses Corsaires*, 112–14, 145–7, 234–6, 298.

175 On the Palache family see García-Arenal and Wiegers, *A Man of Three Worlds*; Bloom, *Economic Activities of the Jews of Amsterdam*; Gans, 'Don Samuel Palache'; Corcos, 'Quelques aspects de la société juive dans le vieux Maroc', 175–6; id., 'Samuel Pallache' (Heb.); Israel, 'The Jews of Spanish North Africa'; Hirschberg, *A History of the Jews in North Africa*, vol. ii, 212–34; Chouraqui, *Histoire des Juifs en Afrique du Nord*, 132, 148; see also SAA entry no. 5075, no. 339, Not. W. Benninck, p. 244, 21 June 1617; also published in *Studia Rosenthaliana*, 11/1 (1977), 95.

176 'Nosos Irmaos de Salee . . . p^{a} socorro de sua nesesidadez hua Baril j nela, a Cravo £ 14[?] . . . e £ 240, a Arroz . . . f 106:15:8; por custo do baril en que vaj f 1:2' (SAA entry no. 334, no. 215, p. 15, 12 Tamuz 5424). For needy Jews from North Africa arriving in Amsterdam in spring 1664 see 'a hum berberisco que chegou neste dia de Salle' (ibid., 19 Nisan 5424); 'o mesmo berberisco para sua grande nesesidade' (ibid., 24 Nisan 5424); 'a tres berberiscos nesesitados' (ibid., 18 Iyar 5424); 'diversos Pobres Berberiscos . . . f 1:4' (ibid., p. 68, 10 Elul 5424). On the wars, anarchy, and famines in Morocco in the 1660s see Israel, *Diasporas within a Diaspora*, 311; Maziane, *Salé et ses Corsaires*, 70; Rosenberger and Triki, 'Famines', 15 (1974), 16–24, 64–5; Bakker, 'Slaves, Arms and Holy War', 35–40; on the sieges of Salé see Caillé, *La Ville de Rabat*, i. 216–23.

177 They were known as *megorashim* (expelled or driven out) as opposed to the *toshavim* (resident, native). On the different backgrounds of North African Jewry see Hirschberg, *A History of the Jews in North Africa*, vol. i, ch. 7; Chouraqui, *Histoire des Juifs en Afrique du Nord*, 130, 138–40; Corcos, 'Quelques aspects de la société juive dans le vieux Maroc', 159–61; id., 'The Jews of Morocco' (Heb.), 300–290; Stillman, *The Jews of the Arab Lands*, 58; Gerber, *Jewish Society in Fez*, 46–51.

178 See the example of David Machorro de Leon in Appendix III.

179 See the following sources in SAA entry no. 334 for Jews from different North African centres. *Tetuán*: 'Jacob Israel de Tituao . . . f 5,–' (no. 219, p. 357, 1 Iyar 5457); 'Mosseh Massiach de Tetuao . . . f 6:6' (no. 217, p. 274, 27 Tamuz 5441). *Algiers*: 'Juda Cohen de Argel . . . f 7:10 p[a] se hir a Berberia' (no. 219, p. 401, 14 Tishrei 5459); 'Aos horfanos de Argel . . . p[a] se yrem para Sale' (no. 218, p. 175, 23 Iyar 5447). *Oran*: 'Eliau Cansiano, forasteiro de Oran . . . f 2:10' (no. 173, p. 146, 11 Tishrei 5411). We also find refugees from Oran, driven away in 1669 (no. 174, p. 863, 22 Av 5429), such as 'Aron Sasportas dos desterrados de Oran' (no. 216, p. 10, 27 Sivan 5430 and 5 Av 5430; no. 216, p. 13, 8 Nisan 5431; no. 216, p. 74, 17 Iyar 5431). See further: 'Sara de Oran' (no. 216, p. 127, 5432–3); 'Judica de Oran' (no. 216, p. 114, 21 Av 5432); 'Simha Judia de Oran' (no. 216, p. 114, 1 Tamuz 5432; no. 216, p. 114, 29 Tamuz 5432).

Jews from Oran also arrived in London, to be sent on by the Portuguese community there to Livorno (L. D. Barnett, *El Libro de los Acuerdos*, 36 (5429). For the expulsion of Jews from Oran to other places of refuge such as Nice and Livorno, see Schaub, *Les Juifs du roi d'Espagne*, ch. 3. For Jews from 'Marrocas' (possibly a reference to Morocco), see 'Joseph Torres de Marrocas . . . f 12,–' (SAA entry no. 334, no. 219, p. 101, 1 Sivan 5452). For Jews from Salé see 'a hu berberisco yrmão de Ely de Medina de Sale . . . f 4,–' (SAA entry no. 334, no. 215, p. 12, 18 Av 5423); 'Merima de Sale . . . f 1:5' (ibid., no. 174, p. 732, 20 Adar 5426); 'Veuva do Gaon de Sale' (ibid., no. 173, p. 20, 1 Kislev 5408); 'forasteiro de Sale' (ibid., no. 215, p. 317, 29 Elul 5429); 'Juda Obediente de Salle' (ibid., p. 11, 2 Tamuz 5423); 'hun forasteiro de zalle' (ibid., no. 216, p. 10, 13 Tishrei 5431); 'a hun forasteiro vindo de salle' (ibid., p. 69, 13 Elul 5431). For Jews from Fez see 'Marianna Vendelac de Fes por estar zega' (SAA entry no. 334, no. 216, p. 10, 27 Sivan 5430).

180 SAA entry no. 334, no. 216, p. 74, 28 Tevet 5432: 'Hua molher de Ourao vinda de Cadix'.

181 For *berberiscos* see 'dois Berberiscos e hu Italiano . . . f 4:10' (SAA entry no. 334, no. 173, p. 239, Rosh Hodesh Tishrei 5413); 'berberisco forasteiro . . . Purim f 1:10' (ibid., no. 174, p. 85, 14 Adar II 5415); 'ao berberisco . . . f 2' (ibid., p. 172, 1 Sivan 5416); 'tres berberiscos nesesitados e forasteiros . . . f 2:6' (ibid., no. 215, p. 15, 18

Iyar 5423); 'Moseh Berberisco . . . p. estar doente . . . f 1:4' (ibid., p. 317, 9 Elul 5429); 'A Efraim Senior Berberisco . . . sem petisao' (ibid., p. 317, 11 Tishrei 5430).

182 On average, 7% over the 17th century: see Appendix I, Table 1.

183 For Salonika see: 'Ysaque Alcama de Salonique . . . f 3,–' (SAA entry no. 334, no. 218, p. 175, 6 Av 5447); 'Abraham Israel Ger de Salonique . . . f 4,–' (ibid., no. 215, p. 117, 8 Tamuz 5425). For Constantinople see: 'Dois forasteiros de Constantina . . . f 25,–' (SAA entry no. 334, no. 219, p. 357, 5 Tamuz 5457); 'Joseph Bar de Constantinopel . . . f 4,–' (ibid., no. 218, p. 175, 6 Av 5447). For Izmir see: 'Meir Uziel q veyo de Esmir' (SAA entry no. 334, no. 219, p. 101, 20 Nisan 5452). For Alexandria see: 'Forasteiros que binieron de Alexandria . . . f 3:3' (SAA entry no. 334, no. 216, p. 172, 6 Iyar 5434); 'a hum forasteiro dos 2 assima de Alexandria p. seu viagem . . . f 12:12' (ibid., 23 Iyar 5434). For Sofia see: 'Jacob Franco Turquia de Sufia . . . f 1:10' (SAA entry no. 334, no. 172, p. 117, 15 Adar 5401). For Jerusalem see: 'Jozeph Lopes p^{a} Jerusalaim a sua caza, ajuda . . . f 30,–' (SAA entry no. 334, no. 215, p. 264, 2 Elul 5428); 'Abraham Sason de Jerusalaim . . . f 15,–' (ibid., no. 219, p. 224, 22 Elul 5454); 'Ishak Lopez de Jerusalaim p^{or} ordem dos ssres do mahamad . . . f 60,–' (ibid., no. 218, p. 386, 7 Tishrei 5451). For Safed see: 'a hu de Sefate . . . f 12,–' (SAA entry no. 334, no. 17, p. 36, 21 June 5390/1630); 'Simon Bar Jaacob Saliah de Saphet p^{a} seu viage . . . f 25,–' (ibid., no. 219, p. 317, 20 Elul 5456); 'Sabatay Semach de Safet . . . f 21:8' (ibid., no. 219, p. 224, 29 Sivan 5454).

184 For *levantinos* see: 'Nove forasteiros italianos e levantinos para ajuda de poderem fazer a pascoa lhes dey por ordem do Mahamad . . . f 16:12' (SAA entry no. 334, no. 173, p. 137, 14 Nisan 5410); 'Sadia levi Levantino . . . 8 £ [*livras* of matzah meal]' (ibid., no. 174, p. 552, 3 Nisan 5423); 'uno de Levante pa irse . . . f 1:16:8' (ibid., no. 216, p. 172, 19 Heshvan 5435); 'judeu Levantino co hua filha . . . 15 [*livras* of matzah meal]' (ibid., no. 172, p. 78, 9 Nisan 5400).

For *turques* see: 'differentes Italianos e Turques . . . oito pesoas em tudo . . . f 14,–' (SAA entry no. 334, no. 173, p. 232, 14 Nisan 5412); 'Jacob Nehemias de Turquia . . . f 1:10' (ibid., no. 172, p. 180, 14 Nisan 5402); 'aos dous velhos de Turquia . . . f 6,–' (ibid., p. 180, 12 Nisan 5402); 'a un Haham de Turquia . . . f 3,–' (ibid., no. 174, p. 219, 12 Nisan 5417).

185 On the poor in the Ottoman empire see Ben-Naeh, 'Poverty'; id., *Jews in the Realm of the Sultan*, 261–80, 390–2; on economic decline among the Sephardim in the empire see Bashan, 'The Rise and Decline of the Sephardi Communities in the Levant'.

186 Nahon, 'Amsterdam and Jerusalem'.

187 SAA entry no. 334, no. 5, p. 149, 29 Tishrei 5382.

188 SAA entry no. 334, no. 217, p. 5, 7 Heshvan 5437: 'p^{a} hua m^{er} com 2 f^{os} vindos de Turquia p^{a} se ajudarem e lhes buscar pouzada'; ibid., p. 62, 27 Nisan 5437: 'a Sara Cohen de Salonique que ten levado por divercas vezes e agora diz vay p^{a} Londrez f 5,–'.

189 On members of the Habilho family see *Encyclopaedia Judaica*, viii. 178–9; on Eli Habilho see SAA entry no. 5075, no. 2207, Not. A. Lock, p. 935, 9 Dec. 1659. No marriage contract could be found in Amsterdam; in 1657 he was given matzot for three people (SAA entry no. 334, no. 174, p. 199, 22 Adar 5417: 24 *livras* of matzah meal; 8 *livras* of matzah meal was the portion usually given to one person; see more on this issue in Ch.3 and there in n. 85). In 1671 and 1682 there was talk of a son (ibid., no. 216, p. 64, 5431; ibid., no. 217, p. 242, 5442: 'Eli e David Habilho'); in 1662 Eli is mentioned as a *shamash* for the first time (ibid., no. 174, p. 481, 14 Adar 5422). The size of his family expanded to at least seven members (ibid., no. 216, p. 142, 5433). He apparently died in 1688; the wife of Eli Habilho is mentioned as a widow and as such supported by the community charity box (ibid., no. 175, p. 404, Rosh Hodesh Nisan 5448).

190 SAA entry no. 334, no. 969, p. 283, 16 Av 5494; the cost of their trip was covered on their arrival in the city; the same applied to the passengers from Izmir: 'por frete de 3 passageiros d'Esmir' (ibid., no. 970, p. 655, 19 Adar 5516).

191 For numbers in the *ondertrouw* registers see, for the 17th century, Swetschinski, *Reluctant Cosmopolitans*, table 2.1 (p. 68), and, for the 18th century, Appendix I, Table 2 below; for people on poor relief not registered in the *ondertrouw* registers in the 17th century, see Appendix I, Table 1 below.

192 On the situation in the Balkans at the end of the 17th century see Stavrianos, *The Balkans since 1453*, 173–7; Palmer, Colton, and Kramer, *A History of the Modern World*, 812–13, 196–200; Spielman, *Leopold I*, 93–168; Sugar, *Southeastern Europe under Ottoman Rule*, 195–202; id., *Nationality and Society*; Kann, *A History of the Habsburg Empire*, 62–7. On the fate of the Jewish population during these years of turmoil in cities such as Buda, Belgrade, and Sarajevo see M. Levy, *Die Sephardim in Bosnien*, 16–18, and Pass Freidenreich, *The Jews of Yugoslavia*; see also Benbassa and Rodrigue, *Sephardi Jewry*; Ben-Naeh, *Jews in the Realm of the Sultans*, 61–2. For the contribution of the Amsterdam Portuguese community in helping Jews taken as prisoners of war by Christian forces in cities such as Buda, Belgrade, and Sarajevo see SAA entry no. 334, no. 20, p. 105, [n.d.] 5447; ibid., no. 176, p. 3, 20 Iyar 5449; ibid., no. 20, p. 131, 9 Sivan 5449; ibid., no. 176, p. 5, 15 Tamuz 5449; ibid., no. 20, p. 131^{v}, 20 Tamuz 5449; ibid., no. 176, p. 17, 1 Heshvan 5450; ibid., p. 134, 12 Heshvan 5450; ibid., no. 20, p. 270, 8 Tamuz 5459.

Some Jews managed to reach other Jewish centres after escape or liberation from captivity. In 1690, for example, Jews from Belgrade were spotted begging in the market in Leipzig (Freudenthal, *Leipziger Messgäste*, 33). Others reached Amsterdam. On the confrontation between these Sephardim of the East and those of the West, specifically with the Portuguese Jews of Amsterdam, see Levie Bernfeld, 'Confrontation entre l'Orient et l'Occident'. For refugees in Amsterdam from Buda after 1687 see 'a hum de Bude se chama Baru . . . f 7:10' (SAA entry no. 334, no. 218, p. 175, 1 Heshvan 5448); 'Abraham Bar Juda escravo de Buda . . . f 1:4' (ibid., p. 168, 5 Heshvan 5448); 'a Rahel de Bude V^{a} de moshe saar . . . f 1:10' (ibid., p. 170, 13 [Kislev] 5448); 'a 4 Pesoas de Bude . . . f 4,–' (ibid., p. 174, 12 Adar II 5448); 'a hua cama p^{a} hum pobre de Buda doente . . . f 16:10' (ibid., p. 323, 17 Tevet 5450). For refugees from Belgrade in Amsterdam after 1687 see 'aos Pobres de Belogrado j otro q recomendou o HH . . . f 1:4' (ibid., p. 170, 20 Kislev 5448). Obadia Hesqia registered from 1689: 'obadia esquiao . . . f 1,–' (ibid.,

p. 298, 13 Nisan 5449). During the Purim distributions in 1690, some from Belgrade are described as captives, or *cativos*: 'a 5. Cativos de Belogrado . . . f 7:10' (ibid., p. 365, Purim 5450); the group is mentioned later on as *belogrados*: 'Segue a Repartisão da Turva . . . Belogrados' (ibid., p. 422, [n.d.] 5450).

193 M. Cohen, *Et sofer*; Abendanon, *Sheloshah sarigim*.

194 Abendanon, *Sheloshah sarigim*, 284–98.

195 On his arrival in Amsterdam see SAA entry no. 334, no. 218, p. 306, 14 Av 5449: 'a Joseph Abendanon de belogrado . . . f 4,–'. On Abendanon's background, his life in Belgrade as a student in the *beit midrash* of Haham Joseph Almosnino and later as the *haham*'s assistant, and his whereabouts until he reached Amsterdam in the Balkan wars see Abendanon, *Sheloshah sarigim*, 284–98. On Abendanon see further Adler, 'Hebrew Elegies', 141–7 (the information Adler gives here is not always correct: Abendanon did not go with Haham Almosnino to Nicolsburg as Adler maintains; 'Hebrew Elegies', 146); Kayserling, *Biblioteca*, 55; Wininger, *Große jüdische national Biographie*, 4.

196 Joseph Sarfati is mentioned by de Barrios as a student in the Gemilut Hasadim yeshiva in 1683 (Pieterse, *Daniel Levi de Barrios*, 121). In 1698 Sarfati, a widower and by profession a brewer, married Ester Foa (SAA DTB 701, p. 4, 7 June 1698). Through this marriage Sarfati became connected to the Amsterdam publishing house of the Foa brothers (he was now Netanel Foa's brother-in-law), and he encouraged them to publish works by *sheliḥim* from Erets Yisra'el; on Sarfati see also the foreword to Abraham Cuenque's *Sefer avak soferim*. Judging from the amount of tax he paid—he was among the lowest taxpayers in the Amsterdam Portuguese community—Sarfati was not particularly rich (SAA entry no. 334, no. 176, p. 190, 26 Adar 5455: '½ finta . . . f 3'). On the assessment of taxes in the community see Chapter 3.

197 In 1692 Abendanon worked in the publishing house of David de Castro Tartas and helped in the publication of an index of abbreviations, published as a supplement to *Sefer peri hadas*, the work of Hesqia da Silva (Kaufmann, 'Joseph ibn Danon', 290; Silva, *Sefer peri hadas*: 'Lu'aḥ resh milin').

198 On Joseph Abendanon going to London see SAA entry no. 334, no. 219, p. 101, 27 Nisan 5452; on his activities in London see Hyamson, *The Sephardim of England*, 51, 78–9, 87, 93, 111, and, further, Lopez Laguna, *Espejo fiel de vidas* (this work was approved by David Nieto and Joseph ibn Danon).

199 Cohen was one of hundreds of Belgrade Jews who had been taken captive and who suffered greatly as they waited to be liberated. Through his letters Cohen not only wanted to inform the Jewish world about the trials he and his fellow captives were going through but also to discover where he might find a safe refuge for himself and his family once he had been set free.

200 M. Cohen, *Et sofer*, 15*b* and 17*a*: questions posed by Moses Cohen in captivity in Osijek to Joseph Abendanon and Joseph Sarfati in Amsterdam, 1689–90. On Cohen's correspondence with Sarfati and Abendanon see also Ginsberg, 'Moses Kohen aus Beograd'. I should like to thank Israel Hershler for helping me analyse Cohen's *Et sofer* and Abendanon's *Sheloshah sarigim*.

201 Cohen, *Et sofer*, 16*b*, 28 Adar 5450: letter from Joseph Sarfati addressed to Moses Cohen.

202 Cohen, *Et sofer*, 16*b*, 28 Adar 5450.

203 Cohen, *Et sofer*; Ginsberg, 'Moses Kohen aus Beograd'.

204 SAA entry no. 334, no. 219, p. 2, [5451]: 'Las Personas que Hay al Prezense de Velogrado . . .'. This group of around forty-five people consisted of the following. There were eight couples with children: 'Meir Cohen su mujer Reyna cohen y zadick; Moseh abenado su muger Rrahel y sara su hijo; Issack Valensin su muger Biola y ribca lamila y deborah; Joseph alcoser y su mujer Judica alcoser y su hija Rrahel; Selomoh Aramay su mujer y lha Criansa; Ab: Levy su mujer sarah lha criansa; Joseph Crespo su mujer Ribca Jayon y lh rapaz; Jacob Malquy y su muger Rrahely lha Criansa'. Two couples came without children: 'Ab: Auby su mujer; Menahem Sulam su mujer Ribca'. There were four women registered as heads of families with children: 'Mazalso y su hija Rrahel y pinqaz', 'Doña Jurada y su hijo eliao Jayon', 'Paloma Vidal y lh ninho', and 'Flor de Pinto y su hija Miriam'. Joya Cahanet was the only lone woman without children. The orphan boys and girls registered on this list were Moses de Minhana, Perla Angela, and Gracia Sulam. Two men came alone from Belgrade to Amsterdam: Abraham Urbaz and Salomon de Cais. A year later the group had grown to about fifty-eight, consisting of nine couples with children, one couple without children, nine single women without children, five orphan boys, one orphan girl, and three single men (ibid., no. 219, p. 26, 25 Kislev 5452).

205 SAA entry no. 334, no. 220, pp. 178, 180, 184, 215, and 234, 26 Av–5 Elul 5462; ibid., p. 234, 18 Adar II 5464.

206 'Despacho de forasteiros e pesoas q vão fora da Terra: . . . a Ester Menasseh p[a] Belogrado f36,–' (SAA entry no. 334, no. 221, p. 17, 15 Heshvan 5465).

207 For Jews travelling from Buda to North Africa see SAA entry no. 334, no. 218, p. 168, 28 Tishrei 5448. For *belogrados* travelling to North Africa (Salé) see the example of Haim Halaim *belogrado* (ibid., p. 386, 17 Kislev 5451). For *belogrados* travelling to London (besides Joseph Abendanon) see Buena Raba (ibid., no. 219, p. 270, 1 Heshvan 5456); Juda Siprut di Gabay, who went there twice, in 1702 and 1707, and who left for Jamaica in 1726 (ibid., no. 220, p. 187, 28 Nisan 5462; ibid., no. 221, p. 103, 10 Adar II 5467; ibid., no. 223, p. 273, 7 Av 5486); Moses Abinun (ibid., no. 221, p. 153, 4 Heshvan 5468). For *belogrados* travelling to Surinam see the son of Angel Vidal (ibid. no. 969, p. 265, 29 Tamuz 5493). For *belogrados* leaving for unknown destinations see David Sid (ibid., no. 218, p. 386, 18 Tamuz 5450: 'a David Sid para hirse. . . f 8:10'); Mordecai Farah *belogrado* (ibid., p. 386, 26 Heshvan 5451); Menahem Sulam and his wife: 'se fue . . . Menahem Sulam su mujer Ribca 2 [almas]' (ibid., no. 219, p. 2, [5451]); Salomon Aramay and Jacob Malquy and their families: 'se fue: Selomoh Aramay su mujer y lha Criansa . . . se fue: Jacob Malquy y su mujer Rrahely lha Criansa' (ibid.); Eliau Abud (ibid., p. 101, 27 Nisan 5452); and Reina Russu and her two children (ibid.). In 1692 a group of twelve *belogrados* left the city to travel to an unknown destination (ibid., p. 101, 4 Iyar 5452: 'a Ishac Oeb para 12: pesoas de Belogrado q se vão . . . f 90,–:

a s^{r} Sara Piloso com 3: filhos, dona franca com 1 filho, Reyna Burla, Hana Burla, Sol Cabeson, Buena Alagem, Mordohay Oeb, Jeudah Benado'). The Portuguese leadership tried to find someone to accompany the group: 'Se ordenou 8 p^{s} p busquem pesoa q acompanha d^{a} gente se deu f 30,–' (ibid., p. 101, 4 Iyar 5452). Other *belogrados* leaving for unknown destinations were Isaac Baruk (ibid., p. 102, 22 Av 5452), who later returned (ibid., p. 204, 9 Nisan 5454); an anonymous refugee from Belgrade (ibid., p. 224, 29 Sivan 5454); David Israel (ibid., p. 317, 26 Elul 5456); and Mordecai Mutalbot (ibid., p. 401, 6 Tamuz 5458).

208 See Levie Bernfeld, 'Confrontation entre l'Orient et l'Occident', 56–9. I found around twenty *belogrados* who were buried in the Portuguese cemetery at Ouderkerk aan de Amstel in the period 1694–1766 (SAA entry no. 334, nos. 421–2, and no. 1329), including Obadia Hesqia (ibid., no. 422, 13 Shevat 5454); Doña Gaon (ibid., no. 1329, p. 135, 11 Adar 5457); Joya Cohen de Belogrado (ibid., no. 421, 17 Elul 5460); Meir Cohen Belinfante and his son Sadik (ibid., no. 422, 19 Adar II 5461; ibid., 18 Dec. 1750); Jacob Sulam and Eliau Hesqia Cohen Belinfante in 1728 (ibid., no. 422, 3 and 23 Tamuz 5488); Abraham Siprut di Gabay in 1733 (ibid., no. 422, 17 Heshvan 5494); Miriam de Minhana in 1744 (ibid., no. 421, 4 Tamuz 5504); and Angel Vidal in 1748 (ibid., no. 422, 28 Iyar 5508). On the Belinfante family see Divendal, 'Mozes Cohen Belinfante'.

209 SAA entry no. 334, no. 17, p. 29, 20 July 5389.

210 SAA entry no. 334, no. 174, pp. 118–19, 6 Elul 5415. On this list we encounter not only the local poor, given charity through a special *nedava*, but also people in distress returning from Brazil ('p. povres da nedaba asima e pesoas menesterozas e vindo de Brazil'). Abraham Azuby, Abraham de Pisa, Abraham de Casseres, and Jacob Abendana, included on this list, were previously registered in the Portuguese community in Recife in Brazil (ibid., no. 1304, pp. 10–14, 1 and 15 Kislev 5409).

211 On Aron de Aguilar see Emmanuel, 'Les Juifs de la Martinique', 511–12. De Aguilar appeared on the charity roll in Amsterdam between 5415 and 5420 (see e.g. SAA entry no. 334, no. 174, p. 118, 6 Elul 5415; ibid., p. 136, 26 Tevet 5416; ibid, p. 250, 11 Adar II 5418; ibid., p. 332, 25 Nisan 5419; ibid., p. 356, 1 Heshvan 5420). In 1659 he had a family consisting of three members including himself. Previously he had studied at Ets Haim, where he received a stipend (SAA entry no. 334, no. 1052, p. 57^{v}, Rosh Hodesh Av 5397 'f 2'; after 1660 he disappears from the welfare roll.

212 SAA entry no. 334, no. 19, pp. 493–4, 27 Av 5421. As early as 1659 there was a suggestion that the situation in Essequibo was difficult (ibid., no. 24, p. 2, 5419). For the situation in these colonies see Oppenheim, 'An Early Jewish Colony', 95–106; Arbell, 'The Failure of the Jewish Settlement in the Island of Tobago'; id., 'The Jewish Settlement in Poomeroon'; id., 'Jewish Settlements in the French Colonies'.

213 SAA entry no. 334, no. 174, p. 428, 1 Nisan 5421. For relations between Martinique and Amsterdam see Emmanuel, 'Les Juifs de la Martinique'.

214 SAA entry no. 5075, no. 1138, Not. J. van de Ven, p. 295, 20 Sept. 1661.

215 SAA entry no. 5075, no. 10711, no. 13, Not. S. Dorper, 16 Jan. 1744.

216 He blamed Ashkenazi Jews for his failure, accusing them of misleading him and calling them traitors (SAA entry no. 5072, no. 711, p. 24, June 1709).

217 Swetschinski, *Reluctant Cosmopolitans*, 120–1; Kellenbenz, *Sephardim an der unteren Elbe*, 45–54; Böhm, 'Die Sepharden in Hamburg'; id., 'Antijüdische Ressentiments'; Whaley, *Religious Toleration*, ch. 3; Braden, *Hamburger Judenpolitik*; Weber, 'Were Merchants More Tolerant?', 85–7.

218 For the high proportion of Portuguese Jews from Hamburg, the German states, and Denmark who registered their marriages with the civil registrar in Amsterdam, especially during the early decades of the 18th century, see Appendix I, Tables 2 and 3; for the numbers of Portuguese Jews registering their marriage at City Hall during the 17th century see Swetschinski, *Reluctant Cosmopolitans*, table 2.1 (p. 68).

219 Pohl, *Portugiesen in Antwerpen*; Salomon, 'The "De Pinto Manuscript"'; Swetschinski, *Reluctant Cosmopolitans*, 65–9, 81–2, 88–9; Révah, 'Pour l'histoire des Marranes à Anvers'.

220 Thus David Baruh, coming from Belgrade, received money for his passage ('passaje'), as recorded in SAA entry no. 334, no. 218, p. 386, 15 Tamuz/7 Av 5450. Eliau Lige stayed in the city for several weeks (ibid., p. 386, 26 Heshvan 5451: 'Eliau Lige Belogrado vindo . . . f 1:10'; ibid., 17 Kislev 5451: 'Eliau Liche Belogrado para hirse . . . f 5,–').

221 Kuijpers, *Migrantenstad*, 84, cites research proving that in 19th-century Europe only a fraction of immigrants settled in a city permanently. A similar assertion could be made about the migration of poor Jews into the Portuguese community of early modern Amsterdam.

222 *Livro longo de cuatro contas* was also the name given to some charity registers after 1729 (SAA entry no. 334, nos. 969–72 and 978–9, contain the so-called *Registro dos despachos*: exit documents for people mentioned in the *Livro longo de cuatro contas*).

223 For routes from the peninsula via Amsterdam to London and in many cases on across the Atlantic to the west, see the case of Abraham Gamboa, who went from Oporto to Amsterdam and then on to London (SAA entry no. 334, no. 218, p. 319, 9 Elul 5449). Jacob Fernandes went from Spain to Amsterdam and continued to Barbados (ibid., no. 220, p. 87, 25 Nisan 5460). David Henriquez arrived with his family from Toledo and set out from Amsterdam to London (ibid., no. 221, p. 18, 1 Shevat 5465). In 1710 Samuel Mendes travelled from Lisbon to Amsterdam and then on to Jamaica (ibid., no. 221, p. 258, 4 Shevat 5470). Daniel Rois left Spain for London via Amsterdam (ibid., no. 222, p. 73, 3 Heshvan 5475). For the route from North Africa to London and then often on to the west via Amsterdam see the case of David and Jacob da Pena, who in 1682 went from Salé via Amsterdam to London (ibid., no. 217, p. 307, 2 Adar 5442). In 1684 a woman from 'Berberia' was paid to continue from Amsterdam to London (ibid., p. 482, 15 Heshvan 5445). See also the case of Jacob Messias, who in 1687 travelled from Tetuán to Amsterdam and set out from there for Barbados (ibid., no. 218, p. 175, 4 Kislev

5448: 'Jacob Messias de Tittuao . . . f 5,- para yr a Barbados'). For routes from south-eastern Europe and the Levant to London and on to the west via Amsterdam see the case of Abraham Calvo, who started out in Turkey and ended up in Brazil, with Amsterdam as his port of transit (ibid., no. 172, p. 49, 23 Tevet 5400). In 1725 Abraham Ries arrived from Belgrade to travel on to London (ibid., no. 223, p. 227, 10 Elul 5485). For routes from Italy to London and on to the west, stopping over in Amsterdam, see the case of Isaac Nunes Henriques, who in 1699 travelled with his wife and children from Venice through Amsterdam and on to London (ibid., no. 220, p. 33, 12 Nisan 5459); David Habillo Nunez also went from Venice to Amsterdam, with a final destination of Jamaica (ibid., no. 221, p. 413, 12 Av 5472: 'David Habillo Nunez de Venetieza para Jamaica f 9,–'). For routes from France to Amsterdam, then on to London and the west, see the boy from France who went to Amsterdam to be circumcised and was sent on to Brazil (ibid., no. 172, p. 49, 22 Kislev 5400: 'A mancebo q vehijo de Franca e se circumcidou e vaj pa o Brazil . . . se despachou f 2:10'); see also Isaac Roiz Lopes, who in 1709 went from Bayonne to Amsterdam and on to London (ibid., no. 221, p. 257, 28 Nisan 5469). Jacob Dias from France continued to Jamaica via Amsterdam in 1726 (ibid., no. 223, p. 274, 24 Elul 5486). For routes from Hamburg to London and on to the west via Amsterdam see the case of Abraham Mendez, who as a young boy went from Hamburg in 1639 via Amsterdam to Brazil and received 9 guilders from the Amsterdam Portuguese community to travel on (ibid., no. 172, p. 43, 10 Kislev 5400). A young boy, the son of Abraham Ger, also travelled in 1640 from Hamburg to Amsterdam, where he received 6 guilders to travel on to Brazil (ibid., no. 172, p. 49, 1 Shevat 5400). In 1669 Eliau Aboab travelled from Hamburg to Surinam via Amsterdam (ibid., no. 215, p. 317, 6 Heshvan 5430: 'Eliau Aboab de Amb° para yrse a Surinhão . . . f 3:3'). See also Abraham Acohen, who in 1711 went from Hamburg via Amsterdam to London (ibid., no. 221, p. 360, 29 Nisan 5471). For the route from Italy to the German states via Amsterdam see Joseph Semah, who travelled from Mantua to Hamburg via Amsterdam (ibid., no. 218, p. 243, 5 Kislev 5449: 'Joseph Semah de Mantua pª Hamburgo . . . f 4'). See also the case of Joseph from Turin, who moved, via Amsterdam, to the German states in 1724 (ibid., no. 223, p. 172, 22 Elul 5484: 'Joseph de Turin . . . f 3, Alemania'). For the route from the Levant to Amsterdam and thence to Hamburg see the case of Abraham Pichi, who went from Constantinople via Amsterdam to Hamburg in 1696 (ibid., no. 219, p. 317, 25 Tishrei 5457); Mordecai Sarfati had taken the same route earlier, in 1688 (ibid., no. 218, p. 242, 12 Av 5448).

224 Cottaar, Lucassen, and Lucassen, *Van over de grens*, 12; Lottum, *Across the North Sea*, ch. 4. For European overseas expansion see also Scammel, *The First Imperial Age*, and titles mentioned in his 'Suggestions for Further Reading', 257–61.

225 Moch, *Moving Europeans*, 47–59.

226 Rachel Rodrigues came to Amsterdam from Spain and continued to France (SAA entry no. 334, no. 220, p. 88, 15 Elul 5460; for help given to her on arrival in Amsterdam see ibid., p. 55, 25 Nisan 5460). In 1737 Abraham Nunes Carvallo was given financial assistance in Amsterdam when he arrived there en route from Portugal to Bayonne (ibid., no. 970, p. 427, 8 Tamuz 5497); Isaac de Almeida travelled from Spain to Amsterdam in 1725 to continue to Livorno (ibid., no. 223, p. 173, 29 Shevat 5485); Abraham Ramos and Samuel Teixeira left Spain for Amsterdam respectively in 1728 and in 1729 to set out for France (ibid., no. 223, p. 381, 5 Av 5488; ibid., p. 382, 9 Shevat 5489). For similar patterns of travel via London see the case of Abraham Furtado, who left Portugal for London to settle in southern France: Cavignac, 'L'Immigration des Juifs portugais à Bordeaux', 128.

227 Two women arriving in Amsterdam from Bayonne in 1699 took their time—six years—to consider migration: in 1705 we meet them again, setting out for Livorno (SAA entry no. 334, no. 220, p. 8, 2 Tamuz 5459; ibid., no. 221, p. 57, 15 Sivan 5465). Isaac Gomes arrived from Bayonne in 1700, also to continue to Livorno (ibid., no. 220, p. 87, 22 Iyar 5460); Jacob Lopes came from France to Amsterdam to travel on to Italy (ibid., no. 223, p. 172, 5 Heshvan 5485); Jacob Palache set out from Salé for Livorno via Amsterdam (ibid., no. 221, p. 413, 12 Av 5472); Samuel Martines came from Tetuán to head on to Livorno or Izmir (ibid., no. 221, p. 413, 3 Kislev 5473). For the route from France to North Africa via Amsterdam see Jacob Pereyra, who came from Rouen to Amsterdam to set out for Tetuán (ibid., no. 222, p. 189, 8 Sivan 5476). For the route from North Africa to Italy via Amsterdam see Salom Cohen, who came from Tunis to Amsterdam en route to Venice (ibid., no. 222, p. 128, 25 Sivan 5475).

228 See the case of David Machorro de Leon in Appendix III. This pattern continued through the 18th century (R. Cohen, *Jews in Another Environment*, 24–34). On Ashkenazi Jews travelling away from home to seek business opportunities and new outlets for their products see the letters described in Arnheim, 'Hamburg/Altona-Copenhagen', and the letter from Jacob Isaks to his wife Jutte (SAA entry no. 5075, no. 7533, Not. J. van Vilekens, pp. 997–9, 30 Sept. 1710).

229 Moch, *Moving Europeans*, 17, 58–9.

230 In 1697 Moses Lopes Nunes travelled from Valladolid in Spain to Amsterdam. He obtained money there to leave for Tunis; one year later he had returned to Amsterdam in order to travel to Salé (SAA entry no. 334, no. 219, p. 357, 16 Heshvan 5458; ibid., p. 401, 25 Elul 5458).

231 For more detail see Appendix III.

232 For the routes David Machorro de Leon took see Appendix III. See also an example of the Palache family's frequent journeys to and from North Africa in García-Arenal and Wiegers, *A Man of Three Worlds*.

233 For Abraham Pinheiro see SAA entry no. 334, no. 215, p. 42, Nisan 5423–4. He left for Guyana, having previously been in Brazil (Wiznitzer, *Jews in Colonial Brazil*, 138), and travelled back and forth. In 1664 his son Daniel was born in Martinique (SAA DTB 694, p. 235, 1 Dec. 1664; see also Emmanuel, 'Les Juifs de la Martinique', 513). He returned from the west to Amsterdam between 1665 and 1668 (see e.g. SAA entry no. 334, no. 174, p. 731, 20 Adar 5426; ibid., no. 215, p. 104, 7 Kislev 5426: rental subsidy; ibid., p. 252, 5428: matzot). In 1668 he apparently left again, leaving his wife and children behind in Amsterdam. His wife died there in 1673. The Portuguese community supported her and their children until her death ('mulher de Abraham Pinheiro') (see e.g. ibid., no. 174, p. 823, Rosh Hodesh Elul 5428; ibid., no. 215, p. 342, 5429: rental subsidy; ibid., no. 216, p. 63, 5431: matzot; ibid., p. 104, 5432: peat; ibid., no. 174, p. 992, Rosh Hodesh Iyar 5433; ibid., no. 216, p. 144, 16 Iyar 5433). Pinheiro returned to Amsterdam in 1674, apparently to take care of his now motherless children. From 1674 until the beginning of the 18th century he received financial support from the Portuguese community (see e.g. ibid., no. 216, p. 165, 4 Adar II 5434; ibid., p. 165, 5434: matzot; ibid., no. 217, p. 520, 5445: matzot; ibid., no. 174, p. 1013, Rosh Hodesh Nisan 5434; ibid. no. 175, p. 220, Rosh Hodesh Nisan 5443; ibid., no. 176, p. 377, Rosh Hodesh Nisan 5461).

David Alvares Torres returned from Brazil earlier (SAA entry no. 334, no. 173, p. 239, Rosh Hodesh Tishrei, Sukkot 5413: 'David Torres Brazil . . . f 3,–'). He was a member of the Portuguese community in Brazil (ibid., no. 1304, p. 14, 1 Kislev 5409; Wiznitzer, *Jews in Colonial Brazil*, 138). After his return from Martinique in 1661 (SAA entry no. 5075, no. 1138, Not. J. van de Ven, p. 295, 20 Sept. 1661), David was supported periodically by the Amsterdam Portuguese community from 1662 until 1668, together with his family of five (see e.g. ibid., no. 174, p. 484, 24 Adar 5422; ibid., no. 215, p. 191, 5426–7: *nedavot*; ibid., p. 238, 5427–8: peat; ibid., p. 293, 5428: rental subsidy). David kept travelling. In 1668 he left for Barbados with his family, including a baby a few months old (ibid., p. 264, 23 Elul 5428: 'David Alvares Torres p[a] irse à Barbados com sua caza e com hua filha de teta de poucos mezes . . . f 100,–'). In 1675 he was apparently back in Amsterdam, and received money to travel again (ibid., no. 216, p. 193, 13 Elul 5435). Thereafter he lived in a number of different locations in the West Indies: his daughters sent applications, from different islands and cities, to participate in the Dotar lottery in Amsterdam. In 1676 he was in Barbados, in 1677 in Curaçao, in 1679 in Jamaica, and in 1681 in London (ibid., no. 1144, p. 229, 5436; ibid., p. 239, 5437; ibid., p. 263, 5439; ibid., p. 291, 5441). Finally, in the spring of 1681, he returned from Barbados to Amsterdam (ibid., no. 217, p. 267, 20 Tamuz 5441). He died in 1684. His daughters continued to receive welfare in Amsterdam, for example in 1684 (ibid., no. 175, p. 255, Rosh Hodesh Nisan 5444: 'Orfans de David Alvarez Torrez').

For Jacob Gabay Correa see Appendix III.

234 In 1697 Salomon do Porto returned to Amsterdam, though we do not know where from, and was sent out again, to another unknown destination (SAA entry no. 334, no. 219, p. 357, 17 Iyar 5457: 'f 5': 'q torno a reseber p[a] sehir'); around eight years later he came back from Venice, only to return once more to Italy (ibid., no. 221, p. 102, 8 Kislev 5467: 'a selomo porto de veneza p[a] Italia f 12,–'). About three years later he was again in Amsterdam, and was again sent to Venice (ibid., p. 360, 3 Av 5471: 'a selomoh Porto para Veneza f 12,–'). A few months later his wife(?) and children left for Venice (ibid., 15 Shevat 5472: 'hana do porto e filhos p[a] Veneza f 5,–').

235 In 1700 Mordecai Lealtad obtained money to travel to Livorno (SAA entry no. 334, no. 220, p. 87, 25 Nisan and 17 Menahem-Av 5460); about two months later he was in Rotterdam, en route for London (ibid., no. 220, p. 88, 18 Tishrei 5461). In 1702 he received money in Amsterdam to go to Livorno (ibid., p. 187, 9 Iyar 5462). In 1703 he was back in Amsterdam en route to London (ibid., p. 237, 20 Sivan 5463). A few months later he returned to Amsterdam en route to Salé (ibid., p. 237, 10 Elul 5463). In 1755 we meet a Mordecai Lealtad again being sent out for five years to an unknown destination (ibid., no. 970, p. 467, 22 Tevet 5515 . . . 'f 3,–').

236 Jona Fresco travelled in the years 1686–1736, but was in Amsterdam in 1687, 1690, 1691, 1700/1, 1721, and 1727 ('Jonah Fresco: para se hir com sua familia para Barbados sem fiança . . . f 10': SAA entry no. 334, no. 218, p. 110, 22 Tamuz 5446; ibid., p. 119, 27 Adar 5447: 'por mortalha cx[a] e barco p[a] hua criança de Jonah Fresco f 6:1'; ibid., p. 323, 8 Tamuz 5450: 'capa e gasto de levar hua criatura de Jona Fresco f 1:8'; ibid., p. 385, 22 Iyar 5450: 'a Jona fresco . . . f 5,–'; ibid., no. 219, p. 23, 11 Tamuz 5451 . . . 'f 8,–'). He left for Venice in 1695 ('Jona Fresco para Venecia': ibid., p. 270, 1 Heshvan 5456). He was back in Amsterdam in 1700 (ibid., no. 220, p. 38, 29 Shevat 5460: 'a yona fresco p. ter em caza d[a] mulata . . . f 3,–'; ibid., p. 54, 8 Nisan 5460: 'Jona Fresco . . . f 0:18'; 'Jona fresco f 0:18': ibid., p. 117, 26 Sivan 5461). In 1707 he left for London ('jona fresco p[a] Londres . . . f 10,–': ibid., no. 221, p. 154, 6 Kislev 5468). In 1711 he left for Hamburg (ibid., p. 360, 6 Iyar 5471: 'a Jona Fresco para Hamburgo . . . f 5,–'). Later he moved to The Hague (ibid., no. 222, p. 355, 21 Kislev 5480: 'jona Fresco para Haya . . . f 40,–'). He was back in Amsterdam in 1721 (ibid., no. 223, p. 15, 21 Iyar 5481: 'Jona fresco f 6,–'). In 1724 he moved to London (ibid., p. 172, 7 Iyar 5484). In 1727 he moved once again to The Hague (ibid., p. 322, 3 Tamuz 5487: 'jonah fresco: haya f 6,–.'). In 1736 he was back in town (ibid., no. 970, p. 9, 17 Sivan 5496: 'a jona fresco f 1:10').

237 See Y. Kaplan, 'The Travels of Portuguese Jews'; id., 'Amsterdam, the Forbidden Lands, and the Dynamics of the Sephardi Diaspora'; Graizbord, *Souls in Dispute*. On this phenomenon see also sermons by Morteira condemning such trips, cited and discussed in Saperstein, *Exile in Amsterdam*, 303–6.

238 SAA entry no. 5072, no. 252, p. 12, 16 Aug. 1736: 'Den Reg[t] is in den jaare 1724 met sijn huyse komen vlugten wegens religie Saken uijt Portugaal en sig neder gesteld te Bayoennen mede brengende tien duyzend Pezos sijnde hollands geld circa drie en twintig duyzend guldens dewelke hij aldaar voor het Grootste Gedeelte heeft verloren en vervolgens op hoop van Beter fortuyn in de Jare 1731 naar holland gekomen met omtrent vier duyzend Guldens, ende alsoo den Req[t] siende sijn Gehele capitael vergaan en den jaare 1733 wederom Geresolveerd is naar Portugal te keren met Eenige coopmanschappen om alsoo sig wederom in staat te stellen dog het fortuyn hem ter contrarie wesende het ongeluk heeft ondergaan naar dat hij hem op 16 Januari 1735 te Portugaal had ingescheept om naar Holland te retourneeren int schip genaamt de twee Gebroeders Cap. Pierre Abadie, mede brengende ses duyzend cruzados zijnde hollandse f 6975: soo in geld als goederen, mistg[s] alle sijn boeken chartres en Papieren in die al omme bekende storm die geweest is op de 18 jan 1735 schipbreuk te lijden sodanig dat sij geslagen sijn tegens de custen genaamd camarin te Galicia alwaar niets van t Gehele Schip is Gesalveerd als eenige Persoonen soo dat den Req[t] alhier voor een notoire schade brengt de Gem. somme van f 6975; voor Extraordinaire Reijskosten van Portugal op Bayoenen Bourdeaux en hollandt ten minsten f 1000.'

239 SAA entry no. 334, no. 13, pp. 7 and 8, paras. 22 and 25, 24 Shevat 5382. On the issue of sending away the poor in the early years of the 17th century see Swetschinski, *Reluctant Cosmopolitans*, 182–3, 185–6, and Bartal and Kaplan, 'Emigration' (Heb.).

240 SAA entry no. 334, no. 13, p. 45, 21 Av 5388.

241 Their number included many who were given money to travel practically every year. For references in the *escamot* to sending off poor Ashkenazi Jews see SAA entry no. 334, no. 19, p. 105/20, Tamuz 5399, pp. 430–1, 6 Iyar 5418, and p. 533, 8 Sivan 5424. For financial surveys see ibid., no. 239, p. 11, 5399–5400: 'despeza feita com tudescos encaminhados p[a] Polonia'; ibid., no. 240, p. 89, 1 Nisan 5419: 'se despenderao . . . en encaminhar pobres tudescos e polacos'; ibid., pp. 121, 124, 1 Nisan 5421; ibid., p. 192, 1 Nisan 5425: 'despendidos com tudescos encaminhadoz p[a] Polonia'.

242 SAA entry no. 334, no. 22, pp. 161–2, 25 Heshvan 5508. For a detailed analysis of the problems and plans see Pinto, *Reflexoens*; R. Cohen, *Jews in Another Environment*, 18–34; id., 'Passage to a New World'; Levie Bernfeld, 'Financing Poor Relief', 88–9. This project is an example of another form of migration known as 'colonizing migration' (Moch, *Moving Europeans*, 17; Canny, 'In Search of a Better Home?'; Scammel, *The First Imperial Age*, ch. 2).

243 For the Portuguese empire see Coates, *Convicts and Orphans*; for England on Georgia see Coleman, *Colonial Georgia*, chs. 1 and 2; for France see Quinn, *The French Overseas Empire*, 51–2, 56, 59; for the German poor in Husum sent off to Holland see Kuijpers, *Migrantenstad*, 63–70.

244 Bruijn, 'Personeelsbehoefte', 226, 241–4, 246; Voorst van Beest, *De Katholieke Armenzorg*, 81–2, 112–20; Hallema, 'Emigratie'; Manen, *Armenpflege in Amsterdam*, 98; McCants, *Civic Charity*, 64–70; Kuijpers, *Migrantenstad*, 204, 209, 298; for sending away poor farming families to Surinam see also *Nederlandsche Jaerboeken* (vol. i, p. 34); for the Reformed Church of Amsterdam see e.g. SAA entry no. 376: no. 8, p. 380, para. 3, 30 Nov. 1651; no. 187, p. 17, 4 June and 2, 9, and 30 July 1693; no. 187, p. 38, 30 Sept. 1706; no. 187, p. 44, 16 May 1709; no. 187, p. 66, 23 Sept. 1717; no. 187, p. 74, 3 Dec. 1722; no. 21, pp. 381–2, 3 Aug. 1741.

245 In 1700 299 heads of families took regular poor relief from the Amsterdam Portuguese community, while 478 heads of families paid the internal taxes (SAA entry no. 334, no. 176, pp. 337–48, 1 Nisan 5460; ibid., no. 220, pp. 79–85, 5461).

246 SAA entry no. 334, no. 22, p. 162, 25 Heshvan 5508.

247 'Tanto por a tibies erepugnancia dos desvalidos quanto por a ineficasia de podelos constringir' (SAA entry no. 334, no. 22, p. 171, 10 Nisan 5510).

248 For France see Nahon, *Les 'Nations' juives portugaises*, 3–7, 13–17, 186–8; for London see R. D. Barnett, 'Dr. Samuel Nunes Ribeiro', and Oliel-Grausz, 'A Study in Intercommunal Relations', 51; for Hamburg see Shulvass, *From East to West*, 28–9.

249 SAA entry no. 334, no. 221, p. 414, 1 Adar 5473: 'Moseh Alvares pago a la cansel Belegin[s] y el escottete y despacho a Liorne asta su enbarque f 62,4,8'.

250 *Handvesten ofte privilegiën*, v. 66. For the contracts signed by poor Portuguese Jews agreeing to leave see the so-called *Registro dos despachos* (SAA entry no. 334, nos. 978–9, 1759–1814).

251 SAA entry no. 5061, no. 705, no. 3, 4–5 Sept. 1759; Emmanuel, *History of the Jews of the Netherlands Antilles*, 777.

252 J. Katz, *Tradition and Crisis*, 35, 86–7.

253 SAA entry no. 334, no. 13, pp. 8–9, para. 29, 24 Shevat 5382.

254 'A Jacob levy que vino de Yerusalaim p[a] se bolver p[a] alla . . . f 37:10' (SAA entry no. 334, no. 217, p. 419, 12 Heshvan 5444).

255 'Ishac Rodriguez Nunes . . . f 20,– . . . vindo de Argel pa se bolver' (SAA entry no. 334, no. 218, p. 15, 13 Tamuz 5445).

256 'Rachel Vaya de Liorne q vai p. tera p[a] italia . . . f 4' (SAA entry no. 334, no. 218, p. 242, 5 Av 5448).

257 SAA entry no. 334, no. 221, p. 257, 21 Kislev 5470.

258 Most Ashkenazi Jews, as we have seen, were sent back to the German states and eastern Europe. For individual cases see SAA entry no. 334, no. 172, p. 59, 26 Shevat 5400: 'Tudesco de Emden . . . p[a] se hir . . . f 1:04'; ibid., no. 215, p. 17, 14 Shevat 5424: 'Jacob van Wourms tudesco p[a] seu viagem . . . f 1:12'; ibid., p. 318, 5 Nisan 5430: 'Tudesco para yrse fora da terra . . . f 0:10'; ibid., no. 217, p. 6, 25 Iyar 5437: 'Por ordem dos ssres do mahamad a 1 polaco p. Papel del s[r] H. Ishack Aboab dizendo que se vay p[a]. fora . . . f 1:18'; ibid., no. 215, p. 17, 20 Sivan 5423: 'Nachum Polaco p[a] ajuda de seu viagem . . . f 2:10'; ibid., p. 269, 10 Av 5428: 'V[a] de R. Pinhas p. Hum socorro p[a] bolver a Polonia . . . f 15:15'.

259 For *forasteiros* see SAA entry no. 334, no. 216, p. 11, 2 Tevet 5431: 'a un forasteiro p[a] se encaminhar . . . f 2:10'; ibid., p. 10, 28 Kislev 5431: 'hum forasteiro p[a] se hir . . . f 3:3'; ibid., no. 218, p. 242, 2 Sivan 5448: 'dous forasteiros q vão p[a] polonia pa se hirem pa turquia '; ibid., no. 219, p. 357, 22 Elul 5457: 'hum forasteiro p[a] se hir a Terra Santa . . . f 2,–'. For *pobres* in general mentioned in these reviews see ibid., no. 216, p. 113, 13 Iyar 5432: 'que dey a huns pobres que se vao p[a] fora . . . f 1:8'.

260 An 18th-century document bears witness to pressure allegedly exerted by the *kahal* (SAA entry no. 334, no. 22, p. 144, para. 4, 28 Adar II 5502; ibid., no. 502, pp. 71–2 [n.d., probably mid-18th century]): in this document the administration of the Portuguese congregation threatened to withhold relief in cases in which suitable candidates for emigration refused to go. See also R. Cohen, *Jews in Another Environment*, 23.

261 For a similar policy elsewhere in Europe see Kuijpers, *Migrantenstad*, 67–8.

262 SAA entry no. 334, no. 17, p. 6, 20 Nov. 5383.

263 SAA entry no. 334, no. 10, p. 1, 3 Sivan 5405. For the payment made to Captain Almquer in 1702 to take Josua Tuby Valensin to Livorno see ibid., no. 220, p. 187, 18 Heshvan 5463.

264 SAA entry no. 334, no. 218, p. 175, 20 Elul 5447: 'a Arao Melina o mestre p[a] o leve a bayona'.

265 SAA entry no. 334, no. 218, p. 15, 16 Sivan 5445: 'f 6:6 . . . para forasteiro . . . se embaracar para berberia'; ibid., no. 219, p. 101, 4 Iyar 5452: 'a Ishac Oeb para 12 pesoas de belogrado q se vão . . . f 90,–'.

266 SAA entry no. 334, no. 220, p. 237, 20 Heshvan/26 Shevat 5464.

267 SAA entry no. 334, no. 13, p. 45, 21 Av 5388; ibid. no. 19, p. 105/20, 30 Tamuz 5399; ibid., pp. 430–1, 6 Iyar 5418.

268 On the *borgbrieven* issued by different institutions or individuals in the Dutch Republic outside Amsterdam see M. van Leeuwen, 'Amsterdam en de armenzorg', 148–54.

269 SAA entry no. 334, no. 217, p. 61, 15 Sivan 5437.

270 SAA entry no. 334, no. 217, p. 62, 5 Tamuz 5437.

271 SAA entry no. 334, no. 218, p. 110, 17 Sivan 5446.

272 SAA entry no. 334, no. 217, p. 62, 13 Sivan 5437.

273 SAA entry no. 334, no. 217, p. 419, 8 Sivan 5443.

274 SAA entry no. 334, no. 218, p. 175, 1 Tamuz 5447.

275 SAA entry no. 334, no. 22, p. 145, art. 8, 28 Adar II 5502.

276 SAA entry no. 334, no. 22, p. 167, 8 Heshvan 5509.

277 SAA entry no. 334, no. 970, p. 459, 2 Iyar 5509.

278 SAA entry no. 334, no. 970, p. 459, 9 Iyar 5509.

279 SAA entry no. 334, no. 970, p. 444, 3 Tamuz 5507.

280 See R. Cohen, 'Passage to a New World', and *Registro dos despachos* (SAA entry no. 334, no. 978). For earlier examples see the case of Abraham da Silva (ibid., no. 217, p. 307, 23 Shevat 5442): 'a ab[m] da silva para sehir a sale que promette restituir enela chegando conbem f 31,10'.

281 SAA entry no. 334, no. 13, p. 31, 11 Aug. 5384.

282 SAA entry no. 334, no. 217, p. 112, 16 Iyar 5438.

283 SAA entry no. 334, no. 217, p. 419, 3 Av 5443.

284 SAA entry no. 334, no. 218, p. 386, 27 Tamuz 5450.

285 SAA entry no. 334, no. 17, p. 2, 8 Apr. 5382.

286 Oppenheim, 'An Early Jewish Colony', 132, and 'An Early Jewish Colony: Supplemental Data'.

287 SAA entry no. 334, no. 215, p. 223, 10 Nisan 5428.

288 SAA entry no. 334, no. 217, p. 61, 12 Elul 5437: 'Por hordem dossres do Mamad a David Lopes Roldao que se torna Pera Bayona de donde veo'.

289 For temporary assistance to him see SAA entry no. 334, no. 217, pp. 94, 148, 190, 241, distributions of matzot for the years 5438–41; for special assistance in the year 5439 see ibid., pp. 154–8, 196, 204.

290 SAA entry no. 334, no. 217, p. 160, 27 Nisan 5439: 'a David Lopez Roldao q vay a Bayona'; the document records that he returned to the city of Amsterdam ('bolviendo'); the travel expenses he was given must have been returned since the amount in the register has been blotted out.

291 SAA entry no. 334, no. 218, p. 15, 7 Heshvan 5446: 'a David Lopes Roldan para seir da terra e nao bolver f 31:10'; ibid., 2 Kislev: 'a dito Roldan Para sehir a Rotterdam e dai a Londrez f 18:18'.

292 SAA entry no. 334, no. 218, p. 111, 2 Elul 5446: 'a David Lopes Roldan para se hir a bordeus'.

293 SAA entry no. 334, no. 217, p. 482, 13/20 Tamuz 5444; ibid., no. 219, p. 23, 13 Sivan 5451.

294 SAA entry no. 334, no. 219, p. 270, 19 Tamuz 5455: 'Isaque Sacuti p[a] Liorne, con condicion que sino se va nole despacharan jamas peticion ninguna'.

295 SAA entry no. 334, no. 24, p. 2, 1 Apr. 5419.

296 SAA entry no. 334, no. 24a, p. 2[v], 5 Adar 5424.

297 SAA entry no. 334, no. 17, p. 47[v], 15 Aug. 1633.

298 SAA entry no. 334, no. 17, p. 27, 20 May 5389.

299 SAA entry no. 334, no. 17, p. 48[v], 10 Sept. 5394/1633.

300 SAA entry no. 334, no. 218, p. 116, 19 Sivan 5446; ibid., 7, 10, and 12 Av.

301 SAA entry no. 334, no. 215, p. 17, 23 Nisan/13 Iyar/9 Sivan 5423.

302 SAA entry no. 334, no. 4, p. 303, 11 Tamuz 5380.

303 SAA entry no. 342, no. 951, p. 129, 9 Mar. 1686; ibid., 21 May 1686; ibid., 18 June 1687; SAA entry no. 334, no. 24a, p. 67, 9 Mar. 5446; ibid., no. 218, p. 116, 8 Sivan 5446: 'aos Regentes da casa dos locos por Mosseh Mendes Carlos do prim[ro] quartel f 25'; ibid., 26 Sivan 5446: 'a duas pessoas por levar o d[o] Carlos a cassa dos locos'; ibid., no. 218, p. 180, 8 Tamuz 5447.

304 In 1688 Moses Mendes Carlos was put on a boat to London (SAA entry no. 334, no. 218, p. 176, 4 Nisan 5448: 'f 20 . . . a Moseh Mendes Carlos . . . para se yr a Londres'). Six months earlier Jacob Mendes Carlos settled down in London (ibid., p. 111, 14 Tishrei 5447); he was apparently Moses' nephew. Jacob Mendes Carlos married in 1685 in Amsterdam; at the time he announced that his parents were no longer alive (SAA DTB 695, p. 33, 25 Aug. 1685). Moses Mendes Carlos did not stay in London permanently, returning to Amsterdam despite the fact that Jacob Namias de Castro had stood surety for his departure. In 1696 he died and was laid to rest in Ouderkerk (SAA entry no. 334, no. 219, p. 275, 29 Tevet 5456).

305 SAA entry no. 334, no. 221, p. 57, 22 Kislev, 3 and 26 Shevat 5466. Several months later, after the winter (and Pesach), Isaac did catch his boat (ibid., p. 102, 27 Nisan 5466).

306 Isaac Gomez Bernal became ill and did not go to London as planned (SAA entry no. 334, no. 221, p. 57, 27 Tamuz–19 Elul 5465). About six months later he changed his destination to Bayonne (ibid., p. 102, 5 Iyar 5466). Abraham Israel do Valle, the father of Dr Saldanha, who in 1729 had arrived from Spain at the age of 56 and who had been circumcised on his arrival, was about to leave from

Amsterdam two years later when he fell ill. He was taken from the island of Texel, where he had to go to embark, back to Amsterdam. For a record of his circumcision see SAA entry no. 334, no. 378, p. 18, 11 Oct. 1729/18 Tishrei 5490. For his departure see ibid., no. 969, p. 158, 19 Heshvan 5492. For his departure from Texel see ibid., p. 163, 8 Tevet 5492; see also ibid., p. 158, 19 Adar 5492; ibid., p. 165, 26 Adar 5492. Samuel Teixeira was paid for taking care of do Valle, who was ill for sixteen weeks (ibid., p. 215, 1 Sivan 5492). Do Valle seems to have left Amsterdam only about three years later, in 1735, as his name appears in the list of people leaving the community ('Abraham del Vale Sardana': SAA entry no. 334, no. 970, p. 424, 17 Tevet 5496).

Moses Roiz and his wife Gracia were about to leave for London and continue their journey from there when the Mahamad decided to keep them in Amsterdam and put them on the roll of people who received a monthly allowance. Maybe they had fallen ill, or maybe there were other reasons. (See SAA entry no. 334, no. 221, p. 57, 27 Tamuz 5465; ibid., 24 Tishrei 5466.)

307 This happened to Jacob Rossa da Costa and his sisters Lea Costa Roza and Judith Costa Roza, to Sara, daughter of Salomon Munis, and to Daniel de Moses Cortissos in 1759. They left on a ship for Curaçao and were supposed not to return to Amsterdam within fifteen years. However, it appears that their ship was wrecked a few months later. Daniel did not survive the disaster. The others were given shelter by the inhabitants of a village close to Amsterdam, Castricum, who gave them clothes, food, and drink (SAA entry no. 334, no. 970, p. 698, 10 Tevet 5520).

308 See Appendix I, Tables 4 and 5.

309 For transmigration in the Dutch Republic see Lucassen, *Dutch Long-Distance Migration*, 26.

310 Moch, *Moving Europeans*, ch. 3; Lucassen and Penninx, *Newcomers*, 137.

311 Calculations based on the figures in Appendix I, Tables 4, 5, and 8.

312 See Appendix I, Tables 4 and 5.

313 On the relative economic decline of Italy see Black, *Early Modern Italy*; Sella, *Italy*. On the poor moving back to Italy see 'Servo Robigo de Veneza p[a] ajuda de bolverse . . . f 3:3' (SAA entry no. 334, no. 215, p. 269, 22 Tamuz 5428); 'Ishac Arroio p[a] ajuda de bolverse a Liorne . . . f 10,–' (ibid., p. 263, 29 Tamuz 5428); 'Italiano . . . 12 pl . . . p[a] se bolver a italia p[a] ajuda do caminho' (ibid., p. 269, 7 Elul 5428); 'Obadia Italiano p[a] irse p[a] Italia . . . f 2:10' (ibid., no. 217, p. 7, 12 Sivan 5436); 'Forasteiro de Roma p. se bolver para sua caza com sua mulher por ordem dos ssres do mahamad . . . f 1:16' (ibid., p. 112, 20 Tamuz 5438); 'Eliezer a Cohem Italiano p[a] Liorne . . . f 2,–' (ibid., no. 219, p. 271, 18 Shevat 5456).

314 For *desterrados de França* moving on to Italy see the case of Jacob Flores *dos desterrados* and his family, who went via France to Livorno in the spring of 1686 (SAA entry no. 334, no. 218, p. 110, 20 Tamuz 5446). He received 75 guilders to make the journey. For Jews travelling from Buda via Amsterdam to Italy see ibid., p. 175, 1 Heshvan 5448; ibid., p. 176, 4 Nisan 5448. For *belogrados* moving from Amsterdam to Italy see 'a Ab: Peres de Belogrado p[a] hir a Italia . . . f 12,–' (ibid., no. 219, p. 23, 20 Sivan 5451); 'Haham Muchachon p[a] Italia . . . f 31:16' (ibid., p.

224, 12 Shevat 5455); 'aSer Zebulun . . . p[a] auda de seu viage a Italia . . .' (ibid., no. 1211, p. 38, 9 Adar 5459); 'A Jeuda Alva para irse p[a] Veneza com sua familia . . . f 10,–' (ibid., no. 219, p. 317, 7 Av 5456). The Juda Alvo mentioned in the last of these records had left four years before for an unknown destination, but returned to Amsterdam (ibid., p. 101, 1 Tamuz 5452); 'Jeuda Alvo p[a] sehir . . . f 3,–' (ibid., 1 Tamuz 5452); 'a Ab[m] Levy p[a] Se hir a Liurne . . . f 4:10' (ibid., p. 401, 6 Tamuz 5458). A year earlier Abraham Levy had left to go to the 'tera santa' (ibid., p. 357, 20 Sivan 5457); 'Belogrados . . . Abraham Levy' (ibid., p. 339, 7 Iyar 5457); 'a Juda Seby p[a] se hir a Veneza . . . f 6,–' (ibid., p. 401, 1 Av 5458); 'a Josseph Levy p[a] se hir a Liorne e seo filho . . . f 7:10' (ibid., p. 401, 12 Heshvan 5459); 'Joseph Levy orpham . . . Estes são osq vierão ultimam[te] de Belogrado e banha . . .' (ibid., p. 26, [Kislev] 5452).

315 For Livorno as an important economic centre of Jewish life in the 18th century, especially in the first half of that century, see Trivellato, *The Familiarity of Strangers*; ead., 'The Port Jews of Livorno'; Filippini, 'La ballottazione a Livorno', 'La Nazione ebrea di Livorno', and 'Le Rôle des négociants'; Toaff, *La nazione ebrea*.

316 SAA entry no. 334, no. 12, p. 22[v], 5397: 'peticoens que se despacharão entrando alguns peçoas que forão p[a] Brazil'; Israel, 'The Jews of Dutch America', 341–2.

317 SAA entry no. 334, no. 172, p. 21, 21 Av 5399. In 1653 he returned to Amsterdam via Rotterdam and was receiving financial support (ibid., no. 173, p. 259, 23 Adar II 5413: 'Jacob Moreno e familia vindo de Rott[m]').

318 SAA entry no. 334, no. 172, p. 21, 7 Elul 5399; for support given to him see ibid., p. 5, 24 Nisan 5399.

319 SAA entry no. 334, no. 172, p. 49, 6 Tevet 5400.

320 SAA entry no. 334, no. 1304, pp. 10–15, 1 and 15 Kislev 5409.

321 Oppenheim, 'An Early Jewish Colony'; Arbell, 'The Jewish Settlement in Poomeroon'; id., *The Portuguese Jews of Jamaica*; see, further, SAA entry no. 334, no. 215, p. 42, Nisan 5423–4. See e.g. the case of Isaac da Costa: we first meet him in Brazil, then in Amsterdam. In 1663 he received money from the Amsterdam Portuguese community to cover his travel expenses for a trip to Guyana. After this we have no record of his whereabouts. Isaac had three daughters: they all tried to get dowries through Dotar, but only one succeeded, in 1697. She married several months later. Isaac's widow was in receipt of welfare continuously between 1687 and 1698. In 1698 she travelled to Surinam at the expense of the community (Wiznitzer, *Jews in Colonial Brazil*, 88, 101; SAA entry no. 334, no. 215, p. 42, 3 Iyar 5423; ibid., no. 20, p. 105, 17 Adar 5447; ibid., no. 176, p. 292, Nisan 5458; ibid., no. 219, p. 401, 17 Iyar 5458; ibid., no. 1144, pp. 290, 428, 446, 449, 451, 5441, 5455, 5457–8).

322 SAA entry no. 334, no. 174, p. 252, 1 Nisan 5418.

323 SAA entry no. 334, no. 174, p. 306, 1 Nisan 5419.

324 SAA entry no. 334, no. 174, p. 369, 1 Nisan 5420.

325 SAA entry no. 334, no. 174, p. 428, 1 Nisan 5421.

326 SAA entry no. 5075, no. 2889, Not. P. Padthuysen, p. 352, 11 May 1660.

327 See SAA entry no. 334, nos. 220–3 and 969–70. For expansion to the west see Goslinga, *The Dutch in the Caribbean*; Emmanuel, *History of the Jews of the Netherlands Antilles*; Israel, 'The Sephardic Contribution to Economic Life'; id., 'The Jews of Dutch America'; Klooster, *Illicit Riches*; id., 'The Jews of Surinam and Curaçao'; R. Cohen, *Jews in Another Environment*. For Curaçao see also Y. Kaplan, 'The Curaçao and Amsterdam Jewish Communities', and, further, Yerushalmi, 'Between Amsterdam and New Amsterdam', and Israel, *Diasporas within a Diaspora*, ch. 16.

328 This tendency confirms the data in Israel, 'The Jews of Dutch America', 336–7, showing an increase of population in Curaçao for the period 1702–89.

329 See the calculations in R. Cohen, *Jews in Another Environment*, 25. Cohen bases himself here solely on the *Registro dos despachos*, while additional data can be found in SAA entry no. 334, no. 970, 5495–5519. Sometimes, and especially in the 18th century, the West Indies authorities expressed their displeasure at being sent immigrants who were of little practical use: see *Jews in Another Environment*, 23–4.

330 For 'resettlement' in England see Hyamson, *The Sephardim of England*, ch. 1; Endelman, *The Jews of Georgian England*, chs. 1–3; D. S. Katz, *The Jews in the History of England*, ch. 3; Y. Kaplan, 'The Jewish Profile of the Spanish-Portuguese Community of London'; E. R. Samuel, 'Portuguese Jews in Jacobean London'; id., 'The First Fifty Years'; id., 'Readmission'; Roth, 'The Resettlement of the Jews in England in 1656'; Wolf, 'Status of the Jews in England after the Re-Settlement'; id., 'Jews in Elizabethan England'.

331 Patinkin, 'Mercantilism'; Endelman, *Radical Assimilation*, esp. ch. 5; id., *The Jews of Georgian England*; D. S. Katz, *The Jews in the History of England*, ch. 3; Hyamson, *The Sephardim of England*. On the relations between the Jews of Amsterdam and London see also Yogev, *Diamonds and Coral*; Oliel-Grausz, 'A Study in Intercommunal Relations'. For the position of England in the 18th century see Palmer, Colton, and Kramer, *A History of the Modern World*, ch. 7.

332 See Israel, *Diasporas within a Diaspora*, 581–2.

333 Lipman, 'Sephardi and Other Jewish Immigrants in England', 43–4.

334 L. D. Barnett, *El Libro de los Acuerdos*, see e.g. pp. 19 (5424), 36 (5429), and 68 (5433); R. D. Barnett, 'Diplomatic Aspects of the Sephardic Influx '; D. S. Katz, *The Jews in the History of England*, 181–2.

335 R. D. Barnett, 'The Correspondence of the Mahamad', 3–4.

336 His travelling companions included his mother-in-law, aunt, and brother-in-law: see SAA entry no. 334, no. 221, p. 413, 15 Elul 5472. On the establishment of Jews in Gibraltar see Benady, 'The Jewish Community of Gibraltar'.

337 On London as the point of departure for Jamaica and Barbados, and as the metropolis behind the new settlements in the west, see Oliel-Grausz, 'A Study in Intercommunal Relations', 54.

338 SAA entry no. 334, no. 218, p. 316, 18 Iyar; ibid., 8 Tishrei 5450. In the summer of 1690 Jessurun was told to leave and never return (ibid., p. 385, 9 Sivan 5450).

339 SAA entry no. 334, no. 221, p. 57, 13 Tamuz 5465.

340 SAA entry no. 334, no. 221, p. 57, 25 Nisan 5465; ibid., 8 Sivan 5465. See also ibid., 27 Tamuz 5465.

341 The leadership of the Amsterdam Portuguese community must have been well informed about, and given close consideration to, strategies adopted elsewhere to deal with the problem of poverty through colonization—for example the Georgia colonization plan. See the undated document in the files of the Amsterdam Portuguese community in which the Georgia plan is elaborated and discussed as a way to get rid of the poor, and in which Surinam is brought up as an alternative: SAA entry no. 334, no. 66a [most likely 1732/3]. It took another fifteen years for the Amsterdam Portuguese community to decide on this matter and to put these schemes into practice. See Kayserling, *Biblioteca*, 92 (citing a fifty-three-page manuscript, 5493/1733'); see also Oliel-Grausz, 'A Study in Intercommunal Relations', 51.

342 Palmer, Colton, and Kramer, *A History of the Modern World*, ch. 7.

343 See here esp. Nahon, 'From New Christians to the Portuguese Jewish Nation in France', 350, 352, and 'Bayonne', 52–3. On the threat of expulsion in 1722 and the expulsion of seventy-eight Jews from Bayonne, Bidache, and Peyrehorade in 1749, see Nahon, *Les 'Nations' juives portugaises*, 8–11, 13–15; id., 'Los *Cristianos Nuevos*'; id., 'Dépêches des Secrétaires d'État', 218–19 (no. 92, 7 Jan. 1749: 'Juifs demandent qu'ils [tous vagabonds] soient chassés du Royaume. Ils citent un exemple en pareilles circonstances en 1684'). In 1761 150 Jews were expelled from Bordeaux (Malino, *The Sephardic Jews of Bordeaux*, 18–19; Arbell, 'Jewish Settlements in the French Colonies').

344 Nahon, 'Los *Cristianos Nuevos*', 598, 604–5.

345 As in the case of Abraham Lopes Refael being sent to Surinam via Amsterdam: cited in Nahon, *Les 'Nations' juives portugaises*, 289 (doc. LXXXVI).

346 SAA entry no. 334, no. 969, p. 102, 2 Av 5490: 'por tres familhas que vierao de fransa f 12:3'; ibid., p. 160, Sivan 5491: 'p. frette de Rica Gomes de fransa f 6:14'. In 1747 a child died on the boat on his way from Bordeaux to Amsterdam (ibid., no. 970, p. 575, 7 Adar 5507).

347 See Appendix I, Tables 4 and 5. The data from the *ondertrouw* registers (see Tables 2 and 3) reveal a similar development. See the case of Jacob Gomez from Bordeaux, who, after spending the winter in Amsterdam and staying a further six months, had to go back to Bordeaux with his wife in 1679 even though he was ill (SAA entry no. 334, no. 217, pp. 105–6, 15 Sivan and 27 Tamuz 5438; ibid., p. 108, 14 Heshvan 5439; ibid., p. 142, 7 Heshvan 5439; ibid., pp. 145, 147, 154, 26 Kislev, 16 Shevat, and 13 Nisan 5439; ibid., p. 139, 5439: for peat; ibid., p. 149, 5439: matzot; ibid., p. 160, 4 Iyar 5439: 'Jacob Gomez e sua mulher . . . q vao a Bordeaux . . . f 24,–').

348 SAA entry no. 334, no. 92, p. 203, 5 Oct. 1747.

349 Some remained in Amsterdam, although to judge by special notes in the *sedaca* books their sojourn was considered temporary: SAA entry no. 334, no. 219, 5451: 'Segue o Rol da Repartição pellos pobrez de França'. On those who left see SAA entry no. 334, no. 218, pp. 175–6, 13 [Heshvan]–24 [Elul] 5448; ibid., pp. 242–3, 4

Iyar–11 [Tamuz] 5448. It was stated that, as a condition of receiving money to cover their travel expenses, these *desterrados* would never again be able to rely on financial support from the Amsterdam Portuguese community if they returned to Amsterdam (ibid., no. 24a, p. 68v, 28 Iyar 5446). Thus Sara Gomes del Valle, the widow of Simon Gomes del Valle, returned to Bayonne with her daughter in 1687 (ibid., no. 218, p. 175, 24 Elul 5447).

350 Nahon, 'Los *Cristianos Nuevos*'; Marzagalli, 'Atlantic Trade'; Malino, *The Sephardic Jews of Bordeaux*; Menkis, 'The Gradis Family'; Butel, *Les Négociants bordelaises*, and id., *Vivre à Bordeaux*.

351 Marzagalli, 'Atlantic Trade', 271; Cavignac, 'L'Immigration des Juifs portugais à Bordeaux'.

352 See Appendix I, Tables 4 and 5.

353 Kellenbenz, *Sephardim an der unteren Elbe*. For Hamburg see SAA entry no. 334, no. 17, p. 36, 9 July 5390 ('Italianno que se vaj pa Amburgo . . . f 2'); ibid., no. 218, p. 243, 5 Kislev 5449 ('Joseph Semah de Mantua pa Hamburgo . . . f 4'). For Jews from Buda to Hamburg and other areas in the German states see ibid., p. 174, 22 [Adar II] 5448; ibid., p. 176, 23 Adar II 5448; ibid., p. 243, [17 Adar] 5449.

354 Sara Lumbrosa, for example, was paid to leave Amsterdam for Hamburg with her granddaughter: 'Sara Lumbrosa y netta para Hamburgo . . . f 12' (SAA entry no. 334, no. 219, p. 270, 11 Iyar 5455).

355 The *belogrado* Jacob Alegem travelled via Hamburg to south-eastern Europe in 1703. The Portuguese community in Hamburg gave him an additional sum of money for the journey (SAA entry no. 334, no. 220, p. 237, 30 Sivan 5463: 'a jacob alegem q se lhe pagou em Hambo pa siguir seu viage f 26').

356 See Appendix I, Tables 4 and 5.

357 Studemund-Halévy, 'Dokumentation Kahal Kadosh Bet Israel', 40 (introduction) and 42 (art. 3).

358 On the mediation of Portuguese rabbis in Amsterdam on a matter of inheritance in Hamburg in 1738 concerning gifts to poor people and widows in the latter city see SAA entry no. 334, no. 118, file 1, 22 Shevat 5498.

359 See Appendix I, Table 5.

360 'A Myrna Cohen Berberisco . . . para Berberia . . . f 68,85' (SAA entry no. 334, no. 17, p. 10, 10 Nov. 5384/1623); see also ibid., no. 217, p. 482, 9 Shevat 5445: 'pa un pasagero de berberia f 5,–'.

361 SAA entry no. 334, no. 220, p. 237, 10 and 13 Elul 5463.

362 For Jews from Buda returning to their home towns in central Europe see SAA entry no. 334, no. 218, p. 175, 20 [Heshvan] 5448; for those from Buda leaving for the Ottoman empire see ibid., p. 242, 1 Tamuz 5448; ibid., 5 Av 5448. On the *sheliḥim* R. Joseph Menasseh and R. Joseph Mataja visiting Amsterdam in the winter of 1701 to ask for money for the restoration of the *kehilah* of Belgrade, which seems to have encouraged *belogrados* to return there, see ibid., no. 25, p. 62, 1 [Shevat] 5461 (the money was granted). For *belogrados* returning to their city of origin see ibid., no. 220, p. 137, 30 Nisan 5461: 'Josseph Crespo pa Belogrado

. . . f 15,–', and 'Eliau Gaon p[a] Belogrado . . . f 6,–'. Earlier (see n. 206 above) we saw that Ester Menasseh returned to Belgrade in 1704. Isaac Adaña returned in 1708 to the city of his birth (ibid., no. 221, p. 205, 29 [Sivan] and 14 [Tamuz] 5468) and Haim Crespo did likewise in 1713 (ibid., p. 414, 1 Adar 5473). When the Austrians took Belgrade again in 1717, emigration thither from Amsterdam came to an almost complete standstill. On the situation in Belgrade see A. Levy (ed.), *Jews in the Ottoman Empire*, 80–1. For those *belogrados* leaving for other places in south-eastern Europe and the Levant see the cases of Joseph Valensin, who left for Izmir in 1693 (SAA entry no. 334, no. 219, p. 167, 22 Oct. 5454); Moses de Minhana, who left for Turkey in 1707 (ibid., no. 221, p. 102, 14 Shevat 5467); and Joseph Hazan, who went to the Levant in 1716 (ibid., no. 222, p. 189, 14 Heshvan 5477). In 1726 one *belogrado* reappeared in Amsterdam and was sent back to south-eastern Europe (ibid., no. 223, p. 228, 8 Adar II 5486).

363 A. Levy, *The Sephardim in the Ottoman Empire*, 78–84.

364 On the emigration of the poor to Erets Yisra'el see also Bartal and Kaplan, 'Emigration' (Heb.). For emigration from Amsterdam to Erets Yisra'el in the 18th century see Barnai, *The Jews in Palestine*, 30.

365 See SAA entry no. 334, no. 13, p. 68, 4 and 6 Iyar 5391. In 1633 Daniel Abensur went with his mother and sister directly to Erets Yisra'el; Ester Gaona left on the same boat, together with her three daughters, and so did Ester Pereyra (ibid., no. 13, p. 97, 14 Sivan 5393). Some months later Sara de Castro and David do Sende also set out for Erets Yisra'el (ibid., p. 106, 18 Kislev 5394; ibid. p. 107, 10 Tevet 5394). The decision by the *imposta* board in 1631 to suspend travel subsidies until further notice because of a shortage of funds, but not to restrict travel to Erets Yisra'el, certainly played a crucial role here.

366 On him and his plan see Loker, 'Juan de Yllan', 23. On other Portuguese Jews leaving at that time see Scholem, *Sabbatai Sevi*, 529–30.

367 See the letters sent in the early decades of the 17th century: SAA entry no. 334, no. 13, p. 60, 25 Elul 5390; ibid., p. 40, 7 Feb. 5387; ibid., pp. 56–7, 17 Mar. 5390; ibid., p. 116, 10 Adar 5395. See also Ya'ari, *Emissaries from Erets Yisra'el* (Heb.).

368 SAA entry no. 334, no. 222, p. 128, 24 Iyar 5475: 'a Viuva de Jacob Pereira, Ribca de Mos Israel Guer, a Rachel Henriques de Liorne . . . a Jerusalaim'.

369 M. Cohen, *Poverty and Charity*, 80, 146–7, 194; for Jewish women migrating in the Middle Ages see Grossman, *Pious and Rebellious*, 235–6, 247, 249–50, 253.

370 Roth, *The House of Nasi*. On Mendes and others see Adelman, 'Jewish Women and Family Life'; see also Kayserling, *Die jüdische Frauen*; Aelion Brooks, *The Woman who Defied Kings*.

371 On Glückl of Hameln see Turniansky (ed.), *Glikl* (Heb.), and Davis, 'Glikl Bas Judah Leib', 14; Richarz, *Die Hamburger Kauffrau Glikl*. Many poor Ashkenazi women arrived in Amsterdam, and up to 1670 they were supported by the Portuguese community: a quarter of the Ashkenazi Jews receiving matzot in 1641 were women (SAA entry no. 334, no. 172, pp. 132–3, 8 Nisan 5401). In most cases these women came from abroad, alone or at the head of a family. We also find many Ashkenazi women on a list of Polish Jews being sent back to Poland:

'rol dos polacos q se vao p[a] polonia' (ibid., no. 1210, [n.d.; 17th century]). On Ashkenazi women in the Dutch Republic see also Egmond, *Underworlds*, 124.

372 As a rule, non-Jewish female immigrants did not travel such great distances as Jewish ones, as most came from other parts of the Dutch Republic, and from the German regions bordering the Netherlands. Many of these found work as servants; a minority who arrived as or ended up working as prostitutes often came from big cities and ports, such as Rotterdam and Hamburg (van de Pol, *The Burgher and the Whore*, 146–7; ead., 'The Lure of the Big City'). On the influx of poor women to Amsterdam in general see also van de Pol and Kuijpers, 'Poor Women's Migration'; Kuijpers, *Migrantenstad*, 100–3.

373 See Appendix I, Table 6.

374 See her application concerning participation in the Dotar lottery: 'Rahel Lopez, orpham de Ant[o] Djas q morou em Cadiz' (SAA entry no. 334, no. 1143, p. 205, 5412; ibid., no. 1151, p. 316 [n.d.; *c.*1652]). The use of Spanish and Jewish names is significant. After joining the Portuguese Jewish community of Amsterdam, the ex-Conversos took Jewish names (whereas on the peninsula they were known only by their Spanish names), though they continued to use their Spanish aliases for business purposes. In this case, the fact that names on a petition addressed to the Portuguese Jewish community are not Jewish ones implies that these people had apparently never joined a Jewish community. Rachel's mother is called Maria, not a common name in the Jewish community to say the least. Most probably she stayed on the peninsula or elsewhere in the Spanish empire. The girl has a Jewish name, which she adopted in Amsterdam; most likely she was known by a different name on the peninsula.

375 SAA entry no. 5004, no. 110 (Calisregisters), p. 125, 24 Aug. 1700; ibid., DTB 702, p. 93, 27 Aug. 1700.

376 See the case of Bernaldo Lopes described in n. 77 above. We find the same phenomenon but in the opposite direction—men returning to their place of origin and later bringing over their families from Amsterdam—in the case of Jacob Alegem, who in 1703 left the city without his family, probably to check what Belgrade was like ('provizionalm[te]') before settling there permanently (SAA entry no. 334, no. 220, p. 237, 15 Iyar 5463: 'A Jacob Alegem p.[a] irse a belogrado provizionalm[te] . . . f 20,–'; ibid., p. 237, 30 Sivan 5463). Alegem returned to Amsterdam seven years later, this time to bring his family back with him (ibid., no. 221, p. 308, 27 Nisan 5470: 'Jacob Alagem con sua familia p[a] Belogrado').

377 For similar groups of poor women from abroad setting out for Amsterdam see Kuijpers, *Migrantenstad*, 79–81.

378 Levine Melammed, *Heretics or Daughters of Israel?*; Huerga Criado, 'Una familia judeoconversa'; Kamen, *The Spanish Inquisition*, 285 and n. 12; Caro Baroja, *Los Judíos en la España moderna*, i. 160; Carrasco, 'Inquisición', 47–8; and López Belinchón, *Honra, libertad y hacienda*, 357–9 and the references cited there. López Belinchón shows that the majority of the people taken by the Inquisition in Cuenca in the period 1650–9 were women (p. 373, table 6). Lucio d'Azevedo's table detailing the number of New Christians sentenced by the Inquisition in

Portugal during the period 1682–91 shows that just over half were women (670 out of 1,329; Azevedo, *História*, 492); Torres Arce, 'Los judaizantes', 675, states that many women appeared before the inquisitorial tribunal at Logroño in the 18th century. See also the case of Beatriz Nuñez, as decribed in Pulido Serrano, *Injurias a Cristo*, 117–22.

379 SAA entry no. 334, no. 218, p. 174, 4 Nisan 5448: 'a Ribca R[s] Nabaro E Rahel Pereyra V[a] vindas da Enquisisão'.

380 On the Jewish identity of Portuguese women in Amsterdam see Levie Bernfeld, 'Mujeres judías hispano-portuguesas', and ead., 'Sephardi Women in Holland's Golden Age', 196–200.

381 SAA entry no. 334, no. 1141, p. 28, 20 Nov. 1615.

382 SAA entry no. 334, no. 1141, pp. 90 and 92, 12 Adar 5378. From 1657 orphans and poor young women from Amsterdam, Hamburg, and Glückstadt were given preference (ibid., no. 1143, p. 284, 6 Tishrei 5418).

383 For an early example, of a woman coming from Spain in 1623, see SAA entry no. 334, no. 17, p. 10, 26 Nov. 1623/5384; for the arrival of women in the mid-18th century see SAA entry no. 334, no. 970, p. 43, 12 Tishrei 5507, on the arrival of Sara de Torres Serrano, who travelled to Amsterdam from Spain via Portugal as late as 1746.

384 Such broken families also existed in Madrid, where older women or widows in charge of children or grandchildren were mostly dependent on charity: López Belinchón, *Honra, libertad y hacienda*, 347.

385 'A Izabel de Campos V[a] e familia, vinda de Esp[a]': SAA entry no. 334, no. 219, p. 394, 11 Shevat 5459.

386 'As quatro mulheres vindas de Espanha q estam juntas e sao da sedaca': SAA entry no. 334, no. 173, p. 259, 23 Adar II 5413.

387 'Lea y Ribca Rs., vindas de Espanha': SAA entry no. 334, no. 219, p. 91, 2 Heshvan 5453.

388 'A Umas Portugezas Vindas de Lx[a]': SAA entry no. 334, no. 173, p. 206, 7 Kislev 5412.

389 'A Raquel Henriq[s] vinda de Portugal f 1:4': SAA entry no. 334, no. 219, p. 390, 12 Heshvan 5459.

390 'p. frete da V[a] de Sara Delgada Rachel Namias & netos vindos de Portugal': SAA entry no. 334, no. 970, p. 22, 5 Av 5499.

391 See the case of Ribca Gomez de Sevilla, who apparently arrived alone in Amsterdam in 1651, where she was supported by the community until her death in 1658 (SAA entry no. 334, no. 174, p. 235, Rosh Hodesh Nisan 5418). In 1656 she appears to have been widowed, though there is no trace of a husband (see e.g. SAA entry no. 334, no. 173, p. 194, Rosh Hodesh Kislev 5412; ibid., p. 260, Rosh Hodesh Nisan 5413; ibid., no. 174, p. 31, 14 Adar 5414: 8 *livras* of matzah meal; ibid., p. 167, Rosh Hodesh Iyar 5416: 'V[a]' (widow); ibid., p. 198, 22 Adar 5417: 8 *livras* of matzah meal; ibid., p. 253, Rosh Hodesh Nisan 5418). Another case is that of Yael, wife of Gideon da Silva, who as both wife and widow was supported by the community from 1645; her husband apparently died in 1651, but without appearing in the city; her entry on the welfare list as 'the wife of' changes to 'the widow of' in 1651, and on the basis of the matzot distribution she received over the years she seems always to have lived on her own. We have no trace of Gideon in any of the sources during the period 1645–56. See e.g. SAA entry no. 334, no. 172, p. 316, 11 Tishrei 5406; ibid., no. 173, p. 19, Rosh Hodesh Kislev 5408: 'Yael da Silva, mulher de Gidon da Silva'; ibid., p. 27, 20 Adar 5408: 8 *livras* of matzah meal; ibid., p. 158, 6 Kislev 5411: 'Veuva de Gidion da Silva'; ibid., no. 174, p. 85, 20 Adar II 5415: matzot (8 *livras* of matzah meal); ibid., p. 190, Rosh Hodesh Kislev 5417. For similar situations among Jews in medieval Egypt see M. Cohen, *Poverty and Charity*, 148–55.

392 See Appendix I, Table 6. For the male majority of immigrants on welfare from the German states and Poland see e.g. SAA, entry no. 334, no. 172, pp. 132–3, 8 Nisan 5401; for the majority of women among the *belogrados*, see the welfare lists on which they are mentioned, e.g. SAA entry no. 334, no. 219, p. 2 [5451].

393 SAA entry no. 334, no. 219, p. 2 [5451].

394 SAA entry no. 334, no. 219, p. 228, 6 Nisan 5455.

395 SAA entry no. 334, no. 219, p. 305, 26 Iyar 5456: 'Dona Jurada por outro nome Viuva de Ishac Gaon'.

396 SAA entry no. 334, no. 1151, p. 316 [n.d., *c*.1652]: 'muy pobre e miseravel'.

397 'A Sara da Fonsequa . . . a ter quatro crianssas con grande necessidade avenda vinda de fora' (SAA entry no. 334, no. 17, p. 5, 12 Oct. 5383).

398 See the petitions of the *desterrados de França* to Dotar: SAA entry no. 334, no. 1152, pp. 451, 453, 462: they stated that they had no remedy, were without means and without shelter, and burdened with many children. For help given to this group see also ibid., no. 217, pp. 520–6, Pesach 5445, and ibid., no. 218, pp. 75–80, 5445.

399 For Europe outside the Dutch Republic see Flynn, *Sacred Charity*, 23–4; the articles in Henderson and Wall (eds.), *Poor Women and Children*; Hufton, 'Women without Men', 361; Jütte, *Poverty and Deviance*, 41, 43–4; Martz, *Poverty and Welfare in Habsburg Spain*, 204–5; Moch, *Moving Europeans*, 46–7; and Norberg, *Rich and Poor in Grenoble*, 103 ff. For the Dutch Republic see van de Pol, *The Burgher and the Whore*, 150–1; Pot, *Arm Leiden*, 263, 266; Schmidt, *Overleven na de dood*, 173; Wijngaarden, *Zorg voor de Kost*, 88; and van der Vlis, *Leven in armoede*, 76–7.

400 As a result many were unable to claim their dowries (SAA entry no. 334, no. 1141, p. 129, 1 and 13 Adar 5380; ibid., no. 1142, p. 8, 5383). In 1627 two girls were given some time to find a partner (ibid., p. 84, 13 Adar 5387). After 1631 girls were given eight years from the time they drew a lot, instead of the three years then in force, to find a partner (ibid., no. 1142, p. 138, 7 Adar II 5391). Starting in 1668, Ester, the daughter of Abraham Mendes Fronteyra, tried to get a dowry through Dotar. Eleven years later, in 1679, she was lucky enough to draw a lot of 500 guilders. However, twelve years later, in 1691, the money reserved for her dowry was moved back to Dotar's capital account. She had presumably been unable to find a partner within this period (ibid., no. 1151, p. 604, 5428; ibid., no. 1144, pp. 120, 146, 180, 189, 229, 262, 264, 390, 5428, 5430, 5432, 5433, 5436, 5439, 5451). Also, many non-Jewish women arrived in Amsterdam on their own and did not marry there, as Lotte van de Pol has convincingly shown (van de Pol and Kuijpers, 'Poor Women's Migration').

401 According to my calculations, between 6% and 28% of emigrants were both female and head of the family unit: see SAA entry no. 334, nos. 215–23 and 969–70 (e.g. no. 218, p. 15, 5445/6: twenty-nine male and two female heads of household).

402 Jan Lucassen, *Dutch Long-Distance Migration*, 20 and 36, states that a quarter of emigrants to the west were accompanied by their families; only a few women from Portugal emigrated to colonies of the Portuguese empire (Guimarães Sá, *Quando o rico se faz pobre*, 16); see also Fauve-Chamoux, 'Femmes qui migrent'. For Jewish emigrants the picture is the same: Wiznitzer, *Jews in Colonial Brazil*, 129–30, mentions only a few women travelling to Brazil; Egmond, 'Contours of Identity', 217–18, observes the same pattern among Ashkenazi Jews—the men travelled for work, leaving their wives at home.

403 SAA entry no. 334, no. 22, p. 167, para. 1, 8 Heshvan 5509.

404 SAA entry no. 5075, no. 351B, Not. W. Cluijt, p. $222^{r–v}$, 16 June 1625; also published in *Studia Rosenthaliana*, 30/2 (1996), 316, and cited in Israel, *Diasporas within a Diaspora*, 294. On this phenomenon in non-Jewish society see the example in Kuijpers, *Migrantenstad*, 66–7.

405 For David Henriques Correones see SAA entry no. 334, no. 174, p. 460, 14 Tishrei 5422; for his wife Sara, from 1653 to her death in 1661, see ibid., no. 173, p. 260, Rosh Hodesh Nisan 5413; ibid. no. 174, p. 24, 2 Kislev 5414: peat: 'a mulher de David Enriq^{s} Corriones'; ibid., p. 474, Rosh Hodesh Kislev 5422.

406 He had a large family and used Amsterdam as a staging post for Brazil (SAA entry no. 334, no. 1304, p. 11, 1 Kislev 5409; ibid., no. 173, p. 28, 20 Adar 5408: matzot (40 *livras* of matzah meal); ibid., p. 49, Rosh Hodesh Menahem-Av 5408; ibid., p. 72, Rosh Hodesh Tevet 5409). His wife and children originally stayed on in Amsterdam for a while, during which time they were supported by the Portuguese community (see e.g. SAA entry no. 334, no. 172, p. 201, Rosh Hodesh Shevat 5403; ibid., p. 206, 14 Adar 5403 (matzot; 36 *livras* of matzah meal): 'Rachel Israel de Pisa e 4 f^{os}'; ibid., p. 289, 1 Adar 5405; ibid., no. 173, p. 49, Rosh Hodesh Menahem-Av 5408; ibid., p. 71, 1 Kislev 5409). In 1648 they appear to have joined him in Brazil: 'p. se aver ido ao Brazil' (SAA entry no. 334, no. 173, p. 72, Rosh Hodesh Tevet 5409; see also Wiznitzer, *Jews in Colonial Brazil*, 138, 175). In 1655 he returned to Amsterdam with his large family (SAA entry no. 334, no. 174, p. 118, 6 Elul 5415). On his living on charity from the *kahal* between 1655 and 1662 see e.g. SAA entry no. 334, no. 174, p. 136, 26 Tevet 5416; ibid., p. 293, Rosh Hodesh Tevet 5417; ibid., p. 190, 1 Kislev 5417; ibid., p. 304, 16 Adar 5419: 60 *livras* of matzah meal; ibid., p. 529, Rosh Hodesh Heshvan 5423. In Amsterdam two of his daughters asked if they could participate in the lottery for a dowry with Dotar in the years 5416–22 (1656–62) (SAA entry no. 334, no. 1143, pp. 255, 274, 289, 299, 307, 320; ibid., no. 1144, p. 63; ibid., no. 1151, p. 373 [n.d.]).

In 1662 he saw an opportunity to cast off the yoke of poor relief by going to Jamaica (SAA entry no. 334, no. 174, p. 529, 4 Heshvan 5423: 'por se lhe aver tirado [do rol da sedaca] p. ordem do mahamad e aver se lhe dado ajuda de custa para se ir pera Jamaica por pettição que fes'; see also Wiznitzer, *Jews in Colonial Brazil*, 175). This turned out to be a short-lived adventure. In 1664 he moved from Jamaica to London (Friedenwald, 'Material for the History of the Jews', 48); in 1666 he appears to have turned up again in Amsterdam, this time accompanied only by his wife. There he stayed until 1671 (see *nedavot*, distributions of matzot, and special distributions over the years 5426–32: e.g. SAA entry no. 334, no. 174, p. 731, 20 Adar 5426; ibid., no. 215, p. 201, 5427: matzot (16 *livras* of matzah meal); ibid., p. 248, 5428–9: *nedavot*; ibid., no. 216, p. 95, 5431–2: *nedavot*; list of people for whom travel expenses were covered: ibid., p. 70, 15 Kislev 5432: 'Ab. Israel Piza p[a] seo viage p[a] despacho . . . f 31:10'). His children had apparently remained behind overseas (Wolff and Wolff, *Dicionário biográfico*, 161; Friedenwald, 'Material', 58; W. S. Samuel, *Jewish Colonists in Barbados*, 44–5); in 1671 he rejoined them, and the family settled down for good in Barbados (*Jewish Colonists*, 44–5, 58, 98, 102; Friedenwald, 'Material', 91; see further Wolff and Wolff, *Dicionário biográfico*, 161; eid., 'Mistaken Identities', 106; Wiznitzer, *Jews in Colonial Brazil*, 138 and 175; W. S. Samuel, 'Sir William Davidson', 69).

407 The husband of Sara Mendes was travelling when his daughters got married in Amsterdam (SAA DTB 681, p. 142, 19 Oct. 1651; ibid., p. 172, 26 Jan. 1652); for Sara Mendes and her daughters in receipt of welfare see e.g. SAA entry no. 334, no. 172, p. 4, 24 Nisan 5399; ibid., p. 77, 9 Nisan 5400 (matzot; 20 *livras* of matzah meal): 'Sarah M[des] e 2 filhas'; ibid., p. 139, 14 Nisan 5401; ibid., p. 206, 14 Adar 5403 (matzot; 24 *livras* of matzah meal): 'Sarah Mendez e duas f[as]'; ibid., p. 293, 14 Adar 5405 (matzot; 32 *livras* of matzah meal): 'Sarra Mendez e filhas e Jenrra'; ibid., no. 173, p. 121, 19 Adar II 5410: 8 *livras* of matzah meal; ibid., p. 206, 7 Kislev 5412: peat; ibid., p. 235, Rosh Hodesh Menahem-Av 5412.

408 When Abigail Salom got married in Amsterdam the whereabouts of her father, David de Moses de Paz, were unknown ('en weet niet waar sig ophout': SAA DTB 715, p. 384, 14 Nov. 1726).

409 Many women and children in early modern Amsterdam were dependent on charity, since their husbands or fathers were working overseas (see the minutes of the administration of the so-called 'Oude Zijds Huiszittenhuis', which mention that women fall into poverty when their husbands are away: 'en soo mannen nae Oost ofte westindien ofte nae andere quartiere buyten s' Lants zijn', SAA entry no. 349, 1.1.1: Books of Resolutions 1639–1703, p. 151, 1639–1703). See further van de Pol, *The Burgher and the Whore*, 149–51, 160, and 'The Lure of the Big City'; M. van Leeuwen, 'Amsterdam en de armenzorg', 152–3 and n. 43; Schmidt, *Overleven na de dood*, 69; Kuijpers, 'De zeventiende-eeuwse migrantenkerk', 44; Haks, *Huwelijk en gezin*, 211. See also Egmond, *Underworlds*, 124, on the position of Ashkenazi women in the Dutch Republic. In the census of 1795 there is still mention of a surplus of women in Amsterdam, among Christians as well as among Jews (Farret, Verster, and van Swinden, *Rapport*, 33–5, and Boekman, 'De bevolking van Amsterdam', 286). In most cities of early modern Europe the majority of the population was female (Vries, *European Urbanization*, 196, 212; Hufton, 'Women without Men', 355–76; Cavallo, 'Conceptions of Poverty', 180); for the situation in the medieval Jewish world see M. Cohen, *The Voice of the Poor*, 84.

410 'A Jeudit Monsanto y ester Gonsales p^{a} Londres . . . f 22' (SAA entry no. 334, no. 222, p. 73, 22 Av 5474); 'Jeudit Gabay Faro e d^{r} Gama e fam^{a} a Londres f 130' (ibid., p. 305, 11 Kislev 5479); Abigail Carvalho left for England with a travel subsidy. She had been in receipt of welfare from the Amsterdam Portuguese community before. In fact, at the same time as she left for England it was confirmed she would be taken off the monthly welfare list (ibid., no. 218, p. 386, 3 Av 5450). Abigail Correa, together with her three sisters, moved to Antwerp in 1670 (ibid., no. 174, p. 889, Rosh Hodesh Sivan 5430); in 1705 Abigail Naar Pardo left for Hamburg (ibid., no. 221, p. 57, 2 Iyar 5465).

411 SAA entry no. 334, no. 222, p. 305, 3 Av 5478: 'Ester de Mattos e 2 criancas a franca f 80'.

412 Ester Lopes Henriques, with her granddaughter, and Judith Peixotto left for Salé in 1699 and 1721 respectively ('A Ester Lopes Henriques p^{a} se hir a Sale e sua neta f 30': SAA entry no. 334, no. 219, p. 402, 9 Adar 5459; ibid., no. 223, p. 15, 4 Kislev 5482). The widow Abigail Savaya left for Izmir in 1738 (ibid., no. 970, p. 426, 1 Elul 5498). Reina Mesias moved to Gibraltar in 1738 (ibid., p. 426, 14 Sivan 5498).

413 SAA entry no. 334, no. 17, p. 34, 10 Mar. 1630.

414 Sara Gomez and Judith, the orphan of Jacob Orobio de Castro, left for Surinam in 1670 and 1711 respectively (SAA entry no. 334, no. 216, p. 3, 15 Elul 5430; ibid., no. 221, p. 360, 17 Nisan 5471); Sara Fermy for Jamaica in 1718 (ibid., no. 222, p. 315, 28 Iyar 5478); Ribca de Mattos and her family for New York in 1720 (ibid., no. 222, p. 401, 1 Tamuz 5480).

415 SAA entry no. 334, no. 220, p. 187, 19 Tishrei 5463: 'p. segunda vez p. Londres e p. ultima'.

416 SAA entry no. 334, no. 223, p. 60, 20 Kislev 5483.

417 SAA entry no. 334, no. 175, p. 303, 6 Tamuz 5445.

418 SAA entry no. 334, no. 220, p. 62, 24 Menahem-Av 5460.

419 See Dekker and van de Pol, *The Tradition of Female Transvestism*.

420 SAA entry no. 334, no. 219, p. 23, 3 Av 5451: 'Aron filho de selomoh levi Maduro p^{a} yr a Salle acompanando sua Yrman f 10'.

421 SAA entry no. 334, no. 217, p. 274, 15 Shevat 5442.

422 SAA entry no. 334, no. 219, p. 101, 4 Iyar 5451.

423 'A Sara Diaz Para sehir a Jamaica assr: em dr^{o} para una vestido f 20; 26 de pano de linho p^{a} camizas . . . f 10:8' (SAA entry no. 334, no. 218, p. 15, 23 Tishrei 5446; ibid., 24 Tishrei 5446: 'a seu genro Ishack Mesia Para sehir a Jamaica . . . f 50').

424 'A molher do haham Riby Jeuda Leb para sehir a Jerusalaim f 30' (SAA entry no. 334, no. 218, p. 316, 1 Tamuz 5449).

425 SAA entry no. 334, no. 222, p. 20, 12 Elul 5473.

426 SAA entry no. 334, no. 218, p. 242, 24 Elul 5448: 'a Rica Nunes Almeida p[a] mandar sua filla q vay a cazar a sirinhao f 20'.

427 SAA entry no. 334, no. 221, p. 308, 17 Nisan 5470: 'rica nunes almeida con sua filha p. Surinam f 150'. Her son(?) Eliau Nunes de Almeida may have followed six months later (see ibid., 11 Tishrei 5471).

428 SAA entry no. 334, no. 217, p. 62, 25 Tishrei 5437.

429 SAA entry no. 334, no. 217, p. 112, 12 Av 5438. Simha Meatob was also told never to return after being given money to leave to London with her husband in 1683 (ibid., p. 419, 3 Av 5443).

430 Sara Saso also agreed not to ask for help from the Amsterdam *kahal* for fifteen years and to return the money if she did well in her new home (SAA entry no. 334, no. 980, p. 4, 29 June 1759).

431 Kuijpers, *Migrantenstad*, 116, notes a similar development among the Lutherans in the city: migrants who became members of the Amsterdam Lutheran Church were the ones who had settled down in the city; however, a large number of migrants lived there only temporarily and never put down roots.

432 Parker, 'Calvinism and Poor Relief', 117, makes the point that confessional groups in Amsterdam assisted the poor in order to keep them in the fold.

433 For a similar policy on the part of the French Portuguese, who sent their poor to the French colonies, see Nahon, 'Bayonne', 52–3.

434 Abendanon, *Sheloshah sarigim*, 294.

435 See also Shulvass, *From East to West*.

3 Demographic Outline

1 M. van Leeuwen and Oeppen, 'Reconstructing the Demographic Regime of Amsterdam'; Nusteling, *Welvaart en werkgelegenheid in Amsterdam*, 31–49, 234–6. London had long ago outstripped Amsterdam, with a population of 200,000 in 1600, rising to 900,000 in 1800 (Lottum, *Across the North Sea*, 101–2); Paris did not lag far behind (Vries, *European Urbanization*, 35). For a comparative overview of population growth in European cities in the early modern period see *European Urbanization*, chs. 3 and 4. The *Statistische Mededeeling* (p. 1, no. 1) puts the Amsterdam population at 217,024 in 1795 and at 200,560 in 1796. It was not until well into the 19th century, however, that the population of Amsterdam exceeded that of early modern Amsterdam (240,000).

2 Israel, 'The Republic of the United Netherlands', 100. The figure of 20,335 arrived at by the census inspectors of 1795 can reasonably be rounded up to 21,000 since the inspectors claimed it was difficult to count all Jews (Boekman, 'De bevolking van Amsterdam in 1795', 19).

3 Israel, 'The Republic of the United Netherlands', 100; Y. Kaplan, 'Amsterdam and Ashkenazi Migration', 44; id., 'The Portuguese Community in 17th-Century Amsterdam and the Ashkenazi World', 35.

4 Nusteling, *Welvaart en werkgelegenheid in Amsterdam*, 24–5, mentions the problem; so does Israel, 'Gregorio Leti', 270. In the Jewish world of those days there were many poor people who operated outside the official Jewish community; see

further Glanz, *Geschichte des niederen jüdischen Volkes*, 130; Egmond, 'Contours of Identity'; ead., *Underworlds*.

5 For the census of 1797 see Bloemgarten, 'De Amsterdamse Joden', 67 and n. 2. For the census of 1798 and of 1799 see Bosch Kemper, *Geschiedkundig onderzoek*, table XI, *f*). For 1796, the *Statistische Mededeeling* (p. 23, no. 19) provided figures of 20,749 Ashkenazi Jews as against 2,800 Sephardi Jews. My thanks to Harmen Snel, senior staff member at the Amsterdam City Archives, with whom I exchanged ideas about the different censuses held at the end of the 18th century.

6 One of these visitors was Francisco Xavier de Oliveyra, citizen of Portugal, who toured Amsterdam in 1741 (Oliveyra, *Memorias*, 56–7, 126–7). In the mid-18th century 38% of the Ashkenazi community of Amsterdam (5,340 people) could be defined as poor and on welfare (Reijnders, *Van 'Joodsche Natiën' tot Joodse Nederlanders*, 41). Israel, 'The Republic of the United Netherlands', 100 (table 3.1), calculates that there were 14,000 Ashkenazim in Amsterdam in 1750.

7 Israel, *Empires and Entrepots*, 359.

8 Leti, *Teatro Belgico*, ii. 336; also mentioned in Franco Mendes, *Memorias*, 94. For more on Leti see Israel, 'Gregorio Leti', 267–84.

9 Israel, 'Gregorio Leti', 270.

10 Israel, 'The Republic of the United Netherlands', 100.

11 Leti, *Teatro Belgico*, ii. 336. Special thanks to Floor Borsboom for her help with the translation of the Italian fragments. See also Israel, *Diasporas within a Diaspora*, 494–5, where he describes the fact that Leti, in 1685, was very impressed by the wealth and cultivated aristocracy of Amsterdam's Sephardi community and did not notice any sign of poverty.

12 See esp. SAA entry no. 334, nos. 172–81, 215–23, and 969–70; for the *Livros de escamot* see ibid., nos. 19–22.

13 For a more detailed description of these taxes see Swetschinski, *Reluctant Cosmopolitans*, 185, 196–8; Levie Bernfeld, 'Financing Poor Relief', 71–5. See further SAA entry no. 334, no. 19, pp. 2^{v}/80, 3^{v}/82, 4/83, paras. 14, 23, 28–9, 28 Elul 5398–28 Adar II 5399; Pieterse, *Daniel Levi de Barrios*, 158–62.

14 Examination of the *Kohier* of 1742 (Oldewelt, *Kohier*) suggests that the percentage varied, but in most cases was around 2%. The highest incomes, of over 10,000 guilders, were taxed relatively less. On the basis of the *Personeele Quotisatie* in 1742 Moses de Chaves was taxed on a yearly income of 40,000 guilders. His annual *finta* payment was 181 guilders (Oldewelt, *Kohier*, ii. 98; SAA entry no. 334, no. 285, p. 13, 5502), 0.45% of his general wealth. With an average tax rate of 2%, the Portuguese community of early modern Amsterdam was relatively flexible in comparison with Jewish communities elsewhere, where the tax burden could be as high as 10% of an individual's wealth. The fact that the Jews in Amsterdam did not have to pay a communal tax to the government might explain the discrepancy between the rates in Amsterdam and those elsewhere (Baron, *The Jewish Community*, ii. 254–6, 261).

15 Saperstein, *Exile in Amsterdam*, 194–5.

16 On the Ottoman empire see A. Levy, *The Sephardim in the Ottoman Empire*, 47;

Bornstein-Makovetsky, 'Structure, Organization and Spiritual Life', 324; Baron, *The Jewish Community*, i. 172–3 and ii. 281–9; *Encyclopaedia Judaica*, xix. 532–57 ('Taxation'). For tax assessment in Venice see Malkiel, 'The Ghetto Republic', 125, 130–1. For France see Cavignac, 'L'Assistance chez les Juifs de Bordeaux', 27–30. For assessments of taxes through a committee, consisting of *parnasim*, treasurers, the almoner of the sick, and seven prominent members of the community among the Ashkenazi community of Amsterdam, see *Handvesten ofte privilegiën*, ii. 481–2, para. 18, 11 Oct. 1737.

17 The rules concerning the age limits for taxpaying purposes are not set out explicitly in the sources (Pieterse, *Daniel Levi de Barrios*, 158, para. 14: 'fintando aos yahidim cabesas de casas'). However, in practice those liable to taxation were married men or those aged 20 years old and over, as laid down in the regulations of admission to *ḥevrot* such as Bikur Holim (Pieterse, *Daniel Levi de Barrios*, 175). In Ets Haim, too, the right to vote was conferred at the age of 20 (SAA entry no. 334, no. 1052, pp. 2^{r-v}, art. 10, 5397). See further J. Katz, *Tradition and Crisis*, 91–2; Baron, *The Jewish Community*, ii. 38, 248–9; on the biblical significance of the age of 20 see ibid. 251. On the provisions of Roman Dutch law concerning the age of majority see S. van Leeuwen, *Het Rooms-Hollands-Regt*, vol. i, para. XII: 'Van Meerderjarige en Minderjarige, Mondige en Onmondige' (pp. 58–60).

18 We find references to individuals who, upon arrival or marriage, were taxed on a lower scale (in this case for the cemetery) because they were poor (Pieterse, *Livro de Bet Haim*, 145: 'Vindos a terra novo, 5376: Moseh Machabeo pobre pago com sua comodidade 2 florin'; 'Dos que cazarem de novo: Jacob Israel barbeiro pobre page com sua comodidade f 1 [*finta*]'; ibid. 146, 5375). On taxation of the poor in Ottoman Jewish society see Rozen, *Jewish Identity*, 104.

19 There are a few references in the administrative records of the Amsterdam Portuguese community stating that people on welfare should be exempt from taxation (for the situation in different Jewish communities in this respect see Baron, *The Jewish Community*, ii. 250–2, 278–9). The articles of the *imposta* tax of 1622, set up to fund sending the poor away, are an example in explicitly allowing exemption for people on welfare: 'exçepto osque forem pobres de sedaka' (SAA entry no. 334, no. 13, p. 5, para. 14, 24 Shevat 5382). For exemption of widows from paying taxes see Pieterse, *Livro de Bet Haim*, 147, 5375: 'das viuvas deste kahal de Bet Jaacob que de acordo se não fintarão'. At the end of the 18th century widows (and other women, apparently) were all required to pay the *finta* tax: for this decision see SAA entry no. 334, no. 30, p. 331, 14 Adar 5551: 'Seresolveu de propor os seguintes . . . 3. de Fintar as V^{as} a respeito de Suas Constituisoems'; for an application of the decision see ibid., no. 290, pp. 1–30, 5554 [1794].

20 Swetschinski, *Reluctant Cosmopolitans*, 197; see also SAA entry no. 334, no. 19, pp. 3^{v}/82, 4/83, paras. 23, 28–9, 28 Elul 5398–28 Adar II 5399; Pieterse, *Daniel Levi de Barrios*, 161–2.

21 Reminders to pay *promessas* are especially frequent in the 18th century. It is clear from the Resolution Books of the community where these reminders appear that the leadership put a lot of pressure on members to pay up (see SAA entry no. 334, no. 21, p. 426, Iyar 5466; ibid., no. 22, p. 184, 18 Tishrei 5512; ibid. p. 210, 9 Adar 5518). In 1762 the leadership explicitly talks about the obligatory nature of *promessas*, and even refers to *offertas obrigatorias* (SAA entry no. 334, no. 22, pp. 238–9, 18 Nisan 5522). We find the same pattern in the Ashkenazi community, where a strict eye was kept on the payment of 'offereren' (*Handvesten ofte privilegiën*, ii. 490, para. 61, 11 Oct. 1737).

22 Travellers who stayed in Amsterdam for a short period and were listed only in the registers of arrivals and departures have not been included in the calculations (SAA entry no. 334, nos. 215–23). Nor have those who, after the mid-18th century, signed a contract to leave the city, registered in the so-called *Registro dos despachos* (ibid., nos. 978–9).

23 SAA entry no. 334, no. 973.

24 In 1650, 27% of the Ashkenazi population of Amsterdam—200–300 people—was supported by the Portuguese community (SAA entry no. 334, no. 173, p. 121, 19 Adar II 5411); in 1670 approximately 16% of their number were on Portuguese welfare (SAA entry no. 334, no. 174, p. 846, Rosh Hodesh Nisan 5429).

25 See Appendix I, Table 8.

26 Besides the middle group mentioned here, *promessas* were also paid by a few well-to-do widows (SAA entry no. 334, no. 173, p. 156, 12 Heshvan 5411). Among the *promessas* group we also find visitors to the synagogue (ibid., no. 277, 5516: 'Ab^{m} Martins . . . Haya; Ab^{m} da Fonseca . . . Londres; Ab^{m} de Ishac Curiel . . . Surinhão').

27 SAA entry no. 334, no. 174, pp. 709–19, 11 Tishrei 5426; ibid., pp. 729–33, 20 Adar 5426; ibid. no. 240, p. 201, 5425–6. Woolf, 'Introduction', 6, also realizes that in times of crisis the level of poverty could rise dramatically.

28 Israel, 'The Republic of the United Netherlands', 100. See Appendix I, Table 7.

29 For an average family size of 4.3 persons, based on the census of 1795, see Farret, Verster, and van Swinden, *Rapport*, 5; Boekman, 'Demografische en sociale verhoudingen', 285. Leti estimated that the average family consisted of six members (Israel, 'The Republic of the United Netherlands', 100 and n. 38). Other sources also give high averages for the size of Jewish families: see e.g. Kracauer, 'Beiträge', 131, which gives an average of 5.42 people per family for Frankfurt in 1703. For the years between 1610 and 1675, Nusteling, *Welvaart en werkgelegenheid in Amsterdam*, 238, appendix 1.3A, calculated that the average number of people in one family among the Portuguese Jews varied from 3.5 to 4. Haks, *Huwelijk en gezin*, 143–50, mentions an average of 4 people per family. For the calculations concerning the period around 1795, the average of 4.3 individuals per family unit was used to calculate the number of individuals of all families headed by males paying *finta* and *promessas*. For the same period around 1795, widows (who paid the *finta* from 1791, and *promessas*) have been assumed to be single-person households, even though they may have lived with others, and to balance the calculations a figure of 3.3 individuals has been used for all other families headed by women (without husbands) paying *finta* and *promessas* since 1791. For people on welfare in the 18th century an average family size of 2.6

individuals has been used. For the average of individuals per family on welfare, see Appendix I, Table 13, and the section later in this chapter entitled 'Family Composition'. Even if we were to assume only one person per family unit for widows and other women for the period around 1795, the total would still be substantially higher than has hitherto been assumed (3,770 instead of 2,800).

30 For the 17th century, an average of 2.75 individuals has been calculated for a family on welfare (for the average of individuals per family on welfare, see Appendix I, Table 13, and section on 'Family Composition' later in this chapter); following Nusteling, an average of 3.5 individuals per family paying *finta* and *promessas* has been used for 1650/1, and an average of 4.0 individuals per family paying *finta* and *promessas* for 1675 (Nusteling, *Welvaart en werkgelegenheid in Amsterdam*, 238, appendix 1.3A).

31 Pinto, *Reflexoens*, 6. See calculations in Appendix I, Table 8.

32 SAA entry no. 349, no. 1.1.7, p. 453, 8 Jan. 1799. See also Bosch Kemper, *Geschiedkundig onderzoek*, table XI, *f*.

33 I disagree with the thesis of Jonathan Israel (*The Dutch Republic*, 1025), who maintains that the number of Sephardim in Amsterdam at the end of the 18th century would have remained stable thanks to the balance brought about by emigration and immigration. In 1794 a total of 329 men paid the *finta* tax—a decline of 88 members (21%) from 1750. The number of women paying the *finta* tax was 160 (66 widows and 94 other women), 33% of the total (SAA entry no. 334, no. 290, pp. 1–30, 5554 [1794].

34 On these problems see also Jütte, *Poverty and Deviance*, 45–61.

35 Israel, *The Dutch Republic*, 360, 1017; M. van Leeuwen, Schoenmakers, and Smits, *Armoede en bedeling*, 4, 15–17; Pot, *Arm Leiden*, 358; J. Faber and M. van Leeuwen, *Amsterdamse katholieke bedeelden*, 21; Wijsenbeek-Olthuis, *Achter de gevels van Delft*, 374 n. 99; Sprunger, 'Mennonites', 146.

36 M. van Leeuwen, Schoenmakers, and Smits, *Armoede en bedeling*, 3–4.

37 Jütte, *Poverty and Deviance*, 51, 53–4, 56; Woolf, 'Introduction', 4–8; Hufton, *The Poor of Eighteenth-Century France*, 21–4; Martz, *Poverty and Welfare in Habsburg Spain*, 118–19; Slack, *Poverty and Policy*, 72.

38 Israel, *European Jewry*, 208.

39 Bolle, *De opheffing*, 46.

40 Rivlin, *Mutual Responsibility* (Heb.), 165.

41 Simonsohn, *History of the Jews in the Duchy of Mantua*, 521. Black, *Early Modern Italy*, 156, says only a few of the Jews of Rome were rich.

42 Simonsohn, *History of the Jews in the Duchy of Mantua*, 519–21.

43 Kochan, *Jews, Idols and Messiahs*, 108–9.

44 Horowitz, 'Charity, the Poor' (Heb.), 209–31; Glanz, *Geschichte des niederen jüdischen Volkes*, 11, 129–30, 166–71, 301 and n. 13; Rivlin, *Mutual Responsibility* (Heb.), 165.

45 M. Cohen, *Poverty and Charity*, 16.

46 A. Levy, *The Sephardim in the Ottoman Empire*, 34.

47 Leti, *Teatro Belgico*, ii. 336.

48 Bennassar, *The Spanish Character*; Kamen, *Spain 1469–1714*, 226–91; Defourneaux, *Daily Life in Spain*; Domínguez Ortiz, *La sociedad española*, 396–402.

49 Abraham Idaña in a letter written in the year 1686 (Teensma, 'Fragmenten', 132, 146).

50 'Sermão Sexto', *Sermões que Pregarão*, 107–8; see also Fuks and Fuks-Mansfeld, 'The Inauguration', 500–1.

51 See e.g. SAA entry no. 334, no. 220, pp. 79–85, 5460–1; for the same pattern of stratification in the Sephardi communities in southern France see Szapiro, 'Le Sud-Ouest', 235.

52 See P. Jansen, 'Het ritme van de dood'; id., 'Poverty in Amsterdam'; Nusteling, *Welvaart en werkgelegenheid in Amsterdam*, 128–39; Vries and van der Woude, *The First Modern Economy*, 607–54. For the development of the consumer price index in the 17th and 18th centuries, see table 2 of Jan Luiten van Zanden's list of data files of historical prices and wages, *Prices and Wages and the Cost of Living in the Western Part of The Netherlands* on the website of the International Institute of Social History (<http://www.iisg.nl/hpw/brenv.php>).

53 Deursen, *Plain Lives*, 7; the cost of living of an older woman in the Dutch Republic has been estimated at 100 guilders a year (Groenveld, 'For the Benefit of the Poor', 204).

54 At 2005 values this would come to €21,000 a year (multiplying it by 70): Zandvliet and Lesger, *De 250 rijksten*, p. xiii. Care is required in making such calculations: it is not simple, or perhaps even possible, to compare two periods so far apart. However, the multiplier gives us some idea of the value of the guilder during the Dutch Golden Age. For salaries and income in the Dutch Republic in general see Noordegraaf, *Daglonen in Alkmaar*; Noordegraaf and Schoenmakers (eds.), *Daglonen in Holland*; Vries, 'The Labour Market'; Noordegraaf and van Zanden, 'Early Modern Economic Growth'.

55 Vries and van der Woude, *The First Modern Economy*, table 12.3; Zanden, *Prices and Wages*, table 3; for an overview of different incomes and professional structure in the Dutch Republic see Vries and van der Woude, *The First Modern Economy*, 561–606.

56 SAA entry no. 334, no. 25, 20 Adar, 5461.

57 His mother was also given some charity, although in the beginning only periodically (SAA entry no. 334, no. 172, p. 205, 14 Adar 5403: 'ao Hazan e molher': 18 *livras* of matzah meal; 'a May do ditto': 8 *livras* of matzah meal; ibid., p. 230, 11 Tishrei 5404 [Sukkot]; ibid., p. 244, 14 Adar II 5404 [Purim]; ibid., p. 262, 12 Nisan 5404 [Pesach]; ibid., p. 267, 5 Sivan [Shavuot], these distributions being respectively 2.10 guilders, 5 guilders, 4 guilders, and 2.10 guilders). Only after 1647, on the death of her son, was the mother put permanently on the register for poor relief (ibid., no. 173, p. 4, Rosh Hodesh Iyar, 5407: 3 guilders). Before this Abraham must have had to take care of most of his mother's expenses.

58 SAA entry no. 334, no. 19, p. 164/249, 3 Tevet 5404. Where the poverty line is drawn precisely it is often defined on an individual basis. Baruch had an important position in the community, and thus could not be allowed to live on charity, as it would damage his prestige and position among the members. In 1651, when the *ḥazan* had already died, the family received 68 *livras* of matzah meal (ibid., no. 173, p. 167, 22 Adar 5411). On the basis of 8 *livras* of matzah meal per person, we can calculate that in 1651 Baruch's family consisted of eight members.

59 Nusteling, *Welvaart en werkgelegenheid in Amsterdam*, 171. See also Vries and van der Woude, *The First Modern Economy*, 627–32, 646, and Nusteling, *Welvaart en werkgelegenheid in Amsterdam*, 101–24, 252–3.

60 The pension was agreed for a period of five years, starting in 1668, after the death of her husband in 1667 (SAA entry no. 334, no. 1328, p. 263, 5427). The agreement was made after the widow, Rachel, complained to the administration of the Portuguese community about the extreme poverty she and her five children were experiencing. The sum given to her by the community was apparently her only source of income, since she told the *parnasim* that she had no one else who could support her: 'nao tendo pessoa nein parente a soccorrese'. The pension was not paid solely from the Portuguese charity box; two of Maimon's ex-colleagues were forced to contribute, giving up part of their salary, a total of 2 guilders a week (SAA entry no. 334, no. 24a, p. 17, 27 Sivan–11 Tamuz 5427; ibid., pp. 18^{v}–19, 26 Iyar 5428). For monthly distributions of charity to Rachel see ibid., no. 174, p. 806, Rosh Hodesh Adar 5428; ibid., p. 823, Rosh Hodesh Tamuz 5428. For rental subsidy see ibid., no. 215, p. 296, 5428–9 (she received a rental subsidy of 10 guilders a year). For the four festivals (Sukkot, Purim, Pesach, and Shavuot) see ibid., p. 292, 5428–9. For matzah meal and peat see ibid., pp. 254, 260, 5428.

When the five-year contract expired in 1672, Rachel tried her luck outside Amsterdam (SAA entry no. 334, no. 216, p. 114, 7 Av 5432). In 1674 she was apparently in Livorno, from where her daughter Ester applied to participate in the Dotar lottery (ibid., no. 1144, p. 208, 5434: 'Ester orphan de Maimon Haya em Liorne'). The widow returned to Amsterdam with her children in 1675, although she travelled again the same year (ibid., no. 216, p. 192, 8 Kislev 5436: 'p^{a} su viage . . . f 1'). That trip must have been a short one. Back in Amsterdam she lived off charity until 1683, when the Portuguese community paid her travel expenses to go to Bordeaux (ibid., no. 217, p. 4, 28 Elul 5436; ibid., p. 336, 11 Nisan 5442; for her departure see ibid., p. 419, 23 Elul 5443).

61 SAA entry no. 334, no. 25, p. 166, 8 Adar II 5489. In the mid-18th century the community paid a yearly income to the widows of the cantors of 180 guilders plus matzot and peat (ibid., p. 285, Sivan 5503; ibid., p. 292, 5505).

62 SAA entry no. 5072, no. 727, p. 21, 14 Nov. 1725.

63 SAA entry no. 5072, no. 696, p. 94, 2 Dec. 1694. Drago was to pay *finta* tax of 10 guilders a year (ibid., no. 176, p. 25, 24 Adar 5450, 5 guilders for half a year, *finta* tax).

64 Vries and van der Woude, *The First Modern Economy*, 564.

65 Zandvliet and Lesger, *De 250 rijksten*, pp. xii–xv. With the same precautions as noted above, 1 million guilders could be valued at €70 million today (Zandvliet and Lesger, *De 250 rijksten*, 37–8).

66 For 1631 see Frederiks and Frederiks, *Kohier van den tweehonderdsten penning van Amsterdam*; for 1631 and 1674 see Vaz Dias, 'Over den vermogenstoestand'.

67 It was Isaac de Pinto whose yearly contribution was 484 guilders (SAA entry no. 334, no. 174, p. 1092, 9 Tishrei 5436).

68 SAA entry no. 334, no. 172, pp. 96–8, 9 Tishrei 5401; ibid., no. 290, pp. 1–23, 5550. In 1640 the amount varied between 4 and 150 guilders. From 1700 to the end of the 18th century the sums varied between 2 and 200 guilders. In 1790 the minimum tax paid was 3 guilders and the maximum 208 guilders. See also Wagenaar, *Amsterdam*, ii. 228.

69 In this connection, Vaz Dias, 'Over den vermogenstoestand', 171, mentions 43%; for the number of Portuguese paying the *finta* tax see Appendix I, Table 8.

70 For the number of Portuguese paying the *finta* tax, see Appendix I, Table 8; see further Oldewelt, *Kohier*, ii. 68–109; also Vaz Dias, 'Over den vermogenstoestand'. Vaz Dias wrongly states that the *Kohier* of 1742 covers people with annual incomes over 800 guilders: the figure should be over 600 guilders. In contradiction to my calculations, Vaz Dias counts 283 Portuguese families in the *Kohier* of 1742. In the calculations relating to the Portuguese mentioned in the *Kohier* of 1742 and the *finta*-paying members of the Portuguese community, only the number of males as heads of families is taken into account. In the *Kohier* of 1742, 279 male heads of family are mentioned, as opposed to 217 male members, who are being assessed among the Portuguese community. The difference of 62 could maybe point to the fact that in the mid-18th century some Portuguese were not affiliated to the community. Another explanation could be the number of adolescents mentioned in the 1742 *Kohier* who did not yet appear in the *finta* assessments.

71 On average, in the pre-industrial cities of the Republic, only 20% of households had an income of 600 guilders or more a year, while only 6–8% had a yearly income above 1,000 guilders (Vries and van der Woude, *The First Modern Economy*, 562–4). Lesger, 'Stagnatie en stabiliteit', 259, table 13, concludes that three-quarters of Amsterdam's population is unaccounted for in the *Kohier*, which is not far from the situation within the Amsterdam Portuguese community. For the financial structure of Sephardi communities in southern France in the 18th century see Szapiro, 'Le Sud-Ouest', 235; for a similar situation in Jewish communities of the Ottoman empire see A. Levy, *Sephardim in the Ottoman Empire*, 91–3.

72 Swetschinski, 'The Portuguese Jewish Merchants of Seventeenth-Century Amsterdam', 404–8.

73 See Appendix I, Table 9.

74 See Appendix I, Table 10.

75 Taxed at between 11 and 50 guilders: see Appendix I, Table 9.

76 Taxed at between 51 and 208 guilders: see Appendix I, Table 9.

77 Taxed at between 11 and 50 guilders: see Appendix I, Table 9.

78 Vaz Dias, 'Over den vermogenstoestand', 169–70, also notices a growth in prosperity between 1631 and 1674. Israel, 'The Changing Role of the Dutch Sephardim', 42–7 and 50, calls the period from 1657 until 1672 the 'Golden Age of the Portuguese Jews'.

79 Swetschinski, 'The Portuguese Jewish Merchants of Seventeenth-Century Amsterdam', 408; id., *Reluctant Cosmopolitans*, 192, table 4.2.

80 Swetschinski, 'The Portuguese Jewish Merchants of Seventeenth-Century Amsterdam', 408, on the other hand, concludes in his analysis of the *finta*-paying members of the Portuguese community between 1678 and 1695 that the community was becoming more polarized and losing its middle-class members. Elsewhere, the growing rift between the rich and the poor did not imply the disappearance of the middle classes; for the Ottoman empire see A. Levy, *The Sephardim in the Ottoman Empire*, 83.

81 Taxed at between 51 and 208 guilders; see Appendix I, Table 9.

82 A strong polarization between rich and poor is characteristic of the social stratification among the population of the Republic in the 18th century in general (Israel, *The Dutch Republic*, 1017). Professor Marco van Leeuwen, *The Logic of Charity*, 41–3, has calculated the incomes of all heads of families in Amsterdam at the beginning of the 19th century. On the basis of his research one can conclude that the majority of the inhabitants of Amsterdam belonged to the lowest income groups and only a fraction enjoyed great wealth.

83 In accordance with Jewish law, orphans were registered separately on welfare lists (M. Cohen, *Poverty and Charity*, 237).

84 See e.g. SAA entry no. 334, no. 4, pp. 146–7, Rosh Hodesh Adar II 5380; ibid., no. 172, pp. 77–8, 9 Nisan 5400. One list even registered the addresses of the people on welfare according to streets and lanes (ibid., no. 173, p. 260, Rosh Hodesh Nisan 5413). As time went by and poverty increased, registration became more concise and organized: see e.g. the list of 1680 (ibid., no. 175, p. 112, 1 Nisan 5440).

85 One *livra* (pound) was equal to around half a kilo; SAA entry no. 334, no. 10, [no page number], 5393: 'O maso se reparte a £ 8 por pesoa benentendido pelos q resebeu.' The measure of 8 *livras* a person was not always strictly observed: in certain cases a little more or less was given (ibid., no. 172, p. 130, 8 Nisan 5401: 'Brattis pintta £ 9'). Still, 8 *livras* of flour remains the starting point and we keep to that. Many German and Polish Jews received matzot through the Portuguese community until 1670, and on this basis we can estimate the number of Ashkenazim on welfare through the Portuguese community. These Ashkenazim were given less matzah meal: mostly 6 *livras* per person, as opposed to the 8 *livras* given to each Sephardi (ibid., pp. 77–8, 9 Nisan 5400). Moreover, the quality of matzah meal given to Ashkenazim was invariably inferior. In 1650 Portuguese and Ashkenazi Jews were still receiving matzah of the same quality (ibid., no. 173, p. 121, 19 Adar II 5410: '£ 3803 p. nossos pobres e £ 1629 a tudescos a placas 3, 3/8' per *livra*. In 1669 *tudescos* got matzot of inferior quality (ibid., no. 215, p. 303, 5428–9: 2⅜ 'placas', a *livra* of matzah meal for German and Polish Jews as against 2¾ 'placas' a *livra* of matzah meal for the Portuguese poor. Even though the poor were assigned an amount of matzah meal they usually received matzot after they were baked and not the meal as such; on the production of matzot for the poor see e.g. SAA entry no. 334, no. 25, p. 257, 23 Heshvan 5501).

86 SAA entry no. 334, no. 974, file D, 1744–5/5505.

87 See Appendix I, Tables 11 and 12.

88 SAA entry no. 5075, no. 3712, Not. F. Tixerandet, pp. 102–3, 6 Dec. 1690.

89 For Jacob Rodrigues Carrion see SAA DTB 687, p. 228, 20 July 1668; SAA DTB 688, p. 101, 13 June 1670; for Rachel Louzada: SAA DTB 691, p. 53, 27 Aug. 1677; for Isaac Baruch: SAA DTB 680, p. 122, 8 June 1649; for Rachel Aboab: SAA DTB 674, p. 264, 30 Sept. 1637.

90 SAA DTB 714, p. 126, 25 Feb. 1724.

91 SAA entry no. 334, no. 172, p. 293, 14 Adar 5405: 'Sarra Thomas e netto . . . 16 [*livras* of matzah meal]'.

92 SAA entry no. 334, no. 215, p. 305, 5429: 'Judit Rodriguez e neta . . . 18 [*livras* of matzah meal]'.

93 SAA entry no. 334, no. 20, p. 177, 7 Adar 5454: 'Judu Valensin con 3 netos'.

94 SAA entry no. 334, no. 217, p. 98, 5 Adar 5438: 'q ter os netos, f[os] de David Cohen de Lara en sua caza'. David Cohen de Lara was apparently related to the Hamburg Portuguese community's *haham* of the same name (on whom see *Encyclopaedia Judaica*, xii. 492–3). In 1669 David Cohen de Lara married Sara Semah da Costa (SAA DTB 688, p. 13, 13 Sept. 1669; at this ceremony Sara was assisted by her mother Rachel Semah).

95 SAA entry no. 334, no. 172, p. 205, 14 Adar 5403: 'Sara Lopez Pitta e dous f[os] . . . 24 [*livras* of matzah meal]'; ibid., p. 292, 5405: 'e tres filhos . . . 32 [*livras* of matzah meal]'; ibid., no. 173, p. 213, 23 Adar 5412: 'Sara Lopez Pita . . . 8 [*livras* of matzah meal]'; ibid., no. 174, p. 609, 12 Kislev 5424: 'Netta de Sara Lopes Pitta'.

96 SAA entry no. 334, no. 173, p. 78, 20 Adar 5409: 'Abraham de Fiqueiroa . . . 24 [*livras* of matzah meal]'; ibid., p. 167, 22 Adar 5411: 'Abraham de Fiqueiroa e familia . . . 34 [*livras* of matzah meal]'; ibid., no. 174, p. 142, 22 Adar 5416: '24 [*livras* of matzah meal]'; ibid., p. 304, 16 Adar 5419: '36 [*livras* of matzah meal]'; ibid., p. 550, 3 Nisan 5423: '30 [*livras* of matzah meal]'; ibid., no. 215, p. 359, 5430: '8 [*livras* of matzah meal]'.

97 SAA entry no. 334, no. 215, pp. 199, 252, 304, 359, 5427–30: '40 [*livras* of matzah meal]'; ibid., no. 216, pp. 62, 111, 142, 5431–3: '40 [*livras* of matzah meal]'; ibid., pp. 165, 188, 209, 5434–7: '16 [*livras* of matzah meal]'; ibid., no. 217, pp. 50, 94, 5438: '16 [*livras* of matzah meal]'. Thus, between 1667 and 1673 Ester's family consisted of five people, if we base ourselves on 8 *livras* of matzah meal per person; however, from 1674 until her death in 1678 the family unit consisted of just two people, including Ester.

98 SAA entry no. 334, no. 172, p. 293, 14 Adar 5405: '40 [*livras* of matzah meal]'; ibid., no. 173, p. 28, 20 Adar 5408; ibid., p. 78, 20 Adar 5409; ibid., p.122, 19 Adar II 5410; ibid., p. 167, 22 Adar 5411, ibid., p. 214, 23 Adar 5412: '40 [*livras* of matzah meal]'; ibid., p. 259, 23 Adar II 5413: '34 [*livras* of matzah meal]'; ibid., no. 174,

p. 31, 20 Adar 5414; ibid., p. 86, 20 Adar II 5415: '34 [*livras* of matzah meal]'; ibid., p. 142, 2 Adar 5416; ibid., p. 198, 22 Adar 5417; ibid., p. 250, 11 Adar II 5418; '30 [*livras* of matzah meal]'; ibid., p. 304, 16 Adar 5419; ibid., 367, 16 Adar 5420; ibid., p. 425, 29 Adar II 5421: '40 [*livras* of matzah meal]'; ibid., p. 484, 24 Adar 5422; ibid., p. 550, 3 Nisan 5423; ibid., p. 620, 1 Nisan 5424: '24 [*livras* of matzah meal]'; ibid., p. 693, 10 Nisan 5425: '32 [*livras* of matzah meal]'; ibid., no. 215, p. 199, 5427: '24 [*livras* of matzah meal]'.

99 For a similar pattern among Conversos in the Iberian peninsula and overseas see Studnicki-Gizbert, '*La Nación*', 81–5.

100 Vries and van der Woude, *The First Modern Economy*, 665–99; Israel, *The Dutch Republic*, esp. pt. 4, 'Age of Decline'; Vries, *The Economy of Europe*; Nusteling, *Welvaart en werkgelegenheid in Amsterdam*. On the tobacco industry, its importance for labour among the Portuguese Jews, and its decay in the 18th century see Roessingh, *Inlandse tabak*, 208, 218, 393–5, 400, 410, 420, 423, 437, 439, 453, 486, 492; id., 'Tobacco Growing'; Israel, *European Jewry*, 147, 150, 203. For demographic structures among the Amsterdam Jews, both Portuguese and Ashkenazi, see Hart, *Historisch-Demografische Notities*.

101 See Appendix I, Tables 11 and 12; we find the same pattern elsewhere, though sometimes a little later. For 18th-century Turin see Cavallo, 'Conceptions of Poverty', 190–3.

102 See Appendix I, Tables 11 and 12. The percentage of women on welfare among the Portuguese was usually higher than elsewhere but this does not always hold: if we compare it, for example, with the non-Jewish community of the city of Zwolle in the 17th century it is almost the same—53.7% (Wijngaarden, *Zorg voor de Kost*, 88–9). In early modern Zamora in Spain, 66.4% of indigent households were headed by single women (Flynn, *Sacred Charity*, 23–4). Norberg, *Rich and Poor in Grenoble*, 106, states that in Grenoble 57% of recipients of charity at the start of the 18th century were women. For a similar pattern of poor women on welfare in a Jewish community see M. Cohen, *Poverty and Charity*, ch. 5.

103 See Appendix I, Table 14. For the high proportion of single women in Europe in medieval and early modern times see Kowaleski, 'Singlewomen'; for a similar general situation in Amsterdam see Kuipers, *Migrantenstad*, 198.

104 See Appendix I, Tables 11 and 12.

105 See also Woolf, 'Introduction', 15 and n. 29; id., 'Charity', 169–70; Gutton, *La Société et les pauvres*, 54–6.

106 See Appendix I, Table 13.

107 See Appendix I, Table 14.

108 SAA entry no. 334, nos. 172–4 (1639–76), 216 (1670–35), and 974–6 (1734–96) (distributions of matzah meal); ibid., no. 172, pp. 130–1, 8 Nisan 5401: 'Reparticão do massod feitta este anno como abaixo se declara . . . Imm^el^ Castiel mulher e 2 f°s 32 [*livras* of matzah meal], Daniel Obidiente e mulher 16 [*livras* of matzah meal], Irman de d^tor^ mercado e 2 f^as^ 24 [*livras* of matzah meal].'

109 Gutton, *La Société et les pauvres*, 54–6, comes to the same conclusion concerning the small-scale character of households on welfare. For Florence at the beginning of the 19th century see Woolf, 'Charity', 169; for the Dutch Republic see Pot, *Arm Leiden*, 263–7, and van der Vlis, *Leven in armoede*, 74–8; for Amsterdam see M. van Leeuwen, Schoenmakers, and Smits, *Armoede en bedeling*.

4 The Organization of Welfare

1 See Goldish, 'The Amsterdam Portuguese Rabbinate'.

2 On social care among the Jews in historical perspective, both in general and in specific countries, see Abrahams, *Jewish Life*; Assis, 'Les Institutions sociales médiévales'; id., *The Golden Age of Aragonese Jewry*; Baer, 'Der Ursprung'; id., 'The Origins of the Organization of the Jewish Community' (Heb.); id., *A History of the Jews in Christian Spain*; Baron, *The Jewish Community*; Bergman, *Tsedakah in Israel* (Heb.); Farine, 'Charity'; Frisch, *An Historical Survey*; Horowitz, 'Jewish Confraternities'; id., 'Charity, the Poor' (Heb.); J. Katz, *Tradition and Crisis*; Kohler, 'The Historical Development of Jewish Charity'; Marcus, *Communal Sickcare*; Neuman, *The Jews in Spain*; Rivlin, *Mutual Responsibility* (Heb.); Ruderman, 'The Founding of a Gemilut Hasadim Society'; Ben-Naeh, *Jews in the Realm of the Sultans*, 164–290; Bornstein-Mazovesky, 'Structure, Organization and Spiritual Life'. For a review on Jewish thought in the 17th century see Twersky and Septimus, *Jewish Thought*. On the upswing of Jewish spirituality in early modern times see Scholem, *Major Trends*, 244–86; Idel, 'Religion'; and id., 'Spanish Kabbalah'. For philosophy and kabbalah in Renaissance Italy see Bonfil, *Rabbis*, 280–98; for the publication of kabbalistic works in Amsterdam such as that of Abraham Cohen Herrera see Swetschinski, *Reluctant Cosmopolitans*, 294–6; Yosha, *Myth and Metaphor* (Heb.).

3 Unfortunately the statutes of the Spanish (Ponentini) community of Venice are not available. It is therefore difficult to make a comparison between the social structures of the Spanish community in Venice and those of the Portuguese Jewish community of Amsterdam. We do know that the dowry organization Dotar, established in 1615, was a copy of an organization founded by the Spanish Jews of Venice two years earlier (Bodian, 'Portuguese Dowry Societies'). Other concrete indications also lead us to southern Europe. In article 2 of the Amsterdam Portuguese statutes of 1639 the Ponentini community of Venice is mentioned: 'segindo ho estilo de Veneza' (Pieterse, *Daniel Levi de Barrios*, 156). Also, the name of the community in Amsterdam is the same as that of the Ponentini community of Venice: Kahal Kados de Talmud Torah. Those laying down the *escamot* of the Spanish Portuguese community of London in 1664 also referred to the fact that the Amsterdam Portuguese community followed the model of Venice: Bodian, 'Amsterdam, Venice'; ead., 'The Escamot of the Spanish–Portuguese Jewish Community of London', 16; L. D. Barnett, *El Libro de los Acuerdos*; Israel, *Diasporas within a Diaspora*, ch. 2; Fuks-Mansfeld, *De Sefardim in Amsterdam*, 59; Oliel-Grauz, 'A Study in Intercommunal Relations'. For the translation of the *takanot* of Valladolid in 1432 into specific Sephardi communal models on the peninsula and their transference, after 1492, to many of the

diverse centres around the Mediterranean see Baer, *A History of the Jews in Christian Spain*, ii. 260–9; Moreno Koch, *Las taqqanot*.

4 SAA entry no. 334, no. 19, p. 162/247, 1 Kislev 5404; Rivlin, *Mutual Responsibility*, 33–86 (Heb.); Ruderman, 'The Founding of a Gemilut Hasadim Society'.

5 For Italy see e.g. Pullan, *Rich and Poor in Renaissance Venice*; id., *Poverty and Charity*. For the Dutch Republic see Parker, *The Reformation of Community*; Prak, 'Armenzorg 1500–1800'; Groenveld, 'For the Benefit of the Poor'. For Spain see Flynn, *Sacred Charity*; Rumeu de Armas, *Historia de la previsión social en España*.

6 For the Jewish world see e.g. A. Levy, *The Sephardim in the Ottoman Empire*, 65–70. For the non-Jewish world see M. van Leeuwen, *The Logic of Charity*, ch. 3; Parker, 'Calvinism and Poor Relief', 113. For France see Cavignac, 'L'Assistance chez les Juifs de Bordeaux'.

7 SAA entry no. 334, no. 1051, p. 1, 48 Omer 5376.

8 SAA entry no. 334, no. 13, pp. 3–9, 24 Shevat 5382; Swetschinski, *Reluctant Cosmopolitans*, 182–7.

9 *Handvesten ofte privilegiën*, ii. 473, 17 Nov. 1670; Swetschinski, *Reluctant Cosmopolitans*, 176, 186–7.

10 Swetschinski, *Reluctant Cosmopolitans*, 190–1, 196; id. 'The Portuguese Jewish Merchants of Seventeenth-Century Amsterdam', 376–8, 391–404; Y. Kaplan, 'The Jews in the Republic', 121–5 ('The Power of the *Mahamad*'). For oligarchic structures elsewhere in the western Sephardi diaspora see Trivellato, *The Familiarity of Strangers*, 92–3; for qualities of Jewish trustees of charitable bodies see Frisch, *An Historical Survey*, 109–15.

11 Baron, *The Jewish Community*, ii. 23; J. Katz, *Tradition and Crisis*, 65–75; Baer, 'The Origins of the Organization of the Jewish Community' (Heb.).

12 See the discussion on this subject in Rozen, *Jewish Identity*, 103–18.

13 Roorda, 'Hollands regentenpatriciaat'; Roorda and van Dijk, 'Social Mobility'; Deursen, *Bavianen en Slijkgeuzen*, vol. i, ch. 5; Prak, *Gezeten burgers*, ch. 2, esp. 106–8. For the ruling classes and the administration of charity in Amsterdam see M. van Leeuwen, *The Logic of Charity*, ch. 1, esp. pp. 11–12. Marco van Leeuwen (ibid., ch. 3) points to a division among the groups of administrators of the poor. His research showed that deacons of the Lutheran and Reformed churches belonged to the higher middle class, while other charity administrators were mostly recruited from the elite. For Geneva see Kingdon, 'Social Welfare'. For Aix-en-Provence see Fairchilds, *Poverty and Charity in Aix-en-Provence*, 38–45. For Grenoble see Norberg, *Rich and Poor in Grenoble*, 296–7. For the phenomenon of co-optation in *misericórdias* in the Portuguese empire see Guimarães Sá, *Quando o rico se faz pobre*, 104.

14 Frisch, *An Historical Survey*, 116–18; Bergman, *Tsedakah in Israel* (Heb.); *Encyclopaedia Judaica*, iv. 569–75 ('Charity').

15 Domínguez Ortiz, *La sociedad española*; Black, *Italian Confraternities*, 170–8.

16 Juan Luis Vives, *De subventione pauperum* (1526); Tomás de Trujillo, *Tratado de la limosna* (1563); Martín Batista de Lanuza, *Tratado sobre el modo de distribuir y* *repartir la limosna con discreción, mérito y utilidad* (1606). Olivera's treatise was copied in Amsterdam in 1686 by the Portuguese Jew Abraham Idaña, together with other pieces (SAA entry no. 15030, no. 130527, pp. 1–11, and Teensma, 'Fragmenten'). See also Cristóbal Pérez de Herrera, *Discursos para el amparo de los legítimos pobres y reducción de los fingidos: y de la fundación y principio de los Albergues destos Reynos, y amparo de la milicia de ellos* (1598), vol. cic; Miguel de Giginta, *Tratado de remedio de pobres* (1579); and Dominguo de Soto, *Deliberación en la causa de pobres* (1545). On these treatises see also Flynn, *Sacred Charity*, 185–6.

17 On classification of the Jewish poor in medieval times see M. Cohen, *The Voice of the Poor*, 107–9.

18 On *pobres de solemnidad*, also in Pisa, see Toaff, *La nazione ebrea*, 601.

19 Olivera, *Tratado de la hobligaçion*, 1–3.

20 Olivera puts beggars on a lower level than the disabled poor, but on the basis of biblical commands (Deut. 14: 29; 15: 7–12), does not exclude them from charity. On giving to beggars see also Baron, *The Jewish Community*, ii. 321–2.

21 The distinction between the deserving and the undeserving poor was not new in the early modern period but stems from earlier days. On this phenomenon in medieval Jewish, Christian, and Muslim society see Safley, *The Reformation of Charity*, 6; Lev, *Charity*, 12; M. Cohen, *Poverty and Charity*, ch. 2. For the same point of view in the Portuguese London community's *El Libro de los Acuerdos* see L. D. Barnett, *El Libro de los Acuerdos*, 9, para. 24, Rosh Hodesh Elul 5423.

22 SAA entry no. 334, no. 93, p. 96, 6 Av 5512.

23 Ashkenazim were taken care of and given charity by the Portuguese community of Amsterdam from the start. Records exist going back to 1617 (SAA entry no. 334, no. 6, p. 194, 5 May 5377/1617: 'f 1:3:8 que tanto dey a hum tudesco q prenderao p[a] se hir'; ibid., 3 June 5377/1617: 'a 3 tudescos').

24 For *pobres da terra* see SAA entry no. 334, no. 6, pp. 192–3, 17 Feb. 5378; ibid., no. 3, p. 6, 1 Iyar 5381. Another name was *pobres ordinarios* (ibid., no. 9, p. 73, 5382).

25 *Passageiros* (SAA entry no. 334, no. 9, p. 98, 5386), *forasteiros* (ibid., p. 12, 5379), *pobres estrangeyros* (ibid., no. 17, p. 38, 30 Jan. 5391/1631), *pobres encaminhados para fora da terra* (ibid., no. 3, p. 5, 1 Adar 5381). After 1622 there were also the so-called *pobres gerais* (ibid., no. 17, p. 32, 13 Jan. 1630), taken care of by the *imposta* board and not (yet) divided among the separate *kehilot*, as opposed to the *pobres particulares* (ibid., no. 5, p. 176, 19 Shevat 5382), who were taken care of by the different Portuguese *kehilot*.

26 Para. 32 of the 1639 statutes (Pieterse, *Daniel Levi de Barrios*, 163; SAA entry no. 334, no. 19, p. 4[v]/84, 28 Adar II 5399).

27 The amount of welfare had to be generous enough to prevent Jews joining Christian congregations in the city: in a few cases the possibility of more assistance was an important consideration, if not the most important one, in the decision to leave the Jewish community (see Ch. 7). The amount of welfare granted was also one of the reasons why some poor people switched their religious allegiance among the different Christian denominations: Groenveld, 'For the Benefit of the Poor'.

28 Pieterse, *Daniel Levi de Barrios*, 156; para. 3 of the statutes of 1639 (SAA entry no. 334, no. 19, p. 1^v/78, 28 Adar II 5399).

29 SAA entry no. 334, no. 381, p. 11 [n.d., apparently 18th century]; see also other documents in SAA entry no. 334, no. 381; for letters from Livorno and Ferrara concerning the Jewish background of the family Franco Vezinho see ibid., no. 118, p. 623, 2 June 1725; ibid, p. 625, 18 Jan. 1726; ibid., pp. 626–7, 7 Tishrei 5487. See also Oliel-Grausz, 'Networks and Communication', 63–4.

30 SAA entry no. 334, no. 381, p. 12, [n.d.; apparently 18th century]. The same name was cited as the person who received money from a legacy of Jacob Mazahod in 1733 (ibid., no. 736, p. 40, 5493: 'Sara Rois Frois f 20,–').

31 SAA entry no. 334, no. 1151, p. 215, 1634.

32 SAA entry no. 334, no. 25, p. 188, 9 Nisan 5489.

33 SAA entry no. 334, no. 1153, p. 371, 5 Shevat 5460.

34 That is to say, all four of Isaac's grandparents belonged to the *nação*. Witnesses for the orphan Ribca Valensin from Belgrade also declared that they knew her father (ibid., p. 144, 24 Adar 5456).

35 The petition of the orphan Rachel Arama to Dotar declared that she was 'da nação portugueza', born in Belgrade and now living in Amsterdam; witnesses confirmed her statement (SAA entry no. 334, no. 1153, p. 53, 25 Adar 5456; ibid., 15 Shevat 5456). Similarly, the petition of Rachel aLevi, orphan of Jomtob aLevi, born in Belgrade and now living in Amsterdam, confirms that she belonged to the Portuguese 'nacão' (ibid., p. 52, 26 Adar 5456). Witnesses of Paloma, daughter of Mayl de Minhana from Belgrade, also declared that they knew her parents were Spaniards ('Espanhoes'); her grandfather used to be the 'sochet y bodek do K.K. de belogrado' (ibid., p. 370, 11 Shevat 5456).

36 SAA entry no. 334, no. 13, p. 121, 3 Nisan 5396: 'Samuel Ramirez que partio de Gelanda pera Italia e como seya noso Portuges aquem temos obrigação de socorrer e avanteyar'; see also money given to the Portuguese Jacob Coronel, 'prezo em ostende . . . f 12:12' (ibid., no. 216, p. 147, 8 Shevat 5434).

37 SAA entry no. 334, no. 13, p. 121, 3 Nisan 5396.

38 See the example of a poor Italian Jew who was sent away with 3 guilders in 1620 (SAA entry no. 334, no. 4, p. 144, 29 Tevet 5380), while Abraham Dalvarenga was paid 260 guilders to set out for Italy in 1623 (ibid., no. 13, p. 28, 20 Aug. 5383). Isaac Bravo was given 100 guilders to go to Guyana (ibid., no. 215, p. 42, 29 Nisan 5423), while in the same period Moses Engel received just 2 guilders for his journey (ibid., p. 11, 26 Sivan 5423). David Alvares Torres and his family got 100 guilders in 1668 to set out for Barbados (SAA entry no. 334, no. 215, p. 264, 23 Elul 5428), while in the same period Salomon Levi Italiano got a little less than 1 guilder to return to Venice (ibid., p. 269, 20 Tamuz 5428). In 1670 the wife of Moses Zacuto got 30 guilders to go to Hamburg with her family (SAA entry no. 334, no. 216, p. 2, 16 Iyar 5430); at the same time a foreigner from Constantina was given 1.10 guilders to leave Amsterdam (ibid., p. 10, 20 Tamuz 5430). See also the case of the Italian Jew being sent to an unknown destination and given 1.10 guilders in 1688 (SAA entry no. 334, no. 218, p. 243, 5 Kislev 5449) as opposed to the 50 guilders granted to David Franco de Almeida for his trip to Livorno (ibid., p. 242, 14 Tishrei 5449).

39 The same sociological phenomenon of a superior attitude or feeling of exclusivity could be observed among other groups leaving the peninsula, for example the *moriscos* who held on to their Iberian world-view as they settled in Tunis in the early years of the 17th century (Ravillard, 'Los Moriscos', 618; Latham, 'Contribution', 42–3).

40 SAA entry no. 334, no. 1322, p. A, 16 Adar I 5375; ibid., no. 1141, p. 3, 14 Adar I 5375; for an overview of the archives of Dotar see Pieterse, *Inventaris*, 68–70; on Dotar see further Révah, 'Le Premier Règlement'; Bodian, 'Portuguese Dowry Societies'; Pieterse, *350 jaar Dotar*.

41 SAA entry no. 334, no. 1186, p. 1, 5385, introduction: 'toda a pessoa necesitada judia'; ibid., p. 40[v], 5437: 'p. sy e p. outros da misva do emprestimo a beneficio de pesoas q nao sao Judeos de nossa nação portugueza e espanhola . . . de oje em diante com pena de herem nemhua pessoa posa tomar p[a] levar nem mandar p outrem a dito emprestimo nenhua prenda q nao seja de Jahid deste K.K.'. See also Pieterse, *Daniel Levi de Barrios*, 181.

42 SAA entry no. 334, no. 1211, 'sobre a escama terseira', p. 3, 12 Adar 5414: 'judeos de nação portuguesa ou espanhola'; for Aby Jetomim see further Pieterse, *Inventaris*, 71, and below.

43 SAA entry no. 334, no. 1189, p. 52, 26 Kislev 5457.

44 SAA entry no. 334, no. 120, file 81, para. 12, 6 Shevat 5494: 'nossa naçam Portugueza, ou Espanhola'.

45 SAA entry no. 334, no. 25, p. 218, 8 Tevet 5495.

46 SAA entry no. 334, no. 25, p. 337, 8 Tevet 5510.

47 SAA entry no. 334, no. 700, Not. P. Padthuysen, pp. 7–9, 30 Mar. 1703: 'y por quanto ella Testadora tiene una acion en la Compania dela India Oriental, en la Camara de Zelanda de quiñentas livras de gruessos de Caudal o principal que ella Testadora estima al presente en doze mil florines, cuija acion esta en nombre della Testadora portanto es que dice ella Testadora querer y ser su expressa voluntad, que los rendimientos dela dicha Acion se empleen en obras pias, es asaber para casamientos de donzellas dela Generacion della Testadora y del dho su marido difuncto en sanguinidad . . . bien entendido que no podra entrar ninguna abalotear y gosar el dho fruto de tres reparticiones sin que tenga la hedad de catorze años cumplidos ij siendo que no aija donsella del parentesco en sanguinidad della Testadora ni del dho su marido difuncto que la pretenda en tal caso serviran las dhas tres reparticiones para casamiento de dos donzellas huerfanos benemeritas delanacion judaica Portuguesa desta Ciudad de Amsterdam, lo que se ira ansi continuando siempre'. For claims to a dowry by the family members of Abigail Dias da Fonseca see SAA entry no. 334, no. 700, p. 36, 14 Heshvan 5480; ibid., p. 56, 19 Tevet 5497.

48 SAA entry no. 334, no. 175, p. 166, 4 Heshvan 5442, dealing with a gift of 500 guilders: 'com condição que não se resgate com elles senão for yudeu espanol ou portugues'.

49 M. Cohen, *Poverty and Charity*, 69; on the concepts of the nobility of the Jewish people and its purity of blood see the Amsterdam rabbis Morteira and Menasseh ben Israel, quoted in Saperstein, *Exile in Amsterdam*, 476–8.

50 Glick, 'On Converso and Marrano Ethnicity'; Graizbord, *Souls in Dispute*, 37–8, 52–3; id., 'Religion and Ethnicity', 43, 46; Schreiber, 'Cristianos Nuevos de Madrid', 554–5; Stow, *Theater of Acculturation*, 24. For exclusion of New Christians in Bahia see Russell-Wood, *Fidalgos and Philanthropists*, 124, 135–45, 181, 183, 278–80; Guimarães Sá, *Quando o rico se faz pobre*, 7–10, 94, 110–11, 184; id., 'Ecclesiastical Structures', 267–9.

51 For the similarly exclusive character of expatriate *morisco* society in Tunis see Latham, 'Contribution'.

52 For the expression 'carriers of culture' see Berghe, *Race*, 85, 147, 150.

53 Hellinger, 'The Emerging Definition of the Poverty Line in Jewish Law'; Brooks, *Support*, 30, 152; M. Cohen, *Poverty and Charity*, 6–7; Horowitz, 'Charity, the Poor' (Heb.); see also Olivera, *Tratado de la hobligaçion*.

54 'Conforme a calidade de seu estado': see *Sermões que Pregarão*: 'Sermão sexto que preegou o Docto Talmid H. Doctor & Philosopho Yshac Vellozino'.

55 See lists of petitions of the so-called 'structural' poor (those who, owing to specific problems, did not work and thus lived in chronic need), registered as 'poor of the country', as opposed to those of urgent cases ('urgensias' or 'urgensias extraordinarias') in the *livros longos* during the 17th and 18th centuries—SAA entry no. 334, nos. 215–23 and 969–70. The so-called 'conjunctural' poor were those people who could normally subsist on their daily income, but who could not manage to build any savings so that, in a crisis, they tended to fall into poverty. On 'structural' as opposed to 'conjunctural' poor as terms in vogue in the early modern period see Mollat, *The Poor in the Middle Ages*, 26; Fairchilds, *Poverty and Charity in Aix-en-Provence*, 73.

56 In the 19th century this preference was recorded in the statutes of the Portuguese community (*Reglement voor de Nederlandsch–Portugeesch-Israelitische Kerkelijke Gemeente te Amsterdam* of 1850: SAA entry no. 334, no. 131, pp. 22–3, 7 Feb. 1850). The poor were divided into two categories: the first category consisted of (*a*) abandoned children or those under 15 who had no parents, and (*b*) people who because of old age or disability were unable to work or earn an income through any other means; the second category consisted of other poor in the Portuguese community in need.

57 See surnames such as 'the blind': Rachel Sega de Espanha (SAA entry no. 334, no. 174, p. 273, 12 Nisan 5418); 'the surd' (deaf): Ester Cohen a Surda (ibid., no. 215, p. 12, 12 Elul 5423); 'the mute': Mudos de Hamburgo (ibid., p. 13, 1 Heshvan 5424); 'the crazy' (mentally disabled): 'Sara Caanet loica' (ibid., no. 172, p. 316, 11 Tishrei 5406).

58 The community considered giving more than 6 guilders to the widow of Eliau Lopes Crespin (in this case 7 guilders and 10 stivers), but decided in her case to

adhere strictly to the rules and not to give more than 6 guilders a month (SAA entry no. 334, no. 21, p. 14, 11 Kislev 5420). Rachel Sega de Espanha, on the other hand, received an allotment of 10 guilders a month, apparently because she was blind (ibid., no. 215, p. 1, 1 Sivan 5423).

59 See e.g. the money given to the *secretos* in 1666 (SAA entry no. 334, no. 174, p. 733, 20 Adar 5426: 'mais dados aos seguintos q por serem secretos se havião sentado aparte em tudo'). Here distributions vary between 6:6 guilders and 100 guilders; also in 1666 the *secreto* Isaac Febos received one extremely large gift of 100 guilders. On the same occasion, Ester Ferão, as a 'mulher encuberta', received 55 guilders (ibid.). In the 18th century levels of distribution to so-called *secretos* were relatively high as the community tried to cope with the rising impoverishment of formerly well-off families. In Jewish tradition the latter were entitled to an allowance that enabled them to maintain their accustomed standard of living. In line with this approach, Abraham Jessurun Espinosa received 350 guilders in 1733, Abraham Touro 400 guilders in 1737, and Abraham Rep: Semah Fero 450 guilders in 1753 (SAA entry no. 334, no. 973, pp. 3 and 5, 12 Iyar 5493, 11 Shevat 5497, 25 Tishrei 5514). On these principles in Jewish law see Frisch, *Historical Survey*, 56–7, 118–21; Brooks, *Support*, 149–50. For the treatment of the genteel poor in Italy see Pullan, *Rich and Poor in Renaissance Venice*, 373–4; Spicciani, 'Poveri Vergognosi'; for their treatment in Spain see Flynn, *Sacred Charity*, 79–80, 93–4. On the phenomeon of the genteel poor in pre-industrial Europe more generally see M. van Leeuwen, *The Logic of Charity*, 593, and the literature mentioned there in n. 3.

60 SAA entry no. 334, no. 217, p. 5, 5438.

61 See e.g. the list of 1696 (SAA entry no. 334, no. 219, p. 269, 1 Nisan 5456).

62 For the separate registration of *belogrados* in 1713 see SAA entry no. 334, no. 221. For *belogrados* placed at the bottom of the charity rolls see e.g. the following in SAA entry no. 334: no. 218, p. 430, 1 Heshvan 5451; no. 219, p. 26, 1 Nisan 5452; no. 219, p. 149, 14 Nisan 5453; no. 219, p. 196, 24 Jan. 1694; no. 219, p. 250, 12 Nisan 5455; no. 219, p. 269, 1 Nisan 5456; no. 219, p. 338, 9 Nisan 5457; no. 219, p. 355, 13 Adar 5458; no. 220, p. 5, 27 Nisan 5459; no. 220, pp. 162–71, 5462. For relations between *belogrados*, Sephardim from the eastern Sephardi diaspora, and those in the west see Levie Bernfeld, 'Confrontation entre l'Orient et l'Occident'. For another example of the unequal relationship see the policy of the division of seats in the Gemilut Hasadim yeshiva: it was decided that during the holidays the seats at the table and the two couches would be reserved for the *ba'ale torah*, or members of the yeshiva. 'Our Portuguese' ('os nossos Portuguezes') got priority, even if they were not brothers of the *ḥevrah*. 'Our brothers from Belgrade' ('nossos irmaos de Belgrado') and Italian and Levantine Jews ('Italianos e Levantinos') could only have a seat if there were any left after the others were seated (SAA entry no. 334, no. 1191, p. 214, 1 Tevet 5459).

63 SAA entry no. 334, no. 19, p. 19/104, 33 Omer 5399. In the 19th century, candidates for *sedaca* were discussed extensively within the administration of the Portuguese community ('het armbestuur'). At that time notes concerning the poor were certainly made (SAA entry no. 334.A, suppl., no. 130: Notulen van de Vergaderingen der Tweede Afdeeling (Armbestuur) van het Collegie van Parnassijns, pp. 20 and 30, 1 Nov. 1877).

64 According to Wagenaar, *Amsterdam*, ii. 222, the Portuguese community would fix the level of charity only once a year. Wagenaar based this estimate on 'information he received and trusted that it was precise and true in most aspects'. Alms papers of poor Jews within the Ashkenazi community were checked twice a year (*Handvesten ofte privilegiën*, ii. 483, para. 25, 11 Oct. 1737).

65 Wagenaar, *Amsterdam*, ii. 160–2. The Reformed Church of Amsterdam decided that the deacons had to visit the poor at home: 'dat de Diaconen sullen gaen ende besoeken de arme lidmaten dije van de gemeene aelmoessen nemen ende henluyden vermanen tot alle t zien dat de arme christenen van node is nae gelegentheyt der persoonen' (SAA entry no. 376, no. 1, p. 13, 7 Apr. 1579); see also Roodenburg, *Onder Censuur*, 111–14; Deursen, *Bavianen en Slijkgeuzen*, 115–17. Concerning the supervision of recipients of outdoor relief in Amsterdam see Wagenaar, *Amsterdam*, ii. 271, 274; M. van Leeuwen, *The Logic of Charity*, 99–103; Groenveld, 'For the Benefit of the Poor'; and Kuijpers, *Migrantenstad*, 303–9, 313. For Grenoble see Norberg, *Rich and Poor in Grenoble*, 104–5.

66 See e.g. Simon do Valle, charged as a *shamash* to go round the houses of the poor distributing welfare (SAA entry no. 334, no. 215, p. 13, 15 Heshvan 5424).

67 SAA entry no. 334, no. 1141, p. 6, 14 Adar I 5375.

68 The founders of the *ḥevrah*, Oneg Sabat, established in 1747 (SAA entry no. 334, no. 25, pp. 315–17, 25 Kislev 5508), had discretion ('a sua discrisão') in deciding who deserved assistance, so they must have known the poor at close quarters; the members of Kisuy Ros decided which poor person or youngster was entitled to receive a jacket or hat and then chose them by lot, so again they must have known these people personally (SAA entry no. 334, no. 25, p. 259, para. 6, 20 Tevet 5501).

69 See the example of Rachel de Sea, daughter of Dr Benjamin de Sea (SAA entry no. 334, no. 20, p. 113, 10 Shevat 5448).

70 SAA entry no. 334, no. 973.

71 Castro Tartas, *Sermões que Pregarão*, 100, in his 'Dedicatoria A o Magnifico Senhor Iahacob Telles da Costa'; see also Fuks and Fuks-Mansfeld, 'The Inauguration of the Portuguese Synagogue'.

72 'Si Vmd[s] visitaran Como deven las Casas de los Pobres supieran quien nessecitaba la cedaca' (SAA entry no. 334, no. 119a, file 20, p. 748, n.d. [1724]).

73 It is well known that the supervisors of the Reformed Church, visiting the poor at home, recorded the details of each individual in so-called visitors' books ('bezoekboekjes'). None of these have been preserved; see e.g. Wagenaar, *Amsterdam*, ii. 160–2.

74 Kuijpers, *Migrantenstad*, 303–9; for fraud in the Jewish community of Mantua see Simonsohn, *History of the Jews in the Duchy of Mantua*, 521.

75 See e.g. the exchange of lists of poor, made up in 1618 by the Bet Israel and Bet Jacob communities, to prevent fraud (Ancona, 'Komst der Marranen', 234, and the notarial deed SAA entry no. 5075, no. 645A, Not. S. Cornelisz., p. 759, 12 July 1619). In 1622 the representatives of the three separate Portuguese *kehilot*, being members of the *imposta* board, put up a list of all the poor in receipt of welfare in the three *kehilot* to get a clear picture of the scope of poverty and also to prevent fraud (SAA entry no. 334, no. 13, p. 11, 26 Shevat 5382). In 1634 the monthly distribution to the poor of the community of Bet Israel was revised after certain individuals received too large an allowance (SAA entry no. 334, no. 10, p. 8, Rosh Hodesh Tamuz 5394).

76 Her fraud was not discovered until several years after her marriage when the first wife of Menasseh, who was thought to have died, appeared in Amsterdam, as mentioned earlier. On Perla Obediente, Moses Vas Mexicana, and Isaac Menasseh see SAA DTB 697, p. 437, 14 Nov. 1692; SAA DTB 702, p. 384, 23 Dec. 1701; SAA entry no. 5004, no. 110 (Calisregisters), p. 146, 10 Jan. 1702; SAA entry no. 334, no. 20, pp. 282, 304, Nisan 5460–1; ibid., no. 176, p. 378, Nisan 5461; ibid., no. 387, p. 18, 5462: *ketubah* of Isaac ben Aron Menasseh. For the distribution of welfare to Perla Obediente as a widow despite her new marriage see e.g. SAA entry no. 334, no. 176, p. 416, 1 Nisan 5462; ibid., no. 177, p. 89, Nisan 5466. Did Perla continue to deceive people about her identity? In 1717 the widow of Mos. Vas Mexicana left for Surinam and received 100 guilders for her trip (SAA entry no. 334, no. 222, p. 246, 20 Tishrei 5478); a person with the same name was back in Amsterdam in 1739 (SAA entry no. 334, no. 970, p. 130, 5 Kislev 5500).

77 See e.g. the letter of Maasim Tobim of 1709: SAA entry no. 334, no. 66, p. 709, 28 Nisan 5469: 'cazo que os não tenhão da Sedaca'; see also Mishenet Zequenim: SAA entry no. 334, no. 25, p. 343, para. 25, 8 Tevet 5510.

78 SAA entry no. 334, no. 1242, p. 3, para. 9, 3 Shevat 5514, refers to the organization Malbis Arumim in The Hague; for the implementation of this rule see SAA entry no. 334, no. 1242, p. 11, 5514.

79 SAA entry no. 334, no. 974, 5512/1752.

80 SAA entry no. 334, no. 174, p. 544, Rosh Hodesh Adar 5423.

81 SAA entry no. 334, no. 174, p. 77, Rosh Hodesh Tevet 5415; ibid., p. 515, 4 Tishrei 5423; ibid., p. 803, Rosh Hodesh Tevet 5428. The widow of Abraham Alvito was also taken off the list of monthly distributions because, according to the leadership, she did not need *sedaca* any longer (ibid., p. 803, Rosh Hodesh Tevet 5428).

82 SAA entry no. 334, no. 174, p. 498, Rosh Hodesh Nisan 5422; ibid. p. 805, Rosh Hodesh Shevat 5428. From 1661 to 1668, Eliau Henriques received monthly distributions in cash, as well as distributions during the three pilgrimage festivals and Purim; he also received a rental subsidy in cash, and peat and matzot in kind. See SAA entry no. 334, no. 174, p. 498, Rosh Hodesh Nisan 5422; ibid., p. 510, 1 Iyar 5422; ibid., p. 567, 3 Nisan 5423; ibid., p. 582, 14 Nisan 5423; ibid., p. 618, 1 Nisan 5424; ibid, p. 651, 1 Iyar 5424; ibid., p. 683, 1 Nisan 5425; ibid., p. 702, 1 Iyar 5425; ibid., p. 750, 1 Iyar 5426; ibid., p. 772, 1 Nisan 5427; ibid., no. 215, pp. 4, 7, 59, 62, 104, 178, 234, 5423–7: rental subsidy, varying between 4 guilders and 3.3 guilders; ibid., no. 174, p. 484, 24 Adar 5422; ibid., p. 693, 10 Nisan 5425: matzah meal, 10 *livras*; ibid., p. 475, 9 Kislev 5422; ibid., p. 674, 12 Kislev 5425; ibid., no. 215, pp. 108, 182, 239, 5426–8: *turva* (peat) 25, 20, and 10 *sestos* (baskets); ibid., no. 174, p. 460, 14 Tishrei 5422; ibid., p. 734, 17 Adar II 5426; for holidays and special occasions, around 2 guilders.

83 SAA entry no. 334, no. 179, p. 13, 4 Tishrei, 8 Heshvan 5489; ibid., p. 357, 26 Elul 5499; ibid., p. 362, 29 Heshvan 5500.

84 SAA entry no. 334, no. 217, p. 27, 5436–7: 'nao selhe deo de Sebuot haver morto o Pay de q^{m} erdou'. A similar case is that of Ester Gomes, the widow of David Gomes, and her daughter Reyna Gomes, the widow of Abraham Melo de Leon, who stated in a request to the States of Holland and West Friesland that their poverty would force them to take weekly charity through the Portuguese community were they not excluded because they had assets of their own, in this case an inheritance (SAA entry no. 334, no. 119a, pp. 447–8 [n.d., apparently 1696]).

85 SAA entry no. 334, no. 175, p. 19, Rosh Hodesh Kislev 5438: 'se despediu'; ibid., p. 91, Rosh Hodesh Kislev 5440.

86 Y. Kaplan, 'Moral Panic', 111.

87 These paupers thus did not disappear completely from the poor-relief list. An example is the case of David da Silva, *forasteiro*. In 1671 he set out for a trip to Erets Yisra'el and provision was made that he would receive financial support each year out of the annual gifts sent by the Amsterdam Portuguese community to Erets Yisra'el (SAA entry no. 334, no. 216, p. 74, 7 Av 5431: 'p^{a} yr a terra samta e la se lhe concedeo plo no Rol em 5 p^{as} cada anno'). Another is that of Judith Nunes de Amsterdam. From 1683 she received welfare in Erets Yisra'el, sent to her from her former base in the Portuguese community of Amsterdam (ibid., no. 20, pp. 56, 75, 88, 95, 104, 112, 127^{v}, 142, 5443–51). We also meet Moses Arary (apparently a *haham*, originally from Izmir) on the list of inhabitants of the Terra Santa, being supported by the Amsterdam Portuguese community (ibid., no. 20, pp. 8, 31, 56, 5441–3; on him see also ibid., no. 217, p. 3, 3 Tamuz 5436; ibid., no. 217, p. 160, 24 Iyar 5439). Joseph Lopes seems to have travelled from Amsterdam to Jerusalem and back again, first in 1668 and later in 1683. From 1684 he was supported in Jerusalem by annual contributions from the Amsterdam Portuguese community (ibid., no. 215, p. 264, 2 Elul 5428; ibid., no. 217, p. 419, 7 Iyar 5443; ibid., no. 20, pp. 75, 88, 95, 104, 142, 176, 5444–54). Similar agreements were also made earlier. On the eve of Jacob Alcalaim's departure from Amsterdam for Erets Yisra'el it was decided that he would get an annual contribution to be paid to him in Erets Yisra'el (ibid., no. 10, p. 89, 4 Nisan 5382); see also ibid., no. 19, p. 14/99, 13 Iyar 5399; ibid., pp. 164/79–165/80, 18 Elul 5400.

88 See the opinion of Raphael Mordecai Malki in Rozen, *Jewish Identity*, 152; id., *The Jewish Community in Jerusalem*, 275 (Heb.); Emmanuel, 'Hakham David Lopes Yeshurun' (Heb.), 90; on Jacob Tirado see Nahon, 'Amsterdam and Jerusalem', 99 and n. 17.

89 SAA entry no. 334, no. 174, p. 606, 1 Kislev 5424: 'Sedaca Repartida por Roshodes deve . . . e averse auzentado Graçia Pinta aquem se davão f 2:10'.

90 SAA entry no. 334, no. 220, p. 137, 10 Iyar 5461: 'Abraham Rodriguez p^{a} Fransa y se quito delasedacka y Bodadahesed turva maso . . . f 45'.

91 SAA entry no. 334, no. 173, p. 209, Rosh Hodesh Adar 5412: 'Debora e Sara Albres o meio de f 5,- que tinha por hua delas estar cazada'.

92 SAA entry no. 334, no. 174, p. 544, 2 Adar 5423: 'Sedaca Repartida por Roshodes deve por o gabbai mosseh de chaves f 491:3 Por tantos que repartij por este mes o roshodes por pobres da terra necessittados na mesma conformidade do passado abattendo f 2:10 de Debora Gomez aver casado'; ibid., no. 1144, p. 69, 25 Sept. 5423: 'Termo do Dotte q se mandou pagen aos[r] David Levy Maduro q casou co Debora Gomez orfan . . . Em 25 de settem[ro] nos foy pedido p. o s[r] David Levy Maduro lhe pagasem os florins quinientos e trinta, ass. os florins quinientos a sorte q sahiu a Debora Gomez orfan e os trinta promezas em o anno 5422 . . . Baraha em Bespora de Rosasana deste anno nesta cidade.' Here, as in many other cases, the couple apparently underwent a Jewish ceremony only and did not register, as they were obliged to by Dutch law, their intention to get married at City Hall. Consequently, no trace of such a registration could be found.

93 Daniel married in 1669 (SAA DTB 688, p. 8, 30 Aug. 1669).

94 SAA entry no. 334, no. 66a, p. 8, para. 4, 10 Nisan 5510.

95 The bride had come from Belgrade to Amsterdam with her parents in 1691 (SAA entry no. 334, no. 219, p. 2, 5451; ibid., p. 26, 25 Kislev and Tevet 5452). Jacob Alegem had come from the same city in the same year to Amsterdam with his mother Buena (SAA entry no. 334, no. 219, p. 26, 22 Elul 5451). For their *ketubah* see SAA entry no. 334, no. 385, p. 93; for their civil marriage see SAA DTB 699, p. 261, 6 Apr. 1696; for distributions of charity see SAA entry no. 334, no. 219, p. 355, 13 Adar 5458.

96 Money was withdrawn from Jacob's salary in order to support his daughter Abigail on a yearly basis until his death in 1675 (SAA entry no. 334, no. 24, p. 13, 4 Kislev 5421; ibid., no. 24a, p. 18, 18 Iyar 5428: 'a sua filha Abigail Nuñez que padesia maior pobreza com 3 filhos'; ibid., no. 215, p. 328, 5429; ibid., no. 216, p. 23, 10 Elul 5430; ibid., p. 87, 8 Heshvan 5431; ibid., p. 123, 24 Nisan 5432; ibid., p. 154, 1 Iyar 5433; ibid., p. 179, 1 Iyar 5434; ibid., p. 200, 28 Nisan 5435). On Jacob Juda Leon Templo see also Offenberg, 'Jacob Jehuda Leon', and also the agreement, forced upon R. Jacob Juda Leon and his son Eliau by the Mahamad, concerning the payment by the father of the rent on his son's house (SAA entry no. 334, no. 24, p. 15, 12 Elul 5422).

97 SAA entry no. 334, no. 20, p. 81, 12 Adar 5444. The same stipulation was made on the appointment of Moses Fernandes Tabago and on that of Isaac Castiel (for Isaac Castiel see SAA entry no. 334, no. 20, p. 102, 15 Kislev 5447; for Moses Fernandes Tabago: ibid., p. 102, 15 Kislev 5447). Ester Coen Crespa was removed from the list when her aunt was given a paid position in the *mikveh*, having promised to support Ester (SAA entry no. 334, no. 24a, p. 65[r], Sivan 5444). Benvenida Rosa, the wife of Imanuel Montel, took over the running of the *mikveh* from her late mother and was given the post on condition that she paid her brother Abraham Baruch Rosa 8 guilders a month for the rest of his life; in addition, she had to agree to employ her sister-in-law Ribca, the widow of Imanuel Semach, as an unpaid assistant (SAA entry no. 334, no. 25, p. 170,

8 Tevet 5488). Isaac Israel de Bagaral agreed, upon the urging of the members of the Mahamad, to support his father Moses Israel Bagaral with a payment of 72 guilders a year throughout the latter's life (SAA entry no. 334, no. 25, p. 125, 1 Apr. 1714).

98 SAA entry no. 334, no. 1191, p. 429, Tevet 5478.

99 J. Katz, *Tradition and Crisis*, 126.

100 SAA entry no. 334, no. 19, p. 4^v/ 84, 28 Adar II 5399, and Pieterse, *Daniel Levi de Barrios*, 163, para. 32: 'os pobres que se ouvrem de admetir a rescodes da sedaqua serão pesoas de boa vida e Custumes'. For earlier examples see the *imposta* deputies, who helped the poor only if they were 'pessoaz benemerjtas' (deserving) (ibid., no. 13, p. 54, 10 Feb. 5390; ibid., p. 25, 22 Omer 5383: 'para poderem dar atte florins doze à casa ou familia que lhe parecer benemerita'). In 1616 poor students of the Talmud Torah school could get support (in terms of clothes and food) on the basis of their need and how deserving they were (ibid., no. 1051, p. 2, 9 Sivan 5376: 'q dellas pareçer a dittos offiçiaes vestirem e alimentarem talmidim pobres e benemeritos deste socorro'). In 1622 Jacob Alcalaim (see above, n. 87) received help to travel with his family to the Holy Land and a promise of support while he was there not only because he was poor, but also because of his respectful personality (ibid., no. 10, p. 89, 4 Nisan 5382: 'Diz jahacob Alcalaim q ele se presente hir p[a] tr[a] santa con sua familia . . . e q ser muito pobre . . . E visto ser ho suplicante Pessoa m[ta] Conheçida e benemerjta Acordou ho Mahamad'). For the same kind of policy in Dutch Christian communities see Deursen, *Bavianen en Slijkgeuzen*, 114–16; Roodenburg, *Onder Censuur*, ch. 3; and Kuijpers, *Migrantenstad*, 309–13. For the Ashkenazi community of Amsterdam see *Handvesten ofte privilegiën*, ii. 483, para. 25, 11 Oct. 1737. For the screening of the behaviour of the (Waterlander) Mennonite poor see Sprunger, 'Mennonites', 149–50. For cases of the screening of Jews who wanted to become Christians seeking admission to the Reformed Church see e.g. the case of Elias Senior Coronel (SAA entry no. 376, no. 12, p. 76, 4 Feb. 1670; ibid., p. 83, 13 Mar. 1670); see also that of Joseph Musaphia (ibid., no. 25, p. 129, 31 Jan. 1765; ibid., p. 132, 14 Feb. 1765; ibid., p. 136, 28 Feb. 1765; ibid., p. 139, 7 Mar. 1765).

101 While it was the custom in Jewish and non-Jewish society to present letters of recommendation, we have little evidence that Sephardim who were in need of help adopted this practice, apart from supplying testimonies to prove their Jewish ancestry or membership of the Spanish and Portuguese nation; witnesses in Amsterdam often confirm the details given by the applicants. Of course, Conversos fleeing the Iberian peninsula had no way of applying for a recommendation from a Jewish community in their country of origin. Proof has been found that in the 18th century the Amsterdam Mahamad issued recommendations of individuals on welfare whom it thought fit to be sent abroad (SAA entry no. 334, no. 25, p. 325, 3 Kislev 5509). For the custom among the Jews in medieval Egypt of supplying letters of recommendation see M. Cohen, *Poverty and Charity*, 78; for letters of recommendation written by the *hahamim* in the Ottoman empire see Ben-Naeh, *Jews in the Realm of the Sultans*, 267–8. For application regulations for the poor with non-Jewish institutions, where witnesses were also taken along, see M. van Leeuwen, *The Logic of Charity*, 99–101; Kuijpers, *Migrantenstad*, 296–7.

102 For a letter of recommendation requested by a poor Ashkenazi woman in Amsterdam see SAA entry no. 5075, no. 7533, Not. J. van Vilekens, pp. 81–2, 17 Jan. 1710: 'Dat sij getuijge Rachel Salomons . . . ten huyse van Salomon Isacks sijnde Pernasen van de hoogduytse Joodsche Natie binne dese Stadt . . . om een Brief van voorschrijvinge volgens het gebruijk van haer natie om eenig soulaas van haer getuijges vrienden die in vreemde plaetsen woonen te genieten . . . waer op Salomon Isacks seijde . . . gij hebt al tien of twaalf schooybrieven gehadt om het land door te trecken.' *Schooybrieven* are letters that give licence to beg (*schooyen* is begging).

103 SAA entry no. 334, no. 217, p. 482, 15 Heshvan 5445: 'pago en rotterdao de encaminhar te Lond[s] uma s[ra] de Berberia recomendada pelo H. H. Sasporta 9:9 e aqui dado f 4 . . . sao f 13:9'.

104 Y. Kaplan, 'Deviance and Excommunication', 110 and n. 35; see also SAA entry no. 334, no. 21, pp. 25–6, 3 Tevet 5473; ibid., p. 26, 10 Heshvan 5477.

105 SAA entry no. 334, no. 19, p. 324, 28 Iyar 5412.

106 SAA entry no. 334, no. 19, p. 308, 25 Sivan 5411.

107 SAA entry no. 334, no. 25, p. 45, 12 Heshvan 5458.

108 SAA entry no. 334, no. 24a, pp. 18[v]–19, 26 Iyar 5428: 'avendo dito seo marido servido com toda satisfação è umildade como lhes era notorio'. Maimon Haiaia was appointed in 1662 (ibid., no. 19, p. 510, 29 Kislev 5423).

109 SAA entry no. 334, no. 247, p. 267, 2 Shevat 5500: 'que se repartirão por pessoas benemeritas fora do Rol da sedaca f 1990,16'.

110 *Memorial dos despachos*: SAA entry no. 334, no. 10, p. 1, 18 Tamuz 5405: 'dizendo se yra p[a] sua caza . . . e parece não se vão pelo que se recomenda cazo que volvão a pedir ajuda p[a] isso a sedaca não selhes de que assi convem para ensino de otros'.

111 SAA entry no. 334, no. 24, p. 19, 23 Nisan 5423: 'En 23 de Nisan se tomo aCordo por os ss[res] do Mamad de não dar Rescodes ni otro socoro e ajuda de pagar caca ni despachar peticão A Sarah moron de luna mientras tiver en sua cassa A Isack Rodriges de Mercado . . . por as Causas . . . que são a ver dito Mercado a ver levado en Sabat a dha neta dela Sarah moron de luna y cebrantado sabat sendo Casado y despois tornar asta Sera Con dita Moza y dar get a sua muller Y Con Todas estes Ocasiois metelo en Caca, Cosa tan mal parecida.' The wedding must have taken place outside Amsterdam, because there is no trace of it in the city archives. The leaders of the Portuguese community, however, were informed about it. Only afterwards, as the record says, did he divorce his first wife, Hester de Leon, whom he married earlier in 1660 (SAA DTB 684, p. 351, 17 Sept. 1660). The threat of a *ḥerem* concerning Sara was not put into effect. The situation apparently resolved itself. It is possible that Isaac left the community and the city for good, for after the 1660s there is no trace of him in either the tax or the welfare registers of the Portuguese community—unless he is the Isaac Rodriges de Mercado who got married in 1674 and 1683, first to Abigail Henriquez (SAA entry no. 334, no. 382, p. 21, 15 Heshvan 5435), then to Ester Henriquez (ibid., p. 253, 4 Tevet 5443).

112 SAA entry no. 334, no. 25, p. 342, para. 21, 19 Tevet 5510.

113 SAA entry no. 334, no. 1220, p. 13, para. 2, 8 Nisan 5510: 'decençia, decoro e honestidade. evitando juramt^{os}, alvorotos e desordems'. *Bom Judesmo* refers to the principles by which Portuguese Jews were supposed to behave within their own community. On codes of etiquette imposed on the Portuguese community both within and outside the synagogue, see Y. Kaplan, 'Order and Discipline'.

114 On complaints about the bad behaviour of an inmate see SAA entry no. 334, no. 1220, p. 34, 10 Tamuz 5512.

115 SAA entry no. 334, no. 25, p. 218, 8 Tevet 5495.

116 SAA entry no. 334, no. 120, file 94, pp. 982–3, Rosh Hodesh Tamuz 5530.

117 Dotar's basic point of view on this subject, as noted in the early days of its establishment, was to give dowries only to girls who were 'de boa vida e costumes, honestas e honrradas, sem notta de vileza' (SAA entry no. 334, no. 1411, p. 12, 15 Adar I 5375/1615).

118 SAA entry no. 334, no. 1143, p. 200, 18 Tamuz 5411; ibid., p. 36, 13 Adar 5400; ibid., p. 26, 17 Adar II 5399; ibid., p. 24, 11 Adar 5399. Referring to this case in 1651, Dotar reiterated the idea that girls had to be 'moças q seijão Donzellas de boa vida e Costumes, honestas e honradas sem notta de vileza' (ibid., p. 200, 18 Tamuz 5411).

119 Ayllon, *Sermon*, 21–2, 24, 26–7.

120 SAA entry no. 334, no. 1145, p. 180, 22 Shevat 5507: 'Termo p^{a} expressar o bom comportam^{to} q devem ter as orphas e Donzellas despois de lhes aver sahido as sortes desta S. C.'; ibid., pp. 311–27, 24 Tevet 5516.

121 Y. Kaplan, 'Moral Panic'; id., 'Deviance and Excommunication'.

122 Abraham Drago, Samuel Pinto, and Salomon Franqo were expelled (SAA entry no. 334, no. 1052, p. 46, Tevet 5411: 'escluzo . . . Abraham Draguo'; ibid., Rosh Hodesh Nisan 5411: 'escluzo Semuel Pinto'; ibid., Rosh Hodesh Nisan 5411: 'escluzo . . . Selomoh Franqo'; see further SAA entry no. 334, no. 1052, pp. 34–5, 10 Nisan 5432).

123 SAA entry no. 334, no. 1211, p. 5, Kislev 5424. Interestingly enough, later on, in 1677, this Abraham Pretto and fellow Aby Jetomim orphan Isaac de Casseres were put into *ḥerem* for four days because they had performed a wedding ceremony without the permission of the parents or presence of the rabbi (Y. Kaplan, 'The Social Functions of the Herem', 136–7 and n. 71).

124 SAA entry no. 334, no. 1211, p. 3^{v}, 8 Elul 5413. See further the following cases: Aby Jetomim withdrew its support for David Castiel because he did not fulfil his obligations (ibid., p. 4, 17 Tamuz 5418: 'e mais despedido nao fazer seu dever') and for Abraham Gadelha for the same reason (ibid., p. 3^{v}, 8 Tishrei 5413). Moses Jessurun Furtado was described as an inconvenient subject: 'por nao ser sujeito conveniente' (ibid., p. 4^{v}, 1 Elul 5420) and Jacob Jessurun was also dismissed because he did not fulfil his obligations: 'não acudindo á sua obrigacão e sendo protestado diferentes vezes sem haverse emendado, se tomou rezolucão de despedido . . . nao tem q pretender oficio' (ibid., p. 19^{v}, 12 Tishrei 5442). See also the case of Joseph Pereyra (ibid., p. 6^{v}, 1 Heshvan 5434).

125 SAA entry no. 5075, no. 7533, Not. J. van Vilekens, pp. 257–60, 12 Mar. 1710, last will of Ester Rodriguez.

126 'Te werden verdeelt onder haer Testatrices bloetvrienden uyt een wettig huwelijk verwekt te weten die van een goet leven zijn en profesie dien van de joodse religie.' She also insisted that if no such person could be found most of the money should go to the *sedaca* box: see SAA entry no. 334, no. 641, Not. C. van Achthoven, 3 Mar. 1724, copy of the last will of Rachel Belmonte alias Schonenberg, para. 7.

127 Kuijpers, *Migrantenstad*, 309–16; Flynn, *Sacred Charity*, 59–60. In the Portuguese community of St-Esprit in France, a distinction was made between 'errants et vagabonds' allowed to stay for a short period and 'personnes distinguées [par leur mérite] et connues', who were entitled to more support (Nahon, *Les 'Nations' juives portugaises*, 186–9, Saint-Esprit 1754); furthermore, anyone in the Portuguese community of southern France who wanted to receive a passport had to obtain a certificate of good behaviour from the leadership (Szapiro, 'Le Sud-Ouest', 245); on this theme see also Y. Kaplan, 'Order and Discipline'; id., 'Gente política'.

128 Para. 32 of the statutes of 1639: 'Os pobres . . . e serão admetidos por busolo e balas': Pieterse, *Daniel Levi de Barrios*, 163; SAA entry no. 334, no. 19, p. 4v/84, 28 Adar II 5399.

129 For petitions see M. Cohen, *The Voice of the Poor*; Würgler, 'Voices'; Nubola, 'Supplications'; Schmidt Blaine, 'The Power of Petitions'; Heerma van Voss, 'Introduction'.

130 SAA entry no. 334, no. 220, p. 188, 7 Tevet 5463: 'a Simao do Valle repartir as Peticoins f 30,–'.

131 See *Encyclopaedia Judaica*, xiii. 217–19 ('Lots'). For procedures of the same kind in other Jewish communities, such as those in Italy, see Baron, *The Jewish Community*, iii, 463. For Venice see Malkiel, 'The Ghetto Republic', 129–30, and id., *A Separate Republic*, 68, 210, 213. For Livorno and Pisa see Toaff, *La nazione ebrea*, 504 (paras. 22–3), 506 (para. 36, Pisa, *Haskamot del Libro Nuevo*, 12 Menahem-Av 5396), 525 (paras. 8–9, Pisa, Rosh Hodesh Nisan/22 Apr. 5373), 555 (para. 8), 558 (para. 10, Livorno, *Escamot e Estatudos do K.K. de Liorne*, 1655), and 594 (para. 1, Livorno, *Parte primera de las escamot tocantes al govierno*, 1677). For Livorno see also Trivellato, *The Familiarity of Strangers*, 77; Rozen, *Jewish Identity*, 124. For Ferrara see Ruderman, 'The Founding of a Gemilut Hasadim Society', 239. For lotteries in the non-Jewish world see (for Italy) F. C. Lane, *Venice*, 259–61, (for Spain) Flynn, *Sacred Charity*, 60, and (for the Portuguese overseas empire) Guimarães Sá, *Quando o rico se faz pobre*, 175. In Spain and Portugal, a child, representing innocence, was allowed to take out the lots.

132 For the procedure for selecting members of the Mahamad see SAA entry no. 334, no. 19, p. 1v/78, paras. 6–7, 28 Adar II 5399; also published in Pieterse, *Daniel Levi de Barrios*, 157. For the election of other administrators see SAA entry no. 334, no. 19, p. 10/95, 11 Nisan 5399; ibid., p. 11, 12 Nisan 5399: election of the administrator for the cemetery and of the administrators of the *ḥevrah* Bikur Holim.

Within the latter organization lots were also cast to elect those who would accompany the dead to the cemetery (ibid., p. 162, para. 3, 1 Kislev 5404). See ibid., p. 12, 3 Sivan 5399, for election for the *parnasim* of the Talmud Torah school. The administrators of the *ḥevrah* Honen Dalim were also drawn by lot (ibid., no. 1186, p. 1, para. 1, 5385; Pieterse, *Daniel Levi de Barrios*, 181). New candidates for membership of the *ḥevrah* Gemilut Hasadim were drawn by lot (ibid., no. 19, p. 162/247, para. 2, 1 Kislev 5404). In 1670 the administrator/treasurer of Abodat Ahesed was drawn by lot (ibid., p. 614, 7 Nisan 5430). A doctor for the *ḥevrah* Bikur Holim was chosen by lot (SAA entry no. 334, no. 21, p. 383, 1 Elul 5486). For the lottery in the Ashkenazi community of Amsterdam to appoint a new administration see *Handvesten ofte privilegiën*, ii. 480, para. 7.

133 SAA entry no. 334, no. 24, p. 15, 20 Nisan 5421.

134 SAA entry no. 334, no. 24, pp. 15a–b, 4 Elul 5421 (and [close to] 12 Elul 5422?).

135 SAA entry no. 334, no. 19, p. 756, 8 Tevet 5437: 'e dispois de se haver discorido sobre as mais nesesitadas desamparadas ebenemeritas serezolveo na Conformidade do Cap[o] 32 dos acordos ... fosem admitidas nelle as pesoas seg[tes]'.

136 See e.g. the request of the widow Beruja in SAA entry no. 334, no. 175, p. 124, [n.d.].

137 SAA entry no. 334, no. 19, p. 790, 8 Nisan 5438.

138 SAA entry no. 334, no. 25, pp. 244–8, esp. p. 247, para. 10, 26 Adar II 5499.

139 SAA entry no. 334, no. 19, p. 812, 24 Shevat 5439.

140 SAA entry no. 334, no. 19, p. 830, 11 Adar II 5440.

141 SAA entry no. 334, no. 736, p. 74, 23 Elul 5511.

142 See the standard formula in a petition such as that of Rachel, orphan of Manuel da Silva (SAA entry no. 334, no. 1152, p. 480, [n.d.], 1686: 'Rahel orpha de Manuel da Silva (q ds aja) de capas ydade para poder cazar; muy humildem[te] suplica a VMs seja posta nas sortes deste anno.' Beautiful boxes were often used to hold the lots, such as the silver ones of Dotar or the leather boxes with silverwork used to choose *kohanim* and *levi'im* by lot (SAA entry no. 334, no. 218, p. 118, 18 Tevet 5447). Abraham Dias, as a gold-, silver-, and coppersmith, had to repair the boxes from which lots were drawn for the *mitsvot* in the synagogue (ibid., no. 217, p. 115, 26 Elul 5438: 'p[a] consertar as caixetas donde se tirao as sortes p[a] as misvot da esnoga').

143 SAA entry no. 334, no. 25, p. 219, para. 6, 8 Tevet 5494.

144 SAA entry no. 334, no. 25, p. 343, 8 Tevet 5510.

145 For Hase Amaharacha see SAA entry no. 334, no. 1234, p. 5, 1 Heshvan 5474; for Kisuy Ros: ibid., no. 25, pp. 258–60, 20 Tevet 5501; for Quetonet Bat Codes: ibid., p. 302, para. 15, 3 Av 5505.

146 The Portuguese community, therefore, often hired people to help the poor at home during sickness or after a death.

147 For the same reason, institutionalization of Catholic welfare in the city was also developed at a later stage (Groenveld, 'For the Benefit of the Poor').

148 In 1715 we meet Sephardi paupers in London begging in the Stock Exchange (Oliel-Grausz, 'Portugais et tudesques', 34).

149 For similar motives behind provisions in other denominations in the city see Groenveld, 'For the Benefit of the Poor', 200, 204–5.

150 On the Mazon Abanot orphanage for girls see SAA entry no. 334, no. 120, file 81, 8 Adar I 5494; ibid., no. 25, p. 213, 19 Adar I 5494; ibid., entry no. 334.A, suppl., no. 204k, 5494–5694/1734–1934, Portugeesch Israelietisch Meisjes-Weeshuis. On the Rehobot almshouse see Franco Mendes, *Memorias*, 103–4. On the Mishenet Zequenim old-age home see Pieterse, *Inventaris*, 72, and SAA entry no. 334, nos. 1220–33; on its establishment see SAA entry no. 334, no. 25, pp. 337–47, esp. art. 31, 19 Tevet 5510; ibid., entry no. 334.A, suppl., no. 191 jjj, 21 Adar I 5513; see also below. On the house for young people with difficulties, erected in the second half of the 18th century, see Y. Kaplan, 'Deviance and Excommunication', 108. Only in the 19th century do we see the emergence of a Portuguese Jewish hospital (including an old-age home for women), called Mesib Nefes (see SAA entry no. 334, nos. 1275–86). On Aby Jetomim's acquisition, in the 19th century, of a building in which boys could be given daytime and night-time care see *Reglement*, 1817, 4.

151 SAA entry no. 334, no. 19, p. 4^{v}/84, para. 32, 28 Adar II 5399; see also Pieterse, *Daniel Levi de Barrios*, 163.

152 These were distributed before Pesach, Shavuot, and Sukkot (SAA entry no. 334, no. 19, p. 22/107, para. 12, 22 Tamuz 5399; for distributions to the poor on Purim see ibid., para. 14).

153 See yearly overviews for these different distributions in the *livros longos*, e.g. SAA entry no. 334, no. 215, pp. 311–14, 5429–30.

154 In times of crisis such as harsh winters, hot summers, epidemics, or wars, extra money was gathered and distributed. See e.g. the distribution to the poor in 1674, during the war which had been raging since 1672 (ibid., no. 174, p. 1011, 2 Adar II 5434: 'para se repartir por Pobres . . . f 380:8'; ibid. p. 1012, 11 Adar II 5434: 'f 494:9'). See also Appendix I, Table 24.

155 See e.g. SAA entry no. 334, no. 215, pp. 267–9, 5428–9.

156 SAA entry no. 334, no. 215, pp. 234–7, 5427–8.

157 See e.g. SAA entry no. 334, no. 216, pp. 61–4, 15 Adar 5431.

158 Peat was given to heat the house. The distribution took place once or twice a year (see e.g. SAA entry no. 334, no. 217, pp. 325–9, 5441–2).

159 On the distribution of clothing see nn. 323–37 below and also Vestiaria (SAA entry no. 334, nos. 1187–8).

160 SAA entry no. 334, no. 1052, p. 75^{v}, 5406: 'Por conserto de livros e algús que se comprarao p^{a} dar a pobres.'

161 SAA entry no. 334, no. 6, p. 357, 16 Aug. 5377: 'Dous pares de Thephilin'; see also ibid., no. 220, p. 140, 5 Iyar 5461: 'a Seml Touro hixo de Mosseh Touro pa un talet y sisith f 1:18'; for new immigrants from Portugal in 1746 receiving *tefilin*, *tsitsit*, and *talitot*: ibid., p. 9, 5506: 'aos seguintes que vierão de Portugal . . . tefilin, talet sisit'.

162 These *mitsvot* had been practised since the initial settlement. For money transferred to Erets Yisra'el through the Portuguese community of Bet Jacob see SAA entry no. 334, no. 6, p. 183, 14 Apr. 5377/1617; for help to captives via the *cativos* organization of Neve Salom see ibid., no. 9, p. 16, 5377; and see other chapters for more examples of help through these organizations. For similar organizations in Venice and London see Carpi, 'The Activities of the Officials of the Sephardi Jewish Congregation in Venice' (Heb.); R. D. Barnett, 'The Correspondence of the Mahamad', 23–33.

163 There were some exceptions: care for the sick through Bikur Holim was given in kind rather than in money (Pieterse, *Daniel Levi de Barrios*, 176; SAA entry no. 334, no. 19, pp. 18/103–19/104, para. 3, 33 Omer 5399). In the later 17th century and on into the 18th, kosher bread was distributed by the Portuguese community to its poor (SAA entry no. 334, no. 219, p. 105, 1 Shevat 5453: 'para pezar o pao oqual se repartiu p. pobres f 2:8'; ibid., p. 226, 30 Nisan 5454: 'p. 23 Paes q reparty p. Pobres f 2:6'); for distributions to other poor people in the city, most often consisting of goods in kind, see M. van Leeuwen, Schoenmakers, and Smits, *Armoede en bedeling*; Manen, *Armenpflege in Amsterdam*, 50.

164 In times of crisis the poor received more money because of the rise in the cost of bread. See e.g. the decision taken by the *imposta* board (SAA entry no. 334, no. 13, p. 65, 8 Heshvan 5391) and that taken by the community of Bet Israel (ibid., no. 11, p. 47, 5391); for Neve Salom see ibid., no. 9, p. 144, 5391. It was during crises that private charities stepped in, especially during the 18th century: as at these times they distributed more in kind than in cash, the pattern of charity among the Amsterdam Portuguese Jews more closely resembled that in the surrounding society.

165 For delivery of money to the poor see SAA entry no. 334, no. 218, p. 382, 19 Adar 5451; for delivery of peat see the record of the person who was paid to distribute it to the house of the poor in 1742: 'por mandar a turva a caza dos povres f 10' (SAA entry no. 334, no. 970, p. 530, 5 Nisan 5502); for delivery of wood to the house of the poor by the Hase Amaharacha organization see SAA entry no. 334, no. 1234, p. 80, 5476.

166 M. van Leeuwen, 'Arme Amsterdamse joden', 60; Sprunger, 'Mennonites', 148. The poor among the Lutherans were given welfare at home: Kuijpers, *Migrantenstad*, 313.

167 The Portuguese community of Neve Salom (which existed until 1639) already had, in addition to a list of poor people receiving monthly distributions, a list of those receiving help on a temporary basis (SAA entry no. 334, no. 9, p. 18, 5378; ibid., p. 32, 5380). Separate lists existed for those receiving peat, matzot, or clothes (ibid., p. 73, 5382; ibid., p. 2, 5376). The genteel poor were mentioned separately, as were passengers, *tudescos*, and foreigners (ibid., p. 18, 5378; ibid., p. 23, 5379; ibid., p. 60, 5381).

168 See e.g. SAA entry no. 334, no. 215, pp. 206–60, 5427–8; ibid., no. 174, p. 805, Rosh Hodesh Tevet 5428.

169 SAA entry no. 334, nos. 220–1.

170 See e.g. SAA entry no. 334, no. 969, 5488: *Livro longo de cuatro contas.* Might the reorganization of welfare have had something to do with the epidemic raging in town, claiming many victims among the Portuguese Jews (Franco Mendes, *Memorias*, 108)?

171 Baron, *The Jewish Community*, i. 125–6, 348–60; id., ii. 170–207; J. Katz, *Tradition and Crisis*, ch. 18.

172 Y. Kaplan, 'Tradition and Change'.

173 SAA entry no. 334, no. 1051, p. 1, 48 Omer 5376. For institutions of Jewish learning of the same name in the Jewish community at an earlier date see Assis, 'Institutions sociales médiévales', 210–15; id., 'Welfare and Mutual Aid', 340–2; Baer, *A History of the Jews in Christian Spain*, i. 236, ii. 261–2; Baron, *The Jewish Community*, i. 356–60; Rivlin, *Mutual Responsibility*, 123–57 (Heb.); Simonsohn, *History of the Jews in the Duchy of Mantua*, 588–9; and Hacker, 'The Intellectual Activity of the Jews of the Ottoman Empire', 108–9. For the importance of study (*talmud torah*), mentioned in the first section of the *takanot* (regulations) of Valladolid in 1432, see Baer, *A History of the Jews in Christian Spain*, ii. 261–2, and Moreno Koch, *Las taqqanot*, 21–35. On the importance of education as one of the improvements introduced in the reform of charity in 16th- and 17th-century Europe, see Vives, *De subventione pauperum*, ii. 64–5 (1973 edn.), and Pullan, *Rich and Poor in Renaissance Venice*, 405–6.

174 Menasseh ben Israel, *Thesovro dos dinim*, second part, ch. 1, p. 92.

175 On the Ets Haim yeshiva, for the size of the classes see SAA entry no. 334, no. 1051, p. 25, 4 Tishrei 5406; ibid., no. 1052, p. 44, 5409; ibid., p. 46^{v}, 4 Sivan 5411; ibid., p. 47^{v}, 1 Sivan 5412; for the curriculum see ibid., no. 19, pp. 3/81–3^{v}/82, para. 22, 28 Adar II 5399; Pieterse, *Daniel Levi de Barrios*, 97–100, 160–1. The number of students grew as time went by. At the end of the 17th century there were 209, divided among seven classes according to age and level with an average of thirty students per class (SAA entry no. 334, no. 1189, 5456). The Portuguese Jewish school had a good reputation in the Jewish world (Swetschinski, *Reluctant Cosmopolitans*, 210–11). It attracted students from abroad (for the arrival in 1677 of students from Bayonne see SAA entry no. 334, no. 24a, p. 42, 12 Av 5437). Moreover, graduates of the Amsterdam Portuguese yeshiva moved on to other Jewish centres to lead communities: Moses Zacuto became *haham* in Mantua (*Encyclopaedia Judaica*, xxi. 435–9: 'Zacuto, Moses Ben Mordecai'; Pieterse, *Daniel Levi de Barrios*, 101), Isaac Naar became *haham* in Verona (Pieterse, *Daniel Levi de Barrios*, 101), and Josia Pardo became *haham* in Curaçao and Jamaica (Pieterse, *Daniel Levi de Barrios*, 102). See further Goldish, 'The Amsterdam Portuguese Rabbinate', 12–14; Lieberman, 'Educational Institutions'; and Paraira and Silva Rosa, *Gedenkschrift*. The structured way of learning followed in the religious schools of the Amsterdam Portuguese community was also a feature of the school system in the non-Jewish world: for the Latin school in the Dutch Republic see Kuiper, *De Hollandse 'Schoolordre'*, 63, and Roberts, *Through the Keyhole*, 107–8; for the education of children in early modern Europe see Ariès, *L'Enfant et la vie familiale*, part 2, 'La Vie scolastique').

176 For the school career of Spinoza see Nadler, *Spinoza*, 64–5, 90–1, 93, 103–15; for Portuguese students at Leiden University see Y. Kaplan, 'The Self-Definition of the Sephardi Jews of Western Europe'.

177 Saperstein, *Exile in Amsterdam*, 478.

178 Bass, *Sefer siftei yeshenim*, 8.

179 SAA entry no. 996, no. 17, 26 Jan. 1699/18 Sept. 1705: last will of Abraham Israel Suasso.

180 Cohen, *Et sofer*: letter of Joseph Sarfati to Moses Cohen, 25 Heshvan 5450. In the early 18th century Rabbi Moses Hagiz was working as a private tutor among the Amsterdam Sephardim (Carlebach, *The Pursuit of Heresy*, 58). For private teachers among the Conversos in Spain see López Belinchón, *Honra, libertad y hacienda*, 258–9; for the same pattern in different Jewish communities see Simonsohn, *History of the Jews in the Duchy of Mantua*, 588–9; Hacker, 'The Intellectual Activity of the Jews of the Ottoman Empire', 107; Baer, *A History of the Jews in Christian Spain*, i. 431–2; Assis, *The Golden Age of Aragonese Jewry*, 32–3; id., 'Welfare and Mutual Aid', 340–1; Nahon, *Les 'Nations' juives portugaises*, 424; id., 'From New Christians to the Portuguese Jewish Nation in France', 356; A. Levy, *The Sephardim in the Ottoman Empire*, 47 and references mentioned in n. 174 there. For the private educational system among the Portuguese of Antwerp see Gomes de Souza, 'Documentos', 20^{v}, para. 25; on private education in the Dutch Republic among well-to-do families see Roberts, *Through the Keyhole*, 99–137; Booy, 'Naar school', 427–8.

181 SAA entry no. 334, no. 218, p. 253, 7 Feb. 5449.

182 SAA entry no. 334, no. 222, p. 17, 22 Kislev 5474: 'a Ab^{m} Fidanque p^{a} ensino dos filhos de Cardozo f 5:17:8'.

183 Horowitz, 'Jewish Confraternities', 35–6; J. Katz, *Tradition and Crisis*, ch. 18; for the non-Jewish world see Cunningham, *The Children of the Poor*, ch. 3.

184 On Salomon Levy Maduro see Ya'ari, *Hebrew Printers' Marks* (Heb.), 88, and SAA entry no. 334, no. 970, p. 532, 12 Av 5502; for the distribution of books, *tefilin*, *tsitsit*, and *talitot* see ibid., no. 1052, p. 103^{v}, 5428: '31 livros de gramatica . . . q alguns repartidos com talmidin pobres'; ibid., 124^{v}, 20 Sivan 5443: '6 livros de reza p^{a} pobres, 14 gramaticas p^{a} pobres do midras del R. Oliveira'; ibid., p. 75^{v}, 5406: 'Por Tales e Sissiot p^{a} algús meninos'; ibid., no. 176, p. 353, 21 Iyar 5460: 'taletot, thephilin q se repartirao . . . talmidim'. In the mid-18th century a book was set up by the *gabai da sedaca* (treasurer of the Portuguese community) to note all the people who received 'taletot, tephilim, sisit e livros de reza' (SAA entry no. 334, no. 989, 28 Adar II 5501; see page 3: 'Aos talmidim do medras de R: Meza, Aharon Cardoso . . . livro sisit'). For the provision of clothing to poor students through the Vestiaria dos Talmidim see below; for similar provisions to poor students elsewhere, for example in Salonika, see Hacker, 'The Intellectual Activity of the Jews of the Ottoman Empire', 108–9.

185 SAA entry no. 334, no. 1052, pp. 1–3, 14 Sivan and 26 Tamuz 5397; Pieterse, *Daniel Levi de Barrios*, 97. When they reached the age of 13, students became eligible to receive a scholarship to study at the Ets Haim yeshiva (ibid., pp. 1–3, 26

Tamuz 5397). For lists of students receiving such scholarships see ibid., p. 44, 14 Sivan 5409. For Jewish education within the Portuguese community of Amsterdam see also Lieberman, 'Educational Institutions', and Paraira and Silva Rosa, *Gedenkschrift*. To be members of Talmud Torah educational institutions Portuguese Jews contributed half a guilder a month and made *promessas* during the year, especially on Shavuot (SAA entry no. 334, no. 1051, p. 1, 48 Omer 5376; ibid., no. 19, p. 84/169, para. 13, 5401).

186 For secular education to the poor see e.g. SAA entry no. 334, no. 215, pp. 32, 34–5, 5423–4.

187 See instructions to teachers David Senior Coronel, Daniel Lopes Arias, Salomon Marques, and Jacob de Casseres by the Mahamad (SAA entry no. 334, no. 19, p. 681, 21 Menahem-Av 5433; also cited in Swetschinski, *Reluctant Cosmopolitans*, 211). They were supposed to teach poor boys secular subjects from 11 to 12.30 a.m. and from 5 to 6.30 p.m. (in winter after the *arvit* prayer: after 4 or 5 p.m., or later). The hours of teaching seem to have been similar to those of the Dutch schools, though shorter than those of the Portuguese. In Dutch schools a normal day was from 7 or 8 a.m. to 11 a.m., and 1 p.m. to 4 or 5 p.m. (Kuiper, *De Hollandse 'Schoolordre'*, 151). In the Portuguese community the teaching of secular subjects was additional and took place after the teaching of religious subjects. In all, the Portuguese community's curriculum seems to have been more demanding than the Dutch one.

188 Reading, writing, and arithmetic also formed the normal basic curriculum in schools of the Dutch Republic. Of course, in Dutch schools the Dutch language was taught rather than Portuguese (Roberts, *Through the Keyhole*, 100; Booy, *De Weldaet der Scholen*, 210–22; id., 'Naar school', 439–40; id., *Kweekhoven*, esp. chs. 1 and 2; Kuiper, *De Hollandse 'Schoolordre'*, 64).

189 Pinto, *Reflexoens*, 30–1. De Pinto refers to the curriculum of French schools, which was fashionable in the Dutch Republic in the 18th century (Roberts, *Through the Keyhole*, 116).

190 SAA entry no. 334, no. 882, pp. 2–4, Rosh Hodesh Shevat 5418; ibid., p. 18, 26 Shevat 5418; Y. Kaplan, *From Christianity to Judaism*, 139–45; for Latin see Jacob Monsanto, learning Latin with Doctor de Prado, 'aprender lati com o Doitor'; see also Révah, 'Aux origines de la rupture Spinozienne', 394.

191 In 1678 the annual salaries of three teachers amounted to 84 guilders (SAA entry no. 334, no. 175, p. 35, 8 Nisan 5438). In 1683 Jacob de Casseres received an annual salary of 42 guilders. In 1688 and 1689 one teacher, Salomon Marques, was responsible for the secular education of poor boys: his salary was 84 guilders in the first year, and rose to 120 guilders in the second (SAA entry no. 334, no. 175, p. 402, 24 Adar II 5448; ibid., p. 446, 17 Adar 5449). For similar salaries given to non-Jewish teachers at Dutch schools see Beck, *Spiegel van mijn leven*, introduction, esp. 10, 16, and n. 10.

192 SAA entry no. 334, no. 13, p. 128, 5396; ibid., p. 119, 10 Kislev 5396: 'que atentando aobem que se fazia nos mosos e considerando tambem sua emposibilidade lhe quizesesem dar desta cx[a] da imposta hua ajuda com aqual seria obrigado ha emsinar todos os mosos da sedaca'; ibid., no. 17, p. 56v, 20 Oct. 5396. The fact that his salary was paid through the charity box could also have to do with the principle that personnel serving the community were considered not employees but volunteers, and therefore were paid through the *sedaca* account. On the relationship of community personnel to the welfare lists see Miriam Frenkel, 'Charity in Jewish Society', 349.

193 For Abraham Machorro see SAA entry no. 334, no. 215, p. 153, 13 Nisan 5426; Barrios, *Triumpho*, p. 759 (Ets Haim/Montezinos Library copy, 2 F 81): 'Dezima'; 'Alos insignes en la flauta y la pluma Abraham Machorro, en la bihuela Ishac Mendez y en la dança y harpa Manuel Pimentel'; 'Con la flauta de Thalia Machorro, eleva al Parnasso en el Poëtico passo'; for his work as a copyist see the manuscript written by Isaac Orobio de Castro: 'Respuesta a un Filósofo Hebreo . . . copiado por Abraham Machorro' (1668: Ets Haim/Montezinos Library 48 C 4).

194 For the inspection by the Mahamad and the rabbinate of secular education see Y. Kaplan, *From Christianity to Judaism*, 138–46.

195 See the case of Isaiah de Souza, who was both on welfare and employed as a teacher: SAA entry no. 334, no. 172, p. 164, 1 Nisan 5402; ibid., p. 223, 1 Sivan 5403: 'mestre de Portugez'; ibid., no. 173, p. 30, 6 Nisan 5408: 'diversos mosos pobres que ijnsinou na sua escola'; ibid., p. 19, 5408.

196 For the two teachers left after 1679 see SAA entry no. 334, no. 175, p. 57, 10 Adar 5439; for the single one after 1687 see ibid., p. 361, 14 Adar 5447.

197 Between 1673 and 1675, and after 1677–8, there is no information available regarding the names and numbers of poor children who had a secular education (SAA entry no. 334, nos. 216–17).

198 Also during the 1690s there were complaints about a lack of interest in education and many students failed to attend the Ets Haim yeshiva (SAA entry no. 334, no. 1052, pp. 144v–5, 2 Elul 5455).

199 For the age of Portuguese students enrolled in Jewish schools for the poor see Y. Kaplan, *From Christianity to Judaism*, 138–46. Orphan children of Aby Jetomim were accepted for three or six years once they reached the age of 10. By then they had apparently finished primary school, as was normal in Europe more widely and in the Dutch Republic in particular (Roberts, *Through the Keyhole*, 100–5). In the 18th century orphans of members of Aby Jetomim were accepted for six years from the age of 8 (instead of 10) and could stay until they were 13; other children were accepted from 9 to 13 (Franco Mendes, *Memorias*, 55–7; Pieterse, *Daniel Levi de Barrios*, 117–19; see further on Aby Jetomim below). In the non-Jewish world children went to university after finishing Latin school at the age of around 17, sometimes earlier (Roberts, *Through the Keyhole*, 110, 124), or went on to learn a trade on a private basis or within the framework of a guild. Isa van Eeghen, *De gilden*, 23–4, mentions 14 as the age at which boys started a professional education.

200 Abraham Bassan was born in 1661 (SAA DTB 693, p. 173, 11 July 1682). He started at the school for poor boys in 1666, when he was 5, and continued until the age of at least 11 (in 1672), and possibly for another two years until his bar-mitzvah. Thereafter, until 1675, no students are named in the documents, and he is not mentioned again (SAA entry no. 334, no. 215, pp. 132–3, 174–5, 230–1, 284–5, 332–3, 5425–30; ibid., no. 216, pp. 25–6, 89–90, 5430–2).

The following are examples of poor boys who started secular education at a rather late age.

Isaac Calvo de Andrade was enrolled in the secular school for poor boys at least from the age of 8 (possibly earlier: we do not have detailed documentation on the years before 5423) until he was 17, from 1663 to 1672 (SAA entry no. 334, no. 215, pp. 34–5, 89–90, 134–5, 176–7, 232–3, 284–5, 332–3, 5423–30; ibid., no. 216, pp. 27–8, 91–2, 5430–2). Then, until 1676, he went on to learn a profession with the bookbinder Huygen (ibid., no. 1211, p. 6, 3 Adar II 5429; ibid., p. 1^{v}, 5432; SAA entry no. 5075, no. 2239, Not. A. Lock, pp. 95–6, 10 May 1672). He was 21 by the time he completed his studies. He got married when he was 23 (SAA DTB 691, p. 164, 14 Oct. 1678).

Moses Dias was 28 when he got married in 1683 (SAA DTB 693, p. 361, 14 May 1683). He went to the school for poor boys at least from 1663, at the age of 8, to 1671, when he was 16 (SAA entry no. 334, no. 215, pp. 33–5, 87–8, 132–3, 172–3, 228–9, 282–3, 330–1, 5423–30; ibid., no. 216, pp. 25–6, 5430–1). He continued in the Ets Haim yeshiva until 5434 (ibid., no. 1052, pp. 36–7, 5434), receiving a monthly allowance of 4 guilders (Pieterse, *Daniel Levi de Barrios*, 104), and finished his school education at the age of 19. On Dias as a printer in Amsterdam see Meijer, *Encyclopaedia Sefardica Neerlandica*, ii. 6.

Abraham Penco became a schoolmaster himself and got married in 1689, at the age of 33 (SAA DTB 696, p. 371, 9 Sept. 1689). He followed classes for secular subjects at the poor school from 1664 to 1673 at least, or perhaps for a further year, which means that he was enrolled in school between the ages of 8 and around 17 (SAA entry no. 334, no. 215, pp. 35, 90, 135, 175, 333, 5424–30; ibid., no. 216, pp. 28, 92, 124, 5430–3).

201 Samuel Nassi left for Surinam (Oudschans Dentz, *De kolonisatie*, 14–16) and Jacob Monsanto for Curaçao (SAA entry no. 334, no. 219, p. 22, 11 Iyar 5451). Both were students of Ribera (Y. Kaplan, *From Christianity to Judaism*: on Nassi pp. 140–1; on Monsanto pp. 141–2). On the appointment of Ribera to teach poor boys see SAA entry no. 334, no. 174, p. 194, Rosh Hodesh Adar 5417.

202 SAA entry no. 334, no. 215, pp. 90, 135, 175, 231, 283, 5424–9; ibid., no. 216, 5430–1.

203 Moses Cohen Belinfante and his sister Sara taught both Sephardi and Ashkenazi girls in the poor school of The Hague Sephardi community in the latter part of the 18th century. Later, Sara seems to have started a girls' school in Amsterdam (Divendal, 'Mozes Cohen Belinfante', 101). For Sephardi girls in England in the midcentury taught by Protestant women teachers see Sutcliffe, 'Identity', 103.

204 In correspondence with the Amsterdam authorities during the early years of settlement, the Portuguese maintained that their young women never went into the street (*Handvesten ofte privilegiën*, ii. 470–1, 15 June 1622). In another source, two Amsterdam Portuguese Jewish girls—Violante Gomes, who was 20 years old, and Aldonsa Nunes, who was 18—declared in 1623, before the notary, that they, being young daughters, according to the customs of Portugal were not used to going out ('sij luyden oock Jonge dochterse weesende na de costume van Portugal niet gewoon zijn uyt te gaen': SAA entry no. 5075, no. 646A, Not. S. Cornelisz., p. 580, 28 June 1623; also published in *Studia Rosenthaliana*, 24/2 (1990), 221). Here we come across an Iberian custom apparently influenced by Islam (Patai, *The Seed of Abraham*, 246–7). On women in the Iberian peninsula see Pescatello, *Power and Pawn*, ch. 2, esp. 27–8.

205 Swetschinski, *Reluctant Cosmopolitans*, 88–90, 284–5, table 2.8; Hart, *Geschrift en getal*, 130–2; Dodde, 'Joods Onderwijs', 70–1; Kuijpers, 'Lezen en schrijven'; Schellekens, 'Determinants', 153, 156–8, and tables 2 and 8. For education given to poor Jewish women in the Middle Ages see Grossman, *Pious and Rebellious*, 159–60. For literacy among women in early modern Europe see Houston, *Literacy*, 21–5, 40, 45–6, 142, 144–6, 157–8, 169–71. On the lack of education for girls in countries of Arab influence see Defourneaux, *Daily Life in Spain*, 146–8; Baskin, 'Jewish Women in the Middle Ages', 103; Levine Melammed, 'Sephardi Women', 130; Patai, *The Seed of Abraham*, 986, ch. 8, esp. 236, 238–9, 243–7, 250, 256; Casey, *Early Modern Spain*, 204–5, 212–13; and Vollendorf, *The Lives of Women*, 169–86. For literacy among the Conversos in Spain see López Belinchón, *Honra, libertad y hacienda*, 255 and n. 27.

206 Swetschinski, *Reluctant Cosmopolitans*, 211, 284–5, suggests the same. Adelman, 'Servants and Sexuality', 82, maintains that in Venice families took orphan girls into the house, taught them to read Hebrew and Italian, and instructed them in needlework and other household tasks.

207 Roberts, *Through the Keyhole*, 102, 107, 116–22, 136; Booy, 'Naar school', 439–40; Kuijpers, 'Lezen en schrijven', 513–14; Heuvel, *Women and Entrepreneurship*, 46–56.

208 Levie Bernfeld, 'Sephardi Women in Holland's Golden Age', 190–1.

209 Ibid., 189–90, 196.

210 Although her father Daniel Lopes Arias was, among other things, a teacher in the Portuguese community and *shamash* of the Maskil el Dal *ḥevrah*, and her brothers studied at the Ets Haim yeshiva, Sara Lopes Arias apparently did not get any formal education. She married a teacher in the Portuguese community in 1683, but could not sign her name in full at the registration of her intended marriage (SAA DTB 693, p. 427, 17 Sept. 1683). On the other hand, the daughter of Isaac Orobio de Castro was able to write (Swetschinski, *Reluctant Cosmopolitans*, 284); see further in Levie Bernfeld, 'Sephardi Women in Holland's Golden Age', 189.

211 See e.g. Levie Bernfeld, 'Sephardi Women in Holland's Golden Age', 189. The rate of illiteracy among girls from the eastern Sephardi diaspora, for example brides from Belgrade in Amsterdam, was equally high. The following *belogrados* girls were unable to write their (first) name in full in Roman letters at the time of marriage: Rachel Alcoser (SAA DTB 699, p. 261, 6 Apr. 1696), Luna Machorro (SAA DTB 706, p. 151, 27 Jan. 1708), Gracia Serrana (SAA DTB 707, p. 375, 20 Nov. 1710), Ora Uziel from Belgrade, the widow of Abraham Aubi (SAA DTB 711,

p. 48, 1 Aug. 1717), and Reina Aubi (SAA DTB 718, p. 336, 5 July 1731). Some of the *belogrados* girls were able to read and write, however: Rachel Levi (SAA DTB 701, p. 256, 28 Aug. 1699), Paloma de Minhana (SAA DTB 703, p. 21, 25 Feb. 1702), and Miriam Aubi (SAA DTB 703, p. 91, 27 May 1702) all signed their names in Roman script.

212 N. Z. Davis, 'Women in the Crafts', 169–72; Schmidt, *Overleven na de dood*, 121–3, 139, 143.

213 Ayllon, *Sermon*, 21–2, 24, 26–7.

214 SAA entry no. 334, no. 613, Not. C. van Achthoven, 28 May 1722, last will of Moses Abrabanel.

215 Menasseh ben Israel, *Thesovro dos dinim*, fifth and last part, 12 Tamuz 5407.

216 SAA entry no. 334, no. 26, p. 296, 25 Iyar 5511. For reform in education in other Jewish communities see J. Katz, *Tradition and Crisis*, 229–31; similar initiatives were being taken throughout early modern European society (Cavallo, *Charity and Power*, 90–1).

217 The same holds true for other Jewish communities of the Dutch Republic. The situation in the non-Jewish world was much better: see Dodde, 'Joods Onderwijs', 68–9. For similar developments starting at an earlier stage in Italian Jewish society see Bonfil, 'Halakhah', 60–1.

218 Exod. 22: 21. See also Maimonides, *Mishneh torah*, 'Hilkhot de'ot', 6: 10: 'a man ought to be especially heedful of his behaviour toward widows and orphans, for their souls are exceedingly depressed and their spirits low' (Twersky, *A Maimonides Reader*, 62).

219 Baron, *The Jewish Community*, ii. 330–3; M. Cohen, *Poverty and Charity*, 237; Epstein, *The Jewish Marriage Contract*, 185–6.

220 Many welfare lists of the community show the item of 'orfão' and 'orfã' or in plural 'orfãos' and 'orfãs' (SAA entry no. 334, no. 174, p. 750, 1 Iyar 5426; ibid., no. 176, p. 24, 1 Nisan 5450; ibid., no. 215, pp. 288–92, 5428–9).

221 For orphan girls housed with families trying to get a dowry through Dotar see 'Judica Rodriges em caza de Abraham Coen Anriques' (SAA entry no. 334, no. 1142, p. 76, 5387). Another orphan was Sara Israel, who was received in the house of Jacob Curiel (ibid., pp. 29, 34, 5384). Judith Fransa was a 'bastarda em casa de Isack Mezurado' (ibid., p. 60, 5386). Judith Lopes stayed in the house of Jacob Palacios (ibid., p. 9, 5383). For contracts made in the 18th century by the Portuguese community on behalf of a deceased mother, confirming the willingness of people to take in and care for orphans in return for payment, see SAA entry no. 334, no. 720, 3 June 1776, 4 and 17 Feb. 1777, which deals with the orphans of Ester Labat Keijzer, David and Moses Cohen Labat Keijzer. For Italy see Adelman, 'Servants and Sexuality', 82.

222 Cited from the Talmud in *Encyclopaedia Judaica*, xv. 483–7, s.v. 'Orphan'.

223 For Aby Jetomim see Pieterse, *Inventaris*, 71.

224 For concepts of 'honour' and 'shame' in early modern Europe see Waardt, 'De geschiedenis van de eer'. For the Dutch Republic see van de Pol, *The Burgher and the Whore*, ch. 2 and literature cited at p. 207 n. 1; Roodenburg, *Onder Censuur*,

244 and the literature cited at n. 58. For Spain see Domínguez Ortiz, *La sociedad española*, 396–402; Bennassar, *The Spanish Character*, 213–48; Casey, *Early Modern Spain*, 170–1; Maravall, *Poder*; Defourneaux, *Daily Life in Spain*, 32–44; and Mendes Drumond Braga, 'Poor Relief', 207–8, 210–11. On the Conversos of Spain see Domínguez Ortiz, *La clase social*, vol. ii, ch. 3; López Belinchón, *Honra, libertad y hacienda*, esp. 226 ff.

225 The inventory of the Amsterdam-based Dotar contained a copy of the *escamot* of the Venetian dowry organization (SAA entry no. 334, no. 1141, p. 171, 28 Feb. 1622; ibid., p. 20, 5383, 26 Mar. 1623).

226 Burns, *Notarial Culture*, 111; Assis, 'Welfare and Mutual Aid', 326; id., 'Les Institutions sociales médiévales', 197–8.

227 Pullan, *Rich and Poor in Renaissance Venice*, 376–94; Black, *Italian Confraternities*, 178–84; Flynn, *Sacred Charity*, 59–62; Russell-Wood, *Fidalgos and Philanthropists*, 173–200; Rumeu de Armas, *Historia de la previsión social en España*, 83, 135–6, 196–7, 212, 241–2, 257.

228 Flynn, *Sacred Charity*, 60; Russell-Wood, *Fidalgos and Philanthropists*, 176, 180–1, 187–9; see also Black, *Italian Confraternities*, 178–84; Klapisch-Zuber, *Women, Family and Ritual*, ch. 10.

229 As mentioned earlier (see nn. 39 and 51 above), *moriscos* expelled from the peninsula and settling down in a new environment took similar Iberian concepts and practices abroad. A dowry organization similar to those in Amsterdam or Venice can also be found among *moriscos* in exile. For such an organization among the *moriscos* in Tunis see Penella Roma, *Los moriscos*, 15; Latham, 'Contribution', 47.

230 Founders and members of *ḥevrot* like Dotar, their descendants, and their families were given priority in welfare. Consequently, newcomers unrelated to the members had fewer opportunities to receive benefits from the organization. For similar patterns in Italy see Orfali, 'The Portuguese Dowry Society in Livorno', 148–9; Horowitz, 'Processions', 242–4. Charitable organizations giving priority to family members seem to have been a common phenomenon in early modern Europe: on the priority given to members in the foundation articles of private Amsterdam almshouses see Eeghen, 'Het Deutzenhofje', 115; Spaans, 'De gift aan de armen', 380–1.

231 SAA entry no. 334, no. 1142, p. 163, 17 Mar. 5392: 'de que não se admetissem por companheiros, Irmaos pobres'.

232 SAA entry no. 334, no. 1142, pp. 193–4, 5395. Similar references are made in other mutual aid societies. The establishment of Hase Amaharacha in 1713 apparently attracted so many people that it was decided in 1729 that poor brothers admitted to the *ḥevrah* could not enjoy the privileges of membership (i.e. the distribution of firewood) until they had belonged to it for three years. For the establishment of this *ḥevrah* see SAA entry no. 334, no. 1234, 1 Heshvan 5474. For the limitations see ibid., p. 35, Kislev 5490.

233 For brides from south-eastern Europe who participated in the Dotar lottery see the example of Rachel, daughter of Joseph Alcoser from Belgrade (SAA entry no. 334, no. 1144, pp. 418–20, 429, 5454). She was placed in the lowest category because of lack of family ties to the members, and after two years of participation had still not managed to get a dowry. She got married nevertheless (SAA DTB 699, p. 261, 6 Apr. 1696).

234 SAA entry no. 334, no. 1151, p. 586, n.d. [1667]: 'Senhores administradors e tezoureiro da santa Irmandade das orfams . . . Clara de Almeida que mora Em bayona, orfam de pai e maim filha de fram[co] Rodriguez almeida que padezerão seos pais em Cordova e Yrmam do martir Isaque dalmeida bern[l] que padezeó em Santiago de galiçia, samtificamdo o nome de el Dio.' In the same year Clara drew a lot of 350 guilders. Six years later she found a partner in Bayonne and got married. After Haham Isaac Israel of the Kahal Kados Nefutsot Yehudah of Bayonne sent a message to Amsterdam to confirm a Jewish wedding ceremony had taken place, the money was paid to Clara's groom (SAA entry no. 334, no. 1152, p. 212, 13 Sivan 5433; ibid., no. 1144, p. 200, 30 Sivan 5433). In Bayonne another dowry organization functioned from 1652 (Nahon, 'Los *Cristianos Nuevos*', 598–9).

235 SAA entry no. 334, no. 1143, p. 284, 6 Tishrei 5418.

236 For other orphans going abroad see the case of the orphan Simha Cahanet from North Africa, who was sent back to Salé, ibid., p. 269, 29 Tishrei 5429.

237 On this foundation, for which Sequeira bequeathed 12,000 guilders, see SAA entry no. 334, no. 1144, pp. 655–6, 5478; see also ibid., p. 680, 15 Adar II 5480. For a similar bequest in Livorno see Trivellato, *The Familiarity of Strangers*, 90.

238 Last will of Rachel de Prado, alias Rachel Gabay Faro, widow of Isaac de Prado (SAA entry no. 5075, no. 7490, no. 18, Not. J. van de Ende, 12 Mar. 1708).

239 For private dowry funds among the Sephardim in Venice see Trivellato, *The Familiarity of Strangers*, 49. Terpstra, *Abandoned Children*, 271, maintains that in Bologna half of the couples marrying from the mid-17th century to the end of the 18th century were subsidized by charitable dowries. For similar patterns in Spain see Flynn, *Sacred Charity*, 59–62; Bilinkoff, 'Elite Widows'.

240 The name is based on Ps. 68: 6.

241 For 'el Padre de Huérfanos' see Arco, 'Una notable institución social'; Rumeu de Armas, *Historia de la previsión social en España*, 171–2; Flynn, *Sacred Charity*, 58–9; Mendes Drumond Braga, 'Poor Relief', 207. For the combination of orphanage and vocational education for poor children in the Dutch Republic see van der Vlis, *Leven in armoede*, 164–6; Eeghen, *De gilden*, 23–4.

242 Wagenaar, *Amsterdam*, ii. 275–301, 319–26, 336–40, 341–4, 345–8; McCants, *Civic Charity*; Groenveld, 'Wezen'; van der Vlis and Rinsema, *Weeshuizen in Nederland*.

243 For orphanages elsewhere in Europe, for example in Bologna and Florence, see Terpstra, *Abandoned Children*.

244 For such a request in a letter from France see Nahon, 'Les Rapports des communautés judéo-portugaises de France avec celle d'Amsterdam', 51–2, 63, 72, 181; SAA entry no. 334, no. 92, p. 145, 9 Kislev 5507.

245 For education offered by Aby Jetomim to *belogrados* orphan boys see n. 252 below.

246 Only at this time was Aby Jetomim completely institutionalized (*Reglement*, 1817, p. 4).

247 For the situation in medieval Egypt see M. Cohen, *Poverty and Charity*, 236–9.

248 The yeshiva was housed in the same building throughout the 17th century; in the 18th century it was moved to another address where the *shamash* lived as well. On the yeshiva with paid students and a *rosh yeshivah* see Franco Mendes, *Memorias*, 56.

249 Apparently the orphanage had a secular school of its own, teaching reading and writing in the Portuguese language (SAA entry no. 334, no. 1211, p. 3, 5414: 'escola de ler y escrever regulase f 7'). For the religious education it offered see ibid., p. 7, 21 Tevet 5435: 'dezejo que tem que ditto seu filho se yzersite na ley divina e aprendim[to] da boa doctrina'. For more on the education of Jewish orphans in medieval times see M. Cohen, *Poverty and Charity*, 238–9.

250 Franco Mendes, *Memorias*, 57. At that time the curriculum included (as well as religious studies) writing, arithmetic, and the Dutch and French languages, followed by learning a trade. In this respect the orphanage was quite modern compared to the educational facilities offered by the Portuguese community. Aby Jetomim adapted its educational system to follow mainstream education in the Dutch Republic and in Europe more generally.

251 McCants, *Civic Charity*, ch. 4. For orphans in the Mennonite Church see Sprunger, 'Mennonites', 152. See also Lieberman, 'Childhood and Family', 159–63.

252 Josua Cohen Peixotto learned the trade of bookkeeper with Daniel da Silva (SAA entry no. 334, no. 1211, p. 18[v], 5437), starting in 1675 (ibid., p. 7, 1 Adar 5435) and finishing three years later (ibid., 1 Adar 5438). Moses de Jacob Machorro (ibid., p. 25, 1 Elul 5454) and Abraham Castro de Oliveros (ibid., p. 8, 24 Elul 5436) learned the same occupation. Joseph de Isaac Baruch (ibid., p. 24[v], 28 Av 5453) learned the job of a broker. Aron Castiel was taught the trade of barber-surgeon by Samuel [de Leon] Benavente (ibid., p. 8, 15 Sept. 1678). Aron Sanches learned to be a wigmaker (ibid., p. 47, 5470). Abraham Preto was placed in the house of Isaac Idaña to learn the craft of *lapidario* (ibid., p. 5[v], 15 Elul 5428); Aron Baruh Alvares was also trained in cutting precious stones (ibid., p. 8, 5437). Moses Coronel was placed with David de Castro Tartas to learn the printing trade (ibid., p. 9, 5442–3). Isaac Calvo de Andrade was trained as a bookbinder (see n. 200 above).

Belogrados orphan boys educated by Aby Jetomim include Pinhas Levy (SAA entry no. 334, no. 1211, p. 18[r], 1 Elul 5457; for his admittance at the orphanage see ibid., p. 24, 29 Av 5452), who studied at the Aby Jetomim yeshiva, continuing at the Ets Haim yeshiva in 1700; Angel Vidal; and Joseph de Minhana (ibid., p. 109[v], 1 Elul 5457; ibid., p. 109[v], 28 Menahem-Av 5459; ibid., p. 40, 5464–8). Mordechai Lumbroso, broker in spices (SAA entry no. 334, no. 1211, p. 38, 13 Tishrei 5460), had learned the profession of cashier four years earlier (ibid., p. 25, 26 Menahem-Av 5455); on his arrival in Amsterdam from Belgrade see ibid., no. 219, p. 250, 12 Nisan 5455: 'Belogrados . . . Mordochay Lumbroso'. Others trained in the same occupations include Aser Zebulun (ibid., p. 25[v], 29 Tamuz 5456) and Pinhas Levy (ibid., p. 18^{v}, 5457–62). For Eliau Gaon's admission as an orphan see SAA entry no. 334, no. 1211, p. 24, 28 Av 5453. Moses de Minhana was trained as a wool broker (SAA entry no. 334, no. 1211, p. 24, 29 Av 5452; ibid., p. 25^{v}, 29 Tamuz 5456; ibid., p. 27, 5456; ibid., p. 38, 13 Tishrei 5460), although on his marriage his occupation was given as teacher (SAA DTB 701, p. 256, 28 Aug. 1699).

Teachers for the orphan boys of Aby Jetomim in the 17th century were mostly of Portuguese background, which implies that Portuguese Jews were able to educate and train the children within their own group. Samuel de Leon Benavente taught the profession of barber-surgeon (SAA entry no. 334, no. 1211, p. 8, 5435); Josua Sarfati taught bookkeeping (ibid., p. 20, 23 Menahem-Av 5440), as did Daniel da Silva (noted above in the case of Josua Cohen Peixotto); Moses Dias taught printing (ibid., p. 12, 16 Elul 5450). Meir de Sadik Cohen [Belinfante], the grandson of the immigrant Meir Cohen [Belinfante] from Belgrade (SAA entry no. 334, no. 219, p. 2, 5451), learned to cut and polish diamonds and was teaching this profession to orphan boys of Aby Jetomim around 1720 (ibid., no. 1211, p. 76^{v}, 1 May 1720; ibid., p. 79, 12 Kislev 5482). There was one Ashkenazi Jew at that time, Isaac de Vries, who taught the profession of barber and surgeon (ibid., p. 7^{v}, 12 Elul 5447): Michael Lopes studied under him. Isaac Calvo de Andrade, as mentioned above (n. 200), learned the trade of bookbinder with the Dutch teacher Huygen.

In the 18th century the situation changed to a certain extent. At this time we find more Ashkenazi Jews involved as teachers, although Portuguese Jews still formed the majority. The Ashkenazi Moses David was hired to teach Abraham Caransa the trade of tailor (SAA entry no. 334, no. 1211, p. 192^{v}, 10 Oct. 1754). Moses Zadok taught Abraham Henriques La Fuente the trade of barber and wigmaker (ibid., p. 209^{v}, 17 Sept. 1757). Learning a trade with a private teacher, often at the teacher's workshop or home, was not a privilege enjoyed only by the orphans of Aby Jetomim. Those Portuguese parents who were able to do so agreed contracts with professionals to teach their children a trade, a practice widely followed throughout Europe, including the Iberian peninsula (Lieberman, 'Childhood and Family', 160). For Portuguese boys put to work as apprentices see the example of Moses, son of Catarina Vaz, who was sent for three years to learn diamond cutting at the house of Joseph Jessurun (SAA entry no. 5075, no. 109, Not. J. F. Bruyningh, pp. 136^{v}–137^{v}, 7 Mar. 1617, published in *Studia Rosenthaliana*, 11/1 (1977), 87); Abraham Senior, about 17 years old, spent three years learning the trade of kaffa worker ('kaffa' denotes a fabric which could be silk, velvet, or Indian cotton) with a Dutch teacher (SAA entry no. 5075, no. 377B, Not. J. and N. Jacobs, p. 328^{r-v}, 29 Aug. 1614, published in *Studia Rosenthaliana*, 7/2 (1973), 270). It seems some children lived at their teachers' houses: for example, the orphan boy Mordecai Gerbon was given shelter in the house of Joseph Ariette, a jeweller and diamond cutter, because of his great poverty ('door de groote armoede die hij hadt'). Ariette was instructed by Aby Jetomim to teach Gerbon the trade of diamond cutting. Mordecai, however, was caught stealing diamonds (SAA entry no. 334, no. 118, file 1, pp. 81–98, 16 Sept. 1718). Also,

Abraham Castro de Oliveros seems to have been living in the house of his teacher Josua Sarfati (ibid., no. 1211, p. 8, 5436). On the other hand it is understandable that Isaac Calvo de Andrade, apprenticed to a Dutch teacher, would not live in his teacher's house if he wanted to be an observant Orthodox Jew. See also Lieberman, 'Adolescence'. For the general practice in early modern Europe of sending boys to learn a trade at the house of a master, both within and outside the guilds, see Rumeu de Armas, *Historia de la previsión social en España*, 191–3; J. Lane, *Apprenticeship*; Munck, 'De disciplinering'; Eeghen, *De gilden*.

253 McCants, *Civic Charity*, 71–2, 74–5.

254 The boys were made to understand that they had to look for work abroad: SAA entry no. 334, no. 1211, p. 20, 5440: 'aver o sobredito orfao em lugar do officio querer fazer hum viagem p[a] Curaçao'; ibid., p. 21, 3 Elul 5441: 'f 30,– . . . p[a] fazer viage a Sale em lugar de off.[o]'; ibid., p. 25, 1 Elul 5454: 'em lugar de oficio . . . va para Jamaica'; ibid., p. 51[v], Rosh Hodesh Sivan 5476: 'de poder ir a Jerusalem'.

255 For similar patterns in the Dutch Republic of sending out orphans see van der Vlis, *Leven in armoede*, 165; Hallema, 'Emigratie'; Eeghen, *De gilden*, 19–24. McCants, *Civic Charity*, 64–70, shows that many orphans from the 'Burgerweeshuis' were sent out to the East Indies to be employed by the VOC (Verenigde Oostindische Compagnie; the Dutch East India Company). For orphan boys in Portugal sent abroad to the Portuguese empire see Coates, *Convicts and Orphans*.

256 Eliau Lopes was 14 years old when he was accepted at Aby Jetomim (SAA DTB 691, p. 22, 4 June 1677; SAA entry no. 334, no. 1211, p. 4[v], 24 Adar 5423). He stayed there for seven years until 1670. Thereafter he studied in the afternoons in the class of Haham Aboab at the Ets Haim yeshiva, at least from 1671–2 until 1678 (ibid., no. 1052, pp. 35–8, 5432–8). Meanwhile, from 1665, he was also a student in the yeshiva of Temime Darech (Franco Mendes, *Memorias*, 63) and apparently also in that of de los Pintos (ibid. 70). He also delivered sermons (SAA entry no. 334, no. 217, p. 11, 8 Sivan, 10 Elul, 8 Tevet 5436–7) at the inauguration of the synagogue in 1675 (Franco Mendes, *Memorias*, 79; Fuks and Fuks-Mansfeld, 'The Inauguration of the Portuguese Synagogue', appendix 'Sermão Quinto'). In 1678 he left for Barbados to be the *haham* of the community there (SAA entry no. 334, no. 1211, p. 18[v], 19 Tamuz 5438; Emmanuel, *History of the Jews of the Netherlands Antilles*, 90–7). David Palache was another orphan who left for Barbados (SAA entry no. 334, no. 1211, p. 19, 8 Elul 5437).

257 For Surinam see Jacob de Gabriel Nunes (SAA entry no. 334, no. 1211, p. 19, 28 Iyar 5447), Salomon Mesiah (ibid., p. 19[v], 24 Tevet 5442), and Aron Uziel Cardozo (ibid., p. 19[v], Tamuz 5442). For France see Abraham Lopez, who left to get married in Bordeaux (ibid., p. 19[v], Elul 5442). For Hamburg see Isaac Zacuto, who left Aby Jetomim and Amsterdam to get married in Hamburg (ibid., 12 Menahem-Av 5438). For London see Jacob Nunes (ibid., p. 18[v], [n.d.] 5438). For Antwerp see Abraham Gomes (ibid., p. 18[v], Elul 5431). For Italy see Isaac Vaez leaving for Livorno (ibid., p. 4, 21 Av 5422). For orphans leaving for Curaçao, Jamaica, North Africa, and Jerusalem see above, n. 254.

258 For an overview of distribution in money and in kind see SAA entry no. 334, no.

1211, p. 2[v], 5414; ibid., p. 91[v], 5448; ibid., p. 208[v], 5517; ibid., p. 193[v], 15 Kislev 5525. In all, Aby Jetomim took in 119 boys during the 17th century (for an estimate of the number of orphans see ibid., p. 3, 5414; ibid., p. 18[v], 8 Elul 5437). For individual cases see Abraham Mayer (ibid., p. 3[v], 29 Av 5411) and Jacob de Casseres (ibid., p. 4, 4 Elul 5416). Total average expenditure per boy in the 18th century was 1,050 guilders over six years (SAA entry no. 334, no. 1211, p. 193[v], 5505–10: the orphan Aron de Jacob Cardozo), that is, 175 guilders a year (including monthly allowances, clothes, expenses for schooling, peat, and matzot, and medical expenses). Expenses for professional training were mostly around 150 guilders over three years in the early modern period, 50 guilders a year (ibid., p. 18[r], 5457; ibid., p. 2[v], 1654). In the 17th century the orphan boys received a monthly allowance of 4 guilders plus clothes and shoes, peat, matzot, and sick care. Costs, including secular and religious education, amounted to 110 guilders a year per orphan (for an overview of clothes given to orphans see SAA entry no. 334, no. 1211, p. 91[v], 5448). In the 18th century the boys got a monthly allowance of 5 guilders plus clothes, peat, matzot, assistance during illness, and extra money to learn a trade (Franco Mendes, *Memorias*, 56).

259 SAA entry no. 334, no. 1211, p. 2[v], 5414; ibid., p. 91[v], 5448; ibid., 1757: 'Copia dos orph[s]: que Ouve Este anno'; ibid., p. 208[v], 5517–18; ibid., p. 193[v], 15 Kislev 5525.

260 MS Ets Haim 48 D 43, 'Memoria delos mosos solteros que ay en la Nacion de 13 Años ariva, en 19 Sivan 5435', pp. 35–8.

261 Pieterse, *Daniel Levi de Barrios*, 119.

262 Franco Mendes, *Memorias*, 50, 55–6; see also SAA entry no. 334.A, suppl., no. 198r [n.d.]. This extension of hospitality was abolished in 1767. It is not clear where the *ḥevrah* of Aby Jetomim accommodated Jewish travellers. Certainly there was no specific building for this purpose. Probably private individuals were hired to provide this service.

263 Pinto, *Reflexoens*, 30–1.

264 Baron, *The Jewish Community*, ii. 332. For a similar society established in London in 1704, see Lieberman, 'Adolescence', 16.

265 SAA entry no. 334, no. 1210, file 81, p. 893, 8 Adar I 5494: 'moveu a algums Zelozos a establecer esta nova Hebrà . . . Mazon abanot á imitação da gloriosa e pia Irmandade de Abi Jetomim, dandolhes vestido, ensino, oficio, e mezadas, excedendo em darlhes alimento na mesma caza . . . E por isso como obra tão agradavel, se constitue sua Divina Magestade Paë de Orphãos'.

266 See the introduction to the foundation of the girls' orphanage (SAA entry no. 334, no. 120, file 81, 6 Shevat 5494).

267 SAA entry no. 334, no. 1210, file 81, p. 910, 8 Adar I 5494. It was only in the 19th century (1840) that it was decided to accommodate the orphan girls overnight as well (*Portugeesch-Israelietisch Meisjes-Weeshuis*, 18).

268 On the male initiators see SAA entry no. 334, no. 120, file 81, p. 891, 6 Shevat 5494, and ibid., p. 919, 8 Adar I 5494; on regulations for female administrators see ibid., pp. 909–14; on regulations for the treasurer see ibid., pp. 906–8. A division of labour between men and women also existed on the boards of non-

Jewish charitable organizations; however, the emphasis on male rather than female authority was much less pronounced (Wagenaar, *Amsterdam*, ii. 279, 284, 287, 313, 323, 337, 339, 343, 346).

269 On the tasks of the *shamash* see SAA entry no. 334, no. 120, file 81, p. 918, 6 Shevat 5494.

270 SAA entry no. 334, no. 120, file 81, pp. 897–8, 8 Adar I 5494.

271 SAA entry no. 334, no. 120, file 81, p. 891, 9 Shevat 5494; ibid., pp. 895–7, 903, 8 Adar I 5494.

272 See the covenant of the girls' orphanage Mazon Abanot of 1734 (SAA entry no. 334, no. 120, file 81, p. 893, 5494: 'por evitar todo genero de liviandade, onde a vista, e debaixo de azilo, amparo e patrocinio das S[ras] Administradoras, aprendão os boms costumes, e proçederes, não vivendo osiozas, senão honestamente com seo trabalho').

273 SAA entry no. 334, no. 120, file 81, p. 891, 9 Shevat 5494; ibid., pp. 910, 912–13, 8 Adar I 5494.

274 SAA entry no. 334, no. 120, file 81, p. 913, 8 Adar I 5494.

275 SAA entry no. 334, no. 120, file 81, p. 895, 8 Adar I 5494; for the city girls' orphanage, the so-called 'Burgerweeshuis', see McCants, *Civic Charity*, 84, 205.

276 SAA entry no. 334, no. 120, file 81, p. 891, 9 Shevat 5494; ibid., pp. 895–6, 914–15, 8 Adar 5494.

277 *Portugeesch-Israelietisch Meisjes-Weeshuis*, 17; SAA entry no. 334, no. 120, file 81, p. 915, 8 Adar I 5494: here it states only 'leer' ('to read').

278 SAA entry no. 334, no. 120, file 81, p. 915, 8 Adar I 5494; see also McCants, *Civic Charity*, 82–8; Kuijpers, *Migrantenstad*, 246. For the peninsula see Mendes Drumond Braga, 'Poor Relief', 207–8.

279 SAA entry no. 334, no. 120, file 81, pp. 904, 911, 916, 918, 8 Adar I 5494.

280 SAA entry no. 334, no. 120, file 81, p. 896, para. 6, 8 Adar I 5494; for a description of her tasks see ibid., p. 912, para. 15; ibid., pp. 915–17. Pescatello, *Power and Pawn*, 27–8, mentions the same subjects for the education of girls at home in Spain, namely 'the traditional household tasks, Christian dogma and embroidery' ('Christian dogma', of course instead of 'Jewish faith').

281 SAA entry no. 334, no. 120, file 81, p. 891, 9 Shevat 5494; ibid., pp. 895, 904, 8 Adar I 5494. For discharge of the orphans with clothes and money see also SAA entry no. 334.A, suppl., no. 1, 120, file 81, p. 875, art. 48, 6 Shevat 5494. For the discharge of orphans in early modern Europe see Terpstra, *Abandoned Children*, 268–70.

282 *Portugeesch-Israelietisch Meisjes-Weeshuis*, 16–17.

283 Cited in Baron, *The Jewish Community*, ii. 327. For the Bikur Holim organization among the Portuguese poor in 17th-century London see L. D. Barnett, *El Libro de los Acuerdos*, 21–3, Elul 5424.

284 On health care in the early modern world see Grell and Cunningham, *Health Care and Poor Relief in Protestant Europe*; Grell, Cunningham, and Arrizabalaga, *Health Care and Poor Relief in Counter-Reformation Europe*; also Friess, 'Poor Relief'.

285 See de Barrios for the Bikur Holim *ḥevrah*, also called simply 'Hebra', established in 1609 (Pieterse, *Daniel Levi de Barrios*, 95; Ancona, 'Komṣt der Marranen', 211). For the co-ordination of the activities of Bikur Holim between the two existing *kehilot* in 1616 see SAA entry no. 334, no. 1051, 48 Omer 5376, and Paraira and Silva Rosa, *Gedenkschrift*, 10–13. See also the activities in different *kehilot* and *imposta* before 1639. For Bet Jacob: SAA entry no. 334, no. 3, p. 22, 7 Nisan 5382: 'por Achebra do K.K.'. For Bet Israel: SAA entry no. 334, no. 11, 5387: 'Despezas deste K.K. . . . gastos da Hebra con doentes pobres'; ibid., p. 35, 5390. For Neve Salom: SAA entry no. 334, no. 9, p. 60, 5381: 'guasto da Quebra'; ibid., p. 73, 5382; ibid., p. 93, 5385. For the cost of caring for the sick poor of the *imposta*: SAA entry no. 334, no. 13, p. 16, 11 Kislev 5383; ibid., no. 17, p. 31, 28 Oct. 5390/1629; ibid., no. 13, p. 86, 25 Tishrei 5393; ibid., p. 128, 6 Iyar 5396; ibid., p. 140, 15 Shevat 5398. For all three *kehilot* in 1639: SAA entry no. 334, no. 13, p. 131, 10 Iyar 5396: 'plos parnasim da habara do Kaal, donde . . .'. For Bikur Holim after the reunion: SAA entry no. 334, no. 19, pp. 17/102–19/104, 33 Omer 1639; Pieterse, *Daniel Levi de Barrios*, 95–7, 175–8. Few documents of the archives of Bikur Holim have been preserved (SAA entry no. 334, no. 294).

286 Although the stipulation was not made explicitly, it seemed that all members of the community were expected to join Bikur Holim and fulfil their duties (SAA entry no. 334, no. 19, pp. 17/102–19/104, 33 Omer 5399; ibid., p. 140/225, 7 Kislev 5403; Pieterse, *Daniel Levi de Barrios*, 175–8).

287 Assis, 'Welfare and Mutual Aid', 325–30; id. 'Les Institutions sociales médiévales', 201–4; Baron, *The Jewish Community*, ii. 327–8.

288 Rivlin, *Mutual Responsibility* (Heb.), 87–103; Marcus, *Communal Sickcare*, 84, 228, 252. For medical treatment of the poor in the Jewish community of medieval Egypt see M. Cohen, *Poverty and Charity*, ch. 8.

289 In the early period before 1639, Bikur Holim provided medical care, nursing, medicines, food, clothes, and shrouds. For doctors see the case of David Farar, who acted as a doctor for Bikur Holim before 1624, healing the poor and giving them charity (Saperstein, *Exile in Amsterdam*, 178). For prescriptions see the case of Abraham Alfarim (SAA entry no. 334, no. 17, p. 33, 13 Mar. 5390/1630). For food and care see the case of Moses Rachao (ibid., p. 5, 11 Sept. 5382). For nursing see the case of Ester Nunes, alias A sega Castellana (ibid., p. 36, 10 June 5390; ibid., p. 41, 24 Aug. 5391/1631; ibid., p. 48, 15 Aug. 5393/1633). For clothes see Ester Nunes (ibid., p. 31, 18 Nov. 5390/1629; ibid., p. 38, 8 Dec. 1630/5391). For watching over the sick and dying see the case of Isabel Correa (SAA entry no. 334, no. 9, p. 154, 5392). For burial see the cases of David Soares (Pieterse, *Livro de Bet Haim*, 97, 17 Dec. 1620) and Dina Ger (SAA entry no. 334, no. 17, p. 58^{v}, 18 Apr. 5396/1636). For shrouds see the case of Lea Gomez (ibid., no. 11, p. 35, 5390).

290 Pieterse, *Daniel Levi de Barrios*, 95–7.

291 See Morteira's sermons from 1619 to 1628 (Saperstein, *Exile in Amsterdam*, 49, 174–80).

292 SAA entry no. 334, no. 19, p. 17/102, para. 1, 33 Omer 5399: 'milhor se acudir aos enfermos pobres de nossa nacão'; ibid., p. 18, ch. 3: 'o que for necessario p^{a} a cura dos enfermos pobres que actualm^{te} stiverem admittidos no rol da Sedaca'.

293 SAA entry no. 334, no. 19, p. 17/102, 33 Omer 5399.

294 SAA entry no. 334, no. 19, p. 4/83, para. 30, 28 Adar II 5399. Anyone who refused to do so was fined ten *placas* (ibid., pp. 17–19, 33 Omer 5399; ibid., p. 140, 7 Kislev 5403). The obligations of the members comprised watching over the sick and dying, accompanying the dead to the cemetery, forming a *minyan* (for prayers) during the *shivah* (the first seven days of mourning), etc. (ibid.).

295 SAA entry no. 334, no. 19, pp. 162/247–163/248, 1 Kislev 5404; ibid., p. 246, 16 Tamuz 5408; Pieterse, *Daniel Levi de Barrios*, 120–2. According to Franco Mendes, Gemilut Hasadim was founded in 1639 as an independent *ḥevrah* to organize funerals because of dissatisfaction over the procedures of Bikur Holim (Franco Mendes, *Memorias*, 50; see also SAA entry no. 334, no. 19, p. 162/247, 19 Heshvan 5404). In 1648 discord resurfaced within this organization, resulting, as noted above, in the formation of Aby Jetomim. For other groups active in dealing with burials see Abodat Akodes in 1705 (SAA entry no. 334, no. 119a, file 23, p. 766 [n.d.]; ibid., no. 25, p. 88, 16 Tamuz 5465; ibid., p. 174, 5 Adar 5488; Franco Mendes, *Memorias*, 51). For organizations with the same name in Italy see Rivlin, *Mutual Responsibility* (Heb.), ch. 1; Ruderman, 'The Founding of a Gemilut Hasadim Society'; Horowitz, 'Processions', 240–1.

296 Paupers suffering short-term illness were looked after by Bikur Holim and received help in kind, such as medicines and food (SAA entry no. 334, no. 19, p. 18/103, para. 3, 33 Omer 5399). For examples before 1639 see the prescriptions for the sick sons of Abraham Peres consisting of butter, meat, eggs, and raisins (ibid., no. 17, p. 35, 9 Mar. 5390); for an example from 1669 see the distribution of meat, chicken, sugar, bread, and eggs by Bikur Holim (ibid., no. 294, pp. 32–43, 1669), and also the prescriptions for meat and chicken prescriptions written by Dr Souza (ibid., no. 990, 25 Av [*c*.1750: no year written on the prescription]: see Pieterse, *Inventaris*, p. 62: SAA entry no. 334, no. 990: 'Stukken betreffende de Hebra (Ziekenverzorging), *c*.1750': 'Carn^{ro} p^{a} Abigael Oeb'; 'Galinha p^{a} Rahel Roza, 2 Av'.

People who were ill for more than two months or who were or became permanent invalids fell directly under the control and supervision of the board of the *kahal* (SAA entry no. 334, no. 19, p. 18/103, para. 3, 33 Omer 5399). They received a weekly monetary allowance for as long as the Mahamad saw fit to support them. At what point the transition was made from temporary to permanent care varied. In 1639 the term was set at two months (ibid.). In 1654 this was reduced to four weeks (ibid., no. 25, p. 31, 19 Tevet 1654). Later we come across more variable terms. Thus we can see that the Mahamad tried to keep a constant eye on the state of the health of the Jewish community (SAA entry no. 334, no. 25, pp. 31–2, 19 Tevet 1654; ibid., pp. 69–70, Menahem-Av 5462; ibid., no. 24a, p. 31^{v}, 26 Heshvan 5434). For an overview of distributions to the poor that were directly under the control of the Mahamad see SAA entry no. 334, no. 215, pp. 101–3, 5425–6: 'Sedaca Repartida por semanas com pesoas doentes'. For specific examples see the child of the widow of Michael Lopes (ibid., no. 216, p. 192, 13 Kislev 5436: 'hijo de la V^{a} de Michael Lopes sele decreto seg^{da} ves por quatro semanas a f 1,10 cada una'): this child's life was in danger from 17 Tevet

5435/1675 (ibid., p. 170, 17 Tevet 5435: '4 semanas estar enfermo de peligro cada semana medio ducatas'), and the weekly distribution was continued until the child died around a year later (ibid., p. 192, 14 Shevat 5436).

297 SAA entry no. 334, no. 19, pp. 17/102–19/104, 33 Omer 5399; ibid., no. 25, p. 31, 19 Tevet 1654; ibid., no. 24a, p. 30^{r-v}, 7 Iyar 5433. For more instructions to the doctors by the Mahamad see ibid., p. 31^{v}, 26 Heshvan 5434. For pharmacists appointed to serve Bikur Holim in Amsterdam see the case of Abraham de Castro (ibid., no. 19, p. 567, 1 Heshvan 5427). For surgeons see the case of Samuel de Leon Benavente (ibid., no. 215, pp. 286–7), who was one of the few surgeons to achieve membership of the Amsterdam surgeons' guild (Silva Rosa, *De geschiedenis van de Portugeesche Joden te Amsterdam*, 105).

298 From 1673 we find women on the payroll of the community for work such as bloodletting, which they had apparently learned to perform (SAA entry no. 334, no. 24a, p. 31, 1 Elul 5433). For Portuguese women assisting surgeons and barbers see ibid., no. 219, pp. 126–7, 5452–3: 'Isaac Tovar, Sel° Sena e Isaac de Mercado por deitar ventozas e ajuda aos pobres f 31:10 e mais f 31:10 por se obrigarem cada hum a ter hua mulher para a asistencia dos pobres em todo f 63,–'. Non-Jewish women in the Dutch Republic were working in similar professions (Koorn and Roodenburg, 'Kopsters'; on these 'kopsters' see also Manuelidis, 'Kopster', and the etching by Cornelis Dusart, *Kopster*, 1695, in Yale Medical Library, Clements C. Fry Collection). On Jewish women elsewhere in the medical profession see Shatzmiller, *Jews, Medicine*, 108–12; Marcus, *Communal Sickcare*; Grossman, *Pious and Rebellious*, 119.

299 For instructions see below and SAA entry no. 334, no. 21, p. 123, 13 Tishrei 5477; ibid., p. 145, 5478; ibid., p. 204, 25 Kislev 5480; ibid., p. 211, 24 Shevat 5480. Concerning complaints made by the poor about their health care see ibid., no. 25, pp. 69–70, Menahem-Av 5462.

300 For the foundation of the Mesib Nefes hospital in 1833–4 see SAA entry no. 334, no. 1275; Silva Rosa, *De geschiedenis van de Portugeesche Joden te Amsterdam*, 161. The so-called Portugees-Israelitiesch Ziekenhuis dates from the early 20th century (Silva Rosa, *De geschiedenis van de Portugeesche Joden te Amsterdam*, 161).

301 See e.g. Baron, *The Jewish Community*, ii. 328–9; Gutwirth, 'Jewish Hospitals in Spain' (Heb.); Backhaus, 'Im Heckhus die Lahmen, Blinden und Hungerleider', 33–9.

302 MS Ets Haim 31, 13 14, 'Proposta feita em Commitee que Se juntou em Consequencia da Resoluçao dos S[res] Velhos de 30 de Tisry 5508 & Methodo Submetido a o Examem de dittos S[res] para estabelecer Hum Hospital ou Enfermaria Para os Doentes Necessitados' (pp. 1–26), 30 Tishrei 5508; see also Hyamson, *The Sephardim of England*, 83; Kochan, *Jews, Idols and Messiahs*, 110; R. D. Barnett, 'Dr. Jacob de Castro Sarmento'; Assis, 'Welfare and Mutual Aid', 330–3; id., 'Les Institutions sociales médiévales', 199–201; Marcus, *Communal Sickcare*, 160–208; Baron, *The Jewish Community*, ii. 327–8.

303 Caro Baroja, *Los Judíos en la España moderna*, ii. 62; López Belinchón, *Honra, libertad y hacienda*, 240–1; Guimarães Sá, *Quando o rico se faz pobre*, 107, 194–5.

304 Pieterse, *Livro de Bet Haim*, 109. Apparently the hospital concerned was the so-called Pesthuis, since this incident took place during the epidemic of 1624 ('se enterrou hu judeu tudesco pobre que faleceo no hospital'). For another case of a poor *tudesco* who died in a hospital ('hu judeu tudesco que faleceo no hospital') being buried at Ouderkerk see Pieterse, *Livro de Bet Haim*, 109, 1 Sept. 1620.

305 SAA entry no. 347, no. 118, p. 48r, 26 Feb. 1670.

306 SAA entry no. 347, no. 119, p. 66v, 11 Nov. 1670.

307 SAA entry no. 334, no. 17, p. 30, 16 Sept. 5389: 'pera levarem a casa da Pesde Sarah . . . e sua comida f 9'.

308 For the so-called 'Lazarushuis' in Amsterdam, an institution for the treatment of leprosy, located close to the Portuguese synagogue (Esnoga) that was completed in 1675, see Eeghen, 'Het Leprozenhuis'. For Portuguese inmates see SAA entry no. 334, no. 222, p. 24, 20 Tevet 5474: 'Aos Lazaros pa curar a cabessa de hum filho de Dd Atas f 3,–; ibid., p. 357, 15 Tamuz 5479: 'curar 3 filhos de Jos. Coen Belinfante aos Lazarus'.

309 SAA entry no. 334, no. 118, file T, p. 32. The need to observe Jewish law was another reason why the leadership of the Portuguese community established the workhouse for Ashkenazim as it was difficult for Jewish inmates in non-Jewish workhouses to observe *kashrut* (for more on this see below).

310 SAA entry no. 5075, no. 942, Not. D. Bredan, 22 Mar. 1633: Dr Paulo de Lena. De Lena left for Rouen, where he became a fervent opponent of judaizing New Christians. For more on him see Révah, 'Autobiographie d'un marrane', 61–2, 72, 74, 80, 112; also Swetschinski, *Reluctant Cosmopolitans*, 234, 274 and notes there. Examples of medical personnel who, in addition to income from medical work, also received charity are Doctor Messiah (SAA entry no. 334, no. 173, p. 114, 1 Tevet 5410: 'Ao doutor mesiah'; ibid., p. 122, 19 Adar II 5410: 'ao Dor messiah e mulher'; ibid., p. 205, 7 Kislev 5412: 'ao dtor Messia') (his widow was also on the charity roll for roughly twenty-nine years, from 1652 (ibid., p. 209, Rosh Hodesh Adar 5412) to 1681 (ibid., no. 217, pp. 237/240, 5440–1) and Doctor Abraham Frois, who was assisted twice for an exceptional reason without further explanation (SAA entry no. 334, no. 217, pp. 57, 104, 5437–8), and received 60 and 63 guilders). In 1697 Dr Frois was accepted as doctor for the 'Hebra' (ibid., no. 20, p. 222, 19 Adar 5457); he completed his doctorate in Utrecht in 1663 (Esso, 'Aandeel der Joden', 672). Moses Falcão *boticario* was a pharmacist who also received welfare: he was given intermittent financial support between 1665 and 1685 (5426–45) for rent, peat, matzot, and the observance of festivals, and to help him when he fell ill (see e.g. SAA entry no. 334, no. 215, p. 212, 3 Tevet 5428; ibid., p. 300, 5429: peat; ibid., no. 216, p. 97, 5432–3; ibid., no. 217, p. 62, 7 Nisan 5437; ibid., p. 236, 5440–1; ibid., p. 304, 5441– 2; ibid., p. 522, 5445: matzot. He was also supported as a *secreto* (SAA entry no. 334, no. 174, p. 733, 20 Adar 5426). For his work as a pharmacist see ibid., no. 217, pp. 23–4, 27 Elul 5436–7; ibid., no. 217, pp. 231–2, 5440–1; moreover, he assisted in the production of *shemurim* for Pesach (ibid., no. 216, p. 1, 5430). Falcão was also a member of the Honen Dalim yeshiva (Pieterse, *Daniel Levi de Barrios*, 124).

311 In 1676 Daniel Lopes kept in his house his sister-in-law, who was mentally disabled, a *cunhada loca* (SAA entry no. 334, no. 217, p. 4, 29 Elul 5436). For that reason he did not have to pay his *finta* tax. On the mentally ill see also Y. Kaplan, 'The Self-Definition of the Sephardi Jews of Western Europe', 134–5.

312 The cost of nursing, clothes, and cleaning had to be paid by the Portuguese community, as was the case for poor members of the Christian community who needed care in the city's mental hospital. For the admission of poor members of the Reformed Church into this mental hospital, which had a so-called 'pest house' as an annexe, and the covering by the Church of the costs incurred by poor inmates who were among its members, see SAA entry no. 342, no. 1059, p. 47^{r-v}, 16 May 1748.

313 SAA entry no. 334, no. 969, p. 222, 6 Nisan 5493: 'ao D^{r} dos locos curar 8/7 a ferra f48,–'. It is unclear whether the doctor consulted was Jewish or non-Jewish.

314 SAA entry no. 334, no. 19, p. 17/102, 33 Omer 5399.

315 SAA entry no. 334, no. 174, p. 499, 4 Nisan 5422; ibid., p. 636, 8 Nisan 5424: 'f 610:10 Pello Repartido com pessoas doentes e outros que não estão em Roshodes'.

316 For barbers and surgeons, hired on a yearly basis, see annual overviews in the *livros longos* (e.g. SAA entry no. 334, no. 215, pp. 232–3, 5427–8: barbers Isaac Baruch, Michael Lopes, and Samuel de Castro; the last-named was given precise instructions in writing). For a pharmacist see the appointment of Abraham de Castro in 1666 (ibid., no. 19, p. 567, 1 Heshvan 5427). Dr David Sarfati was appointed in 1680 on a yearly salary of 150 guilders and given strict orders to help and visit all the poor and prescribe medicines (SAA entry no. 334, no. 20, p. 10, 29 Kislev 5441). For medical services provided without charge see the cases of Dr Orobio de Castro and Dr Daniel Gabriel de Anauia, who offered their services 'por caridade' (for Orobio de Castro: ibid., p. 109, 8 Elul 5447; for de Anauia: ibid., no. 990, p. 35, [n.d., apparently the early 18th century]). Dr Samuel Barreto offered his services to the old-age home without charge (SAA entry no. 334, no. 1220, p. 66, 9 Nisan 5518). For the practice of offering free medical care in other Jewish communities see Marcus, *Communal Sickcare*, 24; Rivlin, *Mutual Responsibility* (Heb.), 90; D. S. Katz, *The Jews in the History of England*, 369.

317 In the early period, medical personnel were paid only for services provided. In 1630 Dr Joseph Bueno was paid 6 guilders for surgery (SAA entry no. 334, no. 17, p. 35, 7 Apr. 1630/5390). Dr Mendo Lopez was also paid (8.14 guilders) for seeing the poor and writing eleven prescriptions (ibid., p. 48, 15 Aug. 5393/1633). For an invoice for 30.10 guilders concerning different prescriptions see ibid., p. 59, 15 June 5396/1636. Dr Daniel Machorro was paid for prescriptions (ibid., pp. 43 and 47, 8 May 5392/1632, and 10 Apr. 1633/5393). For other doctors who took care of the poor see Jacob Bueno and Dr Serrano (ibid., no. 24, p. 15^{v}, 4 Elul 5421). Jacob Moreno was paid 63 guilders for his services to the sick poor (ibid., no. 215, p. 71, 22 Adar 5425). Jacob Israel Mendes, in his role as a doctor, was paid for his services to the poor of the 'Hebra' (ibid., p. 115, 18 Adar 5426), as was Dr Sea (ibid., p. 313, 26 Shevat 5430). For payments to pharmacists for their work in the early period see ibid., no. 17, p. 67, 12 Sept. 5399/1638. In 1627 the pharmacist Samuel

Perez, who prepared prescriptions for the poor, received 5 guilders and 4 stivers for the distribution of medicines and 2 guilders and 7 stivers for the distribution of food (ibid., p. 23^{v}, 15 Aug. 5387). Another pharmacist of the early period working for Bikur Holim was Jacob Coronel (ibid., p. 55^{v}, 20 May 5395/1635). Abraham Israel made medicines for the general poor (ibid., p. 20^{v}, 19 July 5386) (this may possibly be the same person as Abraham Israel Nunes Boticario: ibid., no. 173, pp. 3 and 5, 5407). Bento Sanches also distributed medicines (ibid., no. 17, p. 44, 1 Aug. 1632/5292), and a barber was paid for bloodletting (ibid., p. 51, 25 Mar. 5395/1634).

318 SAA entry no. 334, no. 20, p. 10, 29 Kislev 5441.

319 SAA entry no. 334, no. 20, p. 152, 25 Kislev 5452: Dr Aron Borgas and Dr Abraham de Medina on salaries of 100 guilders each; ibid., no. 25, p. 349, 8 Nisan 5510: Dr Isaac Dias, Dr David del Valle, and Dr Jacob Lopes Sousa.

320 In Christian communities, too, sick care was seen as a duty of the Church and applied through the Church authorities in charge of poor relief. Thus the Dutch Reformed Church also had barber-surgeons, doctors, and midwives of its own: Roodenburg, *Onder Censuur*, 113; Lieburg, 'Geneeskundige zorg'; id., 'Religion and Medical Practice'; Manen, *Armenpflege in Amsterdam*, 86. For health care provided through welfare institutions elsewhere in Europe, e.g. in Aix-en-Provence, see Fairchilds, *Poverty and Charity in Aix-en-Provence*, 47–9.

321 See e.g. the organization of Roffe Holim (SAA entry no. 334, no. 25, pp. 330–1, 13 Tamuz 5509), which gave help to sick poor of 'our nation', and above all to its own members, also organizing their funerals.

322 Deut. 10: 18; Assis, 'Welfare and Mutual Aid'; Baron, *The Jewish Community*, i. 132, 136, 362, ii. 8, 187–90, 306–7, 320, 324.

323 SAA entry no. 5075, no. 2261B, Not. A. Lock, pp. 547–51, 9 Feb. 1660: 'Inventaris van de goederen en middelen naegelaten en metterdoot ontruympt bij Jeronimo Doria van Drada alias Salomon Doria in sijn leven Portugees koopman binnen dese stede.' Clothes of the deceased Isaac Bueno were also given to the poor: 'Inventaris van de goederen ende middelen naegelaten ende metterdoot ontruympt bij Isaac Bueno . . . wat aengaet de clederen van linnen en wolle tot den lijve van de overleeden behoort hebbende dezelve sijn alle gegeven aen den armen' (ibid., pp. 839–44, 5 July 1661; Bonke, 'Portugezen op Vlooyenburg', 37–8). In the will of Miriam Alvares the same intention is formulated thus: 'deixo toda a ropa de servicio e todos meus vestidos se dem a pobres e a parientes q o ajao mister' (SAA entry no. 334, no. 628: 'Papeis tocantes a caza mortuoria de Miriam Alvarez que Ds tem. Miriam Alvarez, N° 4', last will written and signed by Miriam Alvares, 28 Oct. 1678; handed over to Not. F. Tixerandet on 21 November 1678; opened by Not. D. van der Groe 29 Aug. 1685). Mayr a Royo said on his deathbed that, after paying a debt owed to Menasseh ben Israel, leaving a gift to the *talmud torah* of his community Bet Israel, and covering the expenses of his funeral and paying for tombstones for himself and his wife, any remaining money and clothes should be given to the needy poor (ibid., no. 10, p. 141, 24 Shevat 5389 ('E q o demaiz q sobejasse tanto de dr.° como fatto se Repartisse p. Pobrez nessesitados'); ibid., pp. 147 and 148, 11 Sivan 5390).

324 Matt. 25: 35–6. In the Middle Ages the seven works of mercy became a moral code of charitable behaviour in the Catholic Church (Flynn, *Sacred Charity*, 44–9; see also McBrien (ed.), *Encyclopedia of Catholicism*, 853–5, s.v. 'Mercy'). For the distribution of clothes in Amsterdam through guilds see Bos, *Onderlinge hulpverlening*, 17, 145, 276. For the distribution of clothes through the Reformed Church of Amsterdam see Roodenburg, *Onder Censuur*, 113.

325 For private donations of clothes to the poor in Catholic Spain see Flynn, *Sacred Charity*, 47. For patterns in an earlier period, in Castilian society 1150–1350, see Ruiz, *From Heaven to Earth*, 111–12.

326 Will of Abigail Abarbanel (SAA entry no. 5075, no. 2895B, Not. P. Padthuysen, 28 Sept. 1666): 'y enquanto a los vestidos y ropa blanca del cuerpo della testadora quiere ella testadora que su dho marido los de por su alma aquien a el bien le parecieron sin que nadie le pueda decir cosa ninguna'.

327 Bet Israel: SAA entry no. 334, no. 11, p. 4, 5388: 'custo de vestiaria q Se Repartio pelloz pobrez p. chanuqua . . . f 134:8'. For Bet Jacob see ibid., no. 7, p. 109^{v}, 20 Kislev 5391.

328 SAA entry no. 334, no. 174, p. 135, 26 Kislev 5416. For the objects distributed see ibid., no. 17, p. 38, 8 Dec. 5391; ibid., no. 10, [no page number], 5393: list of the poor of the community Bet Israel, to whom clothes were given during Hanukah.

329 For individuals given clothing upon arrival see Abraham Alvito, receiving a piece of fabric (SAA entry no. 334, no. 17, p. 38, 8 Dec. 5391/1630); Samuel Navarro getting shoes, socks, and a piece of fabric (ibid., no. 17, p. 31, 8 Dec. 1629/5390); Jacob Romeiro *forasteiro*, a suit ('para hum vestido': ibid., no. 173, p. 26, 14 Adar 5408).

330 SAA entry no. 334, no. 19, p. 19/104, 33 Omer 5399; see also Pieterse, *Daniel Levi de Barrios*, 178; SAA entry no. 334, nos. 1187–8. Vestiaria is named in 1641 in the last will of David Senior Coronel, drawn up in Pernambuco, Brazil. He set aside an annual sum of 20 guilders to be spent on clothes to be distributed during Hanukah (ibid., no. 19, pp. 98/183–99/184, 15 Tamuz 5401).

331 SAA entry no. 334, no. 1051, p. 2, 5376; ibid., p. 136/201, 16 Heshvan 5403; ibid., nos. 1189–90: Vestiaria dos Talmidim.

332 SAA entry no. 334, no. 19, p. 683, 29 Kislev 5434.

333 SAA entry no. 334, no. 19, p. 481, 25 Kislev 5421. The Vestiaria dos Talmidim reformed its statutes a month later (ibid., p. 483, 4 Tevet 5421). It is possible that the Aby Jetomim orphanage may have been another serious competitor in this field, for it also distributed clothes, though to orphan boys only (SAA entry no. 334, no. 1211, p. 2^{v}, 5414: 'escama 10 da ymstituysao . . . Esta samta Yrmandade admytira mosos orfos aos coays se aja de dar caza, comyd, y vestido por tempo de tres anos'; see also Pieterse, *Daniel Levi de Barrios*, 117).

334 SAA entry no. 334, no. 19, pp. 482–3, 4 Tevet 5421; ibid., no. 21, p. 61, 26 Iyar 5474.

335 SAA entry no. 334, no. 120, p. 940, 5495; ibid., no. 25, pp. 218–20, 8 Tevet 5495; ibid., no. 1242, 3 Shevat 5514.

336 See her last will: SAA entry no. 5075, no. 7619, no. 300, Not. A. Tzeewen, 26 May

1723: 'item aen de broederschap der kleeding van de Portugeesche Joodsche Natie alhier betreckelijck tot de vrouwen de somme van een hondert guldens eens'.

337 SAA entry no. 334, no. 25, pp. 244–8, 26 Adar II 5499. Quetonet Bat Codes distributed shirts to poor people of both sexes, not just to women (no. 25, ibid., pp. 299–302, 3 Av 5505).

338 Malkiel, 'Ghetto Republic', 123, 129; Pullan, *Rich and Poor in Renaissance Venice*, 604–21; id., 'Jewish Banks'; Black, *Italian Confraternities*, 228–30; Ravid, *Economics and Toleration*; Bashan, 'Jewish Moneylending'; Poliakov, *Les Banquiers juifs*. On Jews and moneylending in medieval society see Shatzmiller, *Shylock Reconsidered*, esp. ch. 4; on moneylending by Jews in Erets Yisra'el see Rozen, *Jewish Identity*, 16. The *monte de piedad* arrived in Spain quite late in the 17th century, influenced by its Italian model: Elliott, *The Count-Duke of Olivares*, 63. For New Christians in Spain active in keeping a pawnshop at the beginning of the 18th century see Lera García, 'La última gran persecución'.

339 Pullan, 'Jewish Banks'; id., 'Charity and Usury'; id., *Rich and Poor in Renaissance Venice*, 539–40; id., 'Jewish Moneylending'.

340 Pieterse, *Daniel Levi de Barrios*, 106; Franco Mendes, *Memorias*, 37–8.

341 SAA entry no. 334, no. 644, [no page number], 16 June 1775.

342 Strauss, *Nuremberg*, 198.

343 L. Jansen, *Stads Bank van Lening*, 16–24; Carasso-Kok and van Lakerveld, *De Amsterdamse Stadsbank van Lening*, 19–62. In Rotterdam a loan bank was founded following the example of Amsterdam (Voorthuysen, *Stads-bank van Lening*, 21; Deursen, *Plain Lives*, 59–62). Interest rates varied between 13.5% and 16.25% for less valuable items pawned and 8.66% and 9.6% for more valuable items.

344 SAA entry no. 334, no. 1186, pp. 1–2, 5385; Pieterse, *Daniel Levi de Barrios*, 106, 181.

345 SAA entry no. 334, no. 1186, p. 1, para. 3, 5385.

346 Maimonides, *Mishneh torah*, 'Hilkhot matanot aniyim', 10: 7; see also Baron, *The Jewish Community*, ii. 326–7.

347 Pieterse, *Daniel Levi de Barrios*, 106. On epidemics in the Low Countries see Noordegraaf and Valk, *De Gave Gods*.

348 Pieterse, *Livro de Bet Haim*, 106–15. The death rate in the Amsterdam Portuguese community Bet Jacob during the 1620s reached a peak in 1624. The number of burials in the Portuguese cemetery rose from 56 in 1623 to 77 in 1624, falling back to 54 in 1625, 26 in 1626, and 24 in 1627. There are references to victims of the epidemic in this *Livro de Bet Haim*, for example: 'Hua filha de Abraham Pinto de Bet Israel que morreo de peste' (Pieterse, *Livro de Bet Haim*, 112, 10 Apr. 5385) and 'Ester Lopez . . . morreo de peste' (ibid., p. 114, 4 Tamuz/9 July 5385). On this epidemic see also Commelin, *Beschryving*, 1179–80.

349 SAA entry no. 334, no. 1186, p. 1, introduction, 5385.

350 'He a esmola pela qual diz a escrittura sagrada que escapa de morte violenta e pois por nossos peqados' (SAA entry no. 334, no. 1186, p. 1, introduction, 5385).

351 Saperstein, *Exile in Amsterdam*, 104–5.

352 Horowitz, 'Jewish Confraternities', 15–16; id., 'Processions', 241; Vogelstein and Rieger, *Juden in Rom*, ii. 214; Stow, 'The Good of the Church'.

353 Based on Micah 6: 8; *Samen-spraeck*, 61; for penance through charity in the non-Jewish world see Fairchilds, *Poverty and Charity in Aix-en-Provence*, 54–8.

354 SAA entry no. 334, no. 1186, p. 1, para. 3, 5385; on this principle see Deut. 23: 20–1, Exod. 22: 24.

355 SAA entry no. 334, no. 1186, p. 1, para. 3, 5385; ibid., p. 5, 5390. There was no maximum set on the value of goods pawned at the loan bank of the city of Amsterdam (L. Jansen, *Stads Bank van Lening*, 20).

356 SAA entry no. 334, no. 1186, p. 1^v, para. 9, 5385; L. Jansen, *Stads Bank van Lening*, 21.

357 Teensma, 'Fragmenten', 139. Writing in 1686, Idaña refers to a maximum loan of 50 guilders, as opposed to the maximum of 40 guilders mentioned in a decision taken by the loan bank Honen Dalim in 1630. It could well be that by 1686 the loan bank had raised the maximum, but we cannot find any explicit mention of this as documents on decisions taken by the loan bank in 1686 have not survived.

358 Pieterse, *Daniel Levi de Barrios*, 106, 181–2; Pullan, *Rich and Poor in Renaissance Venice*, 581.

359 SAA entry no. 334, no. 158, p. 222, 5400–50. It is difficult to find out how long the loan bank Honen Dalim continued to function: that it certainly continued well into the 1770s (and even much later: SAA entry no. 334, no. 1027) can be deduced from the inventory of Lea Habilho Benveniste, dated 16 June 1775, in which goods were taken from the so-called Jewish lombard (ibid., no. 644, [no page number], 16 June 1775). Silva Rosa, however, speaks of its ending in 1690 (*De geschiedenis van de Portugeesche Joden te Amsterdam*, 24).

360 According to the articles of 1625 the items to be pawned were brought to the house of the treasurer of the society. One week later, the following Sunday, the owner could get his or her money back from the same place. After 1639 we have little information on the location of the pawn bank. We assume it was still located in the house of the treasurer/administrator. The Portuguese leadership chose a treasurer every year (SAA entry no. 334, no. 1186, p. 1, para. 5, 5385).

361 SAA entry no. 334, no. 1186, p. 1^v, para. 9, 5325.

362 It is said that in 1690 *emprestimo* took place in the building of the community itself (SAA entry no. 334, no. 20, p. 157, 26 Shevat 5450). This indicates that, prior to this date, it took place elsewhere.

363 From 1691 the employee appointed and paid directly by the Portuguese community was Abraham Cohen de Lara (SAA entry no. 334, no. 242, p. 19, 8 Shevat 5451). He had also been the *ḥazan* of the synagogue since 1681, and lived in one of the buildings that surrounded the Esnoga (for his address on his marriage see SAA DTB 693, p. 65, 13 Feb. 1682; on his being chosen as a *ḥazan* see SAA entry no. 334, no. 20, p. 29, 5 Kislev 5442). For appointment of other employees of the loan bank see also ibid., no. 25, p. 74, 14 Kislev 5463; ibid., no. 21, p. 237, 13 Tevet 5481.

364 SAA entry no. 334, no. 1186, p. 40v, 22 Tevet 5437. This restriction was incorporated in the original articles of the association. Loans were intended for poor Jews only (ibid., p. 1, 5385). In those days the Portuguese Jews apparently could not foresee that their community would attract so many Jews from other backgrounds.

365 SAA entry no. 334, no. 22, pp. 211–12, 25 Tevet 5519.

366 SAA entry no. 334, no. 1186, p. 1v, para. 7, 5385; ibid., p. 3, 5386. The loan bank of the city of Amsterdam had similar restrictions, prohibiting the pawning of furniture, beds, or perishable goods (Emeis, *Leentjebuur*, 23–4; based on Exod. 22: 24–6).

367 SAA entry no. 334, no. 13, p. 122, 3 Nisan 5396; ibid., no. 1186, p. 13r–v, 5397; ibid., p. 18v, 5403; ibid., no. 1027, 5450. Before 1775 Lea Habilho Benveniste handed in fabric bags and skirts ('1 saco & saya de Estofa com flores . . . 1 ditto': ibid., no. 644, 16 June 1775). It often happened that pledges were not redeemed (ibid., no. 1186, p. 11, 5396). Perhaps people took the money and left the city.

368 SAA entry no. 334, no. 1186, p. 2r–v, 5385; ibid., p. 40v, 22 Tevet 5437; Pieterse, *Daniel Levi de Barrios*, 106.

369 After the 1670s, however, the prestige attached to administration of the loan bank declined. Around 1645 the administrators of *emprestimo* belonged to the second highest group of taxpayers (SAA entry no. 334, no. 158, p. 26, Tishrei 5405–Tishrei 5406; ibid., no. 172, pp. 313–15, 15 Sivan 5405). With the exception of 1690, after 1683 administrators could only be found among the two least wealthy groups (ibid., no. 175, pp. 305–16, 8 Elul 5445). In 1684 Menasseh Pinheiro de Casseres declined to accept the position of administrator and was fined 200 guilders (ibid., no. 20, p. 86, 29 Elul 5444). Between 1685 and 1689 no administrators are registered and *ḥazan* Abraham Cohen de Lara seems to have taken on the work (ibid., no. 241, p. 119, 5445–6; ibid., no. 158, p. 222, 5446–8: 'Administradores do Emprestimo . . . 5446–5448 . . . não estão notados'). In 1690 the Mahamad decided to stop appointing administrators without salary and turned the post into a paid job (ibid., no. 158, p. 222, 5450: 'Administradores do Emprestimo . . . 5450 . . . em dito anno se extingiu com esta Administração').

370 On the bankruptcy of Samuel de Prado in 1721 a large amount of jewellery belonging to him was taken out of the Bank van Lening (SAA entry no. 5072, no. 639, pp. 121–7, 12 Nov. 1721). In the inventory of Moses de Josua Cohen Peixotto in 1740 a number of letters containing pledges ('lommerdbriefjes') were found; the objects being pledged included gold jewellery, silver objects, and books with gold locks (SAA entry no. 5075, no. 7573B, Not. J. van Vilekens, no. 72, 6 July 1740). At the death of Aron Lopes Colaso in 1774 similar 'lommerdbriefjes' were found in his inventory and only 50% of his debts could be paid off; clearly his trading business (set up by his father) had declined during the 18th century (Pieterse, 'Abraham Lopes Colaso', 5).

371 SAA entry no. 5075, no. 7533, Not. J. van Vilekens, pp. 901–2, 8 Sept. 1710. For women in the Jewish community of medieval Egypt taking loans see M. Cohen, *Poverty and Charity*, 148.

372 SAA entry no. 5075, no. 645B, Not. S. Cornelisz., p. 1119, 17 Nov. 1620; also published in *Studia Rosenthaliana*, 17/2 (1983), 217. We do not know any more about this operation; on Jewish women being active in moneylending see Tallan, 'Opportunities'.

373 One part of the inventory of Lea Habilho Benveniste refers to Jacob Lopes Colaso, who took goods—fabric, bags, and clothes—from her on loan: 'Het navolgende is beleent onder Jacob Lopes Colace voor f 46,3' (SAA entry no. 334, no. 644, 10 July 1775). On similar activity in non-Jewish Amsterdam see the case of Sara Pardoes, who was arrested in 1698 because she kept a pawnshop: SAA entry no. 5061, no. 213, [no page], 18 and 25 Nov. 1698; Voorthuysen, *Stads-bank van Lening*, 44.

374 For Josua de Prado see SAA entry no. 5075, no. 7490, no. 19, Not. van de Ende, 12 Mar. 1708, last will of Josua de Prado, alias Anthonio de Prado: 'En noch ten laetsten aen, en ten behoeve van Elletje Hoogduitse Jodinne des Testateurs gewesene Dienstmaegdt en altans getrouwt met Joseph Levi, de perssen, wielen en gereedtschappen van de Tabakspinderije, bij den Heer Testateur voor haer opgeregt, zoo dat dan ook de rekeningh met den zelven Joseph Levi, wegens de voorschreve spinderije, en de handel van Tabak daer meede of ter dier occasie gedaen op dien voet onder anderen meede geliquideert zal moeten werden.'

For the Amsterdam Portuguese taking loans from family and friends see e.g. SAA entry no. 5072, no. 750, no. 26, [n.d.] Apr. 1748: 'Staat en Inventaris des boedels van Mordechay Semach Aboab'.

375 Baron, *The Jewish Community*, ii. 327; Frisch, *An Historical Survey*, 111; Rivlin, *Mutual Responsibility* (Heb.), 280–5.

376 In St-Esprit in France, for example, Portuguese Jews were taking loans on pledge (Nahon, *Les 'Nations' juives portugaises*, 164).

377 SAA entry no. 334, no. 251, pp. 336, 343–4, 8 Nisan 5535–9 Nisan 5536; see also the loans given to 'Elazar ben Kiki emprestimo f 100,–' (ibid., no. 969, p. 126, 19 Adar 5492), to R. Juda Pisa (ibid., no. 970, p. 630, 9 Nisan 5514), and to Aron Hamis: 'Aaharon Hamis p[a] desempanhar sua roupa' (ibid., no. 222, p. 15, 2 Elul 5473). See also the so-called *Livro de emprestimo* (SAA entry no. 334, no. 1001, 1792–7).

378 SAA entry no. 334, no. 19, p. 340, 25 Sevat 5413; ibid., p. 433, 15 Sivan 5418.

379 SAA entry no. 334, no. 220, p. 75, 6 Adar 5461: 'a Samuel Hamiz Vaz extraordinario selle deo de ordem dos ssres do mahamad prometendo q se ds o favore sese os bolveria a pagar a sedaca f 66'. Concerning repayment of *sedaca* by the poor elsewhere in the Jewish world see Simonsohn, *History of the Jews in the Duchy of Mantua*, 521. Repayment of loans by the poor was a common practice in the non-Jewish world as well; see Hallema, 'Emigratie', 212–15.

380 See *Registro dos despachos*: SAA entry no. 334, nos. 978–9.

381 An orphan in the 18th-century Aby Jetomim orphanage had to agree that if he went on to earn enough as an adult he would pay back the money that had been invested in him. The orphanage produced contracts to this effect that beneficiaries of its charity had to sign (SAA entry no. 334, no. 1211, pp. 47, 49[v], 50, 192[v], 5472, 5474, and 1754): see for example the cases of Joseph Minhana (ibid., no. 1211, p. 50, 1 Nov. 1713) and Moses Pereyra (ibid., p. 51v, Rosh Hodesh Sivan 5475). For Mishenet Zequenim see ibid., no. 1220, p. 5, 'Reglamento tocante o Thezoureyro', art. 3, 8 Tevet 5510.

382 SAA entry no. 334, no. 17, p. 47, 25 May 5393/1633.

383 He was a supervisor of the baking of kosher bread (SAA entry no. 334, no. 28, p. 119, 22 Elul 5535). See also the case of Abraham Alentrino, who was given 225 guilders, to be deducted from his salary: he worked as a 'sangrador da pobreza', assisting the poor with the medical practice of bloodletting (ibid., p. 78, 22 Elul 5534). The practice of providing interest-free loans continued well into the 20th century under the new name of the *Leenfonds* (Silva Rosa, *De geschiedenis van de Portugeesche Joden te Amsterdam*, 24–5).

384 Y. Kaplan, 'The Self-Definition of the Sephardi Jews of Western Europe', 138–9. On the idea of the superiority and nobility of Sephardim see also Graizbord, 'Religion and Ethnicity', 47–8.

385 The most important initiator of the new ideas regarding welfare was himself a New Christian, Luis Vives (*De subventione pauperum*); on him see also Domínguez Ortiz, *The Golden Age of Spain*, 221; id., *Los Judeoconversos*, 218–20, 253, 258; and Bataillon, *Érasme*. Another Spanish New Christian reformer was Cristóbal Pérez de Herrera (on whom see Domínguez Ortiz, *Los Judeoconversos*, 213–14). For an overview of welfare reforms in general and those in Spain in particular see Flynn, *Sacred Charity*, ch. 3.

386 Hallema, *Geschiedenis van het gevangeniswezen*; Spierenburg, *The Emergence of Carceral Institutions*, 9–77; Eerenbeemt, *Armoede en arbeidsdwang*.

387 SAA entry no. 334, no. 19, p. 109/194, introd. and para. 1, 24 Adar I 5402.

388 SAA entry no. 334, no. 19, p. 20/105, 30 Tamuz 5399; ibid., p. 195/280, Av 5404; ibid., pp. 430–1, 8 Iyar 5418; ibid., p. 533, 8 Sivan 5424. See also Y. Kaplan, *From New Christians to New Jews* (Heb.), ch. 4, and id., 'The Self-Definition of the Sephardi Jews of Western Europe', on relations between the Portuguese and the Askenazi Jews in early modern Amsterdam.

389 On prohibitions on begging in the Dutch Republic see Bierens de Haan, *De Nederlandsche strafbepalingen*; Deursen, *Plain Lives*, ch. 3. On laws and views concerning prostitution, especially in the Dutch Republic, see van de Pol, *The Burgher and the Whore*, ch. 3, and ch. 4, esp. 92–3. On the application of criminal law in Amsterdam see Faber, *Strafrechtspleging*, ch. 4; Jütte, 'Poor Relief and Social Discipline'.

390 SAA entry no. 334, no. 19, p. 109/194, 24 Adar I 5402; ibid., pp. 110/195–111/196, para. 8, 24 Adar I 5402. The introduction to the foundation of the new Abodat Ahesed workhouse speaks about taking God's name in vain, the violation of his Holy Law, and the dishonouring of his people.

391 SAA entry no. 334, no. 19, pp. 110/195–111/196, para. 8, 24 Adar I 5402.

392 Calculations based on distributions of matzot (SAA entry no. 334, no. 173, p. 121, 19 Adar II 5411; ibid., no. 174, p. 846, Rosh Hodesh Nisan 5429).

393 SAA entry no. 334, no. 174, p. 846, Rosh Hodesh Nisan 5429.

394 SAA entry no. 334, no. 19, p. 112/197, para. 16, 24 Adar I 5402.

395 SAA entry no. 334, no. 19, p. 116/201, 29 Nisan 5402.

396 SAA entry no. 334, no. 19, p. 109/194, introduction, 24 Adar I 5402.

397 SAA entry no. 334, no. 19, pp. 109/194–110/195, para. 1, 24 Adar I 5402.

398 SAA entry no. 334, no. 19, pp. 110/195, 112/197, paras. 2–4, 18, 24 Adar I 5402.

399 SAA entry no. 334, no. 19, p. 110/195, para. 2, 24 Adar I 5402.

400 SAA entry no. 334, no. 19, p, 110/195, paras. 4–7, 24 Adar I 5402.

401 SAA entry no. 334, no. 19, p. 111/196, paras. 9–11, 24 Adar I 5402.

402 SAA entry no. 334, no. 19, p. 110/195, para. 3, 24 Adar I 5402.

403 SAA entry no. 334, no. 19, p. 112/197, paras. 17–18, 24 Adar I 5402.

404 SAA entry no. 334, no. 19, p. 109/194, introduction, 24 Adar I 5402.

405 SAA entry no. 334, no. 19, p. 116/201, 29 Nisan 5402.

406 On the collection with plates for *tudescos* see SAA entry no. 334, no. 172, p. 117, 15 Adar 5401; ibid., no. 19, p. 116/201, 29 Nisan 5402; ibid., no. 294, p. 19, 5415.

407 SAA entry no. 334, no. 294, p. 19, 5415; Franco Mendes, *Memorias*, 82.

408 In 1643 Joseph Bueno Bivas left 1,200 guilders to the Portuguese community. This produced an annual yield in interest of 36 guilders, of which he stipulated that one-quarter should go to the *ḥevrah* of Abodat Ahesed and three-quarters to Ets Haim, Terra Santa, and *cativos* (SAA entry no. 334, no. 19, p. 143/228, 27 Tevet 5403).

409 SAA entry no. 334, no. 19, p. 259, 6 Tevet 5409.

410 SAA entry no. 334, no. 19, p. 20/105, 30 Tamuz 5399; ibid., p. 533, 8 Sivan 5424. For a similar phenomenon see also the warning from the Lutheran Church (Kuijpers, 'Een zeventiende-eeuwse migrantenkerk').

411 For Ashkenazi inmates of the Rasphuis arrested for begging see e.g. SAA entry no. 347, no. 116, p. 57, 25 May and 24 Dec. 1656: David Slachter ('Joode uit Pals oud 43 jaar weder om sijn beelarij ingebracht'); ibid., p. 102^{v}: Jgeena ('van Cracouw 30 jaar, Jodin . . . in 't werckhuys gebracht om haar bedelarij'). For Jewish children see SAA entry no. 347, nos. 116–19, 1654–75.

412 See e.g. SAA entry no. 334, no. 218, p. 182, 5 Adar 5448; SAA entry no. 347, no. 122, p. 124^{v}, 16 Mar. 1695: 'ontfangen voor een dagh niet te wercken wegens haer Sabbedagh'. For more examples see SAA entry no. 347, nos. 116–25, 1654–1754.

413 SAA entry no. 347, no. 117, p. 220, 14 Jan. 1663. Daniel Pinto also intervened in the cases of Salomon Nachem from Poland, aged 17 (SAA entry no. 347, no. 116, p. 130, 11 Nov. 1657) and Cars Jutte from Poland, aged 13 (ibid., p. 142, 12 Jan. 1658). In 1664, on behalf of the Portuguese community, Daniel Pinto committed himself to a weekly payment of 12 stivers to the gatekeeper of the Willige Rasphuis to prevent poor Jews working on the sabbath and Jewish holidays (SAA entry no. 334, no. 24a, p. 7, 1 Heshvan 5425). In 1670 Daniel Pinto became *parnas* of the Talmud Torah religious school. In that capacity he was present at the inauguration of the Portuguese synagogue in 1675 (ibid., no. 19, p. 59: 'Taboa dos que servirão oficios neste K.K. despois da Junta delle').

414 SAA entry no. 347, no. 117, p. 155, 7 Apr. 1662.

415 SAA entry no. 347, no. 116, p. 166, 17 July 1658.

416 The majority of the group (twenty-seven) were *tudesco* boys. The Rasphuis made a contribution towards travel expenses and also paid for bread and half a *livra* of butter per person (SAA entry no. 334, no. 172, p. 12, 8 Sivan 5399; ibid., p. 9, 12 Iyar 5399). The Rasphuis and Werkhuis also assisted the emigration of Ashkenazim independently of the Portuguese community: Hester Sinder from Poland was allowed to leave the Werkhuis in 1665 on the basis that she would take one son with her to Poland, in consideration of the fact that her other son was about to be enrolled as a soldier in the war against the English ('uyt consideratien dat haer andere soon ten oorlog gaat tegen de Engelsen': SAA entry no. 347, no. 118, p. 62^{v}, 10 Mar. 1665). Sara Isaak from Hamburg, 13 years old, was released on condition that she would go back to Hamburg (ibid., p. 90, 1 July 1667).

417 SAA entry no. 334, no. 172, p. 272, 14 Av 5404; ibid., no. 239, p. 91, 14 Av 5405; ibid., no. 19, p. 215, 13 Heshvan 5407; ibid., p. 237, 1 Adar 5408; ibid., p. 259, 6 Tevet 5409; ibid., p. 275, 25 Kislev 5410; ibid., p. 408, 2 Elul 5416; ibid., no. 240, p. 192, 10 Nisan 5425.

418 A list has been preserved of *polacos* who were sent to Poland via Abodat Ahesed. It specifies twenty-six family units, some with children. Sixteen were headed by men; ten either consisted of single women or were headed by women. See 'q se vao p^{a} polonia' (SAA entry no. 334, no. 1210, p. 40, [n.d.]).

419 SAA entry no. 334, no. 19, p. 613, 14 Adar 5430.

420 A few Portuguese Jews made it to the Rasphuis (SAA entry no. 334, no. 21, p. 2, 5419: 'Sobre o Herera que esta no Raspois'). Jacob Abenacar Pimentel was paid to have a poor person released from the 'Willige Raspoiz' (ibid., no. 218, p. 258, 22 Mar. 5449), though it isn't clear on whose behalf he intervened. See also the case of the son of Zacuto, taken from the Rasphuis in 1713 (ibid., no. 222, p. 20, 11 Iyar 5473: 'Ao filho de Zacuto o q sahiu do Rasphuis . . . f 7, 19, 8').

421 On 21 April 1670 Abraham Moses was released because of a great rush of Jews ('groot aanloop van Jooden'). Two years later, he was arrested for begging for the sixth time; he was let out some months later so that he could enrol as a soldier ('voor soldaet uytgehaald': SAA entry no. 347, no. 119, p. 18^{r}, 21 Apr. 1670 and 28 Mar. 1672). In 1671 Abraham Barents requested the release of Anna Liverman, then 50 years old, from Bamberg (ibid., p. 138, 13 Nov. 1671). In 1674 Hester Isacx, a 46-year-old blind woman from Dobbenesh(?) with a small baby ('suyghent kind'), was released through the mediation of Natan Swaeb (ibid., p. 244, 4 Aug. 1674).

422 Franco Mendes, *Memorias*, 82; SAA entry no. 334, no. 19, p. 613, 1 Nisan 5430; ibid., no. 217, p. 2, 1 Nisan 5436; ibid., no. 1210, pp. 26–7, 5498–9.

423 SAA entry no. 334, no. 19, p. 613, 1 Nisan 5430. Pereyra had been supported since 1666 (ibid., no. 174, p. 732, 20 Adar 5426; ibid., no. 176, p. 377, 2 Nisan 5461). On his work as a barber in the Portuguese community see ibid., no. 215, pp. 286–7, 5428–9. He had a big family (ibid., p. 201, 5427: 40 *livras* of matzah meal, which means his family consisted of around five people).

424 SAA entry no. 334, no. 19, p. 613, 1 Nisan 5430: 2 guilders a month. He had not been mentioned as a teacher since 1670, but we know he taught at the school for poor boys from 1653 to 1669 (ibid., no. 174, p. 26, 1 Tevet 5414: 'f 43:4'; ibid., no. 215, pp. 282–3, 5428–9). His salary in the 1660s varied between 31.4 and 132.12 guilders a year (ibid., pp. 282–3, 5428–9; ibid., no. 174, p. 169, 5421). Mendes also worked at the community preparing for Pesach (ibid., no. 215, p. 310, 5429: '18 plakken'). He had also been supported by the community since 1656 (ibid., no. 174, p. 136, 26 Tevet 5416). For rental subsidy see ibid., no. 215, p. 4, Nisan 5423; for *nedavot*: ibid., no. 216, p. 35, 5430. He seems to have had a large family of five or six members (see the distribution of matzot, ibid., no. 174, p. 620, 1 Nisan 5424: 48 *livras*).

425 SAA entry no. 334, no. 19, p. 613, 1 Nisan 5430: 2.18 guilders a month. Abraham Dias acted as *shamash* for many years. For these duties he was paid 48 guilders in 1672 (ibid., no. 294, p. 45, 5432). In 1694 his annual salary was raised (ibid., no. 1191, p. 168, 5454) to 66 guilders, plus 10 guilders for Purim and 5 guilders for 'asistir nos barcos' (apparently assisting the boats on their way to the cemetery of Ouderkerk). In 1697 he received 76 guilders in annual salary and an additional 15 guilders for Purim (ibid., p. 200, 5457).

426 See also SAA entry no. 334, no. 19, p. 613, 1 Nisan 5430: Samuel Ramirez, 2.10 guilders a month. On him see further Pieterse, *Daniel Levi de Barrios*, 103–4, 125, 131. Abraham Cohen de Lara got 3 guilders a month (SAA entry no. 334, no. 1052, p. 37, 5434).

427 SAA entry no. 334, no. 19, p. 613, 1 Nisan 5430: 'Sarah Lumbroza', 2 guilders a month. For Lumbrosa as a member of the Reformed Church see SAA entry no. 376, no. 9, p. 210, 12 July 1657; ibid., p. 211, 19 July 1657; ibid., p. 215, 6 Sept. 1657; ibid., no. 11, p. 249, 21 Oct. 1666; ibid., pp. 250, 252, 296, 28 Oct. and 4 Nov. 1666, and 28 Apr. 1667.

428 Judith and her family had been on welfare continuously since 1651, with an interruption between Rosh Hodesh Sivan 5417 (1657) and Rosh Hodesh Av 5418 (1658) (SAA entry no. 334, no. 173, p. 189, Rosh Hodesh Elul 5411; ibid., no. 174, p. 223, Rosh Hodesh Sivan 5417; ibid., p. 279, Rosh Hodesh Av 5418). In 1670 she was put on the monthly list of distributions through Abodat Ahesed (SAA entry no. 334, no. 19, p. 613, 1 Nisan 5430). At the same time she was given 18.18 guilders to marry off her daughter (ibid., no. 216, p. 2, 4 Sivan 5430; see further ibid., no. 217, pp. 6–7, 5443; ibid., no. 20, p. 177, 7 Adar 5454). For her children leaving for Italy see ibid., no. 174, p. 514, Rosh Hodesh Tamuz 5422. The departure of her children might have had something to do with the fact that one year earlier the ban on one of her sons, Abraham Vaz, was withdrawn. This son was put into *ḥerem* because of a relationship between him and his sister-in-law (ibid., no. 24, p. 14, 4 Nisan 5421; Y. Kaplan, 'The Social Functions of the Herem', 133, 154). When the ban was lifted he was ordered never to return to the community and synagogue again. Abraham left for Italy less than a year later, apparently together with some of his brothers (SAA entry no. 334, no. 174, p. 514, Rosh Hodesh Tamuz 5422). Before all this, Abraham had been expelled from the Aby Jetomim orphanage (ibid., no. 24, p. 14, 4 Nisan 5421: 'Abraham Vas, fillo de Judiq[a] Enriques de San Lucar'; 'despedido p. não acudir a sua obrigaç[en]' (ibid., no. 1211, p. 4, 5421). He left his mother in Amsterdam, together with his sister, dependent on charity (ibid., no. 217, p. 524, 5445: 50 *livras* of matzah meal were given to Judith Henriques de Sanlúcar, her daughter, and her grandchildren).

429 Marcus, *Communal Sickcare*, 162–70; M. Cohen, *Poverty and Charity*, 105–6, 233–5. In the Dutch Republic, for Delft see van der Vlis, *Leven in armoede*, 45, 56, 151, 254–5; for Friesland see Spaans, *Armenzorg in Friesland*; for Amsterdam see Wagenaar, *Amsterdam*, ii. 75–6, 86, 241–9; Querido, *Godshuizen en Gasthuizen*.

430 For shelter and food given to him see SAA entry no. 334, no. 219, p. 27, 1 Shevat 5452. For his departure to Italy: ibid., p. 101, 27 Nisan 5452.

431 For the hosting of foreigners by Amsterdam Jews see the examples in Chapter 7. For non-Jews hosting Portuguese Jews see Barbara Alberts, wife of Hendrick Jeuriaensz, street labourer ('arbeider aan de straat'), who in 1637 took in Abraham de Mercado from Hamburg as a guest in her home ('in haar huis gelogeerd heeft': SAA entry no. 5075, no. 695B, Not. Jan Warnaertsz., p. 707, 26 Aug. 1637). Sometimes the Portuguese community gave a foreigner money to cover the cost of shelter after the event, as in the case of Salomon Abinum (SAA entry no. 334, no. 216, p. 3, 18 Kislev 5430: 'a Sr Moseh Curiel pelos que pago Selomo Abinum q devia na poissada . . . f 15:2').

432 Nahon, *Les 'Nations' juives portugaises*, 149.

433 Franco Mendes, *Memorias*, 51; Menasseh ben Israel, *De la fragilidad humana*, p. ii.

434 Franco Mendes, *Memorias*, 50, 55–6; Pieterse, *Daniel Levi de Barrios*, 117–18. For Bayert see Wagenaar, *Amsterdam*, ii. 244–5; Querido, *Godshuizen en Gasthuizen*, 14. For an explanation of the significance of the number three in a sermon by Morteira see Saperstein, *Exile in Amsterdam*, 170.

435 SAA entry no. 334, no. 220, p. 16, 17 Heshvan 5460: 'a Gaspar Henriquez Pereira 3 dias de comer e poizada a m[er] de Juan de Mendoza e 10 filhos . . . f 18'; ibid.: 'a m[er] de Juan Mendossa com 10 filhos vindos de Portugal p[a] bolver e hir a Londres . . . f 60'.

436 Guimarães Sá, *Quando o rico se faz pobre*, 29.

437 Toaff, *La nazione ebrea*, 506: Pisa, *Haskamot del Libro Nuevo*, 12 Menahem-Av 5393.

438 L. D. Barnett, *Bevis Marks*, 78–9.

439 Endelman, *The Jews of Georgian England*, 168; for this rule among the Jews in Poland before 1648 see further Baron, *The Jewish Community*, ii. 324.

440 Nahon, *Les 'Nations' juives portugaises*, 186–7, art. xx.

441 SAA entry no. 334, no. 294, p. 19, 5415: 'despendido con pasageiros'.

442 SAA entry no. 334, no. 1191, p. 118, 5448. For the foundation see ibid., pp. 3 and 5.

443 Franco Mendes, *Memorias*, 69. On this *ḥevrah* see also Lieberman, '"Jonen Dalim"'.

444 Pieterse, *Daniel Levi de Barrios*, 125–7; Barrios, *Triumpho* (Biblioteca Rosenthaliana copy, RON A 5252), 288 [pencil], 320 [pencil]; Franco Mendes, *Memorias*, 84.

445 Franco Mendes, *Memorias*, 90.

446 When the *sheliḥim* (emissaries) from Hebron visited Amsterdam in the first half of the 18th century (1719, 1720, 1729, and 1737) Joseph Cohen Belinfante, a descendant of the *belogrados*, was paid for hosting them in his house (SAA entry no. 334, no. 222, p. 358, 7 Kislev and 4 Shevat 5480; ibid., p. 359, 18 Shevat 5480; ibid., p. 402, 17 Sivan 5480; ibid., no. 969, p. 54, 13 Kislev 5490; ibid., no. 970, p. 491, 1 Kislev 5498).

447 Pinto, *Reflexoens*, 10.

448 Ibid. 24–5.

449 As was decided by the Aby Jetomim society (Franco Mendes, *Memorias*, 56).

450 On organizations of the Portuguese community in Amsterdam in the 17th and 18th centuries see Hillesum, 'Vereenigingen'.

451 See e.g. the initiative to establish the loan bank Honen Dalim in 1625 after an epidemic swept through Amsterdam.

452 Pinto, *Reflexoens*, 8. On the growing poverty in this period as a result of war, harsh winters, and economic decline see Israel, *The Dutch Republic*, ch. 36; Palmer, Colton, and Kramer, *A History of the Modern World*, ch. 7, paras. 32–4; Vries, *De economische achteruitgang*; Vries and van der Woude, *The First Modern Economy*, 681–3. For extra help to the poor during this period see the collection of 1740, held because of the harsh winter of 1739/40 (Franco Mendes, *Memorias*, 117; see also SAA entry no. 334, no. 247, p. 267, 2 Shevat 5500).

453 For a society such as the Maskil el Dal to have been founded in 1673 in order to help the poor left out of *sedaca*, there must have been a clear need for its provisions and a gap in the centrally organized system (Pieterse, *Daniel Levi de Barrios*, 125).

454 On this phenomenon elsewhere in southern Europe see Trexler, 'Charity'. M. Cohen, *Poverty and Charity*, 68, maintains that shame prompted people in the Jewish community in medieval Egypt to look for private help.

455 For Italy see Bonfil, *Rabbis*, 176–7, 318–19; Rivlin, *Mutual Responsibility* (Heb.), ch. 4; Horowitz, 'Jewish Confraternities'; id., 'Membership'; Stow, *Theater of Acculturation*, 47, 104–6.

456 See Pullan, *Rich and Poor in Renaissance Venice*, 239–89; Henderson, *Piety and Charity*; Terpstra, *Abandoned Children*; Black, *Italian Confraternities*; Po-Chia Hsia, *The World of Catholic Renewal*, ch. 2.

457 Rumeu de Armas, *Historia de la previsión social en España*, chs. 10, 11, and 14; López Belinchón, *Honra, libertad y hacienda*, 30–1 n. 21; Flynn, *Sacred Charity*; Guimarães Sá, 'Ecclesiastical Structures', 267–9.

458 Guimarães Sá, 'Catholic Charity', 4.

459 Scholem, *Sabbatai Sevi*, 518–45; Y. Kaplan, *From New Christians to New Jews* (Heb.), ch. 10.

460 Carlebach, *The Pursuit of Heresy*. The ideas of spiritual leaders such as Moses Haim Luzzatto could also have had an influence. Luzzatto visited Amsterdam from 1736 to 1743, teaching and writing, and publishing his major works in the city: see Tishby, *Messianic Mysticism*; Meijer, *The Stay of Mozes Haim Luzzatto*; Melkman, *David Franco Mendes*; Ginzburg, *The Life and Works of Moses Hayyim Luzzatto*; Heide, *Messias in meervoud*.

461 For Paame Dalim see SAA entry no. 334, no. 120, file 90, pp. 974–5, 9 Iyar 5516:

'a caridade e hum dos alicerses sobre que se mantem o mundo e nao ignorando nos abaixo firmados a realidade desta tão verdadeira doutrina'. For the phrase in *Pirke Aboth* (Ethics of the Fathers) see 1: 2, p. [40].

462 SAA entry no. 334, no. 25, p. 337, 19 Tevet 5510.

463 For these patterns in traditional *kehilot* in early modern Europe see J. Katz, *Tradition and Crisis*, ch. 16.

464 An example here is the Jadrech Anavim society, established in 1707 by refugees from Belgrade. According to the historian David Franco Mendes this yeshiva was set up 'by some devout people originating from Belgrade' who gathered in a house formerly owned by Jacob Pereyra in Rapenburgerstraat. Besides study, the yeshiva was meant to support the helpless and poor of Belgrade and to assist those in need who were of the same generation as the yeshiva's founders (Franco Mendes, *Memorias*, 103). Apparently this *ḥevrah* did not last long, perhaps because many of the group emigrated. In 1762 we find it again, now managed by people with no connection to the orginal founders (SAA entry no. 5075, no. 10798, no. 847, Not. S. Dorper, 25 June 1762): the signatories of the notarial deed are Abraham da Veiga, Moses Ricardo, and Joseph Henriquez Medina, none of them indicating *belogrado* origins.

465 For conflicts within charitable organizations see Horowitz, 'Jewish Confraternities', 125–6; N. Z. Davis, 'The Sacred and the Body Social'; Rumeu de Armas, *Historia de la previsión social en España*, 252–3.

466 On the schism in Bet Jacob around 1618 see Ancona, 'Komst der Marranen', 228–39.

467 Pieterse, *Daniel Levi de Barrios*, 117, 120.

468 Ibid. 122, 124; Franco Mendes, *Memorias*, 69.

469 Hillesum mentions a hundred in total, but includes societies subordinate to the *kahal*. Study societies, burial societies, and literary societies are also on his list, yet it excludes many other types of society (Hillesum, 'Vereenigingen').

470 See e.g. the *ḥevrot* named for Keter Torah and Tora Hor: Pieterse, *Daniel Levi de Barrios*, 106–11; Lekah Tov: Franco Mendes, *Memorias*, 106, 29 Nisan 5478; Oel Ishack: SAA entry no. 334, no. 25, p. 227, 11 Sivan 5496; Mamlechet Coanim: ibid., p. 304, 5 Heshvan 5506.

471 Pieterse, *Daniel Levi de Barrios*, 106–9, 114–17.

472 Ibid., 122–7, 186–7. Out of the total membership of 270, Temime Darech had 200 female members (74%), which shows how much these women felt the need for some sort of security. Women also constituted the majority in Maskil el Dal—54% of members in 1683 (150 'sisters' out of a total of 275 members).

473 Hase Amaharacha remained quite stable, with around 90 members at the start of the 18th century to about 94 in 1750 (for 1716: SAA entry no. 334, no. 1234, pp. 76–8, 5476; for 1750: ibid., no. 1235, pp. 140–2, 5510).

474 For Dotar and Honen Dalim see Pieterse, *Daniel Levi de Barrios*, 105– 6. For Dotar see also SAA entry no. 334, no. 1163, p. 247, 5504. Honen Dalim had 700 members in 1683, while Dotar had 500 members between 1615 and 1744. Ets Haim had around 800 members between 1659 and 1750 (SAA entry no. 334, no.

1073, pp. 1–9); in 1772 Mishenet Zequenim alone had 256 sisters (ibid., no. 1223, 5532).

475 See e.g. on Maskil el Dal Pieterse, *Daniel Levi de Barrios*, 125–7; Franco Mendes, *Memorias*, 84. For Masmiah Jesuah and Migdal Oz see *Memorias*, 107.

476 *Livros pertenecentes a sancta irmandade de Abi Jetomim*, SAA entry no. 334. A, suppl. no. 195[r].

477 Franco Mendes, *Memorias*, 54. In 1745 Meir Cohen [Belinfante] asked for the new yeshiva, Mamlechet Coanim, to be authorized for the study of Maimonides (Rambam) as well (SAA entry no. 334, no. 25, p. 305, Heshvan 5506).

478 See e.g. the statutes of Honen Dalim-Resit Hochma of 20 Sivan 1741 (SAA entry no. 334, no. 25, p. 277, para. 5, 20 Sivan 5501); see also Paame Dalim (ibid., no. 120, file 90, p. 974, 1 Iyar 5516: 'de cuyo rendimento de repartira sapatos aos povres e desvalidos de nossa nação e ao mesmo tempo nos ocuparem no Estudo da Divina Ley'). Members of Tikvat aJesuah studied the 'Holy Law' (ibid., no. 25, p. 222, 5 Kislev 5496).

479 This *ḥevrah*, which met in the house of Joseph Sarfati, was probably established in 1666 (Franco Mendes, *Memorias*, 107).

480 SAA entry no. 334, no. 25, p. 222, 5 Kislev 5496.

481 SAA entry no. 334, no. 25, p. 277, para. 4, 20 Sivan 5501.

482 SAA entry no. 334, no. 120, file 89, pp. 970–2.

483 See Franco Mendes, *Memorias*, 107. The *ḥevrah* was established in 1721. As well as distributing woollen blankets in wintertime it also provided assistance to brothers and sisters who were sick or dying. In 1724 the board of this *ḥevrah* decided also to distribute meat and bread during the festivals.

484 SAA entry no. 334, no. 120, file 90, pp. 974–5, 9 Iyar 5516. Distributions took place on Pesach and Sukkot.

485 For guilds and mutual aid organizations in the Dutch Republic see M. van Leeuwen, 'Guilds and Middle-Class Welfare'; Bos, 'Beroepsgebonden onderlinges'; id., '*Onderlinge hulpverlening*'; Bos and Stamhuis, 'Begrafenisen weduwenfondsen'. There was a growing number of organizations that protected their members during periods of crisis (Israel, *The Dutch Republic*, 1015). For mutual aid societies in early modern Spain see Rumeu de Armas, *Historia de la previsión social en España*, esp. chs. 11–14. For mutual aid societies among the Jews of Christian Spain see Assis, 'Welfare and Mutual Aid'. For mutual aid societies in Jewish communities in Italy see Rivlin, *Mutual Responsibility* (Heb.).

486 See e.g. a *ḥevrah* such as Asuta Habraya, which helped sick brothers (SAA entry no. 334, no. 1215, p. 2, 5507).

487 On Temime Darech see SAA entry no. 334, no. 1214, pp. 1–18, 1680; Pieterse, *Daniel Levi de Barrios*, 122–4, 186–7; Franco Mendes, *Memorias*, 64, 69, 130; Franco Mendes, *Memorias*, 59, 84, 86–7. For Resit Hochma see Pieterse, *Daniel Levi de Barrios*, 130.

488 It had more women than men as members; on its help to poor widows see Franco Mendes, *Memorias*, 69. See also Lieberman, '"Jonen Dalim"'.

489 Franco Mendes, *Memorias*, 102–3; see also SAA entry no. 5075, no. 6054B, Not.

P. Schabaelje, pp. 1841–4, 30 Sept. 1710: property bought at Muidergracht behind the Portuguese synagogue by Henriques Elias Gabay, the treasurer of the Maasim Tobim association; see also SAA entry no. 334, no. 66, pp. 709–10, 28 Nisan 5469. For deathbed confession in Italy see Horowitz, 'Membership', 37–8.

490 For the establishment of this *ḥevrah* see SAA entry no. 334, no. 1234, 1 Heshvan 5474. For distributions to members and to the poor (there was a different procedure for each category) see e.g. SAA entry no. 334, no. 1234, [no page number], 25 Menahem-Av 5474; ibid., 4 Kislev 5479.

491 SAA entry no. 334, no. 120, file 83, p. 937, para. 3, 16 Tevet 5495.

492 SAA entry no. 334, no. 25, pp. 330–2, 13 Tamuz 5509.

493 Oneg Sabat was established in 1747 (SAA entry no. 334, no. 25, pp. 315–17, 15 Kislev 5508).

494 SAA entry no. 334, no. 1234, p. 2, para. 5, 1 Heshvan 5474.

495 See e.g. Oneg Sabat: SAA entry no. 334, no. 25, p. 317, para. 4, 25 Kislev 5508; Roffe Holim: ibid., pp. 330–2, paras. 3 and 8, 13 Tamuz 5509.

496 Horowitz, 'Jewish Confraternities', 19–57; id., '*Yeshiva* and *Hevra*'; Bonfil, *Rabbis*, 319–20. In the German states and central Europe similar youth societies only arose in the mid- and late 18th century (Marcus, *Communal Sickcare*, ch. 7). For youth organizations in non-Jewish society in late medieval and early modern times see Polizzotto, *Children of the Promise*; Black, *Italian Confraternities*, 47–9.

497 'Como o mundo não pode subsistir sem a meditasão da sagrada ley e caridade nos empregamos em fazer esta pia Irmandade que esperamos no soberano Senhor no de sua aJuda para establesimento desta santa Jesiba' (Hateret Tipheret: SAA entry no. 334, no. 25, p. 268, para. 23, 7 Iyar 5501).

498 This *Caminho de Vidas* was intended to lead his children towards virtue: *emcaminhar a seus Filhos na Virtude* (Saruco, *Caminho de Vidas*, 30–2). Saruco was appointed to teach the children of Imanuel Israel Suasso at his house in The Hague in 1743; he stayed until 1751. For Saruco as the *haham* and *ḥazan* of the Portuguese Jewish community of The Hague after 1751 see Zwarts, *Hoofdstukken*, 204–46.

499 Ishack de Matatia Aboab, *Documentos*. Such educational treatises are also well known in non-Jewish circles (Dekker, *Uit de schaduw*, esp. chs. 1–2).

500 Thus Horowitz, 'Jewish Confraternities', ch. 2, explains the rise of youth organizations in Italy; for the preparation of young people for administrative responsibility through confraternities in Italy see Polizzotto, *Children of the Promise*, 123.

501 See the letter written by Eliasib Sarfati, then 66 years old, on behalf of the members of the Haberim Magsibim *ḥevrah* to the community leaders (SAA entry no. 334, no. 120, file 85, p. 960, 22 Tamuz 5524; SAA DTB 711, p. 47, 13 Aug. 1717). The members for whom he wrote were aged between 12 and 27: Natan Sarfati, 27 years old (SAA DTB 750, p. 152, 20 Feb. 1778); Samuel Meldola, 12 years old (SAA DTB 754, p. 115, 16 Feb. 1784); Salomon Machorro, 16 years old (SAA DTB 746, p. 68, 26 Apr. 1771); Eliasib Meldola, 16 years old (SAA DTB 750, p. 88, 28 Nov. 1777). Meir Cohen Belinfante, then 43 years old, was *rosh yeshivah* of Keter Torah (SAA DTB 714, p. 108, 27 Jan. 1724). In the Haberim Magsibim *ḥevrah*, the above-mentioned Natan Sarfati, aged 27, seemed to be the leader of the younger boys and also took care of the finances in his capacity as treasurer (SAA entry no. 334, no. 120, file 85, p. 962, 22 Tamuz 5524).

502 Pieterse, *Daniel Levi de Barrios*, 113–14, 127–9; Franco Mendes, *Memorias*, 54, 71, 90.

503 Saperstein, *Exile in Amsterdam*, 173–4.

504 For Keter Torah in 1745 see SAA entry no. 334, no. 25, pp. 297–8, 3 Av 5505. For Haberim Magsibim in 1764 see ibid., no. 120, file 85, pp. 958–63, 22 Tamuz 5524.

505 For Tipheret Bajurim see Pieterse, *Daniel Levi de Barrios*, 113–14. For Hateret Bahurim see SAA entry no. 334, no. 25, p. 240, 2 Heshvan 5498. For Keter Torah see ibid., pp. 297–8, 3 Av 5505.

506 For these organizations see Pieterse, *Daniel Levi de Barrios*, 113–14, 127–31. For the date of 1666 for the foundation of Bahale Tesuba see ibid. 91, 130. For Tipheret Bajurim see Franco Mendes, *Memorias*, 71, and for Keter Sem Tob and Sahare Sedek, ibid. 90.

507 For the requirements for membership of Bikur Holim see SAA entry no. 334, no. 19, p. 17/102, 33 Omer 5399.

508 Examples of young men in this age group belonging to Keter Torah in 1745 are: David Naar, 24 years old (SAA DTB 722, p. 267, 22 Feb. 1737); Joseph Haim Azuby, 21 (SAA DTB 727, p. 159, 23 Apr. 1744); Samuel de David Curiel, 24 (SAA DTB 731, p. 288, 19 Mar. 1751); Is. de El. Cohen Belinfante, 20 (SAA DTB 726, p. 420, 28 June 1743); Is. Haim Rodrigues da Costa, 29 (SAA DTB 727, p. 215, 12 June 1744).

509 Pieterse, *Daniel Levi de Barrios*, 131.

510 SAA entry no. 334, no. 1052, pp. 34–5, 10 Nisan 5432; see also Y. Kaplan, 'Secularizing the Portuguese Jews', 107–9.

511 SAA entry no. 334, no. 25, p. 251, para. 9, 7 Heshvan 5500: statutes of Honen Dal; see also ibid., p. 261, 19 Shevat 5501.

512 For Haberim Magsibim see SAA entry no. 334, no. 120, file 85, pp. 958–63, 22 Tamuz 5524. For Kisuy Ros see SAA entry no. 334, no. 25, pp. 258–60, 20 Tevet 5501. For Honen Dal (Menahem Aniim) see SAA entry no. 334, no. 25, pp. 250–3, 7 Heshvan 5500. For Hateret Tipheret see SAA entry no. 334, no. 25, pp. 264–9, 7 Iyar 5501.

513 The Keter Sem Tob society was founded by Abraham Orobio de Castro in 1679. This son of the famous doctor and philosopher Isaac Orobio de Castro was then 13 years old (age based on SAA DTB 699, p. 106, 22 July 1695; on him see also Y. Kaplan, *From Christianity to Judaism*, 107, 208, 304). It is possible that his father and the fathers of the other original members took the initiative to provide suitable occupation for their sons in the period after the barmitzvah. Isaac de Azevedo was born in 1665, so he was 14 years old (SAA DTB 703, p. 154, 20 Oct. 1702). Isaac Gabay Faro was 14 in 1679 (SAA DTB 700, p. 4, 26 Oct. 1696). In Sahare Sedek the average age was also around 13–15, with some exceptions: Isaac Coen Lobato, 14 years old (SAA DTB 699, p. 51, 6 May 1695); Daniel de Paz, 15

(SAA DTB 697, p. 102, 30 Mar. 1691); Moses de Joseph Levi, 13 (SAA DTB 694, p. 150, 23 July 1684); Joseph Capadoce, 13 (SAA DTB 697, p. 166, 16 June 1691); Abraham Lopes Arias, 20 (SAA DTB 695, p. 243, 7 Sept. 1686).

514 For Joseph Franco Serrano see Pieterse, *Daniel Levi de Barrios*, 104, 113, 119, 123, 126, 128, 186. For David Nunes Torres see ibid. 113, 119.

515 For the Belinfantes active in these youth societies see the records of Honen Dal, whose members first met in 1740 at the house of Isaac de Eliau Hesqia Cohen Belinfante, and later in the study rooms of Ets Haim (SAA entry no. 334, no. 25, pp. 250–3, 7 Heshvan 5500; ibid., p. 261, 19 Shevat 5501). (SAA entry no. 334, no. 25, Keter Torah, founded in 1745, had one Belinfante initiator, namely Is: de Eliau Cohen Belinfante, and Sadik Cohen Belinfante as an assistant to the *rosh yeshivah*, who happened to be Meir Cohen [Belinfante] (SAA entry no. 334, no. 25, pp. 297–8, 3 Av 5505). On the Belinfante family see further the literature cited in Divendal, 'Mozes Cohen Belinfante'; also Levie Bernfeld, 'Confrontation entre l'Orient et l'Occident', 50–2, 57–9. On the gravestone of Abraham Siprut di Gabay it is written that he taught every day in his *midrash* (SAA entry no. 334, no. 1329, p. 245, 17 Heshvan 5494). Abraham Siprut di Gabay had also taught the famous poet David Franco Mendes and introduced him to kabbalah (Melkman, *David Franco Mendes*, 36, 133); Abraham is also mentioned as a rabbi of the Somer Holim *ḥevrah* (Franco Mendes, *Memorias*, 103. See also Melkman, *David Franco Mendes*, 36 and n. 25; Pieterse, *Daniel Levi de Barrios*; and on the family see further Levie Bernfeld, 'Confrontation entre l'Orient et l'Occident', 49–52, 58).

516 Pieterse, *Daniel Levi de Barrios*, 113–14, 128–9.

517 Members of Keter Torah met on Friday afternoons and other free days in the *midrash* of Haham R. da Meza (SAA entry no. 334, no. 25, pp. 297–8, 3 Av 5505); members of Honen Dal or Menahem Aniim first met in the yeshiva of Aby Jetomim, then in the house of Isaac de Eliau Hesqia Cohen Belinfante (SAA entry no. 334, no. 25, pp. 250–3, 7 Heshvan 5500), and later in the classrooms of Talmud Torah and/or Ets Haim (SAA entry no. 334, no. 25, p. 261, 19 Shevat 5501). The members of Kisuy Ros also met in the classroom of the religious community academy (ibid.).

518 Pieterse, *Daniel Levi de Barrios*, 113.

519 SAA entry no. 334, no. 120, file 85, p. 960, 22 Tamuz 5524.

520 Franco Mendes, *Memorias*, 54. No mention is made of this group's year of foundation, but it must have been around 1642–3.

521 Franco Mendes, *Memorias*, 90–1; Pieterse, *Daniel Levi de Barrios*, 128–9, 131. Funds to pay for the welfare provided would come from members' monthly contributions.

522 Honen Dal/Menahem Aniim distributed linen to the poor (SAA entry no. 334, no. 25, pp. 250–3, 7 Heshvan 5500); Hateret Tipheret distributed hats and wigs (ibid., pp. 264–9, 7 Iyar 5501).

523 For Kisuy Ros see SAA entry no. 334, no. 25, pp. 258–60, 20 Tevet 5501.

524 SAA entry no. 334, no. 25 pp. 264–9, 7 Iyar 5501.

525 For Honen Dal/Menahem Aniim see SAA entry no. 334, no. 25, pp. 250–3, paras. 3 and 5, 7 Heshvan 5500; for Kisuy Ros see also para. 6 (ibid., p. 259, 20 Tevet 5501).

526 See para. 4 of Haberim Magsibim (SAA entry no. 334, no. 120, file 85, p. 962, 22 Tamuz 5524); see also para. 6 of the *ḥevrah* Kisuy Ros (ibid., no. 25, p. 259, 20 Tevet 5501).

527 Regarding the financial situation of members of Tipheret Bajurim (and their parents), David Bueno de Mesquita, father of Abraham, paid quite a high level of *finta* (SAA entry no. 334, no. 175, p. 308, 8 Elul 5445: 'meia finta f 15,–'); Abraham Mendes da Silva, father of Isaac, was also taxed on a relatively high level of wealth (ibid., p. 306: 'f 18, meia finta'). The young adult members of this *ḥevrah* were not all that young: Abraham de David Bueno de Mesquita was 30 in 1683 (SAA DTB 690, p. 181, 17 Apr. 1676) and paid 'meia finta' of 7.10 guilders (SAA entry no. 334, no. 175, p. 99, 1 Nisan 5440). Isaac de Abraham Mendes da Silva was 26 in 1683 (SAA DTB 693, p. 426, 15 Sept. 1683). Perhaps they were the 'young leadership'.

528 For Sahare Sedek see Mordecai Senior, father of David (ibid., p. 109, 1 Nisan 5440: 'f 15,– meia finta'). Moses Gabbai Henriques, father of Jacob, paid less, 4 guilders 'meia finta' (ibid., p. 108, 1 Nisan 5440).

529 Polizzotto, *Children of the Promise*, 201–3.

530 For Jacob Velho as a child in the poor school see SAA entry no. 334, no. 215, pp. 132–3, 5425–6; for David Cohen Peixotto as a poor man and teacher on welfare since 1666 see ibid., pp. 107, 201, 5426–7; ibid., no. 174, p. 731, 20 Adar 5426; ibid., no. 176, p. 377, 2 Nisan 5461. Sabbatai Roldão was put on the welfare list in 1700 (ibid., no. 20, p. 282, [n.d.] 5460).

531 There were no women among the twenty founders of Dotar in 1615, although they were invited to become members if they were unmarried, widowed, or married with a husband outside the Republic. This was on condition that, if a husband did appear, he would take her place in the *ḥevrah*. The women did not have a vote, but otherwise enjoyed all the privileges of membership for their family and any impoverished descendants (SAA entry no. 334, no. 1322, pp. B–B3, esp. ch. 8, 13 Adar 5375).

532 For Spain see Flynn, *Sacred Charity*, 23–4, 56; Rumeu de Armas, *Historia de la previsión social en España*, 242–4. For Portugal see Guimarães Sá, 'Entre Maria e Madalena'. For Italy see Black, *Italian Confraternities*, 34–8; id., *Early Modern Italy*, 160–2; Terpstra, *Abandoned Children*, 116–32. For female confraternities in western Europe see Hufton, *The Prospect before Her*, 381–90, 490.

533 Rivlin, *Mutual Responsibility* (Heb.), 112–13; Baron, *The Jewish Community*, i. 349; Marcus, *Communal Sickcare*, 135–45; Debra Kaplan, 'Women and Worth', 13. In his last will of 1691 an Ashkenazi Jew of Amsterdam, Joseph Salomons, left a legacy to the sisterhood for clothing poor orphans ('aen het susterschap van het kleeden der arme weeskinderen': SAA entry no. 5075, no. 4242, Not. D. van der Groe, pp. 348–57, 14 June 1692). Horowitz, 'Membership', 38, 51, mentions the declining membership of women in the Gemilut Hasadim society of Ferrara.

534 For the involvement of women in the Aby Jetomim boys' orphanage see SAA entry no. 334, no. 1211, pp. 26^{r-v}, 56–65, [n.d.] 5408–62. According to the information we have, almost the same number of female as male members left legacies to the orphanage (Pieterse, *Daniel Levi de Barrios*, 118); see also Levie Bernfeld, 'Mujeres judías hispano-portuguesas', 146–7, and ead., 'Sephardi Women in Holland's Golden Age', 198. Female members of Aby Jetomim were also mobilized to make clothes for the children (SAA entry no. 334, no. 1211, pp. 2^{v}–3, 5414). Aby Jetomim also had a clause in its founding statutes covering the care of poor widows (Barrios, *Triumpho* (Biblioteca Rosenthaliana copy, RON A 5252), 188 [pencil]: 'a la pobre viudez es apacible'). For the involvement of women in the girls' orphanage see SAA entry no. 334, no. 120, file 81, pp. 909–14, 6 Shevat 5494. For an overview of female members of Mishenet Zequenim, the old-age home, see the lists of female members in SAA entry no. 334, no. 1223, 5532.

535 For Temime Darech see SAA entry no. 334, no. 1214, p. 10, 1672, art. 13: sick sisters would be given assistance, but brothers were privileged. See also the statutes of Mayafu Pehameha Benealim (SAA entry no. 334, no. 25, pp. 244–8, para. 9, 26 Adar II 5499), in which, concerning distribution of shoes to the poor, it is decided that men will be supplied first and women given shoes only if there is enough capital.

536 SAA entry no. 334, no. 172, p. 311, Rosh Hodesh Iyar 5405: 18%; ibid., no. 174, pp. 750–1, Rosh Hodesh Iyar 5426: 25%; ibid., no. 176, pp. 296–7, Rosh Hodesh Adar II 5445: 37%; ibid., p. 349, Rosh Hodesh Nisan 5460: 24%; ibid., no. 974, file a, pp. 1–19, 1734: 24%; ibid., file f, pp. 1–11, 5512: 31%. The percentage of widows is similar to that calculated for cities such as Zwolle, Leiden, and Delft: Schmidt, *Overleven na de dood*, 172–3; van der Vlis, *Leven in armoede*, 77; Wijngaarden, *Zorg voor de Kost*, 88; see also Hufton, *The Prospect before Her*, 221, 246; Norberg, *Rich and Poor in Grenoble*, 106; and Flynn, *Sacred Charity*, 23–4.

537 SAA entry no. 5004, no. 110 (Calisregisters), p. 146, 29 Sept. 1701.

538 The widow of Dr Benjamin de Sea was on welfare continuously from 1677 (SAA entry no. 334, no. 174, p. 1169, Rosh Hodesh Shevat 5437) until her death in 1687 (ibid., no. 175, p. 377, Rosh Hodesh Iyar 5447; for other distributions since 1673: ibid., no. 216, p. 158, 5433–4: *nedavot*; ibid., p. 185, 5434–5: rental subsidy; ibid., p. 186, 5435: peat; ibid., p. 189, 5435: 20 *livras* of matzah meal; ibid., no. 217, p. 8, 1 Iyar 5436; ibid., p. 9, 1 Tamuz 5436). As a widow she was apparently left with two children (ibid., no. 217, p. 52, 5437: 24 *livras* of matzah meal). Her daughter, on her marriage in 1688, told the authorities that her parents were no longer alive (SAA DTB 696, p. 86, 2 Apr. 1688). On this occasion the daughter received a dowry of 802.13 guilders [*sic*] through the legacy of Joseph Soares (SAA entry no. 334, no. 175, p. 422, Rosh Hodesh Iyar 5448). For the widow of the pharmacist Jacob Coronel see ibid., no. 173, p. 258, 23 Adar II 5413. For the widow of Dr Serrano see ibid., no. 216, p. 165, 4 Adar II 5434; ibid., no. 217, p. 158, 2 Heshvan 5440; ibid., p. 329, 5442: peat; a 'Veuva do Dotor' (it is not known which one) was accepted at the monthly lists of welfare distributions (ibid., no. 19, p. 756, 8 Tevet 5437).

539 Rumeu de Armas, *Historia de la previsión social en España*, 360–2. For Italy see Black, *Italian Confraternities*, 206–13.

540 On Rehobot see Franco Mendes, *Memorias*, 103–4; on institutions for women in southern Europe see Guimarães Sá, 'Entre Maria e Madalena', 995; on retirement houses for white Portuguese women in Bahia (Brazil) see Russell-Wood, *Fidalgos and Philanthropists*, ch. 13.

541 Pieterse, *Daniel Levi de Barrios*, 124–5; Franco Mendes, *Memorias*, 69. Later, in 1741, this *ḥevrah* co-ordinated its activities with those of Resit Hochma, distributing food to the poor of the Spanish and Portuguese nation (SAA entry no. 334, no. 25, pp. 275–82, 20 Sivan 5501).

542 For Berit Salom see SAA entry no. 334, no. 25, p. 199, 24 Tamuz 5490. Mispat Abanot (ibid., entry no. 334.A, suppl., no. 195m, 4 Elul 5490) was also a mutual aid society, giving a higher weekly portion of money to members (male and female) of the organization.

543 SAA entry no. 334, no. 25, p. 212, 19 Kislev 5494; ibid., no. 120, file 84, pp. 943–53, 21 Heshvan 5517; Franco Mendes, *Memorias*, 116.

544 For the general political and economic climate in the 1740s see Palmer, Colton, and Kramer, *A History of the Modern World*, ch. 7; Vries and van der Woude, *The First Modern Economy*, 681–7; Israel, *The Dutch Republic*, 998–1018; Vries, *De economische achteruitgang*.

545 Franco Mendes, *Memorias*, 117; see also SAA entry no. 334, no. 247, p. 267, 2 Shevat 5500.

546 For Hesrat Nasim see SAA entry no. 334, no. 25, pp. 270–2, 14 Iyar 5501. For Quesut La Ebion see ibid., pp. 321–4, 24 Menahem-Av 5508.

547 For Parnasad Almanot see SAA entry no. 334, no. 27, pp. 8–10, 7 Kislev 5527. Its statutes of 1767 give sinful behaviour among the Spanish and Portuguese nation as an explanation for the misery of various widows (ibid., no. 120, file 88, p. 965: 'havendo por pecados em nossa nacao Portugeza e Espanhola varias viuvas quais padessem muita mizeria').

548 Guimarães Sá, 'Catholic Charity', 11–12; Pullan, *Rich and Poor in Renaissance Venice*, 276.

549 For Amsterdam see Wagenaar, *Amsterdam*, ii. 241–50, 262, 301–7, 332–6, 340–1.

550 Arede built three houses at the Keizersgracht for this purpose (Franco Mendes, *Memorias*, 103–4). It could be to this establishment that Rica de Leon left money intended for the orphans of Isaac Brandon (for her last will see SAA entry no. 5075, no. 7533, Not. J. van Vilekens, pp. 1197–1202, 31 Oct. 1710).

551 The *ḥevrah* for the care of old people was established on 28 Dec. 1749: SAA entry no. 334, no. 25, pp. 343–6, paras. 24, 31, 19 Tevet 5510; on 17 March 1750 a house was bought in Weesperstraat on the corner of Nieuwe Keizersgracht for the price of 6,000 guilders: SAA entry no. 334, no. 1227, [no page], 19 Adar II 5510; see also ibid., no. 1220, p. 11, 9 Adar II 5510.

552 The initial goal of this pious fraternity was to support 'decent old men and women of our nation so that they no longer have to beg' (SAA entry no. 334, no.

25, p. 337, 8 Tevet 5510; ibid., p. 345, para. 31, 8 Tevet 5510). For the entry into the house of the first inhabitants—'que no ditto mez se Recolherão na Caza Aron de Paz, Selomoh do Porto, Daniel da Silva Solis & Ab[m] Ferro & que Irrevogavelm[te] se admitisão duas velhas p[a] a primeijra ocasião'—see ibid., no. 1220, p. 23, para. 2, 4 Nisan 5511.

553 *Escamot* of the *ḥevrah* Mishenet Zequenim: SAA entry no. 334, no. 25, pp. 343–4, para. 26, 8 Tevet 5510; ibid., entry no. 334.A, suppl., no. 191 jjj, para. 9, pp. 20–1, 5513. The full sequence of priorities was as follows: first, Spanish or Portuguese members of the organization, male or female, living in the city, who had paid their membership fees for six consecutive years; second, Spanish or Portuguese members of the organization, male or female, from abroad, who had been settled in the city for at least one year and had paid their membership fees for six consecutive years; third, Spanish or Portuguese natives of the city who were not members of the organization but who had lived in the city for at least twenty-five years; and fourth, the foreigner ('o estrangeiro') who had been settled in the city for at least six years. Refugees from the Inquisition coming straight from Spain and Portugal would be eligible for entry under the third category.

554 SAA entry no. 334, no. 1223, 5532. For members in Bayonne see also Szapiro, 'Le Sud-Ouest', 238.

555 'Reformação das escamoth': SAA entry no. 334.A, suppl., no. 191 jjj, p. 17, art. 1, 21 Adar I 5513; see also Franco Mendes, *Memorias*, 130. For entry of men to the old-age home see e.g. SAA entry no. 334, no. 1220, p. 43, 4 Nisan 5513; ibid., p. 51, 17 Shevat 5515; ibid., p. 63, 11 Tevet 5518; ibid., p. 97, 15 Tamuz 5525; ibid., p. 153, 9 Adar 5536.

556 SAA entry no. 334.A, suppl., no. 191 jjj, pp. 18–19, art. 5, 21 Adar I 5513.

557 SAA entry no. 334, no. 1220, p. 65, 8 Shevat 5518; ibid., p. 66, 9 Nisan 5518.

558 SAA entry no. 334, no. 1220, pp. 24–5, 12 Nisan 5511: 'Reglamento Renovado . . . para os Velhos & Pays dessa casa'. On the sabbath and on festival days the father of the house should say 'amosi' (the blessing over bread) and the blessings after the meal; he should read the Haggadah and the Megillah and light the 'Hanuquilha' (Hanukah lamp); the mother of the house should light the sabbath candles.

559 SAA entry no. 334, no. 1220, p. 10, 2 Adar II 5510; ibid., p. 12, 8 Nisan 5510; ibid., p. 13, 24 Nisan 5510. For the rules of the yeshiva see SAA entry no. 334.A, suppl., no. 191 jjj, pp. 28–9, 21 Adar I 5513. See also Franco Mendes, *Memorias*, 130.

560 In 1639 it had already been stated that nothing could be ordained or said in the synagogue on behalf of any *ḥevrah* without the approval of the Mahamad (SAA entry no. 334, no. 19, p. 24/109, para. 29, 5399; ibid., p. 482, 4 Tevet 5421). In 1714 the leaders of the Portuguese community declared that it would not be possible to establish any more yeshivot (SAA entry no. 334, no. 25, p. 127, 30 Iyar 5474).

561 SAA entry no. 334, no. 22, p. 260, 17 Tevet 5527.

562 Pullan came to a similar conclusion in reflecting upon the organization of welfare in the Venetian Republic: 'The machinery for the relief of the poor in the Venetian Republic in the 16th and early 17th century was formed by the blending together of old and new institutions, without a clear break with the past.' *Rich and Poor in Renaissance Venice*, 633.

5 Financing Charity

1 For an earlier discussion on this subject see Levie Bernfeld, 'Financing Poor Relief'.

2 This rule was intended to be inviolable and to be observed at all times (SAA entry no. 334, no. 19, p. 5/85, para. 38, 28 Elul 5398/28 Adar II 5399; SAA entry no. 334, no. 19, pp. 1/77–7/89, 28 Elul 5398/28 Adar II 5399; Pieterse, *Daniel Levi de Barrios*, 164).

3 See e.g. the resolutions in 1654 after the end of the first Anglo-Dutch War, or after the year of disaster of 1672, when France, England, and other nations invaded the Dutch Republic (for the wars of the Dutch Republic with England and France during the 17th century see Palmer, Colton, and Kramer, *A History of the Modern World*, 154). Measures were devised to increase revenue: we find the same phrase in 1673 as in 1654, referring to para. 38 of the *escamot* (SAA entry no. 334, no. 19, p. 366, 3 Tamuz 5414; ibid., p. 676, 13 Nisan 5433; ibid., nos. 239–43, 248, 253–4, *Livro grande*). According to the special *sedaca* bookkeeping which forms part of the total survey on income and expenditure, expenditure on welfare and all other items of the *sedaca* account exceeded income in many years (see Appendix I, Table 15).

4 Pieterse, *Inventaris*, 30–4, 44–56 (finances and bookkeeping); SAA entry no. 334, nos. 172–86 (*manual*); ibid., nos. 239–54 (*livros grandes*); ibid., nos. 215–23 (*livros longos*), nos. 969–70 (*livros longos de cuatro contas*).

5 Concerning the management of private accounts see SAA entry no. 334, no. 242, p. 17, 5450.

6 *Livros grandes* (SAA entry no. 334, nos. 239–54).

7 Frisch, *An Historical Survey*, 103 n. 7.

8 See Appendix I, Table 23; Appendix II, Figure 2.

9 Diamond, 'The Community of Resettlement', 147.

10 M. van Leeuwen, 'Liefdadige giften', 417.

11 Until 1670 expenditure also included spending on welfare for Ashkenazim through Abodat Ahesed.

12 See Appendix I, Table 15.

13 Ibid.

14 The term 'nominal' refers to the actual figure in the particular year(s) mentioned, whereas the term 'real' takes inflation rates into account. The calculation is based on tables provided by the International Institute of Social History in Amsterdam (<http://www.iisg.nl/hpw/calculate.php>). For details of the community's income and welfare expenditure through the *sedaca* account see Appendix I, Table 23, and SAA entry no. 334, nos. 239, 240, 242, 248, 254. Calculations of welfare expenditure are based on the amount spent on people in the Amsterdam Portuguese community in receipt of welfare between 1640/1 and 1793/4. These costs in-

cluded expenses on distributions in money and in kind (monthly gifts, welfare distributed before holidays and on other, urgent, occasions, travel and rental subsidies, loans, peat, matzot, clothes, and medical and burial services).

15 Baron, *The Jewish Community*, vol. ii, ch. 15; Frisch, *An Historical Survey*, 100–1, 103–4. For an analysis of the tax system of the Amsterdam Portuguese community see Swetschinski, *Reluctant Cosmopolitans*, 196–8; id., 'The Portuguese Jewish Merchants of Seventeenth-Century Amsterdam', 378–81, 391–411. Unlike Jewish communities elsewhere in Europe, the Jews in the Dutch Republic were not obliged to pay a communal tax to the government authorities.

16 In his sermons Haham Saul Levi Morteira criticized his public for its aversion to paying tax to fund welfare expenditure (Saperstein, *Exile in Amsterdam*, 193–5).

17 The stipulations relating to the *imposta* changed over time. Also, members had to be pressed to pay the tax more frequently as time went by (SAA entry no. 334, no. 19, p. 2/79–2^{v}/80, paras. 8 and 15, 28 Elul 5398–28 Adar II 5399; ibid., pp. 25/110–7/112, 22 Tamuz 5399; ibid., p. 103/188, 27 Elul 5401; ibid., pp. 366–7, 3 Tamuz 5414; ibid., p. 707, 14 Tevet 5435; ibid., p. 715, 24 [*sic*] Rosh Hodesh Shevat 5435; ibid., p. 720, Rosh Hodesh Shevat 5435; ibid., no. 20, p. 139, 4 Tamuz 5450; ibid., no. 22, p. 93, 20 Adar 5492; ibid., p. 125, 4 Adar 5496; ibid., pp. 162–5, 25 Heshvan 5508; ibid., p. 221, 26 Shevat 5520; ibid., p. 222, 28 Adar 5520; ibid., p. 236, 10 Av 5521; ibid., pp. 243–4, 5 Tishrei 5523; ibid., p. 260, 17 Tevet 5527). See also Swetschinski, 'The Portuguese Jewish Merchants of Seventeenth-Century Amsterdam', 379; Pohl, *Die Portugiesen in Antwerpen*, 54–6; Vlessing, 'New Light', 43–75; ead., 'The Portuguese Jewish Merchant Community', 223–43. For the introduction of a similar tax in Livorno in 1665 see Baron, *The Jewish Community*, ii. 265.

18 See Appendix I, Table 16; Appendix II, Figure 4.

19 Baron, *The Jewish Community*, ii. 256–60.

20 See the decision of the *imposta* board to co-ordinate the meat supply (SAA entry no. 334, no. 13, pp. 19–21, 5383). Before 1639 income from the meat hall went to the funds of the *imposta* to support the general expenses of the Portuguese community and to cover expenses on welfare in particular (see the balance sheet of 1634: ibid., p. 110, 11 Nisan 5394).

21 For the financial overviews of the *carniseria* (meat hall) see SAA entry no. 334, no. 18, p. 87^{r-v}, 25 Shevat 5393 and 8 Iyar 5394; on the *carniseria* see also Koen, 'De vleesvoorziening'.

22 SAA entry no. 334, no. 19, pp. 493–4, [27 Av] 5421; see the earlier declaration of 1651 (ibid., p. 308, 25 Sivan 5411). The appeal of 1651 seems to have been successful since the yield of the *promessas* in 1652–3 was higher than that of the year before (see Appendix I, Table 17).

23 For lists of people who did not pay their debts, could not pay their taxes, or were on a lower tax rate see SAA entry no. 334, no. 175, p. 38, 8 Nisan 5438; ibid., p. 447, 24 Adar 5449; ibid., no. 176, p. 350, 1 Nisan 5460.

24 SAA entry no. 334, no. 19, p. 22/107, para. 12, 22 Tamuz 5399: 'Que o sabat antes de cada hua das 3 Pascoas, se fara Nedava de selos peamjm, que o Mahamad repartirá por os pobres de nossa nação'; see also Baron, *The Jewish Community*, ii. 319–25; Frisch, *An Historical Survey*, 104; Swetschinski, *Reluctant Cosmopolitans*, 197.

25 SAA entry no. 334, no. 19, p. 22/107, para. 14, 22 Tamuz 5399: 'Que Dia de Purim se tirarâ por toda a congregacão Ma'ot Purim E p^{a} Sedaca e mais caxinhas como he Costume. E os particulares q qizerem tirar, pedirão l^{ca} aos s^{res} do Mahamad declarando as pessoas p^{a} quem tirão p^{a} que não haja duas tacas p^{a} hua mesmo pobre. E o que renderem as tacas de Maot Purim E Sedaca se repartirá logo, som^{te} por Pobres.'

26 Help was given to the poor during the First Anglo-Dutch War (SAA entry no. 334, no. 174, p. 9, 18 Av 5413). For collection and distribution to the poor in the mid-1740s during the War of the Austrian Succession and a period of extreme need see ibid., no. 180, p. 42, 1 Adar 5501: 'nedaba extraordinaria para se repartir de contado pelos pobres . . . f 1798:6 que se repartirão por ordem dosss^{res} do Mahamad'. An epidemic, for example the one raging in Amsterdam in the years 1655/6, was another reason to gather and distribute to the poor (SAA entry no. 334, no. 174, p. 136, 26 Tevet 5416: 'f 1.016:14 nedaba feitta em 25 de ditto para repartir logo p. pobres vergonçantes e de sedaca pla merçe que el Dio fez escapar seu povo do contagio que ouve na çidade'); on this epidemic see also Commelin, *Beschryving*, 1180–1. Another distribution to the poor took place during the epidemic of 1664 (SAA entry no. 334, no. 174, p. 636, 8 Nisan 5424). For the collection for the poor during the cold winter of 1662/3 see ibid., pp. 537–40, 8 Shevat 5423: 'f 3229:10 . . . por tantos que Importou que se prometteo em 27 de Tebet ultimo passado deste Anno pera a nedaba . . . pera acudir e socorrer a todos os pobres . . . por via de socorro extraordinario por causa do grande e Riguroso Inverno'; ibid., pp. 540–3, 10 Shevat 5423: 'f 3.622, . . . pelloque se a Repartido e Se a de repartir por conta da nedaba q se fes em 27: de Tebet ultimo passado pera os pobres'. For money distributed to the poor because of illness in 1693 see SAA entry no. 334, no. 176, p. 148, 16 Heshvan 5454: 'Moseh de Ab: mocata deve p. Sedaca . . . f 312, = cobrados da nedava asima que Rendeo'; ibid.: 'Sedaka em q^{ta} de Rendim^{to} e despezas . . . f 430,= Repartindo de nedava que se fes p. causa de enfermidades'. Another collection and distribution took place in 1727 because of sickness among the poor: SAA entry no. 334, no. 246, p. 38, 2 Heshvan 5488: 'pelo repartido extra 2/m pela nedaba que ouve f 4008:15'; ibid., p. 38, 10 Heshvan 5488: 'f 1114,– . . . que pagarão . . . da nedaba se fes pelas doensas'. At the time when the epidemic was raging in Amsterdam and when there was another influx of refugees from the Iberian peninsula (1727/8), more peat and matzot were being distributed (ibid., no. 21, p. 425, 25 Shevat 5488). See also the declaration of Abraham de Cordova, in which he says that in 1727 he and his whole family had been very sick for almost eight months (SAA entry no. 5072, no. 731, p. 3, 22 Mar. 1729). For help to the poor in the Portuguese Jewish community in the harsh winter of 1739/40 see SAA entry no. 334, no. 247, p. 267, 2 Shevat 5500: 'que se repartirão pela povreza pelos rois da sedaca, abodad aheset e 6/S: f 2251:6'. See also Appendix I, Table 24. For a comparison with the collections by non-Jewish institutions in Amsterdam, where yields were mostly lower, see M. van Leeuwen, 'Liefdadige giften', 434–8.

27 Thus there was a collection for sick care and clothing for the poor (Vestiaria and Bikur Holim) respectively on Shabbat Hanukah and on Shabbat Mikamokha (the sabbath before Purim in Sephardi tradition) (SAA entry no. 334, no. 19, p. 19/104, 33 Omer 5399: 'A Vestiarya se fará de todas as promessas E rendim^{to} que no dia de Hanukah houver que se aplica tudo p^{a} elle . . . Em Sabat Mi kamoha sé farã nedavah geral p^{a} a despensa desta Sta Hebrah'). On Shabbat Nahamu (the sabbath following Tisha Be'av) one could give money for Erets Yisra'el (Terra Santa): ibid., p. 22/107, para. 13, 22 Tamuz 5399: 'Que se fara Nedavah p^{a} terra s^{ta} por Sabat Nahamuh'. On Shavuot money could be given to the schools of the Portuguese community (Talmud Torah and Ets Haim).

For captives (*cativos*) the administration could collect when necessary: SAA entry no. 334, no. 19, p. 22, para. 13, 22 Tamuz–28 Av 5399: 'e p^{a} Cativos (sendo q as necessidades sobrepuyem ao Rendim^{to} desta Misvah) se fara tambem Nedavah quando pareçer ao Mahamad'. For the celebration of different *ḥevrot* on specific days, common in Jewish Spain, apparently adopting the custom from Christian practices, see Saperstein, *Exile in Amsterdam*, 175 and n. 103.

28 Space must have been found for a variety of separate boxes near the door of the synagogue. Before the union of the three communities in 1639, Bet Jacob had those for contributions to 'Sedaca, Habra e Talmud Thora' and Ets Haim (SAA entry no. 334, no. 1052, p. 1^{v}, para. 2, 26 Tamuz 5397). Apparently during this period there were also boxes for contributions to *tudescos* (ibid., no. 17, p. 43, 8 May 5392/1632; ibid., p. 44^{v}, 30 Sept. 5393/1632). The inventory of the Portuguese community of 5400 gives further information: there is mention of three collecting-boxes which used to belong to the *kahal*, Bet Jacob: one for *sedaca*, one for Erets Yisra'el, and one for *cativos* (SAA entry no. 334, no. 19, p. 52/137). Bet Jacob also transferred to the united Kahal Kados de Talmud Torah a green alms box from which the proceeds were intended to buy wax for Yom Kippur (ibid.); see also Julie-Marthe Cohen, 'The Inventory of Ceremonial Objects', 304–7. Later on, in the united synagogue, boxes for similar purposes could be found. In 1641 there is mention of two other boxes besides the one for *sedaca*, namely one for the Talmud Torah school and one for Bikur Holim (SAA entry no. 334, no. 19, p. 84/169, para. 12, 6 Tevet 5401). Moreover, boxes existed for contributions to Erets Yisra'el and for *cativos* (ibid., no. 19, p. 24/109, para. 30, 22 Tamuz–28 Av 5399). For charity boxes in the Ashkenazi synagogues of Amsterdam see Zwiers, 'Inventory of the Moveable Property', 323, 383, 387.

29 SAA entry no. 334, no. 19, p. 52/137, 5400; ibid., no. 175, p. 298, 1 Nisan 5445. House-to-house collections also enabled women to participate in the *mitsvah* (L. D. Barnett, *El Libro de los Acuerdos*, 22). On collections for the poor on the eve of the sabbath see Maimonides, *Mishneh torah*, 'Hilkhot matanot aniyim', ch. 9: 1.

30 For the yield of the *nedava* for the poor from Brazil in 1655 see SAA entry no. 334, no. 174, p. 89, 1 Nisan 5415: 3,679 guilders. For that for the poor from Poland in 1656 see ibid., no. 240, p. 52, 19 Sivan 5416: 'nedava feita para os Pobres de Polonia': 3,375 guilders; ibid., 6 Av 5416: 72 guilders; ibid., 10 Av 5416: 40 guilders.

31 In the community's financial year Nisan 1685–Nisan 1686, the French refugees were given 4,692.10 guilders (SAA entry no. 334, no. 218, pp. 75–80, 3 Elul 5445–Rosh Hodesh Nisan 5446; ibid., no. 175, p. 305, 25 Menahem-Av 5446: 'nedava p[a] pobres de França': 4,692.10 guilders). On help to the *desterrados* from France see SAA entry no. 334, no. 218, pp. 75–6, 3 and 24 Elul 5445: distribution of linen, blankets, mattresses, dresses, and skirts; ibid., p. 79, 3 Tevet 5446: distribution of a skirt; ibid., 27 Tevet 5446: a cloak, blankets, and linen; ibid., 13 Shevat 5446: skirts and a dress. Assistance was given to a group of some forty families, around 150 people (ibid., p. 80, Rosh Hodesh Nisan 5446). See also Appendix I, Table 24. For relations between the Portuguese community of Amsterdam and that of southern France see Nahon, 'Rapports'.

Money was gathered for the relief and medical treatment of *belogrados*, if not by way of a collection. The surgeon Samuel de Leon Benavente was paid for extra work assisting sick refugees from Belgrade on the orders of the *parnasim* (SAA entry no. 334, no. 219, p. 29, 9 Adar 5452); for further help to *belogrados* in the form of sick care, shelter, support in childbirth, clothes, mattresses, blankets, and money see SAA entry no. 334, no. 218, p. 323, 17 [Tevet] 5450; ibid., p. 323, 24 [Adar] 5450; ibid., pp. 385–6, 5 Tamuz 5450; ibid., p. 386, 11 Heshvan 5451; ibid., no. 219, p. 26, 8 Heshvan 5452; ibid., p. 101, 25 Sivan 5452; ibid., p. 157, 12 Apr. 5454; ibid., p. 202, 28 Mar. 5454; ibid., p. 255, 28 Tamuz 5455; ibid., p. 310, 9 [Heshvan] 5457; ibid., p. 311, 23 Heshvan 5457. Nevertheless, a family from Belgrade received 48 guilders a year, in contrast to the 90 guilders a year given to a refugee family from the western Sephardi diaspora, in this case from France. In 1690 and 1691 965.16 guilders was spent on the poor from Belgrade (SAA entry no. 334, no. 218, p. 430, 2 Nisan 5450–Nisan 5451). There were around twenty families involved, forty-six people in total. On the encounter between Sephardim from the East and those from the West see Levie Bernfeld, 'Confrontation entre l'Orient et l'Occident'.

32 For collections in other Jewish communities, for example that of medieval Egypt, see M. Cohen, *Poverty and Charity*, 224.

33 Breen, 'Collecten te Amsterdam'; M. van Leeuwen, 'Liefdadige giften', 434–8; Wagenaar, *Amsterdam*, ii. 273–4. For collections in the Reformed Church of Amsterdam to help the poor during wartime see SAA entry no. 376, no. 13, pp. 14–15, 30 Nov.–1 Dec. 1673. For help to the French Huguenot refugees see ibid., no. 15, p. 4, 2 Apr. 1683; ibid., p. 21, 30 Sept. 1683. For assistance given by the Reformed Church of Amsterdam to Christian communities abroad see the following examples: collections for the community in La Rochelle (ibid., no. 5, p. 308, 18 Dec. 1625); collections for the poor in the German states (ibid., no. 7, p. 93, 15 May 1635); collections for redemption of captives in Turkey (ibid., no. 8, p. 43, 31 Aug. 1645); money sent to Poland (ibid., no. 9, p. 215, 6 Sept. 1657). For help given by the Amsterdam Lutheran Church to communities abroad see Kuijpers, 'Een zeventiende-eeuwse migrantenkerk', 45. For collections in Friesland see Spaans,

Armenzorg in Friesland. Every year the Portugese community paid a sum of 380 guilders to one of the municipal outdoor relief institutions (the Oude Zijds Huiszittenhuis) to be spent on the poor of the city, to avoid its collectors knocking on the doors of the Portuguese Jews to collect money (SAA entry no. 992, p. 4, 14 April 1644; ibid., p. 1, 5 May 1676).

34 For the year 1675 see SAA entry no. 334, no. 240, p. 302, 5435. For comparison, in 1675 another immigrant church, the Lutheran Church of Amsterdam, had around 9,000 members—perhaps many more—at least three times as many members as the Amsterdam Portuguese community: see Appendix I, Table 7. However, this church had only 3,000 guilders capital to spend on welfare, in addition to proceeds from the ownership of some small houses: Kuijpers, *Migrantenstad*, 106 and 306–7 n. 75).

35 For the year 1750–1 see SAA entry no. 334, no. 249, p. 2, 7 Nisan 5511; Marco van Leeuwen calculated that in absolute terms the capital of the Amsterdam Catholic Church increased fivefold between the end of the 17th century and the end of the 18th century (M. van Leeuwen, 'Amsterdam en de armenzorg', 143–5).

36 SAA entry no. 334, no. 21, pp. 1–2, 11 Nisan 5472; ibid., p. 344, 21 Shevat 5485.

37 Every Shabbat Hagadol (the sabbath before Pesach) the *gabai* (treasurer of the Portuguese community) had to read the balance sheet of income and expenditure, including outgoings through welfare, speaking with great clarity from the *teva*, before the names of the new administration were made known. This was how the *kahal* was informed about the financial situation of the community (SAA entry no. 334, no. 19, p. 22/107, 22 Tamuz 5399). It had been standard practice in traditional *kehilot* since the 14th century for the treasurer to justify the state of the community's finances (Frisch, *Historical Survey*, 111). In addition, after Pesach the Mahamad was obliged to justify all *activa* and *passiva* (assets and debts) of the Kahal Kados before the new members of the Mahamad and make an inventory of them (SAA entry no. 334, no. 19, p. 22/107, para. 10, 22 Tamuz 5399: 'Que o Mahamad seya obrigado dar aos s^{res} novam^{te} ellejtos despois de Pesach conta com Entregas de todos os Effejtos tocantes ao k.k. E depositados nelle por o Inventario q de tudo havera no l^{o}').

38 For income and deficit in relation to expenditure in the *sedaca* account in the first decades, the middle, and the end of the 18th century see Appendix I, Tables 15 and 18. The term 'nominal' refers to the actual figure in the particular years, whereas the term 'real' takes inflation rates into account. The calculation is based on tables provided by the International Institute of Social History in Amsterdam (<http://www.iisg.nl/hpw/calculate.php>).

39 See Appendix I, Table 16; also Appendix II, Figure 4.

40 SAA entry no. 334, no. 22, p. 221, 26 Shevat 5520; ibid., p. 236, 10 Av 5521; ibid., pp. 243–4, 5 Tishrei 5523; ibid., p. 260, 17 Tevet 5527.

41 SAA entry no. 334, no. 19, p. 720, 24 [*sic*] Rosh Hodesh Shevat 5435.

42 SAA entry no. 334, no. 22, p. 260, 17 Tevet 5527. In the 18th century the administration often urged its members to pay the *imposta* (ibid., no. 22, p. 236, 10 Av 5521; ibid., pp. 243–4, 5 Tishrei 5523; ibid., p. 260, 17 Tevet 5527). See also ibid., no. 22, p. 236, 10 Av 5521.

43 SAA entry no. 334, no. 19, p. 561, 20 Iyar 5426. The income from the *imposta* indeed went down that year. The deficit of the *sedaca* account in the year 1665/6 was 6,302.18 guilders (ibid., no. 240, p. 201).

44 It fell from 7,004 guilders in 1671/2 to 2,491 in 1672/3, rising again to 3,704 in 1673/4. See SAA entry no. 334, no. 174, pp. 931–42, 2 Heshvan 5432 (3,079.14 and 3,924.19.8 guilders); ibid., pp. 965–77, 17 Heshvan 5433 (970.15.12 and 1,520.12.8 guilders); ibid., pp. 997–1006, 1 Sivan 5434 (1,657.17 and 2,046.14 guilders).

45 SAA entry no. 334, no. 19, pp. 707–11, 14 Tevet 5435; ibid., p. 715, 24 [*sic*] Rosh Hodesh Shevat 5435. The years 1672/3 and 1673/4 show a deficit on the *sedaca* accounts of respectively 3,674.6.12 and 3,289.19.8 guilders (ibid., no. 240, p. 274, 5432–3; ibid., p. 286, 5433–4).

46 It jumped from 5,188 guilders in 1673/4 to 11,832 in 1674/5 and 13,833 in 1675/6. See SAA entry no. 334, no. 174, pp. 997–1006, 1 Sivan 5434; ibid., pp. 1033–46, 7 Tishrei, and pp. 1053–68, 20 Adar 5435; ibid., pp. 1085–1100, 9 Tishrei 5436, and pp. 1123–39, 1 Nisan 5436.

47 In the years 1693/4 and 1697/8 the total income could not cover the expenditure. The years ended in a deficit of 1,757.7 and 3,417.6.8 guilders respectively. In the 1690s the balance sheet of the *sedaca* ended in credit in only three years (1690/1, 1692/3, and 1695/6); the deficit in other years varied from around 300 guilders in 1691/2 to around 5,000 guilders in 1693/4.

48 Palmer, Colton, and Kramer, *A History of the Modern World*, 182–3. Antonio Alvares refers to this period of war in his last will of 1694 (SAA entry no. 334, no. 616, no. 1, Not. S. Favon, The Hague, 21 Jan. 1694): 'en dat ingeval den oorlog mogte continueeren (dat God vorhoede)'.

49 SAA entry no. 334, no. 20, p. 201, 10 Adar II 5456; ibid., no. 176, pp. 222–35, 1 Nisan 5456: 'f 4.995:10,2 finta dada: f 4.995:10, 1 emprestada: f 9.991'.

50 SAA entry no. 334, no. 22, p. 147, 28 Adar II 5502; ibid., no. 254, pp. 107, 118, 28 Adar 5555.

51 The number of *finta*-paying members rose from 417 in 1750 to 489 in 1794. The growth in numbers is misleading because many of the additional contributors were widows (and apparently other women) assessed for this tax for the first time (SAA entry no. 334, no. 30, p. 331, 14 Adar 5551). For taxing of widows in Ashkenazi communities such as those of Hamburg and Altona see Debra Kaplan, 'Women and Worth', 8–9.

52 1700: SAA entry no. 334, no. 242, p. 168, 4 Nisan 5460; 1730: SAA entry no. 334, no. 247, p. 27, 4 Nisan 5490.

53 On the rise in prosperity in this period see Nusteling, *Welvaart en werkgelegenheid in Amsterdam*, 138–9 and 191. For the rise in tax on meat see SAA entry no. 334, no. 19, p. 740, 1 Shevat 5436.

54 SAA entry no. 334, no. 19, p. 15/100, 10 Sivan 5399; ibid., no. 20, p. 101, 23 Heshvan 5447; ibid., no. 22, p. 89, 13 Adar II 5489; ibid., pp. 278–9, 25 Shevat 5537. The Ashkenazi community, on behalf of its poor, likewise protected the income from its own meat hall and made it clear that all meat should be

slaughtered there, and nowhere else, by the official slaughterers of the community; consequently tax had to be paid before slaughtering the cattle. Revenues from the meat hall were used for the support of the Ashkenazi poor (*Handvesten ofte privilegiën*, ii. 482, para. 20, 11 Oct. 1737; v. 71, para. 5, 8 Oct. 1772).

55 SAA entry no. 334, no. 21, p. 65, 27 Iyar 5443; ibid., no. 22, pp. 115–23, 16 Kislev 5496; ibid., p. 152, 7 Nisan 5503; ibid., pp. 173–4, para. 8, 10 Nisan 5510; ibid., p. 228, 27 Heshvan 5521; ibid., pp. 278–9, 25 Shevat 5537.

56 SAA entry no. 334, no. 22, pp. 196–7, 23 Iyar 5515.

57 See Appendix II, Figure 3.

58 SAA entry no. 334, no. 240, p. 302, 5435. For the same phenomenon in Spain, where merchants in 17th-century Seville invested only 29.4% of their fortune in real estate, see Aguado de los Reyes, *Riqueza y sociedad*, 91–101. For the investments of Dutch merchants see Israel, *The Dutch Republic*, 1003, 1016.

59 SAA entry no. 334, no. 245, p. 226, 5485; ibid., no. 249, p. 1, 13 Nisan 5510; ibid., no. 254, pp. 46 and 56, 5553–4.

60 Dillen, 'Economische positie', 585–91; Israel, *The Dutch Republic*, 1003, 1007–8, 1016; Vries and van de Woude, *The First Modern Economy*, 91–158.

61 SAA entry no. 334, no. 242, p. 174, 5 Nisan 5460.

62 SAA entry no. 334, no. 249, p. 2, 7 Nisan, 5511. The term 'nominal' refers to the actual figure in the particular years, whereas the term 'real' takes inflation rates into account. The calculation is based on tables provided by the International Institute of Social History in Amsterdam (<http://www.iisg.nl/hpw/calculate.php>).

63 See also M. van Leeuwen, 'Amsterdam en de armenzorg', 143–4.

64 SAA entry no. 334, no. 986, pp. 44–50, 25 Jan. 1748: resolution of the 'Staten van Holland en West-Friesland' in answer to a request by the Portuguese community of Amsterdam.

65 For the capital figure in 1750 of 545,245 guilders see SAA entry no. 334, no. 249, p. 2, 7 Nisan 5511; for the capital figure in 1793 of 567,699 guilders see ibid., no. 253, p. 386, 9 Nisan 5553; for the capital figure in 1795 of 586,211 guilders see ibid., no. 254. p. 66, 6 Nisan 5555; for the capital figure of capital in 1796 of 575,500 guilders see ibid., p. 128, 6 Nisan 5556.

66 Dillen, 'Economische positie', 592–3; Israel, *The Dutch Republic*, 1115.

67 Saperstein, *Exile in Amsterdam*, ch. 9.

68 Pinto, *Reflexoens*, 4: 'a causa & os Autores são innocentes; nas outras Republicas, os abusos que se cometen no ministerio, das cousas publicas, se atribue, ordinariamente, à os Ministros, que para satisfazer, seus interesses particulares, sacrificão o do publico . . . As malversações nunca tiverão lugar na administração destas Finanças; o designo, a vontade & o intento dos Directores forão sempre puras, virtuosas & desinteressadas: animados do zelo & temor Divino, procurarão sempre perpetuar este Caridade, do modo que nas circunstancias passadas, parecia o mais conveniente; Porem por grande que fosse a prudencia & penetração de nossos dignos antecessores, não podião antever, certas cousas, que o tempo só podia ensinar.' See also Nijenhuis, *Een Joodse Philosophe*, 15–16; Wijler, *Isaac de Pinto*; R. Cohen, *Jews in Another Environment*, 20–4. De Pinto formulated his analysis during discussions within the administration of the Portuguese community, starting in the 1730s. From 1742 his signature can be discerned at the bottom of clearly formulated plans for reform by the community administration that were issued subsequently. We can therefore assume that de Pinto actively participated in all the discussions of the Kahal Kados de Talmud Torah during that period. The question of the extent to which his ideas, as formulated in his *Reflexoens Politicas* of 1748, were original remains to be resolved; however, it is possible that those ideas were the driving force behind the new policy.

69 Pinto, *Reflexoens*, 6: '& deste modo, insensivelmente, em quatro dias, nós achamos quatrocentos *Jehidim*, carregados com cerca 800 familias, que vivem, ou morrem, a nosso cargo'.

70 Ibid. 8 and 10. By 1773 the Ashkenazi community no longer saw a rise in taxation ('door het verval van veel aanzienlijke Huizen en Familien hunner natie') as a desirable way to cover the rising cost of welfare. Only cost-cutting reforms were introduced (*Handvesten ofte privilegiën*, v. 72–5, 29 Sept. 1773).

71 SAA entry no. 334, no. 19, p. 726, 29 Iyar 5435; see also Y. Kaplan, 'Bans in the Sephardi Community' (Heb.).

72 On Isaac Penemacor see SAA entry no. 334, no. 118, file I, 1675.

73 On the del Sotto affair in 1670 see Swetschinski, 'The Portuguese Jewish Merchants of Seventeenth-Century Amsterdam', 485–99; Ancona, 'De Portugese gemeente', 286; Hagoort, 'The Del Sottos'.

74 SAA entry no. 334, no. 19, p. 727, 11 May 1675/5435.

75 For a extensive discussion on the question of deviance and the ban (*ḥerem*) as a punishment see Y. Kaplan, 'The Social Functions of the Herem'; id., 'Bans in the Sephardi Community' (Heb.); id., 'Deviance and Excommunication'. For Hamburg see id., 'The Place of Herem'.

76 The plea was sent by the Portuguese community to the mayors of Amsterdam in response to a petition by the inhabitants of St Antoniebreestraat, Nieuwe Hoogstraat, and the surrounding area protesting against the influx of Jews into their neighbourhood. On this request by fifty-five merchants to the Amsterdam government to make a special living area or ghetto for Jews see SAA entry no. 334, no. 87, file 20, 1753, *Remonstraçoems e rq*^{a} *aos ss*^{res} *Burgames*^{trs}; Reijnders, *Van 'Joodsche Natiën' tot Joodse Nederlanders*, 75–7.

77 SAA entry no. 334, no. 87, file 20, 1753, *Remonstraçoems e rq*^{a} *aos ss*^{res} *Burgames*^{trs}.

78 See SAA entry no. 334, no. 290, pp. 1–30, 5554, and Appendix II, Figure 3.

79 SAA entry no. 334, no. 22, p. 173, para. 7, 10 Nisan 5510. The plan for this Fundo de Augmento was also described by de Pinto (*Reflexoens*, para. 12, pp. 26–7): 'Meyos para estabelecer o fundo de augmento'.

80 SAA entry no. 334, no. 249, p. 2, 13 Nisan 5510.

81 SAA entry no. 334, no. 22, pp. 196–7, para. 4, 23 Iyar 5515.

82 17,096 guilders in 1776 (SAA entry no. 334, no. 251, p. 341, 8 Nisan 5536) and 11,693 guilders in 1794 (ibid., no. 254, p. 56, 6 Nisan 5554).

83 Pinto, *Reflexoens*, 6, 8, 10, 13, 24–5.

84 SAA entry no. 334, nos. 215–23 and 969–70. For specific overviews see e.g. ibid., no. 216, pp. 68–71, 5431–2; ibid., no. 217, p. 160, 5439–40.

85 In southern France in the mid-18th century the maximum number of Sephardi poor to be supported was fixed: in St-Esprit, for example, it was set at no more than a hundred, any over that was to be sent away; for Bordeaux, only eighty poor families were allowed to stay. See Szapiro, 'Le Sud-Ouest', 237.

86 On the basis of the 1723 plans for reform (SAA entry no. 334, no. 21, pp. 306–7, 27 Sivan 5483) it appears many people other than Sephardim were registered on the charity rolls of the Portuguese community.

87 SAA entry no. 334, no. 21, pp. 506–7, 27 Sivan 5483; ibid., no. 22, pp. 144–7, 28 Adar II 5502; ibid., pp. 161–2, 25 Heshvan 5508; ibid., pp. 167–9, 8 Heshvan 5509; ibid., pp. 171–7, 10 Nisan 5510.

88 For a discussion of the employment of Portuguese Jews in early modern Amsterdam see Swetschinski, 'The Portuguese Jewish Merchants of Seventeenth-Century Amsterdam', esp. ch. 3; id., *Reluctant Cosmopolitans*, ch. 3; Israel, *European Jewry*, index s.v. 'Amsterdam'; id., 'The Economic Contribution of Dutch Sephardi Jewry'; id., 'The Changing Role of the Dutch Sephardim'; id., 'The Sephardic Contribution to Economic Life'; Dillen, 'De economische positie'; Bloom, *The Economic Activities of the Jews of Amsterdam*.

89 After the death of David Abendana in 1672, 48.3.8 guilders were found among his possessions, around 20% of the amount distributed to him since 1664. This money was given back to the Portuguese community (SAA entry no. 334, no. 174, p. 959, 7 Nisan 5432: 'por resto que se acho de David Abendana por sua morte por se aver sustentado da sedaca'). Also in the 18th century, the estate of anyone who had lived on welfare was required to repay the amount they had received if the estate had sufficient funds. Judith Ciudad Real had apparently been quite wealthy—wealthy enough, at least, to own a house in Bayonne at the time of her death. The Amsterdam Portuguese community claimed the revenue from the sale of that house, amounting to 609.11 guilders, to cover the money that had been distributed to her during her lifetime (SAA entry no. 334, no. 90, 19 Aug. 1712; published in Nahon, 'Rapports', 65 and 166). See also the case of the widow of Gabriel Alvares Correa. In 1751, 561 guilders were returned to the community by her estate, based on the money she had received from welfare, 'die zij van de *sedaca* heeft genoten'. A sum of 600 guilders was returned from the estate of Jacob Rodrigues Silva (ibid., no. 249, p. 25, 15 Kislev and 12 Adar 5511). The proceeds of the sale of the household effects of the deceased Rachel Henriques, amounting to 12 guilders, also went back to the Portuguese community (ibid., p. 25, 12 Adar 5511).

In other parts of the Sephardi diaspora similar rules were applied. In Livorno they were even stricter: if a poor person who had received welfare left money or possessions after his or her death, they had to be returned to the Portuguese community, without consideration for the individual's heirs (Toaff, *La nazione ebrea*, 584, para. 76, 26 Oct. 1670).

Similar arrangements existed in other welfare institutions of the city of Amsterdam and could have been copied from them. In a decision of 1530 it is stated that the Huiszittenhuis was entitled to the proceeds of the estate of anyone supported by it who died without heirs (Wagenaar, *Amsterdam*, ii. 273–4, 4 Jan. 1530). In the Reformed Church of Amsterdam a similar decree was not issued until the 18th century (Wagenaar, *Amsterdam*, ii. 163, 15 Sept. 1735).

90 SAA entry no. 334, no. 20, p. 102, 4 Adar I 5494.

91 For details of a wage freeze see SAA entry no. 334, no. 19, p. 676, 13 Nisan 5433.

92 SAA entry no. 334, no. 20, p. 376, para. 1, 5 Adar I 5464. A similar maximum was set on expenses in St-Esprit in 1754: see Nahon, *Les 'Nations' juives portugaises*, 204–7.

93 SAA entry no. 334, no. 21, p. 440, 26 Adar 5467.

94 SAA entry no. 334, no. 21, p. 425, 12 Iyar 5466; ibid., p. 515, 12 Heshvan 5470; ibid., p. 440, 26 Iyar 5488; ibid., no. 22, p. 131, 23 Heshvan 5498.

95 SAA entry no. 334, no. 21, pp. 296–7, 6 Nisan 5483; ibid., pp. 306–7, 27 Sivan 5483; ibid., p. 425, 25 Shevat 5488; ibid., p. 453, 20 Tevet 5489; ibid., no. 22, pp. 144–7, 28 Adar II 5502; ibid., pp. 161–2, 25 Heshvan 5508; ibid., pp. 167–9, 8 Heshvan 5509; ibid., pp. 171–7, 10 Nisan 5510.

96 Expenditure in the *sedaca* account in 1793/4 was 101,392 guilders (SAA entry no. 334, no. 254, pp. 46 and 56, 11 Nisan 5553–9 Nisan 5554). The term 'nominal' refers to the actual figure in the particular years, whereas the term 'real' takes inflation rates into account. The calculation is based on tables provided by the International Institute of Social History in Amsterdam (<http://www.iisg.nl/hpw/calculate.php>).

97 SAA entry no. 334, no. 20, p. 376, para. 2, 5 Adar I 5464.

98 SAA entry no. 334, no. 21, p. 306, paras. 1, 3–5, 27 Sivan 5483.

99 SAA entry no. 334, no. 22, p. 144, paras. 4–5, 28 Adar II 5502; ibid., p. 168, para. 4, 8 Heshvan 5509. In case of illness and at distributions of matzot newlyweds were considered as children of the family.

100 SAA entry no. 334, no. 22, p. 146, para. 15, 28 Adar II 5502.

101 SAA entry no. 334, no. 22, p. 146, para. 17, 28 Adar II 5502.

102 SAA entry no. 334, no. 22, p. 145, para. 10, 28 Adar II 5502.

103 SAA entry no. 334, no. 22, p. 145, para. 11, 28 Adar II 5502; ibid., p. 168, para. 10, 8 Heshvan 5509. Restrictions had already been laid down by 1712: the contribution to Erets Yisra'el was fixed at 13,831 guilders, with the condition that no *sheliḥim* (emissaries) would be received for a period of fifteen years (SAA entry no. 334, no. 21, p. 6, 27 June 1712). Amsterdam was not the only centre to curtail contributions to Erets Yisra'el. For a discussion see Carlebach, *The Pursuit of Heresy*, 57–63; Barnai, *The Jews in Palestine*, 55–7.

104 On the reorganization of the administration to prevent fraud see SAA entry no. 334, no. 22, p. 76, 16 Nisan 5488; ibid., p. 97, 2 Tamuz 5492. The system apparently continued to be confusing: in 1734 orders were given that the demand for matzot and peat be well supervised and the treasurers were instructed to register every week who was taken off the lists, who had died, and who had left the city (SAA entry no. 334, no. 22, pp. 102–3, para. 4, 4 Adar I 5494). The resolutions were repeated in 1752 (ibid., no. 974, 5512, file f) and in 1792 (ibid., pp. 285–91, 24 Adar 5552).

105 SAA entry no. 334, no. 22, p. 167, para. 1, 8 Heshvan 5509; ibid., p. 168, para. 5; ibid., pp. 172–3, paras. 5–6, 10 Nisan 5510.

106 These documents dealt with exemption from tax on peat and on consumer goods (SAA entry no. 334, no. 66, 27 Mar. 1679).

107 SAA entry no. 334, no. 986, pp. 1–3, 18 Apr. 1693.

108 SAA entry no. 334, no. 986, p. 4, 4 Sept. 1681; ibid., no. 20, p. 30, 4 Sept. 1681; ibid., no. 986, pp. 1–3, 18 Apr. 1693; ibid., no. 986, pp. 44–50, 25 Jan. 1748.

109 SAA entry no. 334, no. 87, 30 Oct. 1750, *Req[t] aen Mijne Heeren van den Gerechte.* On the basis of a document from the same file dated 31 Aug. 1748 it appears that both communities were prepared to pay an amount of 10,000 guilders to gain admission to the guilds.

110 SAA entry no. 334, no. 240, p. 284, 5434; ibid., p. 302, 5435. For the average over the 18th century, see n. 116 below.

111 For the bequest of David Vaaz see SAA entry no. 334, no. 19, pp. 277–8, 24 Kislev 5410: 'Termo dos outo mil florins q deixou David Vaaz q ds aja neste kaal kados Para se Sustentar do Rendim[to] hua Yessivah de dez Pesoas em jerusalaim Continuamente como abaixo se declara.' See also the gifts of Abraham Israel Pereyra in SAA entry no. 334, no. 780A, pp. 25–8, Av 5418; no. 782, pp. 10–18, 7 Nisan, signed by Abraham Pereyra 15 Tamuz 5419; ibid., p. 34, 8 Nisan 5419; no. 19, pp. 419–52, 26 Shevat 5419; and in SAA entry no. 5075, no. 2895A, Not. P. Padthuysen, pp. 338–40, 7 Mar. 1666. For the bequest of Moses Franco Drago see SAA entry no. 334, no. 674, portfolio 1–2: will of Moses Franco Drago, Not. J. van de Ven, written 18 Adar 5407, closed 25 Mar. 1647, translated from Portuguese into Dutch by Not. P. Padthuysen (1 Dec. 1670); see also SAA entry no. 334, no. 19, p. 841, 6 Tamuz 5441; ibid., no. 518, p. 26, 5441 ('se fara hua Jesiba Em terra Santa Por nome Jerusalaim aqual mandarao os ss[res] testamenteiros o Interesse dos F.6000 do d.[ro] dos Estados aqual Jesiba sempre sera fixa & dirao na ditta Jesiba sempre aEscava'). For the gift of Jacob Pereyra see SAA entry no. 334, no. 20, p. 166, 21 Adar 5453, and p. 192, 11 Iyar 5455. On the institutions of Abraham and Jacob Pereyra and other yeshivot in Israel see Nahon, 'Amsterdam and Jerusalem'; id., 'Yeshivot hiérosolymites'; id., 'Une source pour l'histoire de la diaspora sefarade'. For the Magen David yeshiva in Jerusalem, established through a legacy of David de Pinto of The Hague in 1750, see id., 'The Hague, Amsterdam, Istanbul, Jerusalem'; see further Benayahu, 'History of the Rabbinical Colleges' (Heb.); Barnai, *The Jews in Palestine*, 65, 166.

112 SAA entry no. 334, no. 19, p. 547, 7 Iyar 5425; ibid., no. 119a, file 37, 7 Iyar 5425.

113 SAA entry no. 334, no. 19, pp. 98–9/183–4, 15 Tamuz 5401.

114 SAA entry no. 334, no. 736, 18 Elul 5481.

115 By means of a letter written in 1714 the New Christian Luis Françisco, living in Oporto, left a bond of 500 Flemish pounds (*livras de grossos*) capital to a *caza de misericordia* in Amsterdam. He died, after being imprisoned by the Inquisition, in 1715. His son Isaac was a member of the Amsterdam Portuguese community at the time. The grant was added to the capital of the community, and annual yields from it were given to Ets Haim and Erets Yisra'el (SAA entry no. 334, no. 21, pp. 114–15, 9 Tamuz 5476).

116 See M. van Leeuwen, 'Liefdadige giften', 423, table 5, on numbers for the 18th century (1725–99); the average donation of Portuguese Jews made to the Portuguese community remained more or less at the same level, namely 1,400 guilders, during the 18th century (SAA entry no. 334, no. 245, p. 226, 9 Nisan 5485; ibid., no. 247, p. 265, 24 Adar 5500; ibid., no. 251, 2 Nisan 5535; ibid., no. 254, p. 331, 6 Nisan 5558).

117 M. van Leeuwen, 'Liefdadige giften', 423.

118 SAA entry no. 334, no. 19, pp. 449–12, 9 Adar 5419; ibid., no. 782, pp. 10–18, 7 Nisan, signed by Abraham Pereyra 15 Tamuz 5419.

119 For legacies to confraternities in Catholic Spain and Italy see Martz, *Poverty and Welfare in Habsburg Spain*, 195–8; Pullan, *Rich and Poor in Renaissance Venice*, 164–5, 184; on donations to the *ḥevrot* in Bayonne see Nahon, 'Pour une approche', 47–80.

120 For legacies to Temime Darech see Johebed de Casseres, 70 guilders (SAA entry no. 5075, no. 3280, no. 74, Not. H. Outgers, 21 Nov. 1685); Sara Torres, 20 guilders (SAA entry no. 5075, no. 3720, Not. F. Tixerandet, pp. 11–14/19ᵛ–21, 23 June 1693). For those to Maskil el Dal see David de Abraham Cardoso, 300 guilders (SAA entry no. 5075, no. 2914, Not. P. Padthuysen, pp. 667–73, 28 Sept. 1687; SAA entry no. 334, no. 518, Not. P. Padthuysen, 21 July 1688). For those to Honen Dalim see David de Abraham Cardoso, 300 guilders; Abigail Dias da Fonseca, 200 guilders (SAA entry no. 334, no. 700, Not. P. Padthuysen, pp. 1–16, 30 Mar. 1703). For legacies to Mazon Abanot see Jacob Abenatar Junior, alias Jacob Abenatar, alias Francisco de Melo Junior, and Ribca Belmonte, 100 guilders (SAA entry no. 334, no. 609, Not. D. van den Brink, 9 Feb. 1750).

121 For Dotar's 'Sacred Capital' of 48,867 guilders in 1675 see SAA entry no. 334, no. 1144, pp. 223–4, 5435. For Ets Haim's capital of 29,183 guilders in the same year see SAA entry no. 334, no. 1116, pp. 156–7, 5435.

122 For Dotar in 1790 see SAA entry no. 334, no. 1170, p. 78, 5550. For Ets Haim in 1790 see ibid., no. 1117, p. 75, 5550. For Dotar in 1700 see ibid., no. 1144, pp. 478–9. For Ets Haim in 1700 see ibid., no. 1116, pp. 303, 307–8, 5460.

123 SAA entry no. 334, no. 1145, p. 25, 5448; ibid., pp. 1–35, Anno 5495, from 5377 to 5507; ibid., no. 1163; see also Pieterse, *Daniel Levi de Barrios*, 105 n. 7.

124 SAA entry no. 334, no. 1073, pp. 1–9. The registration here starts in 1659 (the starting point according to the wall tablets in the winter synagogue).

125 The following legacies were made to Dotar in the period 1615–1700: Sara Cohen de Herrera, 1,000 guilders (SAA entry no. 334, no. 1143, p. 110, 5404); Sara Alvares, 200 guilders (SAA entry no. 5075, no. 2237, Not. A. Lock, pp. 1105–8, 23 Dec. 1671); Abraham Espinoza, 200 guilders (SAA entry no. 1144, p. 245, 6 Kislev 5438); Miriam Alvares, 50 guilders (SAA entry no. 334, no. 628: 'Papeis tocantes a caza mortuoria de Miriam Alvarez que Ds tem. Miriam Alvarez, Nº 4'; the testament was written by Miriam Alvares on 28 Oct. 1678; handed over on 21 Nov. of that year to Notary F. Tixerandet; Notary D. van der Groe opened the will on 29 Aug. 1685); Abraham da Costa de Andrade, 2,000 guilders (SAA entry no. 1144, p. 324, 9 Adar 5445); Jacob Pereyra, a bond of 1,500 guilders (SAA entry no. 1144, p. 388, 25 Sivan 5450); Jacob Aboab Osorio, a bond of 3,000 guilders (SAA entry no. 5075, no. 4263, Not. D. van der Groe, pp. 148–51, 24–25 Apr. 1697; SAA entry no. 334, no. 1144, pp. 448–9, 5457). For an overview of legacies to Dotar, see SAA entry no. 334, no. 1141–4.

For an overview of legacies to Ets Haim, see SAA entry no. 334, no. 1073, pp. 100–2, 5397–5460; ibid., no. 1074. In the 17th century 136 people (27% of whom were women) left money to Ets Haim (Pieterse, *Daniel Levi de Barrios*, 97–105). For examples see Isaac Alfarin, who left one-third of yearly yields of bonds (SAA entry no. 5075, no. 4103A, Not. D. van der Groe, pp. 47–50, 7 July 1682); Abigail Dias da Fonseca, alias Beatris de Caceres, 200 guilders (SAA entry no. 334, no. 700, Not. P. Padthuysen, pp. 1–16, 30 Mar. 1703); Jacob Aboab Osorio, 600 guilders (SAA entry no. 5075, no. 4263, Not. D. van der Groe, pp. 148–51, 24–25 Apr. 1697; SAA entry no. 334, no. 1144, pp. 448–9, 5457); and Jacob Pereyra, 3,000 guilders (SAA entry no. 334, no. 1052, pp. 136v–137, 13 Iyar 5450). For the 18th century see the last will of Aron de Pinto and Abigail de Gracia Nunes Henriques (SAA entry no. 5075, no. 7493, no. 63, Not. J. van den Ende, 10 Aug. 1717); the last will of Joseph Senior (SAA entry no. 334, no. 520A, Not. J. Ardinois, pp. 368–99, 5 Sept. 1719); and the last will of Josua de Prado, alias Anthonio de Prado (SAA entry no. 5075, no. 7490, no. 19, Not. van den Ende, 12 Mar. 1708).

126 See e.g. SAA entry no. 334, no. 1116, pp. 161–2, 5435–6.

127 SAA entry no. 334, no. 1052, p. 24, para. 12, 20 Heshvan 5413.

128 Between 1637 and 1675 sixty-eight people made grants to Ets Haim totalling 23,480 guilders (SAA entry no. 334, no. 1073, pp. 100–3, 23 Iyar 5488). In the same period the *sedaca* account of the Portuguese community received 100 donations totalling 120,000 guilders (SAA entry no. 334, no. 240, p. 302, 5435).

129 SAA entry no. 334, no. 1322, para. 8, 16 Adar I 5375.

130 SAA entry no. 334, no. 1322, para. 8, 16 Adar I 5375. For an example see SAA entry no. 334, no. 1144, p. 624, 10 Adar II 5475, which deals with Joseph Henriques Sequeira.

131 For loans to private individuals see SAA entry no. 334, no. 1141, p. 13 [15], 13 Adar 5375.

132 Concerning financial aid from Dotar to the *imposta* board, formulated as *esmola* (a gift) but bearing interest, see SAA entry no. 334, no. 1168, p. 91, 24 Aug. 5382/1622; ibid., p. 97; ibid., no. 1142, p. 3 [5], 11 Dec. 5383. By 1634–5 the debt of the *imposta* board to Dotar had increased to £858.16.8 (SAA entry no. 334, no. 1168, p. 235, 5394–5). The three Portuguese communities individually also owed money to Dotar (SAA entry no. 334, no. 1141, p. 161, 4 Iyar 5381; ibid., no. 1169, p. 4, 3 Nov. 5396; ibid., p. 22, 5399–5403). During difficult periods such as the early 1630s Dotar even refused support to the *imposta* board as it was in financial trouble and unable to pay (SAA entry no. 334, no. 1142, p. 151, 8 Heshvan 5392).

Three years later that decision was withdrawn (SAA entry no. 334, no. 1142, p. 209, 24 Adar 5395).

133 At the union of the three communities, Dotar conducted an overview of outstanding debts (SAA entry no. 334, no. 1169, p. 22, 5399–5403). Throughout the 17th century the Portuguese community owed money to Dotar; see the financial reports for 1644–61 (SAA entry no. 334, no. 1169, p. 36, 5404–21) and 1661–9 (SAA entry no. 334, no. 1169, p. 93, 5421–9). Between 1661 and 1666 the debt of the Portuguese community to Dotar increased from 18,000 to 28,000 guilders; in 1669 it fell to 23,000 guilders. During the 1670s the Portuguese community took out large loans with Dotar (SAA entry no. 334, no. 19, p. 688, 24 Adar I 5434; ibid., p. 698, 6 Rosh Hodesh Sivan [*sic*] 5434; see also MS Ets Haim 48 D 43, p. 61; 'Dinero que el K,K, q D^{s} Aug^{te} tiene en si de que paga Reditas hasta sabat gadol de 5436'). At the end of the 17th century the debt of the Portuguese community to Dotar was reined in to an acceptable level—2,453.6 guilders in 1688 (SAA entry no. 334, no. 1169, p. 219, 5448). By then the name of the Portuguese community had disappeared from Dotar's accounts: it does not appear again until 1700.

134 See e.g. the case of Judith do Vale who, besides gaining a dowry of 800 guilders, also received 300 guilders as *offertas* granted by three individuals (SAA entry no. 334, no. 1143, p. 322, 15 Adar II 5421).

135 For legacies to Aby Jetomim see Sara Alvares, 100 guilders (SAA entry no. 5075, no. 2237, Not. A. Lock, 23 Dec. 1671; also SAA entry no. 334, no. 1144, p. 283, 20 Adar II 5440); Reyna Gomez: 10 guilders (SAA entry no. 334, no. 119a, file 12, Not. D. van de Groe, p. 444, 21 May 1679); Miriam Alvares: 50 guilders (SAA entry no. 334, no. 628, 28 Oct. and 21 Nov. 1678; 29 Aug. 1685); David de Abraham Cardoso: 400 guilders (SAA entry no. 5075, no. 2914, Not. P. Padthuysen, 28 Sept. 1687; SAA entry no. 334, no. 518, Not. P. Padthuysen, 21 July 1688).

136 SAA entry no. 334, no. 1211, pp. 63–7, 22 Elul 5431–[n.d.] 5462.

137 Pieterse, *Daniel Levi de Barrios*, 118.

138 SAA entry no. 334, no. 1211, p. 27, 5413.

139 Pieterse, *Daniel Levi de Barrios*, 118. The number of original members was said to be forty-two, including eight women, or 19% of the total (Franco Mendes, *Memorias*, 55; SAA entry no. 334, no. 1211, p. 56, *escama* 9, 5408). The maximum membership was later put at 100, but that total was later exceeded. De Barrios mentions a total of 125 members in 1683 (SAA entry no. 334, no. 1211, p. 26, caput 3,5408); see further Franco Mendes, *Memorias*, 56, and Pieterse, *Daniel Levi de Barrios*, 119.

140 For joining fees see the following paragraphs in SAA entry no. 334: for Roffe Holim no. 25, p. 331, para. 7, 13 Tamuz 5509; for Mazon Abanot no. 120, file 81, pp. 874–5, paras. 43–4, 6 Shevat 5494. For monthly and yearly contributions see also SAA entry no. 334: Hesrat Nasim (no. 25, p. 272, para. 10, 14 Iyar 5501); Hase Amaharacha (no. 1234, pp. 1–2, paras. 1 and 3, 1 Heshvan 5474); Hateret Tipheret (no. 25, p. 265, para. 2, 7 Iyar 5501); Honen Dal (no. 25, p. 252, para. 17, 7 Heshvan

5500); Kisuy Ros (no. 25, p. 259, para. 4, 20 Tevet 5501); Mayafu Pehameha Benealim (no. 25, p. 245, para. 2, 26 Adar II 5499); Quetonet Bat Codes (no. 25, p. 301, para. 10, 3 Av 5505); Quesut La Ebion (no. 25, p. 323, paras. 9 and 11, 24 Menahem-Av 5508); Meil Sedaca (no. 25, p. 218, para. 2, 8 Tevet 5495; no. 1242, p. 2, para. 3, 3 Shevat 5514); Sidcat Nassim (no. 120, file 84, p. 951, para. 7, 21 Heshvan 5517); Maasim Tobim–Sidcat Nassim (no. 120, file 84, p. 948, para. 13, 4 Nisan 5518).

For collections see Hesrat Nasim (SAA entry no. 334, no. 25, p. 271, para. 5, 14 Iyar 5501); Hateret Tipheret (ibid., p. 265, para. 2, and p. 268, para. 19, 7 Iyar 5501); Kisuy Ros (ibid., p. 260, para. 13, 20 Tevet 5501); Michse Leani'im (SAA entry no. 334, no. 120, file 89, p. 971, para. 8, [n.d.]); Mayafu Pehameha Benealim (SAA entry no. 334, no. 25, p. 247, para. 8, 26 Adar II, 5499); Quetonet Bat Codes (ibid., p. 302, para. 14, 3 Av 5505); Quesut La Ebion (ibid., p. 323, para. 5, 24 Menahem-Av 5508); Roffe Holim (ibid., p. 331, para. 6, 13 Tamuz 5509); Hase Amaharacha (SAA entry no. 334, no. 1234, p. 46, 17 Kislev 5495: three times a year); Meil Sedaca (SAA entry no. 334, no. 25, p. 219, para. 8, 8 Tevet 5495. For the source of 5514 see ibid., no. 1242, p. 4, para. 14, 3 Shevat 5514).

For boxes at the institutions for contributions see Mishenet Zequenim (SAA entry no. 334, no. 25, p. 341, para. 14, 8 Tevet 5510); Mazon Abanot (SAA entry no. 334, no. 120, file 81, p. 876, para. 49, 3 Shevat 5494).

For income through production see Mazon Abanot (SAA entry no. 334, no. 120, file 81, p. 875, para. 46 and p. 881, para. 8, 3 Shevat 5494).

For fines see Maasim Tobim–Sidcat Nassim (SAA entry no. 334, no. 120, file 84, p. 945, para. 3 and p. 948, para. 6, 4 Nisan 5518); Hesrat Nasim (SAA entry no. 334, no. 25, p. 271, para. 3 and p. 272, para. 14, 14 Iyar 5501); Hateret Tipheret (ibid., pp. 265–6, paras. 5–6, 7 Iyar 5501); Honen Dal (ibid., p. 251, para. 10 and p. 253, para. 21, 7 Hesvan 5500); Kisuy Ros (ibid., p. 258, para. 2 and p. 260, para. 12, 20 Tevet 5501); Michse Leani'im (SAA entry no. 334, no. 120, file 89, p. 971, para. 8 and p. 972, para. 12 [n.d.]); Mayafu Pehameha Benealim (SAA entry no. 334, no. 25, p. 245, para. 3, 26 Adar II, 5499); Quetonet Bat Codes (ibid., p. 300, para. 2, 3 Av 5505); Oneg Sabat (ibid., p. 316, para. 1, 25 Kislev 5508); Quesut La Ebion (ibid., p. 322, para. 3 and p. 324, para. 15, 24 Menahem-Av 5508); Roffe Holim (ibid., p. 331, paras. 4–5, 13 Tamuz 5509); Hase Amaharacha (SAA entry no. 334, no. 1234, pp. 2–3, paras. 6–7, 1 Heshvan 5474); Meil Sedaca (for source of 5514 see SAA entry no. 334, no. 1242, p. 2, para. 2 and p. 4, para. 18, 3 Shevat 5514).

For *offertas* see Hesrat Nasim (SAA entry no. 334, no. 25, p. 272, para. 11, 14 Iyar 5501); Honen Dal (ibid., p. 252, para. 12, 7 Heshvan 5500); Hase Amaharacha (SAA entry no. 334, no. 1234, p. 1, para. 1, 1 Heshvan 5474); Maasim Tobim–Sidcat Nassim (SAA entry no. 334, no. 120, file 84, p. 946, para. 6, 4 Nisan 5518); Mishenet Zequenim (for source of 5510 see SAA entry no. 334, no. 25, p. 340, para. 11 and p. 341, para. 12, 8 Tevet 5510); Mazon Abanot (SAA entry no. 334, no. 120, file 81, p. 874, para. 43, 6 Shevat 5494).

For legacies see Honen Dal (SAA entry no. 334, no. 25, p. 253, para. 22, 7 Heshvan 5500); Mayafu Pehameha Benealim (ibid., p. 246, para. 5, 26 Adar II,

5499); Quetonet Bat Codes (ibid., p. 301, para. 11, 3 Av 5505); Meil Sedaca (for 5495 see SAA entry no. 334, no. 25, p. 219, para. 7, 8 Tevet 5495; for 5514 see SAA entry no. 334, no. 1242, p. 4, para. 13, 3 Shevat 5514); Mishenet Zequenim (for 5510 see SAA entry no. 334, no. 25, p. 340, para. 8, 8 Tevet 5510); Sidcat Nassim (SAA entry no. 334, no. 120, file 84, p. 951, para. 12, 21 Heshvan 5517); Maasim Tobim–Sidcat Nassim (ibid., file 84, p. 948, para. 14, 4 Nisan 5518).

For income from investments such as shares and lotteries see Asuta Habraya (SAA entry no. 334, no. 1215, p. 1, 4 Tishrei 5507).

For expenditure on payment to personnel see Honen Dalim–Resit Hochma (SAA entry no. 334, no. 25, p. 280, para. 17, 20 Sivan 5501); Hase Amaharacha (SAA entry no. 334, no. 1234, p. 73, 5475); Meil Sedaca (ibid., no. 1242, p. 12, 5514); Mishenet Zequenim (for 5510 see SAA entry no. 334, no. 25, p. 342, para. 16, 8 Tevet 5510); Maasim Tobim–Sidcat Nassim (SAA entry no. 334, no. 120, file 84, p. 947, para. 12, 4 Nisan 5518); Mazon Abanot (ibid., file 81, p. 868, para. 11, 6 Shevat 5494); Mishenet Zequenim (SAA entry no. 334, no. 1227, p. 8, 12 Nisan 5512).

For expenditure on transportation see Hase Amaharacha (SAA entry no. 334, no. 1234, p. 73, 5475).

For expenditure on books see Mishenet Zequenim (SAA entry no. 334, no. 1227, p. 8, 12 Nisan 5512).

For expenditure on keeping membership lists see Hase Amaharacha (SAA entry no. 334, no. 1234, p. 73, 5475); Mishenet Zequenim (for source of 5510 see SAA entry no. 334, no. 25, p. 339, para. 7, 8 Tevet 5510); Mazon Abanot (SAA entry no. 334, no. 120, file 81, pp. 873–4, paras. 37–8, 6 Shevat 5494).

For expenditure on boxes see Hase Amaharacha (SAA entry no. 334, no. 1234, p. 73, 5475).

For a complete balance sheet see Mishenet Zequenim (SAA entry no. 334, no. 1230, p. 1, 5510; ibid., no. 1227, pp. 1–5, 5510).

141 For example, the treasurer of Quetonet Bat Codes was obliged to join the *shamash* visiting the houses of all the 'jehidim deste KK q Ds augmente' (SAA entry no. 334, no. 25, p. 302, para. 14, 3 Av 5505); in the Hase Amaharacha *ḥevrah* (SAA entry no. 334, no. 1234, p. 46, 17 Kislev 5495) the *gabai* and *shamash*, assisted by one founder, were to visit the houses of the brothers and the 'Jehidim deste santo Kahal' three times a year. For a description of the activities of other *shamashim* see Hateret Tipheret (SAA entry no. 334, no. 25, p. 265, para. 2, 7 Iyar 5501); Mazon Abanot (SAA entry no. 334, no. 120, file 81, p. 887, para. 2, 6 Shevat 5494).

142 SAA entry no. 334, no. 1234, pp. 72–3, 5475; ibid., no. 1235, pp. 76–7, 5497.

143 SAA entry no. 334, no. 1242, p. 13, 5514.

144 SAA entry no. 5075, no. 2895B, Not. P. Padthuysen, pp. 978–80, 22 July 1666, last will of Rachel Pinta, alias Leonor de Torres, lawful wife of Daniel Pinto: 'Item manda que se repartan entre las parientas mas necessitadas della testadora . . . ducientos florines una vez'.

145 SAA entry no. 334, no. 19, pp. 449–52, 26 Shevat 5419; ibid., no. 782, pp. 10–18, 6–7 Nisan/15 Tamuz 5419.

146 Last will of Abraham Israel Suasso (SAA entry no. 996, no. 17, 26 Jan. 1699–18 Sept. 1705).

147 Last will of Abigail Dias da Fonseca (SAA entry no. 334, no. 700, Not. P. Padthuysen, pp. 1–16, 30 Mar. 1703).

148 For the last will of Sara Torres see SAA entry no. 5075, no. 3720, Not. F. Tixerandet, pp. 11–14/19^{v}–21, 23 June 1693.

149 For a distribution to the poor of 50 guilders see e.g. the last will of Maria Mendes de Pas, alias Chana Aboab, widow of Anthonio de Pas (SAA entry no. 5075, no. 2182, Not. A. Lock, pp. 65–72, 8 Mar. 1677). Moses de Oliveira stipulated in 1662 that his brother was to distribute 125 guilders to the poor of his nation on the anniversary of his death (last will of Moses de Oliveira, alias Gaspar de Oliveira: SAA entry no. 5075, no. 2891B, Not. P. Padthuysen, pp. 1204–5, 16 Sept. 1662). For a gift to the poor of more than 5,000 guilders see e.g. the bequest of a total of 9,000 guilders by Jacob Aboab Osorio (SAA entry no. 5075, no. 4263, Not. D. van der Groe, pp. 148–51, 24–25 Apr. 1697; SAA entry no. 334, no. 1144, pp. 448–9, 5457).

150 See Appendix I, Tables 19–22.

151 See Appendix I, Table 19. The same conclusion was reached by Marco van Leeuwen ('Liefdadige giften', 419–20) in respect of the last wills made by members of the Reformed and Catholic churches of Amsterdam in the 18th century who left charitable bequests.

152 See Appendix I, Table 20.

153 In 1708 Josua de Prado, one of Amsterdam's Portuguese Jewish elite, left 9,200 guilders to charity, and over 75,000 guilders to be divided among certain members of his family and friends. The rest—probably the largest and most valuable part of the inheritance—went to the heirs, his brothers Joseph and Jacob de Prado. See the will of Josua de Prado, alias Anthonio de Prado, SAA entry no. 5075, no. 7490, no. 19, Not. van de Ende, 12 Mar. 1708. For the *finta* tax paid by Josua de Prado see SAA entry no. 334, no. 177, p. 18, 1 Adar 5463: 'Jeosua de Prado 1^{a} finta f 40,=, 2^{a} finta f 50,='; ibid., p. 145, 20 Adar 5468: 'Jeosua de Prado 1^{a} finta f 50,–; 2^{a} finta f 50,–'.

Jacob Marques, a less wealthy member of the *kehilah*, left just 150 guilders to the poor, as against 8,600 guilders to members of his family (see the will of Jacob Marques: SAA entry no. 5075, no. 4089, Not. D. van der Groe, pp. 312–18, 23 Feb. 1679). In 1680 Jacob Marques was assessed as owing 15 guilders in payment of half of the yearly *finta* tax (SAA entry no. 334, no. 175, p. 106, 1 Nisan 5440; ibid., p. 125, 1 Elul 5441: 'Meia Finta f 15,–').

Moses Curiel Rosado, belonging to the lowest tax category, left the poor 1,200 guilders, as opposed to 7,600 guilders to his closest family (see the will of Moses Curiel Rosado: SAA entry no. 334, no. 119a, file 13, 22 Adar 5391; ibid., no. 174, p. 1044, 7 Tishrei 5435: 'Mozeh Curiel Rozado pr.^{a} m^{a} finta *f* 3,=; seg^{a} m^{a} finta *f* 3,=').

154 Last will of Sara Torres (SAA entry no. 5075, no. 3720, Not. F. Tixerandet, pp. 11–14/19^{v}–21, 23 June 1693; see also SAA entry no. 334, no. 176, p. 147, 1 Elul 5453:

'Casa Mortuoria de Sara Torres'). For her charitable gifts see 'Item ala Esiba de Temime darech . . . f[res] veynte . . . Item manda cinquenta f[res] para se repartir . . . p[a] pobres en las tres honras . . . Item dexa a la Sedaca dela nacion portugesa duzientos f.[res] una vez'; see also ibid., no. 20, p. 172, 12 Elul 5453.

155 Last will of Abigail Abarbanel, wife of Pincas Abarbanel (SAA entry no. 5075, no. 2895B, Not. P. Padthuysen, pp. 1378–80, 28 Sept. 1666); her assets to be bequeathed amounted to 3,375 guilders, of which she set aside a little less than 125 guilders for charity. For the will of Isaac Alfarin see SAA entry no. 5075, no. 4103A, Not. D. van der Groe, 7 July 1682. For the settlement of his estate see SAA entry no. 334, no. 175, pp. 197–8, 1 Elul 5442; ibid., p. 104, 1 Nisan 5440: 'Ishac Alfarin, Meia Finta f 4,–'; ibid., p. 122, 1 Elul 5441: 'Meia Finta Ishac Alfarim f 4:–'.

156 SAA entry no. 5075, no. 7493, no. 75, Not. J. van den Ende, 9 Dec. 1717.

157 For the percentage calculated on the basis of wills among the Portuguese in Bayonne see Nahon, 'Pour une approche', 53–4. Norberg, *Rich and Poor in Grenoble*, 118 and 144, describes a growth in charitable bequests from wills in relation to family bequests among the Catholic population, starting at 1% in 1620 and reaching 4% in 1679, while among Protestants the percentage never exceeded 2% for the same period; see also M. van Leeuwen, 'Liefdadige giften'.

158 For gifts in wills of Portuguese women to family and charity, e.g. gifts of widows, see for example the last will of Gracia Senior, alias Doña Isabel Enriques, widow of Duarte Coronel Enriques (SAA entry no. 334, no. 826, Not. P. Padthuysen, 30 Aug. 1673), or that of Rachel Belmonte (SAA entry no. 334, no. 641, Not. C. van Achthoven, 3 Mar. 1724). On Jewish widows in medieval times see Tallan, 'Opportunities'; Burns, *Notarial Culture*, 110. For Portuguese women and their generosity among the Amsterdam Portuguese in the early modern period see Levie Bernfeld, 'Sephardi Women in Holland's Golden Age', 186, 194, 198–9. In the Dutch Golden Age, the generosity of non-Jewish women was mostly greater than that of non-Jewish men (Deursen, *Een dorp in de polder*, 184–6).

159 See Appendix I, Table 22. For a similar conclusion see M. van Leeuwen, 'Liefdadige giften', 423.

160 See MS Ets Haim 48 D 43, p. 61, where for 1676 loans are mentioned, to a value of 98,940 guilders, contracted through three private individuals, the organizations Ets Haim and Dotar, and some unnamed members of the Portuguese community.

161 M. van Leeuwen, 'Liefdadige giften'.

162 Nahon, 'Pour une approche', 54, comes to the same conclusion for Bayonne.

6 The Motives behind Charity

1 This intention seems also to have been present among Conversos on the peninsula: the New Christian Luis Françisco, who left money to a *caza de misericordia* in Amsterdam (see Ch. 5 n. 115 above), had done so in order that 'God would pardon him for his sins' (SAA entry no. 334, no. 21, pp. 114–15, 5476).

2 Lev, 'Charity and Gift Giving in Medieval Islam', 263. On the question of sin and salvation among the Conversos see Altmann, 'Eternality of Punishment'; Yerushalmi, *From Spanish Court to Italian Ghetto*, 21–42. On the relation between charity and reward in Jewish tradition see also Frisch, *An Historical Survey*, 55–8, 66–7, 79, 87–90, and Galinsky, 'Jewish Charitable Bequests', 433. On concepts of sin and redemption in Judaism see also *Encyclopaedia Judaica*, xvii. 150–6, s.v. 'Redemption', and xviii. 621–5, s.v. 'Sin'.

On redemptive almsgiving both in Judaism and in early Christian tradition see Garrison, *Redemptive Almsgiving in Early Christianity*, 46–108.

On concepts of sin and salvation in Catholicism see McBrien (ed.), *Encyclopedia of Catholicism*, 1192–4, s.v. 'Sin', and 1158–60, s.v. 'Salvation'; Magnani, 'Almsgiving'; Ruiz, *From Heaven to Earth*, ch. 6; Rubin, *Charity and Community*, 64–6; Duffy, *The Stripping of the Altars*, 354–62.

On the relation between charity, sin, and reward in Islam, see further Lev, 'Charity and Gift Giving in Medieval Islam'; Sabra, *Poverty and Charity*, 95–100; Y. Frenkel, 'Piety and Charity'; Zomeño, '"When Death Will Fall Upon Him"'; Talmon-Heller, 'Charity and Repentance'.

One of the paintings decorating the walls of the synagogue of Neve Salom before 1639 depicted reward and punishment (*Pajnel do premjo Epena*: for this and the other paintings, depicting biblical scenes, views on Jerusalem, Jewish holidays, subjects from everyday Jewish life, and other aspects of Jewish tradition, once hanging on the walls of the three different Portuguese synagogues and in 1639 sold to members of the Portuguese community, see SAA entry no. 334, no. 172, pp. 38–9, 2 Heshvan 5400).

3 Bird, 'A Comparative Study of the Work of Charity in Christianity and Judaism'; see also on this issue Galinsky, 'Jewish Charitable Bequests', 431–2, who notices the influence of Christian society on the Jewish community of 13th-century Spain. Many Jews at that time were motivated to make charitable bequests by a desire to atone for their sins and ensure the salvation of their souls.

4 The fact that many were strongly preoccupied with death may also be explained in this context. Abraham Israel Torres wrote in his last will of 1661 in Amsterdam that he wanted to be buried in the Portuguese cemetery Bet Haim 'in the hope of the blessed resurrection on the day of the universal Judgment' (SAA entry no. 5075, no. 2890A, Not. P. Padthuysen, pp. 17–19, 10 Nov. 1661). Abigail Semah Cortiços, who in her last will of 1661 asked for forgiveness for her sins, hoped God would save her soul in the hour of salvation and resurrection (SAA entry no. 5075, no. 2890B, Not. P. Padthuysen, pp. 1217–21, 7 Mar. 1661: last will of Abigail Semah Cortiços, alias Clara Gomes, widow of Isaac Semah Cortiços, alias Antonio da Costa Cortiços); see also Levie Bernfeld, 'Caridade'.

5 In his will of 1692 Joseph Salomons, for instance, asked that a *minyan* and a group studying Jewish law assemble in his house every day for two hours, one hour in the morning and one in the evening, for a year following his death. To that end he left a total of 400 guilders to the ten men constituting the *minyan*. He also left money to various organizations associated with his congregation.

In specifying these donations he made no explicit reference to such concepts as repentance or the salvation of the soul (SAA entry no. 5075, no. 4242, Not. D. van der Groe, pp. 348–57, 14 June 1692: last will of Joseph Salomons and his wife). For other Ashkenazi wills see those of Salomon Josephs and his wife (SAA entry no. 5075, no. 4241, Not. D. van der Groe, pp. 403–7, 6 Aug. 1691); of Meijer Josephs and Miriam Arons (SAA entry no. 5075, no. 4241, Not. D. van der Groe, pp. 396–401, 6 Aug. 1691); and of Samuel Coen and his wife (SAA entry no. 5075, no. 6641, Not. G. van der Groe, pp. 959–65, 27 Oct. 1700). For a comparison of the wills of Portuguese Jews with those of Protestants and Catholics in Amsterdam see the wills, signed on the same day, of the Portuguese Jew Abraham Levy (SAA entry no. 5075, no. 4092, Not. D. van der Groe, [no page no.], 15 Nov. 1679, and the Protestant Anthoni des Pommares (ibid.), and the will, signed on the previous day, of Joan Schivelbergh (ibid., [no page no.], 14 Nov. 1679). For a Lutheran will see that of Elsje Adriaans, widow of Pieter Jansz. Noteboom (SAA entry no. 5075, no. 5715, Not. N. van Loosdreght, [no page no.], 28 Sept. 1693). An example of a Mennonite will is that of Sara Spruyt (SAA entry no. 5075, no. 5716, Not. N. van Loosdreght, [no page no.], 7 Dec. 1693). For the wills of Catholics in early modern Amsterdam see those of Eefgen Wijnants, widow of Jan Hendricksz. Buysingh (SAA entry no. 440, no. 253, portfolio 8, Not. L. Lamberti, Nov. 1629) and Elbert Joosten (SAA entry no. 440, portfolio 14, Not. J. van der Hoeven, 9 Sept. 1642). See also Vovelle, *Mourir autrefois*; id., *Piété baroque*; Chaunu, *La Mort à Paris*; Ariès, *L'Homme devant la mort*; Jordan, *Philanthropy*; Norberg, *Rich and Poor in Grenoble*; S. A. Epstein, *Wills and Wealth*; Pugh, 'Catholics, Protestants'. For the Dutch Republic see P. den Boer, 'Naar een geschiedenis'; see further: Levie Bernfeld, 'Caridade'.

6 On methodological problems concerning the interpretation and use of sermons (e.g. those of Saul Levi Morteira) as a historical source see Saperstein, *Exile in Amsterdam*, 47–9, 115–22, 143–4, 182–3, 210, 229–52, 310–11 n. 6.

7 Y. Kaplan, 'El perfil de tres rabinos sefardiés'; Swetschinski, *Reluctant Cosmopolitans*, 286–310; Studemund-Halévy, 'Codices gentium'; H. den Boer, *Spanish and Portuguese Printing*; Goldish, 'The Amsterdam Portuguese Rabbinate', 14.

8 Swetschinski, *Reluctant Cosmopolitans*, 286–97; H. den Boer, *Spanish and Portuguese Printing*.

9 Ashtor, *The Jews of Moslem Spain*, iii. 51–8.

10 Pakuda, *Libro intitulado*. The editor of the book, David Pardo, son of Haham Joseph Pardo, himself became a *haham* of the Portuguese community of Bet Israel in 1618, and from 1639 was one of the *hahamim* of the united Portuguese community.

11 Pakuda, *Hobat Alebabot. Obrigaçam Dos Coraçoens, Livro Moral de grande erudiçaõ & pia doctrina. Composto na Lingua Arabica pello devoto Rabbenu Bahie o Daian . . . dos famosos Sabios de Espanha e traduzido na lingua Santa pelo Insigne Rabi Jeuda Aben Tibon E agora novamente tirado da Hebraica â Lingua Portugueza para util dos da nossa Naçam com estilo façil e intelligivel per Semuel filho de Ishac Abaz de boa memoria* (Amsterdam, 5430 [1669–70]), 4; see also H. den Boer, *Bibliografia*, 15.

12 For the libraries of Haham Morteira and other Amsterdam rabbis see Saperstein, *Exile in Amsterdam*, 65 and n. 67. For the libraries of Amsterdam's Portuguese Jewish merchants see that of Josua de Prado, alias Anthonio de Prado (SAA entry no. 5075, no. 7490, no. 52, Not. J. van den Ende, 28 Sept. 1708: 'Specificatie van den huysraedt . . . op de agtyerkamer boven de sael, omtrent hondert en 't sestig Hebreeuwse en Spaense boeken').

Nahon, 'Le Livre dans la "Nation" juive portugaise', 217, mentions that books on devotion and theology dominate the content of small libraries among the Portuguese in southern France, accounting for 65–69% and 12–32% of the titles respectively. In large libraries such as that of Aron Lopes Colaso, only 9.74% of the books concerned theology, while the major part of the library consisted of books on belles-lettres (33.57%), sciences and arts (7.58%), philosophy (5.58%), and history (30.32%) (on Colaso see also Pieterse, 'Abraham Lopes Colaso'). The pattern for large libraries among the French Portuguese, where books on devotion and theology are less prevalent, is similar to that for libraries among the Dutch Sephardim (Swetschinski, *Reluctant Cosmopolitans*, 302–6); Lunteren-Spanjaard and Wijnberg-Stroz, 'Vreemde luyden- Haagse Sefardim', 39–40 and nn. 52 and 53.

13 H. den Boer, *La literatura sefardí de Amsterdam*, 184, 348. In 1722 a Yiddish version came out in Amsterdam (Berger, 'Ashkenazim', 257–9). Soesman translated the work into Dutch in the mid-18th century (Aboab, *De kandelaar des ligts*).

According to the Amsterdam edition of 5468 [1707/8], the first light concerns 'Departure from evil' or 'de advirtir al hombre la obligaçion que tiene de apartarse del mal camino, y de las superfluidades del mundo' (pp. 1–18ᵛ). It is divided into three tracts. The second light deals with 'the treatise against evil speech' or 'tratado del ablar mal' (pp. 18ᵛ–36ᵛ). It is divided into ten tracts. The third light confirms the observance of the *mitsvot* or 'de afirmar los preceptos' (pp. 36ᵛ–105ᵛ) and is also divided into ten tracts, one of which is the 'limosna' (the seventh tract). The fourth light deals with 'the study of the Torah' or 'del Aprender ley' (pp. 106–24) and is divided into four tracts. The fifth light deals with 'Repentance' or 'de los caminos de la Penitençia' (pp. 124–44) and is divided into three tracts. The sixth light deals with 'Peace' or 'que trata de la Paz' (pp. 144–146ᵛ) and is divided into two tracts. The seventh light, finally, deals with 'Humility' or 'de la umildad' (pp. 146ᵛ–148ᵛ) and is also divided into two tracts.

14 Aboab, *Almenara de la luz*, 81–90.

15 The *Thesovro dos dinim* was published in Amsterdam in 1645–7; for other manuals for this target group see Swetschinski, *Reluctant Cosmopolitans*, 292. A book with similar content and purposes was written for use in southern France by Rabbi Abraham Vaez in Bayonne and printed in Amsterdam in 1692: *Arbol de vidas en el qual se contienen los dinim mas necessarios que deve observar todo Ysrael.*

16 Menasseh ben Israel, *Thesovro dos dinim*, second part, 113–23.

17 Olivera, *Tratado de la hobligaçion*, chs. 6 and 7, esp. pp. 6ᵛ, 7, 7ᵛ; Teensma, 'Fragmenten'.

18 See the lists of books in the library of the Talmud Torah school in 1641 (SAA entry no. 334, no. 1051, pp. 19–20^{v}, 29 Nisan 5401: 'Rol dos livros q se achao nesta Bibliotheca... [p. 19^{v}] Menorat ha Maor... [p. 20] hobat halevavot'; and also ibid., no. 19, pp. 59/144–61/146, 3 Adar 5400); see further the inventory of the library of Ets Haim for 1764: MS Ets Haim 49 B 15. In 1817 the Aby Jetomim yeshiva possessed three copies of the Hebrew version of *Menorat hama'or (Livros pertenecentes a sancta irmandade de Abi Jetomim)*, SAA entry no. 334.A, suppl., no. 195^{r}.

19 Ishack de Matatia Aboab, *Documentos*, 4^{v}, para. 6; H. den Boer, *Literatura*, 113–14; Swetschinski, *Reluctant Cosmopolitans*, 212–13. Mordecai Gutières in Bayonne read his children a commentary on Genesis during the winter nights (*Recreo del alma o amplificacion del verso desde Beresit âsta la salida de hijos de Ysrael de Egipto*). This was a polemical work, establishing the truth of Judaism and written against Catholicism, which was intended to influence Conversos (Nahon, 'Livre', 202, 219). It was read to children from the age of 6.

20 Saperstein, *Jewish Preaching*, ch. 10; id., *'Your Voice Like a Ram's Horn'*; id., 'The Rhetoric and Substance of Rebuke'; on Spanish and Portuguese sermon literature see also H. den Boer, *La literatura sefardí de Amsterdam*, 213–68. For preaching on charity in the non-Jewish world see e.g. Norman, 'The Social History of Preaching', 144–5; Andrew, 'On Reading Charity Sermons'.

21 Saperstein, *'Your Voice Like a Ram's Horn'*, ch. 10.

22 See examples of disparities of views between the spiritual and lay leadership in Saperstein, *Exile in Amsterdam*, 205–7.

23 Cited from Morteira's sermon of 1622 'The People's Envy' (Saperstein, *Exile in Amsterdam*, 192–4).

24 Cited from Morteira's sermon of 1641 'Ha'azinu' for Shabbat Teshuvah (between Rosh Hashanah and Yom Kippur) (Saperstein, *Exile in Amsterdam*, 192–6, 489–526). For this and his other sermons voicing social criticism see also Saperstein, 'Rhetoric', 140–5; id., *Exile in Amsterdam*, 172 n. 91, 196–8, and index s.v. 'charity', 'poverty', and 'wealth'.

25 Isaac Vellozino in Castro Tartas, *Sermões que Pregarão*, 107.

26 For Isaac Aboab da Fonseca see *Prologo a o Lector* by David de Castro Tartas, in *Sermões que Pregarão*, 1.

27 Saperstein, *Exile in Amsterdam*, 124–8, 131, 133–4, 137–9, 378, 384–5, 396–7, 401, 404–6.

28 Nahon, 'Amsterdam and Jerusalem', 111.

29 Silva, *Sermon Moral*, 2–3. I should like to thank Professor Harm den Boer, who drew my attention to this source and allowed me to study the sermons in his collection.

30 In this sermon he refers to the situation in Erets Yisra'el (Silva, *Sermon Moral*, 18–20).

31 Nahon, 'Amsterdam and Jerusalem'. On da Silva's visit to Amsterdam see Fuks-Mansfeld, *De Sefardim in Amsterdam*, 170 n. 37; Rozen, *Jewish Identity*, 32, and the relevant literature mentioned in the notes there. (A portrait of da Silva painted in Amsterdam is now part of the collection of the Israel Museum in Jerusalem; see also Rubens, *A History of Jewish Costume*, 175.) According to Moses Hagiz, da Silva had wealthy relations in Amsterdam (Hagiz, *Sefat emet*), 21; still, he received money from the community to cover the cost of his stay in the city (SAA entry no. 334, no. 219, p. 23, 13 Sivan 5451). On Jacob Pereyra's bequest see SAA entry no. 334, no. 20, p. 166, 21 Adar 5453, and p. 192, 11 Iyar 5455.

32 Baron, *The Jewish Community*, ii. 339–43; Nahon, 'Amsterdam and Jerusalem'.

33 Saperstein, *Exile in Amsterdam*, 138, 192–8, 414–20; on poverty in Catholicism see Weaver, 'Wealth and Poverty'. For a comparative study see Bird, 'A Comparative Study of the Work of Charity in Christianity and Judaism'.

34 See the discussion on this subject in Rozen, *Jewish Identity*, 103–18.

35 Cohen Pimentel, *Questoens*, 45–9, question IX. I should like to thank my teacher Professor Yosef Kaplan for drawing my attention to this source.

36 Nunes Torres, 'Sermam funeral', 7; on Nunes Torres see H. den Boer and Salomon, 'Haham David Nunes'.

37 See e.g. the decision of 1666 (SAA entry no. 334, no. 19, p. 561, 20 Iyar 5426): 'os ssres do Mahamad en Compania do s. H. Ishack Aboab . . . para continuar o socorro dos pobres e otras asistencias . . . e unanimes acordarao'.

38 Saperstein, *Exile in Amsterdam*, ch. 9; see also ibid. 201–2 for a discussion of Saul Levi Morteira's sermon on the weekly Torah reading 'Pinhas' in the 1640s, referring to the incidence of sexual relations between Jews and Christians in past and present: 'If so, how can we wonder at the length of our exile, seeing that this sin always remains among us?' On sexual relations between Portuguese Jews and non-Jewish women in Amsterdam see Lotte van de Pol's 'Amsterdam Jews and Amsterdam Prostitution'.

39 Saperstein, *Exile in Amsterdam*, 193–5.

40 SAA entry no. 334, no. 19, p. 366, 3 Tamuz 5414.

41 On the status of moral discipline among the Portuguese of 18th-century Amsterdam see Y. Kaplan, 'Moral Panic'. Nobody was supposed to play cards or other games in public taverns (SAA entry no. 334, no. 22, p. 88, 5485). Women were admonished to cover their hair, to dress modestly, and to refrain from imitating European trends (SAA entry no. 334, no. 21, p. 257, 8 Heshvan 5482). Admonitions concerning the immodesty of women were not new, but had been expressed many times before in Jewish and Muslim societies, in contrast to Christian societies, where women were accorded more freedom: see e.g. Grossman, *Pious and Rebellious*, 102–22.

42 Ayllon, *Sermon*, 21–2, 24, 26–7.

43 Meza, *Meditaçoens*, 7, 10, 24.

44 Meza, *Sermão moral . . . 28 Tamuz 5510*, 20.

45 Meza, *Sermão moral . . . 26 Tamuz 5512*, 19.

46 Ibid. 23.

47 Abendana de Britto, *Sermão*, 26–8.

48 Pereyra, *Espejo*, ch. 16, para. 1, p. 218. The same verse, cited by Pereyra in Portuguese translation as 'Caridade escapa da morte', is written on marble tablets above a fountain in the so-called Rodeamentos house at the Portugese Jewish cemetery of Ouderkerk aan de Amstel. One tablet is dated 5455 (1694/5), and was apparently added to the wall at a later stage. For the other marble tablet, dated 5465 (1704/5), see Henriques de Castro, *Keur van grafstenen*, 14. On Pereyra see Y. Kaplan, 'Religious World' (Heb.); Méchoulan, 'Abraham Pereyra'; id., *Hispanidad y Judaísmo*.

49 For the use of this phrase, and others based on citations from the Bible, among the Jews in medieval Egypt see M. Cohen, *Poverty and Charity*, 247–8; id., *The Voice of the Poor*, 38–42, 56–7.

50 SAA entry no. 334, no. 1151, p. 121, 15 Shevat 5429.

51 On similar practices in Catholic countries in the Middle Ages see Mollat, *The Poor in the Middle Ages*, 154–5, and also Galinsky, 'Jewish Charitable Bequests', 435.

52 See the will of Miriam Alvares (SAA entry no. 334, no. 628, written and signed 28 Oct. 1678; transferred 21 Nov. 1678 to Not. F. Tixerandet; opened by Not. D. van der Groe on 29 Aug. 1685): 'Em nome do S.[or] Deus de Israel, S.[or] dos exercitos e dos esperitos de toda criatura cuja vida e morte tem nasua mao, digo eu Mirijam del Sotto alias Maria Alvares, que Sou Judia da nacao hebrea e creona leij Santa dado no felise Monte de sinaij, plo S[or] Deus, naqual tenho p Ymfalibel me hey de salvar . . . Deixo ao s[or] Hazan Manuel Abenatar florins cinquenta que me asista de sua Reza quando morer'. Horowitz ('Jewish Confraternities', 58–136) discusses the emergence of a deathbed ritual among Jews in Italy in the 16th and 17th centuries. He explains that the growing participation of the spiritual leadership in that ritual might point to an adaptation to the Catholic environment of those days. Similarly, the concern for the presence of spiritual leadership at the deathbed on the part of the Portuguese Jews of Amsterdam can most probably be ascribed to the Catholic background of many Amsterdam Portuguese Jews. The Amsterdam rabbi Menasseh ben Israel does urge confession as a deathbed ritual in his *Thesovro dos dinim* (second part, pp. 176–8) and bases himself on the *Shulḥan arukh*, 'Yoreh De'ah', 338, 2. However, he does not mention the need for the presence of a spiritual leader at the deathbed.

53 Thus Ester Rodriguez left 15 guilders for prayers for her soul to be said in the Honen Dalim *ḥevrah* and yeshiva (SAA entry no. 5075, no. 7533, Not. J. van Vilekens, pp. 257–60, 12 Mar. 1710). She also insisted on having prayers said in the synagogue (ibid., p. 257). See also the last will of Moses Curiel Rosado, in which legacies to the Portuguese community, Ets Haim, and Aby Jetomim are made on condition that *escavot* are said (SAA entry no. 5075, no. 1563, Not. J. Volkaertsz. Oli, pp. 721–3, 18 Oct. 1678; SAA entry no. 334, no. 119a, file 17: last will of Moses Curiel Rosado). See further the wills of Mordecai Castanho (SAA entry no. 334, no. 520a, Not. J. Snoek, pp. 595–606, 22 Nov. 1730); of Aron de Pinto and Abigail of Gracia Nunes Henriques (SAA entry no. 5075, no. 7493, no. 63, Not. J. van den Ende, 10 Aug. 1717); and of Hester Baruch Alvares, widow of Doctor Jacob de Castro (SAA entry no. 5075, no. 7570, no. 154, Not. J. van Vilekens, 3 Dec. 1737). For requests for an *escava* prayer see also SAA entry no. 334, no. 19, *escamot*, pp. 339, 641, and 689. For charitable donations in exchange for *escavot* prayers see also excerpts from the writings of Menasseh ben Israel in his *Thesovro dos dinim*, second part: *Tratado da Esmola e seu merecimento*, 113–23, esp. p. 117: 'E a Esmola que se promete nas Escavot pellos defuntos, afirmão lhes sirve de beneficio e util'. See also Levie Bernfeld, 'Caridade'. On the situation regarding requests for *escavot* in France see Nahon, 'Pour une approche', 46 and 50–2 (esp. 50 n. 221), and the bibliography there (pp. 115–21).

54 Casey, *Early Modern Spain*, 196; Pike, *Aristocrats and Traders*, 117; Russell-Wood, *Fidalgos and Philanthropists*, 103–4, 151, 167–70; Guerrero Mayllo, *Familia*, 375–8; Flynn, *Sacred Charity*, 35–6, 39; see also the last will of Manuel Teixeira in Lisbon 1505 (Kellenbenz, 'Das Testament von Manuel Teixeira').

55 M. van Leeuwen, 'Liefdadige giften', 425–6.

56 Isaac Alfarin, for example, asked the executors of his will to distribute 200 guilders among the poor after his death, half on the seventh day, a quarter at the end of the month, and the other quarter in the eleventh month following his death (SAA entry no. 5075, no. 4103A, Not. D. van der Groe, pp. 47–50, 7 July 1682; ibid., no. 175, p. 198, 1 Iyar 5442: 'Por la primer repartiçion alos 7/d de sus onras a los pobres f 100; por la segunda repartiçion al mes f 50; por las promesas enla esnoga en sus onras f 7:14'). See also the last will of Rachel Belmonte (SAA entry no. 334, no. 641, Not. C. van Achthoven, 3 Mar. 1724: copy of the last will of Rachel Belmonte alias Schonenberg).

57 SAA entry no. 334, no. 218, pp. 84–6, 24 Heshvan 5446: 'Notta dos f 400: que ofreceo Jahacob de Pintto Para se repartirem Por a menuha de sua may os quais se derão aos Pobres que abaixo Paresse em 24 Heshvan ass[r]. p. maos do Hazan Abraham Coem de Lara, e samas Simon do Vale Por memoria.' On the same occasion Jacob de Pinto also donated money to the poor in Jerusalem; on this see SAA entry no. 334, no. 218, p. 89, 5 Tevet 5446: 'Notta da Reparticão de 100 p. que oferecão Jacob de pinto Para se repartirem em Jerusalaim p. a menuha de sua may Sara de pinta, e se hordenou se dessem aos abaixo como p[e] oje 5 de tebeth a[o] 5446.'

58 SAA entry no. 334, no. 218, pp. 81–3, 6 Shevat 5446: 'Notta dos f 800 que ofresseu em 6 de Sebat assaber f 600 Rachel Lopez Suasso e f 200 seu f[o]. Abraham Lopez Suasso p[a] se Repartirem p. Pobres como se fez dando os aos abaixo no mesmo dia p. mão do Hazan Ab: Cohen de Lara e samas Simon do Vale.' Isaac Israel Suasso was buried at the Portuguese cemetery in Ouderkerk eleven months before this date, namely on 6 Adar II 5445 (1685) (SAA entry no. 334, no. 422). On the Lopes Suasso family see further Swetschinski and Schönduve, *De familie Lopes Suasso*.

59 'e digo primeiram[te] q dexo ao H. Yshac Aboab p. meu universal testamenteiro . . . p.[a] oque dexo 300 florins q o H, e dito meu testamenteiro repartira como milhor lhe pareser . . . Ytem dexo a s[ra] minha maim 10 ducados de ouro, eo quidusin e sendo q ela morra antes o repartira o dito H p. pobres onrados . . . a Daniel Belilhos, p[a] q medisao ogadis, sesenta florins e dusenta florins en mao de dito H p[a] q o reparta como lhe pareser Eo resto da menagem e fato q ficar sevendera p[a] repartir p. pobres pedido ao S[r] Ds aseite minha boa tensão p[a] recolher minha alma com piadade amen' (for the last will of Sara Alvares, wife of Isaac Alvares, see SAA entry no. 5075, no. 2237, Not. A. Lock, 23 Dec. 1671).

60 See also Prov. 20: 27: 'The soul is the lamp of God.'

61 For such a request for a *ner tamid* by Abraham del Prado for the soul of his wife see SAA entry no. 334, no. 19, p. 233, 18 Kislev 5408.

62 For his last will see SAA entry no. 334, no. 119a, file 13, 22 Adar 5391.

63 For the gifts of Abraham Israel Pereyra see SAA entry no. 334, no. 780A, pp. 25–8, Av 5418; ibid., no. 782, pp. 10–18, 7 Nisan/15 Tamuz 5419; ibid., no. 19, pp. 419–52, 26 Shevat 5419; for the donation of Isaac Israel Otsen see SAA entry no. 334, no. 19, pp. 502–3, 1 Elul 5422. His generosity was extended not only to the Portuguese poor and Portuguese welfare institutions, such as the *sedaca* box of the Portuguese community, Ets Haim, *cativos*, Terra Santa, and Dotar, but also to good causes among the Ashkenazi and Polish communities of Amsterdam, and even to the communities of Hamburg and Glückstadt. This individual seems to have been a *ger* (convert), because he set an amount of 600 guilders aside for *gerim* 'de boa vida' (converts who lived a 'good life'): three of them lived in Amsterdam and one in Glückstadt.

64 Salem, *Sermón*, also cited in H. den Boer, *La literatura sefardí de Amsterdam*, 250–1.

65 In their last will, Isaac and Rachel de Prado bequeathed 500 guilders, of which the interest on the capital would go to the students of Ets Haim. In return, *escava* prayers would be said on Jewish holidays, Rosh Hodesh, and the eve of Yom Kippur for them, for the parents of the husband, and for the deceased sons of the couple, in the Esnoga and in the highest class of the yeshiva: 'Em a misva de Eshaim instituida neste nos. K.K. se fara kodes florins quinhentos E em caso q não aja seguido em vida se fara loguo em falesendo coalquer de nos p.[a] se Juntarein ao Cabedal de dita hebra e seu rendim.[to] servir p.[a] os meldantes della com obrig.[cam] de nos botar Escava na Esnogua em os dias da festa dos Parnazes de dita misva, E todos os Roshodes e besporas de quipur no medras grande da mais alta licão a nos Ishack de Prado e Rachel de Prado e a nosos Incurtados filhos Abraham de Prado e Selomoh de Prado: E tambein se botara escava em os ditos tempos em o dito medras a meus SS[s] Paijs Abraham de Prado e Sara de Prado os Coais tein legado em a dita misva de Eshaim de quinhentos florins' (SAA entry no. 5075, no. 3309, p. 42, Not. H. Outgers, 27 Jan. 1691).

66 Benjamin Musaphia (SAA entry no. 334, no. 756, no. 1, pp. 529–52: extract of the testament of H. H. Musaphia, made by Not. H. Outgers on 27 Jan. 1677 of the original will of Benjamin Musaphia, written 4 Dec. 1674; confirmed 5 Dec. 1674 by Not. P. Padthuysen; opened 31 Dec. 1674, Not. P. Padthuysen; ibid., no. 1074, pp. 2[v]–3; ibid., no. 1052, p. 114, 5437. I was unable to locate the original will). The citation is taken from the Ets Haim source (SAA entry no. 334, no. 1052, p. 114, 5437: Copia da Verba do Testamento do S[r]. H. D[r]. Benjamin Musaphia q el D. tem Fol: 103). For further information on Benjamin Musaphia in Hamburg see Kellenbenz, *Sephardim an der unteren Elbe*, 331–8.

67 SAA entry no. 5075, no. 3208, Not. H. Outgers, pp. 166–8, 22 July 1671, last will of Samuel Oeb. For further information on legacies in exchange for *escavot* in Aby

Jetomim see SAA entry no. 334, no. 1211, p. 27, 5413: 'Legados p. q. se deita escava nas eleicoins sao os siguintes'; ibid., pp. 56 ff.: 'Pauta das yrmams'; Pieterse, *Daniel Levi de Barrios*, 117–19.

68 SAA entry no. 334, no. 174, pp. 724–7, 21 Tevet 5426: 'o Gabay Mosseh Curiel por Nedaba feita neste K.K. para socorrer os pobres f 8.345:10 que importão o Rendim^{to} de ditta Nedaba emque offereceram os seguintes'; ibid., pp. 729–33, 20 Adar 5426: 'Nedaba feita neste Kahal p^{a} socorro de pobres . . . que monta como abaixo parece oq Se repartio por duas vezes a p^{ra} em Tebet eaoutra em 15 deste por ordem doss^{res} do Mahamad a saber . . . f 8.345:10.' The establishment of the Gemilut Hasadim yeshiva in 1665 might have been influenced by the same messianic fervour: the founders formulated their intention to set up a yeshiva expressing their hope for a reward if so deserved. God, so they trusted, would have mercy on his people and enable them to put this holy work into practice in the Holy Land (ibid., no. 1191, Rosh Hodesh Tevet 5426). For the developments around Sabbatai Zevi see Scholem, *Sabbatai Sevi*; on the attitude of the Amsterdam Portuguese leadership to the Sabbatian movement see Y. Kaplan, 'The Attitude of the Leadership' (Heb.); on Converso messianism see also Goldish, 'Patterns in Converso Messianism'.

69 Cited in Rozen, *Jewish Identity*, 32.

70 Cited in Carlebach, *The Pursuit of Heresy*, 57–8; see also Goldish, 'Halakhah'.

71 For details of his foundation for the poor set up in 1708 see the last will of Josua de Prado (SAA entry no. 5075, no. 7490, no. 19, Not. van de Ende, 12 Mar. 1708).

72 'Jaarlijx uyt te keeren aan armen en behoeftige menschen de waerde van vijftigh guldens in eetbare waeren' (SAA entry no. 5075, no. 7619, no. 300, Not. A. Tzeewen, 26 May 1723).

73 See e.g. the last will of Rachel Salom de Azevedo, widow of Jan de Paz (SAA entry no. 334, no. 518, pp. 255–6, Not. C. van Achthoven, 16 Feb. 1724): 'aen sedaca van de Portugeese Joodse natie dezer Stadt . . . op de hier onder volgende Conditien . . . voor hunne moeijte en ter benefitie van d'armen hunner natie van de vrugten en revenuen van de . . . door hen t' administreren Capitalen Jaarlijx sullen mogen corten . . . drij p^{r} Cento'. See also the last will of Ester Musaphia (SAA entry no. 334, no. 757, Not. J. Barels de Jonge, pp. 737–49, 19 Aug. 1733), and the last will of Rachel de Spinosa Henriques (SAA entry no. 334, no. 694, Not. Ph. de Marolles, pp. 32–5, 18 Nov. 1736).

74 For this phenomenon in medieval Spanish Jewish communities see Galinsky, 'Jewish Charitable Bequests', 438–9.

75 Last will of Rica de Leon, alias Maria Pereyra, wife of Moses de Leon, alias Roque de Leon (SAA entry no. 5075, no. 7533, Not. J. van Vilekens, pp. 1197–1202, 31 Oct. 1710).

76 SAA entry no. 334, no. 518, Not. J. Barels de Jonge, pp. 387–8, 15 May 1731: last will of Judith Rodrigues Carrion, widow of David de Daniel Rodriguez: 'haar ziel in handen van den Barmhartigen God Israels hem met berouw en leetweesen over haer zonden'.

77 SAA entry no. 5075, no. 7493, no. 63, Not. J. van den Ende, 10 Aug. 1717.

78 Last will of Judith Machado, widow of Samuel Abarbanel Souza (SAA entry no. 5075, no. 8830, no. 777, Not. J. Barels de Jonge, 29 Oct. 1733): 'Eerst en voor alle dingen beval zij Testatrice haar Ziel in handen van den barmhartige God Israels Hem met berouw en leetwesen over haare zonden biddende om dezelven ten tijden wanneer het Hem behaagen zal die tot Zig te roepen, in genaden te willen nemen en haar doode lighaam ter aarde om begraaven te werden op het Bedhaim tot Ouderkerk in het Graf 't geen zij tot dien eijnde heeft voorgeschikt volgens Costume en gewoonten onder die van de Joode Natie alhier gerecipieerd.'

79 Maasim Tobim yeshiva, established in 1707 as a centre for both study and charitable activity directed at taking care of the sick, requested permission from the Mahamad to allow people to assist the dying by reciting psalms and encouraging them to make confession (*viddui*), ask God's pardon, and repent of their sins (SAA entry no. 334, no. 66a, 28 Nisan 5467; Franco Mendes, *Memorias*, 102–3; see also ibid., pp. 943–57, 4 Nisan 5518: Maasim Tobim–Sidcat Nassim). A *ḥevrah* like Michse Leani'im, likewise combining study with charity and thus fighting poverty, used the concept of sin as an explanation of the misery existing among 'our Portuguese and Spanish nation' (SAA entry no. 334, no. 120, file 89, p. 970, n.d. [apparently mid-18th century]; see further Leqah Tov (Franco Mendes, *Memorias*, 106, 29 Nisan 5478); Peri Ets Haim (SAA entry no. 334, no. 25, p. 144, 7 Tamuz 5478; ibid., p. 202, 22 Tevet 5491: name changed to Shevet Achim); Oel Ishack (ibid., p. 227, 11 Sivan 5496); Keter Torah of 1745 (ibid., pp. 297–8, 3 Av 5505); Mamlechet Coanim yeshiva (ibid., p. 304, 5 Heshvan 5506); an unnamed yeshiva (ibid., p. 286, 16 Heshvan 5504).

80 For the influence of an Orthodox core among the Amsterdam Portuguese in the 18th century see Y. Kaplan, 'Secularizing the Portuguese Jews'.

81 SAA entry no. 334, no. 91, p. 89, 6 Shevat 5493, Amsterdam: 'y que desde entonses aun nos he sobre cargado la pobreza que por pecados nos acude de toda parte'.

82 For the family as the prime target of welfare in the Jewish community of medieval Egypt see M. Cohen, *Poverty and Charity*, 190–5; giving priority to family members seems to be a common phenomenon in the history of charitable donation in early modern Europe (Kooijmans, *Vriendschap*).

83 Last will of Gracia Senior, alias Doña Isabel Enriques, widow of Duarte Coronel Enriques (SAA entry no. 334, no. 826, Not. P. Padthuysen, p. 1, 30 Aug. 1673; for a copy of this will see SAA entry no. 334, no. 19, pp. 700–1): 'Declaro q lleve de Dese Sinquenta y quatro mill Cruzados y que dellos no saque mas q lo forcoso para mi Camino Y Como me vine por temores dela inquisision luego q falte Embargo mi hacienda dha ynquisision donde oy esta Con la de Mi Marido padre y hermano que toda estava Junta por loqual noseme puede pedir Cosa ninguna por mi niami por ninguno dellos.'

84 See the last will of Abigail Levi Gomes, alias Doña Blanca Henriques, widow of Antonio Rodrigues Gomes (SAA entry no. 5075, no. 2928A, Not. P. Padthuysen, pp. 29–32, 29 Sept. 1693): 'cuijo testamento, carta de dote ij otros papeles se han quedado en España por aver estado ella testadora ij el dho su hixo francisco presos por la ynquisicion'.

85 On charity among New Christians in the Iberian peninsula see López Belinchón, *Honra, libertad y hacienda*, 276–7.

86 Last will of Gracia Senior, alias Doña Isabel Enriques, widow of Duarte Coronel Enriques (SAA entry no. 334, no. 826, Not. P. Padthuysen, 30 Aug. 1673); see also the last will of Joseph Nahemias Torres, alias Gaspar Nunes Torres (SAA entry no. 5075, no. 633, Not. S. Cornelisz., pp. 134–5, 26 Oct. 1626–10 Jan. 1627).

87 Revised English version by Arnold Pomerans of the de Pinto manuscript translated by Salomon, 'The "De Pinto Manuscript"', esp. pp. 27 and 52, p. 248 n. 354. Isaac de Pina and his large family were assisted by the Portuguese community during the festivals from 1639 until his death in 1672, with supplies of peat and matzot (SAA entry no. 334, no. 172, p. 5, 24 Nisan 5399: 'nedavah de Pesah f 2:10'; ibid., p. 78, 9 Nisan 5400: matzot (40 *livras* of matzah meal); ibid., p. 205, 20 Adar 5403: matzot (50 *livras* of matzah meal): 'Ishac de Pina, molher e 6 f^{os}'; ibid., no. 174, p. 243, 3 Heshvan 5418: peat; ibid., no. 215, p. 111, 8 Tamuz 5425: special help, 'Socorro f 15'; ibid., no. 174, p. 731, 20 Adar 5426: 'f 20'; ibid., 'f 18:18'; ibid., no. 216, p. 130, 1 Kislev 5433: 'cx^{a} p^{a} Izaque Pina . . . f 3:2:8'). Isaac and Aron Cabessão, Isaac Delgado, Rica Delgado, Ester Vaz, and Rica Nunes do not appear on the welfare lists of the Amsterdam Portuguese community.

88 SAA entry no. 5072, no. 695, p. 56, 26 Nov. 1693.

89 'Dho Pires que . . . avia dado y dava a sus hijos cada semana para su mantimiento . . . a dhos sus hijos como limosna por ser pobres y por amor paternal' (SAA entry no. 5075, no. 3684, Not. F. Tixerandet, p. 796, [date of day/month illegible] 1676).

90 'p^{a} q inde remediar a necessidade de sua may' (SAA entry no. 5075, no. 633, Not. S. Cornelisz., pp. 134–5, 26 Oct. 1626–10 Jan. 1627).

91 SAA entry no. 5075, no. 414B, Not. J. and N. Jacobs, p. 542, 16 Dec. 1636, last will of Ester Pinta, widow of Jose Pinto: 'e o rendimento q ouver en cada hu año Repartirao na Vespora de Rosanah por pobres parentes meus nos Coais entrara jacob ferro, Josuah mendes q esta entrevado Semeon franco lagarto e abrao de gouvea q fas pano e outros parentes avendo os aqui'.

92 Last will of Johebed de Casseres (SAA entry no. 5075, no. 3280, no. 74, Not. H. Outgers, 21 Nov. 1685).

93 SAA entry no. 996, no. 17, 26 Jan. 1699.

94 SAA entry no. 5075, no. 6684C, Not. J. Snoeck, p. 677, 6 Sept. 1709.

95 SAA entry no. 334, no. 718, Not. N. Wilthuyzen, pp. 9–10, 19 Sept. 1777: 'Quitansa de Rehuel Labat'.

96 Last will of Abraham Israel Torres, alias Bartholome Fernandes Torres (SAA entry no. 5075, no. 2890A, Not. P. Padthuysen, pp. 17–19, 10 Nov. 1661): 'nombro e instituyo como nombro y instityo por la presente por sus herederos a su hixa Anna de hedad de nueve años poco mas o menos que al presente reside en Osuna en el Reyno de España por la una mitad y'.

97 López Belinchón, *Honra, libertad y hacienda*, 405.

98 Last will of Rachel Pinta, alias Leonor de Torres (SAA entry no. 5075, no. 2895B, Not. P. Padthuysen, 22 July 1666): 'Item manda y dexa a su hermano della testadora llamado Manuel Gomes Torres quien vive en Madrid caso que viniesse aqui al Judaismo la suma de otros mil florines una vez pero si no viniere al Judaismo quiere que no se le de nada.'

99 Last will of Rica de Leon (SAA entry no. 5075, no. 7533, Not. J. van Vilekens, p. 1199, 31 Oct. 1710): 'Item ala dha sobrina dela Testadora Maria Gomes que se halla segun las ultimas notisias Religiosa professa en un Convento en toloza, quientos florines; pero esto en cazo que la dha Maria Gomes en el tiempo delos primeros quatro años despues dela muerta della Testadora, se retirare de toloza a vivir ij observar publicamente la Religion judaica en parte donde lo puede hazer libremente; ij de otra manera queire la suso dha testadora ij est su voluntad quede este legado nulo y ningun valor.'

100 In his last will, Abraham Raphael Rodriguez said he was willing to bestow on the person who helped him flee from Portugal, who became a Jew, and who was now living in Surinam, one-third of his assets on condition he remained a Jew ('item a Joseph Judeo morador em Suriname p otra tersia p[te] . . . y con expresa condision q el dho Joseph Judeo devera de quedar profesando La Ley Judaica y en cazo q el dho Judeo no quedo observando La dha Ley q entonses no gozara alguna coza'). Abraham was willing to grant another third of his assets to his nephew; however, the latter was still living in Oporto in Portugal and would only get his share if at the age of 25 he went to Amsterdam, or to any other part of the world where he could openly declare he was a Jew, and openly profess the Jewish religion ('y al dho sobrino de dho testador llamado Raphael Rod[s] morador no Porto de Portugal p. otra tersia p[te] la q. gozara yncontiniente q. sera llegado en la edad de veijnte y sinco annos y q. q[do] viniere aqui en esta ciudad o en otra p[te] adonde publicamente se declare ser Judio y professa La Ley Judaica y no antes ni de otra suerte': SAA entry no. 334, no. 518, Not. P. Schabaelje, 26 Jan. 1702, pp. 49–51). See also the last will of Dr David de Fonseca-Chacon, residing in southern France, in which his nephews and nieces living in Portugal were given permission to inherit his capital only if they went to France or any other 'country of freedom' (Nahon, 'Bayonne', 49). See also the legacy of Rachel Castro, dated 1788, in Bayonne. She granted her husband, who had gone to Portugal, her domain on condition that he return to southern France. For this example and others see Nahon, 'Pour une approche', 57 n. 251; id., 'Los *Cristianos Nuevos*', 595; see also Y. Kaplan, 'Amsterdam, the Forbidden Lands, and the Dynamics of the Sephardi Diaspora', 36 and n. 9.

101 Nahon, 'Pour une approche', 57 n. 251. Esteban Ares, and Gaspar and Alonso Rodrigues Pasarinos, residents of Seville, declared before the court of the Inquisition in Madrid that they sent money to the Jewish poor of the synagogues in Amsterdam (AHN, Inq. Libro 1107, pp. 163[r]–167[v], 30 Mar. 1635, XI).

102 SAA entry no. 334, no. 25, p. 94, 6 Shevat 5467.

103 SAA entry no. 334, no. 782, p. 34, 8 Nisan 5419.

104 SAA entry no. 334, no. 782, p. 16, written by a scribe 7 Nisan, signed by Abraham Pereyra 15 Tamuz 5419; ibid., p. 34, 8 Nisan 5419.

105 See Pullan, *Rich and Poor in Renaissance Venice*, index s.v. 'dowries'; Hughes,

'From Brideprice to Dowry'; Hufton, *The Prospect before Her*, 68; Russell-Wood, *Fidalgos and Philanthropists*, ch. 8. For dowries in the Jewish communities of Italy see Horowitz, 'The Dowering of Brides'; Rivlin, *Mutual Responsibility* (Heb.), 115–20; Bodian, 'The Portuguese Dowry Societies'. In 1614 Jacob Tirado, a Portuguese Jew in Amsterdam, gave money to the society for marrying orphans in Venice to support orphan girls in Erets Yisra'el (Vlessing, 'New Light', 68 n. 36).

106 SAA entry no. 334, no. 826, Not. P. Padthuysen, pp. 1–4, 30 Aug. 1673.

107 SAA entry no. 5075, no. 633, Not. S. Cornelisz., pp. 134–5, 26 Oct. 1626–10 Jan. 1627.

108 SAA entry no. 334, no. 782, p. 10, para. 1, 7 Nisan, signed by Abraham Pereyra 15 Tamuz 5419.

109 Last will of Miriam Alvares (SAA entry no. 334, no. 628, 28 Oct. and 21 Nov. 1678, 29 Aug. 1685: 'A esta minha sobrinha filha de Joao Alvares nao decha nada por que lepos monga en Italia').

110 SAA entry no. 334, no. 828, pp. 21–36, 15 Nov. 1651, translation from the Spanish by Not. P. Padthuysen, 16 July 1688; see also ibid., no. 19, pp. 523–4, 16 Elul 5423; ibid., p. 527, 24 Kislev 5424.

111 Last will of Joseph Nahemias Torres (SAA entry no. 5075, no. 633, Not. S. Cornelisz., pp. 134–5, 26 Oct. 1626–10 Jan. 1627). For gifts stipulating that family members had priority see also the bequest of Moses Franco Drago, who gave money to establish a yeshiva in Jerusalem on condition that family members would get preference to enter as students (SAA entry no. 334, no. 674, portfolio 1–2: will of Moses Franco Drago, Not. J. van de Ven, written 18 Adar 5407, closed 25 Mar. 1647).

112 In 1644 Sara Cohen de Herrera left 1,000 guilders to Ets Haim for scholarships to poor students, with priority to be given to any among her own family. See SAA entry no. 334, no. 1052, pp. 9v and 10, 20 Elul 5404: 'Termo dos Mil Florins que D. Sara Cahanet Viuva de Haham Abraham Cohen de Herera que Deus aya deyxou a Hebra desKaym com as condicois abayjo declaradas.' Folio 10: 'Ytem dexo mas otros mil florines para La Hebra de Es Kaym que Se Ynstituyo Para sustento de mosos necisitados que asisten en el estudio de La Santa Ley conforme Las constituyciones que sehan Echo, pero con tal condision que sij alguno de mis parientes quisieren usar de la dha Limosna y Renta sele aplicara La dha suma sin ser necesario mas prueba que dezir ellos que lo han menester.' Following her death, on the basis of the wording of her legacy, which stipulated that family members would enjoy preference, Isaac Delgado, a relative of Sara, received an annual scholarship of 35 guilders on top of what he received as a student (SAA entry no. 334, no. 1052, p. 131, 24 Iyar 5448; ibid., p. 133, 1 Av 5448). For the execution of priority given to family members through other legacies see the case of Samuel Palache in the Aby Jetomim boys' orphanage (SAA entry no. 334, no. 1211, p. 7, 21 Tevet 5435).

113 Last will of Miriam Alvares (SAA entry no. 334, no. 628, 28 Oct. and 21 Nov. 1678, 29 Aug. 1685). Miriam left a bond of 5,000 guilders, two-thirds of which was to be used to ease the plight of poor family members: 'Em Primeyro lugar, deixo cinco mil florins em Bilhettes dos Estados, que se porão empoder DoSS[res] do Mahamad, dos quaes, Dos Reditos quese cobraren cada hum anno, separtirão em trez partes, a hua parte de Dittos Redittos disporão Suas Merces emfavor dos pobres dasedaka, desta Cid.[e] de amst.[m] e o outro terco Dos Reditos dos dittos Cinco mil florims se entregarão cada anno, em mãos de Ester Lopez subrinha demeu bem aventurado marido p.[a] Repartir em pobrez desua garacão de Ditto meu marido que Deus tem . . . e o outro terco ultimo de Dittos Redittos se entregarão Ameu Yrmão, Antonio Alvarez para que o repartão entre os pobres de nossa geracão que milhor lhes pareser, e estes trez terços hamde ser Repartidos anualm.[te] todos os annos'. Further gifts were made on her deathbed: 'Deixo dozentos florims, para Se Repartão, entre os pobres deminha garação nahora q eu ijspirar com Otros pobres de nossa nação p mão do Sr Haham nosso, e sé Judica Abenacar Viver, se lhe dem delles florims cinquenta.'

114 SAA entry no. 334, no. 25, pp. 99–100, 7 Heshvan 5473. In 1727 a request was received from Mathias Alvares of The Hague for money to be given to the orphans of Benjamin Vas Martins on the same basis, namely to be taken from the capital Miriam left for poor relatives (SAA entry no. 334, no. 628, 25 June 1727).

115 For the will of Rachel Medina Chamis see SAA entry no. 334, no. 658, 12 Aug. 1738.

116 SAA entry no. 334, no. 658, 15 Apr. 1742.

117 For distribution to the poor among Pereyra's family see SAA entry no. 334, no. 784, p. 52, 1786. For dowries given to family members out of this legacy see ibid., no. 782, p. 26, 5469. In 1707 a grandson of Abraham Israel Pereyra received a scholarship grant of 500 guilders from this legacy (ibid., no. 782, pp. 24–5, 8 Elul 5467).

118 For a similar phenomenon in Italy see Trexler, 'Charity'.

119 See e.g. the last will of Ester Mendez (SAA entry no. 5075, no. 2939, Not. P. Padthuysen, pp. 99–102, 17 Nov. 1698): 'y lo que sobrare quiere ella Testadora y con este nombra y comete ella Testadora por sus albaceas y Executores deste su Testamento a los dhos SS[res] del Mahamad de su nacion en esta Ciudad'; the last will of Joseph Senior (SAA entry no. 334, no. 520a, Not. J. Ardinois, pp. 368–99, 5 Sept. 1719); and the last will of Abraham Raphael Rodriguez (SAA entry no. 334, no. 518, Not. P. Schabaelje, 26 Jan. 1702).

120 Concerning bequests to the Amsterdam Portuguese community see Levie Bernfeld, 'Caridade', 179–204.

121 See e.g. the gift of Abraham Nahar (SAA entry no. 334, no. 119a, file 13, 22 Adar 5391).

122 For the food crisis of the early 1630s see SAA entry no. 334, no. 13, p. 65, 8 Heshvan 5391; ibid., p. 68, 4 Iyar 5391.

123 SAA entry no. 5075, no. 646A, Not. S. Cornelisz., pp. 574–5, 26 June 1623; also published in *Studia Rosenthaliana*, 24/2 (1990), 220–1, no. 2924.

124 Last will of Moses de Oliveira, alias Gaspar de Oliveira (SAA entry no. 5075, no. 2891B, Not. P. Padthuysen, pp. 1204–6, 16 Sept. 1662): 'dixo que al dia de sus honras quiere que se de para repartir entre pobres de su nacion a saber a los siette dias y al mes ciento y veinte florines de a 20 placas cada uno en todo . . . Item dexa ala sinagoga para echarle las escabas acostumbradas sietecientos florines los quales a de repartir.' Moses de Oliveira instructed his brother to act as the executor of his will: 'su hermano Jacob de Oliveira, alias Antonio de Oliveira conforme le tiene comunicado pues dexa enteramente la disposicion dellos a su bien quidado y selo porque le confia que dispondra dellos para el mayor beneficio de sua alma'.

125 Last will of Abigail Abarbanel, wife of Pincas Abarbanel (SAA entry no. 5075, no. 2895B, Not. P. Padthuysen, 28 Sept. 1666): 'y finalmente manda y lega ella testadora al dho su marido . . . para que los reparta entre pobres por la alma della testadora, para comprar sepultura y loque mais fuere necessario'.

126 Last will of Rachel Pinta, alias Leonor de Torres, lawful wife of Sor Daniel Pinto (SAA entry no. 5075, no. 2895B, Not. P. Padthuysen, 22 July 1666): 'que el dho su marido o aya de ser obligado a dar por el espacio de tres años consecutivos e primeros seguientes despues de su fallecimiento, los reditos del dho remaneciente a raçon de quatro por ciento al año a pobres necessitados a saver a los pobres que el dho su marido quisere y eliguere'.

127 Last will of Branca de Pas, unmarried daughter: 'Recommenderen sij testatrice aen de voorn. haere moeder als dan oock uyt te keren aen de Armen van haere natie en tot het doen van pieuse wercken soodanige legaten of & als deselve haere moeder gelieven en goet vinden sal' (SAA entry no. 2181, Not. A. Lock, pp. 162–73, Sept. 1676).

128 'Item los restantes vinte ij sinco florines repartira la S[ra] Sara de Nathan Curiel por pobres na forma que mejor paresiere en las onras de los siete dias ij de los treinte dias' (SAA entry no. 5075, no. 7533, Not. J. van Vilekens, p. 258, 12 Mar. 1710: last will of Ester Rodriguez). The tradition of distributions to the poor at the time of a person's death seems to have been common among Conversos in Spain. For example, on the occasion of the death of Manuel Cortizos, a wealthy Portuguese merchant in Madrid, the female members of his family distributed money among the poor, especially to their own Portuguese people, 'for the soul of the man' (López Belinchón, *Honra, libertad y hacienda*, 346–8); on the complexity of almsgiving in connection with the Cortizos family in Madrid see ibid. 337–65. The Inquisition insisted that it was unusual for Catholics to distribute alms in the streets when someone died, and in this way attempted to expose the Jewish identity of such donors.

129 Last will of Aron Jessurun (SAA entry no. 5075, no. 7701, no. 23, Not. A. Tzeewen, 2 Feb. 1750).

130 'Aan niemand wie hij ook mogen zijn eenige verantwoordinge verschuldigt zijn' (last will of Josua de Prado: SAA entry no. 5075, no. 7490, no. 19, Not. van de Ende, 12 Mar. 1708).

131 'Zodanigh nochtans dat het zal staen aen het believen en goedt vinden van de nagenoemde Executeurs . . . wanneer, aen wie en hoe veeldaer telkens opgebragt en gedistribueert zal werden; zonder dat zij daer van aen iemandt eenige rekenschap zullen behoeven te doen of te geven' (last will of Rachel de Prado, alias Rachel Gabay Faro, widow of Isaac de Prado: SAA entry no. 5075, no. 7490, no. 18, Not. J. van de Ende, 12 Mar. 1708).

132 SAA entry no. 5075, no. 4103A, Not. D. van der Groe, pp. 47–50, 7 July 1682.

133 SAA entry no. 334, nos. 736–7, 18 Elul 5481.

134 See the *Livro de segredos* (SAA entry no. 334, no. 973, 5493–5577).

135 Rumeu de Armas, *Historia de la previsión social en España*, ch. 17; Callahan, 'A Note on the Real y General Junta de Comercio'; Arrizabalaga, 'Poor Relief'; Guimarães Sá, 'Catholic Charity'.

136 On a similar pattern among the Sephardim in Livorno see Trivellato, *The Familiarity of Strangers*, 90. On charity as a matter of prestige in the Jewish community see M. Cohen, *Poverty and Charity*, 227.

137 *Sermões que Pregarão*, 37–8; on Penso see also Pieterse, *Daniel Levi de Barrios*, 107–8.

138 Pieterse, *Daniel Levi de Barrios*, 36–42.

139 Israel, *Diasporas within a Diaspora*, 507–8; Daniel Levi de Barrios describes Belmonte as a person who is *piadoso al pobre* (benevolent to the poor) (cited by Israel, ibid., 508 and n. 72); Swetschinski, *Reluctant Cosmopolitans*, 133–7, 243, 248, 299–302.

140 See the oral orders given by Jacob Pereyra to Haham da Silva in 1696 (Nahon, 'Yeshivot hiérosolymites'; id., 'Amsterdam and Jerusalem', 108).

141 For Mishenet Zequenim see SAA entry no. 334, no. 25, p. 339, para. 7, 19 Tevet 5510; ibid., p. 340, paras. 8–10. Among the expenses of Mishenet Zequenim were the costs of paper and of printing and stitching membership lists (SAA entry no. 334, no. 1227, p. 8, 12 Nisan 5512). For Hase Amaharacha see SAA entry no. 334, no. 1234, p. 73, 5475. Ester Abravanel, widow of David de Samuel Pinto, gave bequests to Aby Jetomim on the express condition that her name, and those of her husband and son, would appear on the brotherhood's lists, which were distributed twice a year (SAA entry no. 334, no. 612, Not. D. van den Brink, 20 May 1754).

142 SAA entry no. 334, no. 25, pp. 339–40, paras. 7–10, 8 Tevet 5510.

143 One list giving the names of brothers and sisters of the *ḥevrah*, one those of the female administrators, one those of the treasurers, and one those of the founders. A separate list was drawn up of all those who left legacies of more than 30 guilders, and another one of heirs of former members who were prepared to continue the monthly contributions of the deceased (Mazon Abanot: SAA entry no. 334, no. 120, paras. 37–8 and 40, pp. 873–4, 6 Shevat 5494). On commemoration of good deeds through tables and rolls in medieval and early modern times see Krausman Ben-Amos, *The Culture of Giving*, 234–36.

144 Besides the lists in the 'wintersnoge', drawn up in 5488 (1727/8), see also SAA entry no. 334, no. 1073, pp. 1–9, 5488; the membership lists start here in 5419 (1658/9).

145 Honen Dalim–Resit Hochma, paras. 12 and 23 (SAA entry no. 334, no. 25, pp.

278, 28, 20 Sivan 1741); Mayafu Pehameha Benealim, para. 5 (SAA entry no. 334, no. 25, p. 246, 26 Adar II 5499); Quesut La Ebion, para. 16 (SAA entry no. 334, no. 25, p. 324, 24 Menahem-Av 5508); Hase Amaharacha (SAA entry no. 334, no. 1234, p. 2, para. 5, 1 Heshvan 5474); Mishenet Zequenim, para. 9 (SAA entry no. 334, no. 1220, 'Reglamento tocante o Thezoureyro', 8 Tevet 5510); Maasim Tobim–Sidcat Nassim, para. 5 (SAA entry no. 334, no. 120, file 84, p. 945, 4 Nisan 5518).

146 Black, *Italian Confraternities*, 108–13.

147 Last will of Gracia Senior (SAA entry no. 334, no. 826, Not. P. Padthuysen, 30 Aug. 1673; see also Franco Mendes, *Memorias*, 56). Although at the start of the 17th century the Portuguese community of Amsterdam issued instructions restricting the number of people accompanying the dead to the cemetery to prevent tensions with non-Jewish neighbours, later records mention no such limitation (Reijnders, *Van 'Joodsche Natiën' tot Joodse Nederlanders*, 31, and SAA entry no. 334, no. 19, p. 26/111, para. 51, 28 Av 5399). For funeral processions in the Jewish community see the example of Venice (Horowitz, 'Processions'). For the importance in Catholic societies of the presence of members of confraternities at a funeral in order to honour the dead and enhance their reputation see Russell-Wood, *Fidalgos and Philanthropists*, 165–7, 201–3; Guerrero Mayllo, *Familia*, 373–5. See also Lieberman, 'Childhood and Family', 162–3.

148 See paras. 4–5 in the last will of Rachel Belmonte alias Schonenberg (SAA entry no. 334, no. 641, Not. C. van Achthoven, 3 Mar. 1724); for similar requests and bequests see the last wills of Jacob Abenatar Junior and Ribca Belmonte (SAA entry no. 334, no. 609, Not. D. van den Brink, 9 Feb. 1750); of Judith de Leeuw (SAA entry no. 5075, no. 7660, no. 721, Not. A. Tzeewen, 17 Sept. 1733); and of Ester Arias Capadoce (SAA entry no. 334, no. 632, Not. Jan Barels de Jonge, 11 June 1745).

149 For the refusal of positions see the *livros longos*. For the 17th century see e.g. SAA entry no. 334, no. 216, p. 177, 5434–5; ibid. no. 218, p. 186, 5447–8; ibid no. 219, p. 411, 5458–9. For the 18th century see SAA entry no. 334, no. 220, p. 244, 5463–4; ibid., p. 421, 5472–3; ibid., no. 226, p. 4, 29 Adar 5511; ibid., no. 157, p. 59, Nisan 5514–15, where a list of several names of *parnasim* is followed by the note 'refuso' ('refused'); ibid., no. 228, p. 4, 5543.

150 For a similar point of view see Cavallo, 'Conceptions of Poverty', 69, 98–9, 254; id., *Charity and Power*, 101, 252; McCants, *Civic Charity*; M. van Leeuwen, *The Logic of Charity*, 83–91.

151 For help to refugees and people in need abroad, paid for by the Amsterdam Portuguese community through its *cativos* organization, see the following (in chronological order):

For the Jews of Mantua see SAA entry no. 334, no. 17, p. 37, 27 Oct. 5391: 2,250 guilders.

For collections made to send to the oppressed in Brazil see SAA entry no. 334, no. 239, p. 115, 27 Elul 5406: 'por as boas novas do Brazil . . . f 198:5'; ibid., p. 115, 1 Shevat 5407: 'que rendeo a nedava p^a o Brazil . . . f 2716:17:8'; ibid., p. 188, 12 Adar II 5413: 'f 1223:18 . . . nedava q se fes para o Brazil em 4 naos'.

For the *nedava* to the persecuted poor in Poland, sent to Poland, see SAA entry no. 334, no. 239, p. 136, 12 Elul 5408: 'nedava p. os pobres de Polonia perseguidos: f 1725:13'.

For help given to thirteen people on their way from Lisbon to Livorno who were seized and taken to Algiers see SAA entry no. 334, no. 174, p. 458, 24 Tamuz 5421: 4,667.14.8 guilders: 'Nedava feita pera resgatte de 13 cativos levados a Argel.'

For participation in international collections to help the Jews in central Europe and the Balkans at the end of the 17th century see the money sent to rescue the Jews of Buda: SAA entry no. 334, no. 175, p. 358, 20 Heshvan 5447; ibid., 21 Heshvan 5447; ibid., no. 20, p. 105, Adar 5447; ibid., p. 108, [4 Sivan] 5447.

A figure of around 600 Jews in captivity after being expelled from Belgrade is mentioned in SAA entry no. 334, no. 176, p. 3, 20 Iyar 5449; for help to this group see also ibid., no. 20, p. 131, 9 Sivan 5449; ibid., no. 176, p. 5, 15 Tamuz 5449; ibid., no. 20, p. 131, 20 Tamuz 5449; ibid., no. 176, p. 17, 1 Heshvan 5450; ibid., p. 134, 12 Heshvan 5450.

For help given to the Jews of Sarajevo see SAA entry no. 334, no. 20, p. 270, 8 Tamuz 5459. For help given in the 18th century to the Jews from Brody, Przemyśl, and Vilnius see SAA entry no. 334, no. 176, pp. 354–5, 24 Iyar and 1 Tamuz 5460.

For help given to Jews in Avignon during the epidemic in 1722 see SAA entry no. 334, no. 21, p. 267, 4 Adar 5482.

For individual gifts by Amsterdam Portuguese to the *cativos* fund, during their lifetime or upon approaching death, see the wills of Isaac Israel Otsen (SAA entry no. 334, no. 19, pp. 502–3, 1 Elul 5422); of Jacob Aboab Osorio (SAA entry no. 5075, no. 4263, Not. D. van der Groe, pp. 148–51, 24–25 Apr. 1697): 'item van vijfhondert gls aan de misva van cativos'); and of Isaac Alfarin (SAA entry no. 5075, no. 4103A, Not. D. van der Groe, 7 July 1682: 'en het resterende sesde part aen Cativos ofte tot lossinge van Joodsche slaven').

See also Swetschinski, *Reluctant Cosmopolitans*, 203; Fuks-Mansfeld, *De Sefardim in Amsterdam*, 166–8. On the priority accorded to the redemption of captives see Maimonides, *Mishneh torah*, 'Hilkhot matanot aniyim', 8: 10; see also Ch. 2 with respect to helping to take Conversos out of the Iberian peninsula through the *cativos* fund. For similar societies and initiatives in the Jewish world see Rivlin, *Mutual Responsibility* (Heb.), 171–3, 280–1, and Baron, *The Jewish Community*, ii. 333–43. Christian churches helped people of their kin abroad as well: for international grants by the Reformed Church to help Protestants in need see SAA entry no. 376, no. 5, p. 308, 18 Dec. 1625; ibid., no. 8, p. 39, 20 July 1645; ibid., p. 40, 27 July 1645; ibid., p. 43, Aug. 1645; ibid., no. 9, p. 215, 6 Sept. 1657.

152 For help given by the community to poor people in Erets Yisra'el see the yearly lists of charity given on behalf of the Amsterdam Portuguese community to be distributed in the Holy Land (SAA entry no. 334, no. 19, p. 738, 22 Tevet 5436); see also Fuks-Mansfeld, *De Sefardim in Amsterdam*, 168–71. For private gifts to Erets Yisra'el see e.g. the will of Jacob Aboab Osorio (SAA entry no. 5075, no. 4263,

Not. D. van der Groe, pp. 148–51, 24–25 Apr. 1697: 'Item van vijfhondert guldens aen de misva van Terra Santa') and the will of Francisco Mendes de Medeiros, alias Isaac Franco (SAA entry no. 5075, no. 615A, Not. P. Ruttens, pp. 435–6, written 23 May 1623 and ratified 31 May 1623: 'p[a] a terra santa o q se achar na caixa em q deixa suas esmolas').

For gifts to *cativos* in combination with gifts to Erets Yisra'el see the last will of Johebed de Casseres (SAA entry no. 5075, no. 3280, Not. H. Outgers, no. 74, 21 Nov. 1685).

153 Saperstein, *Exile in Amsterdam*, 332–3. Rabbi Abraham Broda of Prague reiterated the same principle and put it into practical effect, knowing all too well the usual attitude of the various Jewish communities towards transients. In a letter of recommendation that accompanied Rabbi Hagiz from Jerusalem on his trip throughout Europe in the early 1700s, in the course of which he passed through Amsterdam, he wrote the following: 'I beseech my brethren in the Diaspora not to regard him [Hagiz] as just another passerby . . . it is too shameful for him. Wherever he goes he should be accorded cordiality and hospitality' (Carlebach, *The Pursuit of Heresy*, 60).

154 SAA entry no. 334, no. 20, p. 230, 1 Elul 5457.

155 Idaña in 1683: 'Respuesta a Don Juan mi amigo a la carta que me escrivió' (Teensma, 'Fragmenten', 146–7).

156 See the introduction by Netanel Foa to the work of Abraham Cuenque: 'The Haham the Ba'al, my uncle and brother-in-law, our honoured master and teacher, the late Joseph Sarfati was known for the fact that his house was always wide open for passers-by.' See also Carlebach, *The Pursuit of Heresy*, 69; Roest, *Catalog*, 286. On the printing press of Netanel Foa: Silva Rosa, *De geschiedenis van de Portugeesche Joden te Amsterdam*, 31.

157 Saperstein, *Exile in Amsterdam*, 157–61.

158 Cohen, *Et sofer*, 16*b*, 28 Adar 5450: letter from Joseph Sarfati addressed to Moses Cohen.

159 First published in the 1661 Amsterdam edition of the *Shulḥan arukh*, introd. to 'Oraḥ ḥayim', cited in Y. Kaplan, 'The Portuguese Community in 17th-Century Amsterdam and the Ashkenazi World', 35 and n. 52. It should be remembered that Rivkes was given a job in Amsterdam and had to stay on good terms with the Portuguese establishment. Many of his fellow *polacos* were sent out of the city (SAA entry no. 334, no. 19, p. 408, 2 Elul 5416). See also the account in the *Hollandtse Mercurius* at that time (June 1656), describing the arrival and departure of refugees from Poland: 'Daer tegens quamen tot Amsterdam 3 schepen met 300 joden uyt Polen om den oorlog ontvlucht, seer miserabel gestelt: de joden 't Amsterdam hebben haar eerst in twee packhuysen geleyt en aldaer ververst en verschoont. Naderhand zijn sommige met wooningen en gelegenheden voorsien, andere hebben haer elders verspreyt, eenige togen na Engelandt, met hoop om aldaer te mogen woonen.' For the cost in 1658 of supporting (mostly) Polish Jews, both while they were in the city and to enable them to leave it, see further ibid., no. 240, pp. 69 and 73, 1 Nisan 5418: 'que se gastarao com

Polacos nosos irmaos y despacho para se yrem f 2717,55'; ibid., no. 174, p. 306, Rosh Hodesh Nisan 5419: 'se despenderao no discurso do anno en encaminhar pobres tudescos e polacos nosos irmaos'; see also later: ibid., no. 215, p. 72, 7 Tamuz 5424: 'f 400:17 de gasto de diverssos Polacos encaminhados para Polonia'; ibid., no. 1210, [n.d.: found in Abodat Ahesed archives]: 'Rol dos polacos q se vao p[a] Polonia', a list of twenty-six families.

160 Pereyra, *Espejo*, ch. 18, para. 1, 229–30.

161 Cited in Carlebach, *The Pursuit of Heresy*, 5.

162 For lapses in solidarity among the Conversos in the peninsula see Contreras, *Santo Oficio*, 596–608; Huerga Criado, 'Una familia judeoconversa'; Yerushalmi, *From Spanish Court to Italian Ghetto*, 29–31; Y. Kaplan, 'Amsterdam, the Forbidden Lands, and the Dynamics of the Sephardi Diaspora', 36.

163 López Belinchón, *Honra, libertad y hacienda*, 231 and n. 56.

164 Ibid. 266.

165 SAA entry no. 334, no. 616, Not. S. Favon, The Hague, 21 Jan. 1694. However, he did give to the Talmud Torah school and to the Aby Jetomim orphanage; also, he reserved 10% of the annual yields of two shares of 500 Flemish pounds each in the Dutch East India Company for the poor of the community on condition that the *parnasim* of his community held prayers for his soul.

166 Cohen, *Et sofer*, 16*b*, 28 Adar 5450: letter from Joseph Sarfati addressed to Moses Cohen.

167 Levie Bernfeld, 'Confrontation entre l'Orient et l'Occident', 54–6.

168 He noted this phenomenon in Hamburg concerning the treatment of Ashkenazim by the Portuguese Jews (Studemund-Halévy, '*Senhores* versus *Criados da Nacão*', 355–6).

169 Saperstein, *Exile in Amsterdam*, 321 n. 35.

170 This thesis can be proven on the basis of formulations in last wills, from both 17th and 18th centuries, concerning the distribution of clothes. Here we see a clear line of separation: in general, the oldest clothes were given to the general poor and the more valuable items reserved for the family. The poor here were left unspecified except for one mention of the name of a maid (see the last will of Reyna Gomez: SAA entry no. 334, no. 119a, file 12, Not. D. van de Groe, 21 May 1679: 'Repartiran ocho Camizas las mas usadas para pobres; tengo veinte y dos Camizas buenas las quales se repartiran p Rachel Baruch enriquez, Y sarah Sarphati, Y ester Nahamias, Y Sarah Lopez'). Miriam Alvares decided that all her working clothes and her personal garments ('toda a ropa de servicio e todos meus vestidos') should go to paupers and to poor members of her family (see her last will: SAA entry no. 334, no. 628, Not. D. van der Groe, 29 Aug. 1685). Constantina Levy Duarte reserved her worn-out clothes for the poor as well; her other clothes went to her family and friends (SAA entry no. 334, no. 518, Not. Corn. Den Haan, The Hague, pp. 128–9, 16 Apr. 1699; with an extension: ibid., pp. 130–1, 15 Feb. 1707, last will of Manuel Levy Duarte and Constantina Levy Duarte, p. 124: 'bespreeke ik Testatrice Constantina Levy Duarte alle mijne hembden behalven de slechte, die aan arme menschen gegeven zullen werden, aan voorn. Gracia Alvarez, Isabel Alvarez, de vrouw van David Alvarez en de vrouw van Mathatias Alvarez'). Ester Rodriguez left her everyday clothes to her black servant Mariana, while the rest were to be sent to a relative in London (SAA entry no. 5075, no. 7533, Not. J. van Vilekens, p. 258, 12 Mar. 1710). Gracia Alvares, wife of Isaac de Jongh, handled her bequests in a similar way: she gave most of her clothes to orphans, but left her four best outfits to her daughter and daughter-in-law (SAA entry no. 334, no. 518, Not. A. Tzeewen, 26 May 1723). For similar patterns, already existent in medieval Castilian society after 1200, see Ruiz, *From Heaven to Earth*, 128–9; for the distribution of clothes to the poor by members of other denominations in the city see M. van Leeuwen, 'Liefdadige giften', 425.

171 Last will of Abraham Israel Suasso (SAA entry no. 996, no. 17, 26 Jan. 1699–18 Sept. 1705).

172 SAA entry no. 334, no. 520a, Not. J. Ardinois, pp. 368–99, 5 Sept. 1719.

173 For the last will of Rachel Belmonte see SAA entry no. 334, no. 641, Not. C. van Achthoven, 3 Mar. 1724. For that of Rachel de Prado see SAA entry no. 5075, no. 7490, no. 18, Not. J. van de Ende, 12 Mar. 1708. For that of Abigail Dias da Fonseca see SAA entry no. 334, no. 700, Not. P. Padthuysen, pp. 1–16, 30 Mar. 1703.

174 For the last will of Josua de Prado see SAA entry no. 5075, no. 7490, no. 19, Not. van de Ende, 12 Mar. 1708.

175 Ibid.: 'bij dezelve Heren Parnassims van de Portugese Joodse natie in functie of in dienst zijnde, gerequireert werdende gehouden zullen zijn aen hun E. niet alleen te doen blijken dat de voorschreve distributie met'er daedt en conform des Heer Compts uytgedrukte wille bij hen lieden respectivelijk is gedaen geweest; maer ook . . . de voorschreve distributie aen ende onder de behoeftige menschen door de Heeren Parnassims zelve gedaen zal mogen en moeten werden ten einde dat alzoo d'arme en behoeftige menschen door 't zelve different niet en komen te lijden'.

176 SAA entry no. 334, no. 694, Not. Ph. de Marolles, pp. 11–13, 18 Nov. 1736. For the acquisition of this house in 1709 see SAA entry no. 334, no. 694, Not. W. Sylvius, p. 139, 27 Nov. 1709.

177 SAA entry no. 334, no. 694, Not. Ph. de Marolles, pp. 11–13, 18 Nov. 1736. For references to gifts to the poor see ibid., pp. 4–5, 8–9, 11–15. For reference to the gift to Sara de Tolosa see ibid., p. 14. See also the balance of the assets of Rachel de Spinosa Henriques (ibid., pp. 394–7). For Sara de Tolosa receiving welfare see SAA entry no. 334, no. 974, file a, p. 31, 1734.

178 López Belinchón, *Honra, libertad y hacienda*, 257, 262–6, 274–7, 343–5, 347–9, 360–1. Sometimes poor Portuguese resented the fact that they were dependent on their richer fellows for charity, to the point where the poor were inclined to disclose secrets about wealthy families to the Inquisition. Sometimes money was even distributed in order to appease the poor, although this did not always help. Having been taken by the Inquisition, poor Portuguese widows had little to lose by denouncing rich Portuguese. Before the tribunal, for example, Fernando

Montesinos blamed the envy of the poor for his detention (López Belinchón, *Honra, libertad y hacienda*, 348, 376–7, 379).

179 As the background to all these good deeds, Bahya ben Joseph ibn Pakuda (*Duties of the Heart*, i. 231–7) sets the continuous, endless love of God, which he bestows upon human beings without any self-interest.

7 The Daily Life of the Poor

1 See Hirsch, *Frucht vom Baum des Lebens*, 320.

2 A book of petitions seems to have existed as part of the administration of the Portuguese community of Amsterdam (SAA entry no. 334, no. 970, p. 121, 1 Nisan 5499: 'Repartido como p. menoz do livro das peticoens'). Unfortunately it has not (yet) been found. For petitions as an important source of information on the poor see Schmidt, *Overleven na de dood*, 16–19; see also the different articles in the *International Review of Social History* (Heerma van Voss, 'Introduction'). For petitions in the Jewish world, for example from the Cairo Geniza, see M. Cohen, *The Voice of the Poor*.

3 For the cycle of poverty see van der Vlis, *Leven in armoede*, 78–9.

4 See a fragment in Ishack de Matatia Aboab (H. den Boer, 'Exile', 198–9 and n. 24).

5 SAA entry no. 5075, no. 646A, Not. S. Cornelisz., pp. 814–16, 19 Feb. 1624, also published in *Studia Rosenthaliana*, 28/2 (1994), 205; see also SAA entry no. 5075, no. 646B, Not. S. Cornelisz., pp. 1037–8, 24 Oct. 1624, also published in *Studia Rosenthaliana*, 29/2 (1995), 222. For the Bank of Amsterdam see SAA entry no. 5075, no. 646B, Not. S. Cornelisz., p. 1039, 24 Oct. 1624, also published in *Studia Rosenthaliana*, 29/2 (1995), 223.

6 For Clara Franca Serrana on the welfare lists from 1659 to 1669 see e.g. SAA entry no. 334, no. 174, p. 308, Rosh Hodesh Nisan 5419; ibid., p. 356, 1 Heshvan 5420; ibid., p. 397, 1 Sivan 5420; ibid., no. 215, p. 7, 1 Heshvan 5424; ibid., no. 174, p. 693, 3 Nisan 5425; ibid., p. 729, 20 Adar 5426; ibid., no. 215, p. 244, 5427–8: *nedavot*; ibid., no. 174, p. 842, 2 Adar 5429.

7 'Ester Fonseca de Liorne que aoprezente reside nesta cidade, orfa de pay y de may avendo gozado de felice fortuna em vida de seus pais oje estando em miserable estado sem mejos ninhuns' (SAA entry no. 334, no. 1151, p. 629, 1668).

8 SAA entry no. 334, no. 216, detached sheet, 27 Nisan 5432. Salomon Levy Maduro worked in a printing press (Ya'ari, *Hebrew Printers' Marks* (Heb.), 169 n. 1). From 1651 he was supported periodically, and from 1685 continuously. He had five surviving children (four others died); at least one son, Aron, moved to Curaçao (SAA entry no. 334, no. 218, p. 15, 13 Kislev 5446; ibid., no. 219, p. 224, 17 Iyar 5454; ibid., p. 357, 8 Heshvan 5458). For charity distributions to Salomon Levy Maduro see the following in SAA entry no. 334: peat (no. 173, p. 206, 7 Kislev 5412; no. 215, p. 110, 5426; no. 217, p. 327, 5442); clothes to his children as students of Talmud Torah (no. 1189, p. 7, 5437); help to his wife after giving birth (no. 215, p. 112, 22 Tamuz 5425); sick care (no. 215, p. 103, 8 Adar II 5426; ibid., p. 114, 22 Shevat 5426). For the daughter of Sara Mendes, who was paid to watch over the sick in the house of Salomon Levy Maduro, see SAA entry no. 334, no. 215, p. 114, 2 Adar 5426; ibid., 5 Adar 5426. For the burial of children see SAA entry no. 334, no. 215, p. 14, 21 Shevat 5424; for that of two of Maduro's sons see SAA entry no. 334, no. 216, p. 115, 22 Elul 5432, and for that of yet another son see ibid., p. 169, 14 Nisan 5434. For help on special occasions see SAA entry no. 334, no. 216, p. 145, 11 Sivan 5433; ibid., no. 217, p. 210, 8 Heshvan 5441; *nedavot* (ibid., no. 215, p. 193, 5426–7; ibid., no. 217, p. 301, 5441–2); Purim (ibid., no. 174, p. 737, 17 Adar II 5426); matzot (ibid., no. 216, p. 166, 5434: 50 *livras* of matzah meal, meant to be for six or seven people). In 1681 only enough meal was distributed for three people (ibid., no. 217, p. 242, 5441), while one year later five people must have received it (ibid., p. 318, 5442). In 1683, however, around nine people in Maduro's household were receiving matzah meal (ibid., p. 387, 5443). For rental subsidy see ibid., no. 215, p. 6, 23 Nisan 5423; ibid., no. 217, p. 304, 5441–2; for monthly distributions via Abodat Ahesed see ibid., no. 20, p. 91, Nisan 5445; for a trip Maduro's wife made to Curaçao see ibid., no. 217, p. 160, 27 Tishrei 5440.

9 On this occasion he received 6.6 guilders (MS Ets Haim 48 A 51, 10 Tevet 5439); see also Pieterse, *Daniel Levi de Barrios*, 21–3 and appendix 3; Swetschinski, *Reluctant Cosmopolitans*, 243–9.

10 His request was complied with: from that year, 1694, he received 70 guilders a year for his work as a student (SAA entry no. 334, no. 1191, p. 173, 1 Tevet 5455). Previously, Isaac Ledesma had received 47 guilders a year and 6 guilders for Purim (ibid., p. 168, 5454). He came from Bayonne and on his marriage in Amsterdam in 1686 was described as a schoolmaster (SAA DTB 695, p. 194, 31 May 1686: 'Isaak Ledesma van Bayonne, Schoolmeester op de Houtgracht geassisteerd met zijn vader Moses de Ledesma en Benvenida Salom van Karpentras oud 21 jaar als boven geass. met haar moeder Ribca Salom').

11 SAA entry no. 334, no. 1151, p. 49, [n.d.]. The daughter appears on the lottery list of Dotar in 1621, where it is stated the father has died (ibid., no. 1141, p. 143, 10 Adar 5381: 'filha de Rachel peres, filha do sego dif^{to}').

12 SAA entry no. 334, no. 1152, p. 333, [1685].

13 SAA entry no. 334, no. 381, p. 1 [n.d., around 1718]. Three people signed the petition, namely Salomon de Torres, Isaac Pacheco, and Abraham Gomes Pacheco.

14 SAA entry no. 334, no. 381, p. 11, [n.d.]. The word 'trabalhos' appears in several documents, for example in the *imposta* files ('perseguidos de trabalhos': ibid., no. 13, pp. 8–9, para. 29, 24 Shevat 5382, *Livro de termos*); and even earlier in those of Dotar ('m^{tas} pessoas q . . . se vem aestas Partes ea França perseguidos de trabalhos': SAA entry no. 334, no. 1141, 20 Nov. 1615).

15 SAA entry no. 334, no. 174, pp. 729–33, 20 [Adar] 5426: 'Nedaba . . . o q se repartio . . . mais dado aos seguintos q por serem secretos se havião sentado aparte em tudo a saber' (p. 733); ibid., no. 17, p. 51^{v}, 1 May 5394/1634: 'hua pesoa onrada f 40,–'; ibid., no. 5, p. 118, 5381: 'secretos'; ibid., no. 174, p. 142, 14 Adar 5416: 'A 2 senhoras vergonozas p^{a} o Gabay'; ibid., no. 173, p. 193, 11 Tishrei 5412: 'uma pobre encoberta em mao de Jacob Ergas o velho'.

16 Levie [Bernfeld] and Zantkuyl, *Wonen in Amsterdam*, 53–9; Reijnders, *Van 'Joodsche Natiën' tot Joodse Nederlanders*, ch. 4.

17 This pattern corresponds with that of non-Jews in the city (Levie [Bernfeld] and Zantkuyl, *Wonen in Amsterdam*, 47, 54); see also Wijsenbeek-Olthuis, *Achter de gevels van Delft*.

18 Reijnders, *Van 'Joodsche Natiën' tot Joodse Nederlanders*, 60 and 71. For Delft see van der Vlis, *Leven in armoede*, 94–5; see also Berg, van Leeuwen, and Lesger, 'Residentiële segregatie'.

19 For documents concerning civil marriage see SAA DTB; on the so-called tax 'Middel op Trouwen en Begraven' issued by the 'Staten van Holland en West Friesland' in 1695 and the *Pro Deo* class (literally 'for God', meaning free of charge: this phrase was registered on the document recording the intention of marrying for the poorest people, who were exempted from paying this tax) see Hart, 'Sociale structuur'; on this and other taxes in Holland see Vrankrijker, *Geschiedenis van de Belastingen*, 27–52.

20 SAA DTB 694, p. 216, 27 Oct. 1684.

21 SAA DTB 697, p. 15, 13 Oct. 1690.

22 SAA entry no. 334, no. 173, p. 260, Rosh Hodesh Nisan 5413. One of the poor Portuguese living in Lazarussteeg was Abraham Armandel, who married *Pro Deo* the daughter of Salomon Levy Maduro in 1697 (SAA DTB 700, p. 173, 10 Aug. 1697). Armandel was appointed as a *shamash* in 1700 (SAA entry no. 334, no. 20, p. 292, 12 Menahem-Av 5460). Others were Sara de Tovar (SAA DTB 698, p. 20, 23 Jan. 1693), who was on the monthly charity list through Abodat Ahesed (SAA entry no. 334, no. 20, p. 223, Adar 5457); Ester Cohen Berberisco (ibid., no. 173, p. 260, 1 Nisan 5413); and Ester, the widow of Josua Israel from Hamburg (ibid.), who was on welfare continuously for forty-six years, from 1652 to 1698 (ibid., p. 249, Rosh Hodesh Tevet 5413; ibid. no. 176, p. 292, Rosh Hodesh Nisan 5458).

23 For Markensteeg see the following: Jacob de Oliveira (SAA DTB 691, p. 38, 2 July 1677), who attended the school for poor children (SAA entry no. 334, no. 216, p. 201 (as a student of Jacob de Caceres), 5435–6); Rica Nunes (SAA DTB 695, p. 243, 13 Sept. 1686), who was related to Abraham de Pinto and as a poor family member was supported by him (Salomon, 'The "De Pinto Manuscript"', 27); Ester de Oliveira (SAA DTB 681, p. 150, 24 Nov. 1651), who may have been accepted on to the welfare list in 1682 (SAA entry no. 334, no. 20, p. 51, 26 Elul 5442); Abraham Vas (SAA DTB 677, p. 254, 26 Aug. 1644: 'op de hoek van de Marcussteegh')—there is an Abraham Vas o velho on the charity lists from 1658 to 1668 (SAA entry no. 334, no. 174, p. 246, Rosh Hodesh Adar II 5418; ibid., p. 280, 11 Tishrei 5419; ibid., p. 295, 1 Heshvan 5419; ibid., p. 367, 15 Adar 5420; ibid., no. 215, p. 4, 23 Nisan 5423; ibid., p. 246, 5427–8: *nedavot*); Abraham Vaz o moço (the young one), who only received charity in 1663 (ibid. no. 174, p. 540, 10 Shevat 5423); and Rachel Febos, who lived in 'Markussteegh' and planned to marry the mattress maker Isaac Paiva (SAA DTB 696, p. 425, 13 Jan. 1690).

In Steenvoetsteeg lived Rachel Bondia (SAA DTB 695, p. 79, 16 Nov. 1685), the daughter of Saul Levi Bondia, whose widow had been in receipt of charity since 1661 (SAA entry no. 334, no. 174, p. 511, Rosh Hodesh Sivan 5422); Rachel tried to get a dowry through Dotar from 1675 onwards (ibid., no. 1144, pp. 218, 228, 238, 247, 262, 278, 301, 308, 318, and 327, 5435–45). In the same street was Abraham Mendes Vasques the broker (SAA DTB 687, p. 302, 25 Jan. 1669), who was supported by charity (SAA entry no. 334, no. 174, p. 332, 25 Nisan 5419; ibid., p. 337, 5 Sivan 5419); from 1697 his widow was given 1.10 guilders a month through Abodat Ahesed (ibid., no. 20, p. 223, Adar 5457).

For Turfsteeg see Benvenida Coen Rodrigues (SAA DTB 699, p. 7, 18 Mar. 1695) and Judith Lopes Mellada (ibid. 693, p. 415, 28 Aug. 1683).

24 For Staalstraat see David Ferreira (SAA DTB 686, p. 32, 17 Jan. 1664); he was not paying any communal tax but was not given communal charity either. For Weesperstraat see Isaac Monsanto (SAA entry no. 5072, no. 606, p. 225^{v}, 1 Nov. 1679); he was being supported by the community, having been made bankrupt in 1679; on him see also Y. Kaplan, *From Christianity to Judaism*, 206 n. 120. For Zwanenburgerstraat see Debora Pereyra de Paris (SAA DTB 706, p. 113, 2 Dec. 1707), whose family was in receipt of welfare from 1661 (SAA entry no. 334, no. 174, p. 451, 14 Nisan 5421); Jacob Alegem 'arbeyder' (SAA DTB 699, p. 261, 6 Apr. 1696); and Aron Hesqia Querido, who lived in 'Swanenburgstraet in een gangh' (SAA entry no. 5072, no. 622, p. 92^{v}, 6 Nov. 1698). For Batavierenstraat see Daniel Abendana Mendes (SAA entry no. 5072, no. 601, p. 197, 4 Nov. 1675; SAA entry no. 334, no. 217, pp. 6, 33, 56, 58, 60, 90, 143, 5437–8). For St Antoniebreestraat see Rachel Fernandes (SAA DTB 699, p. 159, 28 Oct. 1695). For Leprozenstraat see Rachel Levy Maduro (SAA DTB 700, p. 173, 10 Aug. 1697). For Lange and Korte Houtstraat see David Israel and Anna Israel (SAA DTB 687, p. 283, 14 Dec. 1668). Was it this David who attended the school for poor students in 1664–6 (SAA entry no. 334, no. 215, pp. 90 and 135, 5424–6) and was requested not to return to study in 1666?

Sara da Rocha lived 'in the fields' ('nos campos': are these maybe the so-called Joden Houttuinen?) (SAA entry no. 334, no. 172, p. 291, 14 Adar 5405). She and her children were supported by the community from 1641 (ibid., p. 141, Rosh Hodesh Sivan 5401); in 1649 she declared that she was no longer going to ask for assistance, 'que nao quer mais' (ibid., no. 173, p. 103, Rosh Hodesh Tishrei 5410). Sara da Fonseca was permanently on welfare from 1639 until her death in 1654 (ibid., no. 172, p. 16, Rosh Hodesh Av 5399; ibid., no. 173, p. 260, 29 Adar II 5413; ibid., no. 174, p. 80, Rosh Hodesh Tevet 5415).

25 Wijsenbeek-Olthuis, 'Woongenot', 222–8.

26 SAA entry no. 5075, no. 7355, no. 1874, Not. J. Valkenburg, p. 637, 13 June 1710. Abraham de Mercado paid 48 guilders for his room, and Abraham Nunes de Carvalho 50 guilders. On the taxes paid by Abraham Nunes de Carvalho see SAA entry no. 334, no. 176, p. 338, 1 Nisan 5460: two *promessa* payments of 3 guilders; two *finta* payments of 6 guilders. In 1710 these two individuals apparently were no longer paying tax as they are not registered on the lists (ibid., no. 177, 17 Adar II 5470). In the mid-18th century the so-called Ververstraat was known as a street where many Portuguese families lived, not only occupying their own houses, but also living in single rooms and even cellars ('zo in huysen als in kamers en kelders'): see the request of the citizens of Amsterdam that the authorities should designate the area a ghetto for Jews, and the Portuguese community's reaction to this suggestion (SAA entry no. 334, no. 87, file 20, 1753, *Remonstraçoems e rq^{a} aos ss^{res} Burgames^{trs}*).

27 SAA entry no. 5061, no. 683, p. 34, 12 Feb. 1670.

28 SAA entry no. 334, no. 1142, p. 172, 13 Adar 5493; previously she was in the house of Josua Jessurun Roiz (ibid., p. 158, 13 Adar 5492).

29 SAA entry no. 5072, no. 614, p. 83^{v}, 2 July 1688.

30 SAA entry no. 5072, no. 622, p. 92^{v}, 6 Nov. 1698; ibid., no. 620, p. 117, 10 Oct. 1696.

31 For the inventory of Ester Barrocas see SAA entry no. 334, no. 218, pp. 155–6, 25 Adar 5447: 'Memoria da Venda da Roupa que se achou de Ester Barocas que Deus tem em virtude da escamah Feita em 15 de Sivan de 5418: se vendeu empregão na camarra dos SS^{res} de mahamad a saber'. For Ester's receipt of welfare from 1661 to 1685 (with intervals) see SAA entry no. 334, no. 174, p. 474, Rosh Hodesh Kislev 5422; ibid., no. 217, p. 524, 5445. Her children left the city around 1677 (ibid., no. 217, p. 87, 5437–8). Her possessions included some linen, clothes, a mirror, two mattresses, two pillows, one blanket, a suitcase, some iron instruments as kitchen utensils, a fruit basket, a wedding ring, and some coins.

32 SAA entry no. 5072, no. 614, p. 150^{v}, 21 Dec. 1688. Besides the paintings, Jacob Argas Henriques' living quarters contained six chairs, one mattress, one day bed, and some earthenware pots. Many poor families had no tables, but there were often a lot of paintings (Wijsenbeek-Olthuis, 'Woongenot', 226–7). Abraham Vasques, who lived in a room in the Vinckebuurt in 1688, also owned some paintings (SAA entry no. 5072, no. 614, p. 90, 20 July 1688); besides these, his few possessions consisted of a day bed, some bedding, a couple of chairs, two small tables, a small wooden chest, a small mirror, a washbasin, and some earthenware pots. Abraham Franco Drago, a tobacco dealer, living in a cellar in Nieuwe Amstelstraat in 1692, owned little more than a bed, some bedding, a few chairs, and a table, with a total value of 22.10 guilders (SAA entry no. 5072, no. 618, p. 36^{v}, 9 Sept. 1692; ibid., no. 694, p. 21, 10 Sept. 1692). He used to pay 5 guilders for half a year's *finta* (see e.g. SAA entry no. 334, no. 175, p. 306, 1 Elul 5445). He later ceased to pay this tax, but we do not find him on the community's welfare lists (SAA entry no. 334, no. 176, p. 23, 24 Adar 5450). Apparently he was supported by family members, as it appears that he and his wife Yael Franco Drago were receiving 45 guilders a month out of a legacy of 6,000 guilders given by Isaac and Jacob Mendes in 1700 (ibid., no. 20, p. 290, 13 Tamuz 5460).

33 SAA entry no. 334, no. 401, pp. 88–89^{v}, 13 Mar. 1698; his possessions included tobacconist's equipment, bedding, linen, tables and chairs, seven paintings, and some crockery (ibid., no. 405, pp. 113^{v}–114, 29 Nov. 1702). Bassan in the meantime had moved from Joden Houttuinen to Rapenburgerstraat; see also Bloom, *The Economic Activities of the Jews of Amsterdam*, 66, and Vaz Dias, 'Een vergeten hoofdstuk'. Bassan did not pay any communal tax in 1690 or 1695 (SAA entry no.

334, no. 176, p. 23, 24 Adar 5450; ibid., p. 182, 26 Adar 5455). In 1700 he paid a minimum amount of *finta* tax—two payments of 1 guilder each—which implies that he belonged to the lowest tax category and that previously he had not even reached that level (ibid., p. 337, 1 Nisan 5460). In 1707 Bassan was given welfare through Abodat Ahesed (SAA entry no. 21, p. 133, 5 Nisan 5477: 'Termo dos que admetirão este ano na sedaca e Abodat Ahesed . . . Abraham Bassan f 4,–').

34 Wijsenbeek-Olthuis, 'Woongenot', and van der Vlis, *Leven in armoede*, 366–8.

35 To get an impression of the wealth of Josua de Prado see his inventory (SAA entry no. 5075, no. 7490, no. 52, Not. van de Ende, 28 Sept. 1708: 'Specificatie van den huysraedt, meublen en Imboedel nagelaten bij den Heere Joshuah alias Anthonio de Prado Zaliger'; ibid., no. 53, 28 Sept. 1708: 'Specificatie van de Juwelen, kleinodien, gout, silver etc nagelaten bij den Heere Josua alias Anthonio de Prado zaliger'). See further the value of the household effects of Joseph and Emanuel Athias, living at Keizersgracht (SAA entry no. 5072, no. 620, pp. 59[v]–64, 30 Dec. 1695–Jan. 1696); that of the possessions of Abraham Senna, living at Oude Zijds Achterburgwal (ibid., no. 610, pp. 105[v]–115, 21 Nov. 1684, worth 735.15 guilders); the inventory of David Ximenes Cardoso, living at Muyder Veer (ibid., no. 608, pp. 182–5, 11 Apr. 1682, value 785.5 guilders); that of Simon Correa, alias Diogo Peres Caminha at Verversgracht (ibid., no. 605, pp. 143–50, 3 Sept. 1677, value 652 guilders). The value of household effects at the home of Isaac Delmonte came to 2,018 guilders (ibid., no. 604, pp. 164[v]–171[v], 14 Jan. 1678). See also the inventory of Joseph Bueno Bivas, alias Ruij Gomes Fronteyra (SAA entry no. 5075, no. 2262A, Not. A. Lock, pp. 149–50, 14 Jan. 1668). Wijsenbeek-Olthuis (*Achter de gevels van Delft*, 141, and 'Woongenot', 217) estimates that in the 18th century the total property of the *Pro Deo* group had a value of less than 300 guilders.

36 Subsidies for rental of apartments occupied by the poor must have already been established in the early 17th century. Traces of the practice can be found in documents from 1616 ('Velho Cego e filha . . . para a caza': SAA entry no. 334, no. 6, p. 2, 19 Nov. 5377/1616), 1621 (ibid., no. 5, p. 161, 1 Kislev 5382), 1622 ('Cat[a] Felipe p[a] aluger da caza . . . f 6,–': ibid., no. 5, p. 274, 20 Tevet 5383; Jonas Jessurun, 'esmola . . . para as cazas . . . f 15,–': ibid., p. 176, 14 Shevat 5382), 1629 ('Dina Gher . . . por ser muyto velho . . . ajuda da caza': ibid., no. 17, p. 29, 5 Aug. 5389), and 1633 (ibid., no. 9, p. 164, 5393). Finally, after 1663, we have yearly reviews of distributions covering rental costs.

37 In 1664 around 183 heads of household (of whom 31% were male and 69% female) received an average of 12 guilders a year each, varying between a minimum of 4 and a maximum of 24 guilders a year (SAA entry no. 334, no. 215, pp. 59–65, 5 Iyar 5424). Later the maximum rental subsidy was 16 guilders, while the minimum of 4 guilders remained the same (ibid., pp. 341–4, 5429–30). Van der Vlis, *Leven in armoede*, 89, calculates the rental subsidy in Delft to be around 3–14 stivers a week, amounting to a minimum of 8 guilders and a maximum of 36 guilders a year (a greater amount than among the Portuguese of Amsterdam).

38 For fluctuations in rental prices of houses, rooms, and cellars see Lesger, *Huur en* *conjunctuur*, 38–92, and Berg, van Leeuwen, and Lesger, 'Residentiële segregatie', 419.

39 Van der Vlis, *Leven in armoede*, 167–8, 254.

40 Some people never had a permanent address and must have stayed in inns: for Abraham Cortissos, a so-called 'loopende persoon' who did not have a household, see SAA entry no. 5072, no. 693, p. 41, 21 Aug. 1691.

41 Grossman, *Pious and Rebellious*, 47.

42 Mitterauer and Sieder, *The European Family*, 31–2; Wijsenbeek-Olthuis, 'Woongenot', 221; Moch, *Moving Europeans*, 32. On extended families among New Christians on the Iberian peninsula living together in multi-generational families, see Carrasco, 'Preludio', 551; Pulido Serrano, *Injurias a Cristo*, 117–18; López Belinchón, *Honra, libertad y hacienda*, 191–216; Studnicki-Gizbert, '*La Nación*', 81–5.

43 Cited in Saperstein, *Exile in Amsterdam*, 193.

44 See the last will of Joseph Mendes da Costa (SAA entry no. 5075, no. 4090, Not. D. van der Groe, [no page], 25 June 1679).

45 See the last will of Josua de Prado (SAA entry no. 5075, no. 7490, no. 19, Not. J. van de Ende, 12 Mar. 1708): 'voorts verklaerde de Heer Testateur aen ende ten behoeve van zijn zeer geëerde en geliefde Moeder Vrouwe Rachel de Prado alias Rachel Gabay Faro . . . de somme van ses duysent guldens Bankgeldt Jaerlijks, haer leven langh geduirende . . . mitsgaders noch de vrije bewoninge van het huys bij den Heer Testateur altans zelfs bewoont, daer Oosterwijk in de Gevel staet staende en gelegen in de Swanenburgerstraet binnen deeze Stadt, mitsgaders met gebruik van alle de huysraedt, meublen en imboedel en 't geene verders tot gebruik of cieraedt van den voorn. Huyse zal hebben gedient.'

46 SAA entry no. 5072, no. 696, p. 56, 26 Nov. 1693.

47 On the dispute between the daughter of Jacob Juda Leon and her husband on the one hand, and the bride's father on the other, concerning the promise of a room in his house after their marriage, see SAA entry no. 5075, no. 2210, Not. A. Lock, pp. 33–4, 7 Jan. 1661; ibid., 119–21, 14 Jan. 1661.

48 SAA entry no. 5075, no. 7667, no. 318, Not. A. Tzeewen, 4 June 1735.

49 In his *Thesovro dos dinim* (v. 24), Menasseh ben Israel recommends that girls who marry as minors should stay with their husbands in their parents' houses until they reach adulthood; for this tradition among Ashkenazim in Amsterdam see Schellekens, 'Determinants', 159, table 11; for this practice elsewhere in Europe in medieval and early modern times (Jewish and non-Jewish circles alike) see J. Katz, *Tradition and Crisis*, 117; M. Cohen, *The Voice of the Poor*, 90; Casey, *Early Modern Spain*, 29.

50 'Mulher de Isaac Penha mora con Leao' (SAA entry no. 334, no. 215, p. 342, 5429–30).

51 For more on this see Levie Bernfeld, 'Sephardi Women in Holland's Golden Age', 183–5.

52 See the last will of Joseph Nahemias Torres, in which he refers to a legacy to the boy Israel who was brought up in his house: 'a Israel o moco q se criou en minha casa e ora esta en Amsterdam casado en Judesmo a vontade de meu irmao e parentes dous mil florins q se contente con eles sen Pretender outra cousa algua en nao se Contentando he minha vontade q lhe não deu nada' (SAA entry no. 5075, no. 633, Not. S. Cornelisz., pp. 134–5, 26 Oct. 1626–10 Jan. 1627, last will of Joseph Nahemias, alias Gaspar Nunes Torres). For the housing of orphans with families in Italy see Adelman, 'Servants and Sexuality', 82. For the situation in the Jewish community of medieval Egypt see M. Cohen, *Poverty and Charity*, 236–9.

53 'Sara Gomes e nettos' (SAA entry no. 334, no. 174, p. 142, 14 Adar 5416; ibid., 22 Adar 5416; ibid., p. 250, 11 Adar II 5418: Purim and matzah meal 56 *livras*); 'Sara Gomes, may do Prado' (ibid., p. 273, 12 Nisan 5418: 2.10 guilders; ibid., p. 281, 11 Tishrei 5419: 2.10 guilders); 'A Gente de Prado' (ibid., p. 305, 15 Adar 5419: 60 *livras* of matzah meal). On the life of Prado see also Y. Kaplan, 'Nueva información'; id., *From Christianity to Judaism*; on Prado's *ḥerem* see Y. Kaplan, 'The Social Functions of the Herem', 144, and Muchnik, 'Juan de Prado'. As mentioned in Ch. 4 n. 92 above, Prado's niece Debora Gomez married David Levy Maduro with a dowry from Dotar. Between 1659 and 1663 Debora was receiving welfare ('Deborah Gomez': SAA entry no. 334, no. 174, p. 340, Rosh Hodesh Tishrei 5420, 2.10 guilders; ibid., p. 544, Rosh Hodesh Adar 5423), but she was taken off the list when she got married. The newlywed couple and their expanding family remained periodically dependent on charity and received among other things rental subsidy, *nedavot*, matzot, peat, and monthly distributions until 1690 (see for example SAA entry no. 334, no. 215, p. 4, Nisan 5423; ibid., p. 108, 5426; ibid., no. 217, p. 325, 5441–2; ibid., p. 520, Pesach 5445; ibid., no. 175, p. 23, Rosh Hodesh Nisan 5438; ibid., p. 376, 1 Iyar 5447; ibid., no. 176, p. 34, 4 Iyar 5450).

54 In 1681 Sara da Rocha married Salomon Senior Coronel, who was born in Brazil. She was then 28 years old (SAA entry no. 334, no. 1144, p. 295, 7 Elul 5441: the couple were granted a Dotar dowry of 900 guilders). The civil marriage, contrary to the regulations, followed some months after the religious ceremony (SAA DTB 693, p. 4, 10 Oct. 1681), at which point it is said that her father was then 'in Westindien'. Her uncle Isaac Furtado acted as witness at the civil ceremony. It seems Sara could not write since she signed with a mark. Ester da Rocha married in 1688, also at the age of 28; her husband was Moses Saruco, a merchant from Hamburg (SAA DTB 696, p. 155, 2 July 1688). Her uncle Benjamin da Rocha was the witness at the wedding. Ester could not write either. For their father Salomon da Rocha, travelling between North Africa and the West, see Appendix III.

Sara and Ester were supported by the community from 1663 to the 1680s, but only on a temporary basis (SAA entry no. 334, no. 174, p. 543, 10 Shevat 5423: 'Sarah e Ester Rocha orphaás'; ibid., p. 732, Tevet–Adar 5426). They also received matzot (from 1665 to 1685; for the last four years, 1682–5, matzot were only given to Ester: ibid., p. 695, 10 Nisan 5425; ibid., no. 217, p. 319, 5442; ibid., no. 217, p. 523, 5445); rental subsidy from 1670 to 1682 (ibid., no. 216, p. 43, 5430–1; ibid., no. 217, p. 304, 5441–2); peat from 1666 to 1682 (ibid., no. 215, p. 125, 5426;

ibid., no. 217, p. 326, 5442); distributions during the holidays (from 1666 to 1682 for both of them, and until 1688 for Ester: ibid., no. 215, p. 192, 5426–7; ibid., no. 217, p. 300, 5441; ibid., no. 218, p. 273, 5448); and poor relief every three months from 1670 to 1682 (ibid., no. 215, p. 316, 23 Adar 5430; ibid., no. 217, p. 316, 3 Nisan 5442). Poor relief in total for the two girls came to 40 guilders yearly, with peat and matzot on top of this. They may also have benefited from an inheritance from their mother. It is reasonable to assume that the father also sent money from Salé and the West Indies, while their uncles Benjamin da Rocha and Isaac Furtado might have supported them as well. The latter, however, were not very well off. Benjamin da Rocha was at the top of the lowest *finta* class, while Isaac Furtado was at the bottom of that same class. They paid the *finta* tax of, respectively, 10 guilders and 2 guilders a year (ibid., no. 175, pp. 101 and 104, 1 Nisan 5440).

55 See SAA entry no. 334, no. 120, file 81, pp. 879–86, 6 Shevat 5494.

56 'Ao rapas q esta com Jacob Ergas' (SAA entry no. 334, no. 172, p. 245, 14 Adar II 5404).

57 'Moseh Roiz q tem em caza f° de Rachel de Castro' (SAA entry no. 334, no. 215, p. 11, 8 Nisan 5423).

58 SAA entry no. 334, no. 17, p. 29, 20 July 5389.

59 SAA entry no. 334, no. 215, p. 114, 2 Adar 5426: 6 guilders 'p. sustentar huo rapaz orfao Aron Gomes ate agora mais de 1/m'. Mordecai was teaching poor children of the Portuguese community (SAA DTB 688, p. 102, 13 June 1670: at his marriage he was already mentioned as a 'schoolmeester'. See further SAA entry no. 334, no. 215, p. 135, 5425–6; ibid., no. 216, p. 195, 6 Nisan 5436). He also worked preparing *shemurim* for Pesach (ibid., p. 1, 5430). In 1676 he was briefly put into *ḥerem* for the 'enormous sin he committed against our Holy Law' (ibid. no. 19, p. 752, 21 Elul 5436). Later he moved to Hamburg (SAA entry no. 334, no. 1153, p. 691, 9 Adar I 5451: 'Hamburgo'). From there he applied for a dowry from Dotar for his daughter (ibid., no. 1153, p. 76, 7 Adar 5456).

60 The wife of Abraham de Castro lived with her daughter and grandchild (SAA entry no. 334, no. 217, p. 349, 5442: matzot, 26 *livras*). The son of the blind Aron del Canho joined his father (ibid., no. 173, p. 121, 19 Adar II 5410). Lea Diaz da Costa, a widow, shared her quarters with at least two sons (ibid., no. 215, p. 237, 5427: rental subsidy; ibid., no. 216, p. 26, 5430–1: education at the poor school for her sons). The mute man from Hamburg lived under the same roof as his brother (ibid., no. 173, p. 121, 19 Adar II 5410). In 1649 the widow Sara Vaz left Seville with her daughter, and they went to live together in Amsterdam (ibid., p. 112, Rosh Hodesh Tevet 5410; ibid., p. 167, 22 Adar 5411: matzot). The widow Sara Rodrigues de Guadeloupe and her sister, also a widow, joined forces (ibid., no. 174, p. 78, 1 Tevet 5415: peat). The widow of David Rodrigues lived with her grandson (ibid., no. 20, p. 177, n.d. [after 17 Adar] 5454; ibid., no. 176, p. 203, Rosh Hodesh Iyar 5455). Three sisters moved in with each other: 'Ester, Judit e Ribca Galenas tres irmans' (ibid., no. 174, p. 250, 11 Adar II 5418: matzot; ibid., no. 215, p. 4, 5423: rental subsidy to 'Galenas tres Irmaas'). Four women from

Spain also formed a self-supporting unit, sharing accommodation (ibid., no. 219, p. 91, 9 Heshvan 5453). The widow Sara Messia lived with her sister (ibid., no. 173, p. 166, 22 Adar 5411: matzot, 16 *livras*). For more examples see 'Izabel da Costa em caza de Costa' (SAA entry no. 334, no. 173, p. 164, 15 Adar 5411); 'Ester e Judit Melo' from Seville (ibid., no. 215, p. 178, 5426: rental subsidy, apparently for a mother and her daughter; ibid., no. 173, p. 28, 20 Adar 5408: matzot: 'Judica de Melo de Sevilla e filha'); 'As Cunhas . . . Branca e Lea da Cunha Dias' (ibid., p. 28, 20 Adar 5408: matzot); 'Mulher de Mosseh da Cunha e Irman' (ibid., p. 45, Pesach 5408). For widows living together in early modern Europe see Hufton, *The Prospect before Her*.

61 Lera García, 'La última gran persecución', 106–7.

62 Caro Baroja, *Los Judíos en la España moderna*, i. 490.

63 López Belinchón, *Honra, libertad y hacienda*, 273–4. Torres Arce, 'Los judaizantes', 674–7, maintains that many judaizers taken by the Inquisition of Logroño in the early years of the 18th century were people of modest means.

64 See the case of the legacy of Luisa Ferro described in Caro Baroja, *Los Judíos en la España moderna*, ii. 119–27; see further López Belinchón, *Honra, libertad y hacienda*, 132, 342–3. The rich merchant Fernando Montesinos was said to give charity to genteel poor Portuguese ('portugueses vergonzantes'): López Belinchón, *Honra, libertad y hacienda*, 277.

65 In some cases goods were hidden: Francisco López asked in a letter in 1733 for assistance which could be reimbursed from the money he had hidden in his house in Sigüenza (Lera García, 'La última gran persecución', 106).

66 López Belinchón, *Honra, libertad y hacienda*, 276. On people becoming impoverished after being sentenced see the examples given in Lera García, 'La última gran persecución', 121–2. On the attitude expressed in rabbinic literature of late antiquity towards rich people who had become poor see Gray, 'The Formerly Wealthy Poor'.

67 SAA entry no. 5075, no. 646A, Not. S. Cornelisz., p. 427, 24 Feb. 1623; published in *Studia Rosenthaliana*, 23/2 (1989), 205.

68 One example of an individual who suffered a series of misfortunes was Abraham de Cordova, who in the early 1700s summarized his experiences as follows. He was trading tobacco to Hamburg. There he was arrested through the involvement of another person and lost a lot of money on his cargo and on legal costs. At first he was unable to leave Hamburg, but finally he returned home to Amsterdam, empty-handed and in great misery. He had no funds at his disposal since he had not received a dowry when he married, and his trading profits had often been low. In addition, he incurred considerable expenses in caring for his children. In 1727 his whole family fell ill for more than eight months, during which time he spent a fortune on doctors, medicine, and food (SAA entry no. 5072, no. 716, p. 4, 30 Nov. 1714; ibid., no. 646, p. 79, 4 Mar. 1729; ibid., no. 731, p. 3, 22 Mar. 1729). Another case of impoverishment is that of Abraham Israel Monsanto (SAA entry no. 334, no. 216, p. 4, 23 Adar 5431: lowering of the *finta* because payment was overdue). In 1665 he twice paid 15 guilders *finta* tax (ibid., no. 174, p. 710, 11 Tishrei 5426), but in 1674 he paid two instalments of only 2 guilders (ibid., p. 1034, 7 Tishrei 5435). In 1680 he is no longer listed as a taxpayer; in fact, from the late 1670s to 1681 he appears on the alms lists (ibid., no. 217, p. 61, 14 Tishrei 5438; ibid., p. 149, 5439: matzot; ibid., p. 209, 13 Tishrei 5441; ibid., p. 256, 22 Tevet 5441). After he died, his widow remained on the alms list (ibid., no. 20, p. 19, 4 Nisan 5441; ibid., no. 217, p. 259, 12 Adar 5441). Another was that of Abraham Rois Carriao, a cotton and tobacco merchant who went bankrupt in 1662 and became dependent on charity in 1680 (SAA entry no. 5072, no. 591, pp. 63–4, 10 Oct. 1662. For further examples see ibid. no. 217, p. 198, 26 Adar II 5440; ibid., p. 269, 10 Elul 5441; ibid., p. 272, 26 Kislev 5442). See also the case of Judith Ciudad Real (above, Ch. 5 n. 89), who still owned a house in Bayonne (SAA entry no. 334, no. 90, 19 Aug. 1712; published in Nahon, 'Les Rapports des communautés judéo-portugaises de France avec celle d'Amsterdam', 65 and 166), so must have known better times in France, though she lived on charity in Amsterdam.

69 'La familia Villegas manifestaba no haberse ido "porque allá no se podía tener officio ni beneficio en que occuparse las personas que habían de ir" por lo que necesitaban reunir aquí una cantidad suficiente, estimada en unos veinte o treinta mil ducados' (López Belinchón, *Honra, libertad y hacienda*, 400 n. 11).

70 Dillen, 'De economische positie'.

71 Jews did enter some guilds, such as those of booksellers and printers, brokers, surgeons, and pharmacists (Dillen, 'De economische positie', 576–7). For professions in Amsterdam organized through guilds see Eeghen, *De gilden*, 137.

72 From the sermon on the weekly Torah reading 'Vayishlaḥ' from the 1630s, cited in Saperstein, *Exile in Amsterdam*, 328–9.

73 Graizbord, *Souls in Dispute*, 84.

74 Ibid. 81.

75 SAA entry no. 334, no. 87, 30 Oct. 1750, *Req[t] aen Mijne Heeren van den Gerechte.*

76 For the professional structure of Conversos in the Iberian peninsula see Domínguez Ortiz, *La sociedad española*, 548; id., *La clase social*, vol. ii, ch. 1; id., *Los Judeoconversos*, 187–98, 209–38; id., *Política y hacienda*, 127 and ch. 3: 'Formaban una población urbana en parte de artesanos pobres, en parte de comerciantes, especuladores y logreros'; López Belinchón, *Honra, libertad y hacienda*, 347, table 8; Pike, *Aristocrats and Traders*, 103–4, 148; Kamen, *The Spanish Inquisition*, 12, 289, 292–3; Graizbord, *Souls in Dispute*, 54–7; Huerga Criado, 'El problema de la comunidad judeoconversa', 483–7.

77 Knowledge of industries was exported to the diaspora. Thus newcomers to Amsterdam set up industries with which they had become familiar in their country of origin, e.g. the processing of chocolate, tobacco, silk, and soap. France offers another example: the continuous influx of poor Portuguese New Christians from the peninsula to southern France enabled the establishment there of workshops in these industries (Israel, *Diasporas within a Diaspora*, 265).

78 The father of Juan de Prado had formerly been a shopkeeper in Lopera, dealing in spices (Y. Kaplan, *From Christianity to Judaism*, 124–5 n. 47). Many new Portuguese immigrants to Spain in the 17th century found work in Spain as shopkeepers or linen merchants (López Belinchón, *Honra, libertad y hacienda*, 273). Lera García, 'La última gran persecución', 102–3, mentions the existence of many small merchants and shopkeepers among the Conversos, dealing in tapes, jewellery, books, and shoes. In Cuenca at the beginning of the 18th century many were also engaged in pawnbroking.

79 For welfare distributions to Dr de Prado see SAA entry no. 334, no. 174, p. 193, Rosh Hodesh Tevet 5417: added to the monthly *sedaca* list for 7:10 guilders: 'Daniel Prado D^or'; ibid., p. 200, Rosh Hodesh Nisan 5417; ibid., p. 219, Rosh Hodesh Iyar 5417; ibid., pp. 192, 243, 5417–18: peat ('10 sestos turva'); ibid., p. 198, 5417: matzot for 'Sara Gomes e D^or Prado' (56 *livras*); ibid., p. 224, 1 Sivan 5417: 'D^or Daniel de Prado f 1:10'; ibid., p. 197, 16 Adar 5417: 4 guilders: 'a Sara Gomez e ao D^tor Prado'. For de Prado as a doctor and teacher in Amsterdam see Révah, 'Aux origines de la rupture spinozienne', 394.

80 Pieterse, *Livro de Bet Haim*, 146 (5375).

81 SAA entry no. 334, no. 216, p. 75, 16 Adar 5432: 'Mulher de astrologo'.

82 SAA entry no. 334, no. 215, p. 18, 29 Elul 5423: 'prateiro Abrao Dias'; ibid., p. 121, 6 Tishrei 5426: 'a Abraham Dias ourivez por consertar 2 lampadas de prata co 1½ on. de prata e feitio f 7:10'. For silversmiths among the Conversos in Spain convicted by the Inquisition see Martínez Millán, 'La persecución inquisitorial', 579, 596.

83 'Abraham Rodrigues de Sevilla, alfayate' (SAA entry no. 334, no. 173, p. 206, 7 Kislev 5412; ibid., p. 214, 23 Adar 5412). Lera García, 'La última gran persecución', 104, mentions that at the beginning of the 18th century 15% of the Conversos in Cuenca were artisans.

84 SAA entry no. 5075, no. 455, Not. P. Mathijsz., p. 54^r–v, 4 Mar. 1613; however, it is not certain that these men are former Conversos, since only their Christian names (Jan Gommes and Christoffel Juan) are known. I should like to thank Eloy Koldeweij, who provided me with this information; see also Koldeweij, *Goudleer*. In the 18th century there is mention of a Sephardi woman, a *belograda*, who repaired gold leather (SAA entry no. 334, no. 223, p. 231, 5 Tevet 5486: 'a Ester Auby por consertar de guadamesins . . . f 5'). Koldeweij, *Goudleer*, 20, explains that in southern Europe the word 'guadameci', 'guadameci', or 'guadamecil' is used for gold leather. The same word was used within the Amsterdam Portuguese community.

85 López Belinchón, *Honra, libertad y hacienda*, 374. For 'costureras', women working as spinners or washerwomen in the peninsula, see Martínez Millán, 'La persecución inquisitorial', 594, 597, 604–6, 608–11. Lera García, 'La última gran persecución', 104, mentions the existence of 'costureras' and 'encajeras' among the Conversos in Cuenca at the beginning of the 18th century. On Jewish women working as seamstresses or embroiderers in the Ottoman empire see A. Levy, *The Sephardim in the Ottoman Empire*, 36. An example of a shoemaker is the father of the Portuguese Manuel Méndez de León, who was working in this capacity in the Iberian peninsula (López Belinchón, *Honra, libertad y hacienda*, 345 n. 24); on a judaizing shoemaker in Spain see also Martínez Millán, 'La persecución inquisitorial', 594. For Sephardi shoemakers living in southern France and being expelled because of their poverty in 1749 see Nahon, *Les'Nations' juives portugaises*, 14.

86 For pedlars see López Belinchón, *Honra, libertad y hacienda*, 37; for Beatriz Rodríguez, ibid. 132.

87 Martínez Millán, 'La persecución inquisitorial', 610. Lera García, 'La última gran persecución', 104, mentions the existence of servants ('domésticas') among the Conversos. For a review of professions held by New Christians in Portugal, including those in trades and arts and labourers, see Lorence, 'Professions'.

88 Swetschinski, *Reluctant Cosmopolitans*, 103, table 3.1. In southern France, too, the poor among the Portuguese nation worked in a variety of professions. Nahon, 'From New Christians to the Portuguese Jewish Nation in France', 344, mentions, among others, 'wholesale and retail merchants, laborers, shoemakers, butchers, painters, dancing instructors, wigmakers, porters, accountants, hawkers, brokers, servants and errand boys'. For a similar professional structure among the Jews in Livorno in the 18th century see Filippini, 'La nazione ebrea di Livorno', 1056–60.

89 Jona Fresco (SAA entry no. 334, no. 218, p. 316, 18 Kislev 5450: 'pª comprar huas cardas pª trabalhar').

90 SAA entry no. 334, no. 217, p. 106, 6 Elul 5438: 'pª orden dos ssres do mahamad pª ajuda de comprar instrumen^{tos} pª fazer fechos pª livros'.

91 SAA entry no. 334, no. 17, p. 46^{v}, 10 Apr. 5393.

92 For the cases of David Machorro de Leon and Salomon da Rocha see Appendix III.

93 Abraham Enriques was given 15 guilders to work in his profession as a shoemaker (SAA entry no. 334, no. 217, p. 489, 29 Adar II 5445: 'sapateyro p. uzar de seo oficio').

94 Jacob Obediente was a teacher (SAA DTB 685, p. 134, 20 Jan. 1662: 'Jacob Obediente van Bayonne de Franse Portugees Schoolmeester'). For his work in the school for poor boys see SAA entry no. 334, no. 215, pp. 89–90, 34–5, 134–5, 174–5, 231, 285, 333, 5423–30; ibid., no. 216, pp. 27–8, 91–2, 5430–2. He was given financial support during his last illness (ibid., p. 69, 26 Av 5431–25 Tishrei 5432). Jacob Rodrigues is mentioned as a teacher receiving welfare periodically (SAA entry no. 334, no. 174, p. 251, 11 Adar II 5418: 'Jacob Rodrigues mestre': matzah meal, 32 *livras*). Apparently he had been living in Brazil as well (ibid., p. 551, 3 Nisan 5423: 'Jacob Rodrigues de Brazil'); he may possibly have been there during the years 5418–24 when his wife was receiving monthly poor relief (ibid., p. 274, Rosh Hodesh Iyar 5418; ibid., p. 652, Rosh Hodesh Iyar 5424), or he may have been travelling somewhere else during that period. It is known that he died in Amsterdam (ibid., no. 215, p. 71, 8 Adar 5425). Isaiah de Souza was mentioned as a 'mestre de escola' (SAA entry no. 334, no. 172, p. 201, 1 Shevat 5403: peat) and a 'mestre dos meninos' (ibid., p. 230, 11 Tishrei 5404: Sukkot). In 1643 he had a wife and one son (ibid., p. 205, 5403: 'Jeshaias de Souza, molher e f^{o}': 24 *livras* of matzah meal). For poor *belogrados* like the Belinfante and Siprut di Gabay

families, well versed in Jewish matters and educated in yeshivot in the Ottoman empire, as teachers in Amsterdam, privately with families, or in the Amsterdam Portuguese yeshivot see Levie Bernfeld, 'Confrontation entre l'Orient et l'Occident', 49–51. For the yeshiva of Belgrade see Pass Freidenreich, *The Jews of Yugoslavia*, 28; Eventov, *A History of Yugoslav Jews* (Heb.); Ben-Naeh, *Jews in the Realm of the Sultans*, 257–61.

95 For Samuel de Casseres as a scribe in 1648 see Pieterse, *Daniel Levi de Barrios*, 151–2. For a description of the work of a scribe see SAA entry no. 334, no. 19, p. 245, 16 Tamuz 5408. De Casseres also looked after the library of Ets Haim (ibid., no. 1052, p. 25[v], 20 Heshvan 5413: 'Samuel de Caceres tivese conta com os livros da bibliotequa'). For Eliau Juda Leon as a scribe see SAA entry no. 334, no. 216, p. 204, 4 Nisan 5436: 'p[a] su trabajo en la obra de letras que se preso en sima la teba'. For Salomon Leon as a scribe see SAA entry no. 334, no. 1052, p. 37, 5434: 'Selomoh Leon sofer'. For Leon as a student in the *midrash* of Haham Aboab see ibid., p. 35, 27 Nisan 5432; he received 4 guilders as a monthly scholarship. For the *belogrado* Meir Cohen Belinfante as a scribe see ibid., no. 422, [no page number], 1701, 19 Adar II 5461; he also wrote *Sefer me'ir ḥayim*, an interpretative work in Hebrew on fragments from the Torah copied by his great-grandson Isaac Cohen Belinfante (MS Ets Haim 47 B 6, pp. 127–43). For Joseph Siprut di Gabay working in the capacity of calligrapher and scribe within the Portuguese community in the period 1724–55 see SAA entry no. 334, no. 223, p. 175, 11 Kislev 5485; ibid., no. 970, p. 552, 24 Av 5504; ibid., p. 559, 2 Nisan 5505; ibid., p. 626, 3 Elul 5513; ibid., p. 648, 11 Tishrei 5516. He apparently also carved the inscriptions on gravestones: see Hagoort, *Beth Haim*, 132, 134–6. For Joseph Siprut di Gabay as a calligrapher and poet see Melkman, *David Franco Mendes*, 32–3, 115–16, 154.

96 Clara and Rachel Belilhos were hired for this purpose. They apparently worked at home; the members of the Mahamad gave them the tools ('hua Planeka ou firma de Cobre q sirve p[a] aestampa') on the strict condition that they followed the instructions of the *hahamim* (SAA entry no. 334, no. 25, p. 243, 27 Heshvan 5499). They were the granddaughters of Haham Isaac Aboab da Fonseca; on their father Daniel Belilhos see Pieterse, *Daniel Levi de Barrios*, 99–100, 109, 123, 125–6, 186. For Jewish women elsewhere operating printing presses see Offenberg, 'Peregrine Printers', 157–8, who mentions the wife of Abraham Conat, a 15th-century Hebrew printer in Italy: 'his wife Estellina was the first woman to be involved in the operation of the printing press'.

97 David Abendana worked with a Dutch baker overseeing the baking of kosher bread (SAA entry no. 334, no. 24a, p. 6, 24 Heshvan 5425). Apparently he had earlier been in Brazil; he was on welfare periodically after his return in 1655 (ibid., no. 174, p. 118, 6 Elul 5415) and continuously from 1665 (ibid., p. 683, Rosh Hodesh Nisan 5425). From 1667 he was given matzot for one person (ibid., no. 215, p. 199, 5427). He may possibly have traded in tobacco at an earlier date (Bloom, *The Economic Activities of the Jews of Amsterdam*, 61). Jacob Rodrigues also worked overseeing the *kashrut* of bread: 'Jacob Rodrigues forneiro q travalha em casa de Tartas' (SAA entry no. 334, no. 216, p. 3, 19 Heshvan 5431); he also worked preparing food (*shemurim*) for Pesach (ibid., no. 215, p. 153, 5426). For an overview of overseers in the 18th century see SAA entry no. 334, no. 25, pp. 92–3, 7 Av 5466. Women would also act as supervisors, much to the annoyance of the Portuguese community, who had delegated these tasks to their husbands (ibid., no. 24a, p. 6, 24 Heshvan 5425). For the involvement of Abigail de Leon, daughter of Rabbi Jacob Juda Leon, in the *mitsvah* around setting aside dough (*ḥalah*) see ibid., no. 174, p. 610, Rosh Hodesh Tevet 5424: 'que assistia em hum forno'; earlier, in 1639, 'Sara a velha do Algarve' had performed this ritual of taking *ḥalah* (Hagoort and Pieterse, *Livro de Bet-Haim*, 17). For work concerning the *mitsvah* of the *ḥalah* see also discussion of Ester de Andrade later in this chapter.

Salomon Azuby was a *shoḥet*. He received charity periodically between 1648 and 1650 (see e.g. SAA entry no. 334, no. 173, p. 26, 14 Adar 5408; ibid., p. 100, 1 Sivan 5409; ibid., p. 137, 14 Nisan 5410). Jacob Querido and Maimon Haiaia were also installed as *shoḥetim* (ibid., no. 19, p. 510, 29 Kislev 5423). Querido, first a student at the Ets Haim yeshiva, received a scholarship from 1645 until at least 1652 (ibid., no. 1052, p. 9, 4 Tishrei 5406; ibid., p. 47v, 5412; ibid., no. 217, p. 98, 12 Adar 5438). For the community covering the cost of the passage of his son when he went abroad see ibid., no. 216, p. 69, 30 Tishrei 5432; apparently he had a large family to keep: ibid., no. 215, p. 254, 5428: 30 *livras* of matzah meal. In addition to his salary as a *shoḥet*, Maimon Haiaia also received peat, matzot, and *nedava* for Purim, like others, such as teachers and rabbis, who performed vital roles in the community (ibid., no. 174, p. 535, 15 Kislev 5423: peat; ibid., p. 553, 5423: 30 *livras* of matzah meal; ibid., p. 616, Purim 5424).

Juda Obediente from Salé worked preparing *shemurim* and *ḥaroset* for Pesach (SAA entry no. 334, no. 215, p. 24, 23 Nisan 5423; ibid., no. 216, p. 169, 5434). In addition he was receiving charity: from 1665 until his death in 1687 he was continuously on welfare, receiving the whole welfare package (ibid., no. 174, p. 683, Nisan 5425; ibid., no. 175, p. 377, Iyar 5447). He was first registered for welfare in 1659 (ibid., no. 174, p. 332, 25 Nisan 5419). He was head of a large family of five or six (ibid., no. 215, p. 199, 5427: distribution of matzah meal). His widow applied to have her daughters accepted for the Dotar lottery (ibid., no. 1153, p. 106, [1696]).

Joseph Hazan also worked preparing food (*shemurim* and *ḥaroset*) for Pesach (SAA entry no. 334, no. 217, p. 103, 5438). He was supported by the community on a temporary basis for several years (ibid., no. 217, p. 93, 5438: peat distribution; ibid., pp. 51, 101, 149, 190, 5437–40: distribution of matzah meal; ibid., pp. 58, 97, 5437–8). He is described as a *forasteiro* and got married in 1679; in this record it is stated that he came from Turkey. His wife was born in North Africa. He signed his *ondertrouwakte* in Hebrew, while his bride seems to have been illiterate (SAA DTB 691, p. 244, 7 July 1679). His daughter applied for a dowry from Dotar (SAA entry no. 334, no. 1153, p. 267, [1698–9]).

98 The widow of David Habilho was paid for the repair of Torah mantles and other ceremonial textiles (SAA entry no. 334, no. 219, p. 29, 1 Adar 5452: 'concerto e feitio de capas e Panos de sepher'); see also the widow Saragal: 'Va de Saragal . . .

p. feitio e concerto de fajas de sepher' (ibid., 8 Kislev 5452). The widow of Is. Templo made or repaired 'talettot e sisit' (SAA entry no. 334, no. 970, p. 536, 21 Heshvan 5503: 'a V[a] de Is. Templo p. sua conta de talettot e sisit f 19:5'; ibid., p. 553, 8 Elul 5504: 'por taletot e tisit a V[a] Templo f 44:17'). Some women were appointed as *mortalhadeyras*, making or repairing shrouds. They also washed the corpses of female members of the community (SAA entry no. 334, no. 218, p. 78, 18 Tishrei 5446; ibid., no. 25, p. 170, 10 Kislev 5488; ibid., p. 209, 14 Heshvan 5492; ibid., no. 912, pp. 127–32, 26 Adar 5515, 11 Iyar 5517, 13 Nisan 5518). For regulations for twelve *mortalhadeyras* appointed in the 18th century see ibid., no. 912, pp. 127–30, 26 Adar 5515.

99 For Rachel Hamis d'Orta and Reyna Buena de Moura see SAA entry no. 334, no. 20, p. 287, 1 Iyar 5460. For the three of the 'New Bath', 'As tres do Banho Novo: Sara Sanches, Judique Ferro, Ester Serrena', see ibid., no. 172, p. 205, 14 Adar 5403: matzot; ibid., p. 48, Rosh Hodesh Shevat 5400: monthly distributions. The latter are also described as widows ('Outro Veuva no banho novo': ibid., p. 117, 15 Adar 5401). Apparently they came from France: 'A Huas S[ras] Veuvas que vierao de Franca . . . se havia despachado p[a] ajuda de fazerem hu Banho' (ibid., p. 21, 6 Elul 5399). According to Abraham Idaña, widows were usually appointed to take care of the *mikveh* (Teensma, 'Fragmenten', 134).

100 Joseph Curiel Franco received a salary for that purpose (SAA entry no. 334, no. 222, pp. 218–19, 5476–7, 220 guilders: yearly salary as an 'administrador do emprestimo'). For *ḥazan* Abraham Cohen de Lara as administrator of the loan bank see SAA entry no. 334, no. 242, p. 19, 8 Shevat 5451; his daughter-in-law, the widow of *ḥazan* Isaac Cohen de Lara, ran the community's pawnshop in 1746 or was the 'directora do lombardo', to use the community members' own description (SAA entry no. 334, no. 974, file 5, p. 19, 5512; ibid., no. 248, p. 214, 13 Nisan 5506). For women and loan banks in the Ottoman empire see Ben-Naeh, *Jews in the Realm of the Sultans*, 325.

101 Abraham Baruch Abarbanel was appointed to watch over the cemetery for a salary of 90 guilders a year (SAA entry no. 334, no. 215, pp. 172–3, 5426–7: 'p. guardar Bet Haim'). His grandson became a barber or 'chirurgijn' (SAA DTB 696, p. 82, 26 Mar. 1688). Abraham Dias and David Fernandes Tabago guarded the synagogue for thirty-two days (SAA entry no. 334, no. 216, p. 194, 6 Elul 5435). Many *gerim* were involved in keeping guard, for example Abraham Ger ('p. guarder a porte a dia de Kipur': SAA entry no. 334, no. 215, p. 218, 11 Tishrei 5428; 'Abrao Ger empacador . . . p. guardar la puerta e dentro en dia de Kipur . . . f 5,–': ibid., no. 216, p. 194, 11 Tishrei 5436; ibid., no. 217, p. 259, 19 Adar 5441: 'f 1:10'). 'Abrao Ger empacador' received temporary financial assistance (ibid., no. 216, p. 188, 5435; ibid., no. 217, p. 50, 5437; ibid., p. 94, 5438; ibid., p. 185, 5439; ibid., p. 241, 5441; ibid., p. 317, 5442).

102 Ribca Lopes Cardoso became such an assistant to the poor in 1735/6 (SAA entry no. 334, no. 25, p. 224, Tevet 5496); Sara de Aguilar earned 24 guilders as an assistant to the poor in 1750 (SAA entry no. 334, no. 181, 13 Nisan 5510). See also Simha de Simson C: Lobatto and Gracia M[r] de Is: Pesach, both employed in the same position in 1794 (ibid., no. 228, p. 309, 5554).

103 For example, Ester, the wife of Salomon Sena, and Sara de Tovar, daughter(?) of Isaac de Tovar, were involved in health-care work as a family enterprise, including surgery, bloodletting, and the like. For such work undertaken by Ester Sena see SAA entry no. 334, no. 219, pp. 126–7, 5452–3; ibid., p. 226, 30 Nisan 5454 ('A estrela Sena quatro sanguesugas f 1:4'); ibid., p. 404, 4 Sivan 5458; ibid. no. 220, p. 92, 23 Elul 5460. For health-care work undertaken by Sara de Tovar see SAA entry no. 334, no. 219, p. 404, 4 Sivan 5458: 'a Sara de Tovar p. huma samechugas a f[a] de Ab. Ramez f 0:12'; ibid., no. 220, p. 92, 23 Elul 5460: 'a Sara de Tovar p. 3 samesugas pa Va de Selomoh Doria f 25'. In the 18th century Ester, the wife of Samuel Lopes, and Debora Vintura were health-care workers in the community (SAA entry no. 334, no. 21, p. 211, 24 Shevat 5480). For Debora Vintura working with Isaac de Tovar and Isaac Israel Bagara in the years 1713–14 see SAA entry no. 334, no. 222, pp. 48–9, 5473–4. Debora Vintura received welfare through Abodad Ahesed in 1708 (SAA entry no. 334, no. 20, p. 476, 5 Shevat 5468). For the education of Jews in the medical professions in the Dutch Republic see Esso, 'Het aandeel der Joden', and Y. Kaplan, 'Sephardi Students' (Heb.). Most women working in this area must have learned their health-care skills from their husbands or fathers and mothers.

104 For Simha de Campos as a midwife see SAA entry no. 334, no. 1329, carton 24, p. 76, no.161: 'S[a] da bemaventurada Simha Partera da naca[o] mulher q foi de Ymanuel do Campos f[o] em 16 Yiar A[o] 5458'. Simha received welfare from the Portuguese community (SAA entry no. 334, no. 215, p. 199, 6 Adar 5427; ibid., p. 348, 5429–30; ibid., no. 216, p. 112, 5432; ibid., p. 127, 5432–3). She was the granddaughter of Haham Isaac Uziel from North Africa and assisted at the birth of Simón, son of Daniel Levi de Barrios. To mark the occasion, the writer penned a sonnet in her honour (Pieterse, *Daniel Levi de Barrios*, 19 nn. 4 and 5). On Rachel de Campos, widow of Daniel de Campos, acting as the midwife of the Portuguese community, and helping in 1685 with the delivery of Jacob Alvares Sotto, see SAA entry no. 5075, no. 7531, Not. J. van Vilekens, p. 141, 21 Feb. 1708. Lea Azuby, wife of Jacob Pereyra, was not only midwife to the Portuguese community during the 18th century but also helped Ashkenazi women deliver children (SAA entry no. 5075, no. 7668, no. 468, Not. A. Tzeewen, 15 Aug. 1735). We come across the profession of midwives among Conversas in the Iberian peninsula as well (Levine Melammed, 'Castilian Conversas at Work'; ead., *Heretics or Daughters of Israel?*). On midwives in the Dutch Republic see Marland, *Mother and Child*; ead., 'The *'burgerlijke'* Midwife'; Frijhoff, 'Vrouw Schaders beroepsjournaal'; Borg, *Vroedvrouwen*; Post, 'De Amsterdamse vroedvrouw'.

105 Sidcat Nassim, whose job was to take care of poor and sick women, chose six capable women of 'good behaviour' to keep watch over sick and dying women (SAA entry no. 334, no. 25, p. 212, 25 Tishrei 5494; ibid., no. 120, file 84, p. 951, arts. 13 and 17, 21 Heshvan 5517). In the Mishenet Zequenim old-age home the tasks of the mother and father of the house were clearly defined (SAA entry no. 334, no. 1220, pp. 23–5, 12 Nisan 5511).

106 For nursing by women from North Africa see the example of Benvenida Halaca below. For women from south-eastern Europe who were active in caring for the sick see n. 113 below. For care by *tudescos* of babies, and of the sick, disabled, and dying among the Sephardi poor, see the case of Ester Barrocas, who was attended at her deathbed by a *tudesca* (SAA entry no. 334, no. 218, p. 156, 5447: 'a hu tudesca que assistiu a difunta'). A *tudesca* also took care of a sick *belogrado* (ibid., p. 385, 5 Tamuz 5450). A *tudesca* was the wet-nurse of the child of one of the *ḥazanim* ('A tudesca que tem a menina do hazan': ibid., no. 173, p. 26, 14 Adar 5408: 5 guilders). Examples of *italianos* looking after the sick include Natan Italiano, who took care of Abraham Ger (SAA entry no. 334, no. 217, p. 8, 11 Nisan 5436), and Sara de Ancona, who looked after a sick daughter of Isaac de la Cuesta (ibid., p. 266, 6 Iyar 5441: 'por trez semanaz asistio doente filha de Izaque de la Cuesta'). Two non-Jewish people who cared for sick Jews were the Dutch woman looking after Dina Ger (SAA entry no. 334, no. 17, p. 49, 25 Oct. 5394/1633) and Elsgen Bruns, also Dutch, who served as wet-nurse and maid at the home of Tomas Nunes Pina for eleven years (SAA entry no. 5075, no. 646A, Not. S. Cornelisz., pp. 171–2, 21 July 1622; also published in *Studia Rosenthaliana*, 21/2 (1987), 200, no. 2673). Salomon Sena was paid for housing the dying Abraham Zacuto, but when the job became too difficult a *tudesco* took over (SAA entry no. 334, no. 216, p. 71, 5 Nisan 5432). From Iyar 1672 a *tudesco* took in Abraham Zacuto in his *pousada* (inn) (ibid., p. 113, 20 Nisan 5432; ibid., p. 147, 25 Sivan 5433). Zacuto was buried on 27 Sivan 1673 (ibid., p. 145, 27 Sivan 5433: 'por a caixa e barco pera Abraham Sacutto').

107 Sprunger, 'Mennonites', 148–9.

108 Commelin, *Beschryving*, 1181. During these crises Portuguese Jews from Amsterdam came together for prayers in places of refuge such as Wijk aan Zee, Maarssen, Maarseveen, and Naarden (see the yield of *promessas* donated there, and also the transportation of *sifre torah* with ornaments and a *yad* to these locations—in 1655 for Wijk aan Zee and for Maarseveen: SAA entry no. 334, no. 240, p. 37, 10 Heshvan 5416; ibid., no. 174, p. 130, 11 Tishrei 5416; for 1664 and 1665 in Wijk aan Zee, Naarden, and Maarssen see ibid., p. 174, 5 Nisan 5425; ibid., p. 192, 10 Nisan 5425; ibid., no. 24a, p. 5^{r-v}, 11 and 15 Tamuz, 10 and 3 Av, 25 Elul 5424). See also Zwarts, 'De Joodse gemeenten', 398, and Y. Kaplan, *From Christianity to Judaism*, 156 and n. 133. To avoid the danger of infection spreading, the Portuguese avoided contact with the Ashkenazi Jews as much as possible, and in the years 1664–5 the latter were sent away in large numbers (SAA entry no. 334, no. 19, p. 533, 8 Sivan 5424; ibid., no. 240, pp. 188 and 192, 1 Nisan 5425; ibid., no. 174, p. 685, 1 Nisan 5425).

109 SAA entry no. 334, no. 24, p. 20, Rosh Hodesh Sivan 5424. For five days, Daniel Lopez Rison took care of Ester Castiel and her son. He buried two sons of Saul Levi Bondia in Ouderkerk, as well as Sara Marques and Rachel Fundao. In addition, he helped in the house of Abraham Castiel. No volunteers were available or ready to help under the auspices of Bikur Holim or Gemilut Hasadim. The Portuguese cemetery had to be expanded in this plague year to deal with the high mortality rate (ibid., no. 240, p. 169, 14 Shevat 5424).

110 Wagenaar, *Amsterdam*, i. 593–4, 605–6. The Reformed Church paid women 6 guilders a week to care for victims of the plague; men received 8 guilders a week (SAA entry no. 377, no. 1, p. 82, 15 Aug. 1655; Lieburg, 'Religion and Medical Practice', 140).

111 SAA entry no. 334, no. 24, p. 21, 24–5 Sivan, 4, 13, and 20 Tamuz 5424; ibid., no. 215, pp. 93–4, 5424–5; ibid., no. 240, p. 192, 1 Nisan 5425: 'f 887:3 pagos as pesoas q assistirao aos doentes'. Following Daniel Lopez Rison, David Oliveira was the second Portuguese employed to look after victims of the plague. He was the uncle of Ester de Oliveira, who came from Vila Real (SAA DTB 681, p. 150, 24 Nov. 1651). Moses de Leon Berberisco, who was of North African origin, gave help to the poor during this same epidemic of 1664/5 (SAA entry no. 334, no. 215, pp. 93–4, 5424–5: 'p. asistir . . . f 9:6'); he left Amsterdam one year later (ibid., p. 217, 28 Kislev 5426) and received 5 guilders to cover his travel expenses. As for Ashkenazi Jews, Ers Samas Tudesco and Salomon Gerson were appointed to help out during this epidemic (ibid., no. 24, p. 21, 25 Sivan and 4, 13, and 20 Tamuz 5424). The salaries paid by the Portuguese community for this work were set at the same level as those paid by the Reformed Church. During the epidemic of 1655 the Portuguese community did not hire extra personnel. However, at that time there was a good deal of criticism concerning the functioning of Bikur Holim, whose adult voting members—all the *yehidim* over the age of 20—were not fulfilling their obligations, such as accompanying corpses to the cemetery and visiting the houses of the mourners, most of them having fled the city (SAA entry no. 334, no. 19, p. 387, 19 Shevat 5415). As a result, the community's leaders seem to have tried a new approach in 1664. The *yehidim* were paying members with the right to vote, as opposed to *congregantes* (non-taxpaying members) and people on welfare, who did not have the right to vote: Fuks-Mansfeld, *De Sefardim in Amsterdam*, 119.

112 SAA entry no. 334, no. 24, p. 21, Rosh Hodesh Sivan 5424. For this dangerous work she received a relatively high salary, namely 3.3 guilders a day and another 20 guilders monthly (SAA entry no. 334, no. 215, p. 94, 5424–5). Benvenida was a poor woman, and had been on the community's charity list since 1665 (SAA entry no. 334, no. 174, p. 680, 12 Adar 5425; ibid., no. 215, p. 191, 5426–7). She was the mother of Joseph Halaco from Salé (SAA DTB 684, p. 377, 16 Nov. 1660).

113 For example, *belogrado* Salomon Levy helped Isaac Gomes Mesquita (SAA entry no. 334, no. 219, p. 404, 9 Tamuz 5458), Isaac Monsanto (ibid., no. 220, p. 36, 23 Nisan 5459; ibid., p. 37, 6 Elul 5459), Moses Vas Mexicana (ibid., no. 220, p. 36, 12 Iyar 5459), Raphael Milano (ibid., 30 Iyar 5459), Jacob Carvalho (ibid., 28 Elul 5459), and Moses Guedelha (ibid., p. 38, 14 Kislev 5460). Another *belogrado* who took care of the sick was Joseph Crespo; in 1693 he kept watch over the dying in the house of Abendana (SAA entry no. 334, no. 219, p. 172, 12 Heshvan 5454); another was Juda Alva, who cared for Moses Barrocas in 1696 (SAA entry no. 334, no. 219, p. 319, 8 Iyar 5456). The *belograda* Doña Jurada watched over a lady called Cardosa (ibid., p. 172, 3 Sept. 5454); *belograda* Paloma Vidal took care of Moses Rodrigues (ibid., p. 361, 11 Tishrei 5458); *belograda* Judith Alcoser helped out in the 'familia de Is. Henriq. Mesq[a]' (ibid., p. 404, 20 Av 5458). For these *belogrados* on the charity lists of the community see SAA entry no. 334, no. 219, p. 2, 5451; ibid., p. 86, 3 Sivan 5452; ibid., p. 251, 12 Nisan 5455.

114 When Torres died, he still owed her money (SAA entry no. 5075, no. 2890A, Not. P. Padthuysen, pp. 17–19, 10 Nov. 1661). One Rachel Lopes received charity in 1681 (SAA entry no. 334, no. 217, p. 256, 1 Shevat 5441). Another woman of the same name applied for a dowry from Dotar in 1652, mentioning that she was without parents (her father had died in Cádiz) and very poor (ibid., no. 1151, p. 316, around 1652). For another Portuguese woman working in care of the sick see the case of Rachel Falcoa watching over a lady called [Sara] da Costa (ibid., no. 216, p. 130, 16 Heshvan 5433).

115 SAA entry no. 334, no. 217, p. 164, 14 Iyar 5439. Nunes Leao also worked for the Portuguese community preparing for Pesach during the years 1663–77 (see e.g. ibid., no. 215, p. 206, 5427). He was given charity on a permanent basis from 1657 until his death in 1681, and his widow continued to receive charity (ibid., no. 174, p. 225, Rosh Hodesh Elul 5417; ibid., no. 175, p. 116, 1 Iyar 5440; ibid., p. 147, 1 Nisan 5441; ibid., no. 174, p. 693, 10 Nisan 5425; ibid., p. 729, 20 Adar 5426). His daughters tried their luck with Dotar (ibid., no. 1151, p. 173, [n.d.]; ibid., p. 253, 5435; ibid., no. 1152, p. 425, 1685).

116 SAA entry no. 334, no. 217, p. 164, 14 Iyar 5439. Isaac Bentancor was sent out to the West Indies in 1663 (ibid., no. 215, p. 42, 4 Heshvan 5424), but apparently returned in 1665. He and his family were periodically on welfare from 1665 to 1684 (ibid., no. 215, p. 112, 28 Av 5425; ibid., p. 201, 5427; ibid., no. 216, p. 100, 5431–2; ibid., no. 217, p. 459, 5444). For many years (1665–72) he also worked to prepare *shemurim* (ibid., no. 215, p. 124, 5425).

117 Debora charged 7 guilders a month (SAA entry no. 334, no. 215, p. 208, Rosh Hodesh Adar 5428); she took care of Rachel Sega until 1682 (ibid., no. 217, pp. 275–80, 316, 5441–2).

118 SAA entry no. 334, no. 219, p. 79, 10 Nisan 5452.

119 SAA entry no. 334, no. 220, p. 95, 27 Adar II 5461. For Ribca Ribeyro assisting Lea Castiel see ibid., no. 222, p. 22, 9 Heshvan 5474. For her assistance to Lea Castiel and the daughter of Abraham Carvalho see ibid., p. 74, 19 Shevat 5474; for Ribca on the charity list see ibid., no. 176, p. 349, 1 Nisan 5460; ibid., no. 974, file a, p. 14, 1734. For more examples see the case of Benvenida Falcoa ('A Benvenida Falcoa p. velar 4/d a Rahel Sacuta . . . f 3': SAA entry no. 334, no. 222, p. 23, 3 Elul 5473; on charity given to her: ibid., p. 51, 5473–4). Apparently she was a divorcee: see ibid., no. 25, p. 94, 2 Dec. 1706. Mariana Sarfati took care of the wife of M: Lopez Cardozo (SAA entry no. 334, no. 25, p. 74, 29 Kislev 5474). The widow Chumaseira assisted the wife of Mattos (ibid., p. 76, 17 Heshvan 5475: 'a V[a] Chumaseira velar 4/ . . . a m[r] de mattos f 3,–'). Sara Abenatar helped the wife of Is. Sacutto: 'Sarah Abenatar p. velar la muxer de Is. Sacutto 5/d y noche f 5' (ibid., no. 220, p. 141, 1 Elul 5461). The widow of Sabbatai de Isay Acohen watched over the widow Gradiz (ibid., no. 221, p. 310, 4 Sivan 5470). For the widow of Moses Abenatar watching over Vintura see ibid., p. 311, 21 Tishrei 5471, and for Roza Lopez Salzeda caring for the widow Sigala see ibid., 25 Tishrei 5471.

120 SAA entry no. 334, no. 220, p. 139, 22 Tevet 5462: 'a Mordohay Rodriguez p. Velar y tener en cassa a Abm Carillo f 16'.

121 'A Is. Franco p. velar 15/8 a Benjamin Preto . . . f 4:4' (SAA entry no. 334, no. 222, p. 23, 3 Elul 5473). For more Portuguese men working in this branch of sick care in the 18th century see ibid., no. 220, p. 141, 4 Elul 5461: 'a Ab. dela Peña por assistir 5/d a Danl Morales f 2:10'; ibid., p. 188, 23 Elul 5462: 'Samuel colon de azevedo p. velar 15/d e noites a yeossuah oliveyra f 7:16'; ibid., p. 239, 6 Kislev 5464: 'a Abm Reffael Forte p. velar 2/d a Mos. Mendez henrq f 1:10'; ibid., no. 969, p. 165, 26 Adar 5492: 'a Saml Teixeira p. ter Ab[m] Israel do Vale por 16/7 por estar doente . . . f 117'.

122 SAA entry no. 334, no. 220, p. 136, 25 Tevet 5462: 'A debora vintura por tener en cassa una q se llama pantaloon f 1:2'; 'a debora vintura por tener en cassa 20/d Mordohay Israel f 1:10'; ibid., p. 135, 18 Adar 5462: 'a debora Vintura p. Tener Maarab enfermo f 2'; ibid., 1 Nisan 5462: 'a Debora vintura y a talano por ter dos pobres enfermos 3/7 f 7:14'. For her activities as a bloodletter see SAA entry no. 334, no. 222, p. 75, 23 Nisan 5474: 'A Debora Vintura 2 chamesugas p[a] Jb Querido f 1:4'; ibid., no. 223, p. 62, 26 Av 5482: 'p. 23 chamesugas a Debora vintura 12 pl f 13:16'; ibid., p. 384, 3 Tishrei 5489: 'a Debora Vintura p. 9 chamesugas f 5:8'. As mentioned earlier (n. 103 above), Debora was also active as an assistant to doctors and surgeons. For examples of women in the wider world, with small infirmaries, see Sprunger, 'Mennonites', 148; McCray Beier, *Sufferers and Healers*, 223.

123 SAA entry no. 334, no. 215, p. 1, 2 Iyar 5423: 'Tudesco que tem cargo do loco Carilho'; ibid., p. 55, 1 Nisan 5425: 'Tudesco q tem o louco Carillo em caza'.

124 SAA entry no. 334, no. 4, 19 and 29 Elul 5379; ibid., no. 5, p. 167, 3 Tevet 5382; ibid., no. 17, p. 2, 26 May 5382; ibid., p. 3, 1 June 5382; ibid., p. 8, 30 Apr. 5383; ibid., p. 13, 1 May and 30 June 5383; ibid., p. 10, 1 Oct. 1623; ibid., p. 6, 23 Oct. 5383; ibid., p. 10, 10 Oct. 5384; ibid., p. 13, 3 Nov. 5385; ibid., p. 19, 15 Mar. 5386; ibid., p. 21, 18 Oct. 5387; ibid., p. 25, 14 May 5388; ibid., p. 26, 11 Oct. 5389; ibid., p. 36, 18 Aug. 5390; ibid., p. 41, 25 Aug. 1631. For the continuation of Masaot's work by his widow see ibid., p. 55, 20 May 5395/1635: 'a molher de Jeremias Mazao dous quartos de Fereyra'; ibid., p. 58[v], 18 Apr. 5396. It is known that Jeremias Masaot payed *finta* of 1 guilder in 1614 (Pieterse, *Livro de Bet Haim*, 160 (5374)). For him receiving welfare see ibid., no. 4, p. 422, 5381; ibid., p. 176, 5382; ibid., no. 17, p. 29, 22 July/Rosh Hodesh Av 5389; ibid., no. 7, pp. 121[v]–122, 5391–2. Masaot lost a son in 1620 (Pieterse, *Livro de Bet Haim*, 97 (11 Oct. 1620)). Between 1615 and 1631 three of his daughters tried their luck at Dotar: in 1630 one succeeded in getting a dowry (SAA entry no. 334, no. 1141, pp. 12, 45, 65, 85, 110, 128, 143, 164, 5375–82; ibid., no. 1142, pp. 9, 29, 43, 61, 77, 94, 110, 124, 130, 140, 5383–91). For the petition written by Jeremias Masaot addressed to the administration of Dotar see ibid., no. 1151, p. 201, 5380. For his daughter Debora receiving a dowry of 240 guilders when she got married see ibid., no. 1142, p. 1187, 13 Adar 5394; SAA DTB 674, p. 60, 11 Oct. 1635; according to this source, at the time of Debora's wedding her mother was ill: 'noch een moeder sieck hebbend'.

125 SAA entry no. 334, no. 969, p. 316, 24 Nisan 5494: 'a Sem[l] Palache p. 1/m da loca ferra f 6,–'; ibid., no. 970, p. 621, 1 Adar 5513; ibid., p. 630, 9 Nisan 5514: 'pago a Jeosua Busnac por Alimento do mes Adar de 5 mulheres, 2 ferras, calo, morales y fortada . . . f 62,–'; ibid., p. 631, 29 Nisan 5514: 'a Jeosua Busnach por alimento de cinco mulheres a saber; a mulher de Calo, a V[a] Furtado, Ester Ferro, Sara Ferro, M[r] de J[b] Morales f 62,–'.

126 SAA entry no. 334, no. 969, p. 316, 8 Nisan 5494: 'a Jeosua Busnaq p. Selomoh Romero privado de Juizo f 3'.

127 'vijff hokken zijnde vier op de kaamer waar de krankzinnege zijn geplasseert en één op de zolder . . . de verhuurster zal gehouden zijn de hokken dienenden tot de krankzinnige staande op de kaamer in zolder voor haar Rekening moeten onderhouden' (SAA entry no. 334, no. 310, 25 Dec. 1781; ibid., 25 Dec. 1783).

128 On these industries see Israel, 'The Economic Contribution of Dutch Sephardi Jewry'; id., 'The Republic of the United Netherlands'; Dillen, 'De economische positie', 561–616; Bloom, *The Economic Activities of the Jews of Amsterdam*, ch. 2; Roessingh, *Inlandse tabak*; id., 'Tobacco Growing'; and Silva Rosa, *De geschiedenis van de Portugeesche Joden te Amsterdam*, 28–32. For Portuguese tobacco industrialists see e.g. Abraham de Aron Dias da Fonseca, who owned a tobacco spinners where the poorer members of the Portuguese Jewish community might have found work (SAA entry no. 5072, no. 620, p. 34, 26 Mar. 1695; ibid., p. 35, 17 June 1695: in his inventory we come across two 'tabackspinne wielen'). Jacob Franco Drago had equipment used in the tobacco industry in his warehouse: 'Voorhuys oft Packhuys . . . dry parssen . . . op de werksolder . . . vijff tabaq werkbancken, een Tabacx Molen, 6 blocken tot molens, een ysere balans met twee houtte Schalen . . . Op de vlieringh . . . Een Tabacsmeulen, 6 d[o] blocken, Een kuyp met swaere ysere banden, dry spinbacken' (SAA entry no. 5072, no. 618, pp. 34[v]–36, 8 Sept. 1692). Jacob de Mercado delivered diamonds and tobacco (ibid., no. 695, p. 17, 5 Mar. 1693). For a chocolate maker who was also on the welfare list see Isaac Monsanto, described as a merchant from Seville (SAA DTB 691, p. 153, 9 Sept. 1678). From 1682, when he was around 37 years old, Monsanto was in receipt of welfare (SAA entry no. 334, no. 20, p. 33, 13 Adar II 5442); he received monthly assistance until 1701 (ibid., no. 176, p. 377, 2 Nisan 5461). For further distributions to him see ibid., no. 219, p. 39, 5451; ibid., no. 176, p. 71, 1 Nisan 5451; ibid., p. 195, 1 Nisan 5455; ibid., no. 176, p. 261, Rosh Hodesh Nisan 5457; he supplied chocolate to the *kahal* (ibid., no. 218, p. 391, 15 Adar 5451).

129 The following are examples of workers in these industries who received welfare payments in addition to their wages. Raphael Montesinos from Venice worked in the sugar refinery ('suikerbakkersknecht') of Abraham Pereyra (Bloom, *The Economic Activities of the Jews of Amsterdam*, 39; SAA DTB 688, p. 259, 28 Aug. 1671; SAA entry no. 5075, no. 2890A, Not. P. Padthuysen, p. 351, 22 Sept. 1661; ibid., no. 2272, Not. A. Lock, p. 46, 23 Jan. 1657). Montesinos also worked preparing the *shemurim* for Pesach (SAA entry no. 334, no. 217, pp. 153, 203, 263, 335, 5439–42). From 1682 he was permanently on welfare (ibid., no. 20, p. 51, 26 Elul 5442). Before this he had been supported on a periodic basis since 1676 (see

e.g. SAA entry no. 334, no. 217, p. 35, 5 Heshvan 5437: peat; ibid., p. 183, 5439: rental subsidy; ibid., p. 236, 5440–1: *nedavot*; ibid., p. 51, 5437: matzot). The rent of his cellar (we don't know whether he lived in it) was paid by the Portuguese community (ibid., p. 23, 1 Dec. 1675; ibid., p. 24, 29 Elul 5436). His daughters applied for dowries with Dotar from 1697 (ibid., no. 1144, p. 444, 5457: Sara). One of them, Ribca, apparently moved in 1700 to Livorno, from where she applied for a dowry while living with an aunt (ibid., no. 1153, p. 364, 1700). Gideon Henriques is mentioned as a tobacco worker in 1697, marrying *Pro Deo* (SAA DTB 700, p. 245, 13 Dec. 1697). He also worked making the *shemurim* for Pesach (SAA entry no. 334, no. 217, p. 335, 5442). He was on the charity lists periodically from 1674 until 1694 (ibid., no. 216, p. 165, 5434, matzah meal; ibid., no. 217, p. 269, 10 Elul 5441; ibid., p. 271, 17 Heshvan 5442; ibid., no. 218, p. 385, 13 Sivan 5450; ibid., no. 219, p. 224, 4 Tamuz 5454). He and his wife are also mentioned as carers for the sick and dying (SAA entry no. 334, no. 219, p. 79, 10 Nisan 5452; for his wife Sara Baesa see ibid., no. 222, p. 76, 6 Elul 5474: 'Sara Baesa p 8/7 velar a ditto [dv. Vintura] f 6,–'). Joseph Azuby worked in the silk industry, being mentioned as a 'sijkaarter' at his first marriage (SAA DTB 695, p. 68, 26 Oct. 1685). Two years later he is mentioned as a *shamash* (ibid., p. 454, 12 Sept. 1687). He attended the school for poor boys for seven years (SAA entry no. 334, no. 215, pp. 133, 173, 229, 283; ibid., no. 216, pp. 28, 92, 124, 5426–33). Jacob de Imanuel Baruch is described as a diamond-cutter in 1668 (SAA DTB 687, p. 161, 10 Feb. 1668). He also worked to produce *shemurim* for the community, yearly from 1674 to 1682 (SAA entry no. 334, no. 216, pp. 169, 190, 5434–5; ibid., no. 217, pp. 1, 55, 103, 203, 263, 335, 5436–42). He received welfare periodically, and permanently from 1673 (ibid., no. 216, p. 142, 5433), and also through Abodat Ahesed (ibid., p. 2, Rosh Hodesh Heshvan). One son died in 1674 (ibid., p. 169, 5 Tishrei 5435). Apparently he still had two children living in 1678 (ibid., no. 217, p. 94, 5438: 32 *livras* of matzah meal). In 1689 his wife travelled abroad (ibid., no. 218, p. 346, 5449: 'se foi fora'). One year later he left Amsterdam as well (ibid., p. 426, 5450–1: 'se foi').

130 Isaac de Abraham Dias worked as a proofreader at the printing house of Moses Dias (Meijer, *Encyclopaedia*, ii. 6, 1718–19; for Moses Dias as a printer see ibid., 2 Feb. 1692; see also Bloom, *The Economic Activities of the Jews of Amsterdam*, 56). On Clara and Rachel Belilhos as printers see n. 96 above. Abraham de Fontes was a bookbinder. In 1679 and 1680 he was paid for the repair of the *Livro de termos* (SAA entry no. 334, no. 217, p. 164, 30 Tishrei 5440; ibid., p. 217, 6 Tishrei 5441). He also worked to prepare *shemurim* for Pesach (ibid., pp. 103, 153, 203, 263, 5438–41). In addition, he was assisted periodically by the community (ibid., pp. 252, 256, 258, 5441). In 1681 he went to Curaçao; he received money from the community to cover the expenses for this trip (ibid., p. 274, 1 Sivan 5441). It is possible that he may have been the Abraham de Fontes who was earlier in Italy (ibid., no. 215, p. 264, 17 Elul 5428) and Curaçao (ibid., no. 216, p. 3, 2 Tevet 5431), and/or that prior to that he was a student at Ets Haim, for which he got a scholarship (ibid., no. 1052, p. 48, 5412). Josua Busnach was also trained as a bookbinder and paid for the binding of (membership?) lists of the old-age home in 1752 (SAA entry no. 334, no. 1227, p. 8, 12 Nisan 5512). For Isaac Calvo de Andrade as a bookbinder see SAA entry no. 334, no. 1211, p. 6, 3 Adar II 5429; ibid., p. 1^{v}, 5432; SAA entry no. 5075, no. 2239, Not. A. Lock, pp. 95–6, 10 May 1672.

131 Kaufmann, 'Joseph ibn Danon', 290; Silva, *Sefer peri hadas*: 'Lu'aḥ rish milin'.

132 Joseph Siprut di Gabay and Juda Pisa, for example, had southern European and Levantine roots and helped to publish *Sefer hanhagat haḥayim. Regimiento dela vida. Libro de mucho erudicion, y doctrina. En el qual como en un Cristalino espejo podrá el hombre corregir sus yerros, y emmendár sus vicios, encaminhandose en la virtud, haziendose en esta vida momentanea merecedor de alcançar la Gloria Eterna*, written by Moses Almosnino in 16th-century Salonika. In 1729 this book was reprinted, having been transcribed in Roman characters from the Ladino in Hebrew characters ('La primera ves que a salido a luyz en caracteres espanoles por industria de Semuel Mendes de Sola, Josseph Siprut Gabay y Jeudah Piza, Amsterdam 1729'). On Joseph Siprut see also Silva Rosa, *Die Spanischen und Portugiesischen Gedruckten Judaica*, 9, no. 34: Hebrew poems of Joseph Siprut di Gabay and David Franco Mendes. Juda Pisa was the son of an immigrant, Haim Pisa, from Constantinople. Like his father, Juda married a girl from a Belgrade family, Luna Aubi (SAA DTB, no. 713, p. 424, 3 June 1723). At the end of the 18th century we still find proofreaders among the offspring of the *belogrados*—for example, Isaac de Eliau Cohen Belinfante. The book Isaac de Eliau Cohen Belinfante was recorded as proofreading is *Sefer tefilot lishe'elat matar*, by Haham Samuel Mendes de Sola with additions by Haham Jacob Lopez da Fonseca, published in 1773 by Israel Mondovi in Amsterdam (Emmanuel, *History of the Jews of the Netherlands Antilles*, 66 n. 18). For yeshivot in the Ottoman empire see Ben-Naeh, *Jews in the Realm of the Sultans*, 257–61.

133 See further Salomon Rison, 'ourives' (SAA entry no. 334, no. 13, p. 84, Rosh Hodesh Tishrei 5392; ibid., no. 17, p. 41, 24 Aug. 5392/1631). The profession was also taught in Amsterdam: Daniel Franco, for example, was placed in the house of a non-Jewish inhabitant of Amsterdam in 1620 to learn the profession of goldsmith (SAA entry no. 5075, no. 611B, Not. P. Ruttens, p. 727, 24 Nov. 1620; also published in Zwarts, 'Joodsche Archiefsprokkels', 412).

134 For more silversmiths see Raphael the silversmith (SAA entry no. 334, no. 219, p. 224, 19 Sivan 5454: 'a Raphael Plateiro f 3'); Abraham Roiz (ibid., no. 378, p. 29, 18 Adar II 5475/23 Mar. 1715: 'hum filho de Ab-m Roiz plateiro: Ishack'); Abraham [son] of David Henriquez, silversmith (ibid., no. 379, p. 135, no. 739, 15 Shevat 5472/23 Jan. 1712: 'Ab^{m} de David Henriq^{z} platero'); Isaac [son] of David Rodriguez, silversmith (ibid., p. 136, no. 767, 18 Adar II/23 Mar. 1715: 'Isaac de David Rod^{z} Platero').

135 For a coppersmith see Abraham Dias: 'por concerto de cobre' (SAA entry no. 334, no. 216, p. 148, 29 Elul 5433). His son Isaac also repaired keys (ibid., 19 Nisan 5433).

136 Joseph Pereyra de Paris was a painter (SAA DTB 693, p. 460, 5 Nov. 1683). He did not pay communal tax, and was on the monthly charity list, if the Joseph

Pereyra mentioned in the following sources is the same as Joseph Pereyra de Paris (SAA entry no. 334, no. 176, p. 291, 1 Nisan 5458; ibid., p. 349, 1 Nisan 5460: 'Josseph Pereyra: f 6').

137 For tailors see Abraham Rodrigues de Sevilla, 'alfayate' (SAA entry no. 334, no. 173, pp. 206–7, 214, 5412); see also D. Is. Alfayate (SAA entry no. 334, no. 6, p. 194, 21 Oct. 5378/1617); Bento Roiz Alfayate (ibid., p. 194, 15 July 5377/1617); Abraham Senior Alfaita (ibid., no. 17, p. 55, 20 May 5395/1635); and Abraham Ger Alfayate (see for example SAA entry no. 334, no. 217, p. 210, 22 Heshvan 5441; ibid., p. 311, 13 Adar II 5442; ibid., p. 520, 5445: matzot). Another tailor, Pierre Nunes de Leon, declared before a notary in Amsterdam that since his arrival in the city he had worked as a tailor to earn a living for his family. He had lived in Portugal for many years and suffered greatly under the Inquisition: all his possessions had been confiscated (SAA entry no. 5075, no. 201, Not. J. Bruyning, p. 75ᵛ, [n.d.] 1624). Tailor 'Azulay' made clothes for the inmates of the old-age home (SAA entry no. 334, no. 1227, p. 10, 12 Nisan 5512). In the 18th century poor orphan boys were taught the trade of tailor (see the case of Abraham Caransa: SAA entry no. 334, no. 1211, p. 192ᵛ, 10 Oct. 1754).

138 For cobblers see Velho Machorro, 'sapateiro' (SAA entry no. 334, no. 4, p. 314, Rosh Hodesh Kislev 5381); Abraham Enriques 'sapateiro' (ibid., no. 217, p. 525, 5445: matzot); Benjamin Dias 'sapateiro' (ibid., no. 173, pp. 26, 45, 48, 59, *nedavot* 5408–9). On his marriage Dias is described as a merchant from Madrid (SAA DTB 683, p. 103, 30 Nov. 1656).

139 Moses Fernandes from Livorno (SAA DTB 694, p. 107, 12 May 1684).

140 For Abraham Nunes see SAA entry no. 334, no. 217, p. 117, 5437–8. Lera García mentions the existence of wax makers in Cuenca at the beginning of the 18th century, describing it as a typical judaizing profession (Lera García, 'La última gran persecución', 104).

141 Isaac Paiva is mentioned as a 'matrassenmaker' (SAA DTB 696, p. 425, 13 Jan. 1690). For welfare distributed to him see SAA entry no. 334, no. 217, p. 40, 18 Heshvan 5437; see also Jona Fresco (ibid., no. 175, p. 444, 6 Shevat 5449: 'a Fresco . . . para fazer colchons').

142 Deursen, *Plain Lives*, 7–10; Panhuysen, 'Gevestigden en buitenstaanders', 154; Kuijpers, *Migrantenstad*, 246; see also SAA entry no. 5061, no. 694, 1747–8, no. 29, petition of bodice-makers and wholesale traders: 'haar werk hebben laaten maaken, meerendeels buitens huys, door knechts op kamers, in kelders en elders, die wederom tot het maaken en naayen en complementeeren van dezelve rijglijven altoos gebruykt en nog gebruyken allerly zoort van vrouwsperzoonen of meyden om een gering arbeidsloon, waar door duyzenden van die vrouwsperzoonen, de kost winnen en haar bestaan hebben'. The same pattern can be found elsewhere in Europe and also in Spain, where women spun at home for the wool and silk industries (Casey, *Early Modern Spain*, 62).

143 For spinning wheels in Portuguese inventories see the following. At the house of Isaac Delmonte alias del Sotto there were 'in 't Portael . . . twee Spinnenwielen' (SAA entry no. 5072, no. 604, p. 167, 14 Jan. 1678); Moses Gabay Isidero had a spinning wheel in the kitchen (ibid., no. 607, p. 201, 26 Mar. 1680); David Ximenes Cardoso also had spinning wheels at home, one in his kitchen and one on the 'Cleerzolder' (ibid., no. 608, pp. 182ᵛ–183, 11 Apr. 1682). When Rachel Pinta Brandon went to live with her nephew Samuel Pinto, one of the things she took with her was a pillow to use while knitting ('una almohada para coser': last will of Rachel Pinta Brandon, SAA entry no. 5075, no. 2894B, Not. P. Padthuysen, pp. 1555–6, 24 Feb. 1665). See also the 'old black pillow to knit' ('een swart oudt nay kussen') in the inventory of Josua de Prado, whose house, as mentioned, was shared with his mother Rachel de Prado (SAA entry no. 5075, no. 7490, no. 52, Not. J. van den Ende, 28 Sept. 1708). Rachel de Spinosa Henriques had a 'Rood Fluweel Naaykussen' (SAA entry no. 334, no. 694, inventory, Not. J. Barels de Jonge, pp. 90–1, 18 Nov. 1737).

144 In 1677 Portuguese women were warned by the Mahamad to refrain from doing this work openly on Sundays and Christian holidays, the magistracy having made the Portuguese community aware of its displeasure (SAA entry no. 334, no. 24a, p. 41ᵛ, 20 Sivan 5437).

145 SAA entry no. 334, no. 217, p. 97, 14 Shevat 5438.

146 SAA entry no. 334, no. 1227, 12 Nisan 5512.

147 Pieter Hannes was the tailor for Jeronimo Doria (SAA entry no. 5075, no. 2261B, Not. A. Lock, pp. 547–51, 9 Feb. 1660: 'Inventaris van de goederen . . . bij Jeronimo Doria van Drada: Lasten van de boedel . . . Pieter Hannes cleermaker . . . *f* 40,–'). Moses Pereyra also had a Dutch tailor, named Coenraet (SAA entry no. 5072, no. 697, p. 74, 16 Nov. 1695). Ester Abrabanel had a non-Jewish seamstress at home (SAA entry no. 334, no. 612, no. 1, Not. D. van den Brink, 20 May 1754, last will of Ester Abrabanel, widow of David de Samuel Pinto: 'Aan Rebecca Jansz Naaijster van Huys').

148 Isaac Ramos got married in 1660 (SAA DTB 685, p. 5, 30 Dec. 1660). At the time he was described as a Portuguese merchant from Zamora in Spain. He also assisted in making *shemurim* for Pesach. He was supported by the Portuguese community from 1663. He left for London in 1668 (see for example SAA entry no. 334, no. 174, p. 543, 10 Shevat 5423; ibid., p. 732, 20 Adar 5426; ibid., no. 215, p. 158, 3 Heshvan 5427; ibid., p. 263, 4 Iyar 5428; ibid., p. 289, 5428–9: *nedavot*; ibid., p. 299, 5429: peat; ibid., p. 265, 12 Tevet 5429: 'pª irse a Londres'). There, in 1673, he was appointed as a broker (D. S. Katz, *The Jews in the History of England*, 186 n. 127).

149 In 1632 it was decided to refuse Jews in Amsterdam permission to practise so-called 'poortersnering'—professional or trade activities requiring citizenship and guild membership, which were closed to all but a very few Jews. This prohibition was especially directed at the craft professions, organized through guilds. The exceptions were tobacco shops, grocery shops, and 'tapperswinkels' (Reijnders, *Van 'Joodsche Natiën' tot Joodse Nederlanders*, 24).

150 SAA entry no. 5061, no. 312, pp. 211–12, 20 Feb. 1659; see also the tobacco shop of Rachel da Zilva: SAA entry no. 5072, no. 589, pp. 263ᵛ–264, 6 Jan. 1662.

151 SAA entry no. 5072, no. 621, pp. 205ᵛ–206, 8 and 11 June 1697; SAA DTB 693, p. 468, 26 Nov. 1683.

152 SAA entry no. 5004, no. 110 (Calisregisters), p. 108, 30 Nov. 1683.

153 SAA entry no. 334, no. 215, pp. 253, 316, 5428 and 5430.

154 SAA entry no. 334, no. 215, p. 313, 2 Nisan 5430.

155 SAA entry no. 334, no. 176, p. 30, 24 Adar 5450; he paid *finta* tax of 4 guilders a year as Josua Jessurun Furtado.

156 SAA entry no. 334, no. 176, p. 350, 1 Nisan 5460. In 1695 his daughter applied for a dowry from Dotar (ibid., no. 1144, p. 429, 5455) and was lucky enough to get one of 720 guilders immediately (ibid., p. 430, 15 Adar 5455).

157 SAA entry no. 5072, no. 591, p. 64, 10 Oct. 1662: 'In 't Packhuys . . . 6 Vaten Snuyf & Vlas . . . Abraham Rois Carriao'. Carriao was supported by the Portuguese community from 1680 to 1681 (SAA entry no. 334, no. 217, pp. 198, 258, 269, 271–2, 5440–2). His widow left for London, having been given money to travel there (ibid., p. 419, 6 Tamuz 5443). His son-in-law, Jacob Rodrigues Carrion, a merchant from Sanlúcar in Spain and Oporto in Portugal (SAA DTB 687, p. 228, 20 July 1668; ibid. 688, p. 101, 13 June 1670), was also on welfare from 1679 (see e.g. SAA entry no. 334, no. 217, p. 158, 5 Tishrei 5440; ibid., p. 264, 11 Nisan 5441; ibid., p. 312, 15 Adar II 5442; ibid., p. 6, 26 Nisan 5443; ibid., no. 20, p. 34, 4 Nisan 5442; ibid., p. 158, Rosh Hodesh Nisan 5452; ibid., no. 176, p. 349, Rosh Hodesh Nisan 5460). He had been receiving financial help from the community since 5 Tishrei 5440; on 22 Kislev 5440 he was given money to go to London, but was back in Amsterdam on 26 Shevat 5440 to receive financial help once more (ibid., no. 217, p. 195, 22 Kislev 5440).

158 Isaac Soeiro is described as a 'toebackkooper' at the registration of his marriage in 1674 (SAA DTB 689, p. 198, 13 Apr. 1674). He attended the school for poor boys as the son of Jacob Soeiro from 1663 to 1667 (SAA entry no. 334, no. 215, pp. 35, 90, 135, and 231, 5423–7; his name for the year 5427–8 on p. 231 is blotted out). Haim Pisa from Constantinople, who married *Pro Deo* in 1702, described himself at that time as a tobacco seller (SAA DTB 703, p. 91, 27 May 1702); two months earlier, he had declared, in his capacity as 'snuyftabackverkooper', that he was without any means: SAA entry no. 5004, no. 110 (Calisregisters), pp. 105^{v}–106, 21 Mar. 1702. For Isaac Menasseh as a tobacco trader in Amsterdam see SAA DTB 702, p. 384, 23 Dec. 1701: 'Pro Deo . . . Isaak Menasse . . . taback&kooper'.

159 Moses Bueno dos Colcoins (SAA entry no. 334, no. 174, p. 485, 24 Adar 5422).

160 SAA entry no. 5072, no. 694, p. 8, 10 Mar. 1692: 'Elias de Medina . . . geleverde stoffen, canten, schoenen, winkelwaren'. Elias de Medina not only dealt in fabrics and shoes, but also had a shop or factory where clothes were made; in 1692 this went bankrupt. He employed a Dutch woman and man as tailors, to whom he owed 20 guilders for 'Cleer mackers loon'. De Medina, who apparently came from North Africa, was supported by the Portuguese community from 1655 until 1675 and again from 1693 (see e.g. SAA entry no. 334, no. 174, p. 131, 12 Tishrei 5416; ibid., p. 736, 17 Adar II 5426; ibid., no. 215, p. 1, 7 Tamuz 5423; ibid., p. 59, 5 Iyar 5424; ibid., p. 108, 5426; ibid., p. 158, 3 Heshvan 5427; ibid., p. 239, 20 Heshvan 5428; ibid., p. 299, 5429; ibid., p. 359, 5430; ibid., no. 216, p. 62, 5431;

ibid., p. 104, 5432; ibid., p. 142, 5433; ibid., p. 165, 5434; ibid., no. 20, p. 167, 28 Adar II 5453). On his marriage in 1658 he had said that he did not have any means. In 1690 the community gave him money to travel to London, but he apparently returned to Amsterdam (SAA entry no. 334, no. 219, p. 17, 1 Tevet 5451: 'a Ely de Medina p. Socorro p[a] yr a Londres f 20,–').

161 Abraham de Castro had a shop where he sold oil (SAA entry no. 5072, no. 605, p. 268[v], 23 Mar. 1678). It is not clear whether he was supported by the community later on, since several 'Ab. de Castros' appear in the records for this period.

162 Joseph Montel had a shop in the 'voorhuys' of his house in Weesperstraat, where he sold candles, spices, linen, material, oil, and matzot (SAA entry no. 5072, no. 701, pp. 212[v]–213, 2 Dec. 1699; ibid., no. 701, p. 67, 9 Dec. 1699). There is no record of him either paying taxes to or receiving charity from the community. The *shamash* Habilho made and delivered wax for candles (SAA entry no. 334, no. 217, p. 490, 2 Heshvan 5445).

163 Jacob Mendes Carels [Carlos] is called a 'cruynier' at his marriage in 1685 (SAA DTB 695, p. 33, 25 Aug. 1685). He apparently moved to London two years later (SAA entry no. 334, no. 218, p. 111, 14 Tishrei 5447). His wife may have received charity on a monthly basis through Abodat Ahesed in 1697 (SAA entry no. 334, no. 20, p. 223, [n.d.] 5457). Aron Baruch Abarbanel sold salt and soap (SAA entry no. 334, no. 218, p. 390, 30 Iyar 5450). At the same time he was a recipient of charity (see e.g. ibid., no. 217, p. 235, 5440–1); besides this, he was paid a salary to take care of the cemetery (ibid., no. 215, pp. 330–1, 5429–30), engrave letters on the gravestones (ibid., no. 221, p. 60, 2 Heshvan 5466), and copy official papers (letters, wills, contracts) for the community (ibid., no. 216, p. 78, 22 Adar II 5432).

164 For his registration of his marriage at City Hall see SAA DTB 694, p. 176, 8 Sept. 1684. He married Ester de Toledo from Paris; he himself was born in Amsterdam.

165 SAA entry no. 5072, no. 694, p. 38, 19 Dec. 1692. He said his wife (see n. 164 above) brought to the marriage 2,000 guilders, which he used to pay off his debts; earlier, in 1679, before his wedding, he had applied for poor relief to the Portuguese *sedaca*. Later, in 1701, his children did likewise. For distributions of charity see SAA entry no. 334, no. 217, pp. 144–7, 5439; ibid., no. 20, p. 304, [n.d.] 5461; ibid., no. 176, p. 377, 2 Nisan 5461.

166 For Isaac Nunez see SAA entry no. 334, no. 174, p. 119, 6 Av 5415. For Pereyra see 'Abram Pereyra muzico . . . f 12,–' (ibid., no. 220, p. 61, 17 Menahem-Av 5460).

167 SAA DTB 695, p. 148, 5 Apr. 1686: a 'speelman op Marcken'.

168 See 'Moses Oeb Trompeter', SAA entry no. 334, no. 222, p. 355, 8 Tamuz 5479: this source records his departure for London.

169 SAA entry no. 334, no. 216, p. 14, 18 Elul 5430. His parents apparently belonged to the 'secret poor' (ibid., no. 174, p. 733, 20 Adar 5426; ibid., pp. 542, 548, 608, 616, 5423–4; ibid., no. 215, pp. 115, 201, 209, 213, 252, 5426–8).

170 SAA DTB 703, p. 21, 25 Feb. 1702: 'taalmeester'.

171 On mail to and from the Dutch Republic see Brink, *De geschiedenis van het postvervoer*, 10–29; see also R. van Gelder's *Zeepost*, 29–31; on written and other forms of communication of Sephardi Jews in Livorno see Trivellato, *The Familiarity of Strangers*, 170–6; on communication between Jews in 14th-century Spain see Gutwirth, 'Hebrew Letters', 269–78.

172 SAA entry no. 334, no. 217, p. 67, 3 Elul 5437. Ereira did not pay *finta* tax but was not in receipt of welfare through the Portuguese community either (ibid., no. 174, p. 1045, 7 Tishrei 5435). His sister did receive charity in 1685 (ibid., no. 217, p. 525, 5445).

173 SAA entry no. 334, no. 222, p. 250, 7 Shevat 5478: 'a Moseh Delgado por portes de cartas f 1:11'; ibid., p. 306, 24 Av 5478: 'a Mos. Delgado por 3 cartas de Londres f 2:15'; ibid., p. 307, 18 Kislev 5479: 'a Mos. Delgado por portes de cartas f 3:17'; ibid., no. 223, p. 61, 1 Sivan 5482: 'Is. Delgado por 3 cartas f 1:7'; ibid., p. 63, 20 Kislev 5483: 'a Mos. Delgado por cartas de Sarinhao e de fransa f 1:16'; ibid., 16 Adar 5483: 'Mos. Delgado cartas de fransa e londres'. For other letter carriers see Isaac da Costa (SAA entry no. 5004, no. 109 (Calisregisters), p. 110, 4 Aug. 1669; SAA DTB 688, p. 2, 16 Aug. 1669), who is also mentioned as a letter carrier in a notarial deed: 'brieven besteller van de joodse natie' (SAA entry no. 5075, no. 3679, Not. F. Tixerandet, p. 985, 21 Aug. 1671). There are several Isaac da Costas mentioned as being on welfare, so it is difficult to identify this individual. For other letter carriers taking letters from Spain, Rouen, and Antwerp in 1623 see SAA entry no. 5075, no. 387, Not. J. and N. Jacobs, 23 Dec. 1623, p. 279$^{r–v}$; also published in *Studia Rosenthaliana*, 27/1–2 (1993), p. 174, no. 3069.

174 SAA entry no. 334, no. 221, p. 17, 23 Tamuz 5464: 'Is. Nunez soldado de ungria p^{a} Lond^{s} . . . f 10'; see also Isaac Lopes de Luna described as a soldier in SAA entry no. 5061, no. 321, p. 19, 2 Mar. 1673; ibid., no. 323, p. 121^{v}, 8 Feb. 1677.

175 Poor Dutch women also earned some money as innkeepers ('logementhouders'): van der Vlis, *Leven in armoede*, 167–8, and Schmidt, *Overleven na de dood*, 74. For the lodging of strangers or relatives in the London Jewish community see Diamond, 'The Community of Resettlement', 145–6. An example of a woman in the Iberian peninsula working as an innkeeper is Isabel de la Mancha, mentioned in Pulido Serrano, *Injurias a Cristo*, 117.

176 SAA entry no. 5061, no. 311, pp. 253^{v}–254^{r}, 6 June 1657.

177 She received 14 guilders for hosting Calvo (SAA entry no. 334, no. 216, p. 10, 16 Iyar 5430). Her husband received welfare from 1663 to 1668. Later she continued to receive charity together with her children. One son, Isaac Farques, was given an education at the school for poor boys. One daughter, Rachel, married Moses Bassan, who at that time (1696) was a tobacco spinner (SAA DTB 699, p. 371, 22 Sept. 1696). See also SAA entry no. 334, no. 215, pp. 13, 200, 253, 263, 267, 269, 5424–8; ibid., no. 174, p. 552, 3 Nisan 5423; ibid., p. 732, 20 Adar 5426; ibid., no. 216, p. 10, 28, 63, 92, 104, 112, 138, 142, 163, 166, 187, 189, 201, 208, 210, 5430–6; ibid., no. 217, pp. 23–4, 36, 52, 93, 100, 139, 149, 189, 199, 248, 5437–40. In 1669/70 Calvo was sent on a journey at the request of the Portuguese community of Hamburg, who paid his expenses (SAA entry no. 334, no. 215, p. 311, 13 Nisan 5429; ibid., no. 216, pp. 10, 27, 13 Nisan–23 Sivan 5430; ibid., no.

174, p. 891, 7 Av 5430). In 1687 he apparently came back to Amsterdam and was sent away again, this time to Bordeaux (ibid., no. 218, p. 175, 14 Sivan 5447).

178 SAA entry no. 334, no. 17, p. 29, 20 July 5389.

179 SAA entry no. 334, no. 217, p. 489, 29 Adar II 5445.

180 SAA entry no. 334, no. 220, p. 11, 12 Elul 5459; ibid., p. 135, 18 Adar 5461. For more work by him in this field see ibid., p. 141, 17 Av 5461.

181 SAA entry no. 334, no. 220, p. 136, 12 Shevat 5462; ibid., p. 135, 4 Nisan 5462.

182 SAA entry no. 334, no. 218, p. 321, 3 Tamuz 5449. In 1701 Alva was once more paid to host *sheliḥim* from Belgrade: R. Joseph Menasseh and R. Joseph Mataja, who visited Amsterdam in the winter of 1701 and stayed at his house for about one month (ibid., no. 220, p. 93, 4 Shevat 5461; ibid., p. 94, 21 Adar II 5461).

183 SAA entry no. 334, no. 220, p. 136, 12 Shevat 5462; ibid., p. 135, 18 Adar 5462.

184 SAA entry no. 334, no. 218, p. 248, 1 Tamuz 5448.

185 For *belogrados* staying with Isaac Talano see SAA entry no. 334, no. 219, p. 26, 8 Heshvan 5452; Isaac Oeb and Isaac Moreno also offered to put up the refugees from Belgrade (ibid., p. 26, 8 Heshvan 5452; ibid., p. 101, 25 Sivan 5452: 'f 9:11'; ibid., p. 101, 7 Av 5452; ibid., p. 102, 14 Av 5452; ibid., 21 Elul 5452).

186 SAA entry no. 334, no. 17, p. 29, 2 Sept. 5389; ibid., p. 31, 28 Oct. 5390/1629.

187 Pike, *Aristocrats and Traders*, 130; Defourneaux, *Daily Life in Spain*, 83–4, 150; Pescatello, *Power and Pawn*, ch. 2; Bennassar, *The Spanish Character*, 103–6, 117–23; Domínguez Ortiz, *La sociedad española*, 398; id., *The Golden Age of Spain*, ch. 11. On the attitude of the Portuguese in India towards 'degrading' work see Schorsch, *Jews and Blacks*, 209, which cites the description of a Frenchman in 1608.

188 Guerrero Mayllo, *Familia*, 343–4. For servants at home see also López Belinchón, *Honra, libertad y hacienda*, 252–3.

189 López Belinchón, *Honra, libertad y hacienda*, 256–7 and n. 34.

190 Bennassar, *The Spanish Character*, 103–6, 117–23.

191 'A mulata de Simão Gomez de Paz' (SAA entry no. 334, no. 216, p. 113, 4 Iyar 5432); 'A negra de Simão Gomez de Paz' (ibid., no. 217, p. 146, 2 Shevat 5439); 'Branca Negra de casa de Simon Gomez' (ibid., p. 195, 22 Tevet 5440). For welfare distributions to Simon Gomez de Paz see e.g. ibid., no. 216, p. 2, 11 Menahem-Av 5430; p. 4, 22 Shevat 5431; ibid., p. 113, 27 Nisan 5432; ibid., p. 146, 3 Adar 5434; ibid., no. 217, p. 60, 19 Heshvan 5438; ibid., p. 257, 28 Shevat 5441. His children, Lea and Sara Gomez de Paz, were on charity, while a 'negra' apparently took care of them: 'una negra q vive con Lea e Sara de Paz' (ibid., no. 217, p. 145, 17 Kislev 5439). For charity given to these girls see ibid., no. 19, p. 756, 8 Tevet 5437; ibid., no. 174, p. 1169, Rosh Hodesh Shevat 5437. As daughters of Simon Gomez de Paz they received a legacy from Gracia Senior (ibid., p. 1051, 18 Tevet 5435: 'Lea e Sarah, filhaz de Simao Gomez de Paz'). They also received a legacy in 1677 from Maria Mendes de Pas (last will of Maria Mendes de Pas, widow of Anthonio de Pas: SAA entry no. 5075, no. 2182, Not. A. Lock, pp. 65–72, 8 Mar. 1677, p. 70: 'aan de twee dochters van Simon Gomes de Pas met namen Lea Aboab en Sara Aboab yder de somme van vijftich gld eens'). The father of Simon Gomez de Paz lived in Madrid in Gracia Senior's house (SAA entry no. 334, no. 826, Not. P. Padthuysen, p. 3, 30 Aug. 1673: 'miguel dias padre de simon gomez de paz que estaba en mi casa en madrid').

192 Nahon cites a case of a woman who in 1656 took her *negra* with her from Portugal to Bayonne (Nahon, 'Bayonne', 48); see also the Alvarès family arriving in southern France from Bragança, bringing with them a 'Portuguese nanny' (Cavignac, 'L'Immigration des Juifs portugais à Bordeaux', 128). Schorsch, 'Early Modern Sephardim and Blacks', 242, maintains that many Jews and Conversos fleeing to eastern lands, especially after 1492, brought their black slaves with them.

193 Cited in R. D. Barnett, 'Diplomatic Aspects of the Sephardic Influx', 216–17.

194 After the death of her mistress she continued to work in service, taking care of the brother-in-law of her former master (Gemeentearchief Den Haag, entry no. 0130-01, no. 319, Not. J. Sijthoff, 27 June 1746, last will of Marie Anne Josephe Therese de Partes, widow of Don Francisco Manrique).

195 SAA entry no. 5075, no. 7533, Not. J. van Vilekens, pp. 1197–1202, 31 Oct. 1710.

196 For personnel employed by the Amsterdam Portuguese Jews see also Levie Bernfeld, 'Sephardi Women in Holland's Golden Age', 188. Sephardi women from the Orient hired for domestic service in Amsterdam had apparently done the same work in their country of origin (Ben-Naeh, *Jews in the Realm of the Sultans*, 349). For *moriscos* arriving in Amsterdam see García-Arenal and Wiegers, *A Man of Three Worlds*, 59–60, 71–3; Y. Kaplan, 'Les Proselytes juifs'; B. Kaplan, *Muslims*. They apparently travelled with their employers from the Iberian peninsula, arriving in Amsterdam in the early period of Jewish settlement there. For *moriscos* as servants in Spain, where black, Moorish, and *morisco* slaves had been a common phenomenon in domestic service since the 16th century, see Pike, *Aristocrats and Traders*, 153, 160, 170, 177. For the good relations between *moriscos* and Jews or Conversos on Iberian soil, in North Africa, and beyond see García-Arenal and Wiegers, *A Man of Three Worlds*, pp. xxii, 9, 88–9. On *tudescos* see also Y. Kaplan, *From New Christians to New Jews* (Heb.), ch. 4. For similar patterns in Hamburg see Studemund-Halévy, '*Senhores* versus *criados*'; Debra Kaplan, 'Women and Worth', 6; Whaley, *Religious Toleration*, 81. For blacks among the Amsterdam Portuguese see also Schorsch, *Jews and Blacks*, 175–8.

197 'Pro Deo . . . Jacob Alexem van Bellogrado Arbeyder oud 24 Jaarn in de Swaanenburgstraat ouders doot geasst. met Salomon Levi en Rachel Alcoser van Bellegrado Oud 17 Jaarn als Voorn. geass[t.] met haar vad.[r] Joseph Alcoser' (SAA DTB 699, p. 261, 6 Apr. 1696).

198 Pescatello, *Power and Pawn*, 30.

199 SAA entry no. 334, no. 518, Not. Ph. de Marolles, p. 349, 12 May 1730: 'Copia do Testamento de d[a] Jeudit Henriques'.

200 SAA entry no. 334, no. 1191, p. 222, 28 Kislev 5460; he earned 18 guilders a year for this job.

201 SAA entry no. 5075, no. 6684C, Not. J. Snoeck, pp. 1012–16, 5 Nov. 1709, last will of Daniel Fresco.

202 SAA 5075, no. 7530, Not. J. van Vilekens, pp. 737–8, 26 June 1707.

203 SAA entry no. 334, no. 826, p. 2, Not. P. Padthuysen, 30 Aug. 1673.

204 SAA entry no. 334, no. 217, p. 60, 3 Kislev 5438. Gracia Levi Victoria also employed a cook, Marianne 'cuzineira' (ibid., no. 175, p. 95, 1 Adar 5440). Ester Ferro did similar work later on (Ester Ferro 'cuzina'): it appears that she had been on the charity roll since 1679, together with Ribca Ferro; after 1687 she appears there alone. In 1699, 1700, and 1704 the records of the Portuguese community give the description 'cuzina' after her name (see for example SAA entry no. 334, no. 217, p. 149, 5439: matzot; ibid., no. 20, p. 33, 13 Adar II 5442; ibid., no. 175, p. 180, Rosh Hodesh Nisan 5442; ibid., p. 362, Rosh Hodesh Nisan 5447; ibid., no. 176, p. 321, Rosh Hodesh Nisan 5459; ibid., p. 349, Rosh Hodesh Nisan 5460; ibid., no. 221, p. 46, 5464: 'Rol da turva e masoth: f 16:8').

205 In the family's will, Sara de Palma was promised a yearly allowance of 80 guilders as well as food, lodging, and clothes. The will also mentions many other maids and male servants, none of them Sephardim, who did not enjoy the same conditions (Gemeentearchief Den Haag, entry no. 0372-01, no. 2077, Not. J. Sijthoff, 16 Jan. 1744, last will of Benjamin Teixeira and Ribca Teixeira).

206 SAA entry no. 334, no. 87, file 20, 1753, *Remonstraçoems e rq*[a] *aos ss*[res] *Burgames*[trs].

207 Hufton, 'Women without Men', 363; Deursen, *Plain Lives*; Kuijpers, *Migrantenstad*, 242. For a similar pattern among the New Christians in Portugal see Lorence, 'Professions', 319–20.

208 SAA DTB 689, p. 250, 31 Aug. 1674.

209 SAA DTB 688, p. 102, 13 June 1670. Abraham Zuzarte was in receipt of welfare from 1679 to 1685 (SAA entry no. 334, no. 217, pp. 195 (15 Kislev 5440), 197 (12 Adar II 5440), 241 (5441), 248 (5441), 317 (5441), 329 (5442), 385 (5443), 458 (5444), 525 (5445)). One or more of his sons moved to Surinam in the years 1691–2 and were given money for their journey (ibid., no. 219, p. 23, 4 Tamuz 5451; ibid., p. 102, 7 Kislev 5453). The widow was given permanent support from 1695 (ibid., no. 20, p. 188, 26 Adar 5455). See also Abraham Zuzarte, registered as an orphan at Aby Jetomim in the years 1653–7 (ibid., no. 1211, p. 3[v], 5413; see further Vaz Dias, 'Vergeten hoofdstuk', 168, and Bloom, *The Economic Activities of the Jews of Amsterdam*, 86). One Abraham Zuzarte was already married in 1648 (SAA DTB 680, p. 20, 14 Aug. 1648); however, this Abraham seems to be the son of David Zuzarte.

210 Moses Bassan married, *Pro Deo*, Rachel Farques, daughter of the widow of Salomon Farques, whom we met above (for their marriage see SAA DTB 699, p. 371, 22 Sept. 1696, where he is mentioned as a tobacco spinner: 'toeback-spinder'); we meet him in 1702 as a grocer ('Moses Bassan kruidenier': SAA entry no. 5075, no. 6677A, Not. J. Snoeck, pp. 145–7, 22 Mar. 1702), and in 1706 there is a record of his bankruptcy (SAA entry no. 5072, no. 629, pp. 96[v]–97, 2 June 1706). For his financial condition see SAA entry no. 334, no. 20, p. 243, 6 Adar 5458, where he asks to be allowed to pay only 2 guilders a year as *finta* tax; he continued to pay *finta* of 2 guilders a year after his bankruptcy (ibid., no. 177, p. 19, 1 Adar 5463; ibid., p. 115, 16 Adar II 5467), as he belonged to the lowest *finta* category. However, by the 1730s he had become more impoverished, and was receiving charity from Abodat Ahesed (SAA entry no. 334, no. 1210, pp. 7–8, 5495–6: 4.10 guilders a month). In 1707 he fathered a child out of wedlock (SAA entry no. 334, no. 377, p. 11, 5467, no. 127 [besnijdenisregister]: 'Jacob filho de Sara Talano dis acomadre aver confesado ser filho de Mosseh Bassan na ora do parto 23: Sivan, 23 Junio dia 5°') and in 1708 he fathered a daughter, Annetje, by a prostitute. He was married at the time (SAA entry no. 5075, no. 7531, Not. J. van Vilekens, p. 449, 28 June 1708).

211 SAA entry no. 5072, no. 700, p. 19, 11 Mar. 1698. Abraham Bassan was a pupil at the school for poor children (SAA entry no. 334, no. 215, pp. 132–3, 174–5, 230–1, 284–5, 332–3, 5425–30; ibid., no. 216, pp. 25–6, 89–90, 5430–2). Later, his widow was supported through Abodat Ahesed in the 1730s, receiving 4 guilders a month (SAA entry no. 334, no. 1210, p. 5, 5495–6).

212 SAA entry no. 334, no. 1191, p. 342, 7 Av 5470.

213 SAA entry no. 334, no. 1191, p. 429, 6 Tevet 5478.

214 SAA entry no. 334, no. 1191, p. 803, Rosh Hodesh Iyar 5506.

215 SAA entry no. 334, no. 1191, p. 677, 5496.

216 Esso, 'Aandeel der Joden', 673; Oldewelt, *Kohier*, ii. 88, 1742: here he is mentioned as 'medicinae doctor'. He acted as a doctor for the poor of the community and received a salary of 200 guilders a year (SAA entry no. 334, no. 21, p. 383, 5486; ibid. no. 974, file a, p. 28, 1734). For his work with private clients see SAA entry no. 334, no. 694, p. 387, 4 Dec. 1737: in September and October 1737 he paid fourteen visits to Rachel de Spinosa Henriques, who was dying; for this he was paid 21 guilders.

217 Simon do Valle asked permission to introduce Isaac Saragal as his successor on condition the latter married his granddaughter (SAA entry no. 334, no. 25, p. 45, 12 Heshvan 5458; ibid., no. 20, p. 288, 21 Iyar 5460; SAA DTB 701, p. 314, 2 Jan. 1700). Simon do Valle was not only working as a *shamash* but also earned an income by selling wax to the community (SAA entry no. 334, no. 217, p. 167, 5439–40; ibid., no. 216, p. 119, 13 Nisan and 7 Menahem-Av 5432; ibid., p. 131, 27 Shevat 5433). For his salary as a *shamash* see ibid., no. 217, pp. 175–6, 5439–40.

218 SAA DTB 705, p. 58, 6 Nov. 1705; SAA entry no. 334, no. 25, p. 87, 8 Kislev 5465; SAA entry no. 5004, no. 111 (Calisregisters), p. 129^{v}, 4 Nov. 1705: at the death of Isaac Saragal his widow declared to the 'Weeskamer' that he had left two children but no means ('dog geen middelen'). See further the case of Eli Habilho, born in Jerusalem: after he died his son David asked the Mahamad for permission to take over his father's work, which it gave (SAA entry no. 334, no. 20, p. 8, 12 Adar 5444). On this same Eli Habilho working for the community as a *shamash* see SAA entry no. 334, no. 215, p. 201, 5427; see also ibid., pp. 280–1, 5428–9. See further the case of the surgeon Samuel de Leon Benavente, who asked the community whether his son-in-law, David Baruch Pardo, could take over his position as a surgeon to the Portuguese community (SAA entry no. 334, no. 25, p. 116, 6 Tamuz 5472).

219 The widow mentioned that she was too old to do the work (SAA entry no. 334, no.

25, p. 83, 25 Adar 5463). For Abraham Nunes at work see ibid., no. 217, p. 117, 5437–8. Abraham and his family were also being supported by the community (ibid., no. 215, pp. 189, 191, 245, and 253, 5426–8: 'Abraham Nunez o cego'; for rental subsidy see ibid., p. 4, 23 Nisan 5423: 'Abraham Nunes q fas a çera . . . f 4,–'; for peat see ibid., no. 216, p. 185: 'Abraham Nunes das candeas'). It is known that the family was related to and supported by the rich de Pinto family (Salomon, 'The "De Pinto Manuscript"', 25).

220 SAA entry no. 334, no. 19, p. 511, 8 Tevet 5423. The family was apparently in trouble before this: in 1652 an inventory of Samuel's household furniture was made when he was declared bankrupt (SAA entry no. 5072, no. 578, p. 201, 18 Dec. 1652). Samuel was supported by the Portuguese community from 1651 until his death in 1662 (see e.g. SAA entry no. 334, no. 173, p. 205, 7 Kislev 5412; ibid., no. 174, p. 427, 29 Adar II, 5421), and so were his widow and his children after his death, from 1662 until 1680 (see e.g. SAA entry no. 334, no. 174, p. 535, 2 Tevet 5423; ibid., p. 608, 12 Kislev 5424; ibid., no. 175, p. 116, Rosh Hodesh Iyar 5440; ibid., no. 217, p. 240, May 5440). The family grew: up to 1672 the widow received 30 *livras* of matzah meal, but in 1673 was granted 40 *livras*, suggesting that somebody had joined the household (ibid., no. 216, p. 112, 5432: matzot; ibid., p. 142[v:], 5433: matzot). In 1679–80 a note is written next to her name on the peat distributions (ibid., no. 217, p. 189, 5439/40): 'away/abroad' ('esta fora'): did she leave?

221 SAA entry no. 334, no. 24a, p. 66a, 15 Sivan 5445.

222 SAA entry no. 334, no. 25, p. 95, 28 Shevat 5467.

223 Schmidt, *Overleven na de dood*, 146, 149–50, 161–2; Hufton, *The Prospect before Her*, 92–5. For a similar pattern among the New Christians in Portugal see Lorence, 'Professions', 319–20.

224 Levie Bernfeld, 'Sephardi Women in Holland's Golden Age', 185–9. For marriage patterns among the Sephardim from south-eastern Europe and the Levant in Amsterdam see ead., 'Confrontation entre l'Orient et l'Occident', 44 and n. 36.

225 Examples are the offspring of the Bassan and Dias families. For Elias Bassan see Oldewelt, *Kohier*, ii. 80; for Daniel Dias see ibid. 86; for Doctor Isaac de Abraham Dias, ibid. 88; and for Jacq and Isaac Bassan, ibid. 96.

226 For similar patterns among the lower ranks of the New Christians in Portugal see Lorence, 'Professions', 326.

227 'Considerando oss[res] do maamad os mutos emuj urgentes nesesidades que cada dia de novo se lhes manifestão de pesoas benemeritos de nosa nasão pedindo os admitão na repartisão dos reshodes eoittros remonstrando p. petisois continuas suas nesesidades' (SAA entry no. 334, no. 19, p. 308, 25 Sivan 5411).

228 See the various applications in SAA entry no. 334, no. 381.

229 SAA entry no. 334, no. 990, p. 35, [n.d., apparently 18th century].

230 The statutes of various charitable institutions in the 17th and, particularly, the 18th centuries show that they too expected written applications, referred to as 'petitions', before providing assistance to the poor. For sick members of the Gemilut Hasadim yeshiva asking for help through petitions see 'p. Petisoens de hums doentes . . . f 4,–' (SAA entry no. 334, no. 1191, p. 489, 5484). In the minutes of Meil Sedaca we read about the requirement for a petition: 'as petisoms se deverão ter emtregado the p[r] de R:H: Kislev' (ibid., no. 25, p. 219, para. 5, 8 Tevet 5495). To apply for help from the Mazon Abanot girls' orphanage, the caretaker had to submit a petition, addressed to one of the founders of this *ḥevrah,* on behalf of the orphan girls (ibid., no. 120, file 81, p. 867, para. 8, 6 Shevat 5494). To be considered for care in the 18th-century Portuguese Jewish old-age home, 'Toda a pesoa da Idade e das Calidades mensionadas poderão presentar sua petisão desde omes de Adar athe Pesah ao tezoureiro ou fundadores' ('those of the age and reputation mentioned above could present a petition to the treasurer or the founders between Adar and Pesach') (ibid., no. 25, p. 342, para. 21, 8 Tevet 5510); similarly, to be eligible for distributions of bread, butter, rice, and vegetables from the Honen Dalim–Resit Hochma society one had to submit a petition (ibid., pp. 277–8, para. 7, 20 Sivan 5501).

231 Hundreds of petitions reached Dotar, not only written by those living in the city itself, but also sent from abroad. Many are still kept in the archives (SAA entry no. 334, nos. 1151–9).

232 For this approach among the poor in the Jewish communities of medieval Egypt see also M. Cohen, *The Voice of the Poor,* 11, and id., *Poverty and Charity,* 16–21. For petitions in the Sephardi diaspora see that of Samuel Valenci, addressed to the administration of the Portuguese community in Pisa (Toaff, *La nazione ebrea,* 526). Petitions were also common elsewhere in the Dutch Republic: for Leiden see Schmidt, *Overleven na de dood,* 11, 16–19; for Delft (where oral interviews were also used) see van der Vlis, *Leven in armoede*; for the Amsterdam Reformed 'Diaconie' see SAA entry no. 376, no. 14, p. 164, 7 Mar. 1680—'versoekende dat alle briefjes die van dezen en geenen aen deze kamer werden geligt om onderstandt te mogen hebben aan de diaconie'—and also the so-called *bedelbrieven* written by poor members of the Reformed Church of Amsterdam (SAA entry no. 376, no. 1, p. 381, 1 Aug. 1741). See further the petition of a couple in distress addressed to the diaconate of the Flemish Mennonite Church (Sprunger, 'Mennonites', 143); the articles on petitions in early modern Europe discussed in Heerma van Voss's introduction to *International Review of Social History*; and, for early modern England in particular, Krausman Ben-Amos, *The Culture of Giving,* 196–205.

233 In the 18th century the submission of petitions remained the normal procedure (SAA entry no. 334, no. 22, p. 167, para. 1, 8 Heshvan 5509: 'que no adiante todos os que entregarem petições para entrar na Sedaca').

234 On the writing of petitions among the Portuguese Jews of Amsterdam see also Berger, *Classical Oratory,* 99–100. In Leiden these requests were written by a notary (Schmidt, *Overleven na de dood,* 16–19).

235 M. Cohen, *The Voice of the Poor,* 8.

236 In 1639 David Pardo submitted a petition on behalf of Moses Sanches (SAA entry no. 334, no. 172, p. 59, 5 Shevat 5400). In 1667 a third person, in this case the *haham,* took the initiative to submit a request on behalf of Sara Lumbrosa:

'q tornou a pedir o Haham p. ella' (SAA entry no. 334, no. 215, p. 209, 3 Sivan 5427).

237 SAA DTB 696, p. 155, 2 July 1688.

238 SAA entry no. 334, no. 1152, p. 403, 1685; ibid., p. 529, 1686.

239 SAA entry no. 334, no. 199a, p. 654, 23 Aug. 1679.

240 On this point see Würgler, 'Voices', 32; Nubola, 'Supplications', 39–40; Schmidt Blaine, 'The Power of Petitions', 58, 62–3, 77.

241 N. Z. Davis, *Fiction in the Archives.*

242 See the various petitions mentioned above and below; see also M. Cohen, *The Voice of the Poor*, 12, 24–5 (petition 3).

243 SAA entry no. 334, no. 216, detached sheet, 27 Nisan 5432.

244 SAA entry no. 334, no. 1151, p. 49, [n.d.].

245 'Ester Fonseca de Liorne . . . suplica a Ums lhe concedam que entre tambem sua sorte com as demais orfans . . . y rogara al Dio pela vida y augmente de todos Ums . . . Vesalom' (SAA entry no. 334, no. 1151, p. 629, 1668). The expression 'Vesalom' is also found in many petitions discussed in M. Cohen, *The Voice of the Poor*, 78–9 (no. 39).

246 SAA entry no. 334, no. 990, p. 35, [n.d., 18th century].

247 SAA entry no. 334, no. 1151, p. 121, 15 Shevat 5429; see also M. Cohen, *The Voice of the Poor*, 18, 22, on the use of religious terms in medieval Egypt.

248 SAA entry no. 334, no. 1152, p. 137, [1670].

249 SAA entry no. 334, no. 1152, p. 333, [1685].

250 See the petition of Branca Dias, asking for her daughter to be allowed to participate in the Dotar lottery and mentioning that she is very poor and has neither possessions nor other help ('Dis branca dias mulher muto pobre . . . e por coanto ela suplicante nao tem poses nem remedio': SAA entry no. 334, no. 1151, p. 42, 5380). For instructions on the information petitions should contain from 1748 see SAA entry no. 334, no. 22, p. 167, 8 Heshvan 5509, para. 1.

251 SAA entry no. 334, no. 220, p. 69, [n.d.]. For similar requests in the non-Jewish world see Würgler, 'Voices', 29.

252 'Senores parnasim | a Viuva Basan | foren servidos | con q poder | seus 5 orfos | de fome ums t | penhar galinhas | foren servidos' (n.d., found as a separate small sheet among the pages of SAA entry no. 334, no. 218).

253 SAA entry no. 334, no. 172, p. 59, 26 Shevat 5400: 'que fez peticão remonstrando suas necessidades. E dever alugel da casa se despachou f 12,–'.

254 MS Ets Haim 48 E 31, [n.d.] enclosed.

255 SAA entry no. 334, no. 13, p. 77, 8 Nisan 5392: 'adevora Jeserum pera pasaje de seu caminho a terra santa como paresse de sua petisão'.

256 SAA entry no. 334, no. 217, p. 106, 11 Elul 5438: 'Abraham Monsanto . . . p. estar muito doente p. petisão de sua mulher'.

257 'Sres Parnases . . . do q.q. de Beth Israel . . . Daniel Montesinos pede a Vms. O admitao a ser semas porqto nao tem outro remedio nem entretenim^{to}' (SAA entry no. 334, no. 10, p. 65, 5381).

258 SAA entry no. 334, no. 10, p. 89, 4 Nisan 5382.

259 SAA entry no. 334, no. 19, p. 417, 11 Nisan 5417.

260 Particularly after 1663, through the very detailed *livros longos*, lists of registrations have been preserved of all those whose petitions were favourably received (SAA entry no. 334, nos. 215–23; ibid., nos. 978–9, *Registro dos despachos*); see e.g. ibid., no. 215, pp. 11–15, 5423–4: 'Despachos de Peticões de pobres da terra e de outros q vao para fora della'.

261 SAA entry no. 334, no. 172, p. 78, 9 Nisan 5400: 'Alem destas pessoas se ha dado à Alguas mais q vierão pedir não stando eu em casa e nem todas se tomarão p. Rool . . . Abraham Pharar'.

262 For references to people elsewhere appearing in person to ask for charity see van der Vlis, *Leven in armoede*, ch. 4; Spaans, *Armenzorg in Friesland*, 125.

263 SAA entry no. 334, no. 24a, p. 118[v], 26 Iyar 5428.

264 SAA entry no. 334, no. 20, p. 113, 10 Shevat 5448. See also her petition to the 'SS[res] Parnasim Y Gabay deste santa Kaal' applying to be allocated money from the legacies of Lopo Soares (ibid., no. 828, p. 167, [n.d.]).

265 She was granted a pension of 130 guilders including peat and matzot (SAA entry no. 334, no. 25, p. 166, 8 Sivan 5485).

266 Maimonides, *Mishneh torah*; Frisch, *An Historical Survey*, 60.

267 SAA entry no. 334, no. 215, p. 317, 9 Elul 5429: 'p. estar doente, sem pitizão'.

268 SAA entry no. 334, no. 215, p. 269, 28 Kislev 5429: 'sem petição p. ter a m[er] doente . . . f 2:10'. For other sick people see ibid., p. 317, 18 Nisan 5429: 'forasteiro doente . . . sein peticao . . . f 1:10'; ibid., no. 217, p. 8, 27 Iyar 5436: 'Jacob Henriques Alvares . . . despacharão os sres do maamad sem petisão p. tempo de 6/7 a f 2 p. cada sem[a]'.

269 SAA entry no. 334, no. 215, p. 266, 22 Adar II 5429: 'vinda de Nisa p. hum socorro sem petição p. mao do Parnas Abraham da Veiga'.

270 SAA entry no. 334, no. 215, p. 265, 15 Shevat 5429: 'sem petição selhe aver queimado sua cama e fato'.

271 SAA entry no. 5072, no. 713, p. 3, 1 July 1711.

272 SAA entry no. 334, no. 5, p. 118, 12 Tamuz 5381: 'particular secreto'; ibid., no. 174, pp. 136–7, 26 Tevet 5416: 'nedaba feitta em 25 de ditto para Repartir logo p. Pobrez Vergoncantes e de Sedaca'; ibid., p. 733, 5426: 'dous pobres secretos'; ibid., no. 216, p. 13, 9 Nisan 5431: 'pobres encubertos por ordem dos SS[res] do Mahamad'; ibid., no. 217, p. 142, 10 Adar 5439: 'Pobre emcuberto com grande familia'.

273 SAA entry no. 334, no. 973. For secret notes on distributions to the poor see also ibid., no. 180, p. 42, 1 Adar 5501: 'nedaba extraordinaria para se repartir de contado pelos pobres . . . f 1798,6 . . . que se repartirão . . . na forma seguinte: pelo Rol da sedaca . . . f 848,10; pelo Rol de abodad aheset f 155; Pelo rol das 6 Semanas f 75,16; a diversos comforme a notisia secreta . . . f 719,–'.

274 SAA entry no. 334, no. 973. For the different distributions given to specific individuals by one *parnas* or the president see e.g. on p. 3: '5493, 12 Iyar: Ab[m] Jessurun Espinosa p. mão do parnas Is: de Sel: Guttieres notado A:S: f 350'. The

initials given here can be found in the *livros longos*, not in the section listing distributions to the poor, but in that on general expenses, *gastos gerais* (see e.g. SAA entry no. 334, no. 969, p. 281, 13 Tamuz 5494, or ibid., p. 283, 2 Av 5494).

275 SAA entry no. 334, no. 737, pp. 1–2, 17 Elul 5481: 'Lista das Piticoims Secretas do legado de Jacob Masahot'.

276 SAA entry no. 334, no. 119a, file 13, 22 Adar 5391. In 1696 his daughter-in-law Abigail Naar from Hamburg applied for money from Nahar's legacy now that, she declared, as a widow with two children she had fallen into poverty. Despite the fact that the will specified that no one was allowed to ask for assistance from Nahar's legacy, either orally or in writing, it was decided to give her a one-off payment of 31.10 guilders because she was related to the legator. However, this was once and for all: the Amsterdam Mahamad ruled that neither she nor her descendants could ever submit another claim against this fund (ibid., pp. 458, 461–2, 13 June 1696, 10 Tamuz 5456).

277 SAA entry no. 334, no. 217, p. 34, 5437: 'nao quiz a 2ª repartição em turva'.

278 SAA entry no. 334, no. 173, p. 47, Rosh Hodesh Sivan 5408: 'q nao quer receber'. In the 1650s her husband appeared again on the list of monthly distributions (ibid., p. 249, Rosh Hodesh Tevet 5413).

279 SAA entry no. 334, no. 216, p. 130, 6 Heshvan 5433: 'q no principio nao quis aceitar'.

280 SAA entry no. 334, no. 218, p. 153, 1 Kislev 5447.

281 See Appendix I, Table 25.

282 M. van Leeuwen, Schoenmakers, and Smits, *Armoede en bedeling*, 8–12; Noordegraaf, *Daglonen in Alkmaar*; Pot, *Arm Leiden*, 303–7; Nusteling, *Welvaart en werkgelegenheid in Amsterdam*, 252–3; Vries and van der Woude, *The First Modern Economy*, 607–64, esp. table 12.3 (p. 620).

283 We have no information on the couple marrying in Amsterdam, since they did not register their intention at City Hall and no *ketubah* documents of that period have survived. Isaac de Andrade must have been away from home for a considerable time—his wife and children lived alone for at least thirteen years. He was in Amsterdam between 1639 and 1640, where he, his wife, and his 'family' were given charity on a temporary basis (SAA entry no. 334, no. 172, p. 5, 24 Nisan 5399; ibid., p. 11, 4 Sivan 5399; ibid., p. 85, 10 Iyar 5400; ibid., p. 77, 9 Nisan 5400: 24 *livras* of matzah meal for 'Andrade, Mulher e familia'). In 1655 a certain Isaac de Andrade payed *promessas*, but it is not certain whether this was the same person (ibid., no. 174, p. 124, 3 Tishrei 5416). Isaac seems to have died around 1650, because at that point his daughter Rachel, asking for permission to take part in the Dotar lottery, presented herself as an orphan (ibid., no. 1143, p. 180, 5410). There is mention of an Isaac de Andrade, originating in Brazil, as a member of Bahale Tesuba in the 1680s. This may possibly have been his grandson (Isaac Calvo de Andrade), by then around 25 years old (Pieterse, *Daniel Levi de Barrios*, 130–1). For Isaac's registration of his marriage see SAA DTB 691, p. 164, 14 Oct. 1678.

284 Ester died on 16 Tevet 5413 (<http://stenenarchief.org/pig/pig_list.php>: row 14, grave 47). She was supported as Isaac de Andrade's wife, together with her three children, for more than ten years ('Mulher de Isack Andrade e tres filhos'), from 1640: see e.g. SAA entry no. 334, no. 172, p. 61, 13 Adar 5400; ibid., p. 121, Rosh Hodesh Nisan 5401; ibid., p. 159, 25 Adar II 5402; ibid., p. 225, 1 Sivan 5403; ibid., no. 173, p. 70, 1 Kislev 5409; ibid., p. 213, 23 Adar 5412; ibid., p. 252, Rosh Hodesh Shevat 5413.

285 SAA entry no. 334, no. 239, pp. 126, 136, 148, 161, 175, 5408–12. For a specific example see ibid., no. 173, p. 27, 14 Adar 5408. For this work she received 30 guilders a year.

286 SAA entry no. 334, no. 173, p. 20, 1 Kislev 5408 (peat): 'Ester de Andrade pr. Sara Coen a douda'; ibid., no. 172, p. 316, 11 Tishrei 5406: 'Sara Coen Loica, cun[a] de Ishac de Pina'. Isaac de Pina seems to have been a member of the de Pinto family and was supported by them. Sara Coen had lived in the house of Isaac de Pina before (ibid., p. 287, Rosh Hodesh Tevet 5405: 'Sara Caanet . . . en cassa de I. Pina').

287 SAA entry no. 334, no. 173, p. 70, 1 Kislev 5409: peat for Ester Coen Surda via Ester de Andrade. For Ester Coen Surda originating in Tunis see ibid., no. 174, p. 750, Rosh Hodesh Iyar 5426.

288 See Appendix I, Table 26.

289 For Rachel's participation in the Dotar lottery see SAA entry no. 334, no. 1143, p. 154, 5408; ibid., p. 164, 5409; ibid., p. 180, 5410; ibid., p. 192, 5411; ibid., p. 205, 5412; ibid., p. 207, 16 Adar 5412; ibid., no. 1151, p. 275, [1651]; ibid., no. 1143, p. 219, 22 Sivan 5413.

290 For Abraham Calvo as a student in Ets Haim see SAA entry no. 334, no. 1052, p. 47[v], 5412; he studied in the class of R. Jacob Juda Leon, with a monthly scholarship of 3.10 guilders. For this Calvo at Aby Jetomim see ibid., no. 1211, p. 3[v], 9 Iyar 5413, where it is stated that he left the orphanage because he got married. Rachel and Abraham did not register their plans to marry at City Hall.

291 SAA entry no. 334, no. 215, pp. 56, 72, 101, 103, 154, 5424–7.

292 SAA entry no. 334, no. 239, p. 188, 25 Tevet 5413.

293 Ibid.: 'q se derao os f[os] de Ester de Andrade por tirar a gala . . . f 22:10'.

294 SAA entry no. 334, no. 174, p. 176, Rosh Hodesh Elul 5416; ibid., no. 175, p. 19, Rosh Hodesh Kislev 5438: 'se despediu'.

295 SAA entry no. 334, no. 175, p. 91, Rosh Hodesh Kislev 5440. It continued until 1683 when her son took over her support (ibid., no. 175, p. 220, 1 Iyar 5443). She returned to the roll in 1687 (ibid., no. 20, p. 105, [n.d.; after 17 Adar] 5447) and remained on it until 1700 (ibid., no. 176, p. 358, Rosh Hodesh Tishrei 5461).

296 For Isaac Calvo de Andrade at school see SAA entry no. 334, no. 215, pp. 34–5, 89–90, 134–5, 176–7, 232–3, 284–5, 332–3, 5423–30; ibid., no. 216, pp. 27–8, 91–2, 5430–2. For Jacob Calvo de Andrade at school see SAA entry no. 334, no. 215, p. 90, 5424; ibid., p. 135, 5425; ibid., p. 177, 5426; ibid., p. 233, 5427.

297 SAA entry no. 334, no. 1211, p. 6, 3 Adar II 5429; ibid., p. 1[v], 5432; SAA entry no. 5075, no. 2239, Not. A. Lock, pp. 95–6, 10 May 1672.

298 Emmanuel, *History of the Jews of the Netherlands Antilles*, 77.

299 SAA entry no. 334, no. 20, p. 81, 12 Adar 5444.

300 For his work as a bookbinder see SAA entry no. 334, no. 1052, p. 122^{v}, 5442; ibid., p. 164^{v}, 3 Iyar 5465; ibid., p. 167, 26 July 5465; see also ibid., no. 220, p. 241, 20 Adar 5464: 'a Ishack Calvo dadrade por 2 livros de papel . . . f 10'. Isaac is mentioned as a merchant at the registration of his marriage in 1678 (SAA DTB 691, p. 164, 14 Oct. 1678). He was active in trade, as well as being a bookbinder and the community's butcher; for his trading activities see the bankruptcy file of Moses Pereyra alias Moreno (SAA entry no. 5072, no. 697, p. 74, 16 Nov. 1695): during 1695, Moses Pereyra paid Isaac Calvo de Andrade 914 guilders for 'trading activities'.

301 Abraham's son Isaac Bueno de Moura mentioned Fronteira in Portugal as the place of origin of the family when he registered his intention to marry in 1671 (SAA DTB 688, p. 287, 13 Nov. 1671). Since he also claimed at that time that both of his parents had died, we presume Sara was his stepmother and Abraham's second wife.

302 SAA Film Ouderkerk: 18 Kislev 5426. For distributions of matzot see SAA entry no. 334, no. 174, p. 368, 5420: 40 *livras* of matzah meal; ibid., p. 426, 5421: 72 *livras* of matzah meal; ibid., pp. 485, 551, 621, 5422–4: 64 *livras* of matzah meal; ibid., p. 694, 5425: 54 *livras* of matzah meal; ibid., no. 215, pp. 200, 254, 5427–8: 54 *livras* of matzah meal.

303 See Appendix I, Table 27.

304 One son, David, was a merchant when he got married (SAA DTB 699, p. 70, 13 May 1695); another, Moses, got married in 1678; at that time his mother Sara was sick (ibid. 691, p. 170, 11 Nov. 1678: 'moeder sieck'); the third son, Isaac, was a translator (SAA entry no. 334, no. 217, pp. 67, 9 Sivan 5437; ibid., p. 164, 26 Adar II 5440; SAA DTB 695, p. 410, 5 June 1687). Isaac was one of the administrators of the Honen Dalim *ḥevrah* until 1682 or 1683 (Pieterse, *Daniel Levi de Barrios*, 124).

305 She lived in the house of Debora Guedelha in 1668 (SAA entry no. 334, no. 215, p. 208, Rosh Hodesh Adar 5428).

306 See Appendix I, Table 28; the cost of living for an older woman in the Dutch Republic has been estimated at 100 guilders a year (Groenveld, 'For the Benefit of the Poor', 204).

307 He worked in this capacity for the Portuguese community from 1663 until the 1720s, repairing candelabra, candlesticks, stamps to mark bread as kosher, keys, and ritual objects such as *rimonim* (SAA entry no. 334, no. 215, p. 18, 29 Elul 5423; ibid., p. 76, 7 Av 5424: 'A Ab. Dias p^{a} conserto de um lampadario f 1:14'; ibid., p. 122, 8 Adar 5426: 'p. 12 marzas p^{a} o pao a Ab. Dias a f 1:10 – . . . f 18,–'; ibid., p. 218, 27 Elul 5427: 'a Abraham Dias p. consertar 2 casticias de prato q estavao quebrados e p. ajudar apendurar o cobre en esnogua p. estar doente o semas Habilho f 4:10'; ibid., p. 320, 9 Shevat 5429: 'a abraham dias por consertar os candeiros dos ssres do mahamad f 0:12'; ibid., no. 219, p. 28, 20 Tishrei 5452: 'a Ab. Dias p. concerto de romanims do kahal f 0:14'; ibid., p. 320, 15 Tevet 5457: 'A Abraham Dias por concerto de trez Rimonim f 1:2'; ibid., no. 220, p. 90, 1 Iyar

5460: 'a abrao dias por a marca que fes para o pao f 1:10'; ibid., no. 222, p. 74, 7 Tevet 5474: 'Ab. Dias: p. duas marcas p^{a} casser f 3: 6'; ibid., p. 131, 21 Shevat 5476: 'A Ab^{m} Dias por consertar hua marca f 0:12').

308 SAA DTB 694, p. 154, 29 July 1684: 'Abraham Dias van Valladolid'; SAA entry no. 5004, no. 110 (Calisregisters), p. 2, 28 July 1684: 'Abraham Dias Spaensse jood'.

309 SAA entry no. 334, no. 174, p. 451, Pesach 5421. Did he come via some part of the New World? He could have been in Brazil, where a certain Abraham Israel Dias was registered among the members of the Portuguese community (ibid., no. 1304, p. 9, 15 Kislev 5409). For Abraham Dias in Brazil see Wolff and Wolff, 'Mistaken Identities', 106.

310 Barrios, *Triumpho* (Biblioteca Rosenthaliana copy, RON A 5252), 251 [pencil]: 'Campean entre los insignes fundadores de la piadosa Yesibá . . . Abraham Dias'.

311 SAA entry no. 334, no. 215, p. 318, 7 Tishrei 5430; ibid., no. 216, p. 1, 5430; ibid., p. 113, 5432; ibid., p. 144, 5433.

312 SAA entry no. 334, no. 294, p. 45, 5432; ibid., no. 1191, p. 168, 5454.

313 SAA entry no. 334, no. 24a, p. 13, 9 Adar 5428; ibid., no. 216, p. 144, 5433; ibid., no. 24a, pp. 69^{v}–70, 2 Heshvan 5447. He earned 2 'plakken' a week (ibid., no. 25, p. 93, 7 Av 5466; ibid., no. 66, 1 Kislev 5439).

314 In the Calisregisters of 28 July 1684 it is said that his deceased wife Rachel Dias left him two young children, but no means of existence. He was remarried in 1684, to Ester Fernandes (SAA DTB 694, p. 154, 29 July 1684).

315 SAA entry no. 334, no. 174, p. 425, 29 Adar II 5421: 20 *livras* of matzah meal.

316 SAA entry no. 334, no. 215, p. 252, 5428: 32 *livras* of matzah meal.

317 SAA entry no. 334, no. 216, p. 111, 5432: 48 *livras* of matzah meal.

318 SAA entry no. 334, no. 217, p. 94, 5438: 60 *livras* of matzah meal.

319 '4 f^{os} de Abram Dias' (SAA entry no. 334, no. 1189, p. 7, 5437, distribution of clothes to students of the religious school of Talmud Torah); 'Ribqua filha de Abraham Dias' (ibid., no. 1144, p. 239, 5437); Ribca participated in the lottery until 1683 (ibid., p. 308, 5443). Sara started to take part in the Dotar lottery in 1684 (ibid., p. 318, 5444).

320 SAA entry no. 334, no. 215, p. 69, 3 Kislev 5425; ibid., no. 216, p. 170, 9 Tevet 5435; ibid., no. 217, p. 312, 14 Adar II 5442.

321 SAA DTB 693, p. 361, 14 May 1683.

322 SAA entry no. 366, no. 65, p. 179, 4 Feb. 1692; see also Silva Rosa, *De geschiedenis van de Portugeesche Joden te Amsterdam*, 31.

323 'A Mos. Dias p. estampar os pregoems f 2:10': SAA entry no. 334, no. 222, p. 130, 30 Nisan 5475.

324 'a Ribca Dias por velar a V^{a} Israel f 1:17:8': SAA entry no. 334, no. 222, p. 76, 22 Av 5474.

325 SAA entry no. 334, no. 66a, 1 Kislev 5439; ibid., no. 217, p. 520, 5445: distribution of matzah meal to Abraham Dias and Moses Fernandes, altogether 48 *livras*.

326 SAA entry no. 334, no. 25, p. 95, 28 Shevat 5467.

327 Jacob de Abraham Dias: SAA entry no. 334, no. 215, pp. 223, 229, 5427; ibid., pp. 283, 285, 5428; ibid., pp. 331, 333, 5429–30; ibid., no. 216, p. 26, 5430–1; ibid., p. 90, 5431–2.

328 For Isaac de Abraham Dias see SAA entry no. 334, no. 1052, p. 166^{v}, 5465. Isaac studied at Ets Haim yeshiva in the class of Rabbi Salomon Juda Leon and received a monthly allowance of 3.50 guilders. In 1670 Jacob Dias, son of Abraham Dias, moved from the poor school to the school of the 'Catellano' (ibid., no. 215, p. 333, 5429–30).

329 'Jacob de Abraham Dias p^{a} hir a Barbados: f 12': SAA entry no. 334, no. 217, p. 212, 13 Iyar 5440.

330 SAA entry no. 334, no. 1191, p. 677, 5496.

331 For the delivery of flour to the community by Isaac Dias see SAA entry no. 334, no. 222, p. 22, 1 Iyar 5473; ibid., p. 248, 23 Nisan 5477; ibid., p. 362, 5479–80. For *derashot* (sermons) see SAA entry no. 334, no. 222, p. 248, 4 Tamuz 5477: 'Isaac Dias d^{or} por hum daras f 15,–'; ibid., p. 249, 29 Elul 5477: 'Isaac Dias por hum daras f 15,–'; ibid., p. 307, 4 Tishrei 5479: 'Isaac Dias por hum daras f 15,–'; ibid., no. 223, p. 61, 1 Sivan 5482: 'Isaac Dias . . . daras f 15'.

332 SAA entry no. 334, no. 19, p. 613, 1 Nisan 5430. This monthly support was extended to 3 guilders in 1694 (ibid., no. 20, p. 177, 17 Adar 5454).

333 SAA entry no. 334, no. 174, p. 540, 10 Shevat 5423, charitable distribution because of the cold winter: 'f 12,–'; ibid., p. 731, 20 Adar 5426, distribution because of Sabbatai Zevi: 'f 20,–'; ibid., no. 215, p. 313, 13 Tevet 5430: 'por petizão . . . f 3,–'. For illness see SAA entry no. 334, no. 215, p. 112, 14 Av 5425: 'f 4,–'; ibid., no. 217, p. 59, 14 Tishrei 5438: 'f 2,–'. For the cost of burying children see SAA entry no. 334, no. 215, p. 69, 3 Kislev 5425: 'f 0,80'; ibid., no. 216, p. 170, 9 Tevet 5435: 'f 4,16'; ibid., no. 217, p. 312, 14 Adar II 5442: 'f 12,–'. For emergencies see SAA entry no. 334, no. 221, p. 54, 9 Shevat 5466: 'a Ab. Dias p. urgensia . . . f 6,–'.

334 See Appendix I, Table 29.

335 His daughters tried their luck with Dotar, but in vain. One daughter, Sara, tried for twelve years (SAA entry no. 334, no. 1144, pp. 179, 188, 206, 219, 228, 238, 248, 262, 278, 290, 301, 308, 5432–43); the other, Ester, tried for sixteen years (ibid., pp. 318, 327, 336, 350, 362, 371, 383, 392, 404, 413, 419, 429, 438, 445, 452, 460, 5444–59). In 1683 Sara married Samuel de Efraim Abarbanel (SAA DTB 693, p. 427, 17 Sept. 1683); like the bride's father, Samuel was a schoolteacher of the 'Jewish church' ('schoolmeester van de Joodse kerck').

336 See e.g. SAA entry no. 334, no. 216, p. 124, 5432–3.

337 Franco Mendes, *Memorias*, 84; Scholberg, 'Miguel de Barrios', 138 n. 52.

338 SAA entry no. 334, no. 24a, p. 33^{v}, 22 Heshvan 5435.

339 SAA entry no. 334, no. 217, p. 203, 5440.

340 SAA entry no. 334, no. 1143, p. 248, 2 Nisan 5415. We have no evidence that Daniel registered his marriage at City Hall.

341 SAA entry no. 334, no. 216, p. 130, 8 Tevet 5433: 'f 2,–'.

342 Pieterse, *Daniel Levi de Barrios*, 186.

343 SAA entry no. 334, no. 1189, p. 7, 5437. See the registration of the intended marriage of one son, Abraham (SAA DTB 696, p. 243, 13 Sept. 1686); on Abraham see also Pieterse, *Daniel Levi de Barrios*, 104, and SAA entry no. 334, no. 1052, p. 36, 5433, *midrash* of Aguilar. Later Abraham was a student in the class of Haham Aboab. He received a scholarship from the legacy of Benjamin Musaphia (ibid., no. 175, p. 72, 8 Nisan 5439; ibid., 1 Nisan 5440). He also seems to have participated in the Sahare Sedek youth society (Pieterse, *Daniel Levi de Barrios*, 129). Abraham Lopes Arias also supplied wax for candles (SAA entry no. 334, no. 25, p. 83, 25 Adar 5463). Another Abraham Lopes Arias is mentioned in the archives, but his name is qualified as 'the old one' ('o velho': ibid., no. 217, p. 33, 5437). In this case we should treat the references in Pieterse with caution (*Daniel Levi de Barrios*, 110, 113, 123, 129). For another son at the Ets Haim yeshiva as an assistant to R. Abarbanel see SAA entry no. 334, no. 1052, p. 164^{v}, 5465.

344 SAA entry no. 334, no. 218, p. 15, 19 Menahem-Av 5445: 'f 6: 30'.

345 See Appendix I, Table 30.

346 SAA entry no. 334, no. 974, file a, p. 17, 1734; ibid., file f, p. 9, 5512.

347 See Appendix I, Tables 25–30.

348 'por senao poder sustentar aqui': SAA entry no. 334, no. 217, p. 61, 17 Elul 5437.

349 SAA entry no. 334, no. 19, pp. 61/146–62/147, 14 Adar 5400.

350 At the end of the 17th century the Purim collection was carried out in the following order (SAA entry no. 334, no. 219, p. 1, 5451):

'El Hordem das Tasas de Purim

PRIMEIRA VOLTA

1. Prezidente para o siclo
2. Gabay da Sedaca
3. O segundo Parnas da Sedaca p^{a} Talmud Tora
4. O terceiro Parnas para a Hebra
5. O quarto Parnas para a fabrica
6. O administrador de Abodad a Hesed
7. Tezoureiro de Es Haim
8. Gabay de Terra Santa
9. Gabay de Cautivos
10. Tezoureiro de Vistiaria
11. Administrador da Vistiaria dos Talmidim
12. O quinto Parnas da Sedaca p^{a} o H.^{n} Abeatar
13. O seisto Parnas da Sedaca p^{a} o H.^{n} Cohen
14. O Prim.^{ro} Parnas da Hebra p^{a} o H.^{n} da Hebra

Os 5 Parnassim de Talmud Tora para os Rubisim

SEGUNDA VOLTA

Todos os Parnasim da Sedaca y Hebra Para Pobres Jerais'.

This tradition was abolished in the 1740s (SAA entry no. 334, no. 22, p. 170, 12 Nisan 5509).

351 SAA entry no. 334, no. 24a, p. 54^{v}, 5 Heshvan 5441.

352 SAA entry no. 334, no. 119a, file 20, p. 748, [n.d., probably around September 1724, as dated on the translation from Spanish into Dutch: ibid., pp. 744–6]: 'Y no Miran ala xente devien . . . pero la sedaca no es Sino para Somiticos, al Caguetes putas y ladrones'; ibid., undated request directed to *parnas* Vega; see also the complete file on Pimentel (SAA entry no. 334, no. 119a, file 20). The Portuguese community asked the Amsterdam police to arrest Pimentel and to put him in prison ('om den voornoemde Pimentel te doen aprehenderen, en confineren': ibid.).

353 SAA entry no. 334, no. 87, file 19, 30 June 1751.

354 SAA entry no. 334, no. 970, p. 444, 29 Heshvan 5508: 'a Ribca Habilho p. 5 @ . . . f 100,–'. (The sign @ is used in the administration books of the Portuguese community to stand for 'anos' or 'años', years.)

355 SAA entry no. 5061, no. 412, pp. 118^{v}–119^{v}, 29 Dec. 1752; SAA entry no. 334, no. 87, [no page no.], 1752.

356 SAA entry no. 334, no. 87, file 19, 29 May 1764; see also the case of Haim Salom, who sent a letter to the *parnasim* in which he criticized them as well as the *haham* of the community. The *parnasim* reacted by requesting the city governors to arrest Haim and put him into prison (ibid., 9 Sept. 1765).

357 SAA entry no. 334, no. 27, 9 Heshvan 5528, p. 45: 'estando informados do pouco cuydado que se tem dos moradores de david de sem.^{l} pinto em que habitão os pobres entre os quais sucedem desordems, se resolveo cometer o s.^{r} de chaves & o s.^{r} gabay p.^{a} tomar inspecsão do comportamen.^{to} dos moradores de d.^{to} Rehobot & fazer raporte do resultado'. It was resolved that hereafter the behaviour of the inhabitants would be inspected.

358 Cited in Rozen, *Jewish Identity*, 108. In other Jewish communities, however, the poor voiced little protest (Simonsohn, *History of the Jews in the Duchy of Mantua*, 523–4).

359 SAA entry no. 5061, no. 198, [no page no.], 22 May 1658.

360 SAA entry no. 5061, no. 208, [no page no.], 12 Jan. 1683. Violent behaviour was not restricted to poor Sephardim. In the records of the Amsterdam court and notarial deeds we meet both poor and well-to-do Sephardim condemned for hitting fellow Jews, their wives and servants, or members of the Dutch population at large. See e.g. SAA entry no. 5075, no. 942, Not. D. Bredan, [no page no.], 4 Aug. 1633, concerning violence caused by Abraham Hamiz. See further the case of Jacob Justo and Gracia da Costa (SAA entry no. 5061, no. 299, pp. 165^{v}–166, 12 Apr. 1633; SAA entry no. 5075, no. 942, Not. D. Bredan, p. 363, 3 May 1633; ibid., pp. 361, 392–3, 395, 421, 20 May, 1 June 1633); several of these documents on Jacob Justo and Gracia da Costa are transcribed by Odette Vlessing in Kistemaker and Levie [Bernfeld] (eds.), *Êxodo*, 68–9. See further the following cases of violence: 'Anthony Rodrigues en zijn zoon . . . over malcanderen gequest te hebben' (SAA entry no. 5061, no. 198, 14 Nov. 1657); 'Samuel de Sousa . . . over Jannetje Libbers in zijn huys opgesloten en groote overlast aangedaan te hebben op Swanenburgerwal bij de 3 Roosen' (ibid., no. 203, [no page no.], 16 Nov. 1666); 'Jacob Iseuron de Spinoza . . . over 't quetsen van David Lopez met een mes in de handt' (ibid., no. 204, [no page no.], 7 Sept. 1669); 'Dr. Salomon Rocamora . . . over 't quetsen van zijn broeder' (ibid., no. 206, [no page no.], 4 Dec. 1674); 'Jacob en Isack Francko gebroeders over 't slaen van een ander' (ibid., no. 208, [no page no.], 12 Jan. 1683); 'Moses Moreno ende Trintie . . . de min van Isaack Corriel over 't slaan en qualijck handelen van Stijntie Jans' (ibid., 14 Sept. 1683); 'Moses Cotinho . . . over het trecken van een houwer het daarmeede aanranden van een joodse prediker sittende in een sleetie en ander gewelt' (ibid., no. 210, [no page no.], 18 Dec. 1691); 'Jacob Lima . . . over dat jmand stootende van zijn stoep daardoor zijn been gebroken heeft' (ibid., 20 May 1692); 'Isaac Cardoza . . . over 't slaan en seer leelijck mishandelen van twee vrouwen' (ibid., no. 211, [no page no.], 17 May 1695); 'Joseph Montes . . . over slaan en mis-handelen van de vrouw van Daniel Fresco' (ibid., 11 Oct. 1695). See also the case of the fighting between Juda Fidanque and Moses Hesqia Oeb in the courtyard of the synagogue, mentioned in Y. Kaplan, 'Deviance and Excommunication', 113–14 n. 14. On discontent and rebellion in the Dutch Republic see Dekker, *Holland in Beroering*; on physical violence among Jews and violence between Jews and non-Jews in England see Endelman, *The Jews of Georgian England*, chs. 3 and 6.

361 Y. Kaplan, 'The Social Functions of the Herem'; id., 'Deviance and Excommunication'; id., 'Order and Discipline'. For his study on *ḥerem* in the Sephardi community in Hamburg see id., 'The Place of Herem'.

362 Y. Kaplan, 'The Social Functions of the Herem', 137, 153 and n. 72; the *ḥerem* lasted from 17 to 23 Shevat 5400/1640.

363 The last date on which he received charity before being put into *ḥerem* was 15 Shevat 5400 [18 Feb. 1640] (SAA entry no. 334, no. 172, p. 59, 15 Shevat 5400: 'doente'; apparently he was sick and had been receiving charity on a weekly basis). He first received charity again a few months later, on 9 Nisan 5400 [1 Apr. 1640] (ibid., p. 78, 9 Nisan 5400). At that time, charity for Pesach was distributed to his wife (ibid., p. 82, 12 Nisan 5400). After this, distributions to him and his large family were continued. No distributions of charity are recorded for his second period in *ḥerem* (28 Av 5402–5 Elul 5402), so no further offences can be proven (the last distribution of charity was in the month of Sivan 5402: SAA entry no. 334, no. 172, p. 182, 5 Sivan 5402; he received financial assistance only during the Sukkot festival in 5403: ibid., p. 197, 12 Tishrei 5403; for distributions after 1639 see ibid., p. 5, 24 Nisan 5399; ibid., p. 43, 8 Kislev 5400; ibid., p. 107, Rosh Hodesh Kislev 5401; ibid., p. 159, 25 Adar II 5402). In 1643 he was put permanently on the charity list (ibid., p. 230, Rosh Hodesh Tishrei 5404). It could well be that *ḥerem*, imposed twice, was only enforced for short periods because he was dependent on charity.

The cases of the paupers Jacob Chamis, Abraham Mendes o Casadinho, and Samuel Marques provide further examples. Jacob Chamis was banned for a short period because he had circumcised a Polish non-Jew. The length of the ban was reduced because of his poverty, but he had to pay a fine of 4 guilders instead (Y. Kaplan, 'The Social Functions of the Herem', 137, 153). I have not been able to trace Chamis on the charity lists of the Amsterdam Portuguese community. Abraham Mendes o Casadinho was released from *ḥerem* in 1639 (Y. Kaplan, 'The

Social Functions of the Herem', 133, 136 and nn. 62, 69). It is not clear when he was put into *ḥerem*, but we can guess it was around 1631–2, when his wife was given charity (SAA entry no. 334, no. 7, 119v, 122, 127, 5391–2: 'mulher de Abraham Mendes Cazadinho'). In 1644 he received a different punishment: neither he nor his wife was allowed to attend synagogue. We do not know how long this punishment was in force. Later in life (especially after 1676) he was supported by the Portuguese community (SAA entry no. 334, no. 217, p. 2 [pencil], 29 Iyar 5436), being accepted for the monthly distribution of 2 guilders by Abodat Ahesed. See further e.g. ibid., p. 45, 14 Adar II 5437; ibid., p. 50, 5437: matzot; ibid, p. 105, 16 Iyar 5438; ibid., p. 245, 5441: peat; ibid., p. 458, 5444: matzot; ibid., no. 20, p. 51, 26 Elul 5442. For charity distributed to his wife ('mulher de Abraham Mendez') see ibid., no. 217, p. 214, 2, 9, 16, and 23 Menahem-Av 5440. It is possible that he received charity before 1677—was he the Abraham Mendes who, as a *secreto*, received 40 guilders (ibid., no. 174, p. 733, 20 Adar 5426)? Was it he who, as a poor man, was given work to prepare for Pesach in 1664–5 and again from 1670 until 1682 (SAA entry no. 334, no. 215, pp. 79, 124, 5424–5; ibid., no. 216, p. 1, 5430; ibid., no. 217, pp. 103, 118, 153, 203, 263, 335, 5438–42)? Apart from Abraham and his wife there must have been two more members of the family, for the household received 32 *livras* of matzah meal in the 1670s and 1680s. The Moses Mendes who was at the secular poor school in 1663–4 (ibid., no. 215, 5423–4) may have been his son. There was apparently also a daughter: Ester Mendes, who, as the daughter of Abraham Mendes, asked to be put on Dotar's lottery list for a dowry and participated in that lottery for twenty-two years, from 1648 to 1670 (ibid., no. 1143, pp. 154, 164, esp. for the years 1648–9; ibid., no. 1151, p. 657: 1669; ibid., no. 1152, p. 94: 1670). Samuel Marques was put into *ḥerem* for adultery in 1646 (Y. Kaplan, 'The Social Functions of the Herem', 136, 154). At the same time, he was told to leave the country before Pesach and never return. He did not do so, but he was treated as if he had: nobody was supposed to talk to him or help him except for his wife, his brother, and his brother-in-law (SAA entry no. 334, no. 19, p. 206, 6 Sivan 5406). We have very little information about what happened to him afterwards, apart from the fact that he was given some peat after his *ḥerem* was withdrawn in 1647 (SAA entry no. 334, no. 19, p. 231, n.d., 5408 [1647]), in the years 1647/9; in addition, from 1647 the records show that matzot, peat, and a gift for Purim were given to his wife and children ('mulher de Samuel Marques'). Perhaps he was simply ignored by the community, even after his *ḥerem* was withdrawn, or perhaps he finally left (SAA entry no. 334, no. 173, p. 20, 1 Kislev 5408; ibid., p. 71, 1 Kislev 5409; ibid., p. 114, 1 Tevet 5410; ibid., p. 122, 19 Adar II 5410; ibid., p. 158, 6 Kislev 5411; ibid., p. 164, 15 Adar 5411; ibid., p. 167, 22 Adar 5411; ibid., p. 211, 14 Adar 5412; ibid., p. 214, 23 Adar 5412; ibid., p. 259, 23 Adar II 5413; ibid., no. 174, p. 31, 20 Adar 5414; ibid., p. 86, 20 Adar 5415).

364 SAA entry no. 334, no. 217, p. 419, 23 Elul 5443; she had left before in 1672 and at that time too received money to cover her travel expenses (ibid., no. 216, p. 114, 7 Av 5432).

365 SAA entry no. 334, no. 24, p. 8, 12 Adar 5420. See also Y. Kaplan, 'The Social

Functions of the Herem', 131 n. 56.

366 See the impression of Francisco Xavier de Oliveyra (1702–83) in his *Discours pathétique*, in which he describes economic need as one reason why Converso fugitives from the peninsula turned for help to Jewish communities abroad (cited in Saraiva, *The Marrano Factory*, 163–4).

367 Parker, 'Calvinism and Poor Relief', 107; Deursen, *Bavianen en Slijkgeuzen*, 124; Roodenburg, *Onder Censuur*, 114.

368 Zwarts, 'De Uriel-Da Costa tragedie'; see further the case of Sara de Pas: SAA entry no. 376, no. 15, p. 82, 14 Dec. 1684; ibid., p. 86, 11 Jan. 1685. For Augustijn Robles see SAA entry no. 376, no. 24, 16 Aug. 1753; ibid., p. 98, 11 Apr. 1754.

369 For this phenomenon see B. Kaplan, *Divided by Faith*, ch. 10.

370 Sara Lumbrosa was a member of the Reformed Church for ten years (1657–66) (SAA entry no. 376, no. 9, p. 210, 12 July 1657; ibid., no. 9, p. 211, 19 July 1657; ibid., p. 215, 6 Sept. 1657; ibid., no. 11, p. 249, 21 Oct. 1666; ibid., pp. 250, 252, 296, 28 Oct.–4 Nov. 1666). However, she finally rejoined the Portuguese Jewish community—possibly because of poor health and a need for support. Sara was given charity by the Portuguese community in 1666, the year in which she returned to Judaism. Before 1670 she was not given charity on a continuous basis (SAA entry no. 334, no. 215, pp. 159, 161, 211, 220, 248, 253, 264, 290, 301, 305, 311, 339, 348, 360, 5427–30). Apparently by then she was living alone, because she only received 8 *livras* of matzah meal for Pesach (ibid., p. 253, 5428). As mentioned earlier, from 1670 she was given charity on a monthly basis through Abodat Ahesed (ibid., no. 19, p. 613, 1 Nisan 5430). In 1688 she was accepted, together with her granddaughter, on the community's official list of recipients of monthly charity (ibid., no. 20, p. 116, 28 Adar II 5448). We lose sight of Sara when, in 1695, she left Amsterdam for Hamburg, together with her granddaughter (SAA entry no. 334, no. 219, p. 270, 11 Iyar 5455); on her see also Eeghen, 'De gereformeerde kerkeraad', 172, and Roodenburg, *Onder Censuur*, 188. On the Reformed Church and the Jews see Roodenburg, *Onder Censuur*, 181–3.

371 See also the case of a Portuguese Jewish woman who joined the Reformed Church in 1695 and thus made herself eligible to apply for a job as a *turfdraagster* (someone involved in the distribution of peat in Amsterdam on behalf of the municipality). This was at a time when there was a shortage of people in this occupation: forty positions had recently become vacant (SAA entry no. 5024, no. 2, p. 296, 27 Apr. 1695). When, in this capacity, she took peat to the Portuguese community, she was verbally abused by them as a traitor, for which they were rebuked by the city's burgomasters. The Portuguese leadership got the message and in its turn threatened its members with punishment to prevent future offences of this kind. As the community leaders insisted, similar behaviour could do a lot of harm to the community's reputation in the surrounding society, whose members treated them 'with so much love and kindness' ('E sendo o Referido tanto em detrimento de nossa Conservacão entre nosos vezinhos de quem . . . somos tratados com todo o amor E Benignidade': SAA entry no. 334, no. 20, p. 195, 28 Menahem-Av 5455). For details of similar attitudes on the part of

Portuguese towards (ex-)Conversos who joined a church in southern France see Nahon, 'Dépêches des Secrétaires d'État', 206 (no. 28), 211 (no. 42), 212 (no. 45), 220 (no. 99); on ex-Conversos going back to Spain and Catholicism see Graizbord, *Souls in Dispute*, ch. 3.

372 On this phenomenon see Y. Kaplan, 'Wayward New Christians'.

373 For these so-called *Confessieboeken* see Faber, *Strafrechtspleging*, 41–2. In these books we find, besides cases of murder and theft, cases of begging, prostitution, adultery, tax evasion, and sexual contacts between Jews and Christians, all considered criminal in the period of the Dutch Republic. The range of offences makes the point that crime is not an absolute concept, but is defined differently by diverse societies in various periods.

374 Faber, *Strafrechtspleging*, 246–9; Egmond, *Banditisme*, 'Crime in Context', *Underworlds*, 106–26, 'Contours of Identity', and *Op het Verkeerde Pad*, 142–67. Todd Endelman, *The Jews of Georgian England*, chs. 5–7, does acknowledge the existence of poor Sephardim in England, but almost never discusses them in the context of crime.

375 Offences of crime against property were found in 51 cases (75%); offences of prostitution were found in 10 cases (15%). Other cases included acts of violence. For Jewish crime in the German states see Glanz, *Geschichte des niederen jüdischen Volkes*. Ulbricht, 'Criminality and Punishment', 54, states that, in the German states too, Jews were mostly involved in crime against property; for an earlier discussion of this topic see Levie Bernfeld, 'Portugese Joden en misdaad'.

376 See Appendix I, Table 8, and Appendix II, Figure 1. The number of crimes committed by Sephardi Jews did not increase proportionately with the increased extent of poverty within the Sephardi community in the 18th century.

377 See Appendix I, Table 31.

378 Faber, *Strafrechtspleging*, 248. In the period 1680–1811, 8.6% of the delinquents were Jews; around 1700, 4%; and around 1730–40 and 1770, 12% or more: Faber, *Strafrechtspleging*, 246–7.

379 After serving under Fullana, in 1677 he joined the regiment of Viscollerido (SAA entry no. 5061, no. 321, p. 19, 2 Mar. 1673; ibid., no. 323, p. 121^{v}, 8 Feb. 1677). On Lieutenant-Colonel Fullana (Nicolas de Oliver y Fullana), alias Daniel Juda, see Kayserling, *Biblioteca*, 101; Silva Rosa, *De geschiedenis van de Portugeesche Joden te Amsterdam*, 68; Raa, *Het Staatsche Leger*, v. 356, 493–4; Lieberman, 'Childhood and Family', 169 n. 51.

380 SAA entry no. 334, no. 216, 130, 20 Tevet 5433: 'f 2,– p. orden do mahamad'.

381 SAA entry no. 5061, no. 323, p. 121^{v}, 8 Feb. 1677; ibid., pp. 127^{v}, 128^{r-v}, 18 Feb. 1677.

382 SAA entry no. 5061, no. 325, p. 204, 19 July 1680: tobacco worker; ibid., no. 327, p. 101^{v}, 8 Oct. 1682: 'parfumer'.

383 Gemeentearchief Den Haag, entry no. 351, no. 106, p. 109^{v}, 6 Apr. 1690. De Luna was found guilty of stealing jewellery, damask, lace, ribbon, coats, and swords (SAA entry no. 5061, no. 321, p. 19, 17 Mar. 1673; ibid., p. 26, 11 Apr. 1673; ibid., no. 323, p. 121^{v}, 8 Feb. 1677; ibid., pp. 127^{v}–128^{v}, 18 Feb. 1677); see also the testimony of his girlfriend and colleague Bregje Henricks (Gemeentearchief Den Haag, entry no. 0351-01, no. 106, p. 116^{r-v}, 6 Apr. 1690).

384 He was apparently working in close contact with David de Solis; on the latter see e.g. SAA entry no. 5061, no. 323, p. 121^{v}, 8 Feb. 1677.

385 Interrogation of Bregje Henricks: Gemeentearchief Den Haag, entry no. 0351-01, no. 106, p. 116^{r-v}, 6 Apr. 1690.

386 Huussen, 'The Legal Position', 33; van de Pol, 'Amsterdam Jews and Amsterdam Prostitution', 173–85.

387 Faber, *Strafrechtspleging*, index s.v. 'overspel'.

388 De Luna was caught several times, whipped, branded, banned, and confined in the house of correction, but he managed to escape and continued his criminal activities (SAA entry no. 5061, no. 321, p. 19, 17 Mar. 1673; ibid., p. 26, 11 Apr. 1673; ibid., no. 323, p. 121^{v}, 8 Feb. 1677; ibid., pp. 127^{v}, 128^{r-v}, 18 Feb. 1677; ibid., no. 325, p. 204, 19 July 1680; ibid., no. 326, p. 44, 12 Jan. 1681; ibid., no. 327, p. 101^{v}, 8 Oct. 1682; ibid., no. 330, p. 4, 1686; ibid., p. 101, 8 Oct. 1687; Gemeentearchief Den Haag, entry no. 0351-01, no. 106, pp. 109^{v}–111^{v}, 6 Apr. 1690).

389 Income from work combined with charity handed out by the Portuguese Jewish community or by a church was certainly less remunerative than crime. For example, in just one robbery de Luna netted around 8,000–9,000 guilders, which he split with two accomplices (Gemeentearchief Den Haag, entry no. 0351-01, no. 106, p. 110^{v}, 6 Apr. 1690, interrogation of Isaac Lopes de Luna). For the level of handouts see Appendix I, Table 25.

390 One such was Abraham Herera. In 1659 he was an inmate of the Rasphuis and is mentioned in that capacity in the documents of the Portuguese community (SAA entry no. 334, no. 24, p. 2, 5419: 'O herera que esta nos Raspois'). Six years later we find an Abraham Herera who received charity through the Portuguese community (ibid., no. 215, p. 71, 5425; ibid., pp. 156–7, 26 Av 5426; ibid., p. 161, 17 Adar 5427). In 1678 we come across a certain Abraham Herera who was being paid by the Portuguese community, together with Aron de la Faia, to look for thieves who had stolen *rimonim* from the synagogue (ibid., no. 217, p. 115, 19 Elul 5438: 'f 10:10'). For Abraham Herera joining the Reformed Church see Roodenburg, *Onder Censuur*, 187, and Eeghen, 'De gereformeerde kerkeraad', 173. David Moreno is another case: he had been responsible for making the *shemurim* for Pesach, but when in 1668 he got married to a Christian girl his name was struck out of the financial administration books of the Amsterdam Portuguese community (SAA entry no. 334, no. 215, p. 206, 5427). He might have been the same David Moreno who married Sara Moreno Monsanto in 1666 (SAA DTB 686, p. 345, 7 May 1666), a marriage which was dissolved by the *hahamim* Isaac Aboab, Jacob Sasportas, and Salomon Oliveira in 1692 (SAA entry no. 5061, no. 210, [no page], 20 May 1692). In 1671/2 a certain Sara Moreno Monsanto is recorded as having received charity (SAA entry no. 334, no. 216, pp. 70, 75, 4 Tevet–7 Adar II 5432). In 1681 the Portuguese community gave one David Moreno 4 guilders a month for a period of six months (ibid., no. 217, p. 1, 9 Iyar 5441), though it is not clear from the records whether this was in fact meant

for his daughter (ibid., p. 267, 1 Tamuz 5441). In another reference to the same name, matzah meal was given to a certain David Moreno in 1684–5 (ibid., pp. 458, 520, 5444–5).

391 SAA entry no. 376, no. 10, p. 55, 8 May 1659; ibid., p. 57, 29 May 1659. In 1659 Samuel Aboab was imprisoned for theft and other 'Godtloosheden' (SAA entry no. 376, no. 10, p. 76, 11 Sept. 1659); see also Roodenburg, *Onder Censuur*, 186–7.

392 See the case of the above-mentioned Samuel Aboab, who also got help from the Portuguese community from 1666 to 1675 (see e.g. SAA entry no. 334, no. 174, p. 733, 20 Adar 5426; ibid., no. 215, p. 160, 12 Shevat 5427; ibid., p. 209, 9 Nisan 5427; ibid., p. 212, 2 Kislev 5428; ibid., p. 253, Pesach 5428; ibid., no. 216, p. 115, 12 Elul 5432; ibid., p. 184, May/Nov. 5434–5; ibid., p. 195, 24 Av 5435).

393 A few did—for example David Belmonte, who stole linen from the Ashkenazi woman he lodged with (SAA entry no. 5061, no. 361, pp. 245^{v}–246, 5 July 1710).

394 David Moreno committed theft with two other men, one of whom—Antonio del Castillo, alias Abraham Santier—was probably a Portuguese Jew (SAA entry no. 5061, no. 326, p. 265^{r}, 9 Jan. 1682: David Moreno).

395 For Sephardim co-operating with Ashkenazim and non-Jews see the case of Daniel Sacoute, Moses Polacq, and Jannetje Jansz. Castenburg (SAA entry no. 5061, no. 362, pp. 92–4^{v}, 5 Nov. 1710; also ibid., no. 364, pp. 180–90^{v}, 11 Oct. 1711). Gracia Baruch was in close contact with several famous Ashkenazi thieves, such as Joseph Cohen, Ansel Praeger, and Barent Polack. For Joseph Cohen see Gemeentearchief Rotterdam, entry no. 15, no. 144, p. 274, 16 Mar. 1712; ibid., p. 434, 19 July 1712; on Andries, alias Ansel Praeger, see e.g. ibid., p. 407, 21 May 1712; ibid., pp. 488–90, 30 July 1712. Barent Polack was accused of stealing from newlywed Portuguese Jews: 'Segt met Isack Snuif tot Amsterdam geen Huysbraek te hebben gedaen bij Nieuw getrouwde Portugiesen, woonende bij de Portugiese kerk' (Gemeentearchief Rotterdam, entry no. 15, no. 145, p. 319, 19 May 1714). For Ashkenazim stealing from Sephardim and selling the stolen goods to a Sephardi Jew see the case of Joseph Cohen, who admitted to having stolen goods from the warehouse of a Portuguese Jew and having sold them on to another Portuguese Jew: 'segt dat Moyses Mester Levi van Praag Isack Boer en hij gev. voorleide winter t' Amsterd. uyt een packhuys van een Portugese Jood twee Baeltjes Bacauw hebben gestoolen, de welke zij van veertig gl. aen een Portugijs genaemt Isack hebben verkogt, welk geld zij onder den anderen hebben gedeelt' (Gemeentearchief Rotterdam, entry no. 15, no. 144, p. 364, 16 Apr. 1712). For close co-operation between Sephardim and non-Jews see the case of Abraham Sinjoor from Constantinople, who was only 16 when he and a Dutch boy robbed a wool warehouse (SAA entry no. 5061, no. 365, p. 105^{v}, 29 Aug. 1712). Another case is that of the musician Abraham Galindo, who together with Isaac Moreno Henriques and Abraham Franco was involved in street violence in the company of Samuel Pietersz. (SAA entry no. 5061, no. 393, pp. 45^{v}–46, 23 Aug. 1735; ibid., no. 397, pp. 240^{v}–243^{v}, 17 Oct. 1738); the last-named was apparently the only non-Jew in a gang of five or more burglars, all of them Sephardim (ibid., no. 393, pp. 24^{v}–28^{v}, 39–41, 124–126^{v}, 128^{v}, 140^{v}–142, 30 June and 3 Dec. 1735). The names mentioned in the interrogation of Samuel Pietersz. van den Berg are Joosje Lopis, Kootie Lopis, Kootie Canelle, Abraham Pavieje, Eusack Moreene, and Moosje Leon. Isaac Lopes de Luna had non-Jewish associates, but co-operated with Portuguese Jews as well, such as David de Solis from Brazil. De Solis also worked with non-Jews, for example one Isaac Bogaert (SAA entry no. 5061, no. 323, p. 121v, 8 Feb. 1677). On the criminal activities of de Solis see SAA entry no. 5061, no. 319, p. 48v, 20 Nov. 1669; ibid., no. 321, p. 153, 30 Dec. 1673; ibid., p. 156v, 15 Jan. 1674; ibid., no. 323, p. 75v, 24 Sept. 1676; ibid., p. 78, 8 Oct. 1676. De Solis also worked with the Portuguese Francisco Pharoni; it is not certain whether Pharoni was a Jew (Gemeentearchief Den Haag, entry no. 0351-01, no. 106, p. 27r–v, 22 July 1675).

396 The Sephardi Jew Abraham Pereyra, for example, went on a crime spree and one night invited the Dutch Samuel Pietersz. to join him. Together they set off to rob people who were asleep in the fields (SAA entry no. 5061, no. 393, p. 141, 3 Dec. 1735: 'of hij een profijtje met hem wilde doen'). Absence of hierarchy and a loose network of criminal associates can also be found among Jews in the German states (Ulbricht, 'Criminality and Punishment', 57). Isaac Lopes de Luna devised a plan to rob a lace shop, together with his girlfriend Bregje Henricks and two other non-Jewish associates, a man named Berckhout and Willem van Meckenum from Brussels. Isaac pretended to be a young baron, the son of the rich merchant Jacob de Pinto. Berckhout played the part of his tutor, while Willem acted as their servant. While the young baron and his tutor inspected the lace, the servant took the key of the shop and had it duplicated, quickly returning the original. Later, when they saw that the merchant had gone out, they returned, opened the shop, and robbed it, taking merchandise valued at 8,000 or 9,000 guilders. Bregje was able to escape with the stolen lace hidden under her skirts (testimony of Bregje Henricks: Gemeentearchief Den Haag, entry no. 0351-01, no. 106, pp. 109–116v, 6 Apr. 1690). In this episode four people, one a Sephardi Jew and three non-Jews, all played a role and divided the loot, the initiator and chief player having been the Sephardi Jew (on Jacob de Pinto see Swetschinski, *Reluctant Cosmopolitans*, 117, 230, 297). In another example, Jacob Moreno worked with a man named Jasparus from Brabant, who had experience with tools used for break-ins, and who had helped a nun escape from a convent (SAA entry no. 5061, no. 372, p. 239v, 13 Nov. 1715). Finally, the records mention Pieter Jensen, who was involved in a robbery with Jacob Asoubie and confessed to having 'received his share of the proceeds' (SAA entry no. 5061, no. 321, p. 91v, 25 May 1672).

397 Many Ashkenazi criminals, too, were first-generation immigrants: Egmond, 'Crime in Context', 84.

398 *Amersfoort*: Sara Olivier (SAA entry no. 5061, no. 342, p. 40, 21 June 1695). *Rotterdam*: David Moreno (SAA entry no. 5061, no. 326, p. 265r–v, 9 Jan. 1682; ibid., no. 337, p. 256v, 6 May 1692). *Brazil*: David de Solis (SAA entry no. 5061, no. 319, p. 48v, 20 Nov. 1669). David was not on welfare, but his mother was (SAA entry no. 334, no. 24a, p. 10v, 28 Menahem-Av 5425). *Flensburg*: Sara Abiatar (SAA entry no. 5061, no. 393, pp. 215v–217, 11 Apr. 1736). *Glückstadt*:

Gideon Henriques (SAA DTB 687, p. 285, 21 Dec. 1668). *Hamburg*: Abraham Herera (SAA entry no. 334, no. 215, p. 71, 5425; ibid., pp. 156–7, 26 Av 5426; ibid., p. 161, 17 Adar 5427; SAA entry no. 5061, no. 312, p. 260[v], 13 Aug. 1659); Jacob Jessurun (ibid., no. 138, pp. 155–6, 23 Feb. 1717); Sara Jacobs Mettera (ibid., no. 349, p. 41, 25 Feb. 1700). *Ritterou* (most likely Rittern or Ritterhude, places in the German states): Abraham Christiaense Mettera (SAA entry no. 5061, no. 351, p. 201[v], 26 July 1702). *Antwerp*: Jannetje de Castro (SAA entry no. 5061, no. 319, p. 252, 15 May 1671) and Jacob Mendes Vas (ibid., no. 335, p. 214[v], 7 Sept. 1690). *Paris*: Isaac Peritie van Parijs (SAA entry no. 5061, no. 319, p. 107[v], 6 Mar. 1670). *Rouen*: Jan Sabbatai Sena (SAA entry no. 5061, no. 341, p. 8, 15 Feb. 1694). *Corsica*: Joseph Drago (SAA entry no. 5061, no. 345, p. 23, 24 Dec. 1697). *Livorno*: Daniel Chavis (SAA entry no. 5061, no. 311, p. 139, 17 Mar. 1656) and Isaac Lopes de Luna (ibid., no. 321, p. 19, 17 Mar. 1673). *Venice*: Eliasar Bassan (SAA entry no. 5061, no. 311, p. 223[v], 9 Feb. 1657) and Jacob Italiaen (ibid., no. 311, p. 194[v], 1 Nov. 1656). *North Africa*: Juda Cohen Berberisco (SAA entry no. 334, no. 17, pp. 5–8, 10–11, 12 Oct.–5 Feb. 5483). *Algiers*: Moses Levy Bentubo (Gemeentearchief Den Haag, entry no. 0351-01, no. 110, pp. 1–6, 14–17 Apr. 1781) and Natan Pays (SAA entry no. 5061, no. 632, p. 6, May–July 1748; ibid., no. 408, p. 25, 4 July 1748). *Salé*: Abraham Pareira (SAA entry no. 5061, no. 400, p. 140[v], 7 July 1740). *Beja*: David de Souza Pimentel (SAA entry no. 5061, no. 632, p. 4, 3 Jan. 1747). *Lisbon*: Abraham Mendes (SAA entry no. 5061, no. 310, p. 24, 23 Apr. 1654). *'Uit Portugal'*: Moses Mendez Caldes (SAA entry no. 5061, no. 631, p. 1, 7 Jan. 1732). *Constantinople*: Abraham Sinjoor (SAA entry no. 5061, no. 363, p. 105[v], 29 Aug. 1712). *London*: Jacob Lopes (SAA entry no. 5061, no. 358, p. 57, 20 Apr. 1708); Mordecai Gabielje (ibid., no. 397, p. 237[v], 2 Oct. 1738); Rachel Mendes (ibid., no. 351, p. 169[v], 6 May 1702). *Curaçao*: David Pretto Henriques (SAA entry no. 5061, no. 406, pp. 204–205[v], 23 Aug. 1746).

399 On this issue see van de Pol, 'Vrouwencriminaliteit'.

400 For female crime among the Ashkenazim see Egmond, 'Contours of Identity', 217–18.

401 Levie Bernfeld, 'Sephardi Women in Holland's Golden Age', 182, 190.

402 See the declaration of the Ashkenazi Jew Joseph Cohen concerning the activities of the mother and wife of Ansel, who bought his stolen goods (Gemeentearchief Rotterdam, entry no. 15, no. 144, p. 475, 23 July 1712: 'seyt dat de moeder en vrouw van Ansel gewoon zijn gestoolen goed te koopen'). As a punishment for begging the Ashkenazi vagabond woman Minke Judas from Memel was confined for eight days and thereafter banned from the area for six years (Regionaal Archief Leiden, entry no. 508, no. 44, p. 3, 19 July 1746). For more on the criminal activities of Ashkenazi women see Egmond, *Op het Verkeerde Pad*, 164, 'Contours of Identity', 217–18, and 'Crime in Context', 88–9, and Ulbricht, 'Criminality and Punishment', 58. Faber, *Strafrechtspleging*, 253–5, concludes that crime in Amsterdam in the early modern period was mostly a male affair.

403 Eliasar Bassan was a poor 28-year-old Jew from Venice, who was brought to court for his aggressive behaviour towards a certain soldier who had converted from

Judaism to Christianity. Bassan had called this soldier a Christian dog, broken his sword into two parts, and knocked him down ('seecker soldaet die vant' jodendom tot Christendom sick heeft geconverteert op straet molestie heeft aengedaen, hem Christen hondt naer geroepen en sijn degen ontweldicht . . . heeft deselve in tween gebroocken en hem met het gevest tusschen hals en neck geslaagen': SAA entry no. 5061, no. 311, p. 223^{v}, 9 Feb. 1657). On Isaac Peritie van Parijs see ibid., no. 319, p. 107^{v}, 6 Mar. 1670.

404 SAA entry no. 5061, no. 329, p. 1, 8 Aug. 1684.

405 Mordecai Gabielje had been caught in the act of stealing four years earlier and was expelled from Amsterdam (SAA entry no. 5061, no. 397, p. 237^{v}, 2 Oct. 1738; ibid., p. 249, 22 Oct. 1738; ibid., no. 391, p. 184^{v}, 25 May 1734; ibid., p. 193, 2 June 1734). For Moses Cohen see ibid., no. 631, p. 3, 21 Mar. 1734: 'Mozes Cohen, Portugeese jood'; for an explanation of the expression 'stoute bedelaar' ('brazen beggar') see Faber, 'Rasphuis', 132.

406 SAA entry no. 5061, no. 390, p. 2, 19 Feb. 1732.

407 SAA entry no. 5061, no. 393, pp. 215^{v}–217, 11 Apr. 1736; ibid., no. 631, p. 4, 1 Feb. 1736: here it says she is an Ashkenazi Jewess, although her name sounds Sephardi. On infanticide in the Dutch Republic see Faber, 'Vrouwen van de rekening'; id., *Kindermoord*.

408 Samuel Aboab was head of a family of six or seven (SAA entry no. 334, no. 215, p. 253, 5428: 50 *livras* of matzah meal was given).

409 On women in the Iberian peninsula working as hawkers see Pescatello, *Power and Pawn*, 27. An example of a Sephardi woman working as a shopkeeper is Rachel Preto. As a sideline, she sold stolen silverware and hired Christian boys to help in her robberies, offering them something to eat and drink afterwards and always remaining the mastermind (SAA entry no. 5061, no. 312, pp. 211–12, 14 and 20 Feb. 1659). Rachel Preto was expelled from the city for a period of three years for theft. She is mentioned as a Jewess; nothing is said of her being black, despite the fact that the name Preto indicates this.

410 Samuel Mendes was a diamond-cutter (SAA entry no. 5061, no. 325, p. 11, 24 Aug. 1679); Manuel da Sylva, a barber (ibid., no. 390, pp. 1–2, 19 Feb. 1732); Abraham Chamis, a tobacco spinner (ibid., no. 342, p. 270^{r-v}, 14 Apr. 1696); Jacob Mendes Vas, a tobacco worker (ibid., no. 335, p. 214^{v}, 7 Sept. 1690); Jonas Josua Henriques, a hatmaker (ibid., no. 393, pp. 190^{v}–191^{v}, 22 Mar. 1736). Abraham Herera was described as a 'bombazijnwerker' (worker in (silk) material: ibid., no. 312, p. 260^{v}, 13 Aug. 1659); Isaac Peritie van Parijs as a cobbler (ibid., no. 319, p. 107^{v}, 6 Mar. 1670); Joseph Abarbanel as a candlemaker (ibid., no. 328, p. 91, 5 Feb. 1684).

411 See e.g. Hester Cordua, said to be a seamstress, cutting bones on the side and doing the laundry for a 'hoerhuis' (brothel) (SAA entry no. 5061, no. 405, p. 140^{r-v}, 3 Sept. 1744).

412 SAA entry no. 5061, no. 342, p. 40, 21 June 1695: Sara Olivier, described as a 'soopiesverkoopster' (drink seller), earned extra income as a madam by soliciting Jews in the street and taking them to her house, where Christian prostitutes were waiting for them. Sometimes Ashkenazi women acted as madams ('hoerewaardinnen') as well (ibid., no. 395, p. 183, 25 Apr. 1737: Branca Marcus).

413 For Ashkenazi prostitutes see the following cases: 'Rachel Jacobs, gewesen dienstmeid en jodin . . . uyt een hoerhuys op de kolck gehaalt te zijn alwaar voor de deur te pronken' (SAA entry no. 5061, no. 346, p. 94, 11 June 1698); 'eene Vrouwe genaemt Rachel wonende op Vloonburgh ende weten, dat sij een hoere is' (SAA entry no. 5075, no. 941, Not. D. Bredan, pp. 749–50, 752–3, 16 July 1632); Terezia Cohen, who was working as a prostitute in a house at Herengracht in Amsterdam (Gemeentearchief Den Haag, entry no. 0351-01, no. 109, pp. 26–7, 16 Aug.–14 Sept. 1759). On the prostitute Anna Margareta Bon, alias Roosje Gabriël Wolf, it was said 'dat zij zich op de straaten door verscheiden manspersoonen als een publijke hoer te laaten gebruiken . . . vagabunderen en pleegen van oopenbare hoererij op 's Heerenstraaten' (Gemeentearchief Den Haag, entry no. 0351-01, no. 110, pp. 15–16, 16 Dec. 1781).

414 Gracia worked in Amsterdam first (for her appearance in an Amsterdam brothel see SAA entry no. 5061, no. 367, p. 168^{v}, 27 July 1713; cited in van de Pol, 'Amsterdam Jews and Amsterdam Prostitution', 184–5). Later she moved to Rotterdam, where she lived in a rented room. Her clients included a so-called 'Oost-Indievaarder' who had promised to marry her—which he did not—and a Dutch soldier named Dirck Bocks, who made her pregnant. In Ghent she had a relationship with an officer whom she robbed of his clothes (for her activities in Rotterdam and Ghent see Gemeentearchief Rotterdam, entry no. 15, no. 145, pp. 82–3, 86–7, 11 and 17 Apr. 1715). For her divorce from David Athias see SAA entry no. 334, no. 221, p. 58, 10 Nisan 5464: 'q pagueij am^{er} de David Athias q^{do} lle deo get . . . f 40,–'. Gracia apparently also lived in London: 'Despachos de forasteiros e pessoas que vao para for a . . . Mulher de D^{t} Atias . . . Londres . . . f 8,–' (ibid., p. 102, 14 Shevat 5467). Francisco Lopes Pereyra left Amsterdam for Livorno because, in his words, his wife Rachel Nunes had an infamous reputation as a loose woman (SAA entry no. 5075, no. 2272, Not. A. Lock, p. 11, 4 Jan. 1657). Hester Cordua was suspected of acting as a whore, although she denied it (SAA entry no. 5061, no. 405, p. 140^{r-v}, 3 Sept. 1744). On Jannetje de Castro 'nachtloopster' see SAA entry no. 5061, no. 319, p. 252, 15 May 1671. On Gracia Moreno see Y. Kaplan, 'The Social Functions of the Herem', 129, 154, and SAA entry no. 5061, no. 310, pp. 56^{v}–57, 63, 64^{v}, 70^{v}, 15 Apr. 1654. For other prostitutes see the cases mentioned in Y. Kaplan, 'Moral Panic', 103–23.

415 Manuel Mercado was a brothel-keeper (SAA entry no. 5061, no. 339, pp. 73^{v}–74, 16 June 1693). David Moreno was a publican outside the Weesperpoort ('tapper buyten de Weesperpoort': SAA entry no. 5061, no. 337, p. 256^{v}, 6 and 14 May 1692). Abraham Mendes, alias Rodrigues Mendes, worked as a ship's cook, and sailed to Brazil, Salé, and Spain (SAA entry no. 5061, no. 310, p. 24, 23 Apr. 1654). For another seafarer see Jacob Lopes (SAA entry no. 5061, no. 358, p. 57, 20 Apr. 1708). For porters see Natan Pays (SAA entry no. 5061, no. 632, p. 6, May–July 1748; ibid., no. 408, p. 25, 4 July 1748: 'kruyer') and Abraham Pareira (SAA entry no. 5061, no. 400, p. 140^{v}, 7 July 1740: 'kruyer'). Convicted of theft, the latter was confined in the Rasphuis for four years and banned from the city for twelve years (SAA entry no. 5061, no. 400, p. 148^{v}, 14 July 1740). For manservants see Isaac Carvalhe (SAA entry no. 5061, no. 378, p. 189, 17 Apr. 1720); David de Solis also called himself 'herenknecht' (ibid., no. 319, p. 48^{v}, 20 Nov. 1669). For street musicians see Isaac Moreno Henriques, who played the *hakkebord*, a stringed instrument played with a small hammer (ibid., no. 397, pp. 240^{v}–243^{v}, 17 Oct. 1738); see also Abraham Galindo (ibid., no. 393, pp. 45^{v}–46^{r}, 23 Aug. 1735; ibid., no. 631, p. 1, 4 Aug. 1735). For small street traders see Moses Levy Bentubo from 'Barbarijen', who traded in watches, linen, and all kinds of other things (Gemeentearchief Den Haag, entry no. 0351-01, no. 110, p. 1, 14–17 Apr. 1781).

416 On David Moreno as a tobacco spinner see SAA entry no. 5061, no. 326, p. 265^{r-v}, 9 Jan. 1682; as a 'tapper' see ibid., no. 337, p. 256^{v}, 6 and 14 May 1692. For sources on Isaac Lopes de Luna as a soldier see SAA entry no. 5061, no. 321, p. 19, 2 Mar. 1673; ibid., no. 323, p. 121^{v}, 8 Feb. 1677; as a tobacco worker see ibid., no. 325, p. 204, 19 July 1680; and as a perfumer see ibid., no. 327, p. 101^{v}, 8 Oct. 1682 ('parfumer'). On Jacob Moreno see SAA entry no. 5061, no. 331, p. 43, 14 Jan. 1687: diamond-cutter; ibid., no. 599, p. 80^{v}, 14 June [1695]: tobacco spinner.

417 Egmond, 'Crime in Context', 88, encounters the same similarity in professions between Ashkenazim involved in crime and those who were not.

418 Egmond, *Op het Verkeerde Pad*, 156, and 'Crime in Context', 77–82.

419 Jacob Moreno stole textiles in Amsterdam at Blauwburgwal (SAA entry no. 5061, no. 329, pp. 228, 231, 1 and 10 Nov. 1685). David Moreno took satin from a house at Nieuwendijk in Amsterdam (SAA entry no. 5061, no. 326, p. 265^{v}, 13 Jan. 1682). Joseph Abarbanel da Cera stole lace in Amsterdam in Hoogstraat and sold it immediately (SAA entry no. 5061, no. 328, p. 91, 5 Feb. 1684). Rachel Cardoose stole a golden chain from a (non-Jewish) woman, passing by in the street; she took it to the goldsmith and sold three pieces that she took from the chain (SAA entry no. 5061, no. 329, p. 1, 8 Aug. 1684). Daniel Sacoute, together with the Ashkenazi Jew Moses Polacq and a non-Jewish woman, stole money and pawnshop receipts (SAA entry no. 5061, no. 362, pp. 92–94^{v}, 5 Nov. 1710). Abraham Messias was accused of taking a golden chain from Sara de Pas, a Sephardi like him, to the pawnshop and keeping the money for himself (SAA entry no. 5061, no. 339, p. 91^{v}, 21 Aug. 1693); David de Solis took stolen silver to sell to a silversmith (SAA entry no. 5061, no. 321, p. 156^{v}, 15 Jan. 1674). On the theft of money by Isaac Moreno Henriques see SAA entry no. 5061, no. 397, pp. 240^{v}–243^{v}, 248^{v}, 17 Oct. 1738. On the theft and sale of various objects by a band of Sephardim together with Samuel Pietersz. see SAA entry no. 5061, no. 393, pp. 24^{v}–28^{v}, 39–41, 124–126^{v}, 128^{v}, 140^{v}–142, 30 June and 3 Dec. 1735. For Ashkenazim operating along the same lines in cities, stealing money, textiles (lace, linen), copper, silver, gold, and watches see Egmond, 'Crime in Context', 77–8.

420 The criminal activities of Ashkenazim on the southern route only started in the last part of the 18th century (Egmond, 'Crime in Context', 92). David de Solis from Brazil committed thefts not only in Amsterdam, but also in The Hague and Rotterdam (SAA entry no. 5061, no. 323, p. 75^{v}, 24 Sept. 1676; Gemeentearchief

Den Haag, entry no. 0351-01, no. 106, p. 27$^{r–v}$, 22 July 1675). Jacob Moreno, alias de Bruyn, travelled about a great deal. He moved from Italy via Brabant through The Hague to Amsterdam. He stole tapestry and stockings, ordered crowbars for his burglaries, and was involved in a knife fight after a wager (SAA entry no. 5061, no. 327, p. 138, 24 Nov. 1682; ibid., no. 335, p. 119^{v}, 4 Apr. 1690). Did he even get help from the Amsterdam Portuguese community in 1704 to leave for Copenhagen? The leadership might have thought to get rid of him in this way (SAA entry no. 334, no. 221, p. 17, 1 Sivan 5464: 'a Jacob Moreno Bruyn p^{a} Copenhagge . . . f 5,–'). Jacob Mendes and Aron Fonseca left Amsterdam via Rotterdam, Antwerp, and Brussels on their way to Paris (Gemeentearchief Rotterdam, entry no. 15, no. 143, pp. 26^{v}–28^{v}, 3 Feb. 1707). Gracia Baruch was accused of stealing clothes in Amsterdam, Rotterdam, and Ghent (SAA entry no. 5061, no. 367, pp. 168^{v}–169^{v}, 27 July 1713). Isaac Lopes de Luna, as has been noted above, was active not only in the Dutch Republic but also in Hamburg and England. The tobacco spinner David Moreno was another thief active in many places. He came from Rotterdam and sometimes stayed with his brother in Brussels. He served sentences in Haarlem and Dordrecht, and was caught stealing linen and satin in Amsterdam (David Moreno, alias de Bruyn: SAA entry no. 5061, no. 326, p. 265$^{r–v}$, 9, 13, 27 Jan. 1682). Years later, in 1692, after two years in the Rasphuis (ibid., no. 335, p. 128^{v}, 17 Mar. 1690) and four years of banishment, he had apparently become a publican outside the Weesperpoort, where he was caught committing adultery with a non-Jewish woman (SAA entry no. 5061, no. 337, p. 256^{v}, 6 and 14 May 1692).

421 SAA entry no. 5061, no. 326, p. 265^{r}, 9 Jan. 1682; on Castillo see also Graizbord, *Souls in Dispute*, 80.

422 SAA entry no. 5061, no. 321, p. 91^{v}, 25 May 1672.

423 For Aron Sanches see SAA entry no. 5061, no. 317, pp. 40–3, 9, 15 Apr. 1666; ibid., no. 318, pp. 214–17, 21 Feb. 1669. In his case, no financial relation between him and the Portuguese community has been found. For Jacob Moreno see SAA entry no. 5061, no. 327, p. 138, 24 Nov. 1682; ibid., no. 331, p. 43, 14 Jan. 1687; ibid., no. 335, p. 119^{v}, 4 Apr. 1690; ibid., no. 599, p. 80^{v}, June [1695]; ibid., no. 372, p. 239^{v}, 13 Nov. 1715.

424 See Egmond, 'Contours of Identity', and ead., *Underworlds*. Ulbricht, 'Criminality and Punishment', 57–8, also notes that, in the German states, Jews involved in crime were mostly observant and traditional.

425 SAA entry no. 5061, no. 339, pp. 73^{v}–74, 16 June 1693. He was not the only Sephardi Jew who had frequent contacts with Christian women and fathered children with them; David Bueno, for example, lived with Marie Barents for seven years and had children with her. This Marie used to be a servant to him and his parents (SAA entry no. 5061, no. 342, p. 2^{v}, 25 Mar. 1695). See also the case of Moses Bassan (SAA entry no. 5075, no. 7531, Not. J. van Vilekens, p. 449, 28 June 1708), and see also van de Pol, 'Amsterdam Jews and Amsterdam Prostitution'.

426 On Isaac Fidanque and Rachel Boena see Gemeentearchief Rotterdam, entry no. 15, no. 149, pp. 249–62, 23 and 26 June 1734.

427 'Johanna Maria van den Berg of op zijn Joods Gracia Baro . . . segt sedert tot Brussel Christen te zijn geworden en aldaer Professie van de R. Catholijke Religie te hebbe gehad en daerom van haer vrinden niet geestimeert te werde' (Gemeentearchief Rotterdam, entry no. 15, no. 145, pp. 82–3, 86–7, 11 Apr. 1715).

428 SAA entry no. 5061, no. 349, p. 41, 25 Feb. 1700; ibid., p. 103^{v}, 22 Apr. 1700. Sara Jacobs Mettera had gone bankrupt and therefore did not pay her rent.

429 SAA entry no. 5061, no. 349, pp. 40–1, 25 Feb. 1700.

430 Gemeentearchief Den Haag, entry no. 0351-01, no. 106, margin of p. 27^{v}, 22 July 1675.

431 See the case of Daniel Montesinos, who in 1625 was released from prison through the intervention of the *imposta* board of the Portuguese communities, which paid 83.4 guilders to the Amsterdam police (SAA entry no. 334, no. 17, p. 14, 17 Jan. 5385). See also the case of Salomon Zuzarte, who, around the time of the appearance of the mystical messiah Sabbatai Zevi, was released from prison at the request of the Amsterdam Portuguese community. Abraham Levi was given 40 guilders to help arrange this, though we do not know how it was accomplished (SAA entry no. 334, no. 174, p. 733, 20 Adar 5426: 'Abraham Levi . . . p^{a} ajuda de sacar da prisão a Selomoh Zuzarte. f 40,–'). In 1698 Salomon Levy (possibly the same person as the *belogrado* who was working in health care: see n. 113 above) was released from prison after the community paid his bail (SAA entry no. 334, no. 219, p. 353, 15 Shevat 5458: 'a Selomo Levy p^{a} ajuda de tiralo da Prizao f 9').

432 SAA entry no. 5061, no. 372, p. 237, 13 Nov. 1715.

433 Roodenburg, *Onder Censuur*, 187, and SAA entry no. 5061, no. 312, p. 260^{v}, 13 Aug. 1659; SAA entry no. 376, no. 10, pp. 68–70, 72, 74, 87, 93, 7, 14, 21, and 28 Aug., 11 Sept., 30 Oct., and 13 Nov. 1659. Herera, apparently, was sent to prison not by the Portuguese Jews ('door het aenhouden der joden'), but at the instigation of the sergeant of the East India Company (Eeghen, 'Gereformeerde kerkeraad', 173). As a result of the 'persistence of the Jews', Herera, who had meanwhile been baptized, ended up in prison in Amsterdam once more.

434 For a decision of 1633 see SAA entry no. 334, no. 13, p. 101, 25 Tamuz 5393. For an earlier case see ibid., no. 17, p. 21, 27 Sept. 5386.

435 SAA entry no. 334, no. 6, p. 2, 19 June 5377/1617: 'que se derao ao escotete que prendeo a hums vellacos p. nosa ordem . . . f 24'; ibid., no. 17, p. 13, 6 July 5384; ibid., p. 21, 27 Sept. 5387; ibid., no. 215, p. 272, 10 Sivan 5428: 'A Pieter Cornelis p. acquietar revoltas de rapazes'. The police were asked to tell one individual from Alexandria not to come to the synagogue and to refrain from hanging around its neighbourhood (SAA entry no. 334, no. 216, p. 174, 23 Tamuz 5434). Often, gifts were given to the police, for example a silver plate (SAA entry no. 334, no. 219, p. 320, 4 Adar 5457: 'por hu pratto de pratta dourada . . . p^{a} mandar ao escotete françes de vroede . . . f 547:7'). For an overview of gifts, such as silver objects, china, and chocolate, given to the police in the years 1662/3 to 1784/5 see SAA entry no. 334, no. 268, 5423–5545. For the common practice of giving gifts as bribes in the early modern world see N. Z. Davis, *The Gift*, ch. 6.

436 SAA entry no. 334, no. 13, pp. 123–6, 11 Apr. 5396. It is not clear whether this policy was put into practice. In those days, however, the Dutch Republic also sent those individuals it wanted to get rid of to the East Indies (Hallema, 'Emigratie', 107).

437 SAA entry no. 334, no. 219, p. 21, 10 Adar 5452. They received 25 guilders. It is not clear where and why their father was imprisoned.

438 See e.g. SAA entry no. 334, ibid., no. 215, p. 265, 14 Kislev 5429; ibid., p. 311, 29 Nisan 5429; ibid., p. 359, 5430: matzot; ibid., no. 216, p. 96, 5431–2: *nedavot*; ibid., p. 138, 5432–3: peat; ibid., p. 164, 4 Adar II 5434; ibid., p. 209, 5436: matzot; ibid., no. 217, p. 30, 5436: rental subsidy. Financial help was continued after their father died in 1676; see e.g. ibid., no. 174, p. 1185, Rosh Hodesh Nisan 5437 ('orfans de Semuel Aboab'); ibid., no. 176, p. 377, 2 Nisan 5461. On Samuel Aboab and his testimonies before the Spanish Inquisition see López Belinchon, *Honra, libertad y hacienda*, 405–8; Muchnik, 'Du judaïsme au catholicisme', 579, 582–4, 588–90.

439 SAA entry no. 5061, no. 308, p. 234, 25 Apr. 1651; Roodenburg, *Onder Censuur*, 187 n. 166; López Belinchon, *Honra, libertad y hacienda*, 405–6.

440 Ester and her family were given charity on a permanent basis from 1652 to 1656 (monthly distribution: SAA entry no. 334, no. 173, p. 249, Rosh Hodesh Tevet 5413). In 1656 she was taken off the list of monthly distributions (ibid., no. 174, p. 190, Rosh Hodesh Kislev 5417). From the distributions of matzot we can tell that the family ('Ester Gedelha e familia') had five members in 1652, and from 1653 to 1657 only four members (ibid., no. 173, p. 214, 23 Adar 5412; ibid., p. 259, 23 Adar II 5413; ibid., no. 174, p. 31, 20 Adar 5414; ibid., p. 86, 20 Adar 5415; ibid., p. 198, 22 Adar 5417). After 1657 there were no more distributions to Ester Guedelha ('Ester Guedelha, mulher do Diabo'); she died in that year, on 14 Tamuz 5417: <http://stenenarchief.org/jpg/00942801.jpg>. Between 1658 and 1668 her daughters Debora and Judith received charity on a permanent basis (SAA entry no. 334, no. 174, p. 273, Pesach 5418; ibid., p. 333, Rosh Hodesh Iyar 5419; ibid., no. 215, p. 208, Rosh Hodesh Adar 5428) and from 1655 they participated in the Dotar lottery (SAA entry no. 334, no. 1143, p. 253, Rosh Hodesh Nisan 5418; ibid., p. 242, 5415: 'Judick e Debora da Costa, filhas de Ester da Costa'; ibid., p. 299, 5419: 'Judique da Costa Gedelha, orphan de Isack da Costa gedelha'). Since Judith da Costa is mentioned as an orphan in 1659, it appears that her father died before that year. Ten years later, Debora was still trying to get a dowry (SAA entry no. 334, no. 1151, p. 92, 5429). On Isaac da Costa Gedelha, alias the 'devil of Vlooyenburg', see also SAA entry no. 5061, no. 308, p. 234, 25 Apr. 1654; ibid., no. 312, pp. 10^{v}–12^{v}, 23 Oct. 1657. The 'devil of Vlooyenburg' is also described as a former messenger-boy of the famous merchant and agent to the Portuguese crown Jeronimo Nunes da Costa, alias Moses Curiel. Apparently he was fired by Nunes da Costa for swindling. He had also been a notary's clerk and had a reputation as an alcoholic (Swetschinski, *Reluctant Cosmopolitans*, 134).

441 In 1633 this Juda Cohen Berberisco was put into *ḥerem* because of bad behaviour ('wegens een slecht leven': SAA entry no. 5075, no. 942, Not. D. Bredan, p. 1205,

16 Mar. 1634,) and criminal activity ('delicten en kwaadaardigheden': SAA entry no. 334, no. 13, p. 102, 11 Av 5393). In 1636 it was decided to send him away for ever, never to return to Amsterdam (SAA entry no. 334, no. 13, p. 57^{v}, 18 Elul 5395; ibid., p. 129, 12 Sivan 5396; Y. Kaplan, 'The Social Functions of the Herem', 131–2 n. 56). His wife Ester Cohen Berberisco and her three children were supported by the Portuguese community in his absence (on the size of this family see SAA entry no. 334, no. 172, p. 205, 14 Adar 5403: 'A do Cohen Berberisco e tres f^{os}'). In 1655 the mother and two children were given charity (ibid., no. 174, p. 86, 20 Adar 5415). Information on further distributions of charity exists for the years 1639–45 (5399–5405; see e.g. SAA entry no. 334, no. 172, p. 5, 24 Nisan 5399; ibid., p. 311, Rosh Hodesh Iyar 5405). In 1645 Ester was taken off the *sedaca* list (SAA entry no. 334, no. 172, p. 315, Rosh Hodesh Elul 5405). Apparently her husband had returned (ibid., no. 10, p. 1^{v}, 5406). In 1648 she was again receiving charity (ibid., no. 173, p. 69, Rosh Hodesh Kislev 5409). In 1652 we find her living in a small alley in the Jewish neighbourhood, the so-called Lazarussteeg (ibid., p. 260, 1 Nisan 5413). Ester was given relief until 1655, after which date charity was stopped by order of the Mahamad, without further detail (ibid., no. 174, p. 132, Rosh Hodesh Heshvan 5416). After this, no trace of Ester or her children can be found in Amsterdam.

442 '14 dagen op water en brood' (SAA entry no. 5061, no. 319, p. 213, 12 Jan. 1671: 'Abram Marcado'); 'twee jaren de stad ontzegd' (ibid., no. 321, p. 13, 18 July 1671: 'Francisco d'Acosta'); 'jaer tuchthuis en een jaar gebannen' (ibid., p. 91^{v}, 25 May 1672: 'Jacob Asoubie'); 'binnen dort noch eens gevangen geweest te sijn en aldaer te pronk gestaan hebben . . . twee jaar Rasphuis en vier jaar verbannen' (ibid., no. 326, pp. 265^{r-v}, 275, 9, 13, 27 Jan. 1682: 'David Moreno'); 'publiek op het schavot gegeseld; 3 jaer in 't tuchthuys geconfinieerd; 6 maanden bij provisie in 't tuchthuys' (ibid., no. 323, p. 127^{v}, 18 Feb. 1677: 'Isack Lopes de Luna'); 'op 't schavot gegeseld en drie jaren gebannen' (ibid., no. 326, p. 44, 23 Jan. 1681: 'Izak Lopes de Loena'); 'twee jaren in 't Rasphuis geconfinieerd onvermindert zijn banissement' (ibid., no. 327, p. 101, 8 Oct. 1682: 'Izak Lopes de Luna'); 'dertig jare in 't tugthuis en dertig jaren gebannen uit Holland en West-Friesland' (ibid., no. 372, p. 234, 13 Nov. 1715: 'Jacob Moreno'). Gracia Baruch was condemned to six years' detention in the workhouse in Rotterdam 'om met haer Handen werck de kost te winne' (Gemeentearchief Rotterdam, entry no. 15, no. 145, pp. 86–7, 17 Apr. 1715); however, she was dismissed and set free after one year: (ibid., 27 Apr. 1717).

443 Hufton, 'Women without Men', 363.

444 Israel, 'Spain and the Dutch Sephardim', 46–56; Schreiber, 'Cristianos Nuevos de Madrid', 555–6. For a combination of religious and economic drives as an explanation for the immigration of New Christians from the Iberian peninsula to 18th-century Bordeaux see Cavignac, 'L'Immigration des Juifs portugais à Bordeaux'.

445 M. Cohen, in his discussion of poor Jews in medieval Egypt (*Poverty and Charity*, 28), does not see the poor as beggars either.

8 Epilogue

1 Vries, *European Urbanization*, 213; Ruderman, *Early Modern Jewry*, ch. 1: 'Jews on the Move'.

2 Menasseh ben Israel, *De la fragilidad humana*, p. ii.

3 Y. Kaplan, 'Political Concepts', 47–9.

4 Swetschinski, *Reluctant Cosmopolitans*, ch. 6. Kenneth Stow, *Theater of Acculturation*, 49, 68, speaks of a specific Roman Jewish subculture in 16th-century Rome.

5 Here I agree with Glanz, who argues that, to avoid jeopardizing its position, the Jewish establishment did not show solidarity with Jewish criminals. On this issue see the discussion in Ulbricht, 'Criminality and Punishment', 62; see also Glanz, *Geschichte des niederen jüdischen Volkes*.

6 For control and survival strategies in welfare see M. van Leeuwen, *The Logic of Charity*, esp. chs. 1 and 6.

APPENDIX III Four Biographical Studies

1 When his sister Luna married in Amsterdam in 1679 she was described as an orphan of Isaac de Leon ('q Deus tem': SAA entry no. 334, no. 1144, p. 268, 19 Tamuz 5439). Her father, Isaac Machorro of Salé (the name 'Sale' is written alongside his name, implying he came from there), visited Amsterdam in 1652 (ibid., no. 173, p. 244, 6 Tishrei 5413: 'Ishac Machorro Sale . . . Promessas: f 24:18'). The fact that in this case he is recorded as paying neither *finta* nor *imposta* means he must have been a visitor, especially since the place of origin is registered here next to his name. Isaac Machorro de Leon was back in Amsterdam in 1674 and received 1.10 guilders for Purim, 3.3 guilders at a special collection on 4 Adar II, and finally, some months later, money to cover travel expenses, namely 20 guilders to return to Salé (ibid., no. 216, p. 146, 13 Adar II 5434; ibid, p. 164, 4 Adar II 5434; ibid., p. 172, 25 Tamuz 5434: 'p[a] se hir a Sale').

2 On David Machorro de Leon see also Silva Rosa, *De geschiedenis van de Portugeesche Joden te Amsterdam*, 33; apparently at one stage he worked on ships as a maritime customs officer. In 1661 David's uncle, his father's brother Salomon Machorro de Leon, became a member of Dotar in Amsterdam (SAA entry no. 334, no. 1144, p. 48, 10 Tishrei 5422; ibid., no. 174, p. 719, 11 Tishrei 5426, list of taxpaying members: 'Salomoh Machoro Leão: promessas 1:12 guilder, meia finta 2:10 guilders, meia finta 2:10 guilders; imposta:–'). Isaac Machorro de Leon took over the membership of Dotar in 1669 (SAA entry no. 334, no. 1144, p. 126, 28 Shevat 5429). Isaac must have been a member of Dotar in Salé, since his name does not appear in either the tax registers of the Amsterdam community or the welfare lists in those years. We know that Salomon Machorro de Leon and Moses Machorro de Leon, David's uncles, travelled to the Iberian peninsula or other 'terras de idolatría', since upon their return they had to beg forgiveness for their actions (Y. Kaplan, 'Travels of Portuguese Jews', 213).

3 SAA DTB 691, p. 244, 7 July 1679. Joseph signed the document in Hebrew. His mother lived in the Ottoman empire, in Turkey. In the registers of the

Amsterdam Portuguese community in 1677 he is registered as 'forasteiro'. He also earned some money within the *kahal* helping prepare the food for Pesach (SAA entry no. 334, no. 217, pp. 51, 93, 101, 103, 149, 153, 199, 5437–40).

4 SAA entry no. 334, no. 1144, p. 167, 15 Adar 5431.

5 SAA entry no. 334, no. 217, p. 104, 11 Nisan, 9 Iyar, and 1 Sivan 5438; ibid., p. 115, 24 Elul 5438 and 24 Tishrei/Rosh Hodesh Heshvan 5439.

6 SAA DTB 694, p. 126, 9 June 1684.

7 SAA entry no. 334, no. 217, p. 160, 11 Iyar 5439; ibid., p. 212, 1 Iyar 5440.

8 SAA entry no. 334, no. 217, p. 253, 3 Kislev 5441.

9 SAA entry no. 334, no. 217, p. 274, 3 Heshvan 5442.

10 SAA entry no. 334, no. 217, p. 160, 11 Iyar 5439; ibid., p. 212, 1 Iyar 5440; ibid., p. 482, 8 Elul 5444; ibid., no.218, p. 111, 2 Av 5446; ibid., p. 175, 5 Av 5447; ibid., p. 316, 22 Tamuz 5449.

11 SAA entry no. 334, no. 217, pp. 255 and 259, 1 Tevet and 12 Adar 5441.

12 SAA DTB 694, p. 126, 9 June 1684.

13 SAA entry no. 334, no. 1144, p. 297, 16 Tevet 5442.

14 SAA entry no. 334, no. 217, p. 482, 8, 18, and 25 Elul 5444.

15 SAA entry no. 334, no. 218, p. 111, 2 Av 5446.

16 SAA entry no. 334, no. 218, p. 175, 5 Av 5447.

17 SAA entry no. 334, no. 218, p. 390, 27 Heshvan 5451.

18 SAA entry no. 334, no. 20, p. 158, Rosh Hodesh Nisan 5452.

19 SAA entry no. 334, no. 1144, p. 78, 5456. David became a member of Dotar in 1683, inheriting the position from his father Isaac Machorro de Leon (ibid., no. 311, 16 Adar 5443). Isaac, as we saw above (n. 2), had taken over the position from his brother Salomon.

20 SAA entry no. 334, no. 1153, pp. 269, 385, 480, 5458–60.

21 For the year 5425 see e.g. SAA entry no. 334, no. 215, p. 71, 16 Shevat 5425; for the years 5428–33 see e.g. ibid., p. 263, 29 Tamuz 5428; ibid., no. 174, p. 995, Rosh Hodesh Menahem-Av 5433. On 'Francos' in the Levant—Italian merchants, mostly of Portuguese origin—and their communities see Barnai, 'The Jews of the Ottoman Empire', 142.

22 Wolff and Wolff, *Dicionário biográfico*, 45.

23 See e.g. SAA entry no. 334, no. 173, p. 239, 5 Menahem-Av 5412; ibid., p. 251, 28 Kislev 5413; ibid., no. 174, p. 30, 14 Adar 5414; ibid., p. 74, 12 Tishrei 5415; ibid., 12 Tishrei 5416.

24 See e.g. SAA entry no. 334, no. 174, p. 77, 1 Tevet 5415; ibid., p. 133, 1 Kislev 5416; ibid., p. 191, 1 Kislev 5417.

25 SAA entry no. 334, no. 174, p. 143, 22 Adar 5416: distribution of matzah meal 40 *livras*.

26 'Sarah, filha de Jahacob gabai correa em Amsterdam' (SAA entry no. 334, no. 1143, p. 227, 15 Adar 5414; ibid., p. 242, 13 Adar 5415; ibid., p. 255, 13 Adar 5416; ibid., p. 274, 13 Adar 5417).

27 SAA entry no. 334, no. 1350, 2 Sept. 1658.

28 SAA entry no. 334, no. 1143, p. 322, 15 Adar II 5421; ibid., no. 1144, p. 92, 18 Nisan 5424. The groom was Jacob Nunes da Fonseca.

29 SAA entry no. 334, no. 215, pp. 35 and 90, 1 Iyar 5423–1 Elul 5424.

30 SAA entry no. 334, no. 215, p. 66, 19 Nisan 5424: 'Jacob Gavai Corea . . . q foi p[a] Cayana f 70,–'; ibid., p. 82, 19 Nisan 5424; ibid., no. 24a, pp. 2[v] and 3, 19 Nisan 5424.

31 SAA entry no. 334, no. 215, p. 157, 26 Elul 5426; Wolff and Wolff, *Dicionário biográfico*, 45.

32 SAA entry no. 334, no. 174, p. 543, 10 Shevat 5423: 'Sarah e Ester Rocha orphaãs'. One of their daughters applied for a dowry with Dotar in 1666 as an 'orfam de maj' (SAA entry no. 334, no. 1151, p. 457, 1666: 'Sara da Rocha, donzela filha de Selomoh da Rocha . . . orfam de maj . . . tem 16 anos de jdade').

33 National Archives, United Kingdom, Court of Chancery 32/218[v], 16 Aug. 1667.

34 SAA entry no. 334, no. 215, p. 211, 15 Elul 5427: 'Selomoh da Rocha . . . p[a]. se ir para Sale'.

35 SAA entry no. 334, no. 215, p. 265, 4 Shevat 5429: 'Selomoh da Rocha . . . vindo de Sale enfermo'.

36 SAA entry no. 334, no. 215, p. 268, 16 Adar 5429; ibid., p. 269, 6 Nisan 5429; ibid., p. 312, 27 Av 5429: 'Selomoh da Rocha . . . para yrse para Serinhao'.

37 'opt schip Jongen Abraham is overgekomen eenen Salomon da Rocha de welke is een persoon van groote naedeel en prejuditje tot welvaeren van onse conservatie en modest leven . . . sich met de eerste gelegenth[t] hier uyt het lant te begeeven' (Nationaal Archief, entry no. 1.05.03, no. 213, p. 383, 22 Nov. 1669/28 Dec. 1672).

38 SAA entry no. 334, no. 216, p. 169, 1 Elul 5434.

39 Oppenheim, 'Early Jewish Colony' (1907), 157–9.

40 SAA entry no. 334, no. 174, p. 543, 10 Shevat 5423: 'Sarah e Ester Rocha orphaãs'; ibid., p. 732, 20 Adar 5426. They also received: matzot from 1665 to 1685—for the last few years for Ester only (SAA entry no. 334, no. 174, p. 695, 10 Nisan 5425; ibid., no. 217, p. 523, 5445); rental subsidy from 1670 to 1682 (ibid., no. 216, p. 184, 5434–5; ibid., no. 217, p. 304, 5441); peat from 1665 to 1682 (ibid., no. 215, p. 125, 5425; ibid., no. 217, p. 326, 5442); distributions during the holidays, from 1666 to 1682 for both of them, and for Ester until 1688 (ibid., no. 215, p. 192, 5426–7; ibid., no. 217, p. 300, 5441–2; ibid., no. 218, p. 273, 5448: *nedavot*); and poor relief, every three months from 1670 to 1682 (ibid., no. 215, p. 316, 23 Adar 5430; ibid., no. 217, p. 316, 3 Nisan 5442).

ARCHIVES CONSULTED

Note on Archive Source

Dates

In the manuscript source SAA entry no. 334, particularly in the sources of the earliest period, dates appear variously in Jewish and Common Era form. This is because immigrants from the territories under Spanish and Portuguese rule were Conversos (people whose forebears had converted from Judaism to Catholicism), and so were not in the habit of using the Jewish calendar; they recorded dates in their most familiar form, or sometimes using a mixture of systems. All dates have been transcribed as they appear in the source.

Page references

Some page references to the archives consist of two numbers: the first is from the time of registration, the second is the number entered by the archivist who organized the records of the Portuguese Jewish community and created an inventory of them. In the notes to the present volume I follow the numbering of the archivist (if added), with the exception of SAA entry no. 334, no. 19, for which both numbers—if appearing (up to p. 214/299, 5406)—are given. For example, 'p. 23/12' in SAA entry no. 19 refers to a single page.

Abbreviations Used in the Notes

AHN	Archivo Histórico Nacional
SAA	Stadsarchief Amsterdam
SAA DTB	Doop-, Trouw-, en Begrafenisregisters (Amsterdam)
SAA Entry no. 334	Amsterdam Portuguese Jewish community
SAA Entry no. 334.A	Amsterdam Portuguese Jewish community, supplement
SAA Entry no. 342	Archives of Municipal Hospitals (Amsterdam)
SAA Entry no. 343	Archives of the Almoners, since 1682
	Governors of the Almoners' Orphanage (Amsterdam)
SAA Entry no. 347	Archives of the Spinhouse and New Workhouse (Amsterdam)
SAA Entry no. 349	Archives of the 'Nieuwezijds and Oudezijds Huiszittenhuis' and of the Governors of the Huiszittenarmen (Outdoor Relief for the Poor) (Amsterdam)

SAA Entry no. 366	Archives of the Guilds and the Brewers (Amsterdam)
SAA Entry no. 376	Archives of the Reformed Church (Amsterdam)
SAA Entry no. 440	Archives of the Roman Catholic Poor Relief Office and of the Roman Catholic Saint Jacob Old Age Home (Amsterdam)
SAA Entry no. 996	Archives of Jac. de Vries Jr. (Amsterdam)
SAA Entry no. 5004	Archives of the Chamber of the Orphan; Burial Registers (Amsterdam)
SAA Entry no. 5024	Archives of Burgomasters; Daily Minutes, Resolutions, Missive Books (Amsterdam)
SAA Entry no. 5061	Judicial Archives: Archives of Bailiffs and Aldermen, of Aldermen and Subordinate Courts (Amsterdam)
SAA Entry no. 5072	Archives of the Governors of the Insolvent Estates Office (Amsterdam)
SAA Entry no. 5075	Archives of Notaries in Amsterdam
SAA Entry no. 15030	Library of the Amsterdam City Archives
Entry no. 1.05.03	Inventory of the archives of the 'Sociëteit van Suriname' (1650) 1682–1795 (Dutch National Archives, The Hague)
Entry no. 0351-01	Judicial Archives (Municipal Archives, The Hague)
Entry no. 0372-01	Archives of Notaries, The Hague (Municipal Archives, The Hague)
Entry no. 0130-01	Portuguese Jewish Community, The Hague (1707) 1708–1941 (Municipal Archives, The Hague)
Entry no. 15	Board of Aldermen of Rotterdam (Old Judicial Archives, Rotterdam)
Entry no. 508	Old Judicial Archives (Regional Archives, Leiden)

Websites

Amsterdam, International Institute of Social History:
http://www.iisg.nl/hpw/brenv.php; http://www.iisg.nl/hpw/calculate.php

Amsterdam, Dutch Jewish Communities (NIK):
http://www.stenenarchief.org/pig/pig_list.php

Amsterdam City Archives (Stadsarchief Amsterdam; SAA)

Entry no. 334: Amsterdam Portuguese Jewish community

Bet Jacob

No. 3 *Livro grande* 1621–3 (5381–3)

No. 4 *Manual da sedaca* 1619–21 (5379–81)

No. 5 *Promessas; fintas* 1618–19 (5378–9)
Manual da sedaca 1621–3 (5381–3)

No. 6 *Promessas e fintas* 1616–18 (5376–8)

No. 7 *Livro das promessas e fintas tocante sedaka do Kahal Kados de Bet Jacob que el Dio aumente e contas de todos os jehidim e as outras . . . No. 25 1631 (5391)*

Neve Salom

No. 9 *Manual* 1616–39 (5376–99)

Bet Israel

No. 10 *Livro de termos* 1618–39 (5379–99)

Nos. 11–12 *Promessas; fintas* 1626–39 (5386–99)

Manual Bet Haim 1639–48 (5399–5408)

Imposta

No. 13 *Libro de termos da ymposta da nação, principiado em 24 de Sebat 5382* 1622–39 (5382–99)

No. 17 *Journal* 1622–39 (5382–99)

Kahal Kados de Talmud Torah

Nos. 19–22 *Escamot*

A 1638–80 (5398–5440)

B 1680–1712 (5440–72)

C 1712–28 (5472–88)

Compendio de escamot 1728–1814 (5488–5574)

No. 24 *Memorial de advertencias* 1659–81 (5419–41)

No. 24a *Memorial de advertencias* 1664–88 (5424–48)

Nos. 25–8 *Livro de memorias* 1688–1773 (5448–5538)

No. 66 *Incoming items* 1643–1810

No. 87 *Privilegios do magistrado da cidade de Amsterdam e outros actos a favor e beneficio deste Kahal Kados* 1630–1797

Nos. 90–3 *Copiador de cartas* 1702–19, 1728–37, 1744–50, 1750–7

Nos. 118–20 *Varios papeis de pleitos findados* (1670–1815)

No. 158 *Livro de eleiçoems do Kahal Kados de Talmud Torah desde a união anno 5399* 1597–1870

Nos. 172–7 *Manual* 1639–1718 (5399–5478)

Nos. 179–81 *Manual A* 1728–58 (5488–5518)

Nos. 215–23 *Livro longo* 1663–1729 (5423–89)

Nos. 239–42 *Livro grande* 1639–1702 (5399–5462)

Nos. 245–6 *Livro grande* 1718–28 (5478–88)

Nos. 247–9 *Livro grande* 1728–58 (5488–5518)

No. 251 *Livro grande* 1767–76 (5527–36)

Nos. 253–4 *Livro grande* 1785–98 (5545–58)

No. 268 *Memoria dos presentes que de parte da Nação Judaica Portugueza se tem feito aos senhores Escotetes desta cidade de Amsterdam* 1663–*c.*1795

No. 277 *Fintas e offertas* 1756–9 (5516–19)

No. 285 *Finta* 1739–43

No. 288 *Finta* 1767–71 (5527–31)

No. 290 *Finta* 1789–95 (5549–55)

No. 294 *Offertas* 1654–72 (5414–32)
No. 310 *Rental contracts* 1733–1865
No. 377 *Copia do livro das circumsisoms* 1693–1725
No. 378 *Notisias de los circunsidadores do jaguidim deste Kahal Kados* 1700–*c.*1740
No. 381 *Certificates* 1731/2, 1734, and undated
No. 382 *Ketubot* 1673–90 (5433–50)
No. 385 *Ketubot* 1695–8 (5455–8)
No. 421 *Burial register* (women) 1616–
No. 422 *Burial register* (men) 1616–
No. 502 *Certificates of birth, marriage, and death* 1663–1857
No. 518 *Livro dos testamentos* 1663–1733
No. 520A *Testamentos e outros actos depositados em poder dos senhores do Mahamad* 1668– 1731
No. 609 *Estate Abraham Abenatar* 1803
No. 612 *Estate Ester Abrabanel, widow of David de Samuel Pinto* 1754; 1759
No. 613 *Estate Moses Abrabanel* 1731
No. 616 *Estate Antonio Alvares alias Joseph Israel Alvares* 1694–1773
No. 628 *Estate Miriam Alvares, widow of Antonio Mendez Sotto* 1685–1742
No. 632 *Estate Ester Arias, widow of Joseph de Abraham Capadoce* 1746–58
No. 641 *Estate Rachel Belmonte alias Schonenberg* 1724; 1741–1814
No. 644 *Estate Lea Habilho Benveniste* 1775
No. 658 *Estate Rachel Medina Chamiz, widow of Joseph Henriques Medina* 1739–65
No. 674 *Estate Moses Franco Drago* 1647; 1681
No. 694 *Estate Rachel de Spinosa Henriques* 1737–1825
No. 700 *Estate Abigail Dias da Fonseca alias Beatris de Caceres* 1703–37
No. 718 *Estate Abraham Labat Keyzer* 1776
No. 720 *Estate Rachel de Abraham Keyzer* 1777–1814
No. 736 *Estate Jacob Mazahod: register of yearly distributions to people on welfare through the official community channels*: 1721–1918 (5481–5678)
No. 737 *Estate Jacob Mazahod: register of yearly distributions to people not provided with welfare through the official community channels* 1721–1865
No. 756 *Estate Benjamin Musaphia* 1673; 1678
No. 757 *Estate Ester de Isaac Musaphia*: 1733; 1736–1886
No. 780A *Estate Abraham and Sara Pereyra* 1659–1828
No. 782 *Estate Abraham and Sara Pereyra: Journal* 1659–1729
No. 784 *Estate Abraham Pereyra* 1780–96
No. 826 *Estate Gracia Senior alias Isabel Henriquez* 1676
No. 828 *Estate Joseph Soares alias Lopo Soares* 1655–1798
No. 882 *Items concerning the ḥerem of Daniel de Prado and Daniel Ribera* 1658
Nos. 969–70 *Livro longo de cuatro contas* 1729–60 (5489 –5519)
No. 973 *Livro de segredos* 1733–1817 (5493–5577)

Nos. 974–6 *Lists of people eligible for welfare distributions in money or in kind (peat, matzot)* 1734–96 (5494–5556)

No. 980 *Requests of the parnasim addressed to the judicial authorities of the city of Amsterdam concerning members of the Portuguese community who received money to travel abroad and nevertheless stayed in the Republic, with dispositions* 1752–59

No. 986 *Privilegio dos senhores Estados de Holanda & Westvriesland & dos senhores do Magistrado de Amsterdam para a isenção do direito sobre a turva para a povresa de Nação e isenção do direito da sisa sobre o trigo para a masot para a povresa* 1681–1805

No. 989 *Register of distributions of talitot, tefilin, and prayer books by the gabay da sedaca* 1741–99 (5501–59)

No. 1001 *Livro de emprestimo* 1792–7

No. 1027 *Lists of pawns* 1690–1824

Hebra (Bikur Holim)

No. 990 *Documents concerning Hebra (Bikur Holim)* c.1750

Talmud Torah school and Ets Haim yeshiva

No. 1051 *Termos de Talmud Torah e de Ets Haim* 1616–1728 (5376–5488)

No. 1052 *Resolutions Ets Haim* 1637–1728 (5397–5488)

No. 1073 *Registers of members Ets Haim; legatees of Ets Haim; decisions concerning different legacies* 1637–1902; initiated 1728

Nos. 1116–17 *Livro grande* 1652–1803 (5412–5563)

Santa companhia de dotar orfas e donzelas

Nos. 1141–5 *Resolutions* 1615–1787

Nos. 1151–3 *Incoming items* 1618–1711 (5378–5471)

No. 1163 *Livro dos irmãos* 1615–1956 (5375–5716)

Nos. 1168–70 *Livro grande* 1615–1733

Honen Dalim

No. 1186 *Regulations; resolutions; membership lists* 1625–84 (5385–5444)

Vestiaria

No. 1187 *Resolutions; Settlement of accounts; lists of names of recipients of welfare* 1753–87 (5513–47)

Vestiaria dos talmidim

No. 1189 *Settlement of accounts; lists of contributors; lists of names of recipients of welfare* 1670–1745 (5440–5505)

Gemilut Hasadim

No. 1191 *Regulations; Resolutions; administration of contribution; lists of treasurers* 1666–1761 (5426–5521)

Abodat Ahesed

No. 1210 *Register of contributions and yearly income and expenditure* 1735–40 (5495–5500)

Aby Jetomim

No. 1211 *Register of orphans, members, administrators and apprentice contracts* 1648 (5408)–1795

Temime Darech

No. 1214 *Regulations* 1672

Asuta Habraya

No. 1215 *Livro grande* 1747–94 (5507–54)

Mishenet Zequenim

No. 1220 *Regulations; Decisions; Minutes* 1750–1843 (5510–5603)

No. 1223 *List of membership* 1772

No. 1227 *Journal* 1759–1842 (5510–5602)

No. 1230 *Livro grande da pia irmandade Mishenet Zequenim* 1750–1842 (5510–5602)

Hase Amaharacha

Nos. 1234–5 *Cashbook of contributions* 1713–59 (5474–5519)

Meil Sedaca

No. 1242 *Regulations; decisions; cashbook of income and expenditure* 1754–1837 (5514–97)

No. 1275 *Documents relating to the foundation of the old women house and hospital Mesib Nefes* 1833/4

No. 1304 *Register for regulations and resolutions on the Portuguese Jewish community in Brazil* 1648–54 (5409–14)

No. 1322 *Copy regulations Dotar* 1615

Nos. 1328–9 *Descriptions of gravestones of cemetery in Ouderkerk aan de Amstel by D. Henriques de Castro c.*1870

No. 1350 *Receipts concerning sale of slaves by the director of the 'Wilde Kust' named Nova Zeelandia, to Michael Dias, Moses Burgos, Jacob Gabay Correa, Abraham Vas, Jacob Machorro, Joseph Lopez and Abraham Rodrigues. Paulo Jacomo Pinto acted as surety* 1659

Supplementary Entry no. 334.A

No. 130: *Minutes of the 'Meetings of the Second Division'—Administration of Welfare (Vergaderingen der Tweede Afdeeling—Armbestuur) of the board of parnasim* 1 Nov. 1877.

No. 191 jjj *Reformaçao das Escamoth, Reglementos, e ordenaçoens para o bom governo da Santa Irmandade Mishenet Zequenim . . . instituida em 19 Tebeth 5510 . . . Amsterdam* 5513

No. 195r *Livros pertenecentes a sancta irmandade de Abi Jetomim* Amsterdam 5577

No. 195m *Mispat Abanot* A° 1730

No. 198r *Aby Jetomim*

No. 204k *The Portuguese Jewish girls' orphanage (Het Portugeesch Israelietisch Meisjes-Weeshuis) 'Mazon Habanot'* 1734–1934 (6 Shevat 5494–5694)

Entry no. 342: Archives of Municipal Hospitals (Archief van de Gasthuizen)

No. 951 *Archives of the 'Dol- or Krankzinnigenhuis', 'Krankzinnigen-boek'* 1640–1745

No. 1059 *Incoming and outgoing items of the 'Gast- and Pesthuis'* 1748

Entry no. 343: Archives of the Almoners, since 1682 Governors of the Almoners' Orphanage (Archief van de Aalmoezeniers, sinds 1682 regenten van het Aalmoezeniersweeshuis)

No. 1 *Register of laws* ('Register van Keuren') 1613–34

Entry no. 347: Archives of the Spinhouse and New Workhouse (Archief van het Spin- en Nieuwe Werkhuis)

Nos. 116–25 *Register concerning entry, discharge or death of inmates of the Workhouse.* 10 vols., 1654–1754

Entry no. 349: Archives of the 'Nieuwezijds and Oudezijds Huiszittenhuis' and of the Governors of the Huiszittenarmen (Outdoor Relief for the Poor) (Archieven van het Nieuwezijds en het Oudezijds Huiszittenhuis en van de Regenten over de Huiszittende Stadsarmen)

No. 1.1.1 *Resolution Books* 1639–1703

No. 1.1.7 *Resolution Books* 1790–9

Entry no. 366: Archives of the Guilds and the Brewers (Archief van de Gilden en het Brouwerscollege)

No. 65 *Registration of newly registered members of the bookseller, book printer, and bookbinder guilds* 4 Feb. 1692

Entry no. 376: Archives of the Reformed Church (Archief van de Hervormde Gemeente)

Church Council (Kerkenraad)

No. 1 *no title* 1578–89

No. 5 *no title* 1621–7

Nos. 7–10 *no title* 1633–63

Nos. 12–15 *no title* 1668–91

No. 24 *no title* 1752–63

Entry no. 440: Archives of the Roman Catholic Poor Relief Office and of the Roman Catholic Saint Jacob Old Age Home (Archief van het Rooms-Katholiek Oude-Armenkantoor en R.K.Bejaardenhuis Sint Jacob)

No. 253

Last wills and legacies to the 'R.C. Oude-Armenkantoor' 1629; 1642

Last will of Eefgen Wijnants, widow of Jan Hendricksz. Buysingh, Not. L. Lamberti, Nov. 1629, portfolio 8

Last will of Elbert Joosten, Not. J. van der Hoeven, 9 Sept. 1642, portfolio 14

Entry no. 996: Archives of Jac. de Vries Jr. (Archief van Jac. de Vries jr.)

No. 17, 26 Jan. 1699–18 Sept. 1705 *Last will of Abraham Israel Suasso alias Francisco Lopes Suasso* 1699; *with codicil* 1705

Entry no. 5004: Archives of the Chamber of the Orphan; Burial Registers (Archief van de Weeskamer; Begraafregisters)

No. 109 (Calisregisters), p. 110, 4 Aug. 1669
No. 110 (Calisregisters), p. 108, 30 Nov. 1683
No. 110 (Calisregisters), p. 2, 28 July 1684
No. 110 (Calisregisters), p. 125, 24 Aug. 1700
No. 110 (Calisregisters), p. 146, 29 Sept. 1701
No. 110 (Calisregisters), p. 146, 10 Jan. 1702
No. 110 (Calisregisters), pp. 105^{v}–106, 21 Mar. 1702
No. 111 (Calisregisters), p. 129^{v}, 4 Nov. 1705

Entry no. 5024: Archives of Burgomasters; Daily Minutes, Resolutions, Missive Books (Archief van Burgemeesters; Dagelijkse notulen, resoluties en missivenboeken)

No. 2 *Resolutions of governing burgomasters and old burgomasters* 27 Apr. 1695

Entry no. 5061: Judicial Archives: Archives of Bailiffs and Aldermen, of Aldermen and Subordinate Courts (Archieven van Schout en Schepenen, van Schepenen en van de subalterne rechtbanken)

No. 138 *Schapenboek*, pp. 155–6, 23 Feb. 1717
No. 198 *Bailiff Account (Schoutsrol)* [unpaginated] 14 Nov. 1657; 22 May 1658
No. 203 *Bailiff Account* [no page] 16 Nov. 1666
No. 204 *Bailiff Account* [no page] 7 Sept. 1669
No. 206 *Bailiff Account* [no page] 4 Dec. 1674
No. 208 *Bailiff Account* [no page] 12 Jan. 1683, 14 Sept. 1683
No. 210 *Bailiff Account* [no page] 18 Dec. 1691, 20 May 1692
No. 211 *Bailiff Account* [no page] 17 May 1695, 11 Oct. 1695
No. 213 *Bailiff Account* [no page] 18 and 25 Nov. 1698
No. 292 *Confession Books (Confessie boeken)*, p. 131, 4 Oct. 1619
No. 299 *Confession Books*, pp. 165^{v}–166, 12 Apr. 1633
No. 308 *Confession Books*, p. 234, 25 Apr. 1651
No. 310 *Confession Books*, p. 24, 23 Apr. 1654; pp. 56^{v}–57, 63, 64^{v}, 70^{v}, 15 Apr. 1654
No. 311 *Confession Books*, p. 139, 17 Mar. 1656; p. 156^{v}, 11 July 1656; p. 194^{v}, 1 Nov. 1656; p. 223^{v}, 9 Feb. 1657; pp. 253^{v}–254^{r}, 6 June 1657
No. 312 *Confession Books*, pp. 10^{v}–12^{v}, 23 Oct. 1657; pp. 211–12, 14 and 20 Feb. 1659; p. 260^{v}, 13 Aug. 1659
No. 317 *Confession Books*, pp. 40–3, 15 Apr. 1666
No. 318 *Confession Books*, pp. 214–17, 21 Feb. 1669

No. 319 *Confession Books*, p. 48^{v}, 20 Nov. 1669; p. 107^{v}, 6 Mar. 1670; p. 213, 12 Jan. 1671; pp. 245^{v}, 246, and 250^{v}, 26 Mar. and 1 May 1671; p. 252, 15 May 1671

No. 321 *Confession Books*, p. 13, 18 July 1671; p. 91^{v}, 25 May 1672; p. 19, 2 Mar. 1673; p. 19, 17 Mar. 1673; p. 26, 11 Apr. 1673; p. 153, 30 Dec. 1673; p. 156^{v}, 15 Jan. 1674

No. 323 *Confession Books*, p. 75^{v}, 24 Sept. 1676; p. 78, 8 Oct. 1676; p. 121^{v}, 8 Feb. 1677; pp. 127^{v}–128^{v}, 18 Feb. 1677

No. 325 *Confession Books*, p. 11, 24 Aug. 1679; p. 204, 19 July 1680

No. 326 *Confession Books*, p. 44, 12 and 23 Jan. 1681; pp. 265^{r-v} and 275, 9, 13, 27 Jan. 1682

No. 327 *Confession Books*, p. 101^{v}, 8 Oct. 1682; p. 138, 24 Nov. 1682

No. 328 *Confession Books*, p. 91, 5 Feb. 1684

No. 329 *Confession Books*, p. 1, 8 Aug. 1684; pp. 228 and 231, 1 and 10 Nov. 1685

No. 331 *Confession Books*, p. 43, 14 Jan. 1687

No. 335 *Confession Books*, p. 119^{v}, 7 Sept. 1690

No. 337 *Confession Books*, p. 256^{v}, 6 and 14 May 1692

No. 339 *Confession Books*, pp. 73^{v}–74, 16 June 1693; p. 91^{v}, 21 Aug. 1693

No. 341 *Confession Books*, p. 8, 15 Feb. 1694

No. 342 *Confession Books*, p. 2^{v}, 25 Mar. 1695; p. 40, 21 June 1695; p. 270^{r-v}, 14 Apr. 1696

No. 345 *Confession Books*, p. 23, 24 Dec. 1697

No. 346 *Confession Books*, p. 94, 11 June 1698

No. 349 *Confession Books*, p. 41, 25 Feb. 1700; p. 103^{v}, 22 Apr. 1700

No. 351 *Confession Books*, p. 169^{v}, 6 May 1702; p. 201^{v}, 26 July 1702

No. 358 *Confession Books*, p. 57, 20 Apr. 1708

No. 361 *Confession Books*, pp. 245^{v}–246, 5 July 1710

No. 362 *Confession Books*, pp. 92–94^{v}, 5 Nov. 1710

No. 364 *Confession Books*, pp. 180–190^{v}, 11 Oct. 1711

No. 365 *Confession Books*, p. 105^{v}, 29 Aug. 1712

No. 367 *Confession Books*, p. 168^{v}, 27 July 1713

No. 372 *Confession Books*, p. 239^{v}, 13 Nov. 1715

No. 378 *Confession Books*, p. 189, 17 Apr. 1720

No. 390 *Confession Books*, p. 2, 19 Feb. 1732

No. 391 *Confession Books*, p. 184^{v}, 25 May 1734; p. 193, 2 June 1734

No. 393 *Confession Books*, pp. 45^{v}–46^{r}, 23 Aug. 1735; pp. 24^{v}–28^{v}, 39–41, 124–126^{v}, 128^{v}, 140^{v}–142, 30 June and 3 Dec. 1735; pp. 190^{v}–191^{v}, 22 Mar. 1736; pp. 215^{v}–217, 11 Apr. 1736

No. 395 *Confession Books*, p. 183, 25 Apr. 1737

No. 397 *Confession Books*, pp. 240^{v}–243^{v}, 17 Oct. 1738

No. 400 *Confession Books*, p. 140^{v}, 7 July 1740; p. 148^{v}, 14 July 1740

No. 405 *Confession Books*, p. 140^{r-v}, 3 Sept. 1744

No. 406 *Confession Books*, pp. 204–205^{v}, 23 Aug. 1746

No. 408, *Confession Books*, p. 25, 4 July 1748
No. 412 *Confession Books*, pp. 118^{v}–119^{v}, 29 Dec. 1752
No. 599 *Justitieboeken*, p. 80^{v}, 14 June [1695]
No. 631 *Justitieboeken*, p. 1, 7 Jan. 1732; p. 3, 21 Mar. 1734; p. 1, 4 Aug. 1735; p. 4, 1 Feb. 1736
No. 632 *Justitieboeken*, p. 6, May–July 1748
No. 683 *Requestbook*, p. 34, 12 Feb. 1670
No. 705, no. 3 *Minute Registers of the Aldermen (Schepenen)* 1759

Entry no. 5072: Archives of the Governors of the Insolvent Estates Office (Archief van de Commissarissen van de Desolate Boedelkamer)

No. 578, p. 201, 18 Dec. 1652
No. 589, pp. 263^{v}–264, 6 Jan. 1662
No. 591, pp. 63–4, 10 Oct. 1662
No. 601, p. 197, 4 Nov. 1675
No. 604, pp. 164^{v}–171^{v}, 14 Jan. 1678
No. 605, pp. 143–50, 3 Sept. 1677
No. 605, p. 268^{v}, 23 Mar. 1678
No. 606, p. 225^{v}, 1 Nov. 1679
No. 607, p. 201, 26 Mar. 1680
No. 608, pp. 182–5, 11 Apr. 1682
No. 610, pp. 105^{v}–115, 21 Nov. 1684
No. 614, p. 83^{v}, 2 July 1688
No. 614, p. 90, 20 July 1688
No. 614, p. 150^{v}, 21 Dec. 1688
No. 618, pp. 34^{v}–36, 8 Sept. 1692
No. 618, p. 36^{v}, 9 Sept. 1692
No. 620, p. 34, 26 Mar. 1695
No. 620, p. 35, 17 June 1695
No. 620, pp. 59^{v}–64, 30 Dec. 1695–Jan. 1696
No. 620, p. 117, 10 Oct. 1696
No. 621, pp. 205^{v}–206, 8 and 11 June 1697
No. 622, p. 92^{v}, 6 Nov. 1698
No. 629, pp. 96^{v}–97, 2 June 1706
No. 646, p. 79, 4 Mar. 1729
No. 693, p. 41, 21 Aug. 1691
No. 694, p. 8, 10 Mar. 1692
No. 694, p. 38, 19 Dec. 1692
No. 694, p. 21, 10 Sept. 1692
No. 695, p. 17, 5 Mar. 1693
No. 695, p. 56, 26 Nov. 1693
No. 696, p. 94, 2 Dec. 1694
No. 697, p. 74, 16 Nov. 1695
No. 700, p. 19, 11 Mar. 1698
No. 701, pp. 212^{v}–213, 2 Dec. 1699
No. 701, p. 67, 9 Dec. 1699
No. 711, p. 21, 24 June 1709
No. 713, p. 3, 1 July 1711
No. 716, p. 4, 30 Nov. 1714
No. 731, p. 3, 22 Mar. 1729
No. 750, no. 26 [n.d.] Apr. 1748

Entry no. 5075: Archives of Notaries in Amsterdam (Archief van de Notarissen ter standplaats Amsterdam)

No. 96, Not. J. F. Bruyningh, p. 100^{v}, 23 Oct. 1603
No. 109, Not. J. F. Bruyningh, pp. 136^{v}–137^{v}, 7 Mar. 1617
No. 131, Not. J. F. Bruyningh, pp. 155^{v}–156^{v}, 4 July 1613
No. 147, Not. J. F. Bruyningh, pp. 29^{v}–31, 1 Feb. 1617
No. 201, Not. J. Bruyning, p. 75^{v}, [n.d.] 1624

No. 258A, Not. J. Meerhout, pp. 16^{v}–17^{r}, 1 July 1610
No. 339, Not. W. Benninck, p. 244, 21 June 1617
No. 351B, Not. W. Cluijt, p. 222^{r-v}, 16 June 1625
No. 377B, Not. J. and N. Jacobs, p. 328^{r-v}, 29 Aug. 1614
No. 383A, Not. J. and N. Jacobs, p. 31, 10 Feb. 1620
No. 387, Not. J. and N. Jacobs, p. 279^{r-v}, 23 Dec. 1623
No. 414B, Not. J and N. Jacobs, p. 542, 16 Dec. 1636
No. 455, Not. P. Matthijsz., p. 54^{r-v}, 4 Mar. 1613
No. 611B, Not. P. Ruttens, p. 727, 24 Nov. 1620
No. 615A, Not. P. Ruttens, pp. 435–6, 23 May 1623–31 May 1623
No. 633, Not. S. Cornelisz., pp. 134–5, 26 Oct. 1626–10 Jan. 1627
No. 645A, Not. S. Cornelisz., p. 514, 17 Feb. 1619
No. 645A, Not. S. Cornelisz., p. 759, 12 July 1619
No. 645B, Not. S. Cornelisz., p. 1119, 17 Nov. 1620
No. 646A, Not. S. Cornelisz., pp. 171–2, 21 July 1622
No. 646A, Not. S. Cornelisz., p. 427, 24 Feb. 1623
No. 646A, Not. S. Cornelisz., pp. 574–5, 26 June 1623
No. 646A, Not. S. Cornelisz., p. 580, 28 June 1623
No. 646A, Not. S. Cornelisz., pp. 814–16, 19 Feb. 1624
No. 646B, Not. S. Cornelisz., pp. 1037–8, 24 Oct. 1624
No. 646B, Not. S. Cornelisz., p. 1039, 24 Oct. 1624
No. 695B, Not. Jan Warnaertsz., p. 707, 26 Aug. 1637
No. 941, Not. D. Bredan, pp. 749–50, 752–3, 16 July 1632
No. 942, Not. D. Bredan, [unpaginated], 22 Mar. 1633
No. 942, Not. D. Bredan, p. 363, 3 May 1633
No. 942, Not. D. Bredan, pp. 361, 392–3, 395, 421, 20 May and 1 June 1633
No. 942, Not. D. Bredan, [unpaginated], 4 Aug. 1633
No. 942, Not. D. Bredan, p. 1205, 16 Mar. 1634
No. 1138, Not. J. van de Ven, p. 295, 20 Sept. 1661
No. 1563, Not. J. Volkaertsz. Oli, pp. 721–3, 18 Oct. 1678
No. 2182, Not. A. Lock, pp. 65–72, 8 Mar. 1677
No. 2205, Not. A. Lock, pp. 357–8, 2 Sept. 1658
No. 2207, Not. A. Lock, p. 935, 9 Dec. 1659
No. 2210, Not. A. Lock, pp. 33–4, 7 Jan. 1661
No. 2210, Not. A. Lock, pp. 119–21, 14 Jan. 1661
No. 2226, Not. A. Lock, pp. 367–8, 14 Feb. 1668
No. 2237, Not. A. Lock, pp. 1105–8, 23 Dec. 1671
No. 2239, Not. A. Lock, pp. 95–6, 10 May 1672
No. 2261B, Not. A. Lock, pp. 547–51, 9 Feb. 1660
No. 2262A, Not. A. Lock, pp. 149–50, 14 Jan. 1668
No. 2272, Not. A. Lock, p. 11, 4 Jan. 1657

No. 2272, Not. A. Lock, p. 46, 23 Jan. 1657
No. 2889, Not. P. Padthuysen, p. 352, 11 May 1660
No. 2890A, Not. P. Padthuysen, p. 351, 22 Sept. 1661;
No. 2890A, Not. P. Padthuysen, pp. 17–19, 10 Nov. 1661
No. 2890B, Not. P. Padthuysen, pp. 1217–21, 7 Mar. 1661
No. 2891B, Not. P. Padthuysen, pp. 1204–6, 16 Sept. 1662
No. 2894B, Not. P. Padthuysen, pp. 1555–6, 24 Feb. 1665
No. 2895A, Not. P. Padthuysen, pp. 338–40, 7 Mar. 1666
No. 2895B, Not. P. Padthuysen, pp. 978–80, 22 July 1666
No. 2895B, Not. P. Padthuysen, pp. 1378–80, 28 Sept. 1666
No. 2914, Not. P. Padthuysen, pp. 667–73, 28 Sept. 1687
No. 2928A, Not. P. Padthuysen, pp. 29–32, 29 Sept. 1693
No. 2939, Not. P. Padthuysen, pp. 99–102, 17 Nov. 1698
No. 3208, Not. H. Outgers, pp. 166–8, 22 July 1671
No. 3280, Not. H. Outgers, no. 74, 21 Nov. 1685
No. 3309, Not. H. Outgers, p. 42, 27 Jan. 1691
No. 3679, Not. F. Tixerandet, p. 985, 21 Aug. 1671
No. 3684, Not. F. Tixerandet, p. 796, [*day/month illegible*] 1676
No. 3712, Not. F. Tixerandet, pp. 102–3, 6 Dec. 1690
No. 3720, Not. F. Tixerandet, pp. 11–14/19^{v}–21, 23 June 1693
No. 4089, Not. D. van der Groe, pp. 312–18, 23 Feb. 1679
No. 4090, Not. D. van der Groe, [unpaginated], 25 June 1679
No. 4092, Not. D. van der Groe, [unpaginated], 15 Nov. 1679
No. 4103A, Not. D. van der Groe, pp. 47–50, 7 July 1682
No. 4241, Not. D. van der Groe, pp. 396–401, 6 Aug. 1691
No. 4241, Not. D. van der Groe, pp. 403–7, 6 Aug. 1691
No. 4242, Not. D. van der Groe, pp. 348–57, 14 June 1692
No. 4263, Not. D. van der Groe, pp. 148–51, 24–25 Apr. 1697
No. 5715, Not. N. van Loosdreght, [unpaginated], 28 Sept. 1693
No. 5716, Not. N. van Loosdreght, [unpaginated], 7 Dec. 1693
No. 6054B, Not. P. Schabaelje, pp. 1841–4, 30 Sept. 1710
No. 6641, Not. G. van der Groe, pp. 959–65, 27 Oct. 1700
No. 6677A, Not. J. Snoeck, pp. 145–7, 22 Mar. 1702
No. 6684C, Not. J. Snoeck, p. 677, 6 Sept. 1709
No. 6684C, Not. J. Snoeck, pp. 1012–16, 5 Nov. 1709
No. 7355, no. 1874, Not. J. Valkenburg, 13 June 1710
No. 7490, no. 18, Not. J. van den Ende, 12 Mar. 1708
No. 7490, no. 19, Not. J. van den Ende, 12 Mar. 1708
No. 7490, no. 52, Not. J. van den Ende, 28 Sept. 1708
No. 7493, no. 63, Not. J. van den Ende, 10 Aug. 1717

No. 7493, no. 75, Not. J. van den Ende, 9 Dec. 1717
No. 7530, Not. J. van Vilekens, pp. 737–8, 26 June 1707
No. 7531, Not. J. van Vilekens, p. 141, 21 Feb. 1708
No. 7531, Not. J. van Vilekens, p. 449, 28 June 1708
No. 7533, Not. J. van Vilekens, pp. 81–2, 17 Jan. 1710
No. 7533, Not. J. van Vilekens, pp. 257–60, 12 Mar. 1710
No. 7533, Not. J. van Vilekens, pp. 901–2, 8 Sept. 1710
No. 7533, Not. J. van Vilekens, pp. 997–9, 30 Sept. 1710
No. 7533, Not. J. van Vilekens, pp. 1197–1202, 31 Oct. 1710
No. 7570, no. 154, Not. J. van Vilekens, 3 Dec. 1737
No. 7573B, no. 72, Not. J. van Vilekens, 6 July 1740
No. 7619, no. 300, Not. A. Tzeewen, 26 May 1723
No. 7660, no. 721, Not. A. Tzeewen, 17 Sept. 1733
No. 7667, no. 318, Not. A. Tzeewen, 4 June 1735
No. 7668, no. 468, Not. A. Tzeewen, 15 Aug. 1735
No. 7701, no. 23, Not. A. Tzeewen, 2 Feb. 1750
No. 8830, no. 777, Not. J. Barels de Jonge, 29 Oct. 1733
No. 10711, no. 13, Not. S. Dorper, 16 Jan. 1744
No. 10798, no. 847, Not. S. Dorper, 25 June 1762

Entry no. 15030: Library of the Amsterdam City Archives

No. 130527 Olivera, Abraham de, 'Tratado de la hobligaçion que todos tienen de dar limosna a los pobres', in Abraham Ydaña, *Tratado de Cosas Particulares . . .* (Amsterdam, 1686), 1–11

SAA DTB: Registers of Baptism, Marriage, and Burial
(Doop-, Trouw- en Begrafenisregisters)

674, p. 60, 11 Oct. 1635
674, p. 264, 30 Sept. 1637
677, p. 254, 26 Aug. 1644
680, p. 20, 14 Aug. 1648
680, p. 122, 8 June 1649
681, p. 142, 19 Oct. 1651
681, p. 150, 24 Nov. 1651
683, p. 103, 30 Nov. 1656
684, p. 377, 26 Nov. 1660
684, p. 351, 17 Sept. 1660
685, p. 5, 30 Dec. 1660
685, p. 134, 20 Jan. 1662
686, p. 32, 17 Jan. 1664
686, p. 345, 7 May 1666
687, p. 161, 10 Feb. 1668
687, p. 228, 20 July 1668
687, p. 273, 10 Nov. 1668
687, p. 283, 14 Dec. 1668
687, p. 285, 21 Dec. 1668
687, p. 302, 25 Jan. 1669
688, p. 2, 16 Aug. 1669
688, p. 8, 30 Aug. 1669
688, p. 13, 13 Sept. 1669
688, p. 101, 13 June 1670
688, p. 102, 13 June 1670
688, p. 259, 28 Aug. 1671
688, p. 287, 13 Nov. 1671
689, p. 198, 13 Apr. 1674

689, p. 250, 31 Aug. 1674
690, p. 181, 17 Apr. 1676
691, p. 22, 4 June 1677
691, p. 34, 24 June 1677
691, p. 38, 2 July 1677
691, p. 53, 27 Aug. 1677
691, p. 153, 9 Sept. 1678
691, p. 164, 14 Oct. 1678
691, p. 244, 7 July 1679
693, p. 4, 10 Oct. 1681
693, p. 65, 13 Feb. 1682
693, p. 173, 11 July 1682
693, p. 361, 14 May 1683
693, p. 415, 28 Aug. 1683
693, p. 426, 15 Sept. 1683
693, p. 427, 17 Sept. 1683
693, p. 460, 5 Nov. 1683
693, p. 468, 26 Nov. 1683
694, p. 107, 12 May 1684
694, p. 126, 9 June 1684
694, p. 150, 23 July 1684
694, p. 154, 29 July 1684
694, p. 176, 8 Sept. 1684
694, p. 216, 27 Oct. 1684
694, p. 235, 1 Dec. 1664
695, p. 33, 25 Aug. 1685
695, p. 68, 26 Oct. 1685
695, p. 79, 16 Nov. 1685
695, p. 148, 5 Apr. 1686
695, p. 194, 31 May 1686
695, p. 243, 7 Sept. 1686
695 p. 243, 13 Sept. 1686
695, p. 410, 5 June 1687
695, p. 454, 12 Sept. 1687
696, p. 86, 2 Apr. 1688
696, p. 155, 2 July 1688
696, p. 265, 18 Mar. 1689
696, p. 371, 9 Sept. 1689
696, p. 425, 13 Jan. 1690
697, p. 15, 13 Oct. 1690
697, p. 102, 30 Mar. 1691
697, p. 153, 25 May 1691
697, p. 166, 16 June 1691
697, p. 437, 14 Nov. 1692
698, p. 20, 23 Jan. 1693
698, p. 183, 6 Nov. 1693
699, p. 7, 18 Mar. 1695
699, p. 51, 6 May 1695
699, p. 70, 13 May 1695
699, p. 106, 22 July 1695
699, p. 159, 28 Oct. 1695
699, p. 261, 6 Apr. 1696
699, p. 371, 22 Sept. 1696
700, p. 4, 26 Oct. 1696
700, p. 173, 10 Aug. 1697
700, p. 245, 13 Dec. 1697
701, p. 4, 7 June 1698
701, p. 256, 28 Aug. 1699
701, p. 314, 2 Jan. 1700
702, p. 309, 26 Aug. 1701
702, p. 93, 27 Aug. 1700
702, p. 384, 23 Dec. 1701
703, p. 21, 25 Feb. 1702
703, p. 91, 27 May 1702
703, p. 154, 20 Oct. 1702
703, p. 233, 23 Feb. 1703
704, p. 290, 6 Mar. 1705
705, p. 58, 6 Nov. 1705
706, p. 113, 2 Dec. 1707
706, p. 151, 27 Jan. 1708
707, p. 57, 6 June 1709
707, p. 375, 20 Nov. 1710
711, p. 17, 28 May 1717
711, p. 47, 13 Aug. 1717
711, p. 48, 1 Aug. 1717
713, p. 147, 30 Apr. 1722
713, p. 309, 7 Jan. 1723
713, p. 424, 3 June 1723
714, p. 108, 27 Jan. 1724
714, p. 126, 25 Feb. 1724
715, p. 384, 14 Nov. 1726
717, p. 418, 14 Apr. 1730

718, p. 336, 5 July 1731
722, p. 267, 22 Feb. 1737
726, p. 298, 1 Mar. 1743
727, p. 215, 12 June 1744
728, p. 475, 17 Feb. 1747
731, p. 288, 19 Mar. 1751
746, p. 68, 26 Apr. 1771
750, p. 88, 28 Nov. 1777
750, p. 152, 20 Feb. 1778
754, p. 115, 16 Feb. 1784

Amsterdam, Ets Haim/Livraria Montezinos

MS Ets Haim 48 D 43 'Dinero que el K,K, q D[s] Aug[te] tiene en si de que paga Reditas hasta sabat gadol de 5436'

MS Ets Haim 48 A 51, 10 Tevet 5439 Request Daniel Levi de Barrios

MS Ets Haim 48 D 9 Aboab, Ishack de Matatia, *Documentos para todo estado e ydade* (1685)

MS Ets Haim 48 D 9 Gomes de Souza, Pedro, 'Documentos a seu filho Bento' (Antwerpen, 1649), in Ishack de Matatia Aboab, *Documentos* (Amsterdam, 5445 [1685]), 18–21

MS Ets Haim 48 B 8 Saruco, Selomoh, *Caminho de Vidas composto por o Hazan Selomoh Saruco Para emcaminhar a seus Filhos na Virtude* (The Hague, 5520 [1760])

MS Ets Haim 48 D 43, pp. 35–8, 19 Sivan 5435: 'Memoria delos mosos solteros que ay en la Nacion de 13 Años ariva, en 19 Sivan 5435', pp. 35–8

MS Ets Haim 31, 13 14, 'Proposta feita em Commitee que Se juntou em Consequencia da Resoluçao dos S[res] Velhos de 30 de Tisry 5508 & Methodo Submetido a o Examem de dittos S[res] para estabelecer Hum Hospital ou Enfermaria Para os Doentes Necessitados', pp. 1–26

MS Ets Haim 48 E 31 [enclosed] Request Semuel Lopes Henriquez [n.d.]

Royal Library (Koninklijke Bibliotheek), The Hague

485 L 20 Vaez, Abraham, *Arbol de vidas en el qual se contienen los dinim mas necessarios que deve observar todo Ysrael /sacados de varios graves autores* (Amsterdam, 1692)

Dutch National Archives (Nationaal Archief), The Hague

Entry no. 1.05.03: *Inventory of the Archives of the 'Sociëteit van Suriname'* (1650) 1682–1795 (1796) (*Inventaris van het archief van de Sociëteit van Suriname* (1650) 1682–1795 (1796))

No. 213 *Incoming letters and documents of the governor* 16 Nov. 1683–31 Dec. 1794

Municipal Archives, The Hague (Gemeentearchief Den Haag)

Entry no. 0351-01: *Judicial Archives* (Rechterlijke archieven)

No. 106, p. 27^{r-v}, 22 July 1675

No. 106, pp. 109–116^{v}, 6 Apr. 1690

No. 109, pp. 26–7, 16 Aug.–14 Sept. 1759
No. 110, pp. 1–6, 14–17 Apr. 1781
No. 110, pp. 15–16, 6 Dec. 1781

Entry no. 0372-01: *Archives of Notaries, The Hague I*
(Notarieel archief Den Haag I)

No. 2077, Not., J. Sijthoff, *last will of Benjamin Teixeira and Ribca Teixeira*, 16 Jan. 1744

Entry no. 0130-01: *Portuguese Jewish Community, The Hague* (1707) 1708–1941

No. 319, Not. J. Sijthoff, *last will of Marie Anne Josephe Therese de Partes, widow of Don Francisco Manrique*, 27 June 1746

Gemeentearchief, Rotterdam

Entry no. 15: *Board of Aldermen of Rotterdam*
(*Old Judicial Archives Rotterdam*) (College van Schepenen van Rotterdam, Oud Rechterlijk Archief Rotterdam)

No. 143, pp. 26^{v}–28^{v}, 3 Feb. 1707
No. 144, p. 274, 16 Mar. 1712
No. 144, p. 364, 16 Apr. 1712
No. 144, p. 407, 21 May 1712
No. 144, p. 434, 19 July 1712
No. 144, p. 475, 23 July 1712
No. 144, pp. 488–90, 30 July 1712
No. 145, p. 319, 19 May 1714
No. 145, pp. 82–3, 86–7, 11, 17, and 27 Apr. 1715
No. 149, pp. 249–62, 23 and 26 June 1734

Regionaal Archief, Leiden

Entry no. 508: *Old Judicial Archives* (Oud Rechterlijk Archief)

No. 44, p. 3, 19 July 1746

Madrid

Archivo Histórico Nacional (AHN)
Inq. Libro 1107, pp. 163^{r}–167^{v}, 30 Mar. 1635, XI

London

National Archives
Court of Chancery 32/218^{v}, 16 Aug. 1667

BIBLIOGRAPHY

Primary Sources

ABENDANA DE BRITTO, ISHAC HAIM, *Sermão exhortatorio pregado no K.K. de T.T. em Amsterdam Por o Doctissimo Senhor Haham Morenu A-Rab R. Ishac Haim Abendana de Britto, Ab Bet Din y Ros-Yessiba do Kahal Kados de Talmud Torah; em Sabat Echa, 4 Ab 5513* (Amsterdam, 1753).

ABENDANON, JOSEPH, *Sheloshah sarigim* (Amsterdam, copy dated 1716), appendix to D. Kaufmann, 'Joseph Ibn Danon de Belgrade', *Revue des Études Juives*, 37 (1898), 284–98.

ABOAB, ISHACK, *Almenara de la luz. Tratado de mvcho provecho para beneficio del alma. Compuesto en lengua Ebraica por el gran sabio Isaac Aboab; Trad. en lengua Bulgar para benefiçio comun por el haham Iahocob Hages* (Amsterdam, 5468 [1707/8]).

—— *De kandelaar des ligts met deszelfs zeven lampen, of het gewoon huisboek der hedendaagsche Joden; bevattende hunnen gantschen kerkelyken burgerlyken godsdienst, met alle deszelfs plegtigheden; en alomme vervuld met fraaye spreuken en gebeurtenissen der Talmudische Rabbynen/eertyds in het Rabbynsch beschreven door den Wereldvermaarden leeraar onder de Portugeesche Joden Isaac Abuabh; thans in het Nederduitsch vert., en met doorgaande aanm. verrykt, door Eliazar Soesman* (Amsterdam, 1756).

ABOAB, ISHACK DE MATATIA, *Documentos para todo estado e ydade* (5445 [1684/5]). MS EH 48 D 9. Ets Haim Library of the Portuguese community of Amsterdam.

AYLLON, SELOMOH, *Sermon, que predicó el Doctissimo Señor Haham Moreno A-Rab R. Selomoh Ailion Ab Bet-Din, y Ros-Yessiba del Kahal Kados de Talmud Torah en dia de Sabath Echá. Año 5483* (Amsterdam, 1722–3).

BARRIOS, DANIEL LEVI DE, *Triumpho del Govierno popular y de la Antiguedad Holandesa* (Amsterdam, 5443 [1683]). Copies in the University Library Amsterdam, Biblioteca Rosenthaliana RON A 5252, and Ets Haim/Montezinos Library 2 F 81.

BASS, SHABBETAI, *Sefer siftei yeshenim* (Amsterdam, 5440 [1680]).

BATISTA DE LANUZA, MARTÍN, *Tratado sobre el modo de distribuir y repartir la limosna con discreción, mérito y utilidad* ([n.p.] 1606).

BECK, DAVID, *Spiegel van mijn leven. Een Haags dagboek uit 1624*, introd. Sv. E. Veldhuizen (Hilversum, 1993).

CASTRO TARTAS, DAVID DE, *Sermões que Pregarão os Doctos Ingenios do K.K. de Talmud Torah desta Cidade de Amsterdam* (Amsterdam, 5435 [1675]).

COHEN, MOSES, *Et sofer* (Fürth, 1691).

COHEN PIMENTEL, ABRAHAM, *Questoens & discursos academicos que compoz e recitou na Illustre Academia Keter Thora* (Amsterdam, 5448 [1687/8]).

COMMELIN, CASPARUS, *Beschryving der Stadt Amsterdam* (Amsterdam, 1693).

CUENQUE, ABRAHAM BEN LEVI, *Sefer avak soferim* (Amsterdam, 1704).

Elogios que zelosos dedicaron a la felice memoria de Abraham Nuñes Bernal, que fue quemado vivo santificado el nombre de su Criador en Cordova a 3 de Mayo 5415 (Amsterdam, 1655).

FARRET, JOHANNES PETRUS, A. G. VERSTER, and JOHANNES HENRICUS VAN SWINDEN, *Rapport over de telling van het volk van Amsterdam, overgegeeven aan de representanten van het zelve volk, op den 20sten october 1795* (Amsterdam, 1795).

FRANCO MENDES, DAVID, *Memorias do estabelecimento e progresso dos judeos portuguezes e espanhoes nesta famosa citade de Amsterdam*, ed. Lajb Fuks and Renate G. Fuks-Mansfeld; commentary Benjamin N. Teensma (Assen, 1975).

FREDERIKS, JOHANNES GODEFRIDUS, and PIETER JACOBUS FREDERIKS (eds.), *Kohier van den tweehonderdsten penning van Amsterdam en onderhorige plaatsen over 1631* (Amsterdam, 1890).

GIGINTA, MIGUEL DE, *Tratado de remedio de pobres* (Coimbra, 1579), ed. Félix Santolaria Sierra (Barcelona, 2000).

GOMES DE SOUZA, PEDRO, 'Documentos a seu filho Bento' (Antwerp, 1649), in Ishack de Matatia Aboab, *Documentos* (Amsterdam, 5445), 18–21. MS EH 48 D 9.

HAGIZ, MOSES, *Sefat emet* (Amsterdam, 1697).

Handvesten ofte privilegiën ende Octroyen mitsgaders Willekeuren, Costuimen, Ordonnantien en Handelingen der stad Amstelredam, ed. Hermanus Noordkerk and Johan Pieter Farret, 5 vols. (Amsterdam, 1748–78).

HERRERA, CRISTÓBAL PÉREZ DE, *Discursos para el amparo de los legítimos pobres, y reducción de los fingidos: y de la fundación y principio de los Albergues destos Reynos y amparo de la milicia de ellos* (Madrid, 1598); ed., with introduction and notes, Michel Cavillac (Madrid, 1975).

Hollandtse Mercurius [newspaper] (1656).

ISRAEL, MENASSEH BEN, *De la fragilidad humana y inclinacion del hombre al peccado* (Amsterdam, 5402 [1642]).

—— *Thesovro dos dinim, que o povo de Israel he obrigado saber e observar*, 5 vols.: vols. i–iv, pp. 1–625 (Amsterdam, 5405 [1645]); vol. v, pp. 1–210 (Amsterdam 5407 [1647]).

LETI, GREGORIO, *Teatro Belgico, o vero ritratti historici, chronologici, politici, e geografici, della sette Provincie Unite*, 2 vols. (Amsterdam, 1690).

Livros pertenecentes a sancta irmandade de Abi Jetomim (Amsterdam, 5577 [1816/17]) (SAA entry no. 334.A, supplement no. 195^{r}).

LOPEZ LAGUNA, DAVID ISRAEL, *Espejo fiel de vidas, que contiene los psalmos de David en verso* (London, 5480 [1719/20]).

MAIMONIDES, MOSES BEN MAIMON, *Mishneh torah*, ed. Nachum E. Rabinovitch, 2 vols. (Ma'aleh Adumim, Israel, 2007).

MEZA, ABRAHAM HAIM DE, *Meditaçoens Sacras ou sermoens varios compostos e recitados neste K.K. de T.T. por o insigne H.H.R. Abraham Haim de Jahacob de Selomoh de Meza. Primeira parte contem XII sermoens* (Amsterdam, 5524 [1763/4]).

—— *Sermão moral que pregou o insigne H.H.R. Abraham Haim de Jahacob de Selomoh de Meza no K.K. de T.T. em Sabath Matot e Masei*, 28 Tamuz 5510 (Amsterdam, 1750).

—— *Sermão moral que pregou o insigne H.H.R. Abraham Haim de Jahacob de Selomoh de Meza no K.K. de T.T. em Sabath Matot e Masei*, 26 Tamuz 5512 (Amsterdam, 1752).

Nederlandsche Jaerboeken inhoudende een Verhael van de Merkwaerdigste Geschiedenissen die voorgevallen zijn binnen den omtrek der Vereenigde Provintien sederd het begin van 't Jaer MDCCXLVII, 2 vols.: vol. i, Jan.–June 1747; vol. ii, July–Dec. 1747 (Amsterdam, 1748).

NUNES TORRES, DAVID, 'Sermam funeral e panegirico A Vida e Virtudes da muy Ilustre Senhora Sara de Pinto, prégado em 2 de Tebeth do Anno 5446, Dedicado Aos magnificos Senhores Iahacob e Moseh de Pinto', in *Sermoens de David Nunes Torres Pregador da celebre irmandade de Abi Jetomim* (Amsterdam, 5450 [1689/90]).

OLIVERA, ABRAHAM DE, *Tratado de la hobligaçion que todos tienen de dar limosna a los pobres . . . Bordeos* (Bordeaux, 5421 [1661]), in Abraham Ydaña, *Tratado de Cosas Particulares . . .* (Amsterdam, 1686), 1–11. MS SAA entry no. 15030, no. 130527.

OLIVEYRA, FRANCISCO XAVIER DE, *Memorias das Viagens de Francisco Xavier de Oliveyra . . .* (Amsterdam, 1741).

PAKUDA, BAHYA BEN JOSEPH IBN, *Duties of the Heart*, trans. from Arabic into Hebrew by Judah ibn Tibbon; trans. into English by David Haberman, 2 vols. (Jerusalem, 1996).

—— *Hobat Alebabot, Obrigaçam Dos Coraçoens, Livro Moral de grande erudiçaõ & pia doctrina. Composto na Lingua Arabica pello devoto Rabbenu Bahie o Daian . . . dos famosos Sabios de Espanha e traduzido na lingua Santa pelo Insigne Rabi Jeuda Aben Tibon E agora novamente tirado da Hebraica â Lingua Portugueza para util dos da nossa Naçam com estilo façil e intelligivel per Semuel filho de Ishac Abaz de boa memoria* (Amsterdam, 5430 [1669/70]).

—— *Libro intitulado 'Obligacion de los Coracones' . . . traduzido, agora de nuevo de Haebraico en lengua Española por David Pardo, hijo del haham Ioseh Pardo* (Amsterdam, 5370 [1609/10]).

PEREYRA, ABRAHAM, *La Certeza del Camino* (Amsterdam, 1666), *see* Méchoulan, *Hispanidad y Judaísmo*.

—— *Espejo de la Vanidad del Mundo* (Amsterdam, 5431 [1671]).

PINTO, ISHAC DE, *Reflexoens Politicas tocante á Constituiçam da Naçam Judaica, Exposiçam do estado de suas Finanças, causas dos atrasos, e desordens que se experimentam, e meyos de os prevenir* (Amsterdam, 5508 [1748]).

Pirke Aboth, ed. with introd. and notes Benzion Dinur (Jerusalem, 1972).

Portugeesch-Israelietisch Meisjes-Weeshuis 'Mazon Habanoth' Amsterdam 5494/1734 6 Sebath 5694/1934, introd. J. Mendes da Costa (Amsterdam, 1934).

Reglement voor het Broederschap van het Weesjongens-Huis der Nederlandsche Portugeesche Israëlietische Gemeente te Amsterdam genaamd Aby Yetomim (Amsterdam, 1817).

SALEM, SELOMOH, *Sermón reprehensible que predico el Doctissimo Sr Haham Morenu Verabenu R. Selomoh Salem Ab Bet-Din, y Ros Jeschiba del K.K. de Talmud Tora En Sabat Echá, 9 Ab, Ano 5525* (Amsterdam, 1765).

t' Samen-spraeck tusschen een Dortsman en een Amsterdammer sijnde den lesten uyt sijn Vader-Stadt gevlucht, wegens de groote, ende af-schrickelijcke pestilentiale sterfte binnen ghemelde Stadt Amsterdam (Amsterdam, 1664).

SARUCO, SELOMOH, *Caminho de Vidas composto por o Hazan Selomoh Saruco Para emcaminhar a seus Filhos na Virtude* (The Hague, 5520 [1759/60]). MS EH 48 B 8.

SILVA, HESQIA DA, *Sefer peri hadas* (Amsterdam, 1692).

—— *Sermon Moral del Fundamento de nuestra ley predicado En esta ilustre Congrega de T.T. en 18 de Hesvan 5451 Por El muy celebre Haham R. Hesqia da Silva, Embiado de Yerusalaim* (Amsterdam, 1690).

SOTO, DOMINGUO DE, *Deliberación en la causa de pobres* (Salamanca, 1545; repr. Madrid, 1965).

Statistische Mededeeling van het Bureau van Statistiek der Gemeente Amsterdam 1894–1934. De bevolking van Amsterdam, ii (*De uitkomsten van tienjaarlijksche volkstellingen van 1830 tot 1930*) (Amsterdam, 1934).

TRUJILLO, TOMÁS DE, *Tratado de la limosna* (Estella, 1563).

VAEZ, ABRAHAM, *Arbol de vidas en el qual se contienen los dinim mas necessarios que deve observar todo Ysrael/sacados de varios graves autores* (Amsterdam, 1692). Copy in Koninklijke Bibliotheek, The Hague, 485 L 20.

VIVES, JUAN LUIS, *De subventione pauperum*, 2 vols. (Brugge, 1526); Latin edn.: Armando Saitta, *De subventione pauperum* (Florence, 1973).

WAGENAAR, JAN, *Amsterdam in zijne opkomst, aanwas, geschiedenissen, voorregten, koophandel, gebouwen, kerkenstaat, schoolen, schutterye, gilden en regeeringe*, 4 vols. (Amsterdam, 1760–8).

Secondary Literature

ABRAHAMS, ISRAEL, *Jewish Life in the Middle Ages*, 1st Dover edn. (New York, 2004).

ADELMAN, HOWARD T., 'Jewish Women and Family Life, Inside and Outside the Ghetto', in Robert C. Davis and Benjamin C. I. Ravid (eds.), *The Jews of Early Modern Venice* (Baltimore, 2001), 143–65.

—— 'Servants and Sexuality: Seduction, Surrogacy and Rape; Some Observations Concerning Class, Gender and Race in Early Modern Italian Jewish Families', in Tamar M. Rudavsky (ed.), *Gender and Judaism: The Transformation of Tradition* (New York, 1995), 81–97.

ADLER, ELKAN N., 'Hebrew Elegies on English Monarchs', *Transactions of the Jewish Historical Society of England*, 2 (1894–5), 141–7.

—— *Jewish Travellers: A Treasury of Travelogues from 9 Centuries* (New York, 1966).

AELION BROOKS, ANDRÉE, *The Woman who Defied Kings: The Life and Times of Don Gracia Nasi—a Jewish Leader during the Renaissance* (St Paul, Minn., 2002).

AGUADO DE LOS REYES, JESÚS, *Riqueza y sociedad en la Sevilla del siglo XVII* (Seville, 1994).

ALTMANN, ALEXANDER, 'Eternality of Punishment: A Theological Controversy within the Amsterdam Rabbinate in the Thirties of the Seventeenth Century', *Proceedings of the American Academy for Jewish Research*, 40 (1972), 1–88.

ANCONA, JOSEPH D', 'Komst der Marranen in Noord-Nederland: De Portugese gemeenten te Amsterdam tot de vereniging (1639)', in Hendrik Brugmans and Abraham Frank (eds.), *Geschiedenis der Joden in Nederland* (Amsterdam, 1940), 201–69.

—— 'De Portugese gemeente "Talmoed Tora" te Amsterdam tot 1795', in Hendrik Brugmans and Abraham Frank (eds.), *Geschiedenis der Joden in Nederland* (Amsterdam, 1940), 270–305.

ANDREW, DONNA T., 'On Reading Charity Sermons: Eighteenth Century Anglican Solicitation and Exhortation', *Journal of Ecclesiastical History*, 43/4 (1992), 581–91.

ARBELL, MORDEHAY, 'The Failure of the Jewish Settlement in the Island of Tobago', *Proceedings of the XIth World Congress of Jewish Studies*, Div. B History, 3 (Jerusalem, 1994), 303–10.

—— 'The Jewish Settlement in Poomeroon/Pavroma (Guyana), 1657–1666', *Revue des Études Juives*, 154 (1995), 343–61.

—— 'Jewish Settlements in the French Colonies in the Caribbean (Martinique, Guadeloupe, Haiti, Cayenne) and the "Black Code"', in Paolo Bernardini and Norman Fiering (eds.), *The Jews and the Expansion of Europe to the West 1450 to 1800* (New York, 2001), 287–313.

—— *The Portuguese Jews of Jamaica* (Jamaica, 2000).

ARCO, RICARDO DEL, 'Una notable institución social: el Padre de Huérfanos', *Estudios de Historia Social de España*, 3 (1955), 189–222.

ARIÈS, PHILIPPE, *L'Enfant et la vie familiale sous l'Ancien Régime*, 2nd edn. (Paris, 1973).

—— *L'Homme devant la mort* (Paris, 1977).

ARNHEIM, ARTHUR, 'Hamburg/Altona-Copenhagen', in *Jewish Studies in a New Europe*, Proceedings of the Fifth Congress of Jewish Studies, Copenhagen, 1994 (Copenhagen, 1998), 39–44.

ARRIZABALAGA, JON, 'Poor Relief in Counter-Reformation Castile: An Overview', in Ole P. Grell, Andrew Cunningham, and Jon Arrizabalaga (eds.), *Health Care and Poor Relief in Counter-Reformation Europe* (London, 1999), 151–76.

ASHTOR, ELIYAHU, *The Jews of Moslem Spain*, 3 vols. (Philadelphia, 1973–84).

ASSIS, YOM TOV, *The Golden Age of Aragonese Jewry: Community and Society in the Crown of Aragon 1213–1327* (London, 1997).

—— 'Les Institutions sociales médiévales: Les Logiques de la charité collective et de l'association', in Shmuel Trigano (ed.), *La Société juive à travers l'histoire*, vol. ii (Paris, 1992), 181–217.

—— 'Welfare and Mutual Aid in the Spanish Jewish Communities', in Haim Beinart (ed.), *Moreshet Sepharad: The Sephardi Legacy*, vol. i (Jerusalem, 1992), 318–45.

AZEVEDO, JOÃO L. DE, *História dos Christãos Novos portugueses*, 2nd edn. (Lisbon, 1975).

BACKHAUS, FRITZ, 'Im Heckhus die Lahmen, Blinden und Hungerleider . . . Die sozialen Institutionen in der Frankfurter Judengasse', in Stefi Jersch-Wenzel, François Guesnet, Gertrud Pickhan, Andreas Reinke, and Desanka Schwara (eds.), *Juden und Armut in Mittel- und Osteuropa* (Cologne, 2000).

BAER, YITZHAK, *A History of the Jews in Christian Spain*, trans. from the Hebrew by Louis Schoffman, 2 vols. (Philadelphia, 1978).

—— 'The Origins of the Organization of the Jewish Community of the Middle Ages', *Tsiyon*, 15 (1950), pp. I–II (Eng.), 1–41 (Heb.).

—— 'Der Ursprung der Chewra', *Zeitschrift für jüdische Wohlfahrtspflege. Herausgegeben von der Zentralwohlfahrtsstelle der Deutschen Juden*, 1 (1929), 241–7.

BAKKER, JOHAN DE, 'Slaves, Arms and Holy War: Moroccan Policy vis-à-vis the Dutch Republic during the Establishment of the 'Alawī Dynasty (1660–1727)', Ph.D. diss., University of Amsterdam, 1991.

BARNAI, JACOB, 'The Jews of the Ottoman Empire', in Haim Beinart (ed.), *Moreshet Sepharad: The Sephardi Legacy*, vol. ii (Jerusalem, 1992), 134–65.

—— *The Jews in Palestine in the Eighteenth Century under the Patronage of the Istanbul Committee of Officials for Palestine*, trans. Naomi Goldblum (Tuscaloosa, Ala., 1992).

—— 'The Jews of Spain in North Africa', in Haim Beinart (ed.), *Moreshet Sepharad: The Sephardi Legacy*, vol. ii (Jerusalem, 1992), 68–72.

BARNETT, LIONEL D., *Bevis Marks Records* (Oxford, 1940).

—— *El Libro de los Acuerdos: Being the Records and Accompts of the Spanish and Portuguese Synagogue of London* (Oxford, 1931).

BARNETT, RICHARD D., 'The Correspondence of the Mahamad of the Spanish and Portuguese Congregation of London during the Seventeenth and Eighteenth Centuries', *Transactions of the Jewish Historical Society of England*, 20 (1964), 1–50.

—— 'Diplomatic Aspects of the Sephardic Influx from Portugal in the Early Eighteenth Century', *Transactions of the Jewish Historical Society of England*, Miscellanies pt. 10 (1977), 210–21.

—— 'Dr. Jacob de Castro Sarmento and Sephardim in Medical Practice in 18th Century London', *Transactions of the Jewish Historical Society of England*, 27 (1982), 84–114.

—— 'Dr. Samuel Nunes Ribeiro and the Settlement of Georgia', in *Migration and Settlement*, Proceedings of the Anglo-American Jewish Historical Conference, London, July 1970 (London, 1971), 82–101.

BARON, SALO W. *The Jewish Community: Its History and Structure to the American Revolution*, 2nd edn., 3 vols. (Philadelphia, 1945).

BARTAL, ISRAEL, and YOSEF KAPLAN, 'Emigration of Indigent Jews from Amsterdam to Erets Yisra'el (Palestine) at the Beginning of the Seventeenth Century' (Heb.), *Shalem*, 6 (1992), 177–93.

BASHAN, ELIEZER, 'Jewish Moneylending in Constantinople and Smyrna during the 17th and 18th Centuries as Reflected in the British Levant Company's Archives', in Ariel Toaff and Simon Schwarzfuchs (eds.), *The Mediterranean and the Jews: Banking, Finance and International Trade (XVI–XVIII Centuries)* (Ramat Gan, 1989), 57–73.

—— 'The Rise and Decline of the Sephardi Communities in the Levant: Economic Aspects', in Richard D. Barnett and Walter M. Schwab (eds.), *The Sephardi Heritage: Essays on the History and Cultural Contribution of the Jews of Spain and Portugal*, vol. ii (Grendon, 1989), 349–88.

BASKIN, JUDITH R., 'Jewish Women in the Middle Ages', in ead. (ed.), *Jewish Women in Historical Perspective*, 2nd edn. (Detroit, 1998), 101–27.

BATAILLON, MARCEL, *Érasme et l'Espagne*, 3rd edn. (Geneva, 1991).

BECKERMAN, WILFRED, 'The Measurement of Poverty', in Thomas Riis (ed.), *Aspects of Poverty in Early Modern Europe* (Alphen aan den Rijn, 1981), 47–63.

BEIER, A. L., *The Problem of the Poor in Tudor and Early Stuart England* (London, 1983).

BEINART, HAIM, 'The Exodus of Conversos from the Iberian Peninsula in the Fifteenth to Seventeenth Centuries' (Heb.), in Robert Bonfil (ed.), *Scritti in memoria di Umberto Nahon* (Jerusalem, 1978), 63–106.

—— 'The Movement of Jews from Morocco to Spain at the Beginning of the Seventeenth Century' (Heb.), in *Salo Wittmayer Baron Jubilee Volume* [Sefer hayovel le-s. r. baron], vol. iii (Jerusalem, 1975), 15–39.

—— (ed.), *Moreshet Sepharad: The Sephardi Legacy*, 2 vols. (Jerusalem, 1992).

BEINART KAPLAN, YAEL, 'A Bibliography of the Writings of Haim Beinart' (Heb.), in Aharon Mirsky, Avraham Grossman, and Yosef Kaplan (eds.), *Exile and Diaspora: Studies in the History of the Jewish People Presented to Professor Haim Beinart on the Occasion of his Seventieth Birthday* [Galut aḥar golah: meḥkarim betoledot am yisra'el mugashim leprofesor haim beinart lemelo't lo shiviim shanah] (Jerusalem, 1988), 583–98.

BEN-NAEH, YARON, *Jews in the Realm of the Sultans: Ottoman Jewish Society in the Seventeenth Century* (Tübingen, 2008).

—— 'Poverty, Paupers and Poor Relief in Ottoman Jewish Society', *Revue des Études Juives*, 163 (2004), 151–92.

BENADY, TITO, 'The Jewish Community of Gibraltar', in Richard D. Barnett and Walter M. Schwab (eds.), *The Sephardi Heritage: Essays on the History and Cultural Contribution of the Jews of Spain and Portugal*, vol. ii (Grendon, 1989), 144–79.

BENAYAHU, MEIR, 'History of the Rabbinical Colleges in Jerusalem in the Seventeenth Century' (Heb.), *Hebrew Union College Annual*, 21 (1948), 1–28.

BENBASSA, ESTHER, and ARON RODRIGUE, *Sephardi Jewry: A History of the Judeo-Spanish Community, 15th to 20th Centuries* (Berkeley, 2000).

BENNASSAR, BARTOLOMÉ, *The Spanish Character: Attitudes and Mentalities from the Sixteenth to the Nineteenth Century* (Berkeley, 1979).

BERG, WILLEM VAN DEN, MARCO H. D. VAN LEEUWEN, and CLEMENS M. LESGER, 'Residentiële segregatie in Hollandse steden: Theorie, methodologie en empirische bevindingen voor Alkmaar en Amsterdam 16e–19e eeuw', *Tijdschrift voor Sociale Geschiedenis*, 24/4 (1998), 402–36.

BERGER, SHLOMO, 'Ashkenazim Read Sephardim in Seventeenth- and Eighteenth-Century Amsterdam', *Studia Rosenthaliana*, 35/2 (2001), 253–65.

—— *Classical Oratory and the Sephardim of Amsterdam: Rabbi Aquilar's 'Tratado de la Retorica'* (Hilversum, 1996).

BERGHE, PIERRE L. VAN DEN, *Race and Ethnicity* (New York, 1970).

BERGMAN, JEHUDAH, *Tsedakah in Israel: Its History and Institutions* [Hatsedakah beyisra'el: toledoteiha umosadoteiha], 2nd edn. (Jerusalem, 5735 [1975]).

BERKVENS-STEVELINCK, CHRISTIANE M. G., JONATHAN I. ISRAEL, and GUILLAUME H. M. POSTHUMUS MEYJES, *The Emergence of Tolerance in the Dutch Republic* (Leiden, 1997).

BIERENS DE HAAN, JACOB, *De Nederlandsche strafbepalingen tegen bedelarij en landlooperij: een historisch, statistisch en kritisch onderzoek* (Utrecht, 1895).

BILINKOFF, JODI, 'Elite Widows and Religious Expression in Early Modern Spain: The View from Avila', in Sandra Cavallo and Lyndan Warner (eds.), *Widowhood in Medieval and Early Modern Europe* (Harlow, Essex, 1999), 181–92.

BIRD, FREDERICK B., 'A Comparative Study of the Work of Charity in Christianity and Judaism', *Journal of Religious Ethics*, 10 (1982), 144–69.

BLACK, CHRISTOPHER F., *Early Modern Italy: A Social History* (London, 2001).

—— *Italian Confraternities in the Sixteenth Century* (1989; repr. Cambridge, 2003).

BLOCKMANS, WIM, 'Circumscribing the Concept of Poverty', in Thomas Riis (ed.), *Aspects of Poverty in Early Modern Europe* (Alphen aan den Rijn, 1981), 39–45.

BLOEMGARTEN, S. E., 'De Amsterdamse Joden gedurende de eerste jaren van de Bataafse Republiek (1795–1798)', *Studia Rosenthaliana*, 1/1 (1967), 66–96.

BLOM, J. C. H., RENATE G. FUKS-MANSFELD, and IVO SCHÖFFER (eds.), *The History of the Jews in The Netherlands*, trans. Arnold J. Pomerans and Erica Pomerans (Oxford, 2002).

BLOOM, HERBERT I., *The Economic Activities of the Jews of Amsterdam in the Seventeenth and Eighteenth Century* (Williamsport, Pa., 1937).

BLUMENKRANZ, BERNHARD, *Documents modernes sur les Juifs, XVIe–XXe siècles* (Toulouse, 1979).

BODIAN, MIRIAM, 'Amsterdam, Venice and the Marrano Diaspora', in Jozeph Michman (ed.), *Dutch Jewish History*, vol. ii (Jerusalem, 1989), 47–65.

—— 'The Escamot of the Spanish-Portuguese Jewish Community of London, 1664', *Michael*, 9 (1985), 9–42.

—— *Hebrews of the Portuguese Nation: Conversos and Community in Early Modern Amsterdam* (Bloomington, 1997).

—— 'The Portuguese Dowry Societies in Venice and Amsterdam: A Case Study in Communal Differentiation within the Marrano Diaspora', *Italia*, 6 (1987), 30–61.

BOEKMAN, EMANUEL, 'De bevolking van Amsterdam in 1795', *Tijdschrift voor Geschiedenis*, 45 (1930), 278–92.

—— 'Demografische en sociale verhoudingen bij de joden te Amsterdam omstreeks 1800', *Vrijdagavond*, 6/5–7 (3, 10, and 17 May 1929), 72–4, 89–91, 103–6.

BOER, HARM DEN, *Bibliografía de los impresos en lenguas española y portuguesa de Holanda c. 1600–1800* (Leiden, 1985).

—— 'Exile in Sephardic Literature of Amsterdam', *Studia Rosenthaliana*, 35/2 (2001), 187–99.

—— *La literatura sefardí de Amsterdam* (Alcalá de Henares, 1995).

—— *Spanish and Portuguese Printing in the Northern Netherlands 1584–1825* (Leiden, 2003).

—— and HERMAN PRINS SALOMON, 'Haham David Nunes Torres (1660–1728), bezitter van het enig overgebleven exemplaar van Uriël da Costa's *Exame das tradições fariseas*', *Studia Rosenthaliana*, 28/1 (1994), 10–49.

BOER, PIM DEN, 'Naar een geschiedenis van de dood; mogelijkheden tot onderzoek naar de houding ten opzichte van de doden en de dood ten tijde van de Republiek', *Tijdschrift voor Geschiedenis*, 89 (1976), 161–201.

BÖHM, GÜNTER, 'Antijüdische Ressentiments gegenüber den Hamburger Sefardim im 17. Jahrhundert', in Michael Studemund-Halévy and Peter Koj (eds.), *Die Sefarden in Hamburg. Zur Geschichte einer Minderheit* (Hamburg, 1994), 89–101.

—— 'Die Sepharden in Hamburg', in A. Herzig and S. Rohde (eds.), *Die Juden in Hamburg 1590–1990: Wissenschaftliche Beiträge der Universität Hamburg zur Ausstellung 'Vierhundert Jahre Juden in Hamburg'* (Hamburg, 1991).

BOLLE, MENACHEM E., *De opheffing van de autonomie der kehilloth in Nederland* (Amsterdam, 1960).

BONFIL, ROBERTO, 'Halakhah, Kabbalah and Society: Some Insights into Rabbi Menahem Azariah da Fano's Inner World', in Isadore Twersky and Bernard Septimus (eds.), *Jewish Thought in the Seventeenth Century* (Cambridge, Mass., 1987).

—— 'The History of the Spanish and Portuguese Jews in Italy', in Haim Beinart (ed.), *Moreshet Sepharad: The Sephardi Legacy*, vol. ii (Jerusalem, 1992), 217–39.

—— *Jewish Life in Renaissance Italy* (Berkeley, 1994).

—— *Rabbis and Jewish Communities in Renaissance Italy*, trans. Jonathan Chipman (Oxford, 1990).

BONKE, HANS, 'Portugezen op Vlooyenburg', in Renée Kistemaker and Tirtsah Levie [Bernfeld] (eds.), *Êxodo, Portugezen in Amsterdam 1600–1680* (Amsterdam, 1987), 32–41.

BOOY, ENGELIN P. DE, *Kweekhoven der Wijsheid. Basis- en Vervolgonderwijs in de steden van de provincie Utrecht van 1580 tot het begin van de 19e eeuw* (Zutphen, 1980).

—— 'Naar school. Schoolgaande kinderen in de Noordelijke Nederlanden in de zeventiende en achttiende eeuw', *Tijdschrift voor Geschiedenis*, 94 (1981), 427–41.

—— *De Weldaet der Scholen: Het plattelandsonderwijs in de Provincie Utrecht van 1580 tot het begin van de 18e eeuw* (Bilthoven, 1977).

BORG, HELENA A. VAN DER, *Vroedvrouwen: Beeld en Beroep. Ontwikkeling in het vroedvrouwschap in Leiden, Arnhem, 's-Hertogenbosch en Leeuwarden 1650–1865* (Wageningen, 1992).

BORNSTEIN-MAZOVESKY, LEAH, 'Structure, Organization and Spiritual Life of the Sephardi Communities in the Ottoman Empire from the Sixteenth to Eighteenth Centuries', in Richard D. Barnett and Walter M. Schwab (eds.), *The Sephardi Heritage: Essays on the History and Cultural Contribution of the Jews of Spain and Portugal*, vol. ii (Grendon, 1989), 314–48.

BOS, SANDRA, 'Beroepsgebonden onderlinges 1500–1800: Gilden- en knechtsfondsen', in Jacobus L. J. M. van Gerwen and Marco H. D. van Leeuwen (eds.), *Studies over zekerheidsarrangementen: Risico's, risicobestrijding en verzekeringen in Nederland vanaf de Middeleeuwen* (Amsterdam, 1998), 91–140.

BOS, SANDRA, *'Uyt liefde tot malcander': Onderlinge hulpverlening binnen de Noord-Nederlandse gilden in internationaal perspectief (1570–1820)* (Amsterdam, 1998).

—— and IDA H. STAMHUIS, 'Begrafenis- en weduwenfondsen, en prebende sociëteiten', in Jacobus L. J. M. van Gerwen and Marco H. D. van Leeuwen (eds.), *Studies over zekerheidsarrangementen: Risico's, risicobestrijding en verzekeringen in Nederland vanaf de Middeleeuwen* (Amsterdam, 1998), 175–82.

BOSCH KEMPER, JERONIMO DE, *Geschiedkundig onderzoek naar de armoede in ons vaderland en de middelen, die tot hare vermindering zouden kunnen worden aangewend* (Haarlem, 1851).

BRADEN, JUTTA, *Hamburger Judenpolitik im Zeitalter Lutherisher Orthodoxie 1590–1710* (Hamburg, 2001).

BREEN, JOHANNES C., 'Collecten te Amsterdam in de Achttiende Eeuw', *Jaarboek Amstelodanum*, 5 (1907), 131–52.

BRINK, EDUARDUS A. B. J. TEN, *De geschiedenis van het postvervoer* (Bussum, 1969).

BROOKS, ROGER, *Support for the Poor in the Mishnaic Law of Agriculture: Tractate Peah* (Chicago, 1983).

BRUGMANS, HENDRIK, and ABRAHAM FRANK (eds.), *Geschiedenis der Joden in Nederland* (Amsterdam, 1940).

BRUIJN, JACOBUS R., 'De personeelsbehoefte van de VOC overzee en aan boord, bezien vanuit Aziatisch en Nederlands perspectief', *Bijdragen en Mededelingen betreffende de Geschiedenis der Nederlanden*, 91/2 (1976), 218–48.

BURNS, ROBERT I., *Jews in the Notarial Culture: Latinate Wills in Mediterranean Spain 1250–1350* (Berkeley, 1996).

BUTEL, PAUL, *Les Négociants bordelaises: L'Europe et les îles au XVIIIe siècle* (Paris, 1974).

—— *Vivre à Bordeaux sous l'Ancien Régime* (Paris, 1999).

CAILLÉ, JACQUES, *La Ville de Rabat jusqu'au protectorat français: Histoire et archéologie*, 3 vols. (Paris, 1949).

CALLAHAN, WILLIAM J., 'Corporate Charity in Spain: The Hermandad del Refugio of Madrid 1618–1814', *Histoire Sociale*, 9 (1976), 159–86.

—— 'A Note on the Real y General Junta de Comercio, 1679–1814', *Economic History Review*, 21/3 (1968), 519–28.

CANNY, NICHOLAS (ed.), *Europeans on the Move: Studies on European Migration 1500–1800* (Oxford, 1994).

—— 'In Search of a Better Home? European Overseas Migration 1500–1800', in id. (ed.), *Europeans on the Move: Studies on European Migration 1500–1800* (Oxford, 1994), 263–83.

CARASSO-KOK, MARIJKE, and CARRY VAN LAKERVELD, *De Amsterdamse Stadsbank van Lening* (Hilversum, 2009).

CARDOZO DE BÉTHENCOURT, L., 'Le Trésor des Juifs Sephardim', *Revue des Études Juives*, 25 (1892), 235–45.

CARLEBACH, ELISHEVA, *The Pursuit of Heresy: Rabbi Moses Hagiz and the Sabbatian Controversies* (New York, 1990).

CARO BAROJA, JULIO, *Los Judíos en la España moderna y contemporánea*, 2nd edn., 3 vols. (Madrid, 1978).

CARPI, DANIEL, 'The Activities of the Officials of the Sephardi Jewish Congregation in Venice for the Redemption of Captives (1654—1670)' (Heb.), *Tsiyon*, 68/3 (2003), 175–220.

CARRASCO, RAFAEL, 'Inquisición y judaizantes portugueses en Toledo (segunda mitad del siglo XVI)', *Revista Manuscrits*, 10 (1992), 41–60.

—— 'Preludio al "Siglo de los Portugueses": La Inquisición de Cuenca y los judaizantes lusitanos en el siglo XVI', *Hispania*, 47/166 (1987), 503–59.

CASEY, JAMES, *Early Modern Spain: A Social History* (London, 1999).

CAVALLO, SANDRA, *Charity and Power in Early Modern Italy: Benefactors and their Motives in Turin, 1541–1789* (Cambridge, 1995).

—— 'Conceptions of Poverty and Poor Relief in Turin in the Second Half of the Eighteenth Century', in Stuart Woolf (ed.), *Domestic Strategies: Work and Family in France and Italy 1600–1800* (Cambridge, 1991), 148–200.

CAVIGNAC, JEAN, 'L'Assistance chez les Juifs de Bordeaux au XVIIIe siècle', *Actes du 108e Congrès national des sociétés savantes: Colloque sur l'histoire de la sécurité sociale*, Grenoble, 5–7 Apr. 1983 (Paris, 1984), 27–35.

—— 'L'Immigration des Juifs portugais à Bordeaux au XVIIIe siècle', in *Les Relations entre le Sud-Ouest et la Peninsula Ibérique, Fédération historique du Sud-Ouest, Actes du 38e Congrès tenu à Pau* (Pau, 1985), 125–38.

CHAUNU, PIERRE, *La Mort à Paris, 16e, 17e, 18e siècles* (Paris, 1978).

CHOURAQUI, ANDRÉ, *Histoire des Juifs en Afrique du Nord* (Paris, 1985).

COATES, TIMOTHY J., *Convicts and Orphans: Forced and State-Sponsored Colonizers in the Portuguese Empire, 1550–1775* (Stanford, 2001).

COHEN, JULIE-MARTHE, 'The Inventory of Ceremonial Objects of the Portuguese Jewish Community of Amsterdam of 1640', *Studia Rosenthaliana*, 37 (2004), 225–307.

COHEN, MARK R., *Poverty and Charity in the Jewish Community of Medieval Egypt* (Princeton, 2005).

—— *The Voice of the Poor in the Middle Ages: An Anthology of Documents from the Cairo Geniza* (Princeton, 2005).

COHEN, ROBERT, *Jews in Another Environment: Surinam in the Second Half of the Eighteenth Century* (Leiden, 1991).

—— 'Passage to a New World: The Sephardi Poor of Eighteenth-Century Amsterdam', in Lea Dasberg and Jonathan N. Cohen (eds.), *Neveh Ja'akov: Jubilee Volume Presented to Dr Jaap Meijer* (Assen, 1982), 31–42.

COLEMAN, KENNETH, *Colonial Georgia: A History* (New York, 1976).

CONTRERAS, JAIME, *Cristianos de España y judíos de Amsterdam: Emigración, familia y negocios*, Diálogos Hispánicos 16 (Amsterdam, 1995), 187–211.

—— *El Santo Oficio de la Inquisición en Galicia, 1560–1700: poder, sociedad y cultura* (Madrid, 1982).

CORCOS, DAVID, 'The Jews of Morocco from the Expulsion of Spain until the Middle of the Sixteenth Century' (Heb.), in id. (ed.), *Studies in the History of the Jews of Morocco*, 318–258.

—— 'Les Juifs du Maroc et leurs Mellahs', in id. (ed.), *Studies in the History of the Jews of Morocco*, 64–130.

CORCOS, DAVID, 'Quelques aspects de la société juive dans le vieux Maroc: Les Prénoms des Juifs marocains', in id. (ed.), *Studies in the History of the Jews of Morocco*, 159–245.

—— 'Samuel Pallache and his London Trial' (Heb.), in id. (ed.), *Studies in the History of the Jews of Morocco*, 256–246.

—— *Studies in the History of the Jews of Morocco* [Yehudei maroco megerush sefarad ve ad emtsa shel ha me'ah hatet-zayin] (Jerusalem, 1976); pp. 1–50 (Eng.); pp. 64–245 (French); pp. 246–342 (Heb.).

COTTAAR, ANNEMARIE, JAN M. G. W. LUCASSEN, and LEO A. C. J. LUCASSEN, *Van over de grens: Gids voor lokaal historisch onderzoek naar immigratie in Nederland* (Utrecht, 1998).

CUNNINGHAM, HUGH, *The Children of the Poor: Representations of Childhood since the Seventeenth Century* (Oxford, 1991).

DAVID, ABRAHAM, 'Fifteenth and Sixteenth Century Pilgrim and Immigrant Journey Routes to the Land of Israel', in *Jewish Studies in a New Europe*, Proceedings of the Fifth Congress of Jewish Studies, Copenhagen, 1994 (Copenhagen, 1998), 163–74.

DAVIS, NATALIE ZEMON, *Fiction in the Archives: Pardon Tales and their Tellers in Sixteenth-Century France* (Cambridge, 1998).

—— *The Gift in Sixteenth-Century France* (Madison, Wis., 2000).

—— 'Glikl Bas Judah Leib: Arguing with God', in ead., *Women on the Margins: Three Seventeenth-Century Lives* (Cambridge, Mass., 1995), 5–62.

—— 'Poor Relief, Humanism and Heresy', in ead., *Society and Culture in Early Modern France* (Stanford, 1975), 17–64.

—— 'The Sacred and the Body Social in Sixteenth-Century Lyon', *Past and Present*, 90 (1981), 40–70.

—— 'Women in the Crafts in Sixteenth-Century Lyon', in Barbara A. Hanawalt (ed.), *Women and Work in Pre-Industrial Europe* (Bloomington, 1986), 167–97.

DEFOURNEAUX, MARCELIN, *Daily Life in Spain in the Golden Age* (Stanford, 1979).

DEKKER, RUDOLF M., *Holland in Beroering: Oproeren in de 17e en 18e eeuw* (Baarn, 1982).

—— *Uit de schaduw in 't grote licht. Kinderen in egodocumenten van de Gouden Eeuw tot de Romantiek* (Amsterdam, 1995).

—— and LOTTE C. VAN DE POL, *The Tradition of Female Transvestism in Early Modern Europe* (New York, 1989).

DETCHEVERRY, ARNAUD, *Histoire des Israélites de Bordeaux* (Bordeaux, 1850).

DEURSEN, ARIE TH. VAN, *Bavianen en Slijkgeuzen: Kerk en Kerkvolk ten tijde van Maurits en Oldebarnevelt*, 3rd edn. (Franeker, 1998).

—— *Een dorp in de polder. Graft in de zeventiende eeuw* (Amsterdam, 1994).

—— *Plain Lives in a Golden Age: Popular Culture, Religion and Society in Seventeenth-Century Holland* (Cambridge, 1991).

DIAMOND, ARTHUR S., 'The Community of Resettlement, 1656–1684: A Social Survey', *Transactions of the Jewish Historical Society of England*, 24 (1974), 134–50.

DILLEN, JOHANNES G. VAN, 'De economische positie en betekenis der joden in de

Republiek en in de Nederlandse koloniale wereld', in Hendrik Brugmans and Abraham Frank (eds.), *Geschiedenis der Joden in Nederland* (Amsterdam, 1940), 561–616.

DIVENDAL, JOOST, 'Mozes Cohen Belinfante: Jew to the Depth of his Soul', *Studia Rosenthaliana*, 31/1–2 (1997), 94–138.

DODDE, NANTKO L., 'Joods Onderwijs in Nederland van 1815 tot 1940', in Hetty Berg (ed.), *De Gelykstaat der Joden: Inburgering van een minderheid* (Amsterdam, 1996), 67–80.

DOMÍNGUEZ ORTIZ, ANTONIO, *La clase social de los conversos en la edad moderna* (Madrid, 1955).

—— *The Golden Age of Spain 1516–1659* (London, 1971).

—— *Los Judeoconversos en España y América* (Madrid, 1971).

—— *Política y hacienda de Felipe IV* (Madrid, 1960).

—— *La sociedad española en el siglo XVII*, 2 vols. (Madrid, 1964–70).

—— 'La sociedad española en el siglo XVII', in R. Menendez Pidal (ed.), *Historia de España. La crisis del siglo XVII: la población, la economía, la sociedad*, vol. xxiii, pt. 3 (Madrid, 1990), 395–593.

DUFFY, EAMON, *The Stripping of the Altars: Traditional Religion in England c.1400–c.1580* (New Haven, 1992).

EEGHEN, ISABELLA H. VAN, 'Het Deutzenhofje', *Jaarboek Amstelodanum*, 52 (1960), 97–123.

—— 'De gereformeerde kerkeraad en de joden te Amsterdam', *Maandblad Amstelodanum*, 47 (1960), 169–74.

—— *De gilden: Theorie en praktijk* (Bussum, 1965).

—— 'Het Leprozenhuis te Amsterdam', *Amstelodanum*, 42 (1955), 85–90.

EERENBEEMT, HENRICUS F. J. M. VAN DEN, *Armoede en arbeidsdwang. Werkinrichtingen voor 'onnutte' Nederlanders in de Republiek, 1760–1795: een mentaliteitsgeschiedenis* (The Hague, 1977).

EGMOND, FLORIKE, *Banditisme in de Franse Tijd: Profiel van de Grote Nederlands Bende: 1790–1799* (Amsterdam, 1986).

—— 'Contours of Identity: Poor Ashkenazim in the Dutch Republic', in Jozeph Michman (ed.), *Dutch Jewish History*, vol. iii (Jerusalem, 1993), 205–25.

—— 'Crime in Context: Jewish Involvement in Organized Crime in the Dutch Republic', *Jewish History*, 4/1 (1989), 75–100.

—— *Op het Verkeerde Pad: Georganiseerde misdaad in de Noordelijke Nederlanden 1650–1800* (Amsterdam, 1994).

—— *Underworlds: Organized Crime in The Netherlands, 1650–1800* (Oxford, 1993).

ELLIOTT, JOHN H., *The Count-Duke of Olivares: The Statesman in an Age of Decline* (New Haven, 1986).

EMEIS, MARINUS G., *Leentjebuur: Bank van Lening 1614 en Stads-Kredietbank 1964. Pandverbeuren* (Amsterdam, n.d. [1964]).

EMMANUEL, ISAAC S., 'Hakham David Lopes Yeshurun and his Journey to Palestine, 5493 [1733]' (Heb.), in *Hommage à Abraham Elmaleh* (Jerusalem, 1959), 90–1.

EMMANUEL, ISAAC S., *History of the Jews of The Netherlands Antilles* (Cincinnati, 1970).

—— 'Les Juifs de la Martinique et leurs coreligionnaires d'Amsterdam au XVIIe siècle', *Revue des Études Juives*, 123 (1964), 511–16.

Encyclopaedia Judaica, 2nd edn. (Jerusalem, 2007).

ENDELMAN, TODD M., *The Jews of Georgian England 1714–1830: Tradition and Change in a Liberal Society*, 2nd edn. (Ann Arbor, 1999).

—— *Radical Assimilation in English Jewish History (1656–1945)* (Bloomington, 1990).

EPSTEIN, MARK A., *The Ottoman Jewish Communities and their Role in the 15th and 16th Centuries* (Freiburg, 1980).

EPSTEIN, LOUIS M., *The Jewish Marriage Contract* (New York, 1927).

EPSTEIN, STEVEN A., *Wills and Wealth in Medieval Genoa 1150–1250* (Cambridge, Mass., 1984).

ESCAMILLA-COLIN, MICHÈLE, 'Les Juifs et l'Inquisition au XVIIe siècle', *XVIIe Siècle*, 46/183(2) (1994), 221–44.

ESSO, IZAAK VAN, 'Het aandeel der Joden in de natuurwetenschappen in de Nederlanden', in Hendrik Brugmans and Abraham Frank (eds.), *Geschiedenis der Joden in Nederland* (Amsterdam, 1940), 643–79.

EVENTOV, YAKIR, *A History of Yugoslav Jews: From Ancient Times to the End of the Nineteenth Century* [Toledot yehudei yugoslaviyah: miyemei kedem ad sof me'ah tesha-esreh], vol. i (Tel Aviv, 1971).

EVERTS, JOHANNES, *De verhouding van kerk en staat in het bijzonder ten aanzien van de armenzorg* (Utrecht, 1908).

FABER, JOHANNES A., and MARCO H. D. VAN LEEUWEN, *Amsterdamse katholieke bedeelden 1750–1850: Een gezinsreconstructie* (Amsterdam, 1987).

FABER, SJOERD, *Kindermoord, in het bijzonder in de achttiende eeuw te Amsterdam* (The Hague, 1988).

—— 'Het Rasphuis: wat is dat eigenlijk?', in Cyrille J. C. F. Fijnaut and Pieter Spierenburg (eds.), *Scherp Toezicht: Van 'Boeventucht' tot 'Samenleving en Criminaliteit'* (Arnhem, 1990), 127–43.

—— *Strafrechtspleging en criminaliteit te Amsterdam, 1680–1811: De Nieuwe Menslievendheid* (Arnhem, 1983).

—— 'Vrouwen van de rekening: kindermoordzaken ten tijde van de Republiek te Amsterdam en in Friesland', in Gert Hekma and Herman Roodenburg (eds.), *Soete Minne en Helsche boosheid* (Nijmegen, 1988), 145–67.

FAIRCHILDS, CISSIE C., *Poverty and Charity in Aix-en-Provence, 1640–1789* (Baltimore, 1976).

FARINE, AVIGDOR, 'Charity and Study Societies in Europe of the Sixteenth–Eighteenth Centuries', *Jewish Quarterly Review*, 64/1 (1973–4), 16–47, 164–75.

FAUVE-CHAMOUX, ANTOINETTE, 'Les Femmes qui migrent au loin 1500–1900: Vie nouvelle ou guillotine sèche?', in *Mesurer et comprendre: Mélanges offerts à Jacques Dupaquier* (Paris, 1993), 195–205.

FILIPPINI, JEAN-PIERRE, 'La ballottazione a Livorno nel Settecento', *La Rassegna Mensile di Israel*, 1 (1983), 199–268.

—— 'La nazione ebrea di Livorno', in Corrado Vivanti (ed.), *Storia d'Italia, Annali 11: Gli ebrei in Italia*, vol. ii (Turin, 1997), 1047–66.

—— 'Le Rôle des négociants et des banquiers juifs de Livourne dans le grand commerce international en Méditerranée au XVIIIe siècle', in Ariel Toaff and Simon Schwarzfuchs (eds.), *The Mediterranean and the Jews: Banking, Finance and International Trade (XVI–XVIII Centuries)* (Ramat Gan, 1989), 123–49.

FLYNN, MAUREEN, *Sacred Charity: Confraternities and Social Welfare in Spain, 1400–1700* (Ithaca, NY, 1989).

FRENKEL, MIRIAM, 'Charity in Jewish Society of the Medieval Mediterranean World', in Miriam Frenkel and Yaacov Lev (eds.), *Charity and Giving in Monotheistic Religions* (Berlin, 2009), 343–64.

FRENKEL, YEHOSHUA, 'Piety and Charity in Late Medieval Egypt and Syria', in Miriam Frenkel and Yaacov Lev (eds.), *Charity and Giving in Monotheistic Religions* (Berlin, 2009), 175–202.

FREUDENTHAL, MAX, *Leipziger Messgäste: Die jüdische Besucher der Leipziger Messe in den Jahren 1675 bis 1764* (Frankfurt am Main, 1928).

FRIEDENWALD, HERBERT, 'Material for the History of the Jews in the British West Indies', *Publications of the American Jewish Historical Society*, 5 (1887), 45–101.

FRIESS, PEER, 'Poor Relief and Health Care Provision in South-German Catholic Cities during the Sixteenth Century', in Thomas M. Safley (ed.), *The Reformation of Charity: The Secular and the Religious in Early Modern Poor Relief* (Boston, 2003), 76–91.

FRIJHOFF, WILLEM TH. M., 'Vrouw Schaders beroepsjournaal: overwegingen bij een publikatie over arbeidspraktijk in het verleden', *Tijdschrift voor Geschiedenis der Natuurwetenschappen, Wiskunde en Techniek*, 8 (1985), 27–38.

—— and MARIJKE SPIES, *1650, Bevochten eenheid* (The Hague, 1999).

FRISCH, EPHRAIM, *An Historical Survey of Jewish Philanthropy: From the Earliest Times to the Nineteenth Century* (New York, 1969).

FUKS, LAJB, and RENATE G. FUKS-MANSFELD, 'The Inauguration of the Portuguese Synagogue of Amsterdam, Netherlands, in 1675', in *Arquivos do Centro Cultural Português*, 14 (Paris, 1979), 489–507.

FUKS-MANSFELD, RENATE G., *De Sefardim in Amsterdam tot 1795: Aspecten van een joodse minderheid in een Hollandse stad* (Hilversum, 1989).

GALINSKY, YEHUDA D., 'Jewish Charitable Bequests and the Hekdesh Trust in Thirteenth-Century Spain', *Journal of Interdisciplinary History*, 35/3 (2005), 423–40.

GAMPEL, BENJAMIN R., *The Last Jews on Iberian Soil: Navarrese Jewry 1479/1498* (Berkeley, 1989).

GANS, MOZES H., 'Don Samuel Palache als Moré en zeerover: Grondlegger onzer gemeenschap', *Opstellen, Opperrabijn L. Vorst aangeboden ter gelegenheid van zijn installatie* (Rotterdam, 1959), 15–23.

GARCÍA-ARENAL, MERCEDES, and GERARD WIEGERS, *Entre el Islam y Occidente, vida de Samuel Pallache, judio de Fez* (Madrid, 1999).

—— —— *A Man of Three Worlds: Samuel Pallache, a Moroccan Jew in Catholic and Protestant Europe* (Baltimore, 2003).

GARRISON, ROMAN, *Redemptive Almsgiving in Early Christianity* (Sheffield, 1993).

GASTER, MOSES, *History of the Ancient Synagogue of the Spanish and Portuguese Jews* (London, 1901).

GELDER, ROELOF VAN, *Zeepost: Nooit bezorgde brieven uit de 17de en 18de eeuw* (Amsterdam, 2008).

GERBER, JANE S., *Jewish Society in Fez, 1450–1700: Studies in Communal and Economic Life* (Leiden, 1980).

GEREMEK, BRONISLAW, *Les Fils de Cain: L'Image des pauvres et des vagabonds dans la littérature européenne du XVe au XVIIe siècle* (Paris, 1991).

—— *Geschichte der Armut: Elend und Barmherzigkeit in Europa* (Munich, 1991).

—— *Inutiles au monde: Truands et misérables dans l'Europe moderne (1350–1600)* (Paris, 1980).

—— *La Potence ou la pitié: L'Europe et les pauvres du Moyen Age à nos jours* (Paris, 1987).

GERWEN, JACOBUS L. J. M. VAN, and MARCO H. D. VAN LEEUWEN (eds.), *Studies over zekerheidsarrangementen: Risico's, risicobestrijding en verzekeringen in Nederland vanaf de Middeleeuwen* (Amsterdam, 1998).

GINSBERG, DAVID, 'Moses Kohen aus Beograd und sein Epistolarium', *Revue Internationale des Études Balkaniques*, 3/6 (1938), 574–81.

GINZBURG, SIMON, *The Life and Works of Moses Hayyim Luzzatto, Founder of Modern Hebrew Literature* (Philadelphia, 1931).

GLANZ, RUDOLF, *Geschichte des niederen jüdischen Volkes in Deutschland: Eine Studie über historisches Gaunertum, Bettelwesen und Vagantentum* (New York, 1968).

GLICK, THOMAS F., 'On Converso and Marrano Ethnicity', in Benjamin R. Gampel (ed.), *Crisis and Creativity in the Sephardic World, 1391–1648* (New York, 1997), 59–76.

GOLDISH, MATT, 'The Amsterdam Portuguese Rabbinate in the Seventeenth Century: A Unique Institution Viewed from Within and Without', in Chaja Brasz and Yosef Kaplan (eds.), *Dutch Jews as Perceived by Themselves and by Others*, Proceedings of the Eighth International Symposium on the History of the Jews in The Netherlands (Leiden, 2001), 9–19.

—— 'Halakhah, Kabbalah and Heresy: A Controversy in Early Eighteenth-Century Amsterdam, *Jewish Quarterly Review*, 84/2–3 (1993–4), 153–76.

—— 'Patterns in Converso Messianism', in Matt Goldish and Richard H. Popkin (eds.), *Millenarianism and Messianism in Early Modern European Culture*, vol. i (Dordrecht, 2001), 41–63.

—— *Rabbi Jacob Sasportas: Defender of Torah Authority in an Age of Change*, MA thesis, Hebrew University of Jerusalem, 1991.

GOSLINGA, CORNELIS CH., *The Dutch in the Caribbean and the Guineas 1680–1791* (Assen, 1985).

GOULVEN, JOSEPH, *Les Mellahs de Rabat-Salé* (Paris, 1927).

GRAIZBORD, DAVID L., 'Becoming Jewish in Early Modern France: Documents on Jewish Community Building in Seventeenth-Century Bayonne and Peyrehorade', *Journal of Social History*, 40/1 (2006), 147–80.

—— 'A Historical Contextualization of Sephardi Apostates and Self-Styled Missionaries of the Seventeenth Century', *Jewish History*, 19 (2005), 287–313.

—— 'Religion and Ethnicity among "Men of the Nation": Toward a Realistic Interpretation', *Jewish Social Studies*, 15 (2008), 32–65.

—— *Souls in Dispute: Converso Identities in Iberia and the Jewish Diaspora 1580–1700* (Philadelphia, 2004).

GRAY, ALYSSA M., 'The Formerly Wealthy Poor: From Empathy to Ambivalence in Rabbinic Literature of Late Antiquity', *AJS Review*, 33/1 (2009), 101–33.

GRELL, OLE P., and ANDREW CUNNINGHAM (eds.), *Health Care and Poor Relief in Protestant Europe* (London, 1997).

—— —— and JON ARRIZABALAGA (eds.), *Health Care and Poor Relief in Counter-Reformation Europe* (London, 1999).

GROENVELD, SIMON, 'For the Benefit of the Poor: Social Assistance in Amsterdam', in Peter van Kessel and Elisja Schulte (eds.), *Rome and Amsterdam: Two Growing Cities in Seventeenth-Century Europe* (Amsterdam, 1997), 192–208.

—— 'De Republiek der Verenigde Nederlanden en haar wezen', in Simon Groenveld, Jeroen J. H. Dekker, Thom R. M. Willemse, and Jane Dane (eds.), *Wezen en boefjes: zes eeuwen zorg in wees- en kinderhuizen*, vol. ii (Hilversum, 1997), 45–251.

GROSSMAN, AVRAHAM, *Pious and Rebellious: Jewish Women in Medieval Europe* (Waltham, Mass., 2004).

GUERRERO MAYLLO, ANA, *Familia y vida cotidiana de una elite de poder: Los regidores madrileños en tiempos de Felipe II* (Madrid, 1993).

GUIMARÃES SÁ, ISABEL DOS, 'Catholic Charity in Perspective: The Social Life of Devotion in Portugal and its Empire (1450–1700)', *E-Journal of Portuguese History*, 2/1 (2004), 1–19.

—— 'Ecclesiastical Structures and Religious Action', in Francisco Bethencourt and Diogo Ramada Curto (eds.), *Portuguese Oceanic Expansion 1400–1800* (Cambridge, 2007), 255–82.

—— 'Entre Maria e Madalena: A mulher como sujeito e objecto de caridade em Portugal e nas colónias (séculos XVI–XVIII)', in *O rosto feminino da expansão portuguesa*, Proceedings of the International Congress in Lisbon, 1994 (Lisbon, 1995), 329–37.

—— *Quando o rico se faz pobre: Misericórdias caridade e poder no império português 1500–1800* (Lisbon, 1997).

GUTTON, JEAN P., *La Société et les pauvres: L'Exemple de la généralité de Lyon 1534–1789* (Paris, 1970).

GUTWIRTH, ELEAZAR, 'Hebrew Letters, Hispanic Mail', in S. Menache (ed.), *Communication in the Jewish Diaspora: The Pre-Modern World* (Leiden, 1996), 257–82.

—— 'Jewish Hospitals in Spain' (Heb.), *Pe'amim*, 37 (1989), 140–50.

HACKER, JOSEPH, 'The Intellectual Activity of the Jews of the Ottoman Empire during the Sixteenth and Seventeenth Centuries', in Isadore Twersky and Bernard Septimus (eds.), *Jewish Thought in the Seventeenth Century* (Cambridge, Mass., 1987), 95–135.

—— 'The Sephardim in the Ottoman Empire', in Haim Beinart (ed.), *Moreshet Sepharad: The Sephardi Legacy*, vol. ii (Jerusalem, 1992), 109–33.

HAGOORT, LYDIA, *Het Beth Haim in Ouderkerk aan de Amstel: De begraafplaats van de Portugese Joden in Amsterdam 1614–1945* (Hilversum, 2005).

—— 'The Del Sottos, a Portuguese Jewish Family in Amsterdam in the Seventeenth Century', *Studia Rosenthaliana*, 31/1–2 (1997), 31–57.

—— and WILHELMINA CHR. PIETERSE, *Livro de Bet-Haim do Kahal Kados de Talmud-Torah Commesado em Pesah do Anno de 5399 em Amsterdam: Het begrafenisregister van de Portugees-Israëlietische gemeente Talmud Torah te Amsterdam 1639–1648* (Amsterdam, 2008).

HAKS, DONALD, *Huwelijk en gezin in Holland in de 17e en 18e eeuw* (Assen, 1982).

HALLEMA, ANNE, 'Emigratie en tewerkstelling van wezen op de schepen en in het gebied der V.O.C. en W.I.C. gedurende de 17e en 18e eeuw: Een bijdrage tot de sociale geschiedenis en inzonderheid tot die van de kinderbescherming in Nederland', *Tijdschrift voor Geschiedenis*, 70 (1957), 204–17.

—— *Geschiedenis van het gevangeniswezen, hoofdzakelijk in Nederland* (The Hague, 1958).

HART, SIMON, *Geschrift en getal* (Dordrecht, 1976).

—— *Historisch-Demografische Notities betreffende de Joden te Amsterdam in de 18e eeuw*, Brochure Stichting Nederlands-Joods Familie-Archief (Amsterdam, 1968).

—— 'Een sociale structuur van de Amsterdamse bevolking in de 18e eeuw', *Jaarboek Amstelodanum*, 65 (1973), 73–84.

HEERMA VAN VOSS, ALEXANDER F., Introduction to id. (ed.), *International Review of Social History*, suppl. 9: *Petitions in Social History* (2001), 1–10.

HEIDE, ALBERT VAN DER, *Messias in meervoud: Het leven van Mozes Chaim Luzzatto (1707–1746)* (Amsterdam, 1984).

HELLINGER, MICHAEL, 'The Emerging Definition of the Poverty Line in Jewish Law', *Jewish Law Association Studies*, 14 (Jerusalem 2002 conference volume), ed. Hillel Gamoran (2004), 127–39.

HENDERSON, JOHN, *Piety and Charity in Late Medieval Florence* (Chicago, 1997).

—— and RICHARD WALL (eds.), *Poor Women and Children in the European Past* (London, 1994).

HENRIQUES DE CASTRO, MZ. DAVID, *Keur van grafstenen op de Portugees-Israelietische begraafplaats te Ouderkerk aan de Amstel met beschrijving en biografische aantekeningen / Selected Gravestones from the Dutch Portuguese Jewish Cemetery at Ouderkerk aan de Amstel with Descriptions and Biographical Notes*, ed. Julie-Marthe Cohen et al. (Amsterdam, 1999).

HEUVEL, DANIELLE VAN DEN, *Women and Entrepreneurship: Female Traders in the Northern Netherlands* (Amsterdam, 2007).

HILLESUM, JEREMIAS M., 'Vereenigingen bij de Spaansche en Portugeesche Joden te Amsterdam in de 17de en 18de eeuw', *Jaarboek Amstelodanum*, 1 (1902), 167–83.

HIRSCH, MENKO M., *Frucht vom Baum des Lebens: Ozer peroth ez chajim: Die Sammlung der Rechtsgutachten Peri Ez Chajim des Rabbinerseminars Ets Haim zu Amsterdam* (Berlin, 1936).

HIRSCHBERG, HAYIM Z., *A History of the Jews in North Africa*, 2 vols. (Leiden, 1974–81).

HOROWITZ, ELLIOTT S., '"And the (Respectable) Poor will be as Your Family": Charity, the Poor and Communal Supervision in the Jewish Communities of Europe between the Middle Ages and the Beginnings of the Modern Period' (Heb.), in Menachem Ben-Sasson (ed.), *Religion and Economy: Connections and Interactions. Collected Essays* [Dat vekhalkhalah: yaḥasei gomlin] (Jerusalem, 1995), 209–31.

—— 'The Dowering of Brides in the Ghetto of Venice: Between Tradition and Change, Ideals and Reality', *Tarbits*, 56/3 (1987), 347–71.

—— 'Jewish Confraternities in Seventeenth Century Verona: A Study in the Social History of Piety', Ph.D. diss., Yale University, microfilm facsimile (Michigan, 1982).

—— 'Membership and its Rewards: The Emergence and Decline of Ferrara's Gemilut Hasadim Society (1515–1603)', in Elliot S. Horowitz and Moises Orfali (eds.), *The Mediterranean and the Jews: Society, Culture and Economy in Early Modern Times*, vol. ii (Ramat Gan, 2002), 27–65.

—— 'Processions, Piety and Jewish Confraternities', in Robert C. Davis and Benjamin C. I. Ravid (eds.), *The Jews of Early Modern Venice* (Baltimore, 2001), 231–47.

—— '*Yeshiva* and *Hevra*: Educational Control and Confraternal Organization in Sixteenth-Century Italy', in Daniel Carpi et al. (eds.), *Shlomo Simonsohn Jubilee Volume: Studies on the History of the Jews in the Middle Ages and Renaissance Period* (Jerusalem, 1993), 123–47.

HOUSTON, ROBERT A., *Literacy in Early Modern Europe: Culture and Education 1500–1800*, 2nd edn. (London, 2002).

HUERGA CRIADO, PILAR, 'Una familia judeoconversa: La quiebra de la solidaridad', *Sefarad*, 49/1 (Madrid, 1989), 97–121.

—— 'El problema de la comunidad judeoconversa', in Joaquin Pérez Villanueva and Bartolomé Escandell Bonet (eds.), *Historia de la Inquisición en España y América*, vol. iii (Madrid, 2000), 441–97.

HUFTON, OLWEN, *The Poor of Eighteenth-Century France 1750–1789* (Oxford, 1974).

—— *The Prospect Before Her: A History of Women in Western Europe*, i: *1500–1800* (London, 1995).

—— 'Women without Men: Widows and Spinsters in Britain and France in the Eighteenth Century', *Journal of Family History*, 9/4 (1984), 355–76.

HUGHES, DIANE O., 'From Brideprice to Dowry in Mediterranean Europe', in Marion A. Kaplan (ed.), *The Marriage Bargain: Women and Dowries in European History* (New York, 1985), 13–58.

HUUSSEN, AREND H. JR, 'De joden in Nederland en het probleem van de tolerantie', in Marijke Gijswijt-Hofstra (ed.), *Een schijn van verdraagzaamheid: Afwijking en tolerantie in Nederland van de zestiende eeuw tot heden* (Hilversum, 1989), 107–29.

—— 'The Legal Position of Sephardi Jews in Holland, circa 1600', in Jozeph Michman (ed.), *Dutch Jewish History*, vol. iii (Jerusalem, 1993), 19–41.

—— 'Legislation on the Position of the Jews in the Dutch Republic, *c.*1590–1796', *Tijdschrift voor Rechtsgeschiedenis*, 69/1 and 2 (2001), 43–56.

HYAMSON, ALBERT M., *The Sephardim of England: A History of the Spanish and Portuguese Jewish Community 1492–1951*, 2nd edn. (London, 1991).

IDEL, MOSHE, 'Religion, Thought and Attitudes: The Impact of the Expulsion of the Jews', in Elie Kedourie (ed.), *Spain and the Jews: The Sephardi Experience 1492 and after* (London, 1992), 123–39.

—— 'Spanish Kabbalah after the Expulsion', in Haim Beinart (ed.), *Moreshet Sepharad: The Sephardi Legacy*, vol. ii (Jerusalem, 1992), 166–78.

ISRAEL, JONATHAN I., 'The Changing Role of the Dutch Sephardim in International Trade, 1595–1715', in Jozeph Michman and Tirtsah Levie [Bernfeld] (eds.), *Dutch Jewish History*, vol. [i] (Jerusalem, 1984), 31–51.

—— *Diasporas within a Diaspora: Jews, Crypto-Jews and the World Maritime Empires (1540–1740)* (Leiden, 2002).

—— *Dutch Primacy in World Trade, 1686–1740* (Oxford, 1989).

—— *The Dutch Republic: Its Rise, Greatness, and Fall 1477–1806* (Oxford, 1995).

—— 'The Economic Contribution of Dutch Sephardi Jewry to Holland's Golden Age 1595–1713', *Tijdschrift voor Geschiedenis*, 96/4 (1983), 505–53.

—— *Empires and Entrepots* (London, 1990).

—— *European Jewry in the Age of Mercantilism 1550–1750*, 3rd edn. (London, 1998).

—— 'Gregorio Leti (1631–1701) and the Dutch Sephardi Elite at the Close of the Seventeenth Century', in Ada Rapoport-Albert and Steven J. Zipperstein (eds.), *Jewish History: Essays in Honour of Chimen Abramsky* (London, 1988), 267–84.

—— 'Jews and Crypto-Jews in the Atlantic World Systems, 1500–1800', in Richard L. Kagan and Philip M. Morgan (eds.), *Atlantic Diasporas: Jews, Conversos, and Crypto-Jews in the Age of Mercantilism, 1500–1800* (Baltimore, 2009), 3–30.

—— 'The Jews of Dutch America', in Paolo Bernardini and Norman Fiering (eds.), *The Jews and the Expansion of Europe to the West 1450–1800* (New York, 2001), 335–49.

—— 'The Jews of Spanish North Africa, 1600–1669', *Transactions of the Jewish Historical Society of England*, 26 (1979), 71–86.

—— 'The Jews of Venice and their Links with Holland and with Dutch Jewry (1660–1710)', in Gaetano Cozzi (ed.), *Gli Ebrei e Venezia: secoli XIV–XVIII* (Milan, 1987), 95–116.

—— 'The Republic of the United Netherlands until about 1750: Demography and Economic Activity', in J. C. H. Blom, Renate G. Fuks-Mansfeld, and Ivo Schöffer (eds.), *The History of the Jews in The Netherlands*, trans. Arnold J. Pomerans and Erica Pomerans (Oxford, 2002), 85–115.

—— 'The Sephardic Contribution to Economic Life and Colonization in Europe and the New World (16th–18th Centuries)', in Haim Beinart (ed.), *Moreshet Sepharad: The Sephardi Legacy*, vol. ii (Jerusalem, 1992), 365–98.

—— 'Sephardic Immigration into the Dutch Republic', *Studia Rosenthaliana*, 23/2 (1989), 45–53.

—— 'Spain and the Dutch Sephardim, 1609–1660', *Studia Rosenthaliana*, 12/1–2 (1978), 1–61.

JANIN-THIVOS TAILLAND, MICHÈLE, *Inquisition et société au Portugal: Le Cas du tribunal d'Évora 1660–1821* (Paris, 2001).

JANSEN, LOU, *Geschiedenis van de Stads Bank van Lening te Amsterdam 1614–1964* (Amsterdam, 1964).

JANSEN, PETER, 'Het ritme van de dood: Sociale conjunctuur in Amsterdam 1750–1800', *Ons Amsterdam*, 25 (1973), 88–91.

—— 'Poverty in Amsterdam at the Close of the Eighteenth Century', *Acta Historiae Neerlandicae*, 14 (1981), 98–114.

JORDAN, WILBUR K., *Philanthropy in England 1480–1660* (London, 1959).

JÜTTE, ROBERT, 'Poor Relief and Social Discipline in Sixteenth-Century Europe', *European Studies Review*, 11/1 (1981), 25–52.

—— *Poverty and Deviance in Early Modern Europe* (Cambridge, 1994).

KAMEN, HENRI, *Spain 1469–1714: A Society in Conflict*, 2nd edn. (London, 1991).

—— *The Spanish Inquisition: An Historical Revision* (London, 1997).

KANN, ROBERT A., *A History of the Habsburg Empire 1526–1918* (Berkeley, 1974).

KAPLAN, BENJAMIN J., *Divided by Faith: Religious Conflict and the Practice of Toleration in Early Modern Europe* (Cambridge, Mass., 2007).

—— *Muslims in the Dutch Golden Age: Representations and Realities of Religious Toleration* (Amsterdam, 2007).

KAPLAN, DEBRA, 'Women and Worth: Female Access to Property in Early Modern Urban Jewish Communities', *Leo Baeck Institute Yearbook* (advance access, 9 July 2010), 1–21.

KAPLAN, YOSEF, *An Alternative Path to Modernity: The Sephardi Diaspora in Western Europe* (Leiden, 2000).

—— 'Amsterdam and Ashkenazi Migration in the Seventeenth Century', *Studia Rosenthaliana*, 23/2 (1989), 22–44.

—— 'Amsterdam, the Forbidden Lands, and the Dynamics of the Sephardi Diaspora', in Yosef Kaplan (ed.), *The Dutch Intersection: The Jews and The Netherlands in Modern History* (Leiden, 2008), 33–85.

—— 'The Attitude of the Leadership of the Portuguese Community in Amsterdam to the Sabbatian Movement, 1665–1671' (Heb.), *Tsiyon*, 39/3–4 (1974), 198–216.

—— 'Bans in the Sephardi Community of Amsterdam in the Late Seventeenth Century' (Heb.), in Aharon Mirsky, Avraham Grossman, and Yosef Kaplan (eds.), *Exile and Diaspora: Studies in the History of the Jewish People Presented to Professor Haim Beinart on the Occasion of his Seventieth Birthday* [Galut aḥar golah: meḥkarim betoledot am yisra'el mugashim leprofesor haim beinart lemelo'ot lo shivi'im shanah] (Jerusalem, 1988), 517–40.

—— 'Between Christianity and Judaism in Early Modern Europe: The Confessionalization Process of the Western Sephardi Diaspora', in Lothar Gall and Dietmar Willoweit (eds.), *Judaism, Christianity, and Islam in the Course of History: Exchange and Conflicts*, Schriften des Historischen Kollegs 82 (Oldenbourg, 2011), 307–41.

—— 'The Curaçao and Amsterdam Jewish Communities in the 17th and 18th Centuries', *American Jewish History*, 72/2 (1982), 193–211.

—— 'Deviance and Excommunication in the Eighteenth Century: A Chapter in the Social History of the Sephardi Community of Amsterdam', in Jozeph Michman (ed.), *Dutch Jewish History*, vol. iii (Jerusalem, 1993), 103–15.

—— *From Christianity to Judaism: The Story of Isaac Orobio de Castro* (Oxford, 1989).

—— *From New Christians to New Jews* [Minotsrim ḥadashim liyehudim ḥadashim] (Jerusalem, 2003).

KAPLAN, YOSEF, 'A Generation of Progress in the Historical Study of Dutch Sephardic Jewry', in Yosef Kaplan, Henry Méchoulan, and Richard H. Popkin (eds.), *Menasseh ben Israel and his World* (Leiden, 1989), 1–6.

—— 'Gente política: The Portuguese Jews of Amsterdam vis-à-vis Dutch Society', in Chaja Brasz and Yosef Kaplan (eds.), *Dutch Jews as Perceived by Themselves and by Others*, Proceedings of the Eighth International Symposium on the Jews in The Netherlands (Leiden, 2001), 21–40.

—— 'The Jewish Profile of the Spanish–Portuguese Community of London during the Seventeenth Century', *Judaism*, 163 (1992), 229–40.

—— 'Jewish Refugees from Germany and Poland in Amsterdam during the Thirty Years War and at the Time of the Chmielnitsky Massacres' (Heb.), in Robert Bonfil, Menachem Ben Sasson, and Joseph Hacker (eds.), *Culture and Society in Medieval Jewish History: A Collection in Memory of Haim Hillel Ben Sasson* [Tarbut veḥevrah betoledot yisra'el be'yemei habenayim: kovets ma'amarim lezikhro shel ḥayim hilel ben-sason] (Jerusalem, 1989), 587–622.

—— 'The Jews in the Republic until about 1750: Religious, Cultural, and Social Life', in J. C. H. Blom, Renate G. Fuks-Mansfeld, and Ivo Schöffer (eds.), *The History of the Jews in The Netherlands*, trans. Arnold J. Pomerans and Erica Pomerans (Oxford, 2002), 116–63.

—— 'Moral Panic in the Eighteenth Century Sephardi Community of Amsterdam: The Threat of Eros', in Jonathan I. Israel and Reinier Salverda (eds.), *Dutch Jewry: Its History and Secular Culture* (Leiden, 2002), 103–23.

—— 'Nueva información sobre la estancia de Juan de Prado en Amberes', *Sefarad*, 35/1 and 2 (1975), 159–63.

—— 'Order and Discipline in the Portuguese Synagogue of Amsterdam', in Albert van der Heide and Irene E. Zwiep (eds.), *Jewish Studies and the European Academic World*, articles from the *Revue des Études Juives* (Paris, 2005), 1–14.

—— 'El perfil de tres rabinos sefardiés a través del análisis de sus bibliotecas', in Jaime Contreras, Bernardo J. García García, and Ignacio Pulido (eds.), *Familia, religíon y negocio: El sefardismo en las relaciones entre el mundo ibérico y los Países Bajos en la edad moderna* (Madrid, 2002), 269–86.

—— 'The Place of Herem in the Sefardic Community of Hamburg during the Seventeenth Century', in Michael Studemund-Halévy and Peter Koj (eds.), *Die Sefarden in Hamburg: Zur Geschichte einer Minderheit*, vol. i (Hamburg, 1994), 63–85.

—— 'Political Concepts in the World of the Portuguese Jews of Amsterdam during the Seventeenth Century: The Problem of Exclusion and the Boundaries of Self-Identity', in Yosef Kaplan, Henry Méchoulan, and Richard H. Popkin (eds.), *Menasseh ben Israel and his World* (Leiden, 1989), 45–62.

—— 'The Portuguese Community of Amsterdam in the Seventeenth Century between Tradition and Change', in Abraham Haim (ed.), *Society and Community*, Proceedings of the Second International Congress for Research into the Sephardi and Oriental Heritage, 1984 (Jerusalem, 1991), 141–71.

—— 'The Portuguese Community in 17th-Century Amsterdam and the Ashkenazi World', in Jozeph Michman (ed.), *Dutch Jewish History*, vol. ii (Jerusalem, 1989), 23–45.

—— 'Les Proselytes juifs dans la communauté portugaise d'Amsterdam au XVIIe siècle: Le Cas de Lorenzo Escudero', in *Actes du septième congrès mondial des études juives, histoire des Juifs d'Europe* (Jerusalem, 1981), 87–101.

—— 'Relations between Spanish and Portuguese Jews and Ashkenazim in 17th-Century Amsterdam', in Shmuel Almog et al. (eds.), *Transition and Change in Modern Jewish History: Essays Presented in Honor of Shmuel Ettinger* (Jerusalem, 1987), 389–412.

—— 'The Religious World of an International Jewish Merchant in the Period of the Renaissance: The Embarrassment of Riches of Avraham Israel Pereyra' (Heb.), in Menachem Ben-Sasson (ed.), *Religion and Economy: Connections and Interactions. Collected Essays* [Dat vekhalkhalah: yaḥasei gomlin] (Jerusalem, 1995), 233–51.

—— 'Secularizing the Portuguese Jews: Integration and Orthodoxy in Early Modern Judaism', *Simon Dubnow Institute Yearbook*, 6, ed. David B. Ruderman and Shmuel Feiner (2007), 99–101.

—— 'The Self-Definition of the Sephardi Jews of Western Europe and their Relation to the Alien and Stranger', in Benjamin R. Gampel (ed.), *Crisis and Creativity in the Sephardi World* (New York, 1997), 121–45.

—— 'Sephardi Students at the University of Leiden' (Heb.), in Jozeph Michman (ed.), *Studies on the History of Dutch Jewry* [Meḥkarim al toledot yahadut holand], vol. ii (Jerusalem, 1979), 65–75.

—— 'The Social Functions of the Herem in the Portuguese Jewish Community of Amsterdam in the Seventeenth Century', in Jozeph Michman and Tirtsah Levie [Bernfeld] (eds.), *Dutch Jewish History*, vol. [i] (Jerusalem, 1984), 111–55.

—— 'The Travels of Portuguese Jews from Amsterdam to the "Lands of Idolatry" 1644–1724', in Yosef Kaplan (ed.), *Jews and Conversos: Studies in Society and Inquisition* (Jerusalem, 1981), 197–211.

—— 'Wayward New Christians and Stubborn New Jews: The Shaping of a Jewish Identity', *Jewish History*, 8/1–2 (1994), 27–39.

KATZ, DAVID S., *The Jews in the History of England 1485–1850* (Oxford, 1996).

KATZ, JACOB, *Tradition and Crisis: Jewish Society at the End of the Middle Ages*, trans. Bernard Dov Cooperman, 2nd edn. (Syracuse, 2000).

KAUFMANN, DAVID, 'Joseph ibn Danon of Belgrade', *Revue des Études Juives*, 37 (1898), 284–98.

KAYSERLING, MEYER, *Biblioteca Española-Portugueza-Judaica*, introd. Y. H. Yerushalmi (repr. New York, 1971).

—— *Die jüdische Frauen in der Geschichte, Literatur und Kunst* (Leipzig, 1879).

KELLENBENZ, HERMANN, *Sephardim an der unteren Elbe* (Wiesbaden, 1958).

—— 'Das Testament von Manuel Teixeira', *Studia Rosenthaliana*, 3/1 (1969), 53–61.

KINGDON, ROBERT M., 'Social Welfare in Calvin's Geneva', *American Historical Review*, 76/1 (1971), 50–69.

KISTEMAKER, RENÉE, and TIRTSAH LEVIE [BERNFELD] (eds.), *Êxodo, Portugezen in Amsterdam 1600–1680* (Amsterdam, 1987).

KLAPISCH-ZUBER, CHRISTIANE, *Women, Family and Ritual in Renaissance Italy* (Chicago, 1985).

KLEINSCHMIDT, HARALD, *People on the Move: Attitudes toward and Perceptions of Migration in Medieval and Modern Europe* (Westport, Conn., 2003).

KLOOSTER, WIM W., *Illicit Riches: Dutch Trade in the Caribbean, 1648–1795* (Leiden, 1998).

—— 'The Jews of Surinam and Curaçao', in Paolo Bernardini and Norman Fiering (eds.), *The Jews and the Expansion of Europe to the West 1450–1800* (New York, 2001), 350–61.

KNOTTER, ADRIANUS, and JAN LUITEN VAN ZANDEN, 'Immigratie en arbeidsmarkt in Amsterdam in de zeventiende eeuw', *Tijdschrift voor Sociale Geschiedenis*, 13/4 (1987), 403–30.

KOCHAN, LIONEL, *Jews, Idols and Messiahs: The Challenge from History* (Oxford, 1990).

KOEN, ELLY M., 'De vleesvoorziening van de Portugese joden te Amsterdam sinds het begin van de zeventiende eeuw', *Jaarboek Amstelodanum*, 62 (1970), 37–48.

KOHLER, KAUFMAN, 'The Historical Development of Jewish Charity', in *Hebrew Union College and Other Addresses* (Cincinnati, 1916), 229–52.

KOLDEWEIJ, ELOY F., *Goudleer in de Republiek der Zeven Verenigde Provinciën: Nationale ontwikkelingen en de Europese context* (Leiden, 1998).

KOOIJMANS, LUUC, *Vriendschap en de kunst van het overleven in de zeventiende en achttiende eeuw* (Amsterdam, 1997).

KOORN, FLORENCE F. W. J., and HERMAN W. ROODENBURG, 'Kopsters: Vrouwen in de marge van de gezondheidszorg', *Spiegel Historiael*, 19/3 (1984), 125–9.

KOWALESKI, MARYANNE, 'Singlewomen in Medieval and Early Modern Europe: The Demographic Perspective', in Judith M. Bennett and Amy M. Froide (eds.), *Singlewomen in the European Past 1250–1800* (Philadelphia, 1999), 38–81.

KRACAUER, J., 'Beiträge zur Geschichte der Frankfurter Juden im 30 jährigen Krieg', *Zeitschrift für die Geschichte der Juden in Deutschland*, 3/1 (1889), 130–56.

KRAUSMAN BEN-AMOS, ILANA, *The Culture of Giving: Informal Support and Gift-Exchange in Early Modern England* (Cambridge, 2008).

KUIJPERS, ERIKA, 'Lezen en schrijven: Onderzoek naar het alfabetiseringsniveau in zeventiende-eeuws Amsterdam', *Tijdschrift voor Sociale Geschiedenis*, 23/4 (1997), 490–522.

—— *Migrantenstad: Immigratie en sociale verhoudingen in 17e-eews Amsterdam* (Hilversum, 2005).

—— 'Een zeventiende-eeuwse migrantenkerk: De Lutheranen in Amsterdam', in Leo A. C. J. Lucassen (ed.), *Amsterdammer worden: Migranten, hun organisaties en inburgering 1600–2000* (Amsterdam, 2004), 35–59.

KUIPER, ERNST J., *De Hollandse 'Schoolordre' van 1625* (Groningen, 1958).

LANE, FREDERIC C., *Venice, a Maritime Republic* (Baltimore, 1973).

LANE, JOAN, *Apprenticeship in England, 1600–1914* (London, 1996).

LATHAM, JOHN D., 'Contribution à l'étude de l'émigration andalouse et à sa place dans l'histoire de la Tunisie', in Miguel de Epalza and Ramón Petit (eds.), *Receuil d'études sur les Moriscos Andalous en Tunisie* (Madrid, 1972), 21–63.

LEA, HENRI C., *A History of the Inquisition of Spain*, 4 vols. (New York, 1906–7).

LEEUWEN, MARCO H. D. VAN, 'Amsterdam en de armenzorg tijdens de Republiek', *Nederlands Economisch Historisch Archief*, Jaarboek 95 (1996), 132–61.

—— 'Arme Amsterdamse joden en de strijd om hun integratie aan het begin van de negentiende eeuw', in Hetty Berg (ed.), *De Gelykstaat der Joden: Inburgering van een minderheid* (Amsterdam, 1996), 55–66.

—— 'Guild and Middle-Class Welfare, 1550–1800: Provisions for Burial, Old Age and Widowhood', *Economic History Review* (forthcoming); published online 26 May 2011, 1–30.

—— 'Liefdadige giften in Amsterdam tijdens de achttiende eeuw', *Tijdschrift voor Sociale Geschiedenis*, 22/4 (1996), 417–42.

—— *The Logic of Charity: Amsterdam 1800–1850* (London, 2000).

—— and JAMES E. OEPPEN, 'Reconstructing the Demographic Regime of Amsterdam 1681–1920', *Economic and Social History in The Netherlands*, 5 (1993), 61–102.

—— JAN SCHOENMAKERS, and FRANS SMITS, *Armoede en bedeling in Amsterdam ten tijde van de Republiek* (Amsterdam, 1981).

LEEUWEN, SIMON VAN, *Het Rooms-Hollands-Regt waar in de Roomse Wetten met het huydendaagse Neerlands Regt . . . over een gebragt werden*, 2 vols. (Amsterdam, 1732).

LERA GARCÍA, RAFAEL DE, 'La última gran persecución inquisitorial contra el criptojudaísmo: El Tribunal de Cuenca 1718–1725', *Sefarad*, 47/1 (1987), 87–137.

LESGER, CLEMENS, *Huur en conjunctuur: De woningmarkt in Amsterdam, 1550–1850*, Amsterdamse Historische Reeks 10 (Amsterdam, 1986).

—— 'Stagnatie en stabiliteit: De economie tussen 1730 en 1795', in Willem Frijhoff and Maarten Prak (eds.), *Geschiedenis van Amsterdam: Zelfbewuste stadstaat 1650–1813*, vol. ii (Amsterdam, 2005), 219–65.

LEV, YAACOV, 'Charity and Gift Giving in Medieval Islam', in Miriam Frenkel and Yaacov Lev (eds.), *Charity and Giving in Monotheistic Religions* (Berlin, 2009), 235–64.

LEVIE BERNFELD, TIRTSAH, 'Caridade escapa da morte: Legacies to the Poor in Sephardi Wills from Seventeenth Century Amsterdam', in Jozeph Michman (ed.), *Dutch Jewish History*, vol. iii (Jerusalem, 1993), 179–204.

—— 'Financing Poor Relief in the Spanish–Portuguese Jewish Community in Amsterdam in the Seventeenth and Eighteenth Centuries', in Jonathan I. Israel and Reinier Salverda (eds.), *Dutch Jewry: Its History and Secular Culture* (Leiden, 2002), 63–102.

—— 'Mujeres judías hispano-portuguesas en el entorno holandés de Amsterdam en el siglo XVII', in Jaime Contreras, Bernardo J. García García, and Ignacio Pulido (eds.), *Familia, religíon y negocio: El sefardismo en las relaciones entre el mundo ibérico y los Países Bajos en la edad moderna* (Madrid, 2002), 137–72.

—— 'Portugese Joden en misdaad in de Republiek', *Pro Memorie*, 8/2 (2006), 208–34.

—— 'Les Sépharades des Balkans à Amsterdam au début de l'époque moderne: Confrontation entre l'Orient et l'Occident', in Esther Benbassa (ed.), *Itinéraires sépharades: Diversité et complexité des identités* (Paris, 2010), 33–61.

—— 'Sephardi Women in Holland's Golden Age', in Julia R. Lieberman (ed.), *Sephardi Family Life in the Early Modern Period* (Waltham, Mass., 2010), 177–222.

LEVIE BERNFELD, TIRTSAH, and HENK ZANTKUYL, *Wonen in Amsterdam in de 17de en 18de eeuw* (Purmerend, 1980).

LEVINE MELAMMED, RENÉE, 'Castilian Conversas at Work', in Marilyn Stone and María del Carmen Benito-Vessels (eds.), *Women at Work in Spain: From the Middle Ages to Early Modern Times* (New York, 1998), 81–95.

—— *Heretics or Daughters of Israel? The Crypto-Jewish Women of Castile* (New York, 1999).

—— 'Sephardi Women in the Medieval and Early Modern Periods', in Judith R. Baskin (ed.), *Jewish Women in Historical Perspective* (Detroit, 1998), 115–34.

LEVY, AVIGDOR (ed.), *The Jews in the Ottoman Empire* (Princeton, 1994).

—— *The Sephardim in the Ottoman Empire* (Princeton, 1992).

LEVY, MORITZ, *Die Sephardim in Bosnien: Ein Beitrag zur Geschichte der Juden auf der Balkan Halbinsel* (Sarajevo, 1911).

LIEBERMAN, JULIA R., 'Adolescence and the Period of Apprenticeship among Western Sephardim in the Seventeenth Century', *El Prezente*, 4 (2010), 11–23.

—— 'Childhood and Family among the Western Sephardim in the Seventeenth Century', in Julia R. Lieberman (ed.), *Sephardi Family Life in the Early Modern Diaspora* (Waltham, Mass., 2010), 129–76.

—— 'Educational Institutions among the Western Sephardim in the Early Modern Period', in Jonathan Cohen (ed.), *Proceedings of the Symposium on Poverty, Welfare and Religion: Family, Gender and Justice*, Hebrew Union College in Cincinnati, 18–20 May 2007 (forthcoming).

—— '"Jonen Dalim," Auto Alegórico de Miguel (Daniel Leví) de Barrios', in Yedida K. Stillman and Norman A. Stillman (eds.), *From Iberia to Diaspora: Studies in Sephardic History and Culture* (Leiden, 1999), 300–15.

LIEBURG, MARIUS J. VAN, 'Geneeskundige zorg als kerkelijke taak: De situatie in de gereformeerde kerk van Rotterdam in de zeventiende eeuw', *De zeventiende eeuw*, 5/1 (1989), 162–71.

—— 'Religion and Medical Practice in The Netherlands in the Seventeenth Century', in Hilary Marland and Margaret Pelling (eds.), *The Task of Healing: Medicine, Religion and Gender in England and The Netherlands 1450–1800* (Rotterdam, 1996), 135–43.

LIPMAN, VIVIAN D., 'Sephardi and Other Jewish Immigrants in England in the Eighteenth Century', in *Migration and Settlement*, Proceedings of the Anglo-American Jewish Historical Conference, London, 1970 (London, 1971), 37–62.

LIS, CATHARINA, and HUGO SOLY, *Poverty and Capitalism in Pre-Industrial Europe* (Hassocks, 1979).

LOKER, ZVI, 'Juan de Yllan, Merchant Adventurer and Colonial Promoter: New Evidence', *Studia Rosenthaliana*, 17/1 (1983), 22–31.

LÓPEZ BELINCHÓN, BERNARDO, *Honra, libertad y hacienda (Hombres de negocios y judíos sefardíes)* (Alcalá, 2001).

LORENCE, BRUCE A., 'Professions Held by New Christians in Northern and Southern Portugal during the First Half of the Seventeenth Century', in Tamar Alexander and Abraham Haim (eds.), *History and Creativity in the Sephardi and Oriental Jewish Communities* (Jerusalem, 1994), 315–26.

LOTTUM, JELLE VAN, *Across the North Sea: The Impact of the Dutch Republic on International Labour Migration, c.1550–1850* (Amsterdam, 2007).

LUCASSEN, JAN M. G. W., *Dutch Long-Distance Migration: A Concise History 1600–1900* (Amsterdam, 1991).

—— 'The Netherlands, the Dutch, and Long-Distance Migration, in the Late Sixteenth to Early Nineteenth Centuries', in N. Canny (ed.), *Europeans on the Move: Studies on European Migration 1500–1800* (Oxford, 1994), 153–91.

—— and MARINUS J. A. PENNINX, *Newcomers: Immigrants and their Descendants in The Netherlands, 1550–1995* (Amsterdam, 1997).

LUNTEREN-SPANJAARD, MARIANKA VAN, and WIJNBERG-STROZ, JOEP, 'Vreemde luyden-Haagse Sefardim in de zeventiende en achttiende eeuw', in *275 Jaar Haagse Snoge: Nieuw elan in eeuwenoud gebouw* (The Hague, 2002), 55–78, 162–9.

MCBRIEN, R. P. (ed.), *The HarperCollins Encyclopedia of Catholicism* (New York, 1995).

MCCANTS, ANNE E. C., *Civic Charity in a Golden Age: Orphan Care in Early Modern Amsterdam* (Urbana, 1997).

MCCRAY BEIER, LUCINDA, *Sufferers and Healers: The Experience of Illness in Seventeenth-Century England* (London, 1987).

MAGNANI, ELIANA, 'Almsgiving, *Donatio Pro Anima* and Eucharistic Offering in the Early Middle Ages of Western Europe (4th–9th century)', in Miriam Frenkel and Yaacov Lev (eds.), *Charity and Giving in Monotheistic Religions* (Berlin, 2009), 110–21.

MALINO, FRANCES, *The Sephardic Jews of Bordeaux: Assimilation and Emancipation in Revolutionary and Napoleonic France* (Tuscaloosa, 1978).

MALKIEL, DAVID J., 'The Ghetto Republic', in Robert C. Davis and Benjamin C. I. Ravid (eds.), *The Jews of Early Modern Venice* (Baltimore, 2001), 117–42.

—— *A Separate Republic: The Mechanics and Dynamics of Venetian Jewish Self-Government, 1607–1624* (Jerusalem, 1991).

MANEN, CHARLOTTE A. VAN, *Armenpflege in Amsterdam in ihrer historischen Entwicklung* (Leiden, 1913).

MANUELIDIS, LAURA K., 'Kopster', *Journal of the History of Medicine and Allied Sciences*, 22 (1967), 82.

MARAVALL, JOSÉ A., *Poder, honor y élites en el siglo XVII* (Madrid, 1979).

MARCUS, JACOB R., *Communal Sickcare in the German Ghetto*, 2nd edn. (Cincinnati, 1978).

MARLAND, HILARY, 'The '*burgerlijke*' Midwife: The *Stadsvroedvrouw* of Eighteenth-Century Holland', in Hilary Marland (ed.), *The Art of Midwifery: Early Modern Midwives in Europe and North America* (London, 1993), 192–213.

—— (ed.), *Mother and Child Were Saved: The Memoirs (1693–1745) of the Frisian Midwife Catharina Schrader* (Amsterdam, 1987).

MARTÍNEZ MILLÁN, JOSÉ, 'La persecución inquisitorial contra los criptojudíos en el siglo XVIII: El tribunal de Llerena (1700–1730); los años de la "gran persecución (1716–1725)"', in Joaquin Pérez Villanueva and Bartolomé Escandell Bonet (eds.), *Historia de la Inquisición en España y América*, vol. iii (Madrid, 2000), 556–656.

MARTZ, LINDA, *Poverty and Welfare in Habsburg Spain: The Example of Toledo* (Cambridge, 1983).

MARZAGALLI, SILVIA, 'Atlantic Trade and Sephardim Merchants in Eighteenth Century France: The Case of Bordeaux', in Paolo Bernardini and Norman Fiering (eds.), *The Jews and the Expansion of Europe to the West 1450–1800* (New York, 2001), 268–86.

MAZIANE, LEÏLA, 'Entre Salé et les Provinces-Unies au XVIIe siècle, une complicité haute en couleur', in Anna Crespo Solana (ed.), *España y las 17 provincias de los Países Bajos: una revisión historiográfica (XVI–XVIII)* (Córdoba, 2002), 257–67.

—— *Salé et ses Corsaires (1666–1727). Un port de course marocain au XVIIe siècle* (Caen Cedex, 2007).

MÉCHOULAN, HENRY, 'Abraham Pereyra, juge des Marranes et censeur de ses coreligionnaires à Amsterdam au temps de Spinoza', *Revue des Études Juives*, 138 (1979), 391–400.

—— *Hispanidad y Judaísmo en tiempos de Espinoza*, edition of Abraham Pereyra, *La Certeza del Camino* (Salamanca, 1987).

MEIJER, JAAP, *Encyclopaedia Sefardica Neerlandica*, 2 vols. (Amsterdam, 5709 and 5710 [1949 and 1950]).

—— *The Stay of Mozes Haim Luzzatto at Amsterdam 1736–1743* (Amsterdam, 1947).

MELKMAN, JOZEPH [JOZEPH MICHMAN], *David Franco Mendes: A Hebrew Poet* (Jerusalem, 1951).

MENDES DRUMOND BRAGA, ISABEL M. R., 'Poor Relief in Counter-Reformation Portugal: The Case of the Misericórdias', in Ole P. Grell, Andrew Cunningham, and Jon Arrizabalaga (eds.), *Health Care and Poor Relief in Counter-Reformation Europe* (London, 1999), 201–14.

MENKIS, RICHARD, 'The Gradis Family of Eighteenth-Century Bordeaux: A Social and Economic Study', Ph.D. diss., Brandeis University, 1988.

MILLÁS VALLICROSA, JOSÉ M., 'Emigración masiva de conversos por la fronterá catalano–francesa en el año 1608', *Sefarad*, 19/1 (1959), 140–4.

MITTERAUER, MICHAEL, and REINHARD SIEDER, *The European Family: Patriarchy to Partnership from the Middle Ages to the Present* (London, 1983).

MOCH, LESLIE P., *Moving Europeans: Migration in Western Europe since 1650*, 2nd edn. (Bloomington, 2003).

MOLL, GOSWIN, *De Desolate Boedelskamer te Amsterdam: Bijdrage tot de kennis van het Oud-Hollandsch failliten-recht* (Amsterdam, 1879).

MOLLAT, MICHEL (ed.), *Études sur l'histoire de la pauvreté* (Paris, 1974).

—— *The Poor in the Middle Ages: An Essay in Social History* (New Haven, 1986).

MORENO KOCH, YOLANDA, *Las taqqanot de Valladolid de 1432: Un estatuto communal renovador* (Salamanca, 1987).

MUCHNIK, NATALIA, 'Du catholicisme des judéoconvers: Rouen, 1633', *XVIIe Siècle*, 58/2 (2006), 277–99.

—— 'Des intrus en pays d'Inquisition: Présence et activités des Juifs dans l'Espagne du XVIIe siècle', *Revue des Études Juives*, 164/1–2 (2005), 119–56.

—— 'Du judaïsme au catholicisme: Les Aléas de la foi au XVIIe siècle', *Revue Historique*, 307/3 (2002), 571–609.

—— 'Juan de Prado o las peregrinaciones de un "passeur de frontiers"', in Jaime Contreras, Bernardo J. García García, and Ignacio Pulido (eds.), *Familia, religíon y negocio: El sefardismo en las relaciones entre el mundo ibérico y los Países Bajos en la edad moderna* (Madrid, 2002), 237–68.

MUNCK, BERT DE, 'In Loco Parentis? De disciplinering van leerlingen onder het dak van Antwerpse ambachtsmeesters 1579–1680', *Tijdschrift voor Sociale en Economische Geschiedenis*, 1/3 (2004), 3–30.

NADLER, STEVEN M., *Spinoza: A Life*, 9th edn. (Cambridge, 2007).

NAHON, GÉRARD, 'Amsterdam and Jerusalem in the 18th Century: The State of the Sources and Some Questions', in Jozeph Michman (ed.), *Dutch Jewish History*, vol. ii (Jerusalem, 1989), 95–116.

—— 'Bayonne dans la diaspora sefarade d'Occident (XVIIe–XVIIIe siècles)', in *Proceedings of the 7th World Congress of Jewish Studies: History of the Jews in Europe* (Jerusalem, 1981), 47–55.

—— 'Los *Cristianos Nuevos* españoles y portugueses en la Francia del antiguo régimen: Solidaridades geográficas', *Príncipe de Viana: Organo oficial de la Institución Príncipe de Viana*, 58 (1997), 212, 589–606.

—— 'Dépêches des Secrétaires d'État des Affaires Étrangères et de la Religion Prétendue Réformée concernant les Juifs (1726–1765)', *Michael*, 4 (1976), 187–247.

—— 'From New Christians to the Portuguese Jewish Nation in France', in Haim Beinart (ed.), *Moreshet Sepharad: The Sephardi Legacy*, vol. ii (Jerusalem, 1992), 336–64.

—— 'The Hague, Amsterdam, Istanbul, Jerusalem: David de Pinto and the *Jesiba* Magen David, 1750–1767', in Yosef Kaplan (ed.), *The Dutch Intersection: The Jews and The Netherlands in Modern History* (Leiden, 2008), 251–78.

—— 'The Impact of the Expulsion from Spain on the Jewish Community of Pre-Revolutionary France, 1550–1791', *Judaism*, 41/2 (1992), 169–79.

—— 'Le Livre dans la "Nation" juive portugaise de Saint-Esprit Bayonne aux XVIIe et XVIIIe siècles', in *IVe centenaire du détournement de l'Adour 1578–1978* (Bayonne, 1978), 201–22.

—— 'Les Marranes espagnols et portugais et les communautés juives issues du marranisme dans l'historiographie récente', *Revue des Études Juives*, 136 (1977), 297–367.

—— 'La Nation juive portugaise en France XVIIème–XVIIIème siècle: Espaces et pouvoirs', *Revue des Études Juives*, 153 (1994), 353–82.

—— *Les 'Nations' juives portugaises de sud-ouest de la France (1684–1791)* (Paris, 1981).

—— 'Pour une approche des attitudes devant la mort au XVIIIe siècle: Sermonnaires et testateurs juifs portugais à Bayonne', *Revue des Études Juives*, 136 (1977), 3–123.

—— 'Les Rapports des communautés judéo-portugaises de France avec celle d'Amsterdam au XVIIe et au XVIIIe siècles', *Studia Rosenthaliana*, 10/1 (1976), 37–78, 151–88.

—— 'Une source pour l'histoire de la diaspora sefarade au XVIIIe siècle: Le Copiador de Cartas de la communauté portugaise d'Amsterdam', in *Proceedings of the First International Congress for the Study of the Sephardi and Oriental Jewry* (Jerusalem, 1981), 109–22.

NAHON, GÉRARD, 'Yeshivot hiérosolymites du XVIIIe siècle', in Gilbert Dahan (ed.), *Les Juifs au regard de l'histoire: Mélanges en l'honneur de Bernard Blumenkranz* (Paris, 1985), 301–26.

NETANYAHU, BENZION, *The Marranos of Spain from the Late XIVth to the Early XVIth Century according to Contemporary Hebrew Sources*, 3rd edn. (Ithaca, NY, 1999).

NEUMAN, ABRAHAM A., *The Jews in Spain: Their Social, Political and Cultural Life during the Middle Ages* (1942; repr. New York, 1969).

NIEROP, HENDRIK F. K. VAN, and RONNIE PO-CHIA HSIA (eds.), *Calvinism and Religious Toleration in the Dutch Republic* (Cambridge, 2002).

NIJENHUIS, IDA J. A., *Een Joodse Philosophe, Isaac de Pinto (1717–1787)* (Amsterdam, 1992).

NOORDEGRAAF, LEO, *Daglonen in Alkmaar 1500–1850* (Haarlem, 1980).

—— and JAN T. SCHOENMAKERS (eds.), *Daglonen in Holland 1450–1600* (Amsterdam, 1984).

—— and GERRIT VALK, *De Gave Gods: De pest in Holland vanaf de late Middeleeuwen* (Amsterdam, 1996).

—— and JAN LUITEN VAN ZANDEN, 'Early Modern Economic Growth and the Standard of Living: Did Labour Benefit from Holland's Golden Age?', in Karel Davids and Jan M. G. W. Lucassen (eds.), *A Miracle Mirrored: The Dutch Republic in European Perspective* (Cambridge, 1995), 410–37.

NORBERG, KATHRYN, *Rich and Poor in Grenoble 1600–1814* (Berkeley, 1985).

NORMAN, CORRIE E., 'The Social History of Preaching: Italy', in Larissa J. Taylor (ed.), *Preachers and People in the Reformations and Early Modern Period* (Leiden, 2001), 125–91.

NOVINSKY, ANITA, *Cristãos novos na Bahia* (São Paulo, 1972).

NUBOLA, CECILIA, 'Supplications between Politics and Justice: The Northern and Central Italian States in the Early Modern Age', in Alexander F. Heerma van Voss (ed.), *International Review of Social History*, suppl. 9: *Petitions in Social History* (2001), 35–56.

NUSTELING, HUBERTUS P. H., *Welvaart en werkgelegenheid in Amsterdam 1540–1860: Een relaas over demografie, economie en sociale politiek van een wereldstad* (Amsterdam, 1985).

OFFENBERG, ADRIAAN K., 'Jacob Jehuda Leon (1602–1675) and his Model of the Temple', in Johannes van den Berg and Ernestine G. E. van der Wall (eds.), *Jewish–Christian Relations* (Dordrecht, 1988), 95–115.

—— 'Peregrine Printers', *Studia Rosenthaliana*, 35/2 (2001), 157–71.

OLDEWELT, WILLEM F. H., 'De Desolate Boedelskamer', *Amstelodanum*, 24 (1937), 157–9.

—— *Kohier van de Personeele Quotisatie te Amsterdam over het jaar 1742*, 2 vols. (Amsterdam, 1945).

OLIEL-GRAUSZ, EVELYNE, 'L'Histoire des Juifs séfarades à l'époque moderne: Éléments pour un bilan', *Revue des Études Juives*, 153 (1994), 133–51.

—— 'Networks and Communication in the Sephardi Diaspora: An Added Dimension to the Concept of Port Jews and Port Jewries', *Jewish Culture and History*, 7, ed. David Cesarani and Gemma Romain (2004), 61–76.

—— 'Portugais et tudesques dans les communautés juives d'Europe occidentale au XVIIIe siècle: Entre défiance et solidarité', *Yod*, 35 (1992), 27–33.

—— 'A Study in Intercommunal Relations in the Sephardi Diaspora: London and Amsterdam in the Eighteenth Century', in Chaja Brasz and Yosef Kaplan (eds.), *Dutch Jews as Perceived by Themselves and by Others*, Proceedings of the Eighth International Symposium on the Jews in The Netherlands (Leiden, 2001), 41–58.

OPPENHEIM, SAMUEL, 'An Early Jewish Colony in Western Guiana 1658–1666 and its Relation to the Jews in Surinam, Cayenne and Tobago', *Publications of the American Jewish Historical Society*, 16 (1907), 95–192.

—— 'An Early Jewish Colony in Western Guiana 1658–1666: Supplemental Data', *Publications of the American Jewish Historical* Society, 17 (1909), 53–70.

ORFALI, MOISES, 'The Portuguese Dowry Society in Livorno and the Marrano Diaspora', *Studia Rosenthaliana*, 35/2 (2001), 143–56.

OUDSCHANS DENTZ, FREDERIK, *De kolonisatie van de Portugeesch Joodsche Natie in Suriname en de geschiedenis van de Joden Savanne*, 2nd edn. (Amsterdam, 1975).

PALMER, ROBERT R., JOEL G. COLTON, and LLOYD S. KRAMER, *A History of the Modern World*, 10th edn. (New York, 2007).

PANHUYSEN, BIBI S., 'Gevestigden en buitenstaanders in de kledingsector: Het Amsterdams kleermakersgilde, 1500–1800', in Leo A. C. J. Lucassen (ed.), *Amsterdammer worden: Migranten, hun organisaties en inburgering 1600–2000* (Amsterdam, 2004), 149–85.

PARAIRA, MOZES C., and JACOB S. DA SILVA ROSA, *Gedenkschrift uitgegeven ter gelegenheid van het 300-jarig Bestaan der Onderwijsinrichtingen Talmud Tora en Ets Haim bij de Portug. Israël. Gemeente te Amsterdam* (Amsterdam, 1916).

PARKER, CHARLES H., 'Calvinism and Poor Relief in Reformation Holland', in Thomas M. Safley (ed.), *The Reformation of Charity: The Secular and the Religious in Early Modern Poor Relief* (Boston, 2003), 107–19.

—— *The Reformation of Community, Social Welfare and Calvinist Charity in Holland 1572–1620* (Cambridge, 1998).

PASS FREIDENREICH, HARRIET, *The Jews of Yugoslavia: A Quest for Community* (Philadelphia, 1979).

PATAI, RAPHAEL, *The Seed of Abraham: Jews and Arabs in Contact and Conflict* (New York, 1986).

PATINKIN, DON, 'Mercantilism and the Readmission of the Jews to England', *Jewish Social Studies*, 8 (1946), 161–78.

PENELLA ROMA, JUAN, *Los moriscos españoles emigrados al norte de Africa* (Barcelona, 1975).

PESCATELLO, ANN M., *Power and Pawn: The Female in Iberian Families, Societies and Cultures* (London, 1976).

PICCIOTTO, JAMES, *Sketches of Anglo-Jewish History* (London, 1875).

PIETERSE, WILHELMINA CHR., *350 jaar Dotar* (Amsterdam, 1965).

—— 'Abraham Lopes Colaso en zijn zoon Aron, kooplieden te Amsterdam en Bayonne van ca. 1700 tot 1774', *Studia Rosenthaliana*, 7/1 (1973), 1–7.

PIETERSE, WILHELMINA CHR., *Daniel Levi de Barrios als geschiedschrijver van de Portugees-Israelietische gemeente te Amsterdam in zijn 'triumpho del govierno popular'* (Amsterdam, 1968).

—— *Inventaris van de Archieven der Portugees-Israelietische Gemeente te Amsterdam 1614–1870* (Amsterdam, 1964).

—— *Livro de Bet Haim do Kahal Kados de Bet Yahacob* (Assen, 1969).

PIKE, RUTH, *Aristocrats and Traders: Sevillian Society in the Sixteenth Century* (Ithaca, NY, 1972).

PO-CHIA HSIA, RONNIE, *The World of Catholic Renewal 1540–1770* (Cambridge, 1998).

POHL, HANS H., *Die Portugiesen in Antwerpen (1567–1648): Zur Geschichte einer Minderheit* (Wiesbaden, 1977).

POL, LOTTE C. VAN DE, 'Amsterdam Jews and Amsterdam Prostitution, 1650–1750', in Chaja Brasz and Yosef Kaplan (eds.), *Dutch Jews as Perceived by Themselves and by Others*, Proceedings of the Eighth International Symposium on the Jews in The Netherlands (Leiden, 2001), 173–85.

—— *The Burgher and the Whore: Prostitution in Early Modern Amsterdam* (Oxford, 2011).

—— 'The Lure of the Big City: Female Migration to Amsterdam', in Els Kloek et al. (eds.), *Women in the Golden Age: An International Debate on Women in Seventeenth-Century Holland, England and Italy* (Hilversum, 1994), 73–81.

—— 'Vrouwencriminaliteit in Amsterdam in de tweede helft van de 17e eeuw', *Tijdschrift voor de Criminologie*, 29 (1987), 148–55.

—— and ERIKA KUIJPERS, 'Poor Women's Migration to the City: The Attraction of the Amsterdam Health Care and Social Assistance in Early Modern Times', *Journal of Urban History*, 32/1 (2005), 44–60.

POLIAKOV, LEON, *Les Banquiers juifs et le Saint-Siège du XIIIe au XVIIe siècle* (Paris, 1967).

POLIZZOTTO, LORENZO, *Children of the Promise: The Confraternity of the Purification and the Socialization of Youths in Florence* (Oxford, 2004).

POST, C. R., 'De Amsterdamse vroedvrouw uit de 18e eeuw', *Bijdragen tot de Geschiedenis der Geneeskunde*, 36 (1956), 1–8.

POT, GERARDUS P. M., *Arm Leiden: Levensstandaard, bedeling en bedeelden, 1750–1854* (Hilversum, 1994).

PRAK, MAARTEN R., 'Armenzorg 1500–1800', in Jacobus L. J. M. van Gerwen and Marco H. D. van Leeuwen (eds.), *Studies over zekerheidsarrangementen: Risico's, risicobestrijding en verzekeringen in Nederland vanaf de Middeleeuwen* (Amsterdam, 1998), 49–90.

—— *Gezeten burgers: De elite in een Hollandse stad. Leiden 1700–1800* (Amsterdam, 1985).

PUGH, WILMA J., 'Catholics, Protestants and Testamentary Charity in Seventeenth-Century Lyon and Nîmes', *French Historical Studies*, 11/4 (1980), 479–504.

PULIDO SERRANO, JUAN I., *Injurias a Cristo: Religión, política y antijudaísmo en el siglo XVII* (Alcalá, 2002).

PULLAN, BRIAN S., 'Charity and Usury: Jewish and Christian Lending in Renaissance and Early Modern Italy', *Proceedings of the British Academy*, 125 (2004), 19–40.

—— 'Jewish Banks and Monti di Pietà', in Robert C. Davis and Benjamin C. I. Ravid (eds.), *The Jews of Early Modern Venice* (Baltimore, 2001), 53–72.

—— 'Jewish Moneylending in Venice: From Private Enterprise to Public Service', in Gaetano Cozzi (ed.), *Gli Ebrei e Venezia: Secoli XIV–XVIII* (Milan, 1987), 671–86.

—— *Poverty and Charity: Europe, Italy, Venice, 1400–1700* (Aldershot, 1994).

—— *Rich and Poor in Renaissance Venice* (Cambridge, Mass., 1971).

—— (ed.), *Crisis and Change in the Venetian Economy* (London, 1968).

QUERIDO, ARIE, *Godshuizen en Gasthuizen*, 2nd edn. (Amsterdam, 1967).

QUINN, FREDERICK, *The French Overseas Empire* (Westport, Conn., 2000).

RAA, FREDERIK J. G. TEN, *Het Staatsche Leger 1568–1795*, 7 vols. (Breda, 1911–50).

RABINOWITZ, LOUIS I., *The Herem Hayyishub: A Contribution to the Medieval Economic History of the Jews* (London, 1945).

RAVID, BENJAMIN C. I., *Economics and Toleration in Seventeenth-Century Venice: The Background and Context of the Discorso of Simone Luzzatto* (Jerusalem, 1978).

—— 'The Venetian Government and the Jews', in Robert C. Davis and Benjamin C. I. Ravid (eds.), *The Jews of Early Modern Venice* (Baltimore, 2001), 3–30.

RAVILLARD, MARTINE, 'Los Moriscos en Berbería', *Nueva Revista de Filología Hispánica*, 2 (1981), 617–29.

REIJNDERS, CAROLUS, *Van 'Joodsche Natiën' tot Joodse Nederlanders: Een onderzoek naar getto- en assimilatieverchijnselen tussen 1600 en 1942* (Amsterdam, 1970).

RÉVAH, ISRAEL S., 'Autobiographie d'un marrane: Édition partielle d'un manuscrit de João (Moseh) Pinto Delgado', *Revue des Études Juives*, 119 (1961), 41–130.

—— 'Aux origines de la rupture spinozienne: Nouveaux documents sur l'incroyance dans la communauté judéo-portugaise d'Amsterdam à l'époque de l'excommunication de Spinoza', *Revue des Études Juives*, 123 (1964), 359–431.

—— 'Pour l'histoire des Marranes à Anvers: Recensements de la "Nation Portugaise" de 1571 à 1666', *Revue des Études Juives*, 122 (1963), 123–47.

—— 'Le Premier Règlement imprimé de la "Santa Companhia de Dotar Orfans e Donzelas Pobres"', *Boletim Internacional de Bibliografia Luso-Brasileira*, 4 (1963), 650–91.

REVEL, JACQUES, 'Au XVIIe siècle: Le Déclin de la Méditerranée?', in Irad Malkin (ed.), *La France et la Méditerranée: Vingt-sept siècles d'interdépendance* (Leiden, 1990), 348–62.

RICHARZ, MONIKA, *Die Hamburger Kauffrau Glikl: Jüdische Existenz in der Frühen Neuzeit* (Hamburg, 2001).

RIIS, THOMAS (ed.), *Aspects of Poverty in Early Modern Europe* (Alphen aan den Rijn, 1981).

RIVLIN, BRACHA, *Mutual Responsibility in the Italian Ghetto: Holy Societies 1516–1789* [Aravim zeh lazeh begeto ha'italkit: ḥevrot gemilut ḥasadim 1516–1789] (Jerusalem, 1991).

ROBERTS, BENJAMIN, *Through the Keyhole: Dutch Child-Rearing Practices in the 17th and 18th Century: Three Urban Elite Families* (Hilversum, 1998).

ROESSINGH, HENDRIK K., *Inlandse tabak: Expansie en contractie van een handelsgewas in de 17e en 18e eeuw in Nederland* (Wageningen, 1976).

ROESSINGH, HENDRIK K., 'Tobacco Growing in Holland in the Seventeenth and Eighteenth Century: A Case Study of the Innovative Spirit of Dutch Peasants', *Acta Historiae Neerlandicae*, 11 (1978), 18–54.

ROEST, MEIJER, *Catalog der Hebraica und Judaica aus der L: Rosenthalschen Bibliothek* (Amsterdam, 1966).

ROODENBURG, HERMAN W., *Onder Censuur: De kerkelijke tucht in de gereformeerde gemeente van Amsterdam 1578–1700* (Hilversum, 1990).

ROORDA, DANIEL J., 'Het Hollands regentenpatriciaat in de 17e eeuw', in *Vaderlands verleden in veelvoud: 31 opstellen over de Nederlandse geschiedenis na 1500* (The Hague, 1975), 232–51.

—— and HENK VAN DIJK, 'Social Mobility under the Regents of the Republic', *Acta Historiae Neerlandicae*, 9 (1976), 76–102.

ROSENBERGER, BERNARD, and TRIKI HAMID, 'Famines et épidémies au Maroc aux XVIe et XVIIe siècles', *Hésperis-Tamuda*, vol. 14 (1973), 109–75; vol. 15 (1974), 5–103.

ROTH, CECIL, 'Abraham Nuñez Bernal et autres martyrs contemporains de l'Inquisition', *Revue des Études Juives*, 100 bis, nos. 199, 200 (1936), 38–51.

—— *A History of the Marranos*, introd. H. P. Salomon, 4th edn. (New York, 1974).

—— *The House of Nasi: Doña Gracia* (Philadelphia, 1947).

—— 'Jewish Art and Artists before Emancipation', in Cecil Roth (ed.), *Jewish Art: An Illustrated History* (London, 1961), 407–538.

—— 'Les Marranes à Rouen: Un chapitre ignoré de l'histoire des Juifs de France', *Revue des Études Juives*, 88 (1929), 113–55.

—— 'The Resettlement of the Jews in England in 1656', in Vivian. D. Lipman (ed.), *Three Centuries of Anglo-Jewish History* (Cambridge, 1961), 1–25.

ROZEN, MINNA, *The Jewish Community in Jerusalem in the Seventeenth Century* [Hakehilah hayehudit biyerushalayim bame'ah ha-17] (Tel Aviv, 1984).

—— *Jewish Identity and Society in the Seventeenth Century: Reflections on the Life and Work of Refael Mordekhai Malki* (Tübingen, 1992).

RUBENS, ALFRED, *A History of Jewish Costume*, 3rd edn. (London, 1981).

—— 'Three Jewish Morality Pictures', *The Connoisseur: An Illustrated Magazine for Collectors*, 134 (1954), 31–3.

RUBIN, MIRI, *Charity and Community in Medieval Cambridge* (Cambridge, 1987).

RUDERMAN, DAVID B., *Early Modern Jewry: A New Cultural History* (Princeton, 2010).

—— 'The Founding of a Gemilut Hasadim Society in Ferrara in 1515', *Journal of the Association for Jewish Studies*, 1 (1976), 233–67.

RUIZ, TEOFILO F., *From Heaven to Earth: The Reordering of Castilian Society, 1150–1350* (Princeton, 2004).

RUMEU DE ARMAS, ANTONIO, *Historia de la previsión social en España* (Madrid, 1944).

RUSSELL-WOOD, ANTHONY J. R., *Fidalgos and Philanthropists: The Santa Casa da Misericordia of Bahia, 1550–1715* (Berkeley, 1968).

SABRA, ADAM, *Poverty and Charity in Medieval Islam: Mamluk Egypt, 1250–1517* (Cambridge, 2000).

SAFLEY, THOMAS M. (ed.), *The Reformation of Charity: The Secular and the Religious in Early Modern Poor Relief* (Boston, 2003).

SALOMON, HERMAN P., 'The "De Pinto Manuscript": A Seventeenth-Century Marrano Family History', *Studia Rosenthaliana*, 9/1 (1975), 1–62.

SAMUEL, EDGAR R., 'The First Fifty Years', in Vivian. D. Lipman (ed.), *Three Centuries of Anglo-Jewish History* (Cambridge, 1961), 27–44.

—— 'Portuguese Jews in Jacobean London', *Transactions of the Jewish Historical Society of England*, 18 (1958), 171–230.

—— 'The Readmission of the Jews of England in 1656, in the Context of English Economic Policy', *Transactions of the Jewish Historical Society of England*, 31 (1990), 153–69.

SAMUEL, WILFRED S., *The Jewish Colonists in Barbados in the Year 1680* (London, 1936).

—— 'Sir William Davidson, Royalist (1616–1689) and the Jews', *Transactions of the Jewish Historical Society of England*, 14 (1936), 39–79.

SAPERSTEIN, MARC, *Exile in Amsterdam: Saul Levi Morteira's Sermons to a Congregation of 'New Jews'* (Cincinnati, 2005).

—— *Jewish Preaching 1200–1800: An Anthology* (New Haven, 1989).

—— 'The Rhetoric and Substance of Rebuke: Social and Religious Criticism in the Sermons of Hakham Saul Levi Morteira', *Studia Rosenthaliana*, 34/2 (2000), 131–52.

—— *'Your Voice Like a Ram's Horn': Themes and Texts in Traditional Jewish Preaching* (Cincinnati, 1996).

SARAIVA, ANTÓNIO J., *The Marrano Factory: The Portuguese Inquisition and its New Christians 1536–1765*, trans., revised, and augmented Herman P. Salomon and Isaac S. D. Sassoon (Leiden, 2001).

SÁRRAGA, MARIAN, and RAMÓN F. SÁRRAGA, 'Early Links between Amsterdam, Hamburg and Italy: Epitaphs from Hamburg's Old Sephardic Cemetery', *Studia Rosenthaliana*, 34/1 (2000), 23–55.

SCAMMEL, GEOFFREY V., *The First Imperial Age: European Overseas Expansion c.1400–1715* (London, 1992).

SCHAMA, SIMON, *The Embarrassment of Riches: An Interpretation of Dutch Culture in the Golden Age* (London, 1987).

SCHAUB, JEAN-FRÉDÉRIC, *Les Juifs du roi d'Espagne: Oran 1509–1669* (Paris, 1999).

SCHELLEKENS, JONA, 'Determinants of Age at First Marriage among Jews in Amsterdam, 1625–1724', *Journal of Family History*, 24/2 (Apr. 1999), 148–64.

SCHMIDT, ARIADNE, *Overleven na de dood: Weduwen in Leiden in de Gouden Eeuw* (Amsterdam, 2001).

SCHMIDT BLAINE, MARCIA, 'The Power of Petitions: Women and the New Hampshire Provincial Government, 1695–1770', in Alexander F. Heerma van Voss (ed.), *International Review of Social History*, suppl. 9: *Petitions in Social History* (2001), 57–77.

SCHOLBERG, KENNETH R., 'Miguel de Barrios and the Amsterdam Sephardic Community', *Jewish Quarterly Review*, 53 (1962), 120–59.

SCHOLEM, GERSHOM G., *Major Trends in Jewish Mysticism*, 3rd edn. (Jerusalem, 1961).

—— *Sabbatai Sevi: The Mystical Messiah 1626–1676* (Princeton, 1973).

SCHORSCH, JONATHAN, 'Early Modern Sephardim and Blacks', in Zion Zohar (ed.), *Sephardic and Mizrahi Jewry: From the Golden Age of Spain to Modern Times* (New York, 2005), 239–58.

—— *Jews and Blacks in the Early Modern World* (Cambridge, 2004).

SCHREIBER, MARKUS, 'Cristianos Nuevos de Madrid ante la Inquisición de Cuenca (1650–1670)', in Joaquin Pérez Villanueva and Bartolomé Escandell Bonet (eds.), *Historia de la Inquisición en España y América*, iii (Madrid, 2000), 530–56.

SELLA, DOMENICO, *Italy in the Seventeenth Century* (London, 1997).

SEN, AMARTYA K., *Poverty and Famines: An Essay on Entitlement and Deprivation* (Oxford, 1981).

SHATZMILLER, JOSEPH, *Jews, Medicine and Medieval Society* (Berkeley, 1994).

—— *Shylock Reconsidered: Jews, Moneylending and Medieval Society* (Berkeley, 1990).

SHULVASS, MOSES A., *From East to West: The Westward Migration of Jews from Eastern Europe during the Seventeenth and Eighteenth Centuries* (Detroit, 1971).

SILVA ROSA, JACOB S. DA, *De geschiedenis van de Portugeesche Joden te Amsterdam 1593–1925* (Amsterdam, 1925).

—— *Die Spanischen und Portugiesischen gedruckten Judaica in der Bibliothek des Jüd. Portug. Seminars 'Ets Haim' in Amsterdam* (Amsterdam, 1933).

SIMONSOHN, SHLOMO, *History of the Jews in the Duchy of Mantua* (Jerusalem, 1977).

SLACK, PAUL, *Poverty and Policy in Tudor and Stuart England*, 2nd edn. (New York, 1993).

SLUYS, DAVID M., 'Hoogduits-Joods Amsterdam van 1635 tot 1795', in Hendrik Brugmans and Abraham Frank (eds.), *Geschiedenis der Joden in Nederland* (Amsterdam, 1940), 306–81.

SPAANS, JOKE W., *Armenzorg in Friesland 1500–1800: Publieke zorg en particuliere liefdadigheid in zes Friese steden, Leeuwarden, Bolsward, Franeker, Sneek, Dokkum en Harlingen* (Hilversum, 1997).

—— 'De gift aan de armen in Friese steden in de zestiende, zeventiende en achttiende eeuw, toegelicht aan het voorbeeld Sneek', *Tijdschrift voor Sociale Geschiedenis*, 22/4 (1996), 375–93.

SPICCIANI, AMLETO, 'The "Poveri Vergognosi" in 15th-Century Florence', in Thomas Riis (ed.), *Aspects of Poverty in Early Modern Europe* (Alphen aan den Rijn, 1981), 119–82.

SPIELMAN, JOHN P., *Leopold I of Austria* (London, 1977).

SPIERENBURG, PIETER C., *The Emergence of Carceral Institutions: Prisons, Galleys and Lunatic Asylums, 1550–1900* (Rotterdam, 1984).

SPRUNGER, MARY S., 'Mennonites and Sectarian Poor Relief in Golden-Age Amsterdam', in Thomas M. Safley (ed.), *The Reformation of Charity: The Secular and the Religious in Early Modern Poor Relief* (Boston, 2003), 137–53.

STAVRIANOS, LEFTEN S., *The Balkans since 1453*, repr. of the 1958 edn., introd. Traian Stoianovich (New York, 2000).

STILLMAN, NORMAN A., *The Jews of the Arab Lands: A History and Source Book* (Philadelphia, 1979).

STOW, KENNETH R., 'The Good of the Church, the Good of the State: The Popes and Jewish Money', *Christianity and Judaism* (1992), 237–52.

—— *Theater of Acculturation: The Roman Ghetto in the 16th Century* (Seattle, 2001).

STRAUSS, GERALD, *Nuremberg in the Sixteenth Century* (New York, 1966).

STUDEMUND-HALÉVY, MICHAEL, 'Codices gentium: Semuel de Isaac Abas, coleccionista de libros hamburgués', in Jaime Contreras, Bernardo J. García García, and Ignacio Pulido (eds.), *Familia, religíon y negocio: El sefardismo en las relaciones entre el mundo ibérico y los Países Bajos en la edad moderna* (Madrid, 2002), 287–319.

—— 'Dokumentation Kahal Kadosh Bet Israel', in Michael Studemund-Halévy and Peter Koj (eds.), *Die Sefarden in Hamburg: Zur Geschichte einer Minderheit* (Hamburg, 1994), i. 37–61.

—— '*Senhores* versus *Criados da Nação*: Portugueses, asquenasíes y tudescos en el Hamburgo del siglo XVII', *Sefarad*, 60/2 (2000), 349–68.

STUDNICKI-GIZBERT, DAVIKEN, '*La Nación* among the Nations: Portuguese and Other Maritime Trading Diasporas in the Atlantic, Sixteenth to Eighteenth Centuries', in Richard L. Kagan and Philip M. Morgan (eds.), *Atlantic Diasporas: Jews, Conversos, and Crypto-Jews in the Age of Mercantilism, 1500–1800* (Baltimore, 2009), 75–98.

SUGAR, PETER F., *Nationality and Society in the Habsburg and Ottoman Empires* (Aldershot, 1997).

—— *Southeastern Europe under Ottoman Rule 1354–1804* (Washington, DC, 1977).

SUTCLIFFE, ADAM, 'Identity, Space and Intercultural Contact in the Urban Entrepot: The Sephardic Bounding of Community in Early Modern Amsterdam and London', *Jewish Culture and History*, 7, ed. David Cesarani and Gemma Romain (2004), 93–108.

SWAAN, ABRAM DE, *In Care of the State: Health Care, Education and Welfare in Europe and the USA in the Modern Era* (Cambridge, 1988).

SWETSCHINSKI, DANIEL M., 'From the Middle Ages to the Golden Age, 1516–1621', in J. C. H. Blom, Renate G. Fuks-Mansfeld, and Ivo Schöffer (eds.), *The History of the Jews in The Netherlands*, trans. Arnold J. Pomerans and Erica Pomerans (Oxford, 2002), 44–84.

—— 'The Portuguese Jewish Merchants of Seventeenth-Century Amsterdam: A Social Profile', Ph.D. diss., Brandeis University, 1979.

—— *Reluctant Cosmopolitans: The Portuguese Jews of Seventeenth-Century Amsterdam* (London, 2000).

—— and LOEKI SCHÖNDUVE, *De familie Lopes Suasso: Financiers van Willem III* (Zwolle, 1988).

SZAJKOWSKI, ZOSA, 'An Auto-da-Fé against the Jews of Toulouse in 1685', *Jewish Quarterly Review*, 49 (1959), 278–81.

—— 'Population Problems of the Marranos and Sephardim in France from the 16th to the 20th Centuries', *Proceedings of the American Academy of Jewish Research*, 27 (1958), 83–105.

SZAPIRO, ELIE, 'Le Sud-Ouest', in Bernhard Blumenkranz (ed.), *Histoire des Juifs en France* (Toulouse, 1972), 221–61.

TALLAN, CHERYL, 'Opportunities for Medieval Northern European Jewish Widows in the Public and Domestic Spheres', in Louise Mirr (ed.), *Upon My Husband's Death: Widows in the Literature and Histories of Medieval Europe* (Ann Arbor, 1992), 115–27.

TALMON-HELLER, DANIELLA, 'Charity and Repentance in Medieval Thought and Practice', in Miriam Frenkel and Yaacov Lev (eds.), *Charity and Giving in Monotheistic Religions* (Berlin, 2009), 265–79.

TEENSMA, BENJAMIN N., 'Fragmenten uit het Amsterdamse convoluut van Abraham Idaña, alias Gaspar Méndez del Arroyo (1623–1690)', *Studia Rosenthaliana*, 11/2 (1977), 126–56.

TERPSTRA, NICHOLAS, *Abandoned Children of the Italian Renaissance: Orphan Care in Florence and Bologna* (Baltimore, 2005).

TISHBY, ISAIAH, *Messianic Mysticism: Moses Hayim Luzzatto and the Padua School*, trans. Morris Hoffman (Oxford, 2008).

TOAFF, RENZO, *La nazione ebrea a Livorno e a Pisa (1591–1700)* (Florence, 1990).

TORRES ARCE, MARINA, 'Los judaizantes y el Santo Oficio de Logroño en el reinado de Felipe V', in Joaquin Pérez Villanueva and Bartolomé Escandell Bonet (eds.), *Historia de la Inquisición en España y América*, iii (Madrid, 2000), 657–93.

TORRES VEIGA, JOSÉ DA, 'Uma longa guerra social: Os ritmos da repressão inquisitorial em Portugal', *Revista de História Económica e Social*, 1 (1975), 55–68.

TOURNEAU, ROGER LE, *Fez in the Age of the Marinides* (Norman, Okla., 1961).

TREXLER, RICHARD C., 'Charity and the Defense of Urban Elites in the Italian Communities', in Frederic C. Jaher (ed.), *The Rich, the Well Born and the Powerful* (Chicago, 1973), 64–109.

TRIVELLATO, FRANCESCA, *The Familiarity of Strangers: The Sephardic Diaspora, Livorno, and Cross-Cultural Trade in the Early Modern Period* (New Haven, 2009).

—— 'The Port Jews of Livorno and their Global Networks of Trade in the Early Modern Period', *Jewish Culture and History*, 7, ed. David Cesarani and Gemma Romain (2004), 31–48.

TURNIANSKY, CHAVA (ed. and trans.), *Glikl: Memoirs, 1691–1719* [Glikl: zikhronot, 1691–1719] (Jerusalem, 2006).

TWERSKY, ISADORE (ed.), *A Maimonides Reader* (New York, 1972).

—— and BERNARD SEPTIMUS, *Jewish Thought in the Seventeenth Century* (Cambridge, Mass., 1987).

ULBRICHT, OTTO, 'Criminality and Punishment of the Jews in the Early Modern Period', in Ronnie Po-Chia Hsia and Harmut Lehmann (eds.), *In and Out of the Ghetto: Jewish–Gentile Relations in Late Medieval and Early Modern Germany* (Washington, DC, 1995), 49–70.

VAZ DIAS, ABRAHAM M., 'Het Amsterdamsche Jodenkwartier', *Gedenkschrift der Stichting Bouwfonds Handwerkers Vriendenkring* (Amsterdam, 1937), 17–40.

—— 'Een blik in de marranenhistorie', *Vrijdagavond*, 9 (16 Sept. 1932), 77–80, 108–10, 122–3.

—— 'Over den vermogenstoestand der Amsterdamsche joden in de 17e en 18e eeuw', *Tijdschrift voor Geschiedenis*, 51 (1936), 165–76.

—— 'Een vergeten hoofdstuk uit de economische geschiedenis der Amsterdamsche Joden', *Vrijdagavond*, 7 (6, 13, 20 June 1930), 151–3, 168–70, 183–5.

VERDOONER, DAVE, and HARMEN SNEL, *Trouwen in Mokum: Jewish Marriage in Amsterdam: 1598–1811*, 2 vols. (The Hague, 1991).

VLESSING, ODETTE, 'New Light, on the Earliest History of the Amsterdam Portuguese Jews', in Jozeph Michman (ed.), *Dutch Jewish History*, vol. iii (Jerusalem, 1993), 43–75.

—— 'The Portuguese Jewish Merchant Community in Seventeenth-Century Amsterdam', in Clé Lesger and Leo Noordegraaf (eds.), *Entrepreneurs and Entrepreneurship in Early Modern Times* (The Hague, 1996), 223–43.

VLIS, INGRID VAN DER, *Leven in armoede: Delftse bedeelden in de zeventiende eeuw* (Amsterdam, 2001).

—— and THIJS J. RINSEMA, *Weeshuizen in Nederland: De wisselende gestalten van een weldadig instituut* (Zutphen, 2002).

VOGELSTEIN, HERMANN, and PAUL RIEGER, *Geschichte der Juden in Rom*, 2 vols. (Berlin, 1895–6).

VOLLENDORF, LISA, *The Lives of Women: A New History of Inquisitional Spain* (Nashville, 2005).

VOORST VAN BEEST, CORNELIS W. VAN, *De Katholieke Armenzorg te Rotterdam in de 17e en de 18e eeuw* (The Hague, 1955).

VOORTHUYSEN, WILLEM D., *Stads-bank van Lening 1614–1989* (Amsterdam, 1989).

VOVELLE, MICHEL, *Mourir autrefois: Attitudes collectives devant la mort aux XVIIe et XVIIIe siècles* (Paris, 1974).

—— *Piété baroque et déchristianisation en Provence au XVIIIe siècle* (Paris, 1973).

VRANKRIJKER, ADRIANUS C. J. DE, *Geschiedenis van de Belastingen* (Bussum, 1969).

VRIES, JAN DE, *De economische achteruitgang der Republiek in de achttiende eeuw*, 2nd edn. (Leiden, 1968).

—— *The Economy of Europe in an Age of Crisis 1600–1750* (Cambridge, 1976).

—— *European Urbanization 1500–1800* (London, 1984).

—— 'The Labour Market', in Karel Davids and Leo Noordegraaf (eds.), *The Dutch Economy in the Golden Age* (Amsterdam, 1993), 55–78.

—— and ADRIANUS VAN DER WOUDE, *The First Modern Economy: Success, Failure and Perseverance: 1500–1815* (Cambridge, 1997).

WAARDT, HANS DE, 'De geschiedenis van de eer en de historische antropologie: Een voorbeeld van interdisciplinaire aanpak', *Tijdschrift voor Sociale Geschiedenis*, 23/3 (1997), 334–54.

WANDEL, LEE P., *Always Among Us: Images of the Poor in Zwingli's Zurich* (Cambridge, 1990).

WEAVER, REBECCA H., 'Wealth and Poverty in the Early Church', *Interpretation: A Journal of Bible and Theology*, 41/4 (1987), 368–81.

WEBER, KLAUS, 'Were Merchants More Tolerant? Godless Patrons of the Jews and the Decline of the Sephardi Community in Late Seventeenth-Century Hamburg', *Jewish Culture and History*, 7, ed. David Cesarani and Gemma Romain (2004), 77–92.

WEBSTER, WENTWORTH, 'Hebraizantes portugueses en San Juan de Luz en 1619', *Boletín de la Real Academia de la Historia*, 15 (1889), 347–60.

WHALEY, JOACHIM, *Religious Toleration and Social Change in Hamburg, 1529–1819* (Cambridge, 1985).

WIJLER, JACOB S., *Isaac de Pinto: Sa vie et ses œuvres* (Apeldoorn, 1923).

WIJNGAARDEN, HILDE VAN, *Zorg voor de Kost: Armenzorg, arbeid en onderlinge hulp in Zwolle 1650–1700* (Amsterdam, 2000).

WIJSENBEEK-OLTHUIS, THERA F., *Achter de gevels van Delft: Bezit en bestaan van rijk en arm in een periode van achteruitgang (1700–1800)* (Hilversum, 1987).

—— '"Woongenot" van armen in de 18e eeuw', in Paul M. M. Klep, Jan Th. Lindblad, Anton J. Schuurman, Jeroen P. J. Singelenberg, and Theo van Tijn (eds.), *Wonen in het Verleden 17e–20e eeuw: Economie, politiek, volkshuisvesting, cultuur en bibliografie* (Amsterdam, 1987), 217–29.

WININGER, SALOMON, *Große jüdische national Biographie* (Czernowitz, 1927).

WIZNITZER, ARNOLD, *Jews in Colonial Brazil* (New York, 1960).

WOLF, LUCIEN, 'Jews in Elizabethan England', *Transactions of the Jewish Historical Society of England*, 11 (1928), 1–91.

—— 'Status of the Jews in England after the Re-Settlement', *Transactions of the Jewish Historical Society of England*, 4 (1903), 177–93.

WOLFF, EGON, and FRIEDA WOLFF, *Dicionário biográfico*, i: *Judaizantes e judeus no Brasil 1500–1808* (Rio de Janeiro, 1986).

—— —— 'Mistaken Identities of Signatories of the Congregation Zur Israel Recife', *Studia Rosenthaliana*, 12/2 (1978), 91–107.

WOOLF, STUART, 'Charity, Poverty and Household Structure: Florence in the Early Nineteenth Century', in id., *The Poor in Western Europe*, 158–97.

—— 'Introduction: The Poor and Society in Western Europe', in id., *The Poor in Western Europe*, 1–46.

—— *The Poor in Western Europe in the Eighteenth and Nineteenth Centuries* (Cambridge, 1986).

WÜRGLER, ANDREAS, 'Voices from among the "Silent Masses": Humble Petitions and Social Conflicts in Early Modern Central Europe', *International Review of Social History*, suppl. 9: *Petitions in Social History*, ed. Alexander F. Heerma van Voss, (2001), 11–34.

YA'ARI, ABRAHAM, *Emissaries from Erets Yisra'el: The History of the Missions from Erets Yisra'el to the Golah, from the Destruction of the Second Temple to the Nineteenth Century* [Sheluḥei erets yisra'el: toledot hasheliḥut meha'arets lagolah, meḥurban bayit sheni ad hame'ah hatesha-esreh] (Jerusalem, 1951).

—— *Hebrew Printers' Marks from the Beginning of Hebrew Printing to the End of the Nineteenth Century* [Diklei hamadpisim ha'ivri'im mereshit hadefus ha'ivri ve'ad sof hame'ah hatesha-esreh] (Jerusalem, 1943); supplementary notes published in *Kiryat sefer*, 31 (1956), 501–6.

YERUSHALMI, YOSEF H., 'Between Amsterdam and New Amsterdam: The Place of Curaçao and the Caribbean in Early Modern Jewish History', *American Jewish History*, 72 (1982), 172–92.

—— 'Conversos Returning to Judaism in the Seventeenth Century: Their Jewish Knowledge and Psychological Readiness' (Heb.), in *Fifth World Congress of Jewish Studies*, vol. ii (Jerusalem, 1972), 201–9.

—— *From Spanish Court to Italian Ghetto: Isaac Cardoso, a Study in Seventeenth-Century Marranism and Jewish Apologetics*, 2nd edn. (New York, 1981).

YOGEV, GEDALIA, *Diamonds and Coral: Anglo-Dutch Jews and Eighteenth-Century Trade* (Leicester, 1978).

YOSHA, NISSIM, *Myth and Metaphor: Abraham Cohen Herrera's Philosophical Interpretation of Lurianic Kabbalah* [Mitos umetaforah: haparshanut hafilosofit shel r. avraham cohen herera lekabalat ha'ari] (Jerusalem, 1994).

ZANDEN, JAN LUITEN VAN, *Prices and Wages and the Cost of Living in the Western Part of The Netherlands*; <http://www.iisg.nl/hpw/brenv.php>.

ZANDVLIET, KEES, and CLEMENS M. LESGER (eds.), *De 250 rijksten van de Gouden Eeuw: Kapitaal, macht, familie en levensstijl* (Amsterdam, 2006).

ZOMEÑO, AMALIA, '"When Death Will Fall Upon Him": Charitable Legacies in 15th Century Granada', in Miriam Frenkel and Yaacov Lev (eds.), *Charity and Giving in Monotheistic Religions* (Berlin, 2009), 217–33.

ZWARTS, JACOB, *Hoofdstukken uit de geschiedenis der Joden in Nederland* (Zutphen, 1929).

—— 'Joodsche Archiefsprokkels XXIII: Portugeesch-Joodsche Industrieën van 1616–1620', *Vrijdagavond*, 6/26 (27 Sept. 1929), 411–12.

—— 'De Joodse gemeenten buiten Amsterdam', in Hendrik Brugmans and Abraham Frank (eds.), *Geschiedenis der Joden in Nederland* (Amsterdam, 1940), 382–453.

—— 'De Uriel Da Costa tragedie van een monnik-biechtvader te Amsterdam (1650)', *Centraal Blad voor Israëlieten in Nederland*, 50/13 (24 May 1934), 8.

ZWIERS, ARIANE, 'Inventory of the Moveable Property of the Ashkenazi Community', *Studia Rosenthaliana*, 37 (2004), 309–97.

INDEX OF PERSONS

There are many identical names in the archives; it should be noted that a shared name does not necessarily indicate a family relationship. Where possible, further characterization of individuals has been supplied.

INDEX OF SUBJECTS

M

Printed and bound by CPI Group (UK) Ltd, Croydon, CR0 4YY

13/09/2026

14961097-0006